Roger Hughart
Christmas 2006 from Lee
R-March 31, 2007

Arch

The Life of Governor
Arch A. Moore, Jr.

Brad Crouser

Published In Beautiful West Virginia by
WOODLAND PRESS, LLC
In collaboration with *Logan Novelties and Books, LLC*

www.woodlandpress.com
www.woodlandgospel.com
ISBN 0-972486-8-X
SAN: 2 5 4 – 9 9 9 9

In memory of my
grandfather,
Harvey S. Crouser
(1897-1976),
who could always tell a good story.

Foreword

The most valid exercise of the biographer's skill must be applied, not toward the denigration of great men, but toward preserving, chronicling, and expositing their greatness. It appears that greatness is a rare commodity among humans and it is invariably lesser men who seek to attack the great, in an ill-fated attempt to bring the great down to their lower level.

In the present work, we have a happy coincidence of a dedicated scholar seeking to immortalize that bright, shining moment in West Virginia's history that was the work of one powerful, catalytic individual, Arch A. Moore, Jr. The author, Brad Crouser, proudly served in the outer circle during the third Moore Administration, and he was an astute observer during the first two, earlier Moore Administrations. Knowing his subject well, Brad knew exactly who to contact and interview, to flesh in the most important political story in the history of this great state. As result, he has given to posterity the story of this very bright, complex, driven and, in some ways, tragic man. He tells us of Moore's life as a warrior, survivor, lawyer, congressman, governor, federal prisoner, husband, father, mentor, and thinker. He describes, not only a very capable, but also a compassionate, emotional leader.

Brad was my student many decades ago and I was impressed by his approach to world, national and state events. He wrote a newspaper column then, and I was also impressed by his continual growth in the journalistic field, which culminated in this biography. He covered a vast pile of documents, television programs, newspaper articles and the like, in addition to conducting exhaustive interviews of Arch Moore's friends, enemies, supporters and detractors, allies and opponents.

It was almost, but not quite, too late when Attorney Crouser began to research this biography. The man closest to Arch Moore during his Congressional service, Bill Loy, had died some years earlier. Many of Governor Moore's associates, admirers, friends, enemies and opponents had begun to age. In another decade, the preparation of this tome would have been impossible.

Perhaps another generation or two will have that great advantage of hindsight that will place the three Moore administrations in better historical perspective. Perhaps, too, later chroniclers will have different perspectives of the good, bad and even indifferent aspects of Moore's life and works.

Crouser provides us with an appropriate amount of detail regarding Governor Moore's formative years. Those who know Governor Moore will tell you that it is nearly impossible to get him to discuss his military experiences. This seems to be true of all men I have known, who had real frontline exposure to war. The author then takes us to Moore's student days and his service to student government at West Virginia University.

Arch Moore served with distinction as the sole Republican in the West Virginia congressional delegation. Moore himself would agree that his tenure in Congress would not have justified the preparation of a biography. It is as the state's only three-term governor that Arch Moore unfolded events that more than requires that a biography be provided.

It is axiomatic that Arch Moore was the first modern governor of the State of West Virginia because he was the first to serve under what is commonly known as the Modern Budget Amendment. Proposed by the legislature, drafted by a commission headed by WVU Dean Carl M. Frasure, Sr., and ratified by the voters, it brought West Virginia government and administration into the Twentieth Century. Heretofore, the state budget was made by a collective known as the Board of Public Works. Because only the governor was barred by law from succeeding himself, he was frequently viewed as a minor and temporary inconvenience. In this sense, Arch Moore was type-forming in West Virginia, much as George Washington was type-forming as the first president under the Constitution. What each did would necessarily influence heavily the practices and procedures of his successors.

Arch Moore had a vision for his home state, a vision which began when he was still a student, the details of which were constantly being honed and perfected. While still a student at WVU, Arch began to mentally record the names and future responsibilities of those he would tap to serve with him in his first gubernatorial administration. The majority of these men had shown excellence in leadership, dedication and loyalty at WVU, with many having been honored with initiation into the ranking honorary, Mountain. In his second administration, he again turned to Mountain's alumnae to staff key administrative positions.

The essence of political greatness may well consist in framing a vision of what one might do if the voters choose to elect one to high office. Lesser men merely seek to honor themselves, adding their names, but rarely accomplishments, to a state's or a nation's history. In Moore's own time we have seen similar visions from England's Margaret Thatcher and America's Ronald Reagan. Each brought about a profound, but nonviolent, revolution. Each had a veritable plethora of detractors, which to the Great merely means that they have successfully offered substance to which a reaction has occurred. Each sought to persuade by and through the mastery of rhetoric, that wonderful philosophical field that substitutes debate for violence.

Many times, my students asked me where Arch Moore stands ideologically. The obvious answer is that Moore was and remains a pragmatist. He has never allowed some ideological consideration to deter him from doing what he believes will benefit his state. Indeed, he could be a hardliner when violence threatened, as during the riots on the WVU campus. He recognized them to be incited by elements foreign to the state and sought to return his alma mater to order, so that education could continue unabated by a tiny minority. He could be as compassionate as any man alive, when reconstituting the state's wholly outmoded mental health facility, which had done little to cure and less to move victims toward independence. He could be just, in ordering a complete restructuring of the Civil Service system so that tests administered were both valid and reliable. And he could be practical, in planning, building and maintaining the highway system, notably the Interstates.

Topping it all, Moore knew every detail of activities going on in the state and nation, in his own administration and throughout the state. Few, past or present, could discourse in such glowing detail, as could Governor Moore. He knew what he wanted and how to get it.

There is no question that Governor Moore's political supporters, open and clandestine, will want to read this book. So, too, will Moore's enemies and detractors. Few will be satisfied with the place Mr. Crouser accords Governor Moore. To some, that place should be so high that Governor Moore would be regarded as the greatest West Virginian of all times. To others, his detractors, most of whom hated Moore long before he ran afoul of the law, there is no place that be named in this world that is sufficiently low. My own guess is that future generations will look at his gravesite and say, "There was once greatness in this man." Let us also hope that, contrary to Shakespeare's observation in Julius Caesar, the good that he did will not be interred with his bones.

— James B. Whisker, Ph.D.
Professor, West Virginia University

Photo courtesy of the Charleston Gazette.

Chapter One
Moundsville

A dynamic, bustling, industrious string of towns and cities made the Northern Panhandle of West Virginia an exciting place to be in the early Twentieth Century. Although imagined now in shades of black and gray, in reality it was a region that greeted the senses with colorful sights, lots of noise and a mix of odoriferous outdoor smells (smoke and pollution) and delightful indoor aromas (ethnic foods).

The only portion of the state north of the Mason-Dixon line, it had more in common and connection with Pittsburgh, Steubenville and Cleveland than Charleston. A relatively prosperous part of the state, normally there were plenty of jobs, lots of action, something always going on. Observed former West Virginia Secretary of State Edgar F. "Hike" Heiskell, residents of Northern West Virginia "were isolated both geographically and culturally from the apple growers and farmers of the Eastern Panhandle, who were barely an hour's drive from Washington, D.C. They also differed from the residents of the far southern end of the state, then a full day's drive away, who were inextricably involved in the mining of coal."

Weirton, Benwood and Wheeling, of course, were smoky steel mill cities. The latter was also a business center and twice the capital (when the state's Republican Founding Fathers were in control). The American steel industry was at its zenith and the mills stayed busy, supplying the nation with sheets of alloys for building cans, cars, equipment, bridges, buildings and appliances.

To the south of them on the Ohio River was the nicely organized town of Moundsville, with its tree-lined streets, cleaner air, Victorian homes and friendly, well-mannered, generally well-educated residents. It was small town, Middle America, as celebrated in the magazines of the day.

The area was also an American industrial center in its prime. Moundsville and nearby Glen Dale derived their prosperity from the Fostoria Glass plant, the Louis Marx Toy manufacturers (largest toy maker in the nation, at the time), the United States Stamping plant (which made ceramic cookware), a smelting plant, and Triangle Conduit & Cable Co., among others. Wheeling had Sylvania Electric and Bloch Brothers, the makers of Mail Pouch chewing tobacco, Marsh Stogies and other cigars. Oftentimes, only standing room was available on the buses that ran between Moundsville and Wheeling every half hour, recalled Jim Cochran, a writer and long-time resident of the area. There had even been a nearby factory in which metal barrel rings were made, a job which apparently did not require high intelligence (hence, the term "hoopies" is still sometimes heard there as a put-down for unsophisticated or intellectually-challenged residents, a northern version of "hillbilly" or "hick").

Adding to the thousands of factory jobs were the many coal mines throughout the area, not only in West Virginia, but also in neighboring Ohio and Pennsylvania. In bustling downtown Wheeling, the 50,000-watt radio station, WWVA, had been beaming country music all over the East Coast and Canada since the 1920s and hosted *The Jamboree*, a live variety show every Saturday night, which was second only to Nashville's Grand Ole Opry in popularity.

The area easily was the most ethnically diverse in the state, adding to the excitement and colorful atmosphere, especially in food, weddings, festivals and other social activities. There remains today a large Italian-American, Polish-American and Eastern European population, especially in Benwood and Follansbee, thousands of whom had been drawn there by the prospect of employment. Less noticed were the Spanish-Americans, who had come to Moundsville by way of East St. Louis, as experts in smelting zinc. They even had their own section of town, called "Spanish Row." The Roman Catholic Church, to which almost all of these immigrant families were devoted members, was a powerful and influential spiritual, political and business force in the Northern Panhandle.

Adding to the color of that section of the state was another factor: organized crime, which provided liquor, gambling and even prostitution, mainly in Wheeling, through which many truckers and others passed. "Bill Lias, owner of the Wheeling Downs horse racing track, was widely accepted as the godfather of the area," remembered Cochran, who worked for *The Wheeling News*. "My editor, Harry Hamm, crusaded against organized crime for years. But Lias was a benevolent guy; he'd done a lot of charity work and took care of people who needed help."[1] Hamm's enthusiasm to clean out the Mafia was not shared by much of the local populace.

Unlike the southern end of the state, the North–at least Ohio and Marshall Counties—had lots of Republicans. With the exception of the northernmost two counties, it was a two-party region, since the days when Northern Panhandle Republicans went to their party's first president, Abraham Lincoln, to seek statehood and separation from Democratic, Confederate Virginia. Moundsville and Wheeling public offices were as dominated by the Grand Old Party as southern West Virginia counties were ruled by the party of Jefferson and Jackson.

FOREST TAYLOR MOORE had been a mover and shaker in the Moundsville area since the turn of the Twentieth Century. Born in 1862, in a log cabin, on what is now Route 250 in Marshall County, he arrived a year before the new state was created and would teasingly insist to his grandchildren that he was "a Virginian." Described by his grandson as a bold, hard working entrepreneur, Moore built scores of homes in the area and cut trees in Webster County, West Virginia (where he owned about 70,000 acres of timber), making the F.T. Moore Planing Mill Company a success and himself a millionaire. At the time, his was West Virginia's largest lumber company. He was elected mayor of Moundsville in 1910, and, along with his son Everett, became a force in the Republican Party. Mayor Moore was known to be generous and helpful to the community. For example, when one of only three African-American men in the town (a Mr. Wade) showed exceptional skill as one of his carpenters, Moore set him up in his own contracting business, which was a great success and a benefit to the area for decades.

"F.T.," as everyone called him, built a row of fine large houses on Fifth Street, known as the Moore Compound (or the F.T. Moore Addition), for himself and several family members. He and wife Eldora Redd Moore[2] had eight children. They included sons, Harry Webster Moore, who would become a chemical engineer at Moundsville's smelter plant; Everett, who became a lawyer and politician; and Saul Moore, who worked as an assistant to his father, F.T., in the lumber business, before becoming a laborer at the Moundsville smelter plant. There were daughters Rose, who worked at Mary Washington College in Virginia and at a West Virginia University fraternity house as a housemother, Virginia and Margaret, who were homemakers, and a third, Iola Moore, who was killed before she was three years old, when she ran out in front of a streetcar.

A fourth son, Arch Alfred Moore, born May 27, 1898, while the family resided in Cowen, Webster County, rounded out the family, a large one, but typical in size for that era.[3] F.T. wanted all his children go to college, which then was pretty much affordable only to upper income Americans.

True roads were almost non-existent in rural Webster County where the family relocated while he was timbering. It was a difficult, albeit temporary, stint for the Moore family in that near-wilderness, frontier-like region of the state. If any of his children needed to go into Webster Springs, for example, F.T. would let them ride the mailman's mule for the long journey "into town," which was then a spa attraction with a grand hotel for tourists. In 1905, F.T. Moore sold his Webster County timber lands to a Col. Bradley of Massachusetts and returned to Moundsville where he enlarged his existing construction businesses which had survived in his absence.

F.T. was a strong-willed, proud, domineering, "my way or the highway" type of patrician not uncommon in the early 1900s. Unfortunately, his strong will clashed with that of an equally stubborn son. Arch was in his second year at Bethany College, on a football scholarship, and had been in love with a pretty girl he'd befriended while in high school. The object of his affection was the vivacious and talented Genevieve Elizabeth Jones (born June 14, 1900), whose father, Zebedee W. Jones[4] and mother, Lucy R. St. Clair Jones,[5] had come to Moundsville from Mannington, West Virginia when she was sixteen, following his job with the B&O Railroad.

"Sis," as Genevieve was known, was an accomplished pianist, the life of the party. Her piano playing accompanied the silent movies at Moundsville's Strand Theater, before the "talkies" came along. "She was a very beautiful young lady," her eldest son would later boast. "She hit town like Lindbergh hitting Paris. But she never showed any interest in anyone but my dad." Even before his college days, Arch, Sr. had been an All-State football player for Moundsville High, nicknamed "Archie" or "Rosie" for some reason no one could recall. Moundsville High's Orospolitan yearbook of 1918 described Arch, Sr. as "an exceedingly quiet fellow who was never known to attend a class meeting. Rather studious and makes good grades. Hobby: watching Genevieve."

Archie had returned from his World War I service in the Army at Ft. Hancock in Georgia, before attending (and playing football at) Bethany. He and Genevieve could wait no longer; they wanted to get married. Even though they were in their twenties, of typical marrying age for that time, F.T. thought they were too young to tie the knot. More importantly, he wanted Archie to finish his education first, so he could be employed, self-sufficient, and support the children who inevitably would follow. In other words, F.T. didn't intend to support his family and his son's family, too.

When the couple refused to back down, and instead went through with a wedding in 1921, F.T. cut off all financial support, including payment of his son's college bills.

Archie and Genevieve were excluded from the Moore Compound. F.T. did build them a house across town in a less affluent section but, unlike for other family members, he didn't give it to them; they took out a mortgage with a local bank and began making house payments.

As the result of being partially outcast, tensions between the young couple and F.T. and Dorie were strained and most of their family socializing, even when children came along, was conducted at the Jones home, not at F.T. and Dorie's. Dropping out of college, Arch, Sr. gave up any thoughts of following his two brothers into a profession. He took a low-paying job as postmaster at the West Virginia State Penitentiary in Moundsville.

Nevertheless, Archie and Genevieve enjoyed a middle class existence in their new home; they even had one of the first radios in town. Archie was a quiet, unassuming, pleasant man, who mainly kept to himself. "He didn't say much, but when he did, it was important and significant," recalled his youngest son. "He was easy-going, but occasionally his temper would explode." Added Jim Cochran, who knew the senior Arch Moore, "He had nothing of the outgoing personality of his brother Everett."

Soon three children were added to the household: Arch Alfred, Jr., born April 16, 1923; Lucy Joycelyn,[6] born on Nov. 20, 1927 (known as "Joy"); and Harry Moore, born June 22, 1929.

Moundsville was an idyllic place in which to raise a family; it provided a life right out of a Norman Rockwell painting. Arch, Jr.'s dad took him to Boy Scout functions (the young Moore would later become part of Troop 79 of the Moundsville Methodist Church). "A lot of volunteering adults positively impacted my life," Arch, Jr. would later recall, with appreciation.

With no car, the family walked a mile to the Simpson Methodist Church each Sunday morning. His mother played piano for the Elk Minstrels and other community groups and became involved in the Moundsville social scene. Sis's family had been active Republicans for generations—a grandfather, Dr. William Jones of Central Station, Doddridge County, had been appointed federal magistrate by President Lincoln. It was just natural for her to become very active in the local women's auxiliary of the Grand Old Party.

"We grew up in a very normal neighborhood," recalled Joy Moore Sievertson, who thought they had been well-behaved. "I don't ever remember us fighting." They also were close-knit. "We had some family dinners at [the F.T.] Moores, but Thanksgiving dinners were always at the Jones grandparents' home." Arch Jr. would remember a "cool" relationship with his paternal grandparents, but his brother and sister saw it otherwise. Harry recalled putting in gardens with his father at F.T.'s home. Despite what had happened between F.T. and Arch, Sr., things were working out pretty well for the young family.

Arch, Jr., his brother and sister attended Third Street Elementary. His father, "who was a great mathematician," helped him do his arithmetic homework at the dining room table by candlelight (the family not having electricity). His mother would later recall that Arch, Jr. "never had low grades. He had almost all A's. His grandfather once said, 'I'll give you fifty cents for every A.' The next month, Arch came home with eight A's. Grandpa said, 'I didn't say *that* many A's!' And Arch said, 'You didn't, Grandpa, but you did say fifty cents each! That's four dollars.' Grandpa reached into his pockets and gave it to him."[7]

"I was probably as spoiled as any first child," Arch, Jr. would concede. But his parents were "solid taskmasters," and the three always had chores to do. The Jones home was where the young Arch Moore "found warmth;" he felt loved and encouraged there. "My Grandmother Jones was probably the strongest person in my life." Harry remembered being at Mrs. Jones's house often when her health declined and she needed help with chores. "Arch (Jr.) was always busy, always looking for projects. He was a good electrician. He had a knack for fixing stuff, it was just something he liked to do."

Apparently a precocious child, Arch, Jr. remembered disrupting a history class when he—and then other students, one by one—began standing, "because the Star Spangled Banner was being played in the nearby band room." When his teacher, Mrs. Lough, asked, " To what do I account for this performance?" Arch replied unapologetically, "I've always been taught to stand when the national anthem is played."

The young Moore told people, from the time he was six or seven, that he was going to be a lawyer. About the same time, when asked by a rotund gentleman one day when Arch was downtown with his father, "What do you want to be when you grow up, sonny?" the first grader had replied confidently, "I plan to be governor of West Virginia!"

From all counts, he was a typical boy—playing ball and running around the neighborhoods with friends, when not in classes. His dad always had a cigarette in his hand or mouth and, like most youngsters, Arch, Jr. tried a homemade, corn silk smoke–one time. "I inhaled flames into my mouth and that was the last time I ever wanted to smoke!"

But things began changing for the Moores, as with many other American families, when the stock market crashed in 1929 and the Great Depression (which actually did not end until defense equipment manufacturing for World War II rejuvenated the economy in the early 1940s) began. It also meant a political change in West Virginia, which until that time had been a healthy, competitive, two-party state. With millions unemployed, Democrats successfully blamed Herbert Hoover, high tariffs, an under-regulated Wall Street and the Republicans for the (worldwide) economic downturn. Theirs became the dominating party in the nation, and especially in hard-hit West Virginia, where it would never again relinquish its hold on the state's political establishment. An increasingly unionized state, its voters began viewing the Republicans as pro-business, and hostile to poor and working class people.

The elder Moore's appointment to the penitentiary staff had been a political one; they all were in those days when there was no civil service protection and almost all state employment was by patronage. Nevertheless, he was able to survive a few months under the new regime. But Arch, Sr. came home one day, the week after Christmas 1933, with his head down, dejected. "I can still picture my dad standing there in the kitchen, giving Mother the bad news," Arch, Jr., then ten years old, would remember. The Democrats had fired Moore from his modest job as prison postmaster, along with other employees who were registered Republican. Work was almost impossible to find, so state jobs must be given to the Democratic faithful. There was no court protection against such political firings. It was just the way the game had always been played.

Mr. Moore's political firing was a devastating blow to the family. "That's when I grew up," Arch, Jr. would recall somberly. "That changed everything. I had to become an adult rather fast." The family would need the young son's help to win their daily bread.

Arch, Sr. would be out of work for about a year ("he had a very difficult time finding something") before landing another low-paying job as janitor/maintenance man for the U.S. Stamping plant, where he would remain until retirement, eventually rising to "safety engineer." The disruption in his income meant the loss of the house that F.T. had built; they couldn't make mortgage payments. Her pride showing in a 1980 interview, Genevieve said, "I want to make it plain, that we were not put out of our home. We weren't foreclosed on, but I'm a worry wart, and instead of worrying about the payments, we just turned the house over to the realty company."

The Moores kept their pride and dignity throughout the financial ordeal; they didn't want any sympathy then or later. "I want it understood perfectly that we were not rich people, that we were not poor people, we were people of moderate means," Arch's mother told the reporter. "And most of that was after the Depression and it hit us so hard." The reporter added, "Just a few minutes into the interview and she wants it understood that she isn't seeking sympathy."

The five moved into a rental home in a less affluent section of town, on Third Street, in which they would remain for twenty-some years. By now, F.T. Moore could not help them even if he wanted to do so; he also suffered a collapse of his timbering, lumber and construction business; the proud patriarch lost most of his fortune.[8]

To supplement the family income, Genevieve Moore would take a job as the pianist for Miss Florence Black's dance studio, accompanying the ballet teacher, as the students practiced and performed. She would work there for the next two decades. As the eldest son, Arch Jr. began delivering *The Moundsville Journal* and *The Saturday Evening Post* under the management of his Methodist pastor, the Reverend Evans. When he got a little older, he began ushering at The Strand and later rose to managing usher at the Park Theater. Moore recalled that, in the summer time, as a promotion, the theaters would offer free, outdoor movies and, "if you were among the first hundred or so in line, you'd get a free candy bar!" He began working long, hard hours, a pattern which would never cease during his lifetime. He became accustomed to being gainfully employed; he found he was happiest when he was being useful, advancing, earning income.

It is clear that, about this time, Arch, Jr. developed a deep-seated, insatiable drive that would define his ambitions and his mission in life. The financial setbacks seemed to help form his personality. Much of that revolved around restoring his family's dignity, given the double setback of being "the black sheep" of the Moore family and later even losing their home due to unemployment. First, it strengthened his identity as a Republican, because of what the Democrats had done to his father. Second, it drove the young Arch's resolve to make some money, help his parents in a big way some day, and to become someone prominent, important and respected, like his grandfather and many other ancestors had been. He determined he would not be someone whose future would be at the mercy of others, of the system. Arch was certain that he did not want to be poor or even just to be "average." He would impose his will on the system, if given the opportunity. He wanted to be someone exceptional. More than others, this period of time molded who he would become.

Arch, Jr. recalled his mother, only minutes before his ride arrived, being able to scrape up five dollars for him to go to a week-long Boy Scout summer camp at Fish Creek. Money was always tight and sacrifices had to be made for the smallest "extra" or luxury. Occasionally, the Moore children would get fifteen cents for a Saturday at the movies. "But nearly everyone was in the same position, so it didn't seem so bad," recalled his sister Joy.

There was time for some fun, as well as work. Arch, Jr. acted in some schools plays. "I had a leading role in one. 'Am I intruding?' was my entrance line." He joined the High-Y Club, the stated goal of which was to promote "Clean Speech, Clean Sports, Clean Living, and Clean Scholarship." He also learned a skill he would use forever, in Speech Club. One teacher, Mrs. McCormick, "insisted that I become a writer," he remembered. He was beginning to realize that he all sorts of skills and talents in many areas.

The Moore brothers, Arch, Jr. and Harry, would acquire the nicknames of "Big Moo" and "Little Moo" from a Scout master, who for some reason wanted to drop the "r" from their name; it had nothing to do with cows.[9] Both boys loved to play basketball and became very skilled at the game; they were natural athletes. With other neighborhood boys, they would gather in "Harler's back yard," a solid dirt "court," and play well into the night, with illumination from a truck's headlights. By digging out ashes under the truck wheels, Harry Moore remembered, they would adjust the lights to point at the right level, and go at it until the battery died. Harry—six feet, two inches tall–big for that era, would become a basketball star at Moundsville High School and later at West Virginia University, one of the first players there to master the jump shot. Arch, Jr. was "vertically challenged," about five feet, seven inches tall.[10]

Despite the height disadvantage, Arch, Jr. also became a high school basketball star. Soon his skills on the court for the Trojans of Moundsville High School were delighting fans and getting noticed by area sports writers. "A one-handed shot from the foul circle by Junior Moore,[11] pint-sized Trojan guard, gave Moundsville a 36-34 triumph over Linsly in sudden death overtime" reported a February 1941 sports page of Wheeling's *Intelligencer.* "Moore, who scored 15 points during the afternoon, hit the hoop freely in the first half when he collected five of his seven goals." Wrote columnist Albert Coxon, "Ball hawks like Junior Moore, Bill Platt and Joe Pelaez make monkeys out of the taller lads. Their ball handling is tops and their passing leaves little to be desired." The team was playing to capacity crowds, even when the wintry Northern West Virginia roads outside were "skating rinks," as one reporter put it.

Another headline read, "Junior Moore's Field Goal Decides Sparkling Fracas," covering another victory. A story noted how Moore could "dart back and forth among the taller [Cameron] Cadets ... Junior Moore cashed four from far out to help the Trojans win ...[He] caught on fire as a sparkplug..." One columnist wrote, "But when orchids are being handed out, pick out a particularly nice one for Junior Moore. The guard, who stands a little better than five feet and probably weighs 115 pounds soaking wet, better than held his own with the taller Cameron cagers..."

In a story about their game with another area rival, the reporter wrote, "Junior Moore ... gained defensive laurels in the contest, repeatedly snatching the ball from the Hundred [High School] attackers to start scoring plays for the Trojans." In one about their defeat of Union, the paper wrote, "Junior Moore's foul put the Trojans ahead to stay..." Another called Arch "Flicker Moore," and raved that his game "was a wild, dazzling scramble from start to finish." The "pint-sized lads" were a "scrappy aggregation," wrote another. Moore's eyes lit up in an interview six decades later, when he recalled that he could make baskets from center court, "and that only got me two points."

Many of his teammates at Moundsville would become All-American and several played basketball in college. His love of the game drew Arch, Jr. close to Uncle Harry W. Jones, who shared his enjoyment of basketball. And it made the young Moore a minor celebrity in the town, someone they'd remember. Arch learned to enjoy the favorable roar of the crowd, applause, the joy of people shouting his name–it was something he'd get used to during most of his life.

Arch, Jr. soon stumbled onto another passion. He helped a friend get elected student body president and discovered his own talent at public speaking, exciting crowds in the high school gym this time, not with his roundball skills, but with his oratory, which was exceptional for a sixteen year old (a photo exists of him giving an early speech, gesturing with his arms). And when the American Legion sponsored Youth in Government, in which students administered the City of Moundsville for a day, he ran for chief of police on the Blueblood Ticket. He made up handbills, which asked potential voters to, "Give us some consideration." His ticket won, with mayoral candidate LeMoyne Blake. The newspaper reported a "stormy" city council session in which the young people voted to repair two holes in two streets. A proposal to raise the pay of councilmen from three to four dollars per session was defeated by one vote.

All this activity had to be worked around an already busy schedule for the high schooler, who kept his grades up. Arch began working at his dad's factory, the U.S. Stamping plant, as a "carrier" on the oven cookware line, starting an eight hour shift at 4:30 after a full day of school and sports. It was a back-breaking schedule he would keep through his junior and senior years of high school, to help the family make ends meet. He became a member of The Enamel Workers Union, a member of organized labor.[12] Junior would be promoted twice during that time, moving up to the chemistry lab. He would remain at the plant even after high school, since he felt it unwise to bother starting college. The attack on Pearl Harbor meant most healthy young men like himself would soon be drafted into the military; it was just a matter of when, not if.

He also discovered romance. Later described by writers as "ruggedly handsome," with his piercing baby blue eyes, thick brown hair and a charming smile and manner, Arch Moore in his senior year began dating–or what passed for it in those days. His first flame was Carol Hearnshaw, daughter of the U.S. Stamping plant's president, Steele Hearnshaw. A "date" usually meant just going over for dinner at her parents' home. "She was the first girl that I was interested in. She was very nice, very pretty. But that didn't work out–she went to WVU and married someone else."

After graduation from Moundsville High, Arch would loved to have gone to Morgantown, too, and quit the grueling, monotonous factory job. But some other adventures, that would keep him occupied for about three years, stood in the way. The calm, if sometimes difficult, years of Moundsville and Arch Moore's boyhood were coming to a close.

Chapter 1 Notes

1. - But Lias' acts were not all benevolent, observed lawyer H. John Rogers. "He was 400 to 450 pounds; they called him 'Big Bill.' He was Greek, not a part of the national mafia; his real name was Liaskakos. He did have alliances with the Toledo mob. His wife was murdered and his successor, Paul Hankish, was called 'No Legs' because, in 1964, his legs had been blown off. Lias was widely suspected in both, but was never prosecuted. He owned the Wheeling police. The government tried to deport him several times, but failed." Roger continued, "Wheeling was wide open to roulette, dice, poker games, and liquor, which was illegal then. But Moundsville didn't get into that." About the Wheeling pollution, he noted, "It wasn't Pittsburgh [which Charles Dickens once called 'hell with the lid off'], but it was working its way there." (Not that anyone much noticed pollution in those days; six out of ten American adults then smoked cigarettes.)

2. - F.T. always called her "Dorie." She would live to be 98 and would live to see grandson Arch elected to Congress three times.

3. - Most of Arch Moore's aunts and uncles on his mother side were also ordinary, working people. An exception was Dorsey Victor "Bull" Jones, who was a catcher for the Chicago Cubs. Donally Jones worked for the B&O Railroad, Harry W. Jones was assistant county clerk for Marshall County for many years and Paul Jones was an orderly at Wheeling Hospital.

4. - Early photos of Zebedee Jones, who was son of a Doddridge County physician, Dr. William Jones, make it obvious that it was from this grandfather that Arch, Jr. would inherit the penetrating, light blue eyes.

5. - Lucy St. Clair Jones was from Flemington,Taylor County, and was believed to be the first female to graduate from an institution of higher learning in what is now West Virginia She had obtained a degree from the now-defunct Flemington College, also known as West Virginia College Institute. Lucy was a descendant of the Shinns, who founded Shinnston, in Harrison Co.

6. - She would become Mrs. Joy Sievertson.

7. - *West Virginia Mountain Messenger*, October 1980.

8. - Arch Moore, Jr. appears to have been slightly embarrassed by the fact that he grew up poor, almost like it was his fault. He rarely mentioned it to anyone, certainly not in a campaign setting as

some candidates are wont to do. It would have made a great contrast when the rich Jay Rockefeller was twice his opponent, but Arch apparently didn't think it appropriate to talk about it. He was proud, however, of how he was able to quickly raise himself from that station of life, as his income grew. He was also very proud of his lineage, the distinguished ancestors he had in both the Moore and Jones sides of his family (too extensive to discuss in this book). "I didn't just get off the raft," he said to this book's author, in discussing how many of his forefathers had helped to settle Northern West Virginia, becoming hard working farmers, businessmen, clergymen, since the late 1700s.

9. - When Arch, Jr. went off to war, he told Harry he could "have" the nickname; he wasn't particularly fond of it. So Harry Moore was known as "Moo Moore" throughout his outstanding college basketball career and the remainder of his life. If one referred to "Moo," you immediately knew who they were talking about.

10 - Regarding his height, H. John Rogers, a New Martinsville attorney and wit who knows Moore, wrote in *Graffiti* that the former governor, sitting behind a desk, "looks like the Colossus of Rhodes, but standing next to you, he looks like a 'munchkin.'"

11. - "Being referred to as 'Junior' sent me up the wall," Arch admitted, 65 years later. He didn't like his other nickname, "Moo," any better. He vowed that no son of his would ever get such a nickname.

12. - "I was the only governor to have been a former union member," Moore believed. When he was running for office, union president Charlie Mills gave him a certificate of membership to the union, telling Arch, "We're gonna make you governor!"

Chapter Two
Suicide Mission

By April of 1943, Arch, Jr. had brought home several hefty pay checks earned while working as a timekeeper for the Bechtel Corporation. The company was laying a twenty four-inch pipeline to transport Texas oil to the East Coast, mainly for military use.[1] Arch had hired onto the project in the previous autumn, when it was working its way through Marshall County. Bechtel's workers and managers, mainly Texans, liked the young Moore and kept him on the job even after it finished in his home county, working on several spreads[2] through Pennsylvania.

One day, having finished a shift, he walked off a spread into the company headquarters in Bedford, Pennsylvania. Arch was handed what he had been expecting for months: his military draft notice. He reported to the Selective Service office in Moundsville on May 15, 1943, then to the Waldo Hotel in Clarksburg for his physical exam. The local newspaper noted that Arch "was inducted into the Army on the twenty-fifth anniversary of the day when his father, Arch A. Moore, Sr., entered the Army for service in the first World War."

Weathered and, at twenty, older than most of the other thirty-nine inductees from the Moundsville area, Arch was appointed by Lt. P. A. Wymore to be their acting corporal. They were loaded onto a train with other draftees for the few hours' trip to Fort Hayes near Columbus, Ohio, where they underwent more exams for assignment purposes, including IQ testing. Given the option of Naval service, Arch chose the U.S. Army, in which his father and uncles had served during World War I. At Camp Joseph T. Robinson in Little Rock, Arkansas, he was selected for Officers Training School. According to records, it was originally intended that he go into medical management.

Casualties in Europe and the Pacific had been so great that, with just more than a year into World War II, the U.S. government was beginning to fear a "brain drain." The nation's college and university campuses almost had been emptied of able-bodied young men after the Dec. 7, 1941, Japanese surprise attack on Pearl Harbor. The unprovoked bombing of our fleet sparked almost unprecedented patriotic feelings. It was suddenly "the thing to do," to help with the war effort in any way possible. As odd as it may now sound, there was some sense of noblesse oblige among the upper income college boys to volunteer to fight—the more dangerous and heroic, the better. As result, potential future leaders like Joseph P. Kennedy,

Jr. were literally being blown to bits. There was serious risk that a whole generation of smart young American men was going to be wiped out.

So programs were created to train "the best and the brightest," those who exhibited talent, special leadership skills and high intelligence, set them aside for leadership, fill vacant areas of expertise, and to prevent them all from becoming cannon fodder.

One of those programs was the Army Specialized Training Program (ASTP). It became the single largest college education program in the nation's history until then, sending more than 200,000 soldiers to 227 colleges to take highly accelerated courses in various disciplines: engineering, medicine, dentistry, personnel psychology and thirty-four different languages.

Col. Herman Beukema, a highly-respected professor of history and government at West Point, was brought to the Pentagon to oversee the program (and defend it against congressional critics who wrongly accused the program of being a means by which sons from wealthy families could safely be kept out of harm's way). He assured congressional investigators that ASTP studies were more rigorous and that it was more "military" than even West Point or the Naval Academy.

With his very high IQ, Arch was selected for the ASTP and was sent to Oklahoma State University in Stillwater for additional exams. Next, he was assigned to Lafayette College, near Allentown, Pennsylvania, which had been taken over completely by the Army's ASTP program. All 350 to 400 uniformed men at Lafayette were there to pursue engineering degrees. Outside the classroom, they paraded and drilled on the football field, reviewed by their cadet corps commander, Arch A. Moore, Jr.

"It was a crash course," Moore explained six decades later. "When I eventually returned to college (at West Virginia University), I had so many credits that I entered as a junior." According to Louis Keefer, who wrote about the ASTP, the cadets were "soldiers first, students second." They were under strict military discipline at all times, wore uniforms, stood in formations such as reveille, were subject to inspections, marched to class and meals, had lights out at 10:30 and "generally behaved–and misbehaved–as much as all other soldiers."

They had a fifty-nine hour work week of "supervised activity," including five hours of military instruction and six of physical education. With their theme song, sung to the tune of "My Bonnie Lies Over the Ocean," the ASTP cadets mocked those who thought they had escaped tough military duty:

Some mothers have sons in the Army,
Some mothers have sons on the Sea;
Take down your service flag, Mother,
Your son's in the ASTP;
Goldbrick, goldbrick, goldbrick for the ASTP!

Then came D-Day, on June 6, 1944. Arch remembered, glumly, "Word came down that casualties were so great that the Army was going to terminate the ASTP and that we were being reassigned to infantry units and special-ops."[3] The high-IQ guys were being sent to the battlefield, after all.

Thus, Arch Moore's government-financed engineering education came to an abrupt and disappointing halt. Gone, too, was his chance of becoming a commissioned officer.

Moore was assigned to Company G, 334th Regiment of the 84th Infantry Division.[4] Calling themselves "The Rail Splitters," they wore arm patches depicting an ax splitting a log. When they reached England, they would be assigned to a newly-created 9th Army.[5] But before being shipped off to Europe, in July and August of 1944, Moore and the other former college students were sent for a "cram course on the art of fighting war" at steamy Camp Claiborne, Louisiana. Among other things, they learned how to pilot gliders, which were being widely used to get troops and supplies to the battlefield.

At Camp Claiborne, Arch became friends with another former ASTP cadet who still had a heavy German accent, his Jewish family having recently fled the Nazis. This stocky young man, who had become an American citizen only in recent weeks, for some reason always seemed to need Arch's help in getting his knapsack on. Arch didn't immediately catch his full name, but decades later it would be known around the world: *Henry Kissinger.*[6]

After completing training, Arch was made a combat sergeant and shipped to Winchester, England. "That country was still being bombed by Hitler's missiles when we arrived," he remembered. Sixty-five days after D-Day, this fresh crop of troops was loaded onto small ships and sailed across the choppy English Channel to disembark at Omaha Beach. Moore's hometown newspaper reported that "Junie, as he was popularly known as a basketball kingpin here ... was an honor student, in fact high man in his class when he left Lafayette."

After landing at the man-made harbor, the troops made their way through France, Belgium and the Netherlands by truck and by foot, fighting off and on, always moving ahead quickly.[7] The 9th was America's northernmost army in Europe, fighting alongside the Canadians and British, which was cause for occasional confusion and "friendly fire." Arch recalled seeing one Brit without a helmet, standing proudly and fearlessly in the turret of a Churchill tank. The Englishman pulled up while the Americans were pinned down by German gunfire. "Hey chap, you need a bit of help?" he shouted down to Sgt. Moore. When Arch responded affirmatively, he used the tank to silence their opponents' gunfire.

THE GOAL WAS to fight their way toward the Rhine River. Moore's unit quickly made it to the northern side of Belgium, parallel to Cologne, Germany. Hot meals were rare at this point and it was common to sleep in damp, cold trenches, foxholes or perhaps in or under a truck. It was normal to be completely exhausted, even for these physically fit young men. They were cheered only by occasional greetings and smiles from those they were liberating, French or Belgian ladies waving small American flags, yelling out to the soldiers. The rare pieces of mail from home were treated like gold. A kind word from mom was more precious than ever before, in this cold, harsh, dangerous, mainly-male world in which they found themselves. A perfumed letter sealed with the lipsticked kiss of the girl left behind was especially treasured.

By mid-October through November, 1944, they were into very heavy combat. "I still can't believe the sheer bravery of soldiers performed before my eyes," Arch later recounted, shaking his head.[8] "But we took a good bite out of the Germans."

The fight was cold blooded killing because the Nazis made it so. Few Germans surrendered even though many probably wanted to; their comrades would shoot them in the back if they tried it. It was kill or be killed for the American liberators. "People of the strength and war-like tendencies of the Germans do not give in," declared the Supreme Commander, Gen. Dwight D. Eisenhower. "They must be beaten into the ground."

Armed with two .45 pistols and an M-1 rifle, Arch found himself "smack-dab in front of the Siegfried Line," as he phrased it. It was the greatest challenge the Americans had encountered in the European theater since the Normandy Invasion. The Siegfried, Germany's last major line of defense, bore no resemblance to the French Maginot Line, through which Hitler's troops easily penetrated in 1940, like a hot knife through melted butter. Military historians have faulted Eisenhower for not simply going around the German fortification, for wasting so many American lives trying to penetrate and destroy it.

In *Citizen Soldier*, author Stephen Ambrose quotes a Captain Cooper.

"The Siegfried Line was undoubtedly the most formidable man-made defense ever contrived. Its intricate series of dragon's teeth, pillboxes, interconnected communication trenches, gun pits and foxholes in depth, supported by an excellent road net and backed up by a major autobahn system that ran back to Cologne, Dusseldorf and other manufacturing sites less than 50 kilometers to the east, provided the Germans with not only an excellent defense system but also a base from which to launch a major offensive." The pillboxes, Ambrose explained, "were half underground, with cannon and machines guns and ammunition storage rooms and living quarters for the defenders, typically about fifteen soldiers." He added, "The U.S. Army had no preparation, no training for attacking the Siegfried Line or driving the Germans out of villages [that were part of the Line in some places]."

What Arch remembered most was all the concrete. About that subject Ambrose wrote, "Hitler, whose faith in reinforced cement never wavered, a result of his World War I experiences, poured a lot of it into the Siegfried in this area." Hitler's concrete was highly resistant to bombs and mortar and made it even more difficult for the American ground troops.

The Germans would also fill the fields in front of the Line with S-mines, or "Bouncing Betties," which could kill, tear off a leg, or—just as fearful—deprive a young soldier of his manhood. "Behind the minefields were the dragon's teeth," Ambrose added. "Interspersed among the teeth were minefields, barbed wire, and pillboxes that were virtually impenetrable by artillery and set in such a way as to give the Germans crossing fire across the entire front. The only way to take those pillboxes was for the infantry to get behind them and attack the rear entry."

To get through those minefields, Sgt. Moore would have his men ride or follow the Churchill tanks when possible. With heavy iron pitches on front of them, the tanks would detonate the mines, making it safe to proceed through the fields.

They would lob grenades into many a German trench, or just kill their enemy with rifle fire. Occasionally, not often, there would be one who would surrender. "One German came to me with terror in his eyes," Arch recalled quietly, his eyes tearing up as he remembered the scene. "He had his gun down, hands up, and he was pointing to his wedding band. I couldn't kill that man. He had a wife and children he wanted to return to. I got him out of there, but we had to wipe everyone else out [in that area]."

Sgt. Moore lost several of his men, as the weeks of battle with the Germans took their toll. But for some, it wasn't death or physical injury that allowed their exit from the battle zone. One Alabama soldier "was just mean as hell," Arch remembered, laughing. "He promised that Hitler was never going to meet a guy like him. If he didn't like what someone said, he'd just pop 'em in the jaw!" But surprisingly, when the bullets started flying, the Southern boy was found "crouched in a trench, in convulsions," Moore recalled, shaking his head. "He just lost his mind." The Alabama soldier had to be sent to the rear.

A couple of fresh new soldiers arrived to replace the ones lost from Moore's platoon. One was a barrel-chested, second generation Italian-American boy, just eighteen and from Arch's mother's hometown of Mannington, to whom Moore took an immediate liking. Lester S. "Leck" Regillo also felt the same way about his new "Sarge."[9]

"We were buddies," Regillo smiled, sixty years later.

The Sergeant wasn't so sure about Leck's fighting capabilities, however. The replacement troops were green, untested, unproven in battle. Although just twenty-one himself, Arch then thought "they were so young!" Oftentimes the "old guys" wouldn't even talk much to the new men; they didn't want to get attached to them because they often did something careless and got themselves killed early on. But, after a few firefights, the new soldiers showed what they were made of, and Sgt. Moore and the "veterans" were glad to have them along. They bonded quickly.

On October 9, 1944, Arch was able to send his parents a rare telegram: "God bless you. All well and safe. All my love = Arch Moore."

Author Bevin Alexander explained the "big picture" of what was going on at the time. "Patton's 3rd Army was to drive through the Saar to Frankfurt, while, north of the Ardennes, Courtney Hodge's 1st Army and the new 9th Army under William Simpson [the Army in which Sgt. Moore served] were to thrust eastward from Aachen to Cologne and Bonn," he wrote. "Patton gained Metz on December 13, but was stopped cold at the Siegfried line short of the Saar. In the effort, Patton's army lost 27,000 men."[10]

IT WAS NEAR THE VILLAGE of Geilenkirchen, Germany, close to Thanksgiving Day, that "we got into the hard stuff," Moore remembered. "At first, the colonel let my men have a five day rest, because we'd been in such tough fighting. But two days into it, they said, 'Sarge, we're going to need your platoon.' We were brought back into the front line." Arch continued, "I put them on the back of a half dozen Churchills. The Germans were firing 88 mm artillery shells at us, which would lift those big tanks right off the ground, making it difficult to hang on."

On November 20, 1944, Sgt. Moore's thirty-six-member platoon jumped into a trench for the night, not far from the face of the Siegfried Line. "I told them we would cut out at dawn; that 'when I give the signal, I am going to be the first man out of these trenches. I hope we can carry out our mission without too much damage to us, but we may never see each other again.'" Sixty years later, Moore could still picture the scene in his mind, the fear and apprehension in the eyes of his men. Some, however, were gung-ho to get on with it, get it over with, even knowing the odds for survival were not good. This promised to be an old-fashioned, brutal, bloody, frontal attack, just like ancient wars of the Roman era, the beaches of Normandy or the fields of Gettysburg had been. The Germans were hidden, well-dug in, and they could cause fatalities very quickly, without warning. It was almost certain to be a suicide mission.

Nerves didn't allow for much, if any, sleep in the trenches. The American boys were thinking of family and home, a turkey dinner they would miss that week, and hoping they would make it back home, that they would have something for which to be thankful on that day. They hoped that they could just perform bravely, as trained, and not disgrace themselves. These, after all, were just boys—tough as they had become—scared and more than a little homesick. Some were nauseated, with knots in their stomachs and in cold sweats.

Most of Moore's platoon was armed with M-1 rifles fitted with bayonets. They also carried hand grenades. Sgt. Moore put a soldier with his lone 50-caliber machine gun on his right, another with the lone automatic Browning rifle on his left.

When dawn broke the next day, they got word that the attack was to begin. "I started moving through the trenches," Arch reminisced slowly, softly and sadly. "Some were crying. Some were anxious to go; they went with joy. Some had utter fear in their eyes; they went with great trepidation. It wasn't easy to get them to leave the safety of the trenches."

But with great bravado and encouragement to them, Sgt. Moore formed a stirrup with his hands, ordered each to put his foot in it, and threw them out of the trench, one-by-one, onto their bellies, rifles poised.

"Then I yelled, 'Follow me!' and up we went, on our feet, firing like mad and [the Germans] are firing back! We were running, crawling, ducking, and standing up again.

"We hadn't gone fifty yards when my machine gunner took a bullet between the eyes. I lost my firepower then and there." He continued, "It was a fierce battle. We were losing men left and right. But we had no choice but to continue." As they made forward progress, a few yards at a time, all they could sometimes see of the Germans–secluded in their concrete bunkers, pillboxes and buildings–were flashes of firepower aimed at them.

WHEN THE BATTLE had progressed another hour after the loss of his machine gunner, what was left of Arch's platoon was walking quietly and cautiously across a German farmer's sugar beet field. In the cold, wintry, November rain, their boots broke the silence with repeated "squish, squish, squish" sounds in the mud.

Momentarily, Sgt. Moore turned his head to check on his Browning rifleman when, without warning, the silence was broken by a "RAT-a-TAT-TAT!" It was German machine guns firing at them.

A hot bullet tore through Arch Moore's face. It ripped through his tongue, exiting the left side of his jaw, with blood, bone, teeth and flesh spraying from his head, and knocking him violently and instantly onto the clumps of the muddy German soil. "Had I not turned my head just at that moment, it would have struck me directly [through his mouth, into his spinal column] and killed me," Moore believed.

His buddy from Mannington, Pvt. Regillo, was standing next to him when Sgt. Moore was struck by the machine gun bullet. "Two German machine guns caught us in a crossfire," Leck explained. Amazingly, he said, despite the fact that part of his face had just been blown away, *Arch Moore kept trying to get back up and charge ahead.* "Blood was spurting out of him. It looked to me like he'd been hit in the neck and it was a fatal wound." Moore was bleeding profusely; it didn't look good for Leck's friend. "I said, 'Arch, stay down, you've been hit bad!' I had to physically hold him down. I guess he was in shock. I kept saying to him, 'You gotta stay down! If you get up they'll cut you in two!'" Bullets were flying above them from, forcing the platoon to hug the ground; they couldn't get any lower.

When asked sixty years later why he insisted on trying to get up and keep fighting the Germans after taking such a hit–what was going on in his mind at the moment–whether it was just an adrenaline rush pushing him onward–Moore had an explanation. *"I had other people to worry about."* He was nearly killed, but he was still thinking about the men who had been entrusted to his command. Moreover, he confessed, he had no idea how badly he'd been wounded. "I couldn't see myself. I didn't realize the side of my face was gone. I was as numb as can be."

After falling, Arch could only remember hearing, "They hit the Sarge!" From that point, he drifted in and out of consciousness. The numbness quickly wore off, replaced by intense, unbearable pain. The Army had provided these front line soldiers with capsules of morphine for just such occasions, so Arch injected himself with it more than once. "There was no way they could get medics in there to us [immediately]. Even with a Red Cross armband, the Germans would shoot them."

Regillo recalled that, soon after Sgt. Moore was struck down, the position on the shanties from which the shots were fired was "called in" and American artillery made quick work of it. The Germans who had shot Moore were killed. "Then we had to go on [and leave the dead and wounded behind]. We had to take another village. We called for medics [to help Sgt. Moore] but I didn't know when they would get there. We couldn't wait on them. From the look of his wound, I expected him to die before they got to him." Leck would not see Arch for several years thereafter. "In fact, I said to another guy from our outfit after the war, 'I guess Arch Moore didn't make it,' and was really surprised when he told me Arch had survived."

Moore lay on the soggy, wintry-cold German beet field, with his face torn apart and severe blood loss, for several hours that day. At some point, his two decades of life flashed in front of him, as if he was going to die.

Many did die. *Thirty three of his 36-member platoon would be killed that day.*

Before his fellow troops could rescue him, the Germans temporarily retook the area in which he and others lay. They moved about, inspecting American bodies to make sure they were all dead, ruthlessly shooting them if there was any sign of life. They didn't want to face them again in some future battle. When a German kicked Sgt. Moore, rolling his body over with his boot, Arch did what any sensible and prudent person would do: *he played dead*. The brutal German soldier walked away and he was safe for a time.

Finally, to his great relief, Sgt. Moore heard a voice shout out in English, "Do we have anybody else here?" But with a torn tongue and weak from blood loss, Arch could not even speak a reply.

Fortunately, another nearby survivor yelled, "I think the Sarge is still alive." A medic crawled over to Moore, grabbing his trembling hand. He realized when he saw Arch's terrible condition that he couldn't talk, but assured him, "You'll be all right. I'll have you out of here." Then, moving with difficulty on their stomachs, the medic dragged Arch into a concrete gutter, "the belly of one of the Siegfried Line fortresses," for temporary safety from the Germans. Soon the Jeep ambulance, with no windshield and two stretchers, was bouncing along, transporting Sgt. Moore and another wounded soldier to the regimental hospital. As the medical Jeep was getting him to treatment and safety, Arch could still hear and feel artillery fire around him.

Arch would discover that the soldier on the other cot was Max Henderson, of Sharples, West Virginia. Unable to respond verbally, Sgt. Moore enthusiastically pointed his thumb to his chest, as to say, "I'm from West Virginia, too!"[11]

At the field hospital, Arch was tagged "Z-1," meaning that he was destined to return to the Zone Interior, the United States, for treatment as soon as possible. The West Virginia connections continued, however: Moore would later discover that his attending surgeon was from Elizabeth, West Virginia, and "a good Republican."

BACK HOME in Moundsville, it was a week before Arch's family would learn of his dire situation. Telegrams were the means by which bad news, such as a son being killed, injured or missing in action, was announced to the family. Neighbors would know something terrible had happened when they would see a Western Union messenger bicycling to a family's home during the war.

"I was at the ballet school," remembered Arch's mother, Genevieve. "I went to this little restaurant for lunch." The owner of the restaurant bought her an extra-special meal, telling her she wanted Mrs. Moore to "eat a real good dinner." Arch's mother thought to herself as she returned to the ballet school, "Why did she do that? She had never done it before. I thought she wanted to be nice to me. But at the school, a neighbor phoned and told me she had seen a Western Union messenger at our house.

"Meanwhile, Miss Florence Black told our big class of 16- and 17-year olds–whom we'd had since they were four-year-olds, 'Mrs. Moore will be back in a little while. There's been a telegram about her son Arch, from whom she hasn't heard in weeks. Now, don't any of you let on when she comes into the room.' But the minute I went in the door, they all broke down and cried. They couldn't help it." Sis ran home as quickly as she could; good or bad, she wanted to know. Her heart was pounding as she ran into the house and tore open the awaiting message from the Army.

The telegram could have been much worse. At least it didn't read, "We regret to inform you..." But it wasn't good. It told the family that their son and brother had been severely wounded. That may mean he wouldn't be coming home, that he might be one of thousands of American boys buried on a foreign battlefield, but at least there was a glimmer of hope. There were no details, however, so the anxiety of not knowing was very intense. What had happened? Where were his wounds? Would he make it? Had he lost limbs? Imagination can be even worse than reality in such situations.

While his wife was still at the dance studio, expecting the worst, Arch, Sr. had gone to get neighbors, friends and relatives to share their grief and give them comfort, as if it was a wake. For all they knew, it could be; Arch, Jr. may be dying or dead by now; news from Europe and the Pacific traveled slowly. "When I got home, my living and dining rooms were filled with my wonderful neighbors," continued Mrs. Moore. "Harry, our son and Joy, our daughter, came in and they looked killed. I sank in the chair."[12]

"I came home from basketball practice," remembered brother Harry. "My mother met me at the door, holding the telegram. It devastated the whole family, especially Mom and Dad, not knowing what's happening over there."

In brief articles, the Moundsville and Wheeling newspapers reported that the son of Mr. and Mrs. Arch Moore of Third Street, "a stellar Trojan basketball performer of a few seasons back," had been "severely wounded."

Sgt. Moore was transferred to division headquarters in Liege, Belgium where that West Virginia native and surgeon, Col. Tom Davis, gave him personalized, special attention. "Sergeant, you're slated to go back to the States but if you waive that right, I believe I can make you good as new," he offered Arch.

"On the battlefield you want to live," Moore observed, philosophically, "and if you're wounded, you want to be good as new." He readily accepted the offer and Dr. Davis artfully fulfilled his promise. He restructured Arch's face, laced it with copper wiring, anchoring it to his teeth so it could heal. He reconstructed his jaw which had been "broken completely," and sewed up his tongue, securing it for several weeks to a stationary platform of sorts, to hold it in place while it healed. Moore had lost three teeth from the force of the bullet. Another tooth was removed by the doctors so he could be tube-fed a liquid diet. He was transferred to Bassingbourn Air Force Base in England for a long recovery period. It would be many weeks before he could speak a word.

And public speaking would eventually be part of his therapy. During those months of recovery and rehabilitation, with some difficulty and sounding like he had a mouthful of cotton, he gave speeches to American soldiers still arriving in France and then in the medieval city of Marburg, Germany. "I had 'been there and done that,' so I was somewhat of a local hero."

The wound would leave Arch with some permanent disability, including lifelong paralysis of the left side of his face that few would notice. Some metal dental work could always be noticed if he smiled widely. But he did indeed look "good as new," as his surgeon had promised. Six decades later, Arch Moore would see a Divine hand in his protection and survival, and not only on that battlefield. "My Lord saved my life three times," is how he described it.[13] "I always felt my Maker saved my life by getting me out [of the war] when He did," Moore added. "Because, within ten to twelve days [of being evacuated], the Battle of the Bulge began and our whole division was overrun."

Arch Moore may have been remembering this difficult chapter of his life when he made a Veterans Day speech as governor on Nov. 9, 1985. He spoke of the indebtedness the nation had to those who fought, died or were wounded to keep our nation free. "We who have known war up close ... scorched battlefields ... fallen comrade ... fear ... weariness ... anger ... we do not ... we cannot ... forget." In what sounded autobiographical, the Governor added:

> Is there a veteran among us, who as a young person in combat ... physically exhausted, ill, or injured ... did not ask, "What am I fighting for? Is it worth it?" At those moments, a vision of a home ... a family ... somewhere in the mountains of West Virginia ... filled our minds. We knew what we were fighting for and it was worth the sacrifice. Although the ultimate price was not required of us, it was required of many ... The cost of freedom is always high.

Shelley Moore later would quote her husband as saying that this near-death experience had a profound impact on him. Having survived the ordeal, Arch dedicated the remainder of his life to serving others. Apparently, he made God a promise as he lay bleeding in that German beet field. He felt his life had been spared for a reason, for some appointment with destiny. (But he would "never trade on any" of his war hero record in his future political campaigns, his friend Tom McCoy would note; Moore would not mention his war experience on the campaign stump, even when he was up against opponents who had avoided military service.)

As with President Eisenhower, whose admiration of Hitler's autobahn system spawned America's Interstate highway system, Arch Moore brought back some attractive concepts from the technologically advanced, if morally depraved, Fatherland. "I obtained some of my bridge-building ideas from Germany," he later confessed. "The stayed-girder bridges in Germany inspired my design for the ones we built in Huntington and Weirton." And, without question, the leadership skills and the coolness and calmness under pressure which Arch would later exhibit in times of challenges and tribulation, were honed on the battlefields of Europe. Later crises, of which there would be many, would pale in comparison to lying in the mud with a bullet hole through one's face.

IN JANUARY 1946, a Moundsville paper reported, "Junior Moore wrote that his only desire is to get home before the basketball season closes so he can see brother Moo play."

But it would be March of 1946 before the military shipped him home, through Baltimore. His uncle, Harry Jones, picked up the returning war hero at the Wheeling bus station. "Arch came to Grandma Jones's house first," recalled his brother. "She was so excited! His face looked good—you had to look closely to even see any scar."

Arch Moore was now a fully mature, battle-seasoned man. He returned with a Purple Heart, a Bronze Star for valor and three campaign stars, "medals representative of three bloody fights." He was glad to be alive.

The smiling young man relaxed and rested up, catching up on family and friends for a couple months. But things had changed since he was gone, he could not go back to the way it was, nor did he want to do so. He'd learned a lot about himself, about the world; he'd gained a lot of confidence in his own ability and leadership skills. His mind and body were toughened by what he'd been through. Arch would not be returning to the pipeline work or the factory. He wanted to attack life with enthusiasm and do something great.

Specifically, he wanted to pursue that dream of becoming a lawyer. In June, he enrolled in summer school at West Virginia University (then the state's only university), attending on the G.I. Bill, as were tens of thousands of returning American servicemen and women.

Chapter 2 Notes

1. - The pipeline, sometimes called "The Big Inch Pipeline," is still in use today, transporting natural gas.

2. - "Spreads" were what they called a stretch of pipeline, usually several miles in length.

3. - Actually, the War Department had made the decision earlier, on Feb. 18, 1944, that 110,000 ASTPers would be returned to the line of duty by April 1, according to Keefer.

4. - Commanded by Gen. Alexander Bolling.

5. - Commanded by Gen. William Simpson.

6. - An ASTP roommate said Kissinger "didn't just read books, he devoured them. He'd be slouching over a book and suddenly explode with an indignant, German-accented, 'Bull s–t!' blasting the author's reasoning. Then he'd tear it apart, explosive words prevailing, and make sense of it." Other ASTP alumni who later had illustrious careers, besides Moore and Kissinger, included New York Mayor Ed Koch, think-tanker Herman Kahn, CBS news man (and the History Channel's) Roger Mudd, sports commentator Heywood Hale Broun, author Gore Vidal, actor/producer Mel Brooks, and four-star Gen. James Harlinger, retired NORAD commander. Kissinger would not forget the classmate who'd helped him with his knapsack. In 1974, as Nixon's top foreign affairs assistant, he arranged for then Gov. Moore to go to China on a trade mission, one of the first Americans permitted to do that.

7. - Wrote Keefer, "Despite great credentials, extremely few [of the ASTPers] gained the chance to attend Officers Candidate School, and practically none got non-commissioned officer ratings until they reached combat zones, where heavy casualties created vacancies for them to fill." He continued, "If anything, the green ASTPers were given an extremely hard time by the oldline regulars who considered them a bunch of smart-ass college kids wanting to steal their stripes and obviously needing to be taught what the 'real' Army was all about. The ASTPers made it worse for themselves by sticking together like glue. As one surprised company commander put it, 'What kind of soldiers deal out bridge hands during their ten-minute training breaks?' Once in combat, however, such prejudice generally disappeared."

8. - Like most other World War II veterans, Moore preferred not to talk about his war experiences and rarely spoke of it. Certainly, no one heard him ever boast of his exploits, on the campaign trail or elsewhere. It was only with much prying that he finally revealed his story for this book, occasionally choking up with emotion as he relayed it.

9. - Regillo would become a lifetime supporter of Arch Moore, and was his unofficial congressional campaign manager in the Mannington area, where he worked as a bartender for the local Moose Club. Regillo and his four brothers, also brave veterans, would get a bridge named for them.

10. - *How Hitler Could Have Won World War II,* Copyright 2000 by Bevin Alexander.

11. - When Henderson and Moore saw each other the next time, it was on High Street in Morgantown, where they were attending WVU. They did what few men dared to do in those days–they embraced. "I was president of my fraternity (Beta Theta Pi) and Max was vice president, but no one knew about our relationship [on the battlefield]," Arch fondly recalled of his friend. Max would become an executive with the U.S. Steel Corporation.

12. - *West Virginia Mountain Messenger,* October 1980.

13. - The second time Arch's life would be spared was in the late 1960s, when, as a congressman on an inspection tour in Vietnam, his chopper was hit by Vietcong gun fire but landed safely. The third was a well-publicized crash on a Sunday afternoon before the November 1968 election, when his helicopter struck a pole and slammed down, causing him injury. He keeps a souvenir piece of the tail rudder in his office, to date.

Chapter Three
WVU and Shelley

The West Virginia University of 1946 would be almost unrecognizable to today's students.

The entire school was restricted to one downtown campus, nestled atop the Morgantown hills, overlooking the green Monongahela River. Opened in 1867, as one of President Lincoln's land grant institutions, WVU had recently doubled its size to six thousand because of the sudden influx of veterans like Arch Moore, who were returning from Europe and the Pacific. As result, classrooms were tight and many of the faculty had to teach a few subjects outside their normal field. It was still small enough that one could become acquainted with many of his classmates, if he chose to do so.

The greatest difference was the way in which campus life was conducted. Sororities and fraternities dominated; more than half of the students were loyal members of one. For most, the frat houses were where they resided, took their meals, socialized and made lifelong friends. Campus politics was split between the Student Party, representing the Greek organizations, and the Independent Party, with whom the non-Greeks aligned.

It was a more sophisticated, genteel time on all college campuses in those days, including Morgantown's. The administration rigidly controlled student behavior to the extent possible. According to Ed Flowers (Class of '52, student body president and later WVU vice president), Dean of Women Edna Arnold was especially strict with coeds. "Women had to be back into their rooms by seven o'clock each evening unless they had a pass to go to the library, in which case they had to wear a long raincoat. Both sororities and fraternities had to have Dean Arnold's permission to sponsor a social function." To the Homecoming Games, male students wore sport jackets and ties, and women dressed formally, with heels. Arch Moore remembered that some coeds even wore fur coats to the games. "We did that out of respect to visiting alumni," laughed Flowers. "We behaved ourselves better on that weekend."

In a commencement address given there on May 19, 1985, Moore would note several of the differences when he was on the WVU campus, including the fact that students could not wear shorts. He remembered building floats for parades and "burning midnight oil the night before exams." He told the graduates, "Our student union was a salvage building from World War II. The whole campus was downtown and Evansdale was nothing but a farm. The medical school, the Creative Art Center, a new Coliseum, the law school building, the School of Engineering and Agriculture Buildings, the P.R.T., the Mountainlair and a new football stadium were only dreams."[1]

An array of extracurricular activities were open, including drama, a debate team, the YMCA, women's honoraries, and all sorts of service organizations. A senior honorary, called Mountain, was open by invitation only to those who had proven themselves in other clubs or student government. "The one who actively sought it was likely to be denied forever," Flowers explained. Two years of ROTC was then mandatory for males and another two years was required if one actually wanted to enter the military as an officer.

HAVING HELPED his nation defeat Hitler and make Western Europe safe for democracy, Arch Moore landed on the WVU campus with equal enthusiasm. He entered school as a junior, with the hours of credit he was able to transfer from Lafayette. Since he planned to go on to law school after completing his Bachelor's degree, he majored in political science, attending most of his classes in WVU's most familiar and second-oldest building, Woodburn Hall. He soon found himself to be an extremely popular, well-known, heavily-involved member of the student body.

With no car, he spent most of the next five years on campus, occasionally hitchhiking or catching a ride with friends back to Moundsville to see his folks. His brother would eventually join him on campus, becoming even better known than Arch, because Moo would become an exciting WVU basketball star (he still holds the career foul shot record).

Arch was eager to see a WVU coed from Glen Dale who'd corresponded faithfully with him during his service in Europe. He was crushed when she told him she'd found another, whom she planned to marry.

In the first few weeks, Arch roomed in a dormitory but, by autumn, roommate Joe Roberts asked him to pledge his fraternity, Beta Theta Pi. This decision would prove to be a significant one. Moving into the Beta House, Arch was elected its president the next year.[2] Fellow Beta Bill Ritchie remembered that there were still lingering effects of Moore's terrible war wound—his speech was still imperfect.

As he'd done in high school, Arch managed a successful political campaign, helping to elect a student body president. He became the "emperor" of Sphinx, a junior honorary service and leadership organization. In his senior year, would become the Summit of Mountain, the invitation-only honorary of honoraries. Arch was president of the Council of Fraternity Presidents. He wrote the first WVU student body constitution.

A Mountaineer statue, in buckskin and with his musket, was a dream of Moore's. He organized a carnival at the Field House which raised $6000 to have it sculpted. His original plan was to erect the symbol atop the WVU Library where it could be seen by all, but that idea was not well received ("I think they feared that it would be a hazard to aircraft there," he joked).[3]

Said Flower, "Everybody [on campus] knew Arch Moore. He ran everything." Arch was always into extra-curricular activities, helping people, encouraging them, doing favors, putting projects together, getting things done. He was not universally loved, however. Even then Moore had a "big ego," Flowers recalled, which sometimes put him at odds with other student activists.

As Summit, Moore would also draw the ire of Dean Arnold and President Irwin Stewart by starting a new tradition on campus. In the autumn of 1947, he initiated "Mountaineer Day," which evolved into Mountaineer Week.

Why? "Because I felt we didn't have unity on the campus and I wanted something fun, to bring us all together," Moore recalled. "We had freshmen, upperclassmen and a vast number of veterans who had served in the war. There just wasn't much interaction between the groups."

On campus for Mountaineer Day, remembered Arch, "Everyone wore straw hats, jerseys, bib overalls, blackened their teeth," as if they had just come down out of the hollow or off the ridge. Noted Flowers, "Today, it is a cultural heritage thing. Then, it was the students' weekend to 'let it all hang out,' when you dressed in hillbilly garb." He laughed, "The administration was trying to shed the [hillbilly] image, and here Arch comes with this!" In fact, Dean Arnold scolded the future governor, "Arch Moore, you have ruined in one day everything I've worked on!"

The students and faculty thought otherwise, however; they greeted Moore's idea with great enthusiasm. The October 28, 1947, issue of *The Daily Athenaeum* quoted a professor saying, "It's pleasing to see the student body show such a manifestation of spirit. We haven't seen enthusiasm of this extent since pre-war days." A November 1, 1947, editorial in that student paper called Mountaineer Day "one of the most successful programs initiated in recent University history."

Ira "Sandy" Latimer, Jr. was a WVU freshman in 1949. His first encounter with Arch was at a "thuse," or pep rally, the night before one of the Mountaineer Days. "It was at a bonfire on the drill field, where the

Mountainlair now stands. [Arch] was already a powerful speaker, firing the student body up for the big football game the next day." That year, the first beard-growing competition started.

"We knew [Mountaineer Day] was a success when two fabricated outhouses were rolled onto the football field," Arch told *The Mountaineer Spirit* magazine in a 2002 interview. "When the first full roll of toilet paper made it up to the 20th row of the bleachers, everybody was in an uproar. We had a great time."

"Arch was a happy-go-lucky guy," recalled classmate Richard Rundle. "He was one of those charming people everybody liked. He was very popular." Others, though, began observing another side of Arch Moore–a Ferris Beueller type character–a handsome, magnetic and charismatic young man, but one who could be a bit of a con artist—yet one whose "victims" didn't object, still being very much attracted and sympathetic to him. Despite his mischievousness, his sometimes manipulation of them, they wanted to like him and wanted him to like them in return. He was developing a trait that would propel him through many years in political life.

A story illustrative of that aspect circulated in Arch Moore lore for years, and it was traced to Charleston carpet store owner Bill Smith. "We were suite mates at the Beta Theta Pi house. Arch gave me a great deal of my education; he taught me about people, life. He was three or four years older than me. My dad worked at a Charleston warehouse and would send me tubes of toothpaste. But every time I needed to brush my teeth, I had to go to Arch's room to retrieve it [because Arch had swiped it from his room]," Smith recalled. "And Arch would always say, 'What are you doing, taking my toothpaste?'

"Being the brainiac that I am, I finally took a nail file and carved an X into the cap. But when I went that evening to Arch's room to again retrieve my toothpaste, as usual he insisted, 'That's *my* toothpaste!' But I said, 'No, Arch, I've got ya this time—I filed an X in the top so I'd know it's mine.'

"Arch looked me right in the eye and replied without hesitating, '*I* filed that X!' My head just dropped; I was beaten to a pulp," Bill Smith chuckled.

On other occasions, Bill would go to Moore's closet to recover his tuxedo shirts, even a white dinner jacket that Arch had "borrowed." His suite mate had even marked out Smith's name and written his own on the label. (Despite those incidents, Smith remained Moore's lifetime friend and supporter, through thick and thin. "He's still West Virginia's greatest governor.") Moore could be an extremely persuasive individual even then,

Smith reiterated. "He could be telling me something and my mind would be saying, 'No, no, no,' but my head would be nodding up and down. I knew he was wrong, but I had to agree." Smith continued, "But he did this sort of thing to rile me, I guess–to have fun. He had a great deal of fun getting the best of somebody, with his pranks."

UPON COMPLETION OF his Bachelor's degree at WVU, Arch turned his attention to the next venture. He'd go to law school.

Said classmate Gary Joe Triplett, "I think it was Arch's mother who influenced him to pursue a legal career more than anyone else. I think she compared his dad's career in the factory to the successful law practice of his Uncle Everett Moore. His mother thought Arch could also do well as a lawyer. From the time he was young, I think she pushed him toward following his uncle's path."

In recent decades, law schools have sorted out applicants through a selective admissions process; it reflects poorly on that system if a student later flunks out. Those who demonstrate that they are qualified to be successful in the classroom and as lawyers—by LSAT scores, grade point averages and interviews—are admitted, usually about a third to half of those who apply.

But in the 1940s, public law schools pretty much admitted all who applied, especially in-state applicants. That was how the WVU College of Law, then located downtown, handled admissions. And then, after a rigorous, demanding, humbling first year, the faculty intentionally flunked-out two-thirds of those who entered. Only one test was given per class, upon which one's entire semester grade depended. The professors allowed the scores to sort out those who couldn't hack it. Remembered Huntington lawyer Dick Tyson, a contemporary of Moore's: "On the first day of class, new law students were warned by their professors, 'Look to your left and right. Only one of you will be here at the end of the year.' Which is precisely what happened. We started with 150 students on the first day—you could get into law school then with a C-plus average—and only fifty of us graduated. The trick was staying in; they tried to weed you out."[4]

Law school was and is taught by the Socratic method, meaning that students would study classic court cases each night and expect to be "put on the hot seat" the next day in, when a professor might ask you to stand and "brief the case" for your fellow students. For a grueling fifteen or twenty minutes, he might pelt you with questions, challenge your conclusions, sometimes even in a harsh, sarcastic, needling manner, trying to ruffle you, treat you like a judge may do in a court room someday. Get you to "think like a lawyer," to see all sides of an issue, to become analytical, even cynical.

As Arch Moore entered law school in the autumn of 1948, he had been accustomed to challenges, and the gruff, demanding law professors were nothing compared to some of the military officers under whom he had recently served. He had breezed through his undergraduate degree with no problem. His intelligence level was well above most of his fellow students. But in law school he nearly got into trouble because of his overly confident attitude.

It would have been difficult, if not impossible, to adequately study law in a rowdy, noisy frat house, so Arch moved into a dorm, becoming one of its "proctors."[5] He and a few other proctors, including Jack Whiting,[6] decided the dorm needed a television (which was a major expense in those days, even for the small, grainy black-and-white screen that was available). So they all began fund-raising. For his part, Arch made and sold baloney sandwiches to dorm residents. When enough money was raised by the group, he announced that he would handle the purchase. The residents soon discovered why he wanted to do so. It was delivered with a metal plaque on it, reading, "Courtesy of Arch A. Moore, Jr."[7] The future politician already was learning how to take personal credit for a joint effort.

As a first year law student, Arch did not initially terminate his extracurricular activities. "Once they know you'll do it, people keep calling you, they seek you out," Moore remembered about his continued campus leadership during law school. "And you can't hide it [from the faculty] because [the activities] are published in *The Daily Athenaeum*." But the law school faculty thinks a student should be devoting one hundred percent of his or her time to the study of law; they frown upon any outside activity. "I found out early that the study of law was like polishing golf skills," recalled Moore. "Law school will not tolerate being neglected. 'The law is a jealous mistress,' as they used to say."

Because he was spending so much time doing more interesting things, Arch's law school grades began to suffer. In most law classes, a student must spend the previous night reading and outlining dozens of supreme court cases, analyzing the rules of law illustrated by each; he must be prepared to answer the professor's questions about those cases or face embarrassment, even a "black mark," if he's unprepared. Classmate Richard Rundle recalled Arch as a "good student," but one who sometimes came to class unprepared. "He might walk into the classroom and casually ask, 'Dick, you got that case for me?'" Rundle recalled with a laugh.

Triplett, an excellent student and editor of Law Review, remembered an opposite incident, when Arch saved his skin one day. Joe was "on the stand" before Dean Thomas Porter Hardman in his tough Evidence class in which he wasn't satisfying Hardman with "yes" or "no" answers. Joe's brow was beginning to perspire. "Arch whispered to me, 'Tell him, it depends.' And that was exactly the answer the Dean wanted to hear—'it depends' being the answer to most legal questions.

"It was already obvious that Arch possessed a brilliant, analytical mind, an outstanding memory. However, I don't remember him being an outstanding law student," continued Triplett. "But that may have been because he was still so active on campus."

Moore agreed, a little more bluntly: "I was a mediocre law student."

The situation deteriorated to the point to which Arch was summoned to the Dean's Office. Dean Hardman, a Rhodes Scholar in his fifth decade at the school, wore tweeds and gold watch chains and smoked a pipe—the stereotypical professor of the era. "Mr. Moore," he said in his English accent, "the faculty has had a discussion about [your law school grades]. We think you have the capacity to be a great lawyer. But you have a decision to make. You must either study law or run this University. The decision is entirely yours."

Arch gulped and responded, "I get the message, sir." He ceased all campus activities and devoted himself to law school until he graduated in May of 1951. "I did keep a 'low profile' job," Moore confessed. "I kept time and checked equipment in new buildings for [WVU] Buildings & Grounds."

Arch could not resist participating in a few more ventures for his university, however. One was the Mountaineer statue project which started during Mountaineer Week in 1950. The other involved something much more significant. The legislature approved a penny-per-bottle tax on soda pop to build the state's first medical school. Both Charleston and Morgantown were vying for it, since it would be an economic boon to the areas. Moore joined a delegation of campus leaders who made the long journey to the capitol to personally petition Governor Okey Patteson to locate the med school at WVU. "Governor Patteson received us very nicely," Arch remembered. "One of the reasons I wanted it at WVU was because Pitt was beating us in football almost every year, and they were drawing men (onto the Pitt team) who wanted to go on to medical or law school. I wanted us to compete." Their lobbying efforts were successful; in 1951, Patteson announced that it would go to the northern site.[8]

WITH HIS FORCED departure from campus politics, Arch began to develop an interest in "real" politics. On Feb. 9, 1950, he attended a Women's Republican Club fund-raising dinner in Wheeling for Congressman Francis Love. A 41-year-old U.S. senator from Wisconsin was the guest speaker. No one knew it at the time, but the speech would launch the "McCarthy Era" of American history, a near-decade long crusade against Communists in U.S. government and public life, one liberals still believe was an era of fear and unnecessary suspicion, of unmerited damage to the reputation of many on the Left, a modern day witch hunt.

U. S. Senator Joseph McCarthy—a deteriorating alcoholic, an Irish Catholic who was close to Ambassador Joe Kennedy and formerly a Democrat himself—told the Wheeling crowd that America was in an "all-out battle between communistic atheism and Christianity" and that our democracy was at risk of being destroyed by "enemies from within." Most sensational, he held up a list claiming, "I have in my hand fifty-seven cases of individuals who would appear to be either card carrying members or certainly loyal to the Communist Party, but who nevertheless are still helping to shape our foreign policy..." The charge was headline news everywhere the next morning.

"Is the Truman Administration full of people loyal to the Soviet Union?" people asked themselves. The speech resonated with an American public which had been shocked to see an ailing, exhausted FDR cede half of Europe to Soviet domination at Yalta, Truman's stagnant, no-win policy in the Korean War, the loss of China to Maoist Communism, the Rosenbergs' smuggling of atomic bomb secrets to Stalin, and a general feeling that America was losing the Cold War. Despite McCarthy's abusiveness, eventual disgrace and Senate censure for his recklessness, it was proven by KGB records in the 1990s that there *were* dangerous spies working for the Soviets out of the Roosevelt and Truman White Houses in the 1940s, most prominently Alger Hiss and Harry Dexter White.

A few of Moore's contemporaries were also getting into the political arena. A. James Manchin, a friendly, flamboyant, outgoing student, was already becoming a caricature of himself. "A. James was always a candidate for some office on campus, student body president or something," remembered Flowers, with a laugh. "But he never won. He would imitate FDR or Churchill, wearing a Hamburg hat, smoking a cigar. His were always interesting campaigns." Female students threw eggs at Manchin when he was parading on Maiden Lane, near Stalnaker Hall, Flowers recalled. "No one knew whether it was something he set up to get sympathy votes." Off campus, in his nearby Marion County, A. James (known then as "Tony" or "Jimmy") got elected to the House of Delegates in 1949. It would be for only one term, however—Manchin was too far ahead of the white voters there, in his vocal support of civil rights and desegregation. The racial equality issue temporarily killed his political career.

Another who would play a major role in the Arch Moore story was a charming young man named Cecil Underwood. In 1945, while Arch was overseas, Cecil began his first term in the House of Delegates, as a Republican from Tyler County, at age twenty-two. He was an immediate hit with the Republicans, with his sharp mind, dry wit, model good looks, and smiling, easy manner. But, noted Loren Archer, an old friend of Underwood's, "He was very much still a farm boy when he first went to Charleston. He arrived in a dark suit, black dress shoes and white socks. Others had to coach him on how to dress."

At a 1946 Huntington convention, Underwood was elected president of the West Virginia Young Republicans. A teacher at Marietta College in the summer of 1947, he decided to cease working on his Master's degree and instead buy his first car to tour the state, recruiting GOP candidates for public office. He began keeping elaborate file cards on everyone he met who was interested in politics, a resource that would come in handy when he ran for governor nine years later.

Arch's Uncle Everett Moore was House Minority Leader but Cecil succeeded him in that post in 1949, at a time when there were only sixteen Republicans in the lower house. Underwood got organized, holding GOP luncheon meetings each day, uniting the few votes they controlled. "We had people who weren't even attending committee meetings. I made sure our people were well-informed and that they became more active in their committees."

Yet another who would later dominate the stage during Moore's era was getting his start. A meat cutter, gas station attendant and welder from North Carolina, Robert C. Byrd joined the Ku Klux Klan near Beckley. Later, he would say he did it so he could get into politics.[9] He got himself elected to the House of Delegates in 1946 and 1948, then the state senate for two years before becoming a congressman in 1952. He would remain in Congress until 1959, when he became a U.S. Senator, one of the longest-serving in history. Until he began seeking party leadership positions in the 1970s, Byrd would vote consistently with the Southern segregationists. He found success by taking the path opposite of Manchin's on the racial equality issue.

BUT ARCH WAS BEGINNING a new phase of his life, entering something more important and enduring than law or politics. He was about to meet his lifetime partner, who would share his hopes and dreams, make them a reality, and who would stick with him with him through good times and bad.

A few months after he hit campus, Arch's friend Zack Sterate told him, "I have a date tonight with a beautiful girl, Shelley Riley. Why don't I ask her if she has a sorority sister she can fix you up with, and we'll make it a double date?" Arch agreed and Zach phoned Shelley. She mentioned another Uniontown girl, Ann Watson. "I don't know if she'll go on a blind date or not," Shelley cautioned.

Ann ("a very attractive girl, the 'campus beauty queen,'" according to Arch) agreed to the date, however, and the four went to a movie and then Comuntzi's Restaurant on High Street for a Coke.

"But I was soon paying more attention to Shelley Riley than my own date," Arch said. "I thought, this girl is a tremendously interesting person! She was intelligent, a great conversationalist, and showed that she had a strong mind and a strong will. She was also very pretty and skinny as a rail!" Like Arch, Shelley was quite active in campus organizations and was president of the Women's Athletic Association at WVU.

Zach and Arch escorted the ladies back to their Alpha Xi Delta sorority house, but it wasn't long before Arch was on the phone to his new friend Shelley Riley. "I asked her to go to another movie and she said, 'Sure!' And we've been going to movies ever since!"

On her end, Shelley told Ann, "Hands off, I want this one!" She was as attracted to Arch ("Moo," as she and others then called him) because "he was so outgoing, and I felt an attraction to him, and him to me." About early their dating, she added, "He loved to dance and I did, too."

The relationship, he said, has been "one of intense loyalty" ever since, a statement with which all who knew the Moores agreed. Shelley, who had been on campus two years before Arch arrived, had been dating a young man from Beckley but, from that day forward, she and Arch dated no other. "She didn't look [for others] and I didn't look," Arch emphasized.

SHELLEY WAS originally named "Sadie Shelley Riley," but the first name was dropped when she began school. She was born in 1926 to Jacob Lewis and Sadie Wardlow Wellons Riley, in Miami, Florida. Her parents were Southern Baptists who grew up in Perry, Georgia. When Shelley was six weeks old, a hurricane unexpectedly blew through Miami. Her family could hear furniture blowing out of the apartment above them. Her older brother sat on the family's refrigerator during the storm, for some reason singing, "I'm sitting on top of the world." As result of the storm, "I almost died," said Shelley, explaining, "My mother was breast feeding me at the time and, the storm frightened her so much, she 'went dry' and they realized I wasn't getting nutrition."

Noticing that her brother was nine years and sister twelve years older than her, Shelley once asked her mother, "Was I adopted?" Sadie Riley replied negatively but added, "You might have been an accident."

Her father was in the tailoring business most of his life and the family moved twenty six times over the years. He moved them to Uniontown, Pennsylvania when Shelley was two or three years old. Working for Henderson Peoples of Cincinnati (who owned the Mr. Peoples retail clothing store in Charleston and in other locations), Jacob Riley would take wool swatches to coal camps throughout the tri-state area. "The miners, who were accustomed to buying from company stores, loved to get those custom-made suits," Shelley noted. It was an era in which men still got "dressed up," wearing fine business suits to church, weddings, funerals, school functions and other social events.

When Shelley was in the third grade, the Rileys moved to Morgantown. The Depression was in full force and Shelley's older brother and sister could get in-state tuition at WVU. When they finished (and Shelley was an eighth grader), the family returned to Uniontown. "I never felt lonely," Shelley remembered, about being uprooted for five years. "I made a lot of friends [in Morgantown], many of whom I stay in touch with to this day."

She played some intramural basketball in high school back in Uniontown. The 1944 edition of the Maroon and White yearbook shows a pretty young lady who looked a lot like Lucille Ball. It listed a host of activities for Shelley Riley, including the Dramatic Club, National Honor Society, Spanish Club, Student Senate, Beta Tri-Hi-Y, the student newspaper, and many others, including "office assistant." About the latter, "They teased me about being Assistant Principal John Dunn's pet."

As a WVU student, Shelley would be just as busy, pledging her sorority in 1944, and serving as president of the Women's Recreation Association.

After Shelley and Arch completed their undergraduate degrees in 1948 (his a B.S. in political science, hers in education with a math major), Shelley taught a year at a Fairchance, Pennsylvania public school. "I taught seventh, eighth and ninth grade math and algebra. I was scared to death and they knew it. It was tremulous times for me—I had trouble with discipline." She remembered one disruptive student with whom she had to deal. "I found a big leather paddle in my desk drawer. I called him to the front of the room and told him to bend over. The student was ten inches taller than I was and said, 'I will not!' I took him to the principal who just let him sit in the office."

Arch and Shelley were married in August of 1949, during his second year of law school at the Great Bethel Baptist Church in Uniontown and had their reception up on the nearby mountain at The Summit. They did not yet have a car of their own, so they borrowed one from a relative and left the reception for their honeymoon. Shelley laughed, "I was always the worry wart, so I cautioned, 'Moo, don't go too fast down this mountain.' But then he was going so slow and I said, 'Well, you can go faster than that.' Arch said, 'I'm driving it as fast as it will go!' We discovered that someone had removed several of the spark plug wires as a prank."

They spent their first night as a married couple in Pittsburgh and then flew down to Virginia Beach for three days.

Shelley's siblings had both married Georgians. Her mother liked Arch, but noted all the changes marrying him meant for her daughter. After politics became part of their lives, Sadie teased her, "You married a damn Yankee, switched from Baptist to Methodist, and Democrat to Republican. What next, are you going to sell your soul?" (Shelley, who would keep her soft, genteel, gracious Southern style and many of her Baptist principles throughout her life, assured her mother "I was not going to completely abandon the Democrats. I just had to register Republican to vote for my husband in the primaries.")

After returning from their honeymoon, the couple rented a small, third floor (South Park) Morgantown apartment as their first marital home. Shelley would never return to teaching full-time (she thereafter would substitute occasionally). She worked their first year of marriage in the film section of the WVU Library.[10]

West Virginia University would always hold a very special place in the hearts of Arch and Shelley, according to their daughter. "Both of my parents said those were the best four years of their lives," noted Shelley Moore Capito. "I always remember them taking us to the Beta House during WVU Homecoming." They loved the memories of the campus, the events in which they'd participated, and the hundreds of lifetime friends they made while in Morgantown. "It was a great time to be there, after the war," Capito added.

Arch finished his education in May of 1951 (L.L.B.) and was immediately admitted to the West Virginia Bar with his classmates, state bar exams then being waived for in-state graduates. "There was never any question what he would do next," remembered Mrs. Moore. They would move back to Moundsville where Arch would practice law with his uncle, Everett Moore.

Chapter 3 Notes

1. - *Third Term The Official Papers of the Honorable Arch A. Moore, Jr.*, copyright 2002 by the State of West Virginia.

2. - He would later stock his gubernatorial administration with fellow Betas.

3. - It would be more than two decades before fund-raising permitted the erection of the statue. As governor, Arch Moore, along with Mountaineer mascot Bob Lowe, would unveil the Mountaineer Statue at its current location, in front of the WVU Mountainlair, in October of 1971.

4. - Dick Tyson, Sept. 6, 2005.

5. - When asked the name of the WVU dorm in which he resided, Arch, in his eighties by now, could no longer remember. But he could not resist some sarcasm, "Oh, it's probably been renamed The Robert C. Byrd Dormitory by now, like everything else in this state!"

6. - Whiting was another decorated war veteran, of both World War II and, later the Korean War, flying 32 combat missions as a bombardier/navigator in the 8th Air Force, earning the Distinguished Flying Cross.

7. - Frances Whiting interview, July 27, 2004.

8. - This would be the first of several times Arch Moore would help decide the location of a West Virginia medical school. He would later start one at Marshall University, in Lewisburg and, with a million dollars in seed money from a Charleston philanthropist, eventually would bring a WVU Med School branch to the capital, as well. He would appoint former Governor Patteson to the newly-created Board of Regents in 1969, upon becoming governor himself.

9. - According to *The Washington Post* and Byrd's own autobiography, he recruited 150 of his friends to form a chapter of the Ku Klux Klan in Crab Orchard, where he was working as a butcher. The Beckley-area Klan elected him their "Exalted Cyclops" and later, as a Kleagle, he continued recruiting for the Klan. Byrd always insisted that his Klan activity had not been racist, but had been simply to meet important and powerful people and, interestingly, it was the national Klan leadership that got him into politics. He continued showing his true colors, however, when he fought Truman's desegregation of the military in the late-1940s. Byrd wrote to one of the Senate's most notorious segregationists, Theodore Bilbo (D-Miss.), that he would never fight in the armed forces "with a Negro by my side." In the letter, which was typical of his attitude, "Rather I should die a thousand times, and see Old Glory trampled in the dirt never to rise again, than to see this beloved land of ours become degraded by race mongrels." –June 19, 2005, *The Washington Post.* Of course, Byrd hadn't even served in the military with whites or dark-skinned Americans: when he was eligible for the draft during World War II, he went off to the Norfolk, Virginia shipyards to work, which gave him a deferment. He not only did not "die a thousand times," but didn't even face death once in service of his country.

10. - In their retirement years, the Arch and Shelley Moore Foundation would contribute heavily to the WVU Library, one of their chief donations.

Chapter Four
Uncle Everett

Everett F. Moore was a leading figure in the Northern Panhandle. A graduate of the University of Virginia and the WVU College of Law, he became a Moundsville attorney in 1906, at the ripe old age of twenty-one. As part of a successful practice, he served as city attorney from 1913 to 1925. Earlier, he had jumped into politics, first being elected to the West Virginia House of Delegates in 1908, and serving off-and-on through 1948. He was elected minority leader of the House on three occasions, and served as chairman of the Judiciary Committee from 1919 to 1920, when the Republicans were in the majority. He helped his father, F.T. Moore, get elected mayor of Moundsville.

Everett was a stout, balding man, and photos show him in the three-piece suits common for a gentleman of the era. "He was flashy, he always had the biggest car on the block," recalled his nephew Arch. "He was probably five feet, ten and weighed 280 pounds. He was jovial, loveable and the smartest man I ever met–his mind was like a trigger." Everett's wife had died in the late 1930s and they had no offspring, so he just threw himself into his practice and his hobby, politics. Those two activities dominated his life. If he had a "son," it was nephew Arch.

In 1941, James Weir wrote in a local paper that Everett Moore was a great legislator who represented Marshall County well. Weir noted that the delegate had "never been partisan," nor had he tried to "punish the minority nor to take advantage of the weakness of [the Democrats] to accomplish partisan or his own ends." He was someone who did not sacrifice principle. His speeches in the House were "without rancor," but ones which drew respect and support to his positions. His "broad grin" was "not put on," Weir thought, but rather "a very sincere smile of friendship and good will."

"I got to know Everett Moore very well," said Cecil Underwood, who succeeded him as House minority leader. "He was a very astute attorney and political leader, a very effective leader when he was there. He knew the legislative process extremely well, and made effective use of parliamentary procedure. He enjoyed considerable respect by a majority of those in the Legislature." But, Underwood noted, Del. Everett Moore had a problem. "He had a drinking problem. He didn't even show up the last two weeks of his final session."[1] It was only logical and natural that Arch Moore join his well-known, well-established uncle when he finished law school in the spring of 1951. He hadn't given consideration to any other alternative. "Arch's mother had always held up his Uncle Everett as an example to him, his profession something to aspire to," thought Joe Triplett. "She didn't want him to end up in a factory all his life, like his father had done. I think that was one of the reasons he went into law." His uncle was pleased to take him under his wing.

But if Arch thought his uncle was going to make it easy for him, he was mistaken. "Uncle Everett was a strange individual," observed Harry Moore. "All he offered Arch was a desk and a chair. Arch had to find his own cases–deeds, divorces, general practice work. By the time Arch joined him, Uncle Everett was getting out of the legislature and was in the coal business as a consultant, mainly." Arch agreed. In those early days of his practice of law he admitted, "I took anything that came through the door."

Nevertheless, Arch remembered his uncle more generously and affectionately. "I was proud of my Uncle Everett from the time I was very young. He was a political identity in the county. He let me have an office[2] and the agreement was that I would give him half of every fee I took in." Because his uncle had no wife or children, Arch reiterated, "he worked all the time."

Shelley Moore also commended Everett Moore. Her husband "felt [Everett's] zeal for serving in the legislature," she noted, and "he was very good with Arch, teaching him the practice of law." Uncle Everett, more than anyone else, formed Arch Moore's public and professional personality, she thought.

Arch and Shelley rented a nearby house on Fifth Street, Moundsville, at fifty-one dollars a month. He had never owned a car in his life ("I used the thumb a lot") and walked to work. Soon after joining Everett's practice, he had his first set of wheels when he bought a 1945 brownish-red, two-door Plymouth from an estate he handled. "It had a big old hump on the back. We drove it for six months." He also used some of his newly-earned income to begin buying some fine business suits and began a lifelong habit of dressing immaculately, stylishly. ("My dad would have worn a jacket and tie even if he hadn't been a lawyer," laughed his son, years later. "He's a real clothes horse.")

Shelley noted that "Arch knew everybody" in Moundsville. Integrating into the town was a challenging experience for her, though. "But they all took me in like a sister." She added that her relationship with Arch's mother was always a good one. Shelley Moore said she soon "joined a girl's bridge club and the Junior League in Wheeling." She was listed on the substitute teachers list in Marshall County, "but they didn't call me much," and she wasn't too upset about that.

As most new lawyers do, coming right out of law school, Arch took on some criminal defense work. "The first case I had, my client was charged with murder. He lived in a trailer and there had been drinking and loud conversations with another guy. Threats were made and my client shot and killed him. I based my defense on, 'Every man's house is his castle.'" But, " I lost it," Moore deadpanned. "The jury found him guilty [only] of assault and battery." He was acquitted on the murder charge. Arch discovered he had the skill for which law school doesn't necessarily prepare one; he could organize the presentation of his evidence and persuade a jury.

The young attorney got his first big financial break when his uncle made him an offer. Everett had sold a large tract of coal property in Wetzel County to the B&O Railroad but the company's counsel, Howard Hardesty, had alleged that there were title problems with it. He couldn't get payment for the full value with defects hanging over the title. "My uncle told me, go do the title work on it and, for all that you prove that I own, I'll give you the profit from it." Remembered Arch, "I couldn't clear it all, but I cleared enough title to earn seven thousand dollars!"[3]

The Fifties and Sixties were decades in which most Americans of means traded cars (only farmers, plumbers and construction types drove trucks, and SUVs and vans were not yet on the scene) every year or two. A new car was a status symbol. Plus, the styles changed drastically each year and rust came quickly to the fenders. A successful young lawyer couldn't be seen in an "old" Plymouth! With his newfound wealth burning a hole in his pocket, Arch took his uncle with him to Cornell Chevrolet in Wheeling to help him pick out a new car. They chose a two-tone blue 1952 Chevy. He took Shelley back to see it, beaming, "I want to buy this for you." She was thrilled and readily agreed to the purchase. They gave the Plymouth to his parents, who had never owned an automobile.

Among his largest clients, Everett had represented B&O and Pittsburgh Plate Glass, who had a plant near New Martinsville. Everett took Arch with him to PPG meetings in Pittsburgh and they became comfortable with the young associate, realizing that he was handling most of the grunt work in the practice. The PPG executives referred the Monsanto company to Arch Moore. Monsanto wanted to join with Bayer (a German company which, by terms of a World War I treaty, could not own a factory in the U.S. without a partner) to create a new company called Mobay. Mobay wanted to put a facility on the Ohio River and needed nearby PPG's hydrogen. Hydrogen was a waste product to PPG, so they were happy to sell it.

But there was a problem. The owners of the land between the PPG facility and the proposed Mobay plant didn't want a pipeline going through their property. Everett knew them well and warned Arch, "That family is stubborn as the devil. They won't sell."

So Arch strained his brain to think of a solution, tossing and turning in bed before "sleeping on it." As sometimes happens, the answer is apparent when you awake. The next morning he asked his uncle, "Who controls the right-of-way for the railroad?" (There was a railway connecting PPG and the proposed Mobay site.) The Moores discovered that a state authority controlled the land on which the rails were laid. (If they could use the railroad right-of-way, they wouldn't need one through the property owned by the "stubborn" family.) "I had Uncle Everett call the Governor and explain to him that there was an opportunity for 500 to 750 new jobs, and within a day the Governor was calling back, telling us we were authorized to lay the [Mobay] pipeline." The plant was built and thousands of families would for decades benefit from the good-paying jobs that Arch Moore's ingenuity and problem-resolution skills made possible.

It was then that people in the area first began talking about Arch Moore as someone who "could get things done." He would represent Mobay as its lawyer until he took office as governor in 1969.

In 1951, the Moores were blessed by the birth of their first child. The couple had already decided that a son would be named Arch III, but as there were already two Arch Moores in the family, it was getting confusing, and they knew a nickname for the boy would be inevitable. "I never liked being called Junior or Moo," Arch, Jr. noted, "so Shelley decided that we would choose the nickname and not leave it to others. We liked the Kim Sisters, of Korea, a popular singing group in our time. But I also knew a guy from Fairmont, who'd been in a competing fraternity at WVU, named Kimberly Godfrey. He went by 'Kim,' and we liked that. So we called our son Kim from the day we brought him home, and that's still what we call him." Kim Moore noted that he didn't even know he had another name until later years.[4]

Kim was "all boy," recalled his mother, "a little rascal." Family friend Dr. Carl Roncaglione remembered when he and Kim lay on their backs on the floor, shooting a dart gun (which Roncaglione bought for him in Pittsburgh) at the ceiling of the Moore's new house, a few years later. The rubber suction tips "left marks all over that new ceiling," Roncaglione laughed. "I don't think Arch appreciated us doing that at all."

In 1953, their first daughter, named Shelley Wellons Moore, was born.

(Her father would call her "Sis," "Sister," or "Shelley 2," even after she was elected to Congress.) The family rounded out with the birth of Lucy in 1956. Shelley, Sr. gave up thoughts of returning to the classroom full-time, devoting herself to family and her husband's career, instead. "I was quite busy taking care of my husband and children," recalled Mrs. Moore, who added that she never regretted not pursuing a career outside the home.

Arch also got heavily involved in the community. In addition to his attendance at his family's Simpson Methodist Church in Moundsville, he joined the Elks, the Eagles, the American Legion and became a Rotarian.

His wife also immersed herself further into the social scene. In addition to her other activities, Shelley became a Grey Lady of the American Red Cross, a Girl Scout commissioner, and a director of the Cerebral Palsy Foundation. But more and more, she was a stay-at-home mom, as most married women were in that day. She tried to learn to play golf and even took lessons after moving to Moundsville, but quickly discovered "this game ain't for me." One lady commended her score until she found out she had played a nine, not an eighteen-hole course, Shelley laughed. She and her husband would begin playing a lot of tennis, which they enjoyed into retirement years.

IN 1952, THE twenty-eight-year-old Arch Moore, Jr. launched his own political career, winning his uncle's former seat in the West Virginia House of Delegates without much difficulty. After having a tough time deciding which ticket on which to run, five star General Dwight D. Eisenhower, still very popular for leading D-Day and defeating Hitler, chose the GOP and proved he had long coat tails for the party which had been out of power for more than two decades. Ike, with his wide grin, won by a huge landslide, sweeping Republicans into Congress with him, creating a GOP majority for the first time since the 1920s. The Democrats held onto West Virginia, however.

In his very brief career in the legislature, Arch would serve with Delegates William W. "Wally" Barron of Elkins, William T. Brotherton of Charleston and Cecil Underwood of Tyler County. He also served with another delegate who would fit into his career in a most negative way: William E. "Ned" Chilton III, a liberal Democrat, an Ivy Leaguer who would publish the *Charleston Gazette*. "He was an odd, high-feeling person," was how Arch remembered Delegate Chilton. (Ned was telling the people the same about this young delegate from Marshall County, at least the "high-feeling" part. Their paths would cross again, many times.)

Oce Smith, then head page for the House of Delegates, met Moore for the first time. Arch "was a very young man, indeed," Oce recalled, and given that he was also in the minority party, did not make a big mark in his one, brief term in the legislature. "He only got one single bill through the legislature, and that was to establish a 4-H camp in Marshall County. He seldom spoke from the floor." Nothing was unusual about any of that, considering that Moore was a freshman, Smith added.

Moore discovered a new and addictive passion, though. He dearly loved the political lifestyle. While many would like to serve, few are willing to do what it takes to get elected: the hand shaking; the speech making; hearing complaints at all hours of the days and in unexpected, inconvenient settings; the fund raising; being "on" 24/7. Those who take government and politics seriously are truly public servants. It is hard work and one must take a certain degree of abuse from a demanding public, which sometimes outweighs the few honors. It certainly is not an ideal life for most people. But Arch didn't mind any of it–he took to it like a fish to water. When a favor-seeker, years later, used the word "politics" in a disparaging fashion, as if it was always a filthy, corrupt, evil practice, Moore, who was offended by the inference, corrected him. "When you help someone in need, that's politics," he told the man. "When you walk across the street to greet someone you know, that's politics."[5]

Observed lawyer/author/politician Richard Neely, grandson of the legendary governor and U.S. Senator, Matthew M. Neely, "There are people who love politics for the sake of campaigning, going to parades, attending meetings, socializing with people, attending receptions, having a drink at a party, or driving through the woods with friends to Moorefield, because it gives them a chance to chat with their friends. But then there are some who are interested in policy; most of those people end up in appointed, rather than elective office." Arch Moore, Neely thought, "was somebody naturally good at politics. He's extremely bright. He always had some scheme to make the world a better place." Moore's reason for entry into the political world was to accomplish a brighter, better life for the people in his state, Neely said.[6]

Moore also discovered that he had a talent few possess, an absolutely priceless asset in politics: *he could remember names, occupations, families details, with phenomenal accuracy.* It was just how his brain was wired; it was as if he had a mental computer. "It was something he was born with," thought his wife.[7] This asset Moore possessed would help him immensely because, as Dale Carnegie emphasized in his books, there is no sound sweeter to one's ear than his or her own name. Successful sales people often repeat a customer's name. That Arch could remember them and cause them to feel important made his constituents feel like he was their friend which, in many cases, was true. Being able to remember names and faces without fail "is a talent that cannot be learned," admitted Richard Neely.

How did he do it? He had taken no memory classes, no one would "brief" him prior to going out, and he used no "black books," Arch insisted; it was just something with which he was blessed from birth. But such retention is also due to how he meets and greets people, he explained. "Most politicians just go down the line and don't really catch people's names. I always made a point of listening when they told me their names. I look them in the eye, I focus my eyes on theirs. I make them repeat it, if necessary. I'll even ask, 'How do you spell that?' if I haven't heard them (which is embarrassing when they answer, 'S-M-I-T-H').

"Then I associate that name with the geographical location in which I've met them. The quickest way to throw me a curve is for someone who is from Bluefield to say hello in Wheeling. That confuses my mind. You should never have someone from Bluefield showing up in Wheeling," Moore laughed. But if that happened, "I'd give him some leading questions until he'd say, 'I was working in Bluefield and then moved up here...' And then it clicks and I'd say, 'Hi, Stan, how are ya?'" Because of his reputation for possessing a phenomenal memory, Moore said he often was tested. "Sometimes someone would come up to me, smile over his shoulder and wink to his friend, saying, 'I'll bet you don't remember who I am.'" But, using his techniques, Arch rarely was stumped.

Although he had high ambitions and a healthy ego, people discovered that Moore really did care deeply about the well being of those he served. Many politicians "put up with" the public just so they can gain power or prestige. But Arch had a gift lacking in others: he simply loved people. He enjoyed talking to them, exchanging information and ideas, attending weddings, funerals, graduations, just being a part of the lives of his constituents, throughout his long career and even into retirement. He never seemed to tire of any of it, constantly thirsting for personal relationships and information. As important to Arch as issues and government accomplishments were, the people was the part of it he seemed to most enjoy. It mattered not their station in life; he could talk gently and patiently to the poorest and least-educated West Virginian as comfortably as he could to the CEO of a large, international company or the president of the United States, which he often would do.

His two-year term in the Legislature was too short, especially for one in the minority party, to make much impact. It was a training ground, primarily. Cecil Underwood remembered Moore's service favorably, however. "Arch had a lot of personality, a fantastic memory and a great grasp on detail. He was a very capable, effective leader, especially on the Judiciary Committee." As Minority Leader, Underwood would have daily luncheon meetings with his fellow GOP members, to get reports on what was going on.

"Those days, unless there was a special session, the legislature met only sixty days, in the first year of the two-year term," laughed Arch. "A member received nothing extra for expenses, including lodging, food, travel, so I lost money on the $500 they paid. But I broke even in the second year, when we didn't meet and I still got the $500."

In the meantime, the Moore & Moore law practice continued to prosper. "I've been tremendously fortunate as a professional and public man," Moore gratefully acknowledged.

With their growing family, the Moores needed more space and their income permitted a larger residence. So, from July of 1954 until March of 1955, contractors were building the young Moore family a new brick home (from the street, a modest-appearing, one story, but the rear view revealing three stories, "a typical politician's home," Arch joked) in a new development in nearby Glen Dale, where they would be near friends. Although they would twice add on to the structure, the elegant, comfortable home they built would be their primary residence for the rest of their lives, the center of family gatherings and holidays and a refuge from Charleston in later years.

(Arch would, henceforth, use Glen Dale as his designated residence. There was no more mention of Moundsville, perhaps because it was known as the location of the state penitentiary, as Weston was known as the locale of the state mental hospital. To most West Virginians in those days, "going to Moundsville" meant you were looking at a prison term and "going to Weston" meant you'd lost your mind. Being threatened with "going to Pruntytown," the lone juvenile lockup for boys, was what parents used to warn errant sons.)

There was a generation gap in Moore & Moore, regarding fees. Everett had been on a long-time retainer with PPG, and hadn't raised his fees in decades even though inflation, rampant during the Truman Administration, had diminished their value. Arch handled a large legal matter for PPG in which they bought a coal company. When he took his proposed fee to his uncle for approval, Everett about had a heart attack; he thought it was much too high. "You can't do this! You're going to get me fired!" he shouted at Arch.

But his nephew countered, "You're still charging five dollars for deeds while other lawyers are charging fifty dollars. Times are moving on, Uncle Everett! This is Class Double-A work I did for PPG." Everett let him submit the "large" bill, but with great apprehension and reluctance.

Two days later, PPG's in-house counsel called the Moore attorneys into his office in Pittsburgh and Everett feared the worst. He sat glaring at Arch as the PPG attorney started, "Mr. Moore, we have received your statement."

"When he said somberly, 'We're going to give you a letter,' I thought my uncle was going to die," laughed Arch. "But instead of what we feared, he smiled, commended us for a thorough job, and handed over a check for the $18,000 I had billed."

With his $9000 share, Arch and Shelley bought both sets of parents new cars as Christmas presents.

Former classmate Richard Rundle remembered the lawyer Arch Moore to be a good one, but sometimes unconventional and unorthodox. "At a workers' compensation hearing, Arch announced to the hearing examiner that he was appearing on behalf of both the claimant and the employer [normally adverse parties in litigation]. The examiner asked Moore how he planned to do that. 'Watch and learn,' Arch replied with a smile. He then presented a closing argument on behalf of the claimant, got up, walked around to the other side of the table and stated, 'On behalf of the employer, we agree with that statement and are prepared to submit for a decision.'" He had been retained by both, and they were in agreement.

It was through his practice of workers' compensation law that Moore became a life-long friend of David Yoho, M.D., a Moundsville family practitioner. "He told me that, if I'd testify for his client, a comp claimant, he'd buy me a bottle of whiskey. I'd have testified for him regardless–he was my patient. Arch has been buying me Chivas Regal ever since," laughed Dr. Yoho. Betty Jane and David Yoho and the Moores would eventually live across the street from each other in Glen Dale and start an informal Saturday night bridge club.

FRANCIS LOVE, a Wheeling lawyer, had served one term in the Congress from the First District, the Northern Panhandle of West Virginia. In 1950 and 1952, he had failed to defeat his Democratic opponent, however, despite a comeback by Republicans elsewhere. Robert Mollohan, a protege of fellow-Fairmonter Matthew M. Neely, held the seat in 1954. In an era in which party organization was everything, Neely was the Democrats' strong state party boss. Heartened by their national successes, Republicans thought they might have a chance to retake the seat if they could find a candidate stronger than Love. It became "anybody but Love," for the First District's Grand Old Party.

"Love was good one-on-one, but was not a great orator," thought Cecil Underwood. Recalled H. John Rogers, who also knew him, Love was "a wonderful, sweet old guy, but he didn't have that killer instinct. He lived upstairs in the McClure Hotel and, as I realized later, he had a drinking problem. Plus, he was a hanger-on, just not a forceful guy. He was a chipmunk-looking fellow, an office lawyer who did wills and deeds, mainly."

A study done by the national Republicans revealed that the First was a swing district. Ohio County alone was identified as containing 23,080 swing voters which would mean 6.2 percent district-wide. The district was 59.7 percent urban, 28.7 percent rural non-farm and 12 percent farm. It was "primarily a manufacturing area employing 34,103 of the 99,476 working group." There were 9000 African Americans and more than 13,000 foreign born people in the district, it said. The research concluded that the correct Republican could win the seat.

"Walter Hallanan, the Republican National Committeeman, who had a lot of respect with the national party, held a meeting of the Republican leaders at the Moundsville Country Club on a Saturday afternoon" in 1954, Arch Moore recalled. "They were looking around for a candidate" for the First District, one who could get some Democratic votes in the seven counties. They raised some money for the project, formed a recruiting committee and Ned Davidson from Wellsburg paid Delegate Arch Moore a visit in his office, asking him if he would run. They wanted someone "that the party could really get behind." It was rare for political parties to get involved in a primary race, Moore added. The committee also encouraged Uncle Everett to allow his young associate to take on Mollohan. "He was very interested but thought it might be a step taken too soon," recalled Arch, noting that his only public service at that point had been the sixty day session in the House of Delegates. "But he loved politics and was supportive of me doing it."

So, after defeating a Wheeling lawyer in the GOP primary, Arch became the 1954 nominee for Congress in the First District. He began a grass roots, "street-walking, hand-to-hand campaign," and the reaction was so positive that wife Shelley thought there was no way they could lose. Moore's main argument for unseating the incumbent Mollohan was to run against Senator Neely. "I argued that Neely didn't deserve two votes, one in the Senate and one in the House of Representatives," Arch laughed, describing his way of telling voters that Mollohan was Neely's puppet. "I compared them to Edgar Bergen and Charlie McCarthy [a popular screen, radio and TV puppeteer of the time]."

He also tried a medium new to politics, television. "I could get air time on WTRF in Wheeling from 11:30 to 1 a.m. for only $300," Moore chuckled. So he would have call-in shows during that late hour, which proved to be popular, "especially since I had a nice looking young lady who would hand me the questions people would call in." Lawyer Frank O'Brien would host the shows. "I did it twice a week," said Arch, noting that it was somewhat risky taking questions live and unrehearsed. But Channel 7 viewers liked this young candidate and agreed with most of his responses. He was getting to know them, and they him, through this new medium.

His campaign brochure was titled, "Elect Arch Moore in '54." The trifold showed Arch with President Eisenhower, House Majority Leader Charles Halleck, Agricultural Secretary Ezra Benson, Speaker Joseph Martin and others. The unspoken message seemed to be, "Moore is a Republican who can better work with the Republicans, who are now in charge of Washington." He advertised himself as one who would represent the First District "24 hours a day," and "not a part-time, but a full-time congressman."

His "platform," it said, was supporting President Eisenhower, higher protective tariffs "to protect the working man," taxation "on the ability to pay," anti-communist laws, reduction of foreign aid, reducing social security retirement to age sixty, serving the "forgotten farmers," help for veterans, "emergency stop-gap measures to halt any recession," and new and diversified industry. He promised to "bring government closer to the people," and said he was opposed to sending American troops to countries "who refuse to defend themselves." It promised that, with Moore in Congress, "You'll know he's there–working for you–full time!" Photos on the last page depicted "Moore the lawyer," "Moore the Legionnaire (with his cap)," and "Moore, the Family Man," with Shelley and their two children on a flowered sofa.

The candidate began calling on relatives, including his mother's cousin who ran Stewart Granite Works in Mannington, a strong Democratic leader there. The Jones cousin was in his bib overalls, sitting near a pot-belly stove, chatting with friends when the young Arch Moore arrived unannounced, to ask for support for his congressional race. "So you're Sis's boy?" he asked, looking him up and down. The cousin, and others in Arch's extended family, helped him win supporters throughout the district, mainly with old-fashioned, one-on-one convincing.

Outside of Moundsville and Wheeling, there was a lot of hostility to any Republican in the First District (and throughout West Virginia, for that matter). The nation was only thirteen years or so away from ending the Great Depression, a harsh economic disaster which many of that era would always blame on the Grand Old Party, even though the economic collapse had been world-wide. Moreover, unions in the steel mills, coal mines, construction, trucking, railroads, factories and elsewhere, were at their peak strength and they credited their rights and growing prosperity to the Democratic Party. Many of those union members would never, ever see the need for a two-party system or even a need for government to be fair to business and industry, not understanding from whence came their employment. It was common for them to vote the straight Democratic ticket until their dying day. They didn't have the foresight to realize supporting candidates in both parties would solidify and strengthen their own interests; they took the British, Labour Party approach.

Accordingly, most in Moore's political party sought their votes elsewhere and stayed far away from organized labor. But Arch had been a union member himself; it was a huge and growing group; he shared many of their interests and felt a kinship to them; and he loved a challenge. So he did not write off those working families as potential supporters. At first, unions would not allow the young Republican to speak at their meetings at all; he was not welcome simply because of his political affiliation. "I was running against Herbert Hoover, not Bob Mollohan," said Arch. Heavily unionized Marion County, in the southern end of the district, and Mollohan's home base, was especially difficult. Arch recalled campaigning at the Farmington No. 9 Mine and holding out his hand to greet miners leaving the bath house at the end of their shift. "Some of them spit on my hand."[8] Arch would take it in stride. "Sorry you feel that way," he'd tell the rude miners. "You'll find out it's a pretty good hand."

Despite his wife's confidence that they would prevail in this first bid, Arch did not win his 1954 race for Congress. He lost, but only by only 5,410 votes, to Congressman Mollohan. (Arch won only Republican Ohio, Marshall and Taylor of the seven counties in the First District.)

It was not the best year for a young Republican to make his debut. Nationally, the Republicans lost nineteen seats and their control of the House of Representatives, which they had held for only two short years (a repeat of what happened in 1948; they lost it in 1950). There were several factors likely responsible for the poor showing: for decades, the party in the White House always lost congressional seats in off-year elections; Ike's coattails were not available in 1954; and the unions, Democrats' strongest supporters, were on the rise. Moreover, the public was discovering that these Republicans were not much different than the Democrats they replaced–Eisenhower's internationalist foreign policy and big government domestic policy were derided as "me too-ism" by conservatives like Senator Robert Taft. Also going against Moore was his youth, that he was relatively unknown outside Marshall County, and that Bob Mollohan had the strong support of the M.M. Neely Democratic machine, perhaps at its apex in power.

But Arch was encouraged by the good showing and his appetite for the job was whetted, not satiated. "Among Republicans, we did the best race in the nation against an incumbent in 1954." He would try it again, as many were urging him to do. In fact, he would just keep on campaigning non-stop, throughout the next two years.

Chapter 4 Notes

1. - Perhaps because of his uncle's weakness, nephew Arch Moore rarely drank and rarely was seen in public with even a soft drink in his hand.

2. - The same three-story, brick building, at the time of this writing, in which Arch Moore keeps his consulting office today.

3. - The national average wage in 1951 was $2,799.

4. - When he went out west, his employer gave him a name badge, "Archie," and that was how he was known in Nevada and by his wife for many years. Governor Moore would ask his son, "Why did you let them do that?" Arch, Jr. knew he didn't like it when he would receive Christmas cards addressed to "Archie Moore" or "Archibald Moore." Kim's son, who would be named Arch Alfred Moore, IV, became known as "Alfie." Said Kim, "When our son was small, we'd tell him, 'Your name is really Arch,' and he'd reply, 'I not Arch, I Alfie!'"

5. - Kevin Sikora, 2003.

6. - Richard Neely, Aug. 26, 2005.

7. - "I've known only one other West Virginia politician who could match him," laughed Marion County Commissioner Jim Sago. "Bob Byrd could remember names and sometimes would also memorize your phone number."

8. - Added Moore in a 2005 interview, "When I later was elected to the Congress, at that same coal mine, some would then grin and shake hands. Others would tease them, 'Are you gonna shake his hand this time?' And, when the mine exploded [in 1968, right after Moore was elected governor for the first time and soon after his helicopter crash] I went up there to grieve with the families. Because of my injuries I had to go in a wheelchair. They were all over that chair, thanking me for being with them. They realized I was their friend."

Chapter Five
Capitol Hill

Having lost his first race in 1954, Arch continued to campaign non-stop for the First District congressional seat through the following year, attending events, constantly introducing himself to potential voters in Weirton, Wheeling, Fairmont, Mannington and elsewhere. He had come too close to beating Bob Mollohan to give it up. This time, he would get him!

But something unexpected—some might say serendipitous—occurred in 1956. Likely at the request of organized labor, the state's Democratic boss, Senator Neely, decided to place Mollohan in Charleston to consolidate his own power; he would run him for governor.

Suddenly Arch Moore was seeking to fill a vacant seat, normally much easier to accomplish, especially for a Republican in West Virginia.

Perhaps Boss Neely thought Mollohan was vulnerable to a second challenge by Moore and wanted to move him for that reason, too. But if he thought putting the Congressman into the Governor's Mansion was going to be a slam-dunk, he was in for a rude surprise; his lieutenant carried a lot of baggage from past political jobs. In the final weeks of the gubernatorial campaign, it was disclosed that Congressman Mollohan had accepted $20,000 in payments from a coal operator who stripped coal from land at Pruntytown's West Virginia Industrial School for Boys, when Mollohan was its superintendent.[1]

Mollohan would face an unexpectedly tough opponent in the young House minority leader, Cecil Underwood, who referred to him as "Bicycle Bob," for darting around the issues and avoiding questions about his ethics. This time, Eisenhower would carry even heavily Democratic West Virginia and his coattails (and questions about Mollohan) helped make Underwood the youngest governor in the state's history and its first Republican since before the Depression.

The First District Democrats would nominate as their candidate for Congress C. Lee Spillers, "well known and very well liked by both Republicans and Democrats," according to Moore. "Lee had refereed high school football and basketball games throughout the Ohio Valley, so lots of people knew him." Spillers had been a state senator, Ohio County prosecutor and U.S. Attorney.

But Arch was getting to be well-known and well-liked, too. He had been active in the VFW and American Legion, chairman of the Mohawk District Boy Scouts and a member of the board of stewards of Moundsville's Simpson Methodist Church.

The two conducted one of the most civil, cordial debates ever, at the McClure Hotel in Wheeling. "I told them that Lee Spillers was an outstanding individual but that there was one vote he could not cast, and that was for a Republican to be Speaker of the House." Moore was anticipating that Eisenhower would be re-elected in 1956, pulling in a Republican Congress as he had done four years earlier. "Lee came right back and said, 'I'm not going to introduce myself, you all know me ... But if you elect Arch Moore, you'll have yourself a fine congressman.'" Arch was shocked at the generous comment. "How can you run against someone like that?"

Something that was "not good" in both the 1954 and 1956 races, from Arch's standpoint, were the "live ballots" (as he called them—they're often referred to as "chain ballots"), which the Democrats had going in Marion County. It was a system that would operate efficiently for the majority party for many decades. In each precinct, at the beginning of election day, an inside Democratic poll worker would (illegally) allow someone to sneak out a blank, un-voted paper ballot. A Democratic poll worker, seated outside in a vehicle, would then mark an X in their party's straight-ticket box. A voter willing to be paid for his vote would pick up the marked ballot from the outside worker, fold and hide it in his jacket, cast it, and bring back out the blank one that had been given to him inside, take it to the outside worker and collect his payment. That second blank ballot would be marked by the outside worker, handed to the next voter willing to sell his vote for cash and/or whiskey. The process would be repeated all day, until the polls closed. Often the Democratic Machine would later reward these crooked Election Day workers for getting high numbers of straight tickets out of their respective precincts. "There were a lot of straight [Democrat] tickets in Marion County," Arch recalled, which would cause him to lose that county in his first two congressional elections.

Further, the Democrats had every public employee out on election day, using state and county trucks and cars owned by the taxpayers, to haul friendly voters to the polls. Those who failed to get their quota of Democrats out to vote could expect to lose their jobs. Additionally, the Democratic ticket was funded by "flower funds," in the Statehouse and county court houses (more about that later). It was swimming upstream for any Republican candidate; the odds were heavily against his chances of success.

Moore hired a press representative for the first time, borrowing Weirton Steel's public relations man. "He'd write press releases, quoting me as saying this or that. I'd tell him, 'I can't say that!' and he'd respond, 'But if you don't say it nobody will.'" He had a brightly painted tractor trailer, dubbed the Arch Moore Bandwagon, which was taken from town to town for parades and rallies.

As in '54, the campaign was a family effort. "My dad (Arch, Sr.) was a very quiet man, but he would touch base with old friends on my behalf," recalled Arch. "It was hard for them to say no to him–he was a whale of a nice guy. My mother worked her phone constantly." Shelley campaigned tirelessly with her husband. "We worked as a team," she said. "I went whenever and wherever [Arch] wanted me to go, if I could get a babysitter." Arch's brother and sister would also join the effort. Harry "Moo" Moore made several speeches at Lincoln Day dinners for his brother, such as one at Weirton, when schedule did not permit the candidate to be there. "Mom and Dad would sit around and worry when the [Democratic] papers would say something critical about Arch," recalled Harry. "They took it to heart. They'd ask Arch, 'Did you read this article? Isn't that terrible?' He'd have to reassure them." Said Shelley Moore about her in-laws, "They knew that [Arch, Jr.] was top of the line. His parents and sister and brother were thrilled to death. His dad was quite reserved but his mother was right out front with her pride."

A growing base of supporters were caught up in the Moore family enthusiasm, all the way to Election Day, November 6, 1956. They liked this smiling, friendly, handsome young man who seemed so much brighter and open than politicians they'd known in the past.

Oce Smith of Fairmont was supporting the straight Democratic ticket as usual. "Spillers' campaign wasn't the most prudent in the world," he observed. "First, Lee thought he had it won before he started. Second, his thirst overcame him many times–it appeared he couldn't leave the 'hoo-hoo water' alone."

This time, Arch was victorious, but by a mere 762 votes. He won in Republican Marshall, Ohio, Taylor and Wetzel Counties, but lost heavily Democratic Brooke, Hancock and Marion Counties.[2]

Arch, Shelley, brother Moo and others had gathered at the Moore & Moore Moundsville law office on election night, which was Arch's tradition from 1952 through his last race in 1988. "I had people in each county calling in the results, and we knew we'd won by four or five in the morning." Shelley had already gone home, so Arch and Moo walked across the street to Kreglow's Restaurant to have breakfast and let what happened sink in. They were a bit numb from lack of sleep, but the adrenalin of victory was keeping them pumped up.

Mr. Moore was going to Washington!

"The next day, Lee called and said 'congratulations,' and it was done," Arch recalled. The victory was rather anticlimactic, after all he and his team had done to get there. It had been a long, exhausting, uphill battle for the 33-year-old lawyer. "I had campaigned from 1954 through 1956, non-stop." Surprisingly, his win received almost no national attention. The only congratulatory phone call he could remember was one from Congressman Bob Wilson of California, who chaired the GOP Congressional Campaign Committee.

Despite his suffering a heart attack in 1955, raising health concerns, it had been another national Eisenhower landslide over Adlai Stevenson. When the President carried West Virginia, it was the first time a Republican had done that since Hoover had won its electoral votes in 1928. Eisenhower's coattails even pulled Chapman Revercomb into the unexpired, two-year U.S. Senate term caused by the death of Harley Kilgore earlier in 1956. Revercomb, of Charleston, had been in the Senate from 1943 to 1949. The Democrats held onto the Senate and House, however.

How did it feel to have just been elected to Congress where so many distinguished Americans had served? Recalled Arch, "We knew it was a big jump for a young man."

Shelley had become comfortable with their lifestyle in the past few years and there was some fear of the unknown. What kind of disruption would this bring to their young, happy family? "When he went to Washington six months of the year, It was tough for me," she admitted. Their settled routine was interrupted. "He came home on weekends but was on the road a lot [even when in West Virginia]. We had hired [domestic] help, but not overnight. I had to manage the house and children by myself during those times. I knew what it meant to him and I was very happy for him. But I was worried, too—we were a young family and there were a lot of things we'd have to change. I like to keep things as-is," she said, laughing at her life-long cautious and conservative nature.

The family was in the galleries to watch him being sworn into the 85th Congress in January 1957. He was assigned to the Judiciary Committee, which suited him well, plus the Select Committee on Small Business and the Joint Committee on Immigration and Naturalization Policy, the latter which would give him multiple opportunities for world travel. His expectation that he'd be part of a Republican Congress were dashed, however—the GOP had gained fifty-three seats—still twenty short of reaching a majority.

"A lot of us [who had been elected for the first time to Congress] were neophytes," said Arch. "Some of us had been in state legislatures. One new member had been Speaker of the Michigan House. On Capitol Hill, it's difficult to monitor everything that's going on in committees. So we had a group called 'Marching and Chowder.' It had been around a while—Presidents Nixon and Ford had been in it during their first terms. Also, twenty of us fifty-three freshmen met every Monday night. We called ourselves the 'Acorns' (because we hoped to grow into mighty oaks). We educated ourselves, turning from one committee's agenda to the next, so when the bill came to the floor we'd know more about it.

"Other Acorns included George Bush [Sr.], John Lindsay, who became mayor of New York, and future governors of New Jersey and Connecticut. We had acorn cufflinks. Years later, when I saw (then-National GOP Chairman) George Bush at a dinner given by Vice President Spiro Agnew, he showed me his cufflinks—he was still wearing the acorns."

Because 762 votes "wasn't a landslide by any means," the Moores played it cautiously and did not relocate their young family to Washington at first, at least not year-around. "Congress then usually adjourned for the year in August," Arch noted. "So we bought a house in Springfield, Maryland which we would use half the year and then lease it to an ambassador or his staff the other half. The children would go to school in Maryland the first half of the year and Glen Dale the second half. "That was difficult" for son Kim, he remembered, explaining, "They taught surface [cursive] writing in West Virginia the first semester and in Maryland the second half, so our son was never taught how to write his letters. I've told him, 'Son, you were born to be a doctor,' because his handwriting is so bad to this day!" (Unlike his son's, Governor Moore's handwriting has always been as perfect and beautiful as a first grade teacher's.)

Arch sought to be the best congressman anyone ever had. He started by setting up one of the most efficient congressional offices in Washington. (When the Republican National Committee had prospective or new members of Congress, Moore was subsequently asked to train them on how to set up their offices.)

Most new members of Congress hired staffers from their own district, people who had helped get them elected. But he did it differently. "I felt I had to learn as fast as I possibly could. I wanted people on my staff who had long experience on the Hill, who could hit the ground running," he said. "I got a list of people who had worked for outgoing senators and congressmen. I hired as my chief of staff Keith Jakes, who'd worked for a U.S.

senator. I could hire seven people; today they have twelve to thirteen staff members. They all had acquaintances in other congressional and senate offices, they knew how to get to the top and get answers. I found two who were experts in the Defense Department and Commerce, which then contained the Department of Energy, two sensitive areas to the seven counties of my district." Only two staffers were West Virginians. One, Alice Jane Dunn of Wheeling, attended a WVU-Maryland football game with Arch's brother Harry. She soon became the other Mrs. Moore.

As would be true when he became governor, Moore was able to attract highly qualified and motivated people, who then made him look good. His congressional staff "turned out to be the best on the Hill," Moore noted. "They remained with me until I ran for governor. They didn't miss a lick."

Residents of the First District became pleasantly surprised at how quickly and thoroughly Rep. Moore's staff would respond to their questions or needs. "If someone wrote or talked with Arch Moore, he or she had every reason to expect that we would take the ball and run with it or get back to them as soon as possible," he noted. "A member of Congress is voting on legislation that affects the whole world, but he's also the intermediary between that constituency and its government." If a problem–local, state or federal–would arise, one often would hear, "See if Arch Moore can help!" Some would affectionately call him "Uncle Arch." His name quickly became a household word.

His staff would cull from the newspapers in the district—then the primary source of news—a photo of a student who had received an award or recognition, a member of a fraternal organization, an elderly person who'd had a birthday, a couple who had been married, just about any news items of note. They would mail that, sometimes laminated, to the individual, with a congratulatory, hand-written note from Congressman Moore. This attention to people's lives made them feel special and honored and it worked like a charm, much to the Democrats' dismay.

Moore never used a signature stamp or machine in his entire career. He signed everything personally, almost unheard-of in politics, and a task which expended dozens of precious hours each week. "A lot of times we'd get petitions, often regarding issues affecting organized labor. If there was a thousand coal miners' names on a petition, I replied to every one of them and signed each letter." He would often strike their formal salutation and ink-in a nickname, or add a personal, hand-written note at the end as a P.S.[3]

"He knew his people," recalled Oce Smith, who usually opposed

Arch but begrudgingly admired his relationship with constituents. "He remembered them in times of tragedy and in happiness. If someone in his district died, especially in a large Italian family, they would receive a long, beautiful letter of condolence from the Congressman or perhaps even a basket of flowers. An old friend of ours who'd been extremely active in the Democratic party told me when his father passed away the first large remembrance of flowers was from Arch Moore, for whom none of them had ever voted or met in their lives. There is little doubt but what that changed a few loyalties on election day.

"Today these responsibilities are pretty much normal throughout the political world but, those days, it was something new. He wrote the primer on full-time campaigning," thought Smith. "He was extremely adept at picking out people who had applied for social security or a visa, phoning them, and telling them how good he felt that he could arrange this for them...when in fact, it was a routine project which simply came through on its own. The Democrats always wondered who it was in these departments who notified him about these applications just in time for his personal intervention but they never seemed to learn who it was.

"He sent Christmas cards to [people] who had never received a Christmas greeting from an officeholder before that time. It meant something to them; they were very proud. And they kept the card hanging on the mantle of their home throughout the year, feeling they knew Arch and Shelley personally and closely, not realizing that thousands of those went out all over the state."

But it wasn't all just PR; Moore genuinely tried to help constituents at every opportunity. For example, his office would work hard to get young men (no women in those days) from the First District into the military academies. Charleston lawyer Tom Sweeney, then a Weirton high school student, would remember his contact with Moore in the late Sixties when he applied for entrance into the U.S. Naval Academy. Sweeney wanted to be a Navy fighter pilot. "I missed the deadline to take the admissions test but Moore set it up for me to take it in a library. When I passed but couldn't become a pilot, due to less-than-perfect vision, Moore asked for a waiver. He was communicating with me, sometimes by telegram. To a high school senior, the son of a steel mill worker, getting a telegram from your congressman was a big deal."[4] And there were literally thousands upon thousands of Arch Moore stories similar to Sweeney's.

Moore had his techniques for remembering people, which were discussed in the last chapter. Another factor that assisted him in remembering names and details was the fact that he signed all his correspondence and often added a hand-written note about their children or "events in their lives." As a result, people around the district and, eventually, the entire state, "began to look at Mrs. Moore and I as if we were part of their family. They shared their lives with us in private letters," Arch said.

Brenda Nichols-Harper, who later would work for Moore, noted he was able to make some personal inquiry to almost anyone he met. "How's your mother doing since her surgery?" or "What's your son doing, now that he's graduated?" She thought, "What a gift! I've never seen anyone who could work a crowd like he could. He just had an amazing ability–he always seemed to know everyone in the room."

Another place he was making friends was on college campuses. He "touched base with Fairmont State, West Liberty, Bethany and Wheeling-Jesuit College presidents and with the young people of those colleges." Moore recalled, "I wanted to get a handle on problems with education, even in the public schools. Every Spring, I'd lecture at Bethany."

He also started a very popular summer Congressional internship program and accepted two college students each year (among whom were David and Susan Hardesty)[5] to work in his Washington office. Soon other congressmen and senators were doing the same. It was a system which developed future leaders, kept Arch in touch with young people, and raised his own profile in the district.

As result of his effort, many otherwise partisan Democrats were simply pretending he was one their own. "I was in Colasessano's[6] in Fairmont one Saturday," laughed Huntington lawyer Dick Tyson, "and it was like the Democratic headquarters in there. All the Democratic candidates, including the Kennedys, came through there. But, between the photos of Franklin Roosevelt and John F. Kennedy, hung a portrait of Arch Moore. I asked them, why this Republican? And they'd only say, 'That's Arch Moore—he's our congressman.' They wouldn't admit he was Republican. But, by god, they were for him!"

The Congressman would return to Glen Dale every Thursday evening to attend to business throughout the First District. During times the family was staying in Maryland, he would return to Washington on Saturday, usually attending church with them on Sunday mornings. At first, he relied on TWA's flights from Washington National (now Reagan) to Wheeling. "More times than not" he would be late getting to the airport and his plane would be on the tarmac at National, nearing take-off. "Jennings Randolph[7] was working for the airlines at the time and I'd have my secretary phone him to tell him I was running fifteen minutes late and ask if he could hold it," Arch laughed. "He'd tell her, 'Well, you know, I think that plane may need to be held up for fifteen minutes for maintenance.' I had a congressional license plate and in those days there were no fences, you could drive right up to the tarmac. I'd park the car, run across the grassy knoll and get to the plane just in time. [Ohio Democratic Congressman] Wayne Hayes, who would often be fuming in that muggy, humid Washington heat, waiting for the plane to leave, never did figure out that it was me who was always holding up those flights to Wheeling."

Members of Congress then received reimbursement for only two trips to their district each year. Beyond that, it came out of his or her own pocket. It became expensive for Arch to come home every weekend, and he was already paying to keep two houses, but he knew the frequent trips were necessary to meet his constituents' needs and to win election every two year.

To ease the transportation problem, Arch would purchase his own twin engine Beechcraft. "The way I could afford it was that I let the pilot, Floyd Graham, have it through the week for his own charter flights. I didn't pay him to pilot it and he didn't pay me for use of the plane. But I had priority when I needed it." Said his son, Kim Moore, "Dad was really into time management—he was way ahead of his time on that. And use of a plane was one of the ways [he saved time]."

If the family was staying at their Glen Dale residence, the Congressman would phone his wife to let her know he was on his way home from the nation's capital. Recalled daughter Shelley Moore Capito, "To let us know it was time to pick him up, he'd buzz the house. My grandfather [Arch, Sr.] would take me with him to that grass landing strip[8] down near the Marx Toy factory by the Ohio River at Glen Dale." Her Congressman father would almost always return home in the evening, after dark, and there were no lights at the field. "So Granddad would point the headlights of his car at the landing strip so the pilot could see to land. And in they'd come!" (She noted that, as governor, her father later had the runway at Glen Dale paved and lighted.)

Unlike her sister and mother, Lucy Moore enjoyed the family plane; she was fearless. But she admitted that the family, "all crowded in there," flew through some life-threatening storms. "The pilot, Floyd Graham—what a character! He could fly through anything, land anywhere."

Not just Glen Dale, but any of the landing strips Congressman Moore used, such as the one in Kingmont, Marion County, were just dirt—bumpy and scary places to land. "When you landed there, you had communication with your Maker," Arch remembered, noting that as soon as he became governor, he made sure that many of those landing strips were paved and extended.

The aircraft was a major convenience for her father but "I hated that plane," Capito confessed. "I just didn't like flying. We flew in a lot of bad weather and there wasn't efficient weather reporting in those days. We would use it to fly to Savanna, Georgia and then on to Miami, Florida at Christmas time to visit family on my mother's side. It would take us twelve or fourteen hours to get down there!" The Moores could get their entire young family aboard their plane, along with their beloved collie, Missy, who "was a good traveler," according to Capito. Kim Moore liked the plane but agreed that at times it was "crazy." He remembered that the family "went through thunderstorms that, by all rights, we shouldn't have made it through. Mom hated it."

Living in a congressman's household often afforded educational lessons for the children, up close and personal. "We lived through some historic times," said Shelley Moore. "I tried to include the children in it, partly so they'd know why their dad wasn't home as much as some dads. I'd take them out of school if I thought it was something important or historical." (An example of that would occur when the Moore family stood quietly along Pennsylvania Avenue to watch the caisson bearing the flag-covered casket of President Kennedy pass by, on its way to Arlington Cemetery, in November 1963.)

Capito didn't remember it being a problem to have her father away from home so often. "I remember when he was there, not when he was not there," she explained. "Mom did a great job caring for our every need. Family was his hobby; he didn't play golf then, for example." The Congressman enjoyed household chores. His daughter mentioned, as an example, that "he was very fastidious about his yard. He always enjoyed mowing the grass and sweeping the driveway." Daughter Shelley said she looked forward to each summer when her parents would host a picnic at their Glen Dale home for those who worked in his office, which included the college students who were interning.

Years later, Capito reminisced in a Father's Day article in a Charleston paper about the closeness she'd felt to her father. "When I was really little and going to school, in the mornings when it was really cold I would eat breakfast, then go back upstairs and get into bed with my dad and he would keep me warm." She continued, "He used to take us to work with him [when he was in Congress]. He'd let us sit on the floor [of the House] and we got to meet a lot of important people." Riding in parades with him and attending events, "He always made us feel that we were a real important part of his campaigns." But there were other times that were tough being a public figure's child, she said. Her girls' school in Washington would hold annual father-daughter dinners and, "in my five years, my dad never came because of his job–he couldn't. In my senior year, he said he couldn't come again and I was really disappointed, but played the martyr role. At the end, he cancelled a trip and came. It meant a lot to me."[9]

Arch developed a delightfully newsy letter, mailed to all of his First District constituents a few times a year. Along with a couple photos, he would offer opinions on timely issues, have a Q&A section about social security and other federal programs, and then reserve a corner for some personal items. In a 1962 issue, while he was in a heated race against redistricted Congressman Cleve Bailey, Arch noted, "Our family has lost the greatest friend we had. There's no way we're going to get over it."

He told readers that their collie, Missy, had died of cancer ("probably because she was pure-bred," Arch speculated). "We were a dog family. That just killed the kids, Shelley and me," he recalled. To replace the lost family member, Mrs. Moore "went out and got a Heinz 57, mixed-breed miniature collie from the dog pound in Washington." In the meantime, the mention of the loss of their pet in the newsletter resulted in over four thousand sympathy letters from constituents. "*The Wheeling News Register* [a Democratic paper] wrote, 'Cleve, please get a dog!'"

The new dog, whom they named Sandy, proved to be a smart one. Arch laughed, "When we would go to our plane, that dog would resist the leash and go ahead of us. The airport personnel would stop and have people watch. The dog would go out, look for our plane and then run toward it. As soon as he would get in it, he would lie down and put his nose up to the vent."[10]

Arch would take his plane, or go by car, to almost every town in the district when he was home on Fridays or during the recess, which usually began in August. "I met constituents in post offices and city halls. In Hundred, West Virginia, they put me in the jail for our meetings." Generally, people came to see Moore about social security, welfare, immigration or military, VA benefits, other problems, almost anything touched by the federal government. "Sometimes they would have children in the [military] service who'd been hurt and they hadn't heard from." Other times, he would receive petitions or requests regarding labor union issues pending before the Congress.

"I tried to stay away from state politics," he recalled about those town hall meetings. "I might kick a letter down to the state–but I didn't have the pull, the connections, that I had with the federal side."

The "bread and butter issue was job loss to foreign countries, even bigger than today," Arch noted, of his early days as the First District's representative in Washington. "We had thirty seven glass plants and we're now down to three. I became a proponent of fairness to the American worker.

"At first, unions would not let me attend their meetings. After I touched them, helped them, they became convinced. They would let me talk ten minutes but not respond to questions. If I had ten minutes, though, I'd get some votes out of that meeting."

Normally a freshman member of Congress, certainly one in the minority party, is to be seen, not heard, and rarely has any success with his legislative proposals. Not so with Rep. Moore. Remarkably, he immediately began sponsoring bills and getting them passed. In April of 1957, he sponsored H.R. 7102, which increased personal income tax exemption from six hundred to a thousand dollars and also provided exemptions for a spouse, dependents and additional exemptions for old age or blindness.[11]

H.R. 8441 had to do with registration of trademarks. H. R. 10826 prohibited charging the public for any television program. *The New York Times* mentioned on July 21, 1957, that Rep. Moore had been appointed to a Judiciary subcommittee that drafted legislation to counter recent Supreme Court decisions which allowed criminal defendants access to FBI records by witnesses who testified against them. Moore's successful bill restricted the records to a trial judge's review, requiring the judge to decide which records were relevant.

In 1958, he would sponsor successful legislation that had a major impact on social security disability, allowing awards when a worker lacked the ability to "engage in any substantial gainful activity by reason of any medically determinable physical or mental impairment which can be expected to result in death or to be of long-continued and indefinite duration." Under another bill, an applicant needed only one quarter to get social security, rather than twenty quarters of employment and payment into the system, to be eligible for disability benefits and it required a monthly check of at least thirty dollars.[12] A bill he introduced in June of 1958, allowed a retiree to draw social security as early as age sixty. H.R. 10866, another Moore bill, prohibited government contractors or suppliers from practicing age discrimination when they hired employees.

According to Oce Smith, who was then working in the office of Senator Neely, "Arch had been in Washington practically no time at all when it was talked about on The Hill that he was something of a wheeler-dealer. He was the slickest wheeler and dealer and con artist in the political system. One of our [Democratic] friends once remarked that Arch 'must have missed a meal someplace along the line,' because he always was pursuing money."

Smith acknowledged, however, that Congressman Moore "was beloved by the staff from the lowest level to the highest in the House, by the officers, the hired help, the youthful pages and by congressmen who [didn't] run the show because he never forgot them. He always called them by name and said something to them about their personal life. Very often, he'd do little favors for them which meant so very much to them."

John Roberts worked for the Democratic leadership in Congress and knew everyone from John F. Kennedy and Lyndon Johnson to Sam Rayburn, on a first-name basis. When Moore asked him for a new carpet for his office, Roberts' first thought was that freshmen congressmen didn't get new furnishings, particularly Republican freshmen congressmen. "I was ready not to like Arch Moore," admitted Roberts, a partisan who now serves as Doorkeeper for the West Virginia House of Delegates.

"He said, 'John, my rug's a mess–can't I get one?' I just couldn't help but like him. I simply liked the guy. It's a real gift [Moore has]. I went back and told the House Clerk that it was terrible and wrote up an order for one."[13]

With success came some inevitable inter-party rivalry with the new Republican governor, Cecil Underwood and, as can be imagined, the bone of contention often was money. Cecil had won the GOP nomination in 1956 with only $19,000 (against Charleston Mayor John Copenhaver, who was much better financed) primarily because of all the grass roots work he'd done as a Young Republican since 1949. But money was badly needed in Cecil's autumn campaign against Mollohan. "Walter Hallanan was the boss of the [West Virginia] Republican party then," recalled Underwood. "He worked for Plymouth Oil Company and raised a lot of money for the party, mainly from the Wheeling area. After Arch Moore and I were elected, there was less industry in the state and, as result, less money for Republicans. Most of that remaining money went to him [Arch Moore]." The two would compete for the next three decades, for votes and for scarce campaign donations.

Moore would continue to keep in touch with his constituents. A 1957 newsletter invited applicants to the military academies and announced that Arch had been appointed by Speaker Sam Rayburn to the Select Committee on Small Business. An April 1957 questionnaire asked whether his constituents approved of President Eisenhower's foreign policy; whether they wanted to reduce the federal debt before lowering taxes; whether they approved an increase in postage rates to provide better buildings and services; and whether they wanted legislation to restrict imports. Another asked opinions on foreign trade, labor reform, education, a natural gas bill, pay TV, tax reductions, social security increases, and extensions of unemployment benefits. They boasted of Moore's role in building new post offices, armories, community facility projects, water and flood control projects, aid to colleges and public schools, housing credits, roads and highways and aid to business and industry.

The Congressman would sometimes get teased during this period about having the same name as a much more famous light-heavyweight champion boxer, Archie Moore. "Although some persons say the Congressman doesn't weigh that much," joked the *Wheeling News-Register.*

The pressing national issue in the late 1950s was the fear of Soviet expansion and a growing sense that the Russians were moving ahead of the U.S. militarily and technologically. That proved to be an illusion (John F. Kennedy used the theme of Soviet superiority to defeat Nixon for president in 1960), but it was widely believed at the time. "One of my classes at WVU had been on the subject of the Soviet Union. I studied Russia quite a bit," remembered Arch. "They had a rigid government that wouldn't tolerate five minutes of dissension—they'd take you out to a firing squad; there was no such thing as a day in court." Moore remembered that there were many in his district who had served in the military in World War II, and now saw the Soviet Union as a threat. "Communism was on everyone's mind. Many of them were just not going to tolerate the Soviets controlling the world. Keep in mind that they controlled a large land mass. We had Communists like Alger Hiss in our own government, which scared the daylights out of us. People would say, 'Thank God we have two oceans to protect us,' which was true until 9-11."

Moore would always have a fascination with the Soviet Union, however, and visited the country on seven occasions, both as congressman and later as governor. After his public career, the Moores took all of their grandchildren to Russia for an educational vacation. St. Petersburg was his and Mrs. Moore's favorite. "I can remember walking those snowy streets in November; it was absolutely beautiful," said Arch. [14]

While a congressman, he got to meet Premier Nikita Khrushchev, who gave him a (somewhat ugly) flowered vase, which he keeps in his Moundsville office. At the height of that empire's power, "I saw a country in which society was maintained with an ironclad fist. Only two percent of the people were Communists, and they lived the most lush and rich lifestyles. The other 98 percent were born and raised in poverty. As a tourist, you could visit an American-style department store, the Gum

Department Store, in Moscow, to buy souvenirs, but there was always a long line."

Once, when he was visiting the Kremlin, he recalled, "Russians loved to engage in conversation. They would follow me and ask, 'USA? USA?' I'd give them a thumbs-up. They were fascinated with John Kennedy. The State Department wouldn't let me go far, or talk to them long, however." On a trip to Ukraine, the Moores had a KGB officer accompany them and dine with them. He would say, "I love the U.S.," Arch recalled. "I told him, 'My plane will be [at a certain location]. You come with Mrs. Moore and me, and we'll get your family out later.' He replied, 'I dream of it, but I cannot leave.'"

Through the State Department, the Moores were furnished an interpreter whose father had been a diplomat during Czarist Russia. "She and her family were pro-U.S. but they could not show that." Arch also befriended the Soviet Ambassador, Anatoly Federovich Dobrynin. "We have always kept six seats on the 50-yard line at RFK Stadium [for Washington Redskins games]. We took Federovich to a Redskins game and he left us, went down to watch the scantily clothed cheerleaders until they were finished with their routine. He asked with a smile, 'How many Sundays do you get to come see football?'"

On one of his trips, Moore and two other congressmen were able to secure the release of five Soviet Jews who wanted to emigrate to Israel. Although they discriminated against them, the Communists did not want to release the millions of Jews there who wanted to leave. "It was a big cave-in for the Soviets," to release even a few to Israel, Arch explained. The modest number released that day eventually resulted in hundreds of thousands of Jews subsequently being allowed to escape; it opened a gate to freedom.

Another contact Arch had with the Communist regimes during the Cold War occurred on a trip to then-West Germany in 1961, when he was on a fact-finding mission, due to the flood of refugees coming in from Soviet-dominated East Germany. "I was the first congressman to penetrate the Berlin Wall," recalled Moore. "I had asked to go over into the east to see Sputnik, which they had displayed in the museum, but was told it was too hazardous to go over there." But Moore had faced hostile Germans with guns seventeen years before. He insisted that he wanted to see the world's first satellite, so West Berlin Mayor Willy Brandt sent a car to deliver him to the Wall. "I walked right through and went to the museum. The East Germans were good to me. I did ask, as I went in [to the East Berlin zone], 'You're going to let me out, aren't you?'"

DURING MOORE'S first term as congressman, one incident endeared him to ethnic voters in the district and caught headlines around the world.

Airman Marion Musilli of Benwood, West Virginia, just north of Moore's hometown of Glen Dale, was driving an Air Force car on a highway near the Athens Air Field in Greece when it struck and killed General Stephanous Saraphis and injured his English wife. The two had been crossing the road in route to the beach. His death set off a firestorm in the Greek press, because Saraphis had been a popular Communist underground leader against the Nazis in World War II and was a member of the Greek Parliament. Because of the anti-Communist fervor in the U.S., the Greeks were whispering that the death was no accident.

Musilli was arrested and was to be tried by three Greek judges without a jury, likely facing at least five years in a Greek prison for involuntary manslaughter. The U.S. State Department was willing to sacrifice the 22-year-old American serviceman, just to keep peace with Greece at a time when the U.S. was trying to keep them from drifting into the Communist, Soviet bloc. "The Communists were very active in Greece," Arch recalled, "and the State Department discouraged me from getting involved. They said there was too much sensitivity–that whatever happens to the young man, happens. They worked on me for ten days."

But that did not suit Airman Musilli's congressman. Arch had been in Europe as a member of the U.S. military himself; he did not fancy the thought of someone like himself being abandoned by his own government just to placate a nation we were protecting from the Soviets by the presence of our base. Arch Moore announced that he would go to Greece and act as the man's lawyer himself. "I took the position that the American flag went with the American soldier, and American law [protections] went with him. I pled his case. I won his case." (Actually, the airman was found guilty but his sentence was reduced due to Moore's intervention. Musilli was sentenced to ten months in prison but eight months were deducted for time served. The West Virginian was allowed to pay a fifty dollar fine in lieu of the remaining two months. Arch paid the fine for him.) Moore was quoted at the time as saying the sentence was "fair under Greek legal practices."

Moore's presence initially had stirred up some hatred in the Greek press. Like the French, many Greek nationals resented America's military presence in their country to begin with. Arch wore an overcoat and hat during the trial but was recognized on Athens' streets and treated somewhat cooly by the populace. "I made the front page of every one of their twenty six newspapers," he recalled. But the evening after the verdict, "I went to visit the Parthenon and everywhere I went I was well received. The State Department went to bed happy. The Air Force gave him to me and I delivered him to his parents in Washington." The Veterans of Foreign Wars of West Virginia passed two resolutions in their mid-winter conference, commending Moore's intervention and assistance in the trial. "And I won most of the Benwood vote in the next election," Arch smiled.

About the incident, *The New York Times'* Tom Wicker admiringly wrote that Arch had "a knack for dramatizing [his] personal service ... He brought the young man home to his mother amid great civic acclaim." (But Wicker noted it wasn't just the high profile constituents who received their Congressman's attention, that Moore "looks after a former serviceman's complaint about his disability pension ... as though the man was a paying client.")

As result of the incident in Greece, Rep. Moore sponsored House Joint Resolution 371, which provided "for the revision of the Status of Forces Agreement and any other treaty or international agreement to which the United States is a party or the withdrawal of the United States from such treaties and agreements in order that foreign countries will not have criminal jurisdiction over American military personnel stationed within their boundaries." He didn't want a repeat of what Musilli had to endure while in the service of his nation. "These boys have no control over where they're going," he explained about his bill. "I was upset that American soldiers were subject to the laws of the countries they were stationed in."

Most of the legislation he pushed in his first two years "had impact on individuals," rather than corporate, union or governmental interests, he noted. His success could be attributed to his skill in rapidly making friends, even among those in the Majority, the Democrats. "As a member of Congress, I spent a lot of time gaining the confidence of my fellow members. They didn't know who or what you were when you came up there, so I tried to constantly make myself a better congressman."

But Arch Moore certainly could not be accused of pandering to First District voters in two other endeavors he pursued aggressively as a congressman, because there were few of either group among his constituency. He fought hard for the rights of Jews and African-Americans during his years in Congress, an effort which probably did not win him many votes back home. "I came [to Congress] in a year when the nation was examining our prejudices," is how he put it, five decades later.

Moore's work in easing immigration and travel laws also won him the gratitude of the Italian government. The president of that nation gave him the two highest medals possible to bestow on a non-Italian. That honor was mentioned prominently in campaign literature in a district full of Italian-Americans. Arch also published a photo of his and Mrs. Moore's private meeting with the Pope.

Senate Majority Leader Lyndon Johnson had decided in 1957 that it might be time to release some type of civil rights legislation for African-Americans, who were still segregated in schools and every part of society in the South, despite the Supreme Court ruling in *Brown vs. Board of Education* in 1954. Only Johnson, with his strong ties to the Southern congressmen and senators, could get such legislation started. It was always unclear whether Johnson (who used the "n-word" privately) really felt sympathy toward blacks, or whether he just saw it as a potential benefit to the Democrats and his own national ambitions. He claimed to be offended by the fact that his black driver could not use public restrooms throughout the South. More than any leader since Lincoln, LBJ made civil rights for black Americans a reality. For all his flaws, history has begun to acknowledge Johnson's role in liberating the descendants of slaves.

What has seldom been recognized, however, was that Congressman Arch Moore also was a key player in evolving civil rights legislation in the 1950s and 60s, as part of his role on the House Judiciary Committee.

Why did he, with an almost all-white constituency and as a Northern Republican, take an interest in the issue? "At that time of my life, I'd gone through World War II and WVU and had never interfaced with many African-Americans," he admitted. Until the Depression reduced their income, his parents had an African-American housekeeper, Mandy Thompson. As he grew up in Moundsville, black children had all been bussed to segregated schools in Wheeling. "But I'm an avid reader and was well-aware of their plight. President Eisenhower did some of the first movement [toward providing civil rights legislation], as did Presidents Kennedy and Johnson. I could not criticize the black man if I didn't give him a chance to get an education, a meaningful job and the right to vote."

Moore claimed he "tied up the Judiciary Committee for two months" because he felt the Civil Rights Act they were considering in 1957 was "in name only," and " not sufficient in relieving" what he saw as restrictions preventing blacks from enjoying the same rights and privileges as white Americans. The Southern Democrats "had watered it down until it was meaningless." Arch "spoke to the Republican caucus about the bill. The Republicans were in the minority and the Democrats were split between the north and south." Eventually, Moore helped get Rep. Emanuel Cellers' bill out of Judiciary, however, and it was passed. Washington's biggest muckraker, columnist Drew Pearson, had falsely written in *The Washington Post* on September 18, 1959, that Moore and Rep. Charlie Halleck had held up and watered down the civil rights bills and also incorrectly wrote that Moore came from a district with a "strong Negro" vote that would get him defeated because he had sided with Southern Democrats on the issue.

The NAACP sent Moore a telegram, thanking him for his part in the success of the bill. *The New York Times* would asked in an editorial, "Why all of this from a West Virginian?" as if the concept was unimaginable. "There was no political benefit," agreed Moore, regarding his role in the civil rights legislation, which continued to evolve through the late 1950s and early 1960s. "It was just a question of fairness."

HAVING LOST the governor's race and his image damaged by ethics issue raised by Cecil Underwood in the 1956 race, Robert Mollohan decided he would like to recover his congressional seat and announced that he would seek to regain it. Apparently referring to Moore's support of the Eisenhower Administration's policies, Mollohan said it was time to end the "rubber stamp" Congress.

"This time, I had the advantage of incumbency," noted Moore. "Although the second time is when you're most vulnerable. They come at you full bore that second time." Arch ran just as frantically as he had in the past two election cycles, as if he was behind all the way. "We just kept building our base. I had confidence that we had it under control."

One of the criticisms the Democrats lodged against Rep. Moore was that his party affiliation was nowhere to be found in any of his literature. They accused him of trying to trick First District voters into thinking he was a Democrat. (As if they wouldn't figure it out when they got into the voting booth.)

Mollohan would also file formal complaints with the U.S. Justice Department's Civil Rights Division over what he contended were unfair campaign practices. Anonymous pamphlets, designed to resemble the *United Mine Workers Journal,* were circulating throughout the district, repeating charges Underwood had made in 1956 against Mollohan. They said, among other things, that Mollohan had worked as a sales representative for the Mason Brothers, a non-union (gasp!) Taylor County coal company, in the 1940s which of course was an absolute no-no for a politician in that heavily unionized era. The paper also attacked the Democrat's overall labor record. He and his supporters were livid. The leaflet was "called something like the *United Miners Journal,*" recalled Mollohan friend

Oce Smith of Fairmont. "I don't recall the exact masthead. Right across the top of the fake journal was a blazon headline endorsing Arch Moore, all of which was of course totally illegal."

When Mollohan struck out with Taylor and Brooke County grand juries in his quest to get Moore supporters indicted for alleged distribution of the literature, he pursued his allegations with the feds. Assistant Attorney General W. Wilson Whitehead subpoenaed employees of the City of Fairmont (then controlled by Republicans) and a Marion County liquor store (then controlled by Republican Governor Underwood) to testify before a federal grand jury in Washington, a process which extended through 1959 and caused Congressman Moore some consternation and anguish. Moore himself was never implicated personally, and nothing ultimately came of the investigation, but it left a bad taste in the GOP congressman's mouth about the Republican Eisenhower Administration, to which he had been intensely loyal during his first term in Congress. He would become a little more discriminating in his support of the Republican positions in the future, perhaps as the result of this perceived betrayal by Eisenhower's Justice Department, in allowing the Mollohan investigation.[15]

One who would work hard against Moore in that 1958 race was an up-and-coming Democrat committeeman from Farmington, by the name of John Manchin. He would help coordinate Mollohan's effort, especially in Marion County.

The nation was drifting into the "Eisenhower Recession" and Republicans were getting blamed for job losses in West Virginia (unemployment rose locally because coal mining jobs were being lost due to automation of the mines and the rebuilt Japanese and German steel mills were giving the Ohio Valley plants some competition). "The smokestack industries in the Northern Panhandle were really having problems," recalled Ken Hechler, the transplanted New Yorker who defeated Republican Congressman Will Neal, the Huntington physician, to gain the Fourth District seat that year. Nevertheless, Arch increased his vote margin. He defeated Mollohan with a comfortable 9,351 margin this time, losing Marion County by a thousand votes and Hancock by 400, but winning the other five counties. The big win demonstrated that voters were very happy with this energetic young congressman, no matter on which ticket he ran.

The New York Times, noting that Senator John Hoblitzell lost the two-year unexpired term for the U.S. Senate and that Rep. Robert Byrd defeated Senator Chapman Revercomb for the six year term (by three-to-two margins), took notice. "The lone Republican survivor [in West Virginia] was Arch Moore...who demonstrated what year-round campaigning can do, even for a Republican in a normally Democratic district. He defeated Robert Mollohan, a former House member, who two years ago had been tarred by a ... scandal involving a state job he had held. The accusations reappeared in the closing days of this campaign although they were not traceable to Mr. Moore." The article added, "Mr. Mollohan was backed by John L. Lewis."[16]

Hechler agreed. "Arch Moore bucked the trend. West Virginia was in a very desperate condition with the highest unemployment rate in the nation. Many had run out of unemployment benefits. A lot of people were hurting." Hechler added, noting it was a compliment, "Moore was a master of PR. He knew how to approach damage control."

Moore developed a shrewd policy, but one which required him to swallow his pride. He believed in bringing one's enemies into his political camp whenever possible. Easier to watch them up close, he thought. Plus, his compassion often crossed party lines. Remembering how his father had lost his job in the middle of the Depression due to his party affiliation, Arch vowed he'd never do that to people. During the campaign, the Congressman heard that John Manchin—who had worked so hard against him—desperately needed a business loan. Most politicians would have taken pleasure at the financial loss of an opponent and been glad to see them removed as a player. But, after the dust had settled from the '58 election, Arch picked up the phone and called John, to ask if he could help him.

"I was shocked," recalled Manchin. "Here he was calling me, and I'd just worked against him as hard as I could. None of the Fairmont bankers would give me a loan to help me keep my [furniture and carpet] business open. They didn't like Italians.

"Arch asked how much I needed and I told him it was twenty-some thousand dollars. He said, 'Meet me at the Bridgeport airport tomorrow afternoon.' He flew in there, got off the plane and handed me a check. He'd borrowed it on his own name from the credit union over at the capitol. I could never, ever work against a friend like that. He saved my business."[17]

After the 1958 victory, the Moores felt more comfortable and confident that they could retain the seat and began making family decisions accordingly. Lucy and Shelley were placed in Holton Arms, a Washington area prep school which had been attended by Jacqueline Kennedy. Kim was placed in Harker. They sold the Maryland house they'd been using six months of the year and bought a beautiful, white brick home in upscale Potomac Falls, Maryland, with a two-and-a-half acre wooded lot and a split rail fence. "In fairness to the children, we had to light somewhere," Arch explained. The couple felt it was too much of a burden on their children to continue to split their school year between Maryland and West Virginia and that it might hurt them academically.

"All of our children were athletically inclined and all three participated in sports," he remembered. "We were all horsemen, especially Lucy. We would go on rides together as a family. We tried to expand their education in every way possible." The Moore children attended school with the children of *Time* magazine editor Hugh Sidey and they became friends. In the 1960s, former All-American, All-Pro Otto Graham moved in across the street from the Moores and they, too, became close friends. When Graham became coach of the Washington Redskins, Arch became a lifelong fan, keeping six coveted 50-yard-line seats throughout his life. Graham "could play a piano like nobody else," recalled Arch. "And his basement was full of trophies like I've never seen." (Fifteen couples from the neighborhood would attend Moore's inauguration when he became governor in 1969.)

But during the congressional recesses in the autumn, the Moores often would return for visits to their Glen Dale home. "I got the city to pave our [graveled] street," Moore said. Every year the extended family has filled the Glen Dale home at Christmas. "We call one of [the largest rooms] our Christmas Room." Mrs. Moore has a large Christmas tree put up in front of the window facing Jefferson Avenue each season.

Arch continued to cultivate friendships in Washington. He was happy to assist even the new Democratic congressman across the hall from his capitol office, whose views on many subjects were opposite his own. Congressman Hechler said he found Arch to be "extremely outgoing and courteous. We got along well together." He and Arch had in common their service in Europe during World War II ("Arch was a genuine war hero," noted Hechler, who interviewed Hermann Goerring and even wrote a best-selling book about the Bridge at Remagden). The new congressman (who'd run as "Dr. Ken Hechler" to woo voters and defeat his physician opponent), especially liked Moore's summer internship program for college students and wanted to copy it, "except Hechler wanted to keep the students for just three weeks and rotate others in." He asked Arch if he would reserve a few hours to speak to each group of his interns and, of course, he readily agreed. Arch rather liked this former historian—who wore the legs of his eyeglasses up high above his ears. Hechler had worked briefly for President Harry Truman, knew lots of key national

Democrats and had the story-telling ability of the Marshall College professor he had been.

But all was not lovey-dovey between the two, by any means. "I later got imbued by all that anti-Republican philosophy–the Democrats told us our majority was tenuous," Hechler admitted. Although the two would never oppose each other in an election, party rivalry outweighed personal friendship.

Accordingly, Hechler said he tried to put Arch in his place when he got an opportunity. He found that Moore's forensic skills were not to be challenged or upstaged, however. "Every year, the West Virginia delegation would breakfast with all the union leaders who would come to Washington. There was always pro-union legislation they wanted introduced and passed. They wanted to strengthen the NLRB, for example. But that was being held up in the Rules Committee by conservative Democrats and Republicans. They finally had got it discharged from the committee and the Democrats [from West Virginia] all voted for it, but Congressman Moore voted against it.

"At the breakfast, I told the union leaders present that I wanted Arch Moore to explain why he voted against it.

"He got up and gave one of the cleverest rebuttals I've ever heard. I remember the vigor, dedication and enthusiasm of his remarks, rather than any substance. Basically, he told them that the delegation needed someone to watch the domineering Democrats. He said it in such a persuasive way that he got a standing ovation! [The union leaders] thought it was remarkable. I think they were one hundred percent in favor of his actions! He refused to be caught," Hechler laughed. "I learned not to tangle with him in debate."[18]

ON JANUARY 18, 1958, Senator Neely had died in office after months of decline. The elderly Democrat had been in and out of the Senate (defeated once by a Republican, and resigned to become governor in the 1940s) since 1922. "I was in Paris attending a conference on taxation when someone knocked on my hotel door and gave me a telegram," recalled Arch. "Keep in mind, [Neely] was one of my constituents [because he resided in Fairmont]."

Governor Underwood had the privilege of naming Neely's replacement. Remembered Moore, "I was asked to attend a meeting of the state's Republican hierarchy, such as it was, at the Mayflower Hotel [in D.C.]. Walter Hallanan and others urged him to appoint this one or that one. I said I'd support whoever the party wanted. But Governor Underwood said, 'No, I feel strongly it's my prerogative as governor to make my own choice.' I had just beaten Bob Mollohan and had several supporters for the position. But Cecil chose John Hoblitzell, who was fine. He was very likeable, had been Eisenhower's chairman in West Virginia, had been state party chairman. They thought he could retain the seat."

It was likely another case of Underwood's jealousy of Moore, even fear of him, however, that prevented the logical choice of a Senator Arch Moore. Perhaps he genuinely was concerned about the "Wheeling connection," the fact that as a lawyer, Arch had represented gamblers, which was a no-no in his mind. Clearly, in the 20-20 vision of hindsight, Arch would have been the better choice, would have had a better chance of keeping the seat for the Republicans (Hoblitzell lost the seat in the next election). But the Underwood-Moore rivalry apparently had already become so intense that it caused common sense to be set aside. (What is even more puzzling is why Underwood did not appoint himself; he sought a Senate seat in 1960, only to be defeated by Jennings Randolph.) Arch always saw the feud as "one way," however. "If a rivalry existed, it was the best-run, one-way rivalry that ever existed," he insisted.

IN 1959, MOORE received criticism from a Democrat newspaper, *The Fairmont Times,* for voting to sustain President Eisenhower's veto of a public works appropriation bill (which Ike had opposed because it was a budget-buster and full of congressional pork-barreling). Arch's "fidelity to his party" had made it doubtful that the Opekiska Lock & Dam could be started on the Monongahela River, the paper's editorial complained. Moore had been the only member of the West Virginia congressional delegation to vote with the Administration but, then, he was its only Republican at this point. The paper opined that the vote killed Arch's chances of being elected governor in 1960, which was being discussed more frequently as a possibility.

"Every four years [while Moore was congressman] rumors would fly recklessly around the state that Arch was getting ready to run for governor," recalled Democratic pol Oce Smith. "He would generally feed those rumors with great design. Then, on the last night of the filing deadline, he would decide that there was still too much left for him to do for his people in the 1st District and that he would stick it out to finish his work."

But Smith was wrong about it all being Arch's doing. There were many who truly wanted his leadership in the state's capitol. After front-runner Charleston Mayor John T. Copenhaver died in 1960, the *Charleston Daily Mail's* Bob Mellace had been suggesting that Moore would be a good candidate to succeed Underwood as governor, noting that the Congressman was "a hard, magnetic campaigner, he can get Democrat votes, he is a family man with a fine war record and he comes from Northern West Virginia where Republican registration is heaviest."

Mellace added, however, that Underwood had put out the word that he wanted Harold "Punchy" Neely, of his administration, to be the candidate. (Except for the familiarity of the electorate to the Neely name–from M.M. Neely–it was puzzling as to why Governor Underwood chose that particular candidate.) In another column, Mellace wondered whether Moore would oppose Underwood in the primary for the 1960 nomination for U.S. Senate. Moore and Underwood were still submitting different nominees to fill federal judgeships, the writer noted. "If either of Moore's two choices get the job, it will appear he has scored a victory over the governor of his state and he will gain stature within the party. This cannot make Underwood very happy." He added that "differences between the Republican governor and the state's only GOP congressman have been pretty well concealed, although those close to both knew they existed." Mellace added that Moore and Underwood were "growing cooler and cooler toward each other."

Underwood, considering it five decades later, thought the struggle between him and Moore to name federal and state judges was a cause of their increasingly hot feud. He attributed the beginnings of the battle to another incident, though. Soon after taking office as governor, Underwood had decided to clean up the Northern Panhandle which, due to its proximity to Cleveland, Steubenville and Pittsburgh, was considered a center of organized crime. State governments were still decades away from making billions from gambling and giving it an air of legitimacy, acceptance and value. Gaming of all kinds was then controlled by organized criminals–not necessarily Mafia–and still had a stigma similar to prostitution or drug dealing. Most of it was "numbers," or "parlay cards" in which small-time gamblers could put a dollar or two on some sporting events at the local barber shop or bar, nothing too significant. It was considered a harmless, if illegal activity, by most. But there was pressure by Protestant churches, particularly, to clean up illegal alcohol sales ("liquor by the drink" was not yet legal, either) and gambling, which they contended hurt the wives and children of the [mainly male] gamblers and drinkers. Police "vice squads" would sometimes raid both.

He would be a hero if he could clean up organized crime so, in 1957, Governor Underwood ordered all available state police to the Wheeling area, where organized, daytime raids were simultaneously made of all known gambling establishments. Machines and cards were seized and owners and bar tenders were arrested and taken to justices of the peace. "But every time we moved on somebody, their attorney was Arch Moore [by then a congressman]. We took them to court and did not get a single indictment. So we backed off, deciding that wasn't a good use of the state police," said Underwood. But it left a bitter feeling with the new governor, a distrust of Arch; there was a stigma attached to a lawyer representing gamblers, as there would today perhaps to one who defended drug dealers.

"That's when [the Underwood-Moore feud] began," said Governor Underwood. "Not a single one of them was indicted!" Cecil was disgusted and suspected Moore from that time forward. While there was no lawful reason why Congressman Moore could not maintain a law practice, nor why he could not seek to have charges against his clients dismissed, Underwood felt betrayed—he took it personally. (*Author's note:* Moore denies that he ever represented any gamblers.)

Fights over patronage kept the fire stoked. The Governor began trying to fill federal judge vacancies with his choices. "I tried to appoint George Seibert, who followed me as House minority leader, but he didn't survive FBI scrutiny because of his family's ties to gambling," he remembered. So he came up with another candidate but discovered that Congressman Moore was supporting a rival for the Northern District vacancy. "I was told by the U.S. Attorney General's office that I could veto anybody, but I might not get my candidate. I found out that Arch told the Attorney General, 'Strike every name Underwood proposes.'" Whether true or not, Cecil was incensed when he heard that one.

It was around this time that Arch did something that he probably regretted a few years thereafter—he rescued the *Charleston Gazette*. The paper, which then had a much lower circulation than its rival, the Clay family's Republican-leaning *Charleston Daily Mail,* had teetered on business failure a few times. To secure both financially, they entered into an agreement by which they joined for the purpose of publication, to share printing presses, distribution and physical plant. Trouble was, a similar arrangement in Arizona had been ruled by the federal courts to be in violation of anti-trust and other laws. They couldn't legally do it, and one Charleston paper might have to go. Since it was the lesser circulating paper at the time, the *Gazette* was the probable victim. But the Clays also wanted the arrangement, because sharing overhead costs would help them, too.

Bob Mellace was sent by Lyle Clay to Congressman Moore to see if he could help. "Bob was a Beta," Arch noted (being a former fraternity brother always helped). With his position on the Judiciary Committee, Arch had excellent relations with the Justice Department, and "felt there was some merit" to their request for an exemption from the law. Charleston needed two papers, he thought, and he knew that they remained competitors, despite sharing facilities.

He succeeded in getting the U.S. Attorney General to issue a letter, exempting the two papers from any federal prosecution, an exemption under which they have operated their "single printing house," through several publisher-owners, to date. "I saved for posterity the *Gazette* and the *Daily Mail*," Arch laughed.

During his congressional years, Arch had no real complaints against the *Gazette*. "Harry Hoffman [then their editor] was from the Wheeling area and had liked my Uncle Everett. He played me straight down the middle when I was congressman." Hoffman even endorsed Arch Moore for re-election in 1958, when Mollohan tried to re-take the seat.

In July of 1959, Moore received a flurry of correspondence following an appearance of young Robert F. Kennedy on the popular Jack Parr's *Tonight Show*. Serving as counsel on his brother's (Senator John F. Kennedy's) Senate Labor Committee, Bobby was advocating support of legislation banning racketeering in unions, particularly Jimmy Hoffa's Mafia-ridden Teamsters Union. Business was supporting Republican versions of labor reform bills, however, not Kennedy's.

Few would have guessed it, but the Kennedy family was about to invade West Virginia, changing its political landscape forever and, some might say, not for the better.

Chapter 5 Notes

1. - *Charleston Gazette*, July 15, 2005. Mollohan was never criminally prosecuted. He became a multi-millionaire during his years in various public offices, but few ever questioned how he became so rich. The Fairmont Democrat would try very hard to get Arch Moore indicted for a campaign pamphlet that was issued in the '58 congressional campaign, however, taking it to local prosecutors, the House of Representatives and the Justice Department when that didn't work. After he retired and gave his seat to son Alan, Bob Mollohan would become Democratic chairman of Marion County.

2. - Moore defeated Spillers by 65,096 to 64,334 votes. Others elected to the House of Representatives that year from West Virginia included a Republican physician, Dr. Will Neal of Huntington in the 4th District, and Democrats Harley Staggers in the 2nd District, Cleveland Bailey in the 3rd, Elizabeth Kee (the former congressman's widow) in the 5th and Robert C. Byrd in the 6th District.

3. - When Moore returned to the governor's office in 1985, he discovered that Governor Rockefeller's staff had left behind his signature machines. "I had Jay Rockefeller's signature machines!" Moore laughed in a 2005 interview. "I could have broke the Bank of New York! But I had

them secured and sent them to him."

4. - He didn't go to the academy but it was by choice, not because Arch Moore didn't try to get it arranged. Sweeney saw no more of his congressman until he'd nearly finished Kenyon College and WVU, but Moore did not forget him. Five or six years later, at a convention at which Moore was speaking along with Ronald Reagan in Washington, he stuck out his hand to the then-Governor and began to introduce himself. Arch interrupted him with, "You're Tom Sweeney of Weirton!" And, as with thousands of others, Moore gained a lifelong fan through the personal attention he gave and his phenomenal retention of names, faces and circumstances.

5. - Found among Moore's congressional papers was a research memo dated July 17, 1967, "The West Virginia Highway System," co-written by intern David Hardesty, the future president of WVU.

6. - For years, Colasessano's family-run bar in the Bellview section of Fairmont was home to the world's best pepperoni buns and wonderful, thick-crust pizza before it was fashionable.

7. - Randolph had lost his congressional seat for bravely supporting the Taft-Hartley Act, which greatly angered his union supporters. After they caused his ouster, he worked in the airline industry, for Capital Airlines, almost a decade until he was elected to the U.S. Senate in 1958.

8. - Where Charles Lindbergh in 1928 landed his *The Spirit of St. Louis,* to the thrill of thousands crowded to see it.

9. - *Charleston Daily Mail,* June 16, 1978.

10. - The Moores would bury their first dog in a Wheeling pet cemetery and Sandy in a Hurricane, West Virginia pet cemetery, and would visit the graves for years to come.

11. - Digest of Public General Bills and Selected Resolutions, 85th Congress, 1st Session, 1957, The Library of Congress.

12. - H.R. 10844 and 10845.

13. - Roberts would recall that, twenty five years later, when he was out of a job, he went to Moore for help. "I had a beard, but he knew immediately who I was. He had his assistant call me about a job opening. These are the things that make a friend for life," Roberts said, although he denied he'd ever voted for Moore. "I asked him, when he was released from prison, "Governor, is there anything I can do to help you? He replied, 'Just take care of Shelley [Capito].'"

14. - "I had to borrow $1000 on a note from the Mercantile Bank [in Moundsville] to be able to go to Russia the first time," remembered Arch. "Mr. Resiker of the bank always wanted to know why you needed to borrow money and I told him I was taking Mrs. Moore with me to the Soviet Union. He had me to go get Uncle Everett's [co-]signature, before he'd give me the loan." Apparently the bank president was afraid Arch wasn't coming back. "The next time I went, he didn't require a co-signature."

15. - A *New York Times* article of November 26, 1958 reported that Mollohan also took his complaint to his fellow Democrats, to a Special House Committee created to investigate elections in Kentucky and West Virginia. "Mr. Mollohan, a former member attempting a comeback...charged that literature distributed during the campaign violated the Corrupt Practices Act," it said.

16. - *New York Times,* Nov. 7, 1958.

17. - John Manchin, October 1984.

18. - Ken Hechler, Sept. 16, 2004.

Chapter Six
Kennedy Cash

Thirteen-year-old Joe Manchin was working on his go-cart downstairs in the family's Farmington garage apartment in April of 1960, when his mother yelled down to him, "I want you to meet someone." He protested that his hands were too greasy, but she insisted that he come upstairs. His father, John Manchin, had some political guests, which was not an unusual occurrence in their very political household.

Wiping his hands on a rag, he ran up the stairs. He found, crowded into the small family kitchen, Senator John F. Kennedy and brothers Teddy and Robert Kennedy, "with their entourage," eating his mother's spaghetti and salad. "They were just common and ordinary," Joe smiled, recalling the event forty-four years later.

John Manchin would have the honor of driving JFK in a Fairmont parade in the family's 1958 white Chevy Impala convertible. Joe added that his "family was very much involved" in Senator Kennedy's quest for the Democratic presidential nomination, of which the West Virginia primary election was deemed so critical. West Virginia was considered important because its voters were ninety-five percent Protestant and JFK was a Roman Catholic. The only other Democratic Catholic candidate, Gov. Al Smith, of New York, had been thumped by Herbert Hoover in 1928, so the perception was that Kennedy would need to win big in a heavily Protestant state to demonstrate that he could defeat the Republican, likely Vice President Richard Nixon, in the November election. Growing up in North-central West Virginia, which is heavily populated by second-generation Italians, Poles and other Eastern Europeans, young Joe Manchin didn't even realize until then that Catholics were in the minority in the Mountain State.

Although the Kennedy clan was dining with his father, it was actually the future governor's uncle, A. James Manchin, they were wooing. Jimmy Manchin, a former Marion County delegate, then a teacher at Jackson Junior High School, by the force of his gregarious personality was "high profile" in the state party organization, despite the fact that he no longer held office.

The handsome Jack Kennedy[1] appealed to West Virginia voters, as he promised to "get the country moving again," and made specific proposals of what he wanted to do to help many in the region who were dirt poor, their plight largely ignored by a Washington which was sinking millions into fighting the Cold War.

As a genuine war hero (he rescued one of his crew after their patrol boat was cut in two by a Japanese destroyer), Kennedy also appealed to the state's many veterans, unlike his opponent, Sen. Hubert Humphrey, who had not served in the military. Congressman Ken Hechler had been making speeches criticizing the Eisenhower Administration's failure to locate any military installations in West Virginia, despite the fact that natives of the state lead the nation in per capita military service and casualties. "I always said, 'First in war, first in peace, but last with the Pentagon!' Kennedy liked that line and began using it. He promised more federal contracts for the state, which he did do as president, including an aviation plant," said Hechler.

JFK brought fellow veteran Franklin Roosevelt, Jr. into the state to campaign against Humphrey. "Roosevelt just sounded like his father," remembered Hechler. "And that was a time when the New Deal was still very popular—many West Virginia homes had pictures of Jesus Christ, John L. Lewis and Franklin D. Roosevelt, hanging side by side."

And unlike any candidate before or since, JFK exuded star-like sex appeal to female voters. Many would come just to see him, touch him, and were thrilled if he spoke to them. As Tom Brokaw said, Jack Kennedy was "the first rock star politician."

And he knew how to make each potential voter feel like a close friend, much in the fashion Arch Moore used in West Virginia. "He had two stenographers follow him around and, if he spoke to you, they would ask your name, address, and a little about you," said Hechler. "In a few days, you'd get a nice, personalized, letter signed by Kennedy. That was really impressive to many voters."

But there was another, critical reason why Kennedy, with very little legislative record to support a presidential bid, was leaping ahead of other Democratic presidential contenders like Senate Majority Leader Lyndon Johnson. House Speaker Thomas P. "Tip" O'Neill, who knew the Kennedys very well, having served with them for years in Massachusetts, explained it without hesitation. "Money was the long arm of politics. Money is the mother's milk of politics. Joe [JFK's wealthy and controlling father] knew that before anyone else came along. You know, you can be a candidate, you can have the issues, you can have the organization, but money does miracles and that [Joe Kennedy] money did miracles in that campaign."

MONEY HAD LONG driven politics in the Mountain State, perhaps more blatantly than anywhere but in the big city Democratic machines. A few candidates, by their stature in the communities, could remain independent, above the fray, and still get elected. But far more had to play the money game, pay to get onto party or party faction slates, if they were to have any hope of being elected to office in West Virginia. And that was the culture, in April of 1960, into which the Kennedys moved and operated like pros, as they blitzkrieged Sen. Humphrey out of the race for the presidential nomination.

Raymond Chafin, head of the Democratic Executive Committee and a Democrat Machine boss in Logan County for decades, like other party bosses, suddenly and "mysteriously" switched allegiance from Humphrey to Kennedy in that famous West Virginia primary. When Bobby and Teddy Kennedy made their rounds and began to generously distribute their father's money, it opened all kinds of doors which previously had been closed to their brother's candidacy. It wasn't just the big bosses who were wooed by the green. With a smile, one precinct captain told Peter Maas of *The Saturday Evening Post*, "My workers each got $20 and I got $150. We're for Kennedy." (The average daily wage in 1960 was about $15.)

As Joe Manchin correctly noted, "Slates and vote buying didn't start with the Kennedys." But some could argue that the Kennedy clan took it to an entirely different level, the success of which would be noted and copied by subsequent millionaire candidates for governor and senator. *The 1960 Democratic primary changed the political landscape in West Virginia forever; many believe for the worse.* The machinery was already in place long before 1960. They just infused more cash money into it than it had ever seen before.

Richard Neely agreed that, in the three decades in which his grandfather controlled the state's Democratic machinery, "you organized. You paid [voters for their votes]." He added that M.M. Neely "even sent the State Road trucks out to pick up voters" and if a State Road employee "didn't have a load [of Democratic voters in his truck], it was his ass, the day after the election!"

Vote buying in those days could take different forms, Chafin recalled. "A woman might need ten dollars to pay her electric bill. The sheriff would give her that money, and she'd deliver her entire family's vote to him and his candidates. The money got out to the people, not like today when [most of the campaign money] is spent on radio and TV. [The campaign dollars] don't get out to the people now, into the communities where they can do some good." Richard Neely agreed that vote solicitation has changed. "Today, they send [the donations] to some schmuck in New York, who makes up the ads." Three to four cases of whiskey, usually half pints brought in from Kentucky liquor stores, were distributed to each precinct, Chafin remembered. "The sheriff would know where the best moonshiners were. He was usually in on it [moonshining], too. You'd buy at least forty gallons for election day. Sometimes he'd even send out his deputies or constables to pick it up and distribute it." When interviewed in 2004, Chafin still found no flaw with this system. "The people got better service out of [their government] then because [elected officials] were dependent on them. We got good voter turn-out. Nowadays, when people don't get paid to vote, they don't vote as much." (He did not mention what type of government service was received by those who didn't support their slates.)

Larry Tucker, who would head the Young Democrats before getting elected to the legislature, added, "Election day in West Virginia was a social event. There'd be people selling food [at the precincts]; it would be a great time. Sure, we gave voters bottles of whiskey or maybe five bucks to haul some voters to the polls. Everyone operated that way; you didn't get elected if you didn't. But then they took the fun out of it by changing the laws. Ken Hechler [as secretary of state] got all those [election reform] laws and he'd been one of the worst when he ran for congress in Southern West Virginia. Now all that [campaign] money goes to radio and TV stations, not the people!" [2]

"It was wide open [throughout the 1960s]," said Johnie Owens, who served as Mingo County's State Road superintendent from 1961 until 1969, later as a controversial sheriff and Democratic party chairman of that county, before going to prison for vote buying and various felonies related to his office. "I don't know where the feds were back in those days, but they didn't bother us." Throughout all the "heavily Democratic counties," it was more common than not to buy votes for two dollars each, said Owens. "You'd be surprised—even the business people, the white collar voters, would [sell their votes for two dollars]." Vote buying was done in various ways. One was to go around and buy absentee ballots, he explained. "In some elections, a candidate would have three thousand absentee ballots before the polls opened. Sometimes, whole precincts voted absentee. A fellow came to vote one time and the election worker told him, 'You go on home, you've already voted!'"

In counties using voting machines, vote-buying was as easy as those with paper ballots, according to Owens. "They called me and my brother the Lever Brothers," explaining that the two worked in tandem in their precinct to buy votes, as was occurring all over Mingo and many other

West Virginia counties in every election. "He'd be the outside man, the precinct captain—he'd 'control the grounds.' I'd work inside the precinct. He'd give a voter the paper with the slate of approved candidates, the voter would say to me, "I need assistance in voting,' and I'd make sure he pulled the lever for the correct candidates. Then I'd put a check-mark on his slate to let my brother know he'd voted the right way. And the voter'd go outside and collect his payment by showing it to my brother."

How did Democrats get the few Republican inside election workers to go along with their crooked scheme? "A lot of 'em would just turn their heads—they didn't care what we did," said Owens, adding, "We always gave the Republicans one seat on the Board of Education. That kept them on board." They sold out just that cheaply, probably afraid that if they complained, they would get nothing. Since the prosecutors, sheriffs and judges were all part of this corrupt Democratic machine, who was going to listen to their complaints, or do anything about it, anyway? Owens' organization was extremely effective, he said. "In a precinct with 500 voters, we'd get 480 of them. The Democrat chairmen controlled those precincts."

Vote buying was just part of an overall corrupt political system, admitted Owens. Until at least the 1980s, he said county sheriffs sent their deputies around each month to shake down area bars for cash "donations," which were taken back to the court house and split 50-50 between the sheriff and the Democratic county chairmen. "It went into their pockets," he claimed. Further, the "flower funds" were prosperous: "When I was State Road superintendent, I would collect ten or fifteen dollars in cash per month from each road worker and take it to the Democrat county chairman. It stayed in the county," he thought. "And that happened in the liquor stores, the court houses and everywhere. They all collected cash and took it to the chairmen."

Another political veteran wrote to Franklin Roosevelt, Jr. in April of 1960, "As I told you last time you were down here, most of these coal-field counties are for sale. It is a matter of who gets there first with the most money." Author Theodore White explained, "Politics in West Virginia involves money–hot money, under-the-table money, open money."[3] A recent Kennedy biographer, Robert Dallek, wrote, "The payoffs involved a system of slating, which was a form of legalized bribery ... It was all very simple: The candidate who paid the most to the county Democratic boss (under the conceit of subsidizing 'printing' costs) would have his list of backers identified as the 'approved slate.'" Dallek noted that Hubert Humphrey was not above playing this dirty game. The future vice president said, "We would pay it, but we don't have the money." Dallek quoted JFK's Kenny O'Donnell as saying the system did not bother "the earthy and realistic people of West Virginia, who were accustomed to seeing the local candidate for sheriff carrying a little black bag that contained something other than a few bottles of Bourbon whiskey."[4]

Noted Edgar F. "Hike" Heiskell, who served as West Virginia's secretary of state from 1973 to 1975, vote buying in Southern West Virginia likely became significant in the 1920s when "outside coal and timber interests provided the foundation for it." It was those companies that "got the cash out in bags and made sure you voted right. They started the process of watching you vote, until that was finally outlawed." After the unions came into power in the 1930s and 40s, the local Democratic party chiefs picked up where the company bosses left off. Noting that vote-buying is rare "north of Route 60," Heiskell, a Republican from a prominent Morgantown family, said it was a "rude awakening" for him to discover just how corrupt the southern eight counties really were. "I was a babe in the woods. I'd tell Northern West Virginia people that their votes were being cancelled out by votes being bought in Mingo and Logan Counties," said Heiskell. "When I'd describe it to them, they didn't seem to know what went on."

JOE KENNEDY, the Senator's father, had made millions of dollars by bootlegging whiskey across the Great Lakes from still-wet Canada during Prohibition. Not part of the Mafia, Joe nevertheless worked very closely with organized crime. He had added to his fortune through success in New York banking, through insider trading in the stock market and investment in the movie industry. In today's money, he was nearly a billionaire as result of his legal and illegal endeavors. Old Joe, or the Ambassador, as he was known, was calling the shots in his son's campaign, as he had always done, which included assuring that the national news media were giving him proper coverage (he reportedly "bought" a *Time Magazine* cover for Jack by giving publisher Henry Luce a $75,000 horse) and framing the "issues" to favor his son.

Significant to the West Virginia primary, Joe called in favors from friends he had made in the bootlegging business, which included the Chicago Mafia. Reportedly, at Joe's request, and through the help of Frank Sinatra who was working hard for JFK,[4] mobster Sam Giancana provided two million dollars for the Kennedy vote-buying in West Virginia, about $11 million in today's money, in addition to untold millions from the Kennedy coffers.

Judith Campbell Exner, a girlfriend shared by JFK and Giancana, reported that Sam's aide, Paul "Skinny" D'Amato, delivered Mafia money to be spent for Kennedy votes, via West Virginia Democratic sheriffs. Tina Sinatra, Frank's daughter, said the mafia also used its union and business connections to distribute JFK vote buying in West Virginia.[5]

A Boston real estate tycoon, Eddie Ford, also acted as a bagman, distributing "$3000 here, $5000 there, throughout West Virginia villages" to help "this young Kennedy boy." Wrote O'Neill, "[A] couple of weeks before the primary in West Virginia, [Ford] filled a suitcase with cash and drove through the state in a big Cadillac with Illinois plates. He'd pick out a sheriff who was powerful, and he'd say, 'I'm a businessman from Chicago, and I'm on my way to Miami. I think this young Kennedy would be great for the country, and I'd like to give you this three thousand dollars to see if you can help him. I'll be coming back this way, and I'll be happy to give you a bonus if you're able to carry the town.'"[6]

While most of the cash paymasters were Kennedy or Mafia subordinates, or even Bobby or Teddy Kennedy, the future president was not above handling cash himself. O'Neill recalled a fund raiser in Missouri in which he witnessed brewery millionaire August Busch meeting John F. Kennedy in a men's room to discuss the "take." Busch told the future president that $17,000 in cash had come in and another $12,000 in checks. "Great," O'Neill quotes Jack Kennedy as replying, "Give me the cash and give Kenny O'Donnell the checks." O'Neill recalled thinking, "Geez, this business is no different if you're running for ward leader or president of the United States." O'Neill mentioned that, when he ran for Congress in 1952, he raised $52,000 "and I don't recall seeing a single check. It was just custom to give cash."[6]

Nor was Kennedy's soon-to-be running mate above playing the cash game. In fact, Lyndon Johnson may have played it better than anyone in U.S. history. According to most of his biographers, LBJ used bagmen Bobby Baker and John Connally to shake down oil millionaires and other businessmen for cash "donations" in exchange for favorable votes in the Senate, which he controlled with an iron hand. While much of the cash reached Democratic coffers, some did not. LBJ became a very wealthy man while supposedly subsiding on a relatively small Senate paycheck. Another convenient way to win his favor was for businesses to buy advertising on his TV and radio stations back in West Texas. Even after Johnson became vice president, Jack Whiting, a Democrat politico in Charleston, recalled personally transporting envelopes containing tens of thousands of dollars in cash to LBJ's office, the "tribute" paid by West Virginia

Democrats, fully expected if any favors were to be forthcoming from Washington. Democratic politics was a money pyramid scheme, with the White House at the top.

But it was more than just money that won Kennedy the primary, thought Ken Hechler, although he admitted its importance. "They asked Sid Christie, the Democrat boss in McDowell County in 1960, how he'd carried that county for Kennedy, and he said, 'Well, I think we had a bunch of Catholic voters in the county,'" Hechler laughed.[7]

To Hechler, it was organization, Kennedy family dedication, and JFK's personal "charisma" that made him win big over Humphrey, as much as the money. "Hubert was an old-time orator who went too long. And he wasn't as prepared as Kennedy," he recalled. "He made a big gaffe while campaigning in Cabin Creek. Someone yelled out, 'You should get Jerry West to help you!' and Humphrey asked, "Who's Jerry West?' On the other hand, Kennedy was always well-briefed before he spoke anywhere."

After a Beckley courthouse speech, Hechler was invited by Senator Kennedy to fly over to Washington with him for a strategy meeting, although Hechler was not endorsing either candidate (Humphrey had taken the unusual step of endorsing him in a tough primary fight in 1958, against local Democrats, because Hechler was considered the most liberal). "At eight a.m., through different doors, burst Ted Kennedy, Robert Kennedy, Sargent Shriver and Eunice Kennedy Shriver. They'd been working different parts of the state. They were in such agreement, trusted each other so fully, that they didn't even bother saying hello," he remembered. "They just started jostling for JFK's attention, 'Here's what we need in Martinsburg,' 'Here's what we need in Bluefield,' and so forth. Their unity, loyalty to each other, their organizational skills, really impressed me."

The next night, Hechler accompanied Sen. Humphrey to a ballroom in Madison for a big speech. "In the elevator, he turned to an aide and asked, 'Bill, do we have a table set up for our literature?' I knew then and there that Kennedy was going to win. What a contrast!"

Pete Thaw, a long-time Democratic politico and Kennedy volunteer that year, agreed with Hechler. "Bob McDonough [JFK's manager in West Virginia], Tom Godby and other Democrats and I had been meeting at ten a.m. every Sunday morning at the Blennerhassett Hotel [in Parkersburg] for two years to plot [JFK's] campaign. We had every county well-organized [for Kennedy] for a year. Humphrey just came in here and got ambushed. They said it was money, but we were just much better organized."

There was no real ideological battle between Senators Humphrey and Kennedy on social or domestic issues; both were liberals. In fact, Humphrey argued that the fact he'd grown up in relative poverty made him more empathetic to the plight of the poor than the wealthy Massachusetts heir. The squalor JFK saw in coal camps, especially in Southern West Virginia, reportedly shocked him. He'd never seen anything like it except in Third World countries. With Republicans arguing that the economy had never been better (which was pretty much true for the nation as a whole), Kennedy told West Virginia audiences: "Let them tell that to the four million people who are out of work, to the three million Americans who must work part time. Let them tell that to those who farm our farms, in our depressed areas, in our deserted textile and coal towns. Let them try to tell it to the five million Americans who live on a surplus food diet of thirty dollars a month."[8] Senator Kennedy promised that, within sixty days of his election, he would submit a "complete program to restore and revive the economy of West Virginia."

WEST VIRGINIA Democrats were not unanimous in their support of the young senator from Massachusetts, however. A *New York Times* article of April 11, 1960, noted that Sen. Robert Byrd, an "avid supporter of Senator Lyndon Johnson of Texas" was urging a "Stop Kennedy" coalition, warning West Virginia Democrats that the state's primary would be their last chance to stop JFK's steamroller. The paper was cynical about Byrd's opposition to the Catholic Kennedy, noting that "the old Ku Klux Klan was strong in West Virginia and Senator Byrd acknowledged membership in it many years ago. By a whispering campaign, Protestants are being urged to mount an efface to counter Senator Kennedy's primary victory in Wisconsin last Tuesday."

Thaw, who was mayor of Sistersville at the time, agreed. "Byrd opposed John F. Kennedy because he's a racist, anti-Catholic, anti-black, anti-Jewish. With Byrd, it was, 'You're for [Lyndon] Johnson, or get out of the way.' He took a lot of organization from us, but it was in name only. West Virginia Democrats quietly supporting Kennedy couldn't admit they were for him because of Byrd's opposition, so it was an illusion that we [Kennedy forces] weren't going to win."

During the course of the battle, Kennedy forces employed Franklin Roosevelt Jr. to release a copy of Humphrey's draft records to the media (he'd obtained a deferment). The Kennedy people even flew William Marland in from Chicago, where the alcoholic former West Virginia governor was driving a taxi cab. They flew him back to Illinois when he fell off the wagon five days later.[9]

Ken Hechler was reminded of the lingering effect of Kennedy cash six years later, as he campaigned in Logan County for re-election. The Congressman drove his red jeep up in a hollow near Chapmanville, to the home of Ernest "Red" Hager, the Democratic chairman of that county. Red asked him if he'd brought his black bag. When Ken asked what he meant, Red's lieutenant, lawyer Bernard Smith, spoke up:

> We control the houses [polling places] and we control most of the voters. Why, we can tell you within fifty votes of how many you'll get on Election Day. To do that takes money. We have to set up our organization, hire drivers, work the grounds and invest financially in the votes of some voters. Why, we even get the few Republican votes in the county. Every one of our Democratic candidates makes a cash donation to help our machine stay oiled. Been that way for years. John F. Kennedy gave, Robert C. Byrd gave, Jennings Randolph gave and you're no different. If you want Logan County's votes, you'll have to bring us that little black bag."

When the maverick Hechler told Smith and Hager that he refused to buy votes they were selling, Smith told him, "Well, you won't carry Logan County, you can bet on that. If you're not on our slate you won't get ten votes down here, just wait and see."[10]

Richard Neely observed that vote-buying among Marion County Democrats was still going strong at least as late as 1980. "I visited my friend Harper Meredith [the circuit judge who ran that county's Democratic machine from the 1940s until 1984] after the election and he gave me a couple cases of whiskey miniatures left over from the election, stacked up in his house. It was still common practice."

About reforms and arrests made in recent decades, Neely was not optimistic those will succeed in ending vote buying and corruption. "The problem with money and politics is like water on a cement floor: it will always find every single crack."[11]

CONGRESSMAN Moore was pretty much staying out of the fray in 1960, concerned with his own re-election effort. *The New York Times,* noting that Arch's First District contained nine-tenths of the state's Catholics, opined that "the swing toward Senator Kennedy" had "created some worry" for the Republican congressman. Moore's election "had seemed certain" because he enjoyed "considerable popularity among Democrats" and had "substantial union aid," even though the AFL-CIO endorsement had yet again gone to his opponent, but the reporter thought there was a chance Arch could be upset that year. "The Democrats acknowledge that Mr. Moore will run well ahead of Mr. Nixon," the paper reported. "However, they are hopeful that Mr. Kennedy's appeal will prove so great that Mr. Narick [the Democrat] will be carried in with him."[12]

Vice President Richard M. Nixon, who was almost as young as Kennedy but far more experienced, was expected by most experts to pull it off in the end and defeat Senator Kennedy. (He probably would have done so, but for his haggard appearance for their first TV debate, a very lukewarm endorsement from his boss, President Eisenhower, and the fact Kennedy was able to position himself to the right of Nixon on issues like Cuba and the so-called missile gap.)

Nixon briefly, but seriously, considered Governor Underwood as his running mate in 1960. Cecil Underwood probably would have helped the GOP ticket far more than Henry Cabot Lodge of Massachusetts, who proved to be a dud. Instead, Nixon asked Underwood to run for the U.S. Senate against Jennings Randolph, who by then had been in office a few months. "He told me, if anyone can win, you can," Underwood recalled. (He did not; Randolph was re-elected.) The Vice President promised him that if he ran and lost, Underwood would be appointed Secretary of Interior in a presumed Nixon Administration. "I declined the vice presidency of the University of Texas to run for the Senate," Underwood recalled.

In May, Arch Moore spoke at the Wyndham County Women's Republican Association in Connecticut, urging them to support Nixon. The six-year-old photo of Moore with President Eisenhower was published in most papers throughout the district in May of 1960. Arch had led a fight for the Administration's redevelopment bill. But at the same time, the young congressman was showing some independence, announcing on May 19, for example, that he would vote to override Eisenhower's anticipated veto of the Depressed Areas Bill, which was expected to inject millions into the West Virginia economy, by helping its poorest citizens. He also voted to override the President's veto of a pay raise for postal workers.

Part of Moore's departure from strictly following the Republican

Party line was for obvious reasons: he served in a district in which Democrats held the most votes, and the state's needs were not being fully met by the GOP's national policies. Increasingly, he was finding himself philosophically to the left of his party.

He demonstrated independence on another of the President's initiatives. Arch voted with several other members of congress against statehood for Alaska in 1959 and Hawaii in 1960, which Eisenhower had supported and signed into law. Some in Washington didn't think either had enough of a tax base to be self-sustaining, but there were other reasons for opposition, too. Hechler remembered taking a group of students to the capitol during the debate. "They heard Senator Tom Connally of Texas speak against Hawaii becoming a state. He said, 'Why, they don't even speak English there!" But Moore's reasons for objection were different. He believed that only territories that were contiguous with the forty-eight states should be considered. "I didn't want to expand," he explained without apology. "I felt we were setting a bad precedent and there would be others like Puerto Rico and Guam that would want to come in. The commonwealth system has worked quite well. Look at Samoa."[13]

Arch was fortunate to have a little known Democrat opponent, since no one of any stature, including Bob Mollohan, was willing to take him on. Steven Narick, who had graduated two years ahead of Moore from the WVU College of Law, and a former Marshall County prosecutor, had frequently faced Arch as a criminal defense lawyer in Moundsville. Their law offices almost adjoined. He won the Democratic nomination and the "honor" of challenging the increasingly invincible Arch Moore.

As he had for years, Moore spoke frequently to veterans groups, where he remained very popular, and newspapers continued to publish photos of him on the U.S. Capitol steps, with visiting women's groups, students and others. (Because one would open a newspaper on a pleasant Sunday afternoon, more often than not, to find a picture of Congressman Moore with a throng of local Scouts, safety patrols, or some civic group, smiling at the camera, it was hard not to have positive feelings about him; he became a comfortable entity. To people of the First District, he was "our friend in Washington.") Throughout the summer, he would ride in supporters' convertibles in parades and crown fair queens, a custom he followed his entire political career.

Moore continued to generate publicity by appointing nominees to the U.S. military academies, a pleasant task, because there were usually enough slots for all who wanted one and could qualify. He also continued to be the featured speaker at innumerable Lincoln Day dinners.

Despite their growing differences, Gov. Underwood assigned him license plate No. 5 (Attorney General W.W. "Wally" Barron held No. 6.), there being no special plate for members of Congress as there are today.

Arch kept bringing home the bacon. He was able to obtain a half million dollars to start construction on the Opekiska Lock and Dam between Morgantown and Fairmont, for example. He generated a lot of publicity in that area by helping Mannington Pottery to reopen, returning jobs to seventy-five employees. *The West Virginian* saluted "Congressman Moore, who intervened effectively in the reopening."

The Grafton Sentinel expressed appreciation for Moore's help in getting a $250,000 SBA loan to renovate the former Hazel-Atlas plant for new use to Taylor County industry and area jobs. It would never have happened "if it had not been for the unceasing devotion of Rep. Moore. It has been Congressman Moore who has led the way to overcoming such problems," the editor wrote.

He also generated some headlines by fighting the dumping of radioactive waste into the Ohio River, which many residents thought was causing a higher than average rate of cancer among Wheeling residents. He joined Reps. Hechler and Slack in voting for the Landrum-Griffin Labor Reform Bill, which unions complained was too tough on them, and employers decried as not tough enough on union abuse and crimes. Arch fought, perhaps harder than any of West Virginia's congressional delegation, against trade agreements that would erode protective tariffs, forcing glass, pottery and other West Virginia jobs overseas. He had almost no success in that regard, however. Even then, "globalization" was at work, although it was not yet identified in those terms.

In these pre-food stamps days, the poorest West Virginians often had to subsist on what was known as "commodities." These were American surplus food products, such as cheese, rice, dried beans, canned meats, cereals, powdered milk, flour, corn meal and similar staples, the distribution of which helped the hungry while keeping food prices high for U.S. farmers. Arch vigilantly pursued more of this free food for his constituents and, in 1960, was able to announce that ten additional train carloads of dried eggs, valued at $300,000, would be made available in the First District.

Likely smarter than the majority of the members there, and certainly more diligent than most, Arch continued to be a player on Capitol Hill. It helped, too, that he had the close friendship of the House Minority Leader, Gerald "Jerry" Ford, and that he was respected by several of the Democratic committee chairmen. That he had chosen experienced, well-connected staff members also helped, because they are a congressman's eyes, ears and hands, in many situations. He had become the fifth ranking member on the House Judiciary Committee and the ranking minority member on the Subcommittee on Immigration and Nationality. He expressed particular satisfaction with the latter appointment, coming from a district heavy in "hyphenated Americans."

He was finally gaining some respect from his former adversaries in the unions, winning the endorsement of The Common Laborers Union and the Brotherhood of Railroad Trainmen and Brotherhood of Local Engineers. *The Logan Banner* noted in 1960 that Moore was one of only nine Republicans in the entire Congress to receive the endorsement of the United Mine Workers. The endorsement "came about because Moore's voting record on labor issues is virtually the same as the state's Democratic congressmen," admitted the *Gazette's* Harry Hoffman, who nevertheless expressed his hope that Arch's opponent, Narick, could still pick up the votes of the UMW "rank and file."

The *Williamson Daily News* admitted that Moore was a "hard worker," and "kept close to his constituents and has made himself of service to them." They quoted one Democrat's grumble, "You'll never convince a lot of people in Grafton that it wasn't Arch Moore himself that got the new toy factory for the town." The paper noted that Moore spent a day in every major community of his district, each time Congress adjourned. They had to recognize hard work when they saw it.

As usual, many Democrats remained loyal to their Republican congressman. One of those was the Farmington businessman whose furniture business he had saved with the loan. John Manchin stuck with Arch, despite the fact that he was increasingly prominent in the Marion County Democratic party. Party bosses "called Manchin on the carpet," according to a Fairmont paper, but he told them he "intended to stand by his guns" and that his support for Arch "was a matter of conscience." The party backed off, for the time being, from ousting the brave Democrat committeeman, but did censure him. *The West Virginian* defended and championed Manchin. "Never mind the candidate's qualifications, never mind the traditional two-party system; there must be no independent thinking or acting!" Editor Dick Parrish wrote with sarcasm about the Dems. "There must be no move which might weaken the strangle-hold of the Courthouse Machine on the people of Marion County."

One leading Democrat remained persistent in his criticism of Moore, perhaps fearful that his seat would someday be targeted by the young Republican. Moundsville's *Daily Echo* reported that Sen. Robert Byrd had downplayed Moore's help to his constituents. "Remember the decisions on veterans or disability cases are not made by your congressman but by the agencies themselves," Byrd growled. "You owe nothing to any congressman–all he does is refer your letter to the proper governmental agency. My secretary can do that!"

Arch joined Vice President Nixon and "Punchy" Neely on a stage to address an overflow crowd at the Charleston Civic Center on Sept. 27. But the state was JFK's.

With a campaign chest which would be dwarfed by subsequent races, Arch spent only $4,472 to be re-elected, mainly on billboards, with Narick spending $3,926. Moore's largest contributions were $3635 from the Republican Congressional Committee, $500 from A.C. Stifel of Wheeling and $200 from businessman and banker Glen Harmon of Grafton.

The political machines or factions thereof controlled elections to a great degree in the First District, just as they did in Southern West Virginia. Moore insisted that he never paid to be listed on Democratic slates in any congressional races. He admitted that his name was on many as he ran for re-election to Congress, but insisted that they were voluntarily put there by the slate makers, not purchased. "With the small budgets I had to spend, I couldn't have afforded to [buy onto Democrat slates] if I had wanted to," he laughed.

Campaign fund records of the time indicate that most of Moore's contributions continued to be of the five, ten, twenty dollar type, from common people who just loved him. They were mainly civic-minded individuals who wanted nothing in return except his good will and, perhaps, his recognition when they ran into him at a dinner or on the street. They liked investing in him, putting their money on the winning horse. Some also appreciated the fact that he was keeping the Republican Party alive in the area, even though he was becoming less and less partisan.

These were the days when a retiree might be subsisting on no more than a forty or fifty dollar check from Social Security each month, but even they wanted to help Congressman Moore. "I received a $15 donation from a person on social security, whom I knew could not afford it," Arch recalled. "She put a note in with it to the effect, 'I believe in you.' I mailed it back to her with a thank you letter, asking her to just speak for me instead. She sent it back with a note, insisting, 'I want my name on your [donors'] list!' I learned a lesson then and there. I later warned my daughter [Congresswoman Capito] to be careful not to insult a contributor, even when you know that small contribution is too much for them to give."

Although they appeared on stage together a few times during their respective campaigns, the relationship between Gov. Underwood and the First District congressman had cooled to the point in which neither really tried to help the other. They continued to battle over patronage. Underwood, of course, controlled all of the state government jobs which were not under civil service, but he wanted to fill federal positions with his people, too. A federal district court vacancy demonstrated the rift between the two Republican rivals. Gov. Underwood had nominated a Clarksburg lawyer for the post. Moore's nominee, Charles Paull of Wheeling, got the seat and was confirmed by the U.S. Senate. Earlier, Moore had hosted five congressmen, including (future New York Mayor) John Lindsay and Robert Michels of Illinois, at Oglebay Park. Underwood was conspicuously absent.

November 8, 1960, was a crisp and clear day with temperatures in the mid-50s in the Mountain State. Colorful leaves had begun falling a couple weeks earlier; it was perfect for a big voter turnout. In the voting machine counties, "lever brothers" like the Owens pair were working hard. In the paper-ballot counties, Democrats used their whiskey and dollars to buy chain ballots, as usual. They were pushing Kennedy, Randolph and Wally Barron, along with their local candidates.

The nation would not know until late the next morning who their next president would be, but JFK squeaked out one of the closest wins in U.S. history, over Nixon (a few thousand votes the other way in three or four key states would have thrown it to the Vice President). Moore ended the 1960 election effort with another big win. He defeated Narick by 80,458 to 53,480, carrying all seven counties, despite the fact that five of them were carried by Kennedy over Nixon. *The Morgantown Post* wrote: "Mr. Moore's victory ... proved that his first election in 1956 and re-election in 1958 were no flukes, but represented a strength at the polls in the First District which almost certainly later make him the logical candidate for the Republicans to select in some future year for governor or senator." Several papers had headlines about the lone GOP winner (Underwood and Neely lost their races by large margins) such as: "Arch Moore is West Virginia Political Phenomenon." He was making a believer out of the Democratic press.

After winning re-election, Arch left for Geneva, Switzerland on November 25, as one of two congressmen serving on the U.S. Delegation to the International Conference on Emergency Migration. This would be one of many trips the Moores took to Europe, officially and as ordinary tourists.

He returned to work, with rumblings in the news media that he would be targeted to lose his congressional seat due to partisan-tilted redistricting (gerrymandering) which occurred as result of the U.S. Census every ten years. In a few short months, he would face one of the most interesting, if toughest, political challenges of his career. His brown, slicked-back hair was prematurely turning gray. By the end of 1962, it would be completely white.

Chapter 6 Notes

1. - "JFK would come in here to campaign with his Palm Beach tan in late winter, making us all feel pretty pale," laughed Fairmont lawyer Harry Cronin, now deceased.

2. - Johnie Owens agreed: "Hechler was two-faced. He once gave me $500 in cash [to put him on the slate]. I wouldn't accept nothin' else. And then, at the end of the year, he sent me a 1099 [form to report it as income tax]!"

3. - Theodore White, *The Making of the President, 1960,* Atheneum, 1961. 4. - Robert Dallek, *An Unfinished Life: John F. Kennedy 1917-1963,* Little, Brown, 2003.

4. - Charleston lawyer Robert Elkins confirmed this out-of-state pressure, recalling that a client of his phoned him, complaining that a Chicago businessman was "leaning on him" to convince his work force to support Kennedy in West Virginia.

5. - *Man of the House, The Life and Political Memoirs of Speaker Tip O'Neill,* O'Neill, 1987.

6. - O'Neill, Ibid., p. 98. Reportedly, during this time, Joe Kennedy had a deal with Cardinal Cushing, of Boston, in which he would remove $900,000 in cash from church offerings in exchange for which he'd write the church a check for a million dollars. He would thereby gain the tax write-off for himself as if he'd donated the full million, plus obtain valuable, untraceable cash with which to operate the John F. Kennedy campaign. Cushing came out $100,000 ahead and also was helping elect the first Catholic president, considered reward enough for the deceit and crime.

7. - Against the strong recommendations of the Bar associations, Kennedy later appointed Christie U.S. District Court Judge in the Southern District of West Virginia as reward. By all reports, Christie was a good judge, however.

8. - Arthur M. Schlesinger, *A Thousand Days,* 1965.

9. - Robert Rupp, *Charleston Gazette,* May 9, 2005.

10. - Robert Nelson, the *Charleston Gazette,* May 16, 2005. Nelson was then Hechler's congressional aide and would later serve as state senator and mayor of Huntington.

11. - Neely, Aug. 26, 2005.

12. - *The New York Times,* Nov. 1, 1960.

13. - Moore, July 1, 2005.

Chapter Seven
The Presidents vs. Arch Moore

Through the 1960 election, West Virginia had six congressional districts. The exodus of 145,000 West Virginians in the Fifties, mainly due to the automation of the coal industry, plus the relative growth of other states, caused the West Virginia delegation some anxiety, however. The results of the 1960 U.S. Census made it clear that the state must lose one of its seats. No one was retiring, so someone had to go.

Immediately, the pols and pundits settled on the three most likely victims. The most obvious was Arch Moore, the lone Republican. If at all possible, the Democrats in the legislature would have carved up his district, inserting heavily Democratic counties, pitting him against a popular Democratic congressman. Trouble was, geographically it was nearly impossible to gerrymander Rep. Moore out of his seat. Because of its location, he was almost guaranteed to keep the Northern Panhandle counties where he was secure with the electorate. They couldn't put Republican Marshall and Ohio Counties in other districts, for example, and leave him Brooke and Hancock; it wouldn't be logical. So they did not have a clear-cut way to get rid of Arch.

The second one on the legislators' list for possible extinction: Ken Hechler. The Huntington congressman was from an upstate New York Republican family, but his time at Columbia, Princeton, and with President Harry S Truman certified him as a dyed-in-the-wool liberal Democrat. He had chosen to teach at Marshall University so that he could run for Congress and it was located in a "swing district" that promised to be good for a Democrat. But Hechler was somewhat of a gadfly, a maverick, an intellectual, without wife and family, felt he was too ethical to buy votes, and generally was distrusted and unloved by the party bosses. He had made a lot of enemies within his party, not only because he was to the left of most of them, but because he had defeated several of the locals in the 1958 primary in the Fourth District who felt he was a carpetbagger. There was a lot of talk about somehow pitting him against Moore, with a new district that snaked along the Ohio River, but that admittedly was unrealistic.

Hechler had a strong ally in Bob McDonough of Parkersburg, who had managed JFK's successful primary in West Virginia, however, and Bob, now state Democratic chairman, was a power behind Wally Barron's throne. When Governor Barron called a meeting of the Democratic congressmen to decide on a strategy to rid the state of the Republican anomaly, McDonough "carried the water for me," Hechler recalled. Instead of pitting him against Moore, Bob removed Ritchie and Tyler Counties from the Fourth, both heavily Republican, and gave Ken a solidly Democratic county, Logan, to help him (previous to these changes, the district had been so two-party that Nixon beat Kennedy in it). "Curt Trent was in on [the redistricting strategy] but it was ultimately Gov. Barron's decision," Hechler said.

So in the 1961 session, the Democratic Legislature decided on a third course: they concluded that Rep. Cleveland M. Bailey was the most expendable. They would combine his district into Moore's.

Born in 1886, Bailey had been a high school principal in Clarksburg, was an AP editor of *The Clarksburg Exponent*, served as state budget director, and then was elected to Congress in November of 1944. He had been a party stalwart, voting exactly as the leadership and the unions instructed him to vote. His loyalty apparently wasn't enough to keep the Statehouse Machine from choosing him to stand up to Arch Moore in the redistricting effort, however. It was musical chairs and Cleve was likely the one to be standing when the music stopped. Of the three different gerrymandering proposals, they ended up accepting one that added his Harrison, Doddridge, Lewis, Gilmer, Calhoun and Braxton Counties into a new First District—at 408,794 population, making it the largest of the five districts. The six remaining counties in Bailey's former district were redistributed to others. "Cleve recognized that the Legislature had done him in" said Hechler, who nevertheless recalled no "conspiracy" to sacrifice Bailey to Moore.

According to a Fairmont newspaper, the Democrat "courthouse gang" in Marion County shook down its 50 to 100 employees in a "flower fund" to help defeat Moore, which meant it surely was occuring in other, solidly Democratic counties in the newly-formed district. In a front page article in *The West Virginian,* readers were informed that "State Road employees are being maced for as much as 4 percent of their pay," and that courthouse workers were being assessed 1.5 percent of their annual salary to support the Democrats. The same "flower fund" existed at the State Capitol, where in each election cycle there was a shake-down of all state workers for the Democratic party. "We gave you your job, now you keep us in power," was the unspoken command. Payment of the involuntary wage tax for Democratic candidates, the "flower fund," was not optional. And, of course, Republicans had to raise their own money and it was almost impossible to match such huge funds through private contributors, particularly when most were ten and twenty dollar donations.

The merging of his and Moore's districts did not make Bailey a bit happy. "They virtually dismembered my district," he complained. "It has made it an almost certain Republican district." (Actually he was wrong: the new district would be 150,000 Democrats to 99,000 Republicans in registration.) Bailey's problem with Arch was not Republican voters, however. As Moore proved four times, he was capable of carrying a large portion of the Democratic vote, as well as almost all of his own party's vote.

Like a prize fighter or wrestler before the big bout, Bailey engaged in some braggadocio, maybe to convince himself as much as others. He told the news media that his "ace in the hole" was the President, whom he had helped with the Massachusetts union vote in 1952, in a tough U.S. Senate race against incumbent Sen. Henry Cabot Lodge. "When the time comes, Jack Kennedy will speak for me at a 40,000 [person] rally on Wheeling Island. I know Mr. Moore's record and if it becomes necessary, I will take him apart and not put him together again." Bailey falsely accused Moore of having one of the worst anti-labor voting records in Congress.

On the other side, Arch expressed confidence to a UPI reporter. Calling the redistricting "essentially fair," Moore said, "I feel I have a fighting chance to keep my seat. Considering that both houses of the legislature are controlled by the opposition, I could not have asked for fairer treatment." He announced that he would open an office in Clarksburg ("so that the residents can meet and discuss matters on a person-to-person basis with their congressman") and that he had "taken immediate steps to make himself familiar with the six new counties and people" in the newly created district. Arch had been on the GOP dinner circuit and other venues for several years, in and out of his district. He had become a known quantity, with some star quality, and it was worrisome to the Democrat bosses who didn't want their lock on power and money threatened.

In retrospect, Moore thought they did him a favor. "They expanded us, even though I had not been asked to be expanded." He was particularly excited by the fact that he now represented Braxton which, although heavily Democratic, was only "one county away from the capital," meaning he would get exposure in the Charleston press, so important for his future should he ever seek statewide office.

Arch actually welcomed the fight of his political life. "He's competitive by nature," noted his son.[1] Moore, of course, had also done his homework for years, producing results for his constituents, regardless of their party affiliation or whether they supported him. He was the "go to man" in Northern West Virginia. Those for whom he had built post offices, obtained grants for sewer and water systems, cut through federal red tape for benefits due them, appointed their sons to military academies, and done all sorts of miscellaneous favors, were not going to abandon him now. The loyalty would be reciprocated, even in what would prove to be another good year for the Democrats.

Arch had another advantage. At thirty-nine, he was full of energy and vitality, not yet at the peak of his career. He bounced around the district tirelessly, like it was all great fun, rarely showing fatigue. His hair was just now beginning to turn white. He had become a dynamic orator, one who could speak eloquently without a note.

Recalled Frances Whiting, whose late husband Jack was Bailey's campaign manager, "I first met Arch Moore at a labor union meet-the-candidates rally in Sutton. He was working the crowd and was young, dynamic—he was just full of himself. He had a straw hat on. I was very, very impressed with him. Jack also was impressed with Arch, how personable he was. It kind of shook us up."

Bailey, by contrast, looked even older than he was; the 76 years had not been kind to him. "I think they had to give him a daily dose of formaldehyde to keep him propped up," laughed Fairmont's H. Gerald Warren, when he spoke of the election ten years later. "He was getting up in years; he didn't have a whole lot of life left in him," agreed Frances Whiting. "Cleve would slouch and Jack and I would have to urge him to sit up straight. He was always hanging onto a cigar all the time, dropping ashes on his shirt and tie. Jack would have to clean him up before he met people." *The New York Times* put it succinctly, that Bailey was a "gnarled political veteran of 76 who is no match for his opponent in the photogenic department."

In his book, which mentions the Moore-Bailey race, Huge Sidey of *Time* called Cleve "a stooped, bald little man who had once taken a swing at Harlem's Congressman Adam Clayton Powell, but he did not connect solidly enough to do damage."[2]

The elderly congressman was "a hot tempered little guy," Frances Whiting admitted. Bailey was often photographed sitting down; he appeared tired and worn out. His suits looked too large by a size or two, like he'd been sick and lost weight. His speaking manner was old school, not appealing to the electronic media or even to many live crowds. Cleve didn't want to be seen next to the very dynamic, lively young Arch Moore, although the latter got Bailey into a convertible with him in at least one parade, according to a newspaper photo.

Maybe because of incidences like the one with Powell, there were rumors that Bailey had an alcohol problem. But Frances Whiting did not know about that, if true. Instead, she said, despite the fact that Bailey "was so old he could hardly get around," he was nevertheless "known for his girlfriends." She recalled a campaign luncheon in which she sat with a few of Cleve's ladies. "One was an attractive, auburn-haired young lady who identified herself as Bailey's 'librarian.' But she was his girlfriend. She was bragging to us all about how close she was to the Congressman. When I identified myself as the campaign manager's wife, she immediately got up and ran out." Frances continued, "The Democratic Executive Committee had been onto Cleve for bringing those women into the district. The party officials told him to get her back to Washington. I never saw her again."

"Bailey had been in Congress for twenty years," Moore noted. "He had built a respectable base in his territory, as I had in mine. So we spent a lot of time in each other's territory. I went into Shinnston [in Moore's "new" county of Harrison], a town which had been founded by my great-great-grandfather. It was a [campaign meeting held in the] Moose ballroom. Many were seeing me for the first time, sizing me up. They had a question and answer session. I didn't know who was Republican, who was Democrat. One guy raised his hand and asked, 'What kind of president do you think Harry Truman was?' There was a lot of controversy over that, at the time. One thing about West Virginians, they watch your eyes; they know if you're being honest. I answered, 'Obviously, Harry Truman was not of my political persuasion. But looking at him from a historical perspective, Harry Truman will be looked upon as a greater president than we think today.'" It seemed to be a satisfactory answer for the times, and later proved to be prophetic. Arch added, "West Virginians can see through you pretty fast. They don't necessarily give you their friendship unless you prove by your actions that you deserve it."

KNOWING THAT THEY were coming at him with full force, Arch went on the offense, launching a partisan attack on the Democrats for the first time in his career. In a gutsy move, he first targeted the top of their pyramid, the popular President John F. Kennedy. At the Young Republican convention in Charleston on July 21, 1961, he had told the crowd that President Kennedy could repay his debt to West Virginia with "a stroke of the pen."

In a "ten point plan" to help the state's economy, Congressman Moore called upon JFK to help the state by placing tariffs on imported glass, ceramic tile, and rayon; negotiate with Britain and Canada for sale of the state's coal; have the Defense Department purchase West Virginia coal for military installations in Europe; award defense contracts to West Virginia companies; force the Small Business Administration to provide assistance in depressed areas; give the state maximum benefit under federal housing legislation; and build a north-south Interstate highway through Morgantown, Clarksburg and Fairmont. (The Democrats made no reply; these were all excellent points.) West Virginia had "handed [JFK] the presidential nomination on a silver platter," Arch told the enthusiastic crowd. "But the only thing thus far forthcoming has been the addition of some items in the surplus commodity food program and ... a pilot program ... for the use of food stamps."

In another venue, Moore also criticized the Kennedy Administration for the oil depletion allowance, which gave the big oil companies tremendous tax advantages. He called it a "callous disregard for the plight of the coal mining area," pointing out that for every one million barrels of oil the nation imported, it deprived the coal industry of $4.5 million worth of business. "It is absolute and utter selfishness of some oil tycoons [and a] threat to our nation's security," Arch said, prophetically.

In August of that year, he also scored some points with voters and raised a valid issue, by vocally opposing a $95 million nuclear power plant in Hansford, Washington, supported by Hechler, Byrd and Randolph. Arch noted that nuclear power also meant less coal jobs and accused the West Virginia Democrats of selling out by supporting government funding for the project. The best interests of coal miners and the coal industry "were traded for peanuts on the floor of the U.S. Senate," Rep. Moore charged. Randolph countered that Arch was being "narrow and provincial." Byrd didn't reply; he was talking about the 24 and 25 percent unemployment rates in Taylor and Webster Counties, but proposed no solution.

The West Virginian, Fairmont's newspaper, spoke enthusiastically of Arch. It noted House Minority Leader Charlie Halleck's comments at an April 25, 1961, Wheeling fund raiser (in which Rep. Robert Michel of Illinois also attended), that Moore "has earned the respect of his colleagues on both sides of the aisle and the respect of the voters of both parties." The editor wrote that Moore was "West Virginia's No. 1 Republican. People in communities turn to him almost by instinct for help and he doesn't fail them, regardless of politics. 'Let's call Arch' is an expression used throughout the First District when the chips are down. And he responds, quickly, and effectively. And the people remember."

Moore adopted a campaign slogan for the '62 race: "Arch Moore: He Gets Things Done for You!" His opponent issued "The Bailey Report," in a tabloid newspaper format, with a prominent photo of the old man standing next to a contrasting, youthful President and another photo with Vice Pres. Lyndon Johnson.

For the first and only time in his congressional career, Moore had to spend a lot of money to win, at least a lot for those days—about $45,000, all told. Some of that was raised at a major event in Wheeling.

Despite a cloudburst and storms that turned Wheeling streets into rivers, and kept Moore and his party from Washington circling the Pittsburgh airport for 35 minutes, a very enthusiastic crowd of 450 (which included former Gov. Underwood) had turned out for that fund raiser. Telegrams praising Moore, from former Pres. Eisenhower, former Vice Pres. Nixon, Sen. Barry Goldwater and others, were read. Halleck said that Moore was "one of the hardest-working members of Congress, Democrat or Republican. No member of Congress has more interest in the people of his district." Nixon said Moore deserved "special recognition many times over ... for his dedication as a public servant," and that he spoke for West Virginians and Americans "who put their abiding trust in the creative enterprise of the free people. We are all in debt for his leadership in the fight to preserve and extend America's freedom."

The 1960 Primary had focused America's attention on poverty in West Virginia, and Democrats nationwide had used it as a call for greater spending programs for the poor in Appalachia. The state was the "poster child" for that effort. But Arch and his fellow Republicans did not like the negative attention. While they did not oppose government assistance for the needy, they preferred an approach that brought jobs into the area, rather than just handouts. *The Washington Post* covered the Wheeling event. It noted the Republican speakers' complaints that Democrats were picturing West Virginia as "a man on ragged knees with a cup in his hand." The *Post* reported that the Wheeling speakers had charged that the Democrats "were embarrassing the state by holding it up as an example of hunger and want ... Rep. Moore told the crowd that the state had become the conversation piece of everyone, in a negative way. 'We're shamed on every front page of every newspaper in the United States. Imagine, the governor of West Virginia posing for a picture handing out surplus pork and gravy to an unfortunate citizen!'" This poor-mouth, Appalachia image was not the one the Republicans wanted to portray to the nation.

Of course, despite the ferocious re-election campaign which extended for about eighteen months, Moore continued with government duties. He spent Easter 1961 in Hong Kong, studying the flow of Chinese refugees from the Communist mainland into that city (then a British colony). He announced construction of a lock and dam above New Martinsville, on the

Ohio. Newspaper articles praised Moore for bringing a civic auditorium to Wheeling. He announced construction of a $300,000 National Guard Armory in Fairmont. As they always had, scores of photos ran in newspapers of the Congressman posing with scout troops, school patrols and women's groups, usually on the steps of the Capitol.

That summer the Moores also slipped away to Grandview State Park to see the new outdoor play about West Virginia's beginnings, "Honey in the Rock." It was enough to make Harry Hoffman of the *Gazette* speculate that Moore was "thinking of going after the senate seat now held by Robert C. Byrd." (Of course, there was no truth to that, whatsoever.) The fear of Moore being a future opponent, however, made Byrd want to drive a stake through Moore's heart in 1962. He campaigned feverishly for Bailey, and continued to belittle the strong communications efforts Moore's staff had with constituents. He particularly lambasted the fact that Moore's office routinely mailed newspaper clippings to people in the district, with hand-written notes of praise from Arch Moore for their particular achievement or honor. That Arch Moore custom of recognition, widely appreciated throughout the district by those who'd celebrated an anniversary, been honored at school, in sports, or in a civic organization, just drove Byrd up the wall for some reason. Rather than copy the successful campaign methods, Byrd criticized it to audiences, as if it was the most terrible thing a congressman could do.

In August of 1962, WJBY TV offered Moore and Bailey an opportunity to debate on the air. Moore wired back, "Happy to accept your offer. I shall adjust my schedule to be available when my opponent is." Bailey, as expected, weakly declined. "I have certain outstanding commitments between now and the election and to break any of these would be extremely embarrassing ... the uncertainty as to when the Congress will adjourn makes it impossible to discuss the matter at this time," he replied, transparently.

But by summer, the Democrats began revealing their plans to bring in the "big guns" to destroy Arch Moore once and for all, to rid this Republican scourge from "their" land. The Wheeling *Intelligencer* opined that the Democrats' plan to oust Moore in '62 should be called "Operation Abolition." Moore was quoted, "I understand the Democratic high command will put on a big push to defeat me and I welcome that challenge." And he was correct–the national Democrats pulled out the stops, engaging in the greatest effort in the history of the state to defeat a Republican officeholder. Undoubtedly, there have been few efforts to match it in national history, anywhere.

Kennedy's Secretary of Labor, Arthur Goldberg, had already campaigned in several northern West Virginia towns in January of 1962, always accompanied by candidate Bailey. Goldberg may not have helped much. *The New York Times* thought Moore's labor record might hurt him, but wrote that Arch was "a good-looking, 39-year-old lawyer whose emphasis on person-to-person campaigning, personal service in his office and his appeal to women voters, tends to overshadow a voting record in Congress that would ordinarily be difficult to defend in a labor area such as this."[3] The newspaper mentioned that West Virginia's per capita income was only $1690 compared to the national average of $2263, and personal income was growing 4.4 percent in the state under Kennedy, compared to 6.9 in the rest of the U.S. The warm feelings of West Virginians for President Kennedy "derives more from affection than from economics," Joseph Loftus wrote. "The random Democrat on the street says the job and money situation is probably no better than it was two years ago..." The state's unemployment rate during the Kennedy years, at 10.3 percent, was "nearly twice the national average."

House Speaker John McCormick and Majority Leader Carl Albert (a future Speaker) spoke on Aug. 25, 1962, on behalf of Bailey at the Weirton Community Center, sponsored by the Brooke County Democrats.

Cleve let others do most of his speaking for him, but at a September 1962 dinner in Fairmont he called Arch Moore a "political kleptomaniac." He told the crowd of 500 that Moore had been "trying to claim everything since the resurrection" and that "it is time for people to stop him." He defended himself against the charge of being a "do-nothing congressman," contending that he was known as "Battling Bailey" on Capitol Hill. Bailey said he was "amused" when "the young eager beaver tried to get into the act when Pres. Kennedy and Gov. Barron announced approval of the north-south highway [I-79]." Other speakers at the dinner included Carl Albert and Sen. Byrd, who called Bailey the "Old Warrior." The very partisan Gov. Barron called for a statewide effort of Democrats to rid the state of the lone Republican congressman. Even Tax Commissioner Howard Hardesty spoke for Bailey (but had nothing bad to say about his old friend Arch Moore).

In an attempt to capture the ethnic vote, Bailey took Reps. John Dent (D-Pa.), an Italian-American, and Roman Pucinski (D-Ill.), a Polish-American, to Weirton to campaign with him.

On September 21, Franklin D. Roosevelt, Jr. came to Benedum Airport in Bridgeport to campaign for Bailey. FDR, Jr. also campaigned at the Wheeling airport, at the Weirton Steel gate, toured a plant in Follansbee and spoke at a luncheon at the Masonic Temple in Wellsburg, after which he went to the Beech Bottom plant and to a rally at St. John's Auditorium. His brother, Rep. Jimmy Roosevelt, also campaigned for the aging congressman in Wheeling. Jack Kennedy had put FDR, Jr. to good use in his campaign and the Democrats thought the charm might work again to defeat Arch Moore.

When the Democrats sponsored a "free beer rally" for Cleve at Oglebay Park on October 1, things got a bit rowdy. A heckler jumped onto the stage and grabbed the microphone away from Congressman Bailey. When an Ohio County deputy sheriff attempted to remove him, the heckler struck him with a beer bottle, drawing blood and requiring 17 stitches. But the event drew two thousand beer drinkers.

On October 5, 1962, former Pres. Harry S Truman gave a speech for Bailey at the Grafton High School football field. Truman said it was "bad for Republicans to have control of the country," apparently forgetting that the Democrats and the liberals had a firm grip on all three branches of the federal government. "Bailey looked much older than Truman," recalled David Bartlett, a teenager at the time, who watched them parade through the Grafton streets. At the Nathan Goff Armory in Clarksburg, Truman asked, "What's the use of having any other congressman if you've got Bailey?" The partisan former president called Bailey "one of the greatest congressmen who ever served." Give-em-Hell-Harry told the crowd, "Do your level best to get out and vote and send Cleve Bailey back to Congress!" Truman also took a swing through Fairmont to help the Jimmy Durante look-alike congressman.

The AFL-CIO, the railroad workers and the UMWA endorsed Bailey even though Moore had one of the best union voting records in the nation, especially among Republicans, had been a union member himself, had received the union's endorsement before, and had stood up for the West Virginia coal jobs when the Democrat congressional delegation was aiding big oil and nuclear power. AFL Pres. Miles Stanley campaigned in Brooke County against Arch Moore and sent out thousands of flyers commanding their membership to defeat Arch. (*The New York Times* noted that Arch had voted "wrong," according to the AFL-CIO, seven out of eleven issues dear to the unions in the past term and Bailey with only one "wrong" vote.)

When the polls showed no improvement, the state Democrats were getting desperate, but they wouldn't concede the seat to the Republican from Glen Dale. Vice Pres. Lyndon B. Johnson made a "whirlwind tour" of Chester, Weirton and Parkersburg, traveling with Bob McDonough on

October 17, 1962. The opposition was pulling out all the stops to defeat Arch. "They did everything but get a gun and shoot him," said Dick Tyson. "But Arch was always resilient and optimistic."

Bailey charged that Arch Moore was "trying to fool the public" because, as usual, Moore's campaign billboards did not mention his political affiliation.

But the *piece de resistance*, in the Democrats' scorched earth method of ridding the world of this Republican from their turf, was the sitting President of the United States. As Bailey promised from the outset, JFK agreed to repay his former colleague in the House, who helped him beat Sen. Henry Cabot Lodge. Harry Hoffman, the unapologetic partisan Democrat political editor of the *Gazette*, speculated hopefully that Kennedy's popularity would rub off on Bailey and "provide some insurance against a light vote" that he feared would help Moore. He alleged that "the glamor has gone from the Moore camp" and that miners in Marion County would come out in large numbers to vote against him, and for Bailey.

Kennedy was a real threat to Arch Moore. In 1962, with the Bay of Pigs fiasco behind him, the space program (which he inherited from Eisenhower) providing excitement, the economy picking up a bit, the Peace Corp and a national fitness program catching on, and his Vietnam War not yet killing Americans, the handsome young president was very popular throughout the nation. It cannot be overemphasized how much the Kennedy clan, especially the First Lady, [4] had brought glamor and excitement to the White House. But he was especially popular in West Virginia, where Democrats who helped him win the 1960 primary felt they had launched his successful bid for the presidency.

So Kennedy agreed to come to Wheeling for Bailey on September 28. The 40,000-strong crowd Bailey had predicted earlier in the year was lowered to an estimate of 20,000, but Democrats were expressing confidence that having the President speak for their man would finally put him over the top, that the voters just couldn't resist a personal plea from JFK.

The Arch supporters took the presidential visit calmly, however. If anything, it just added to the growing image that the Dems were "ganging up on him." There's sometimes value to being on the receiving end of overkill—it makes the victim appear to be an underdog, with whom many relate. Harry Hoffman quoted a worker in Moore's Wheeling headquarters saying, "We consider this visit of the President a great compliment to Mr. Moore. It shows what the Democrats think of Arch Moore." When asked whether Arch would counter with an appearance by former Pres.

Eisenhower, she replied confidently, "Oh no, we love [Ike] but we don't need him."[5]

Something interesting, almost surreal, happened. On the very day on which he was coming into West Virginia to campaign against Arch Moore, the President had the audacity to phone him and ask for a special favor. Perhaps it was his way of needling him a bit, or the irony had not occurred to him. Congressman Moore was in his Washington office when the secretary said, "The White House is on the phone."

Arch Moore picked up the receiver and heard the distinctive Boston accent: "Ahhch, how ah you? Larry O'Brien[6] tells me you're the only one who can help me with something. I have an immigration bill which is important to my program. It's stuck in your Judiciary Committee and there aren't enough votes to get it out [to the floor for a vote]. Could you help me?"

A bit taken aback, but responsive to a direct presidential request, Moore told JFK that he would "do everything" he could to make it happen. Then Arch took advantage of the phone call to speak his mind to the Chief Executive.

"Can I now ask you a question, Mr. President? You felt comfortable in asking me for something and I'm happy to do it. But tonight you're going into my district and campaigning against me. Did you ever give any thought to this inconsistency?"

Kennedy paused for a moment and then politely but revealingly replied, "Ahhch, you do some things because you want to, and some things you do because you have to."

It was dark and raining hard that September night when Air Force One touched down in Wheeling at about 7:10 p.m.[7] The band played "Hail to the Chief," "Anchors Aweigh" and "Happy Days Are Here Again," as the President deplaned. Caravans of faithful Democrats had been bussed in from counties all over the district. On the way to Wheeling Island Stadium, the presidential motorcade (with Bailey sitting next to the President in his car) stopped at Warwood where Kennedy jumped out of his bubble-topped limo to shake some hands. Wrote Huge Sidey, "Along the highways of this state, which in the 1960 primary election had launched him toward the White House, the people showed some of the old frenzied adulation of two years ago."[8]

The entire rally at the stadium lasted no more than thirty minutes, with only Senators Byrd, Randolph and Rep. Bailey making brief remarks (Gov. Barron and Rep. Hechler were there but did not speak). Only about 4000 to 6000 braved the rain, standing in the field, nothing even close in size to the crowd predicted. ("It was a miserable evening," recalled Mrs. Whiting about the weather.) In his ten minutes of remarks, standing before the party faithful, without a hat or overcoat, Kennedy told the West Virginians, "I feel as if I was coming home. After all, this is the state which sent me out into the world and you are the people who made me the Democratic candidate for president of the United States."[9]

The President charged that the Eisenhower Administration had left West Virginia "on the beach to decline, to rot," during the Fifties. He described Bailey as an "experienced man with young ideas," (but did not elaborate on what those ideas were) and a "valued friend" (the two had served together on the House Education Committee). JFK also accused Congressional Republicans of opposing national financing of unemployment compensation, the area redevelopment bill, and increasing the minimum wage to $1.25 per hour. He reminded the crowd that he doubled the state's allotment of surplus farm products for the needy. Wrote Sidey:

> He did some bragging about what he had done for West Virginia, but it was subdued. Then he settled into the routine that he would use in one form or another in most of his coming stops. "Two years ago I said that it was time to get this country moving again. In the past two years, we have made a start, but just a start. But we have begun to act, for no Congress in a generation has passed as much affirmative and constructive legislation as the present Congress."

Kennedy scowled, shook his clenched fist into the rain, and finished his attack: "This is the issue in this campaign. We want to finish the job that we have started here in West Virginia, Ohio and Pennsylvania!"

Then came the climax of the special evening, perhaps of the entire First District congressional campaign, in which the President was to give his fellow Democrats their marching orders for Election Day. "I've got to have people in Congress I can rely on," Kennedy shouted to the drenched crowd. "So I want you to go out and re-elect ARCH MOORE to Congress!" JFK quickly corrected himself, "... uh, Cleve Bailey!"

"There was an audible gasp," said Pete Thaw, who was among the faithful in the crowd. Remembered Frances Whiting, "The crowd booed at the mistake. They were in shock! At first, they thought he was trying to be funny."[10]

Was the President's gaffe a Freudian slip, something left over from his phone call to Congressman Moore earlier that day, a subconscious feeling of obligation? Most (including Moore himself) believed Kennedy just made a slip of the tongue; but some, like the *Gazette's* Harry Hoffman, denied that it even happened, [11] especially with the Republican newspapers chortling all over the state about the President's "endorsement" of Arch Moore. Snorted *The Fairmont Times'* Democrat editor Bill Evans, "It takes either an infantile or a perverted sense of humor to twist this slip into an 'endorsement' of Arch Moore ... [Any] idea of 'endorsing' the Republican candidate from the 1st District was ... far from his mind." But, within days, bumper stickers were popping up around the district: "The President endorses Arch Moore and so do I!"

Ken Hechler recalled that Rep. Francis Walter, a Democrat and chairman of the House Judiciary Committee, asked him the next day, "Is it true that the President endorsed Arch Moore last night?" Said Hechler, "Walter, who had a good working relationship with Arch, was amused by it." Hechler thought that Kennedy's slip of the tongue was due to the fact that "all he'd heard coming down here was Arch Moore. He just considered him part of the West Virginia delegation, along with me, Kee, Slack and the others."

COME NOVEMBER, all the "piling on" did not stop the touchdown. Arch Moore wiggled free and ran it into the end zone again. He defeated Congressman Bailey by 97,556 to 65,328, a comfortable 32,228 margin (and, undoubtedly, overcoming a lot of court house ballot mischief by the opposition). *The New York Times* reported: "Mr. Moore, a 39-year-old lawyer, won despite the fact that Democrats outnumber Republicans by 53,000 in the 13-county district."[12] His Democratic friends throughout the district had remained loyal to their excellent congressman and Bailey was put out to pasture.[13]

Moore couldn't resist having a little fun with the Democrat newspapermen. Unbeknownst to them, he had someone at the Kennedy rally taping the speeches, so he had proof that the faux pas had actually occurred. He and Kim Moore went into a local studio and made a limited edition 45 record which was mailed to about fifty of his tormentors, to taunt them a bit, including Harry Hoffman and Harry Hamm. "We want to wish everyone a Merry Christmas," father and son said. "And now I want to include the words of our President at Wheeling Island," after which JFK's "endorsement" was played.

AS A FOOTNOTE, after Bailey died at age 78 in July of 1965, his widow called Congressman Moore and asked him to speak to her son who, at six feet two, looked nothing like his diminutive father. Before he passed away, Cleve had told his wife, "If you have any problems with my pension or settling the estate, take it to Arch Moore. He'll help you." She remembered that and, accepting no fee, Attorney Moore did what was necessary to get her financial affairs in order and income sufficient to get her through the remainder of her days.

Likewise, Moore never took offense to any of the '62 battle. "Cleve was just doing what was proper. He'd developed friendships in the Congress and strength through seniority. He wanted to stay there, but they pitted the two of us together. He was a patriarch of the House, one of its longest serving members. I never knew why, but he took a liking to me, early on. He told them about me in the [Democratic] cloakroom, 'You keep your eye on that young man.' Our friendship lasted until that 1962 campaign and then he came charging out of the bin.

"He ran a heckuva campaign!"

Chapter 7 Notes

1. - Arch also had a temper that has its limits, Kim added. Moore's son remembered hearing about an incident in which his father and "a buddy were driving in West Virginia. Some guy comes up behind them at the stop light and taps his car against their bumper, shoving them forward. My dad looks in the rearview mirror to see if there were gestures or if it was someone he knew but he didn't. The guys bumps his car again. So Dad threw it in reverse and lambasted him!"

2. - *John F. Kennedy, President,* copyright 1964 by Huge Sidey. On Sept. 28, 1962, *The New York Times* wrote about Bailey, "He is a scrapper...In 1955 ... he got into an argument with Rep. Adam Clayton Powell in a closed committee meeting over Mr. Powell's sincerity in his legislative maneuvers on racial desegregation. Mr. Bailey threw a hard right to the jaw of his larger opponent and knocked the Manhattan Democrat off his equilibrium."

3. - *The New York Times,* Oct. 7, 1962.

4. - For about a decade, Jackie was on the cover of national magazines almost every week; her photo sold copies like none other.

5. - Ike would make a brief appearance for all state Republican candidates, at Charleston's airport, on Oct. 27, 1962, bemoaning the fact that JFK had so many Harvard grads running the White House.

6. - Kennedy's legislative assistant.

7. - The President had insisted that Air Force One, a 707 jet, land at the nearby Ohio County Airport, rather than in Pittsburgh, because it was quicker. "The Kennedys always wanted to land locally, to save time," explained Pete Thaw. The large plane used up all the runway, and then went into the mud at the end of the landing strip.

8. - Sidey, Ibid.

9. - *New York Times,* Oct. 7, 1962.

10. - Before departing the stadium, the President went into a special communications trailer the government had set up for him, so he could remain in contact with his brother Robert and others, concerning the ongoing, intense, almost-nuclear-warfare Cuban Missile Crisis. When he exited the mobile office, Frances, who had been typing Secret Service documents for two weeks, got her chance to see Kennedy again (she'd met him the first time in 1960 as a candidate). She treasures a photo of that handshake, just her, presidential aide Kenny O'Donnell, Congressman Bailey and the

President with rain-drenched Secret Servicemen surrounding him. JFK was to have autographed it for her; it was on his desk, yet unsigned, on Nov. 22, 1963.

11. - That they tried to deny it was foolish, because the speech was carried live by area TV stations and thousands had heard it with their own ears.

12. - *New York Times,* Nov. 7, 1962.

13. - Today, you can still find Bailey's bust, displayed prominently in the state capitol rotunda, perhaps a consolation prize by the Democrats for having pitted him against the young lion. Arch Moore's bust, displayed in the Cultural Center, was boarded off by a Democratic successor. There are unconfirmed rumors that Governor Caperton had Moore's bust ripped out, despite the fact it was anchored into the floor.

Chapter Eight
"Judge" Moore

Coming off his big 1962 win, Arch began considering a career move beyond the House of Representatives to something like Bob Byrd's Senate seat.

In politics, they say there are only two good ways to run—unopposed or scared—and the thoughts of Moore on his tail scared Byrd more than a little. Granted, he was popular with his own party and Republicans, but Byrd knew this Moore guy was sharp, charming and unpredictable. Arch had far more education and arguably had a better grasp of facts. Byrd wrote in his autobiography:

> *Congressman Arch A. Moore, Jr., a Republican, had hinted in early February of 1963 that he might be a candidate against me ... in 1964. Moore, in Charleston for a Lincoln Day speech, said future developments would determine whether he would seek the Republican nomination for governor in 1964, and indicated he might get some idea which way to turn after he made twenty-three scheduled speeches outside his own First Congressional District.*[1]

Apparently the feedback Moore received, and the increasing popularity of President Johnson, told him that 1964 would be the wrong year for a Republican to make a statewide bid of any sort. Staying in the House proved to be a wise choice. As had been the case in the 1958 election which was so disastrous for his party, Arch would be the lone Republican survivor in '64 in heavily Democratic West Virginia. He was so secure in his seat by then that he allowed himself the freedom of international travel in the weeks before that election.

In fact, for a couple of hours in mid-October 1964, Congressman Moore found himself to be the new leader of the Soviet Union. Well, sort of ... in the minds of several hundred Muscovites.

Nikita Sergevich Khrushchev, the irascible premier and First Secretary of the Communist Party who had led that empire through glorious but tense days, through the height of the Cold War, Sputnik, the U-2 incident, the Cuban Missile Crisis, pounding his shoe on the United Nations table, telling Eisenhower, "We will bury you," and Soviet military movements into Africa, had embarrassed his country enough. He was suddenly deposed by the Stalinist faction of his party.

Congressman and Shelley Moore were in Moscow that week. "Khrushchev's photo had been everywhere," he remembered, "on billboards, even in the men's rooms. But the next morning, I noticed his picture was nowhere to be seen. I asked the State Department person who accompanied us, 'Is there something I don't know?' and he responded, 'Mr. Khrushchev resigned and is no longer premier.'"

Through the Kremlin, the Moores had obtained seats to the opera that night, to see a performance of Carmen. "They liked to boast that it was the largest opera house in the world," Moore smiled. "It held six thousand people. It had been built by French masons, and other craftsmen from different nations."

The couple walked the cobblestone street to the opera house and, because they were visiting American dignitaries, were shown to the curtained Premier's Box for the performance. When the orchestra struck a tune and the curtains of the box were drawn open, "The crowd stood on its feet and applauded. They didn't know who was leading them. I began bowing to the crowd," Arch recalled, laughing as he told the story.

"Shelley asked, 'What are you doing?' and I in my tux whispered, 'Just follow my lead. They don't know if I'm the one.'" Because the Moores were in the Premier's Box, the crowd assumed that Moore was their new premier. "So I was head of the Soviet Union for five minutes," Arch joked.

He had opportunities by this time to observe how a nation's leader conducted himself and realized there was no mystique to it. In all, the Moores became personally acquainted with every president from Eisenhower to George W. Bush, although they were closer to some First Couples than others.[2] Congressman Moore's relationship with the first President under whom he served had started off on the wrong foot.

Elected as leader of the freshman class of Republicans in the House of Representatives in 1957, Arch sat next to Dwight Eisenhower at a White House breakfast the President hosted for them. It was within two years of Ike's heart attack and his doctors had him on a strict diet. "They brought him four paper cups, one of which contained juice and the others full of pills," Arch remembered. "That was his breakfast." During the course of the conversation with the new members of Congress, the President had told them that he planned to soon meet with Soviet Premier Khrushchev, which was major international news because the Cold War was at it peak and there had been no Soviet-American leaders' conference of the sort since Truman met with Stalin and Churchill at the end of World War II.

When Arch and the other members of Congress exited the White

House, a group of national reporters greeted them. One asked what the President had to say.

Without thinking, Arch spoke up, "He told us he will soon meet with Premier Khrushchev." The flash bulbs popped and reporters started darting toward phones. Arch's friend from Hancock County, Edwin Flowers, was in Europe on business and heard Moore's name on the radio everywhere he went and even saw his photo in newspapers, as result of the announcement.

But the White House was furious. "The President's press aide called me as soon as I got back to my office," Moore remembered, still cringing about the blunder years later. "He yelled, 'You almost got me fired! You don't speak for the President!' But the reporter had asked and, as the group's spokesman, I'd simply answered his question."

John F. Kennedy had already graduated from the House to the Senate by the time Arch came to Capitol Hill but the two had met before he was elected president. Nevertheless, the Moores were subject to the charm of Jack and Jackie, and the Camelot mystique, the same as most Americans. "I loved attending White House functions and anything ceremonial," recalled Shelley of their congressional days. "Maybe it was just the country girl in me, but when I'd hear other congressmen's wives complaining about having to go to this or that function, I couldn't understand it." They were cautioned, as they went through the receiving line during a Kennedy White House reception for members of Congress, to keep it quick because so many would need to shake the President's and Jacqueline Kennedy's hands. As the line moved along, Shelley silently and nervously practiced, over and over, what she would say to Kennedy when she got to the end of the line. When she finally made it to the President, she was dazzled by his good looks. "I said, 'Mr. Pleasure, it's a President.' Arch asked me, 'What did you say?' but I don't think Kennedy even noticed, he just went on to the next one."

Arch and the rest of the West Virginia congressional delegation would meet in the Rose Garden with President Kennedy in May of 1963, to kick off the state's centennial celebration. Former President Truman (who slipped and called the state "Virginia," and then added, "Well, that's what it *should* still be") and Kennedy were on hand on a rainy June 20, for the state's 100th Birthday.

After the tragic assassination in Dallas, it was a larger-than-life, dynamic, energetic and ambitious man who loved to manipulate Congress and get things done (after whom Arch Moore seemed to pattern himself) who resided in the White House. Lyndon Johnson would usher in another era of activist, big government, an extension of what FDR had started in the 1930s. Despite the difference in their political parties, Congressman Moore couldn't help but like the Texan and his style. The feeling seemed to be mutual. "Johnson and [Speaker] Sam Rayburn always called me 'Judge' for reasons I never knew," recalled Arch, "perhaps because I served on the Judiciary Committee."

One evening in March of 1964, Shelley had phoned her husband at his office. "Are we going to this White House black tie thing tonight?" Neither knew what it was about, just that they had received an engraved invitation. It had instructed them only to enter through the main, Pennsylvania Avenue, gate. "The only times I'd been to the White House, I'd always entered through the back gate," noted Arch. Mrs. Moore asked if a certain gown would be appropriate and Arch agreed. She brought his tux to his office where he changed and off they went in their car.

The guard waved them through as they drove up to the gate, Arch recalled. "He directed us up the driveway to the main door of the building, where we'd never entered before. There were no cars to be seen anywhere in the driveway. A Marine came out and took our car and another, very good-looking, sharply dressed Marine offered his arm to Shelley, to escort her. She came from a military family (her brother was an officer at Fort Benning, Georgia) so she loved that! She loved a uniform! I followed them into the White House."

The Moores looked at each other in puzzlement as they found no one on the ground level, where they'd usually been entertained. Instead, the escort took them to the elevator and, to their surprise, to the President and Mrs. Johnson's private quarters, where few were allowed. As the door opened, there was Lyndon Johnson, who smiled widely and bellowed out his usual greeting to Arch, "Hello, Judge!"

"I remember that it was a beautiful yellow room we entered and it had a great view of the memorials," Arch recalled forty years later. The President directed Shelley Moore to Lady Bird Johnson and he stood talking to Arch, the only congressman who had been invited to the party, for over twenty minutes, non-stop, gripping him with his large hands, as had been LBJ's style since his days as majority leader. He riveted his attention on Moore, even as others such as members of the cabinet, the Supreme Court, and even the Vice President entered ("Hubert, you and Muriel go over there and talk to Bird and Shelley!" Johnson barked to Humphrey).

For reasons known to himself, most of the conversation—or monologue, to be more precise–consisted of LBJ pouring out his heart to Arch about how he feared that he, like JFK, would be assassinated, and how difficult the transition from the Kennedy Administration had been. Johnson had just returned from a trip to New York City and felt particularly vulnerable there, he told Moore. Someone had jumped a security fence to get to him, he said, which gave him a scare. "I just don't know if I'm up to this job sometimes," he lamented. The monologue went on and on as other dignitaries filled the room. Shelley eased back around and scolded Arch for dominating the President's time, but he whispered to her, "He won't let me *go!*"

The purpose of the get-together was finally revealed: it was a surprise birthday party for Chief Justice Earl Warren. "The waiters burst into the room with wine for all, and toast after toast was made," Moore remembered. "Then our group of about fifty people was escorted down the staircase to the State Room, where about 400 other guests had gathered. The Marine Band was playing." As they walked down the staircase with the other guests, Arch allowed himself a fantasy. He reached over and whispered to Shelley, "Do you think we'll ever make it here?" Although the Johnsons were very gracious to Arch and Shelley, they never had a clue why they had been invited. He had some time with President Johnson on other occasions, including a flight to New York's Ellis Island regarding immigration law and he, with the rest of the West Virginia congressional delegation, rode to Morgantown in Air Force One with LBJ. "Johnson was always interested in my views," recalled Moore. "He would look over and ask, 'Judge, what do you think?'" (The Lyndon Johnson Library has corroborative photos in which LBJ appeared to be intensely tuned in to what Rep. Moore was telling him.) Because Arch had traveled to Vietnam on several occasions, LBJ talked to him about that subject almost every time he saw him.

As the treatment he received from the President suggested, Arch Moore was becoming a significant member of Congress, despite the fact that he was a member of the minority. He was being taken seriously by the Democrats who ran Capitol Hill. Even the U.S. Supreme Court would acknowledge his role in significant legislation, such as co-sponsoring the Immigration and Nationality Act, which among other things, afforded some rights to alien deportees.[3]

Sometimes Arch would be in the extreme minority on an issue, but his position would be proven to be prescient. When $91.5 million (a huge sum in those days) was being sought for a nuclear reactor in California, the West Virginia congressman phoned Admiral Hyman Rickover, the Navy's nuclear power authority, for advice. Rickover told him it wasn't practical, that it simply wouldn't work. That opinion, plus Moore's natural hostility to nuclear power (he preferred to use coal), caused him to vote against the proposal, although all 352 other members of Congress voted for it. He proved to be a majority of one. After spending $50 million on the project, the Atomic Energy Commission admitted that the proposed reactor would not work, that the taxpayers' money had once again been wasted.[4] The incident enlarged Moore's reputation as one who "did his homework."

Arch was particularly proud of his work on The Criminal Justice Act of 1963. Among other things, it required indigent criminal defendants to be provided with legal counsel and planted the seeds of what would eventually be a public defender's office. Most states already had such a system, but Moore's bill extended such rights to federal courts. Arch's authorship and advocacy of the complex legislation was so extensive that it was gratefully recognized by members of the opposition party. House Judiciary Chairman Emanuel Celler, a Democrat of New York, told the press, "[This] bill, in a major way, has been the work of [Arch Moore]. He rendered a yeoman service in fashioning of this vital bill and honor is due him. I hope that this bill will be called 'the Moore Bill.'" Attorney General Robert F. Kennedy wrote to Arch, "Especially, I want to thank you for your efforts on behalf of the Criminal Justice Act. The continuing benefit which this measure will be to the people of our country should give you a great sense of accomplishment."[5]

A November 21, 1963 article in *The New York Times* reported that the House Judiciary Committee on which Rep. Moore served had reported out President Kennedy's civil rights bill. "The bipartisan measure reported favorably today calls for a national ban on employment discrimination and segregation at hotels and restaurants," the *Times* continued. "It would speed up voting cases and allow the Justice Department to bring school desegregation suits." The article noted that "Arch A. Moore, Jr. of West Virginia...had supported a broader bill in committee [and expressed] personal views" in the report to the full Congress, as did two other congressmen on the committee.[6] Essentially, the legislation was providing rights that supposedly had been granted to African-Americans one hundred years ago. Two days later, Kennedy would be killed and the task of shepherding the legislation would be his successor's.

The Civil Rights Act of 1964 may have been the most significant legislation passed during Moore's tenure in the House. As the *Times* article had hinted, Moore and Chairman Celler had created a stronger bill, but the Southern Democrats had succeeded in watering it down in committee. An infuriated Arch Moore arose to address the full House, complaining about the "heavy handed and politically motivated manner that is presently being attempted," which he called a "disservice to the democratic process and a disservice to all citizens." He cautioned, "The right to be free from all forms of racial intolerance is so fundamentally the privilege of each and every citizen of the United States that it cannot be made the plaything of politics. The shame of our times, however, is that the subject of civil rights has from the early days of the 88th Congress been made the butt of political opportunism." In harsh terms, Arch condemned the bill that the Southern Democrats (who then ruled the Congress) had "sprung upon the [Judiciary] Committee from out of the night. Where it came from, or who were its benefactors, remains to this day a deep, dark secret. The bill reported was conceived in segregation, born in intolerance, and nurtured in discrimination."[7]

All of the West Virginia delegation would end up voting for the finalized bill. All except Senator Robert C. Byrd, that is. Apparently wanting to continue the old, segregated and discriminatory South, which his Klan had earlier defended, Byrd would filibuster it in the U.S. Senate, speaking non-stop for fourteen hours to try unsuccessfully to kill the legislation. Interestingly, around the time Congressman Ken Hechler was marching in Selma with the Rev. Martin Luther King, Senator Byrd was summoning FBI Director J. Edgar Hoover's assistant, Cartha DeLoach, to his office, ominously suggesting to the Bureau that it was time Dr. King "met his Waterloo."[8] Despite the fact that senators from the former Confederate States, to whom Byrd was strongly allied, had opposed the legislation based on their old argument of States Rights, it passed by 290 to 130 in the House and then passed the Senate with the strong leadership of Senator Everett Dirksen, Republican of Illinois, a flowery and melodious orator. Without the support of the party of Lincoln, Johnson's bill would have been handily defeated; in fact, it wouldn't even have been released from any committee without Republican advocates.

Congressman Moore was one of the bill's architects who stood behind the President's table in the White House with Martin Luther King, Robert F. Kennedy, Hubert Humphrey, Dirksen and the others who made the Civil Rights Act a reality. In his normal fashion, Lyndon Johnson used many pens to put pieces of his signature on the bill, handing the pens to a couple dozen or so congressmen and senators who had sent the legislation to him. He handed one of those pens to Arch Moore. It is a memento he treasures to this day, a reminder of a time when bipartisanship could accomplish something of greatness.

Within months of the passage of the Civil Rights Act, Dr. King was back at the White House, asking the President for legislation to force the

South to allow African-Americans to vote. Black Americans were being denied the right to register based on poll taxes or ridiculously difficult tests that few whites could have passed if similarly mistreated by Southern (Democratic) courthouse clerks and registrars. "He was asking Johnson for legislation that provided for federal registrars to go into these states to ensure that blacks could be registered to vote," explained Ken Hechler. "Johnson told King, 'It's impossible to get two civil rights bills through the congress in one year.' King was determined to defy Johnson, however. So the President called him back and basically said, 'You do what you have to do to force me to do what I need to do.'" It was after that the Selma march made headlines that LBJ called for passage of what would be called the 1965 Voters Rights Act.

Again, the entire West Virginia delegation would support the act in its final form. Again, except for Robert C. Byrd, who filibustered and did everything he could do to prevent it from becoming law. "Congressman Moore voted for a Republican amendment which would have exempted counties which were in compliance, which was not a bad vote," remembered Hechler (whose memory, even at age 90, about the details of such legislation was remarkable). "But [the Democrats] preferred a bill that looked at the entire state of Alabama, for example, instead of individual counties, so the Moore amendment was defeated." Then, on August 3, 1965, a conference report came up, Hechler added, and "Congressman [Robert] McEwen, a Republican of New York, offered an amendment that would allow any state to apply for judicial relief [from the requirement of having federal voting registrars] if fifty percent of the blacks in that state were voting. Moore voted yes on that amendment but it, too, was defeated."

Hechler saluted Arch's bravery and statesmanship in the civil rights movement. "Moore was influenced by the intellectual arguments through his service on the Judiciary Committee," speculated Hechler, "and he was always on the liberal side of civil rights."

But even Arch had his limits, as additional legislation pushed the federal government's power into seemingly every transaction of life. When the 1966 Civil Rights Bill came to the floor, it narrowly passed the House, but he voted against it. Explained a historian:

> A large number of moderates, critical of Title IV, voted against the bill. Congressman Arch Moore of West Virginia, for instance, had voted for the Civil Rights Acts of 1957, 1960, 1964, and 1965, but he could not

> endorse this bill. "The average American," [Moore] noted, "tends to look upon his right to sell realty as being absolute, and I believe that attitude is steeped deep in the traditions of this nation. Legal measures taken to assure equality of housing opportunity necessarily, I believe, constitute an interference with individual property rights."[9]

The New York Times reported, in a front page story of August 10, 1966, that "a motion by Arch A. Moore, Jr., a Republican of West Virginia, to strike the open housing section of the bill," had been defeated by a 222 to 190 votes by the House. But the story indicated that Moore's position would probably be adopted by the Senate, where Senator Dirksen also opposed the provision. (A compromise was worked out and the provision remained in the act.)

Arch Moore would co-sponsor successful legislation in his last years in the Congress that extended social security benefits to those applicants who could prove themselves to be disabled and unable to work. Although it would prove to be a very costly program that would often be abused because of the liberal way it would be administered, it meant financial salvation for millions of Americans.

There was little or no political gain to be had for a Republican by creating and passing legislation that helped African-Americans who traditionally vote about 90 percent Democratic ("And only four or five percent of West Virginia's population is black," noted Hechler), the disabled, or indigent criminal defendants. Many of the beneficiaries of these acts probably would not vote in any election and certainly not for Moore if they did. And, for better or worse, his work on these bills almost went unnoticed by the folk back home. Most West Virginians of the time probably couldn't have cared less whether a person with dark skin had to travel a hundred miles to find a restroom he or she was allowed to use. They probably didn't care whether a criminal defendant wrongfully went to prison because he could not afford to hire a lawyer, or that an alien was deported without due process. They probably didn't care that a blind or lame person would have to sit on the streets and sell pencils to scrape up some rent money (as was often seen in West Virginia towns in those days). Supporting such legislation certainly did not endear a congressman to the Southern conservative Democrats who ran the House and Senate. But for Arch Moore, it was simply the right thing to do. To him, it was the way a civilized, decent nation, that was rooted in Christian principles, should treat those considered the least fortunate of its people. His mother would say of him, years later, "A poor man or a man with a million dollars is the same to Arch."[10]

LEGISLATION WHICH had an even greater effect on West Virginians was the result of Johnson's "War on Poverty." He had campaigned in West Virginia and poor sections of Eastern Kentucky, Ohio and Pennsylvania in 1964, chatting with people on the front porches of their weathered shacks, promising to carry on President Kennedy's efforts to wipe out poverty in Appalachia. And everyone knew that, unlike JFK who had little luck with liberal programs, the former iron-fisted boss of the Senate, LBJ, could get legislation through congress.

Social scientists of the time—on college campuses, think tanks, news media and government itself—were arguing with all sorts of statistics that, if enough tax dollars were spent, poverty could be eliminated in America, everyone would have a job, crime would disappear, and all would be happy. Utopia would arrive. They would prove to be wrong, of course—billions of dollars later. Christ's prediction, "The poor you have with you always," would be validated once again. They didn't take into account such factors as indolence, abandonment of wives and children, character flaws, low intelligence, dependence on government programs, mental illness and drug and alcohol addiction, which are the root causes of poverty in the majority of cases. But it was a fashionable and noble cause to fight poverty, not simply a vote-getter for the Democrats. And even if only a small portion of the poor were rescued, if some children could be fed and clothed, it might prove worthwhile. (And it could be argued that the social programs certainly were no more of a waste of tax dollars than the billions we were spending to fight a losing war in Southeast Asia, to defend ungrateful Europeans against the Soviets, or on foreign aid to third world nations which despised us.)

Federal government public works projects had begun as result of the Great Depression, ostensibly for flood relief or electrical power generation, but ultimately to create jobs and stimulate the economy. Herbert Hoover and, then to a much greater extent, Franklin Roosevelt arranged for public funding of projects which were previously considered within the sole domain of the private market. Among those was a regional program, the Tennessee Valley Authority, which brought jobs and electricity to Alabama and Tennessee. President Kennedy had wanted a regional program like that solely for West Virginia, but ended up accepting a multi-state program for depressed areas called the Area Redevelopment Administration, which he signed into law in May of 1961. It became very unpopular with many segments of the Congress, however. Although hundreds of millions had been spent under ARA, it had "utterly failed to get off the ground and [was] leaving in its wake a shameful record of mismanagement, stodginess and waste," according to liberal Rep. John Lindsay, a future New York mayor.[11]

When he took office, Lyndon Johnson first considered revamping the ARA to fit into his War on Poverty but, because of these concerns, it was dying a quick death in the Congress. On April 9, 1963, President Kennedy created the Appalachian Regional Commission, chaired by the governors of those states and by Undersecretary of Commerce Franklin D. Roosevelt, Jr. It reported to the White House a year later, months after JFK's assassination. Its report described a region in decline, impoverished and desperate, where the per capita income was less than 75 percent of the national average and unemployment was forty percent higher. The study concluded that, before private enterprise could expand in the region, a major, expensive program of public investment was needed for highways, education and training, water and sewer, timber and coal development, expanded health care facilities, more low-income assistance, including food stamps and free school lunches, and federal programs to fund community development corporations.

With the demise of the ARA, Johnson would use the ARC as his regional anti-poverty vehicle and, with the help of Senator Jennings Randolph and others, it came on line in 1965, as one of the nation's largest and longest-lasting public works projects of all times. The ARC was to be an independent agency, funded by the federal government, with its own staff and a board comprised of a federal co-chair, appointed by the president and reporting to him, and the governors of all the states in the region. Johnson also replaced the ARA with another new agency, the Economic Development Administration, which would work in conjunction with the ARC.

Governor Hulett Smith's administration never fully recognized the potential opportunities afforded West Virginia by the ARC and did not tap into the millions of dollars it offered. *But the governor who succeeded Smith would wring every dime out of it he could.* Senator Byrd would also make use of it to fund tens of millions of dollars of new, Appalachian Corridor highways, in the 1980s and 1990s. To a large extent, the ARC would be West Virginia's TVA. It would play a significant role in the revitalization of the state from 1969 into the early Seventies.

But even before the ARC and other agencies began trying to rescue West Virginia from its poverty, there were other Kennedy programs in place, which were bringing recent college graduates in to try to help, just as the Peace Corp was doing in Africa and poor nations in other regions. One of those programs was called VISTA. It was in vogue for college grads (part of JFK's "ask what you can do for your country") to spend a few months in the Peace Corp or VISTA, advertised as "The toughest job you'll ever love." It was rather like secular missionary work, economic and cultural, rather than religious.

NINETEEN SIXTY FOUR had been a year in which a such a figure—who would play widely in Moore's future—arrived in West Virginia. Six feet, seven inches tall, twenty seven-year-old John D. Rockefeller IV, a VISTA volunteer, arrived in the small community of Emmons, on the Kanawha-Boone County line, in his Land Rover.

The New York scion of the Rockefeller (mainly oil) fortune was a giant of a man, particularly as he got older and put some weight on his frame. There was a slump to his shoulders–unclear as to whether it was a postural or spinal problem, or just out of habit, since he had to look down at most people due to his height. His arms were long and he would reach out wide and shake hands with two people at once. He had a wide, friendly grin and his already squinting blue eyes would twinkle and crow's feet wrinkles at the edges would appear in a charming way. Despite being much more shy than his uncles, he dominated a room with his presence and his friendliness seemed genuine.

Jay, as everyone called him, was born in New York in 1937, the only son of John D. and Blanchette Ferry Hooker Rockefeller. Born into one of history's wealthiest families, he had the best the material world has to offer. He and his cousins spent much of their time at the family estate at Pocantico Hills, New York. His family also had homes on Fifth Avenue, at Beekman Place in Manhattan, a ranch in Venezuela and a mansion in Hawaii. Described by his mother as a quiet, studious child, Jay had skipped a grade at a Washington elementary school before going on to the prestigious Phillips Exeter Academy, a New Hampshire prep school. Then it was Harvard, where he joined the most exclusive clubs and, with his height, was a natural for the basketball team.

In the Sixties, most young people were caught up, at least a bit, in the "revolution," the rebellion against the status quo, The Establishment. The Rockefeller cousins were no different, even though by privilege of their birth they were very much a part of that Establishment. Some were so embarrassed by their riches that they changed their last name and dropped out of their high society lifestyle. Jay was different from his three sisters and cousins, in that he was proud of who he was and was not ashamed to be rich. "Jay accepted it from the beginning," his mother recalled in a 1982 newspaper interview. "Most of the others have wanted to live like church mice. Jay enjoys luxury. He's really the only one of them who is normal."[12]

But Jay also had what some might call a hole in his soul; he wanted something more in life than enlarging and enjoying the fortune left to him by his grandfather. "Jay's a good person; his heart's in the right place. He's an honorable person," thought Edgar "Hike" Heiskell, the Republican who followed Rockefeller as secretary of state.[13] The Rockefellers had been great philanthropists, but that prospect alone didn't excite him. He enjoyed his studies (and teaching English) in Japan, learned the language and, for a time, considered a career there. His Uncle David was one of the world's great power brokers and king makers, a founder of the highly influential Trilateral Commission and the Council on Foreign Relations, but that, too, did not appeal to Jay. He'd have to wait much too long to inherit any of those duties, for one reason. And, reportedly, Jay's intellect did not yet impress the elders in his family enough for them to turn the reins of the empire over to him, to any great extent.

It was the anti-poverty movement started by the Kennedys that really caught Jay's imagination. After serving a brief stint in the Peace Corp and his time in Japan, Rockefeller had begun considering work with the American poor and following the Kennedys (and his Uncle Nelson, who was a four-term, very liberal Republican governor of New York) into politics. When he shared his thoughts with Bobby Kennedy, the former attorney general (running for U.S. Senate in New York) reportedly urged him to "go to West Virginia." Bobby knew there was plenty of poverty in the Mountain State and also knew it was fertile ground politically for a wealthy Democrat, as his brother had learned in 1960. Jay changed his registration to Democrat and made arrangement to follow RFK's advice.

So it was off to Emmons. That small community was backward, even by Appalachian standards. Their Southern West Virginia twang was so heavy that it was sometimes difficult for outsiders to understand. The men still wore bib overalls. Automation of area coal mines had put many local miners out of work and, as is too typical in Southern West Virginia, few ventured out of state to seek employment or to even search for local alternative occupations. Thus, many Emmons families were on public assistance, living in substandard housing.

Like many Appalachian communities, Emmons didn't trust outsiders, strangers. They were wary of someone with a last name like

Rockefeller. Hadn't the original Rockefeller made his money by taking advantage of people like themselves? Besides, they may be poor but they were also proud people—what could this young, preppy guy from New York, who'd never got his hands dirty, have to offer them? There's got to be a catch to it. Jay had a long, tough time finding acceptance in Emmons. Like a missionary or anthropologist in a far off Third World jungle, he tried hard to gain their confidence. He started playing ball with the children, even showed them a slide show of his ritzy life, and finally began getting invitations to dinner. Before long, he was involved in building projects (including a park named Rockefeller Center), getting their road fixed, driving mothers and children to medical and dental treatment, trying to find the young men jobs and establishing a Little League team. Before long, he'd won most of them over with his sincerity.

Rockefeller would later say, "Emmons really changed me and stamped me. It made me a fighter for the underdog. It defines me."[14] Among other things, the two years in the rural community convinced the future Senator that a comprehensive national health care system was needed in the U.S., a goal he would pursue passionately throughout his career.

Those near him in those days in the 1960s, and even when he became secretary of state, told funny stories of how out-of-touch Rockefeller was with reality, the common man, because of his extremely protected, wealthy background. For example, lawyer Ed Rebrook told how Jay had no idea what a Coke cost (twenty five to fifty cents), giving him a dime one day to go to a vending machine, and quietly putting the nickel "change" back into his pocket that Ed returned to him (to see if he'd even notice). An aide remembered laughing him to scorn when Jay confessed ignorance that people voluntarily reported their income to the government and paid taxes on it. Reporter Richard Grimes wrote that Jay believed everyone had a financial portfolio. Early supporter Raamie Barker remembered paying for gas with Jay's Exxon credit card. It had no numbers on it, just "John D. Rockefeller IV," since Jay's family were part owners of Standard Oil. Rockefeller did give up his Jaguar sports car he'd tooled around in during his D.C. days, driving the more proletariat Ford Mustang when he came to West Virginia. His naivete, his new perspective, was sometimes refreshing, but more often it got him and his projects into trouble, because he had never had to struggle or worry about having income.

The politics would come quickly, for Jay was in a hurry. A group of Charleston Republicans visited Jay once they were certain he was in the state for the purpose of seeking public office. Pointing out that his Uncle Nelson had functioned quite well as a liberal Republican, they tried to persuade the younger Rockefeller to return to their ranks. But he politely refused. He had switched to Democrat and would stick with West Virginia's majority party.

The Kanawha County Democrats welcomed him with open arms and he was elected to the House of Delegates in 1966. He would win the secretary of state's race in 1968 in a landslide. Many West Virginians were totally convinced the handsome young Rockefeller was on his way to soon becoming president. Sen. Edward Kennedy predicted it in the early Seventies. Jay privately admitted that he wanted to be president by 1980—that was his schedule. Some were even mentioning 1976. His progress toward that quest was to be slowed, however, by a man from Moundsville.

AS THAT FIGURE who would play into Arch's future (Jay) came onto the stage, one who was so important to his past left it. His beloved mentor, Uncle Everett Moore, died. "It was a marquee event," noted daughter Shelley, who recalled the family traveling from Maryland back to West Virginia for the funeral. "It was the first time I ever heard my dad's voice crack with emotion," the Congresswoman recalled, "when he was putting us in the car, telling us about him." Capito remembered with pleasant nostalgia "the holidays—visiting Uncle Everett and Dad's family."

The Moores continued their difficult act of balancing a time-consuming career with managing and nurturing a family. "Growing up in Glen Dale, you always had a sense of Dad's position," remembered Kim Moore. "The town in general was very proud of him and he didn't forget his roots; Mom and Dad were always loyal to the Ohio Valley." For himself, Kim admitted, "In grade school, I was more arrogant than I needed to be but the teachers put me in my place and sat me back down."

Most of their neighbors didn't get to travel much, so "Mom and Dad shared their experiences with the townspeople. When they went to Japan, for example, they brought back souvenirs." Mrs. Moore went to his grade school, bringing souvenirs to all the students and telling about the trip in all the classrooms in which she was welcomed. "They were always sharing," repeated Kim. "They understood the value of their unique experiences and tried to share them with others." When the scout troops would visit the nation's capital, many would stay at the Moore residence in Maryland.

Moore's work meant he was busy 24/7, his son recalled, but "I understood his job and understood that meant sharing him. But when he was home, it was 'me and you.'" Nevertheless, Kim sometimes felt neglected.

Kim played a lot of basketball and soccer. "I can only remember one of my games that he attended." But he hastened to add that almost all of his were away games, and that his father had reminded him, "You told me not to come, that I'd jinx you." Kim had the comfort of knowing "he'd have been there if I'd asked him to be."

As Kim would become a teenager later on, "it was tough, an anti-Establishment time," and he needed some fatherly attention at times, but felt ignored. "He irked me sometimes," Kim admitted. "He was always a voracious newspaper-reader and I had to 'talk through the newspaper' many times." He admitted that his father was good at multi-tasking, but there were times he wanted to talk face-to-face, without any distraction. (About Arch's reading habits, Kim said he never once has seen his father reading a book—he gathered his wealth of knowledge from magazines, newspapers and TV news, he said, "Although he has a house-full of books and I'm sure he's read them at some time or another.")

Generally, Kim had great memories of growing up in the Moore household and of his political father, though. "He's a great storyteller. On numerous Scout outings, he'd mesmerize them with stories about snipe hunting. Then we'd go out into the woods with our flashlights and paper bags to hunt for snipes. Only one of us claimed to find a snipe and, of course, that was Dad," he laughed.

Kim clearly maintained a deep and abiding respect for his father. "He's a man's man," he said of Arch Moore. "He's a great athlete, he has an understanding of economics, of world history, a sense of what happened before and what can happen again ... a grasp of facts, even today ... there are not many left like that ... He's always had a hero's image to me."

The Congressman would "make me feel important, part of it," his son recalled. "He would say, 'Come on, we're going to ride in a convertible in a parade in Shinnston and you're going to help me throw bubblegum. I'd say, 'I don't want to,' but he'd say, 'You're coming!' On election nights, he'd always have me go to the (nearby) courthouse to get an accurate count of the vote. He probably already had it by the time I came back to his (Moundsville) office to report, but he never told me if he did." Kim also remembered participating in flag ceremonies at the 1968 Republican convention in Miami and serving several times as a page in the House of Representatives, thanks to Dad.

What many didn't know about his father is that he has a great sense of humor, Kim thought. "He loves to laugh, loves to hear a joke, and he's a great practical joker type guy." Repeated for years, but apparently never picked up by the victim, are prank phone calls Arch makes to his brother,

Harry "Moo" Moore. "Dad would call him up and ask him questions, using disguised voices each time—a deep, or shrill voice, maybe with an Asian or a clipped Italian accent—and then he'd hang up, slap his hands together and laugh. 'I got him again!' he'd say."[15]

THE 1964 Democratic landslide would only add to the Arch Moore invincibility legend. Johnson was at the peak of his popularity. His opponent, Arizona Senator Barry Goldwater, was labeled a kook who would use nuclear warfare, a conservative when liberalism was still in its ascendancy, someone who would roll back the federal social programs to pre-FDR days. The Republican would carry his own state and the old Confederacy (due mainly to the unpopularity of the civil rights and voting rights legislation), but otherwise it was "All the way with LBJ!" The President won West Virginia by a two-to-one margin, and Robert Byrd defeated his opponent with 67.6 percent of the vote. Hulett Smith, former Democratic state chairman, who nearly defeated Barron in the 1960 primary and then served as his Commerce commissioner, easily defeated Cecil Underwood for governor. The only major Republican to survive was Arch Moore, who won an even greater victory than in previous years.

THE VIETNAM WAR loomed over American politics like no other issue in the late 1960s. Arch Moore was having serious doubts about U.S. involvement in Southeast Asia from very early on, having first visited South Vietnam in 1963. He spent more time in that war zone than any other congressman.

In an August 9, 1965, letter to a constituent in Triadelphia, Arch admitted that he shared the man's "misgivings about the President's proposed solution." First, he thought Americans had "overextended ourselves," and deserved some help from other nations to fight the spread of Communism. Arch expressed particular outrage that our so-called allies were continuing to trade and supply the North Vietnamese, "even as our own servicemen were being killed" by them. The French rubber plantation managers were the only ones who could use the highways without fear of ambush from the Viet Cong, he noted. Moore thought President Johnson should "exert some leadership by calling on our allies to stop their trade with the North Vietnamese and the Red Chinese," and also demand from them troops and money to help with the war. He also told the correspondent that he thought America should "simply stop the foreign aid to our allies who persist in doing business as usual with the enemy." He thought American allies should "realize that they too have an obligation to defend...freedom."

In 1966, Congressman Moore spent twelve days in that war-torn nation and had his second brush with death. "I would go to headquarters to get briefings. I was there because refugees were pouring into the south from North Vietnam." While there, the helicopter ("They called it the American Aviation Company. I later discovered it was part of the CIA's airlines") in which he was a passenger was struck by Viet Cong rifle fire, disabling the rotors ("We lost the propeller completely") and forcing it to land. The pilot had been hit by a bullet, but neither Moore nor any other passenger suffered more than a bruise or abrasion from the hard landing ("We weren't that high in the air"). He explained why they were in danger: "There was no way you could identify lines; there were no military lines [as in conventional warfare]. They were coming out of the woods and we didn't know where they were." What impressed him, stuck in his memory, was the fact that Department of Defense and State Department personnel rushed to his Maryland residence to assure Mrs. Moore that he was safe. [16]

He would make numerous trips to the country during the war, in part because of his role in the House Immigration Committee. "There were thousands of refugees fleeing from the north to the south and they didn't know what to do with them," he explained. "There was the added problem, as in Iraq, that we didn't know who [was trying to kill Americans or not]." (Photos of him—inspecting troops, giving speeches there, sometimes in military fatigues, other times dressed in suit and tie—have been sold on eBay.) Moore enjoyed meeting soldiers and Marines from West Virginia, who were equally thrilled to see him and get some news from back home. He was shaking hands and campaigning, taking care of constituents, even there.

Arch remembered dining, out in the field, with a South Vietnamese officer. "They gave us chop sticks and served raw liver, which they considered a delicacy," he recalled. "I said through my interpreter, as diplomatically as I could, that my delicate digestive tract was not up to eating that. The officer simply reached over and took my plate and ate mine after finishing his own."

The conflict had belonged to the French Colonialists in the 1950s after the Japanese had been driven from Southeast Asia. When the French wilted and withdrew, Eisenhower and Kennedy had sent in American advisors, then troops, to keep the South from falling to a Communist dictatorship. "Soviet Communism was expanding to cover the globe and I, along with others at the time, subscribed to the Domino Theory," remembered

Arch. "We believed that if one nation fell to the Communists, it was just a matter of time before the country next to it went Communist." Vietnam became Lyndon Johnson's war in the public mind and was rapidly losing support in the U.S., as thousands of boys were returning in body bags, with no obvious goal being attained by our efforts. We couldn't seem to respond to Ho Chi Mihn's guerilla warfare any better than the French had done. The village peasants who welcomed and smiled at American troops by day were lobbing hand grenades or shooting mortars into their camps at night. Most didn't care if Ho was Communist; their lives couldn't be much more miserable and they saw the war as a revolution, one of liberation from the foreigners, a continuation of their earlier struggle against the Japanese and French. But few Americans understood those sentiments.

Congressman Moore's newsletter to his constituents often had question and answer columns on topical subjects. In his November newsletter to constituents Moore repeated his earlier theme that the U.S. should not be going at it alone. "The problem in [Vietnam] remains as unfathomable today as it did some ten months [ago] when I was there. If this truly is a cause in which freedom and liberty are at stake, are we not justified in asking other free nations of the world what they are willing to do for that cause?" Arch argued that other nations should "make a significant contribution to our endeavors" in pursuing the war. He added, obviously skeptical about the war's prospects: "A tremendous effort would have to be exerted further to conclude this conflict in the not too distant future. Failure to aggressively pursue its conclusion, I have every reason to believe that my own 15-year-old son would possibly see service in Vietnam."

Arch seemed to enjoy his visits with the military. Toward the end of his last term in Congress, while in Naples, Italy, he was invited to visit an aircraft carrier in the Sixth Fleet, which was in the Mediterranean. He was a little apprehensive about landing on a moving ship ("I'm not good in water," he told them),[17] but agreed to sit in the cockpit of a fighter jet. The pilot demonstrated how he could hide the plane in clouds and "then he darted out of the sky" and landed on deck. "A tail hook caught us. Here I was, a little hoopie from Moundsville, on deck of the U.S.S. John F. Kennedy which had five thousand people aboard."

They put him in Admiral John McCain Jr.'s[18] suite on the ship (It was so large, "You could set up housekeeping there!" joked Arch). After going below and greeting three sailors from West Virginia, he learned that McCain was going to be his host for dinner that evening, but was not yet aboard. How he came aboard amazed the congressman. "It was dark, we were going full speed and the Admiral's ship came up beside the carrier, racing along with it. They shot a wire up to the deck of the carrier [making a pulley system between the ships, in a method called "high-lining"] and harnessed him up in a boatswain chair, transferring him from one ship to the other as we raced along. The band is on deck and starts playing a song, greeting their Admiral. I'm short," admitted Arch, "but he was almost a head shorter than I am. They called him 'Cat McCain.'

"We had a beautiful candlelight dinner. Then the Admiral jumped up and said, 'Congressman, I'm going home.' He saluted, clicked his heels. They got him strapped up again and, using the pulley, started him back across to the other ship. But the two ships got too close together, only forty or fifty yards apart, the line sagged and Admiral McCain got dipped into the water!"

AN ONGOING controversy in the U.S. Senate captured the nation's attention in the late 1960s, and did not escape Congressman Moore's notice. His archived official papers reveal that his office had their clipping service send them numerous article about it. Senator Thomas Dodd, a Democrat from Connecticut, they reported, had accepted about $200,000, a huge sum of money at the time, in "testimonial gifts" from lobbyists, political allies and constituents.

Congressmen and women were being paid salaries of $30,000 a year in the Sixties and the government now paid for six trips to their respective districts per year. Beyond that, they had to find other sources for their expenses, unless they were independently wealthy. A number of congressmen, including Ken Hechler, received $1,000 each for personal expenses from the AFL-CIO's Committee on Political Education (COPE). Former Vice President Nixon nearly had been dropped from the Republican ticket in 1952,[19] when it was revealed he had a "slush fund" to pay for such personal travel, clothing and other needs, prompting the "Checkers Speech" which saved his career. A former aide of the Connecticut senator charged that he had misappropriated hundreds of thousands of dollars and Dodd's son was even called to testify. Dodd was investigated by the Senate Ethics Commission, mainly to determine whether he should have paid taxes on proceeds from fund raising dinners, not whether acceptance of the fees was ethical. *The Washington Post* and other media used the hearings to spotlight the problem, however, of whether federal legislators should even be accepting what could be viewed as legal bribes.

AS THE DECADE wound down, the war in Southeast Asia dragged

on endlessly and with bloody consequences; over 50,000 American lives would be lost in the conflict and hundreds of thousands more wounded or scarred by their involvement. Almost everyone in West Virginia had a family member or friend who had been wounded or killed in the jungles or rice paddies of Southeast Asia. "As a former soldier, my sympathy was always with the soldiers," remembered Arch. "I visited the wounded when I could.

"They wouldn't let us win [the Vietnam War]. I never felt you went to war without finishing the job. But as with Iraq, you could never ascertain, never knew who you were dealing with. I was over there seven times between 1966 and 1968. I'd made up my mind that the decision to win or lose had already been made [by the military brass and the White House]. If you're going to lose, you need to get the troops out as quickly as possible."

In retrospect, should we even have been involved in that war? "I felt it was in our best interests to prevent expansion of Communism," Moore opined, in a 2005 interview. "It was a legitimate undertaking. Subsequently, all that [American military resistance] paid off during Reagan's term [when Soviet-backed communist expansion collapsed]. The will to win was not there; we did not have enough help from the South Vietnamese. The impact of public sentiment was another reason we did not win. The greatest tragedy was that our military was risking their lives, doing the best they could, and then came home to an America which practically disowned them. It was not their fault—it was our leadership's fault. Lyndon Johnson had a hard time wrestling with it." Moore thought, when he would visit the war-torn country, "If I ever have any say about it, we will do this all the way or get out." He added, "And ultimately, Nixon began to get us out of it."

AS HE CONTINUED his service in Washington, Moore also maintained a lucrative law practice, something that came under increasing scrutiny as ethical standards evolved. He certainly was far from being the only congressman or senator who continued to have a practice or business on the side—some of the nation's most prominent legislators had done the same thing. "Martindale Hubbell showed that he represented PPG, Mobay, Weirton Steel and others, the entire time he was in Congress," H. John Rogers noted. "He had no associate (to whom work could be referred). He was up for hire that entire time." Rogers added, "It was perfectly legal–nothing wrong with it. But I wouldn't want a congressman to represent the UMWA or Consol while they were serving as our representative. It's a conflict of interest on its face." But such retainers were lucrative and difficult to give up.

Interestingly, congressional ethics would dominate the last years of Arch's service in Washington. In 1967, Moore became involved in his last high-profile project as a member of the House of Representatives, as the Congress became involved in an effort to oust one of its own members, Adam Clayton Powell, an African-American Democrat who represented Harlem. Arch was appointed as the Republicans' leader by House Minority Leader Gerald Ford on a special committee of the House Ethics Committee to sort out the charges and make a recommendation. The deck was stacked by the Democratic leadership; *The New York Times* noted that "all five Democrats named to the committee belong, in a sense, to a pro-Powell minority group," which included liberals Emanuel Celler, a 78-year-old from Brooklyn, James Corman, Claude [Red] Pepper, John Conyers and Andrew Jacobs.[20]

The charges were that Congressman Powell had his wife and a domestic servant on the congressional payroll, that he took Mrs. Powell and another woman for a two-week vacation to Bimini on government funds, that he had been held in contempt of court for failing to pay a libel judgment obtained against him, and other assorted ethical violations. At first he was stripped of the chairmanship of the Education and Labor Committee, then the Congress held hearings to determine if he could even be seated. Powell, an eleven-term congressman who was very popular in his district, played the race card to the max. He compared his plight to the crucifixion of Jesus and denounced the inquiry as "a conspiracy of white power."

Powell's behavior likely would go unnoticed today but, in that time, he rubbed his fellow members of Congress the wrong way, to say the least. As previously noted, Cleve Bailey once struck him with his fist, so upset he was with something Powell had done or said. Arch rather liked him, however. "He was flamboyant outside, but inside the halls of Congress he was always a gentleman. He had been a Baptist minister."

The special committee which Rep. Moore helped lead actually voted to seat Powell, finding that his actions were not sufficient to throw him out of the House. Again, such a vote would not be a popular one back in the First District; Arch was just voting his conscious.

But, he recounted, Rep. Tom Curtis of Missouri "offered an amendment to the committee's report which held that, yes, Adam Clayton Powell had violated the law and he should be refused entry as a member of the House. Curtis' motion prevailed and the House proceeded to unseat him."

After Congress refused to re-seat him (in a resolution offered by House Minority Leader Gerald Ford), on a 364-to-64 vote,[21] the New York Democrat told a crowd of supporters, "You are looking at the first black man who was ever lynched by Congress." Powell would take a phone call from President Johnson with, "Hello, baby!" and wore brightly colored shirts and handmade alligator shoes, with a beauty queen on each arm, a half-smoked cigar in his mouth, looking like a pimp, admonishing his boosters to "keep the faith, baby!" Admittedly, white members of Congress were not overly fond of him.

But Powell called his accusers "the biggest bunch of hypocrites" ever assembled, saying he was a martyr to a noble cause, surrounded by "about 120 Judases." When reporters would interview him he sat among them, ostentatiously reading a current book, *Washington Expose'*, which reported on a number of crooked congressmen. Robert F. Kennedy, who owed his New York senate seat to the black vote, said he was "disturbed that [the refusal to seat Powell] was taken before the adoption of any uniform code of conduct applicable to all members of Congress."

Powell appealed his ouster to the U.S. Supreme Court. Congressman Moore orally argued before the court, advocating the position his special committee had taken, and in opposition to the vote of the full House. Moore's position won; the high court seated Powell.

Certainly, Powell had not been alone in the sleazy atmosphere of Capitol Hill. And *The Washington Star* admitted that "there [was] virtually no effective ethical or legal standard to measure congressional behavior in this area."[22] Loopholes in federal laws allowed unions and lobbyists to contribute to congressmen and senators without reporting much of it. To bolster their $30,000 salaries, congressmen such as Morris Udall, Democrat of Arizona, were accepting $30,000 testimonial dinner gifts to underwrite their trips back home. The *Star* noted that Democrat Reps. Paul Krebs of New Jersey and William Hathaway of Maine and Senator Quinton Burdick of North Dakota, had created committees to underwrite their personal expenses. Senator Birch Bayh, Democrat of Indiana, admitted that he had accepted "honorariums" so that he could afford to pay for his children's education. As a senator, Hubert Humphrey had taken speaking fees, totaling about $171,000 in 1964, complaining that he couldn't make ends meet with a growing family. Senator Thomas Dodd had accepted $100,000 to $200,000 in "testimonial gifts" from constituents, political allies and lobbyists and paid taxes on none of it. Senator Willis Robertson, Democrat of Virginia (and the Rev. Pat Robertson's father), was criticized for relying on the banking interests to fund him. Others, like Senator Jacob Javits, of New York, and Senator Everett Dirksen of Illinois, Republicans, got theirs through a law practice on the side, through which favor seekers could endear themselves by becoming paying clients. Other senators and congressmen had suspicious real estate deals going.

It seemed they all–Democrats and Republicans alike—were "on the take" to one degree or another, some more legally than others, but all beholding to various interests to boost their personal incomes. And the "golden rule of government" ("He who has the gold makes the rules") prevailed, as it had since the nation's foundation and even before; the special interests largely obtained what they wanted in exchange for subsidizing the members of Congress.

This way of life was defended by those congressmen and senators, however. They believed they did not receive adequate pay and travel allowance, so they were entitled to take money from those who sought to influence them. "You could live in an eighty-dollar-a-month apartment and buy cheap clothes," said Senator Daniel Inouye, Democrat of Hawaii, "but your constituents expect more of you. They would think it below the dignity of the office to live that way." Senator Warren Magnuson, Democrat of Washington, was quoted as saying, "When people make contributions, they aren't trying to buy anything. They are simply trying to keep in office people who think the way they do."

It was a way of life that none of them wanted interrupted. In fact, having your supporters and special interest groups subsidize you as a member of Congress–pay for your new suits, your travel to and from your district, even to help put your kids through college–was almost considered a perquisite of the job, an entitlement. Ethics never had been much of a consideration on Capitol Hill. Few refrained from participation. Perhaps it was no different than it had been decades past, but it seemed a bit sleazier during the Johnson era, perhaps because the man in the White House had, himself, become so wealthy while serving there. (With Bobby Baker, John Connally and Abe Fortas as his bagmen, Senator Lyndon Johnson went from poverty to becoming a multi-millionare.)

Arch was getting a bit tired of it all. Maybe even a bit bored. Yes, he had enjoyed serving six terms in Congress, had a great degree of success and certainly enough adventures for a lifetime. But the constant campaigning (facing re-election every two years), non-stop fund-raising, always being in the Minority, frequently away from his wife, weekly trips back and forth, being tour guide to endless entourages from back home, and all that went with service in Washington, was making the young congressman feel a little stagnated. He was ready to move on to something else, a new challenge. He decided he would give up his seat to run for some other office in 1968.

Did he ever have any regrets that he left the House seat when he did? Did he subsequently wish that he would have stayed in a relatively safe seat, continuing to build seniority?

"No. It was time. By then, I'd been an eight-year member of the Republican National Committee (taking over after Walter Hallanan died). I got to the point where I had the same frustrations personally as most West Virginians [with a poor economy]. I'd interfaced with all fifty-five counties." The economic situation in the Mountain State was not improving to any significant degree; the state needed more leadership than a congressman in one district could provide.

Chapter 8 Notes

1. - *Robert C. Byrd Child of the Appalachian Coalfields,* copyright 2005, WVU Press.

2. - When interviewed for this book in April of 2005, Mrs. Moore showed the author some handwritten note cards she'd just recently received from Barbara Bush, her favorite of all. One mentioned the partisan criticism of Mrs. Bush's son during the 2004 presidential campaign, adding, "They forget we didn't attack anyone. We were attacked [on Sept. 11, 2001]."

3. - The Court looked to what Rep. Moore had said, in an attempt to discover legislative intent, in *Foti v. Immigration and Naturalization Service,* Dec. 16, 1963.

4. - *Outstanding West Virginians,* 1969-1970, by Richard Kelly.

5. - The Moore Collection, West Virginia University Library

6. - *The New York Times,* Nov. 21, 1963.

7. - *United States Code Congressional and Administrative News,* 88th Congress–Second Session 1964.

8. - *Final Report of the Select Committee to Study Governmental Operations With Respect to Intelligence Activities of the United States Senate,* April 23, 1976.

9. - James R. Ralph, Jr., *Northern Protest: Martin Luther King, Jr., Chicago and the Civil Rights Movement,* 1993, Harvard University Press.

10. - *West Virginia Mountain Messenger,* September 1980.

11. - *Congressional Quarterly,* June 1963.

12. - *Jay Rockefeller, Old Money, New Politics,* by Richard Grimes, copyright 1984 by McClain Publishing Co.

13. - "But if you look back on his two terms as governor and then as senator," Heiskell added, "Jay ought to be embarrassed that he hasn't done more for the state. To his credit, at least he hasn't asked that anything be named after him."

14. - *Charleston Daily Mail,* June 23, 2004

15. - Arch A. Moore III, July 15, 2005.

16. - Moore, Aug. 22, 2005. Arch would have one more helicopter crash, the second one in West Virginia, a couple years later. He attributed his survival in this and two other potentially fatal incidences to Divine protection, not in an egotistical or flippant sense but, rather, with thankfulness.

17. - Actually, Moore never learned how to swim. "He sinks like a rock," laughed his son.

18. - U.S. Senator John McCain's father.

19. - Nixon saved his skin by doing something new: he went on TV to give his side of the story, telling viewers in an emotional speech that his wife Pat wore a plain cloth coat, not an expensive fur like the Truman Administration's wives, and that, no matter what, he wasn't going to give back the cocker spaniel, Checkers, which a supporter had donated to his daughters. There was a front page photo of then-Senator Nixon in Wheeling, sobbing on the shoulder of Senator William Knowland, after being assured by Eisenhower that he would not be kicked off the ticket. His candidacy had been saved by a positive response from the public to the "Checkers Speech," and by the conservative Taft wing of the GOP which liked the young Communist-hunter Nixon had become. But that Nixon had such a personal fund courtesy of private donors was never really disputed; it was commonplace for members of Congress to supplement their pay with such "donations." The practice had not begun, nor would end, in 1952. Many believed it was a not-so-subtle form of bribery.

20. - *The New York Times*, Jan. 19, 1967.

21. - Article I, Section 5 of the Constitution provides that "each House shall be the judge of the elections, returns and qualifications of its own members..."

22. - *Star*, June 12, 1966.

Chapter Nine
Victory Over a Former Governor

In 1960 and 1964, newspaper columnists and supporters had touted Arch Moore as the kind of dynamic leader West Virginians needed at their state capitol—they wanted him to run for governor. His sense of timing and political instincts told him those were not the years to take such a risk, however, and there was no use in sacrificing one's congressional seat. He didn't close the door to that interesting prospect, though. Either Cecil Underwood or his protege had been the candidate in the last three gubernatorial elections, so perhaps it was time for someone new. Cecil was telling friends he would not run again in 1968, but Arch was putting out feelers.

"We were driving from Las Vegas to Phoenix through the desert, on our way to visit the president of Fostoria Glass, when Arch asked me, 'Dave, what would you think if I'd run for governor?'" Dr. David Yoho recalled. "I told him, 'You'd be a damn fool!' But he said, 'I think I could be elected. And there are three things I want to do: improve schools, roads and the park system.'"

Arch always weighed his options right up until the last minute;[1] but, by mid-1967, the forty-four-year-old First District congressman decided he would take the plunge, jumping into the race to become his state's chief executive. Chances were nil that the Republicans would take control of the House of Representatives in the foreseeable future, which would provide his chance for a committee chairmanship, the only real power on Capitol Hill. His career could stagnate if he stayed in Congress. Plus, Arch felt he was up to the job of governor, that he had much to offer and that he could be more valuable in Charleston than in Washington. He looked around and realized he was more qualified than most who wanted the job. Plus, he'd become knowledgeable about increasingly available federal funds and knew that the Democrats in the congressional delegation and Governors Barron and Smith simply had not tapped into a fraction of those. Given a chance to lead, Moore knew that he could and would obtain millions of federal dollars into West Virginia, to help get the state on its feet.

Corruption had been rampant and widespread at the state capitol, where in the hallways state contracts were being exchanged for color television sets (which then were worth two or three months' salary) and other bribes. Flower funds were continually shaking down state and local public employees for contributions to the Democrats. The cronyism, the state's lack of progress in relation to others, the exodus of thousands of West Virginians seeking jobs, and a general crisis of spirit, instilled a cry for fresh new leadership. There was an interest in seeking a candidate outside the usual Southern West Virginia "Statehouse gang," someone with a fresh approach and new ideas. Maybe even someone who knew the ins and outs of Washington, who could bring a new perspective. Someone, in fact, like Congressman Moore.

Arch was telling audiences in Charleston and elsewhere that he thought the state had squandered money permitted by the 1948 and 1964 road bond issues. He strongly suggested that there had been something crooked, some "manipulation" of those funds by the Democrats, because there was little to show for the hundreds of millions of dollars the bonds had provided. The *Gazette's* Harry Hoffman was writing that $617 million was needed to complete the Appalachian four lane highway system, but Arch was arguing that it was cheaper to do it now on borrowed and federal matching funds, rather than wait until the state had that kind of money in the bank.

The national mood had changed considerably since 1964. Race riots were burning down sections of America's cities. There was increasing discontent with the thousands of fatalities and our lack of purpose in the Vietnam War; a decreasing number felt it was a cause worth dying for. The drug culture had swept among American youth (the first time it was so widespread in the history of Western civilization); thousands upon thousands were "dropping out" of normal American culture and society, as Harvard's drug-abusing guru Timothy Leary had urged them to do. The Supreme Court had removed prayer from American schools, a highly unpopular edict from the judicial monarchy, and one which some thought made society less settled, more violent and drug-infested. The Sixties, although perhaps the most colorful and creative decade in history, had ushered in a confusing, great cultural upheaval, the drug and sexual revolution being only part of it. The country was polarized between the Left and Right, black and white, old and young, long-haired and short, hedonist and religious, and by regions, like never before. Television's evening news was full of angry, screaming faces and cities on fire caused by rioters and looters. Marches, "sit-ins," campus office takeovers and other forms of rebellion were the norm. Popular leaders were being assassinated. It was a decade of great change and not all for the better, by any means.

Conservative Americans—labeled "The Great, Silent Majority" by presidential candidate Richard Nixon—began to question whether the Great Society was working. They didn't like what they were seeing and hearing. West Virginia, which sometimes seemed a million miles from some of the turmoil, and often blessed by being twenty years behind times, nevertheless shared in the national anguish and discontent. There was a backlash against the fruit of what were perceived as the excesses of The Great Society; it looked like '68 could be a Republican year, for a change.

Nonetheless, running for office in fifty-five counties, versus eleven, would be a whole new ball game for Congressman Moore. To make a statewide run, Arch would need someone on his staff who was politically astute and connected statewide, not just in the North. He found such an assistant in thirty-four-year-old William Loy. Bill Loy would need to leave a successful law practice (with state Sen. Bill Oates) in the old mountain town of Romney. Bill knew hundreds of people as result of his 1963-64 term as statewide president of the Jaycees. He had many friends in the GOP whom Arch needed. If former Governor Cecil Underwood, then West Virginia's "Mr. Republican," was running again as might occur (despite his denials), Arch might just have a tougher time in the primary than in the general election. Moore had never faced significant opposition in his own party.

After some arm-twisting by Moore, Loy joined his congressional staff in 1967, and uprooted his family of seven, moving them to D.C. The Army veteran would work hard, stressful, endless hours at low pay to serve Arch Moore faithfully from that date until he departed in 1973 to run for Congress.[2]

Loy, with his large facial features, dark penetrating eyes and black bushy eyebrows and wide smile, was very good for Arch. He may have been Moore's best personnel decision ever. "Bill loved politics," recalled Hoy Shingleton, Jr., who was Loy's law partner in Martinsburg after his public service, and also a long-time family friend. "He was outgoing. He was a helluva lawyer. Ethical. Didn't drink. His strength was that he could size up a person within half an hour and discover what they really wanted, versus what they said they wanted. He could talk to a janitor or a corporate president with equal ease."

Nelson Robinson, a Loy protege, agreed. "He was a good listener. Bill Loy would sit, rocking his chair and smoking that pipe. But when he responded, it was something wise, worth listening to. He was a good motivator; Bill was persuasive, he could talk people into doing things. He had you believing you could accomplish the task before you. You could fully trust him–if he told you something, you could take it to the bank."

Bill Loy was an asset to Moore for another, very important and unique reason. "Every politician needs someone off whom they can bounce ideas," observed Shingleton. "Arch Moore is no shrinking violet; he was always difficult to say 'no' to." But Loy, who quickly gained Moore's confidence because of his skills, confidentiality and ability to put working coalitions together, was one of very, very few who could talk back to Moore and get away with it. He was not a yes man. "Bill would say to Arch, 'Let's do it another way.' He told him what he needed to hear, not necessarily what he wanted to hear. He was not afraid to give [Moore] unpleasant news." Agreed Robinson, "No one ever had the relationship with Arch Moore that Bill Loy had. And Loy was as loyal as they came."

The two men probably argued a lot, Shingleton speculated, but kept their disagreements private. "Bill probably talked [Moore] out of things that were popular at the time, but which were not good for the state, or good politically." Loy quickly became Arch Moore's "right arm," a sounding board and his "no" man, running his gubernatorial campaigns in '68 and '72, and would advise him, unofficially, until his death.

Some even felt that his six years of service to Arch shortened Loy's life. "If ever there was a 'Type A personality,' Bill Loy was it," thought Robert Elkins, a Charleston attorney who knew him. "They always said that he'd 'had a nervous breakdown and was going to have another one.' But he could get things done. He'd often handle two telephone conversations at a time and never miss a beat."[3]

Audrey Toler, a secretary who came aboard the Moore team in 1968, thought Loy "was like a cyclone, a whirlwind, doing a hundred things at once." She admitted that Bill was "very difficult to work for," because he "was constantly on the phone and you couldn't talk to him, pin him down on anything; he kept everything in his head." She would stay at the office late in the evenings, just to get a few minutes for Bill's direction on matters of urgency, she said. "But he was probably the smartest political person I've known in my life," Audrey added.

Even with good people like Loy working for him, running for governor meant that Arch Moore was leaving a safe congressional seat for something far riskier. Said a March 1967 editorial in *The Republican Delta:*

> *Representative Moore would be a shoe-in to return to his present office in Washington if he were to seek it again. Even the Democratic politicians will acknowledge this privately. But there's a bigger challenge and Arch Moore's fac-*

ing up to it now. He feels very strongly that there's a need to clean up the mess in Charleston and he has his eye upon the governorship. He feels with the deepest of conviction that someone must stick his neck out to restore the good name of West Virginia. The thought of having a 100 percent honest man in the Governor's Mansion would scare the daylights out of a great many on the other side.

CECIL UNDERWOOD, also forty-four years old, was even more restless than Arch at the time. After leaving office, his close friend Senator Byrd had helped him land a well-paying position as a seven-state lobbyist for Monsanto. But the position meant that the former governor did most of his work in the nation's capital, making it difficult to see his young family in Huntington very often. He said, reflecting back, "I didn't want to be a lobbyist all my life, so I resigned. I always had an interest in state government and thought 1968 would be a good year for Republicans." So, reversing his earlier position, Underwood decided to seek his former office. For months, he had told friends like Dick Tyson of Huntington that he would not be running for governor this time. "Cecil and I had been friends for a long time and, since his family was living in Cabell County, I'd probably have committed to him, had he told me otherwise." So Tyson, and undoubtedly many others, had urged Arch Moore to get into it, pledging their support to him, instead.

Soon after he had won re-election in 1966, Congressman Moore phoned the former governor, telling Underwood, "My family and I have decided to make a run for governor. I'm going to announce it in November of 1967 and we'd like to have your support." But he wasn't going to get that support. The two spoke again by phone, advising they were running for governor and neither offered to back down; each was confident the other would lose. Actually, pitting the two against each other in a rare Republican primary race was the culmination of the feud–sometimes friendly, sometimes not—a struggle for domination, a fire that had been smoldering for years.[4]

Cecil remained well known throughout the state. Arch was not; at this point he was the maverick, an outsider, a reformer in the eyes of many. Underwood had been building a strong network of loyal supporters throughout all fifty-five counties since 1947 when he'd visited all of them as state Young Republicans president. In addition to his youthful, good looks, which were a huge asset, Underwood had a dry wit; he was an excellent, humorous after dinner speaker. He also had a smooth one-on-

one style and was charming to all who met him, especially the ladies. Although he was a skillful player of politics, rewarding his friends and punishing enemies,[5] no one had ever really questioned Cecil's integrity. He may well have been the most honest governor to have served until that point in state history, an attribute which likely caused him to lose a few elections.

But Underwood's hold on Republican voters was somewhat tenuous by now. He had lost his most recent two races, against Jennings Randolph for U.S. Senate in 1960 while still the incumbent governor, and against Hulett Smith for governor in the Goldwaterloo of 1964. His choices for governor and U.S. Senator had all failed to win or retain their offices. Moreover, Underwood had the bad luck to serve as governor during the severe recession of the late 1950s which was accelerated in West Virginia, where the coal mines were being automated and thousands of miners were fleeing to Akron and Cleveland for jobs.

He had a terrible struggle with a hostile Democratic Board of Public Works and legislature which cut him no slack and, although he ran a clean, respectable administration, he hadn't accomplish much. His had been a rather typical, average turn at the helm, so there were few nostalgic feelings about his four years in office. Moreover, Underwood had begun to remind some of another politician of the era, Harold Stassen, who kept running for president, despite loss after loss. Even loyal friends who loved him were not so sure Cecil could beat a Democratic opponent if given the nomination again.

On the other hand, Moore had just come off a 70 percent landslide in his northern district in 1966, proving yet again that he was very popular with members of the majority party; he drew cross-over voters; he was electable. His team decided that his strong point in the primary was his electability. Arch's campaign radio jingles for the primary campaign would be (in the style of JFK's 1960 TV commercials done by Frank Sinatra) a popular, upbeat tune, "Let a Winner Lead the Way!"

The *Gazette's* Harry Hoffman began to sour on Moore at this point, likely upon instructions of his publisher, Ned Chilton. Hoffman wrote that Arch had been "very edgy" since it "dawned on him" that Underwood would challenge him for the Republican nomination for governor in 1968. Hoffman quoted Moore as asking, "What's he trying to do–just prevent me from being governor?" Hoffman wrote that Arch had referred to Underwood as "cheap" and a "losing" candidate, which he found offensive.[6] If Moore actually said those things about the former governor, it may have been due to his long-time suspicion that Cecil Underwood was a front man for Senator Robert Byrd. Further, he undoubtedly felt that Cecil had his turn and now it was his. But Underwood saw the same opportunity as Moore did in 1968; he was not about to bow out. Plus, this might be a chance to put a stop to his rival Arch Moore once and for all.

Since Arch had made the mistake of disclosing to Underwood that he would be announcing his candidacy for governor in November of 1967, Underwood decided to beat him to the punch and announced his own candidacy a few weeks before the date Moore had set. He'd one-upped him, but Arch learned a lesson. Two could play the game, as Cecil would soon discover.

AT THE McCLURE Hotel in Wheeling on Nov. 11, 1967, Congressman Moore announced his intentions. He noted that many had urged him to remain in the Congress, that he should "forget ... the governorship ... because it isn't worth it–that the state is beyond the ability of any man to help, and that politics in the state of West Virginia is dirty, and that they don't want us to get involved in this type of situation." But others thought the "state needs strong leadership and that it must be provided immediately." Both groups had "revealed a low regard for their state government."

Moore particularly decried the fact that state officials had failed to avail themselves of funds made available to West Virginia by virtue of federal programs. By "reason of the lack of leadership," the state had "failed to effectively take advantage of this legislation," he accurately charged. The failure of the Democrats since 1930 to build the Mountain State's economy was evident if one "traveled outside [the state] and noted the progress, prosperity and advancement of adjoining states."

Moore's announcement was reminiscent of a forty two-year-old Senator John F. Kennedy's promise to "get the country moving again," when he announced for president eight years earlier. Arch told the news media representatives gathered in Wheeling that his decision had "not been at all difficult," when he realized that a great opportunity to get the state moving awaited a governor who was committed to create jobs for young people, improve education and overcome the lack of roads. That person "must do something to reshape the image of our state in such a way that industry would be desirous of coming in and locating within our boundaries," Moore said, in what would be common theme for him, through the 1980s.

"To simply criticize, I am fully aware, requires no special talent. If one is to criticize, then I believe it requires vision and courage to conceive new and positive and comprehensive programs to lead West Virginia forward, and to assure it and its citizens the opportunity to share in the potential that all of us know is here. This I am dedicated to do."

The 1968 campaign for governor had begun.

A group of Charleston area supporters helped him set up a headquarters on Kanawha Boulevard. "We had a group of Republicans I called 'The Boy Scouts,'" recalled Elaine Davidson of the fresh-faced, young idealistic group who wanted to elect Moore. "They included Elmer Dodson, whom we later elected mayor of Charleston; lawyers Tom Potter, Bill Mohler and Stanley Deutsch; Robert Q. Jones of Smith Barney and Johnny Thomas of Thomas Field wholesale dry goods. I was their den mother." Jones, who had been Barry Goldwater's state chairman in 1964, would serve as Moore's treasurer. Deutsch supervised the headquarters. Upon her husband's recommendation, Davidson had hired a 19-year-old secretary, Audrey Toler, whose military husband was stationed in Panama. It would possibly be her most important hire.[7]

They set out finding volunteers to do the day-to-day work required of a statewide campaign. "You almost had to teach them how to stamp an envelope," laughed Davidson, "but we gave them a lot to do." And their boss, Bill Loy, "was the best political tactician I ever knew," she added. "He knew people, he knew politics, he was a tireless worker and loyal, loyal, loyal."

It was months before Elaine ever met the candidate, however. Arch "was still in Congress and was in Washington a lot during this time," she recalled. "When he came to Charleston, he didn't know any of us who were on his campaign staff. It took him a while to realize that we were trustworthy. We had to prove ourselves, which is a good thing. We worked hard, but [Moore] is a workaholic, a perfectionist." The headquarters would perk along until after the May 1968 primary, would close during that summer and then reopen in the fall. "We tried to have lots of volunteers in there working hard any time Arch would come to visit," laughed Davidson.

A MONTH after he announced his candidacy, on December 15, 1967, the Silver Bridge next to Point Pleasant, Mason County, collapsed, dumping dozens of vehicles into the icy water below. Forty six people were killed. Congressman Moore and an assistant spent time with the survivors while trying to find out what happened. It was clear, from what he learned, that it could happen elsewhere if precautions were not taken to replace dangerous bridges around the state that had long been neglected. (As governor, Moore would obtain Appalachian Regional Commission funds to build a large, safe replacement bridge and, importantly, would start an inspection system to prevent it from happening again elsewhere.)

As Arch began getting out of his congressional district to campaign, it was not merely an opportunity to introduce himself to potential voters. It began a re-education process for himself. "The First District, from Wheeling down into Fairmont and Clarksburg, was relatively prosperous," he pointed out. "But I was greeted by some junior high school children in Preston County who were already missing teeth. I became exposed to some real poverty for the first time and was greatly troubled by what I saw. I decided, then and there, that we would offer some free dental care to those who couldn't afford it, if I was elected."[8]

As concerned as he became about the plight of the poor, Arch did not believe that the Great Society programs should simply arm special interest groups to impose their leftist agendas on communities. With the increased awareness of poverty in the region, universities in the North and elsewhere were sending their graduates into Appalachia, as do-gooders, set out to build a new and (in their view) more just society. Office of Economic Opportunity Chairman Sargent Shriver (a JFK brother-in-law, held over by President Johnson) sent an August 1, 1967, letter to Congressman Moore, assuring him, "Community Action does not mean control by poor people–and it is not designed to challenge what some people call 'the establishment.' Community Action must be broadly representative of the community and not just one isolated segment."

Arch talked increasingly about the longing of West Virginians for positive change. He told people that "the tide has run against the growth, strength and vitality of West Virginia and left it in a state of crisis. I know from my own travels throughout the state that the people yearn for a change–for a chance to be optimistic, but all they get is one uncomfortable jolt after another." He told them the state was "undergoing a crisis in confidence" and the time was ripe for "challenge and change."

He undoubtedly was referring to the recent headlines. On February 14, 1968, former Governor W.W. "Wally" Barron was indicted on federal charges of bribery and conspiracy involving state contracts. (After a fifteen-day trial in August of that year, he would be acquitted, but later convicted for bribing jurors in the earlier trial and was sent to prison. The Barron-Smith Highway commissioner, Burl Sawyers and his assistant, Vincent Johnkoski, Barron's money man Bonn Brown, and Alfred Schroath, a Clarksburg auto dealer, were indicted in the ring and convicted. Barron's Finance commissioner, Truman E. Gore, was freed on a mistrial.)

For the first time, though, there was a lot of "dirt" slung at Arch. He was accused of secretly representing a company within his district. Underwood also charged that, while Moore was "trumpeting himself to be a full-time congressman, he maintained a secret law practice and played power politics with the now-exposed Statehouse machine!" The former governor also charged that Lawyer Moore played politics with the Smith administration to get a $400,000 tax reduction for a corporate client. Then, as now, lawyers were not the most popular members of society and Underwood played that "issue" to the max.

The most enduring of those stories would be one from a few years earlier, when, as an attorney, Arch had represented an elderly recluse, W. G. Taylor, who had no wife or children. Moore had handled an awkward land sale transaction for him and the old man was so pleased that he asked him to prepare his will and become executor of his estate. "He'd been an oil and gas man, and really liked me for some reason," said Arch. "He took me on as a son." When Mr. Taylor died, Arch said he was pleasantly surprised to learn that Taylor had left in his bank lock-box a document conveying 900 shares of Standard Oil (Exxon) stock to him, with the remainder of his small estate being willed to the local Odd Fellows lodge.

When Cecil Underwood began seeking some "dirt" to use against his opponent, his investigator (whom Moore described as a South Charleston unemployed "shuffler," an Odd Fellow himself) discovered the transaction in a search of courthouse records "and ran to Cecil with it." Underwood brought the topic up in a debate, suggesting it was scandalous and, for decades thereafter, the *Gazette* would cite it as Exhibit A of their litany of complaints against Arch Moore. The paper contended that Arch took advantage of the old man. Another story the paper published revealed that, earlier in 1967, property Moore had bought from three heirs and sold to Mobay, had provided one of the three, a mentally incompetent person, with about $7000 less of the proceeds than the other two heirs, and ended up giving him a profit. Arch called the stories a political smear. "That's when my problems [with accusations of ethical lapses] began," Moore noted, ruefully. He blamed Underwood for starting it all.

In 1968, the state's capital had two strong rival, colorful, daring newspapers, unafraid to speak out, even against each other. The *Gazette* was, and is, one of the most partisan Democratic newspapers in the nation—loved by liberals, hated by conservatives.

All of the state's newspapers were not "insipid," as *Gazette* owner Ned Chilton would later complain. There were many partisan publications around the state, even Republican ones, which would present a counter view to the state's prevailing politics. *The Charleston Daily Mail,* owned by the philanthropic Clay family, was one of those. It was a gutsy, lively paper at the time, not afraid to stand up to the *Gazette*. As result, it became the favorite of Charlestonians, circulating over 50,000 copies. Pulitzer prize winning Bob Mellace was one of its colorful, hard-working editors, unafraid to do investigative work, unwilling to just run with the pack, as so many reporters lazily do. In a November 1, 1968, column, he would answer the accusation against Moore:

> *The truth of the matter is: Arch Moore never cheated any incompetent anywhere out of a dime. Arch Moore never represented the mentally incompetent person in this case. Arch Moore never told any court, anywhere, a lie about any property he was buying as the legitimate agent for the corporation that wanted the property.*
>
> *In the land transaction, it was the brother and sister of the mentally incompetent who contracted with Moore to sell their property for one price. It was the brother who came around to Moore later and said he and his sister wanted more for their two-thirds interest. At that stage, Moore and his client had a decision to make. They could sue the brother and sister for non-performance of the contract they had signed, or they could accept the new higher price and buy the property. It was the client's decision to pay the price rather than sue for non-performance.*

Mellace said he polled numerous lawyers of both parties and they were unanimous: "Moore might have made a mistake in judgment but by no stretch of the imagination did he violate any professional ethic as an attorney."

There was no indication that the State Bar had taken disciplinary action against him or even investigated the situation.

One might assume that Underwood did most of the mudslinging against Arch, since he had the most to gain. And certainly he played hardball in his quest for a third opportunity to be his party's nominee for governor. But, in a 2004 interview, he insisted that he had nothing to do with the personal attacks on Congressman Moore's character. "It was a third [Republican] candidate, Peter Beter [yes, that was his real name, a delight for adolescent boys to repeat], who slung dirt at Arch," Cecil insisted. "We had a series of debates. Beter showed up at the Channel 8 (Charleston TV station) debate with a briefcase, claiming it was full of [politically damaging] Arch Moore stuff." Beter, "who was a trial lawyer and self-financed, would always appear at functions wearing a tuxedo, claiming it showed respect for the office," Underwood chuckled.

In April, Peter Beter demanded to know whether "Archibald A. Moore" was "under criminal investigation for violations arising out of [his] misuse of office in Congress ... for financial gain," adding, "The rumors about Moore are everywhere." Beter publicized a March 25th letter which he'd sent to Moore, demanding a yes or no answer to: whether he was under investigation by the FBI, whether he was receiving additional income during his term as congressman, whether he had received money from Consolidated Coal Co., and whether he knew C. Howard Hardesty, the former tax commissioner and CEO of Consol (as if any of that proved anything).

Beter added, "Believe me, the above questions and rumors about you are everywhere. I await and all of West Virginia awaits your immediate answer." Cecil Underwood chimed in with not-so-subtle suggestions that Moore's representation of Mobay as a lawyer during his service in Congress had not been ethical.

Arch normally didn't respond to such attacks. Truth was, he had brought in considerable income as a lawyer during his congressional years. He'd worked closely with Hardesty at various points in his career but, again, there was nothing unusual or illegal about any of that. Undoubtedly, Moore had clients and fees that would not have come to him without the clout he had in Washington but, again, that was very common practice for the day among members of Congress who still considered their representation to be a part-time job, allowing for other career activities.

But because the Beter (and Underwood) ethical charges were being given prominent coverage by the *Gazette* and others, and gaining some traction, Moore issued an answer on April 25. "At no time have I ever indicated that I was not a practicing attorney." He freely acknowledged that he had been Mobay's attorney since 1954. To Underwood's accusation that he was conducting "a secret law practice," he responded, "How this could ever be accomplished and be successful under secret conditions is a mystery to me! Everything I have ever done in my law practice has been carried on in the full light of day and under the same code of ethics governing other lawyers in West Virginia. If anyone has any valid evidence of wrong-doing on [my] part in any respect, I would suggest it be presented to an appropriate prosecuting attorney." But he noted that he also had been fully devoted to his service in the Congress and had one of "the highest voting presence records of any member."

Moore said that Underwood's attack for his legal representation of Mobay "should serve notice on any industry that would desire to locate in West Virginia. That if they can be used to further the political ambitions of Cecil Underwood, they will be used, they will be abused, and their motives will be misrepresented." He pledged to continue to exert "great restraint" in refraining from "personal criticism of my opponents" throughout the campaign (and it appears he kept that promise).

The attacks on his legal work were a sign that his opponent was "getting desperate," Arch told the news media. He sent Underwood a telegram, "It won't work, Cecil."

Three days before the primary, the heat intensified enough that Arch produced records and cancelled checks at a press conference, in support of his denial of a conflict of interest between his work as a lawyer and as congressman. He presented copies of his income tax returns (although reporters complained that he didn't allow them to actually inspect them closely or make copies). He issued copies of a personal income statement which had been certified by an accounting firm for the past decade. The latter showed that his total congressional salary from 1957 through 1967, minus $169,075 in expenses, netted him $98,925. His law practice, minus expenses of $102,425, totaled $85,047, the statement indicated.[9] This statement did not jive with what his accusers had claimed, i.e., that Moore had become a millionaire while juggling a successful law practice with his government service. It was an effective campaign tool for Underwood, though, and it helped him defuse Moore's image as Mr. Clean, the outsider and reformer.

But the Congressman was a slick campaigner; he had defeated a few more Democratic nominees than Cecil had. Underwood thought Arch Moore "was difficult to debate. He'd pull a figure out of the air, and sometimes not the correct figure. And so I had a choice—do I correct him? If so, I come off looking negative and then have no time to say what I'm for." One example occurred at a Weirton High School debate, Governor Underwood recalled, in which Moore claimed he lowered the 60 percent vote required to pass a school bond, to a simple majority. "I did point out to that audience that Arch didn't do that. But most, I just let go by." About one remark at a Jackson County Lincoln Day dinner, Cecil wrote Arch a letter dated Feb. 18, 1968, scolding him for not knowing that Republicans had passed a law requiring an annual audit of the State Road Commission. "I realize you may be out of touch with events in West Virginia due to your twelve years in Congress in Washington. I think, however, you should join me in praise for the effective work of our Republican legislators, rather than try to reap some personal political benefit through the use of completely misleading statements."

Underwood also had an ongoing grudge against Moore involving the issue of campaign funds. It would be a complaint repeated by another Republican adversary in the 1980s. "When I worked in Washington [as a lobbyist] a lot of D.C. people would ask me, 'Why didn't I get a thank-you note for my contribution to your [1960 and 1964] campaigns?'" Underwood recalled. "I'd respond, 'Because I didn't get it.' They'd say, 'Well, we gave it to your Republican National Committeeman (Arch Moore).' But I hadn't seen a penny of it!" Arch had soaked it all up for his own campaigns and projects. Added Democratic politico Oce Smith, "Arch absolutely controlled the finances, period. [His team members] never knew where they were going or had gone, but knew that they had no say in them ... and that [Moore] never, but never, used his own exchequer for anything." And, "Arch treated Cecil like the hated stepchild of the GOP. There were times [when Moore was congressman] that he didn't even support Underwood."

His Washington friends continued to come out in support of Moore, as they had in the congressional races. Sen. Everett Dirksen, the highly respected orator and a father of the Civil Rights Act, wrote, "Arch Moore is a man of historic eminence. Above and beyond all these things, he is that type of individual of whom I can proudly say that it was nice to have met along life's way." The Illinois senator said that Arch had "performed with the highest degree of statesmanship, dignity and dedication," and was a "man of unique competence, integrity and courage. His utter devotion to his people has been illustrated time and time again in Congress."

House Minority Leader Gerald R. Ford endorsed his candidacy. "As a personal friend of Arch Moore for many years I was pleased to be asked to be the Honorary Chairman of the Moore for Governor Committee," Jerry Ford said. "This support for Arch Moore is a personal decision developed out of admiration for him...Arch Moore has been a most effective and constructive member of the House." Ford asked West Virginians to join in electing Moore, who was "a man of complete honesty and integrity," for whom he and colleagues had "the highest regard and esteem." He said Moore had the best chance of leading the party to victory in November. Jerry Ford's endorsement was effective. The future president was loved and respected by Republicans everywhere and had a lot of recognition, having co-hosted Sunday afternoon Capitol Hill talk shows for years.

Understandably, Underwood was furious. He fired off a "nastygram" to Ford:

> What business do you have in injecting yourself into a West Virginia Republican primary? As a member of Congress from Michigan, what do you know about West Virginia problems or who will make the best Republican candidate for governor? You are not a citizen of West Virginia. You can't vote here unless you plan to join the dead voters who have voted in the past, the kind of election corruption I am fighting to destroy. You should be concerned with electing Republicans to Congress. You should have tried to keep my opponent in Congress where he has 12 years of experience, unless you have some reason for not wanting him there. Your actions can do nothing but split the Republican party when we need unity ... Will you please advise me and the people of West Virginia how many more dollars from the Congressional campaign fund and the Republican National Committee I am going to fight in this election? I demand an immediate explanation from you for your unorthodox actions. Cecil H. Underwood, Republican candidate for governor.

NORMAN YOST was a seasoned newspaperman, in a day when newspapers were the chief source of news. Unable to afford higher education, he'd dropped out of WVU to go to work, but he did quite well in journalism. He'd been editor of several publications, a Florida paper and a couple large military magazines, including the Army-Navy Journal. In his home state, he'd edited Wheeling's *Intelligencer*, Morgantown's *Dominion News, The Moundsville Echo,* and *The Fairmont Times*; he had even done stints at the *Gazette* and *The Washington Post*.

At the *Intell*, as they called the Wheeling paper, Yost had broken the Joe McCarthy "Communists in government" story nationwide in 1950, as a stringer for the AP. Norm had been reporting in Havana when Castro marched in with his army and he barely escaped with his life. Not everyone liked Norm; he could be the stereotypical crusty newsman of the day, hammering away on a typewriter, caring less whether one liked him; and he didn't suffer fools easily. But he was good at what he did.

By 1967 Yost, too, was ready for something different in his work. A speech writer for three District of Columbia commissioners [Washington was then run by the Congress], he had applied to become press secretary for a congressman. Before the interview, he dropped in on Arch Moore, whom he knew from growing up in Moundsville. When he asked Moore to put in a good word for him, Arch replied, "Well, if you're going to work for anyone on Capitol Hill, it will be me," and hired Yost on the spot.

If Bill Loy was Arch Moore's right arm, Norm Yost became his left. A father of four, Norm would stick with Moore for a decade.[10] Norm began preparing press releases, writing at least half of Moore's speeches, and traveling with him almost constantly. He even became an "uncle" to the three Moore children, picking them up at airports and looking after them at times.[11]

Arch was already into campaign mode by the time he'd added Loy and Yost to his staff. The gubernatorial race had begun for real in late 1967. "He had a plane and we were in West Virginia three or four days a week, politicking," Yost recalled. "He seldom looked at a speech I wrote for him until he delivered it. If he didn't like it, he would just ad lib."

Yost and Moore had grown up poor, worked hard to move up the ladder, were over-achievers, had gone to the same high school, were within five years of age, and knew many of the same people. They quickly bonded and trusted each other's instincts. With Loy, a great team had been created to run a statewide campaign, maybe even a state government.

Loy and Yost would campaign for their boss by car, putting in frequent sixteen-hour days—arduous, tiring labor in those days before four lane highways. So frequent and distant were Loy's travels that the Moore staff called him "Bill the Roadmap Kid." A lot of what they did was set up an Arch Moore organization from scratch, one capable of fighting a well-financed, well-entrenched, statewide Democrat Machine. It was not an easy task to oppose a political establishment which had ruled the state almost unhindered since 1930. It was often difficult to find men and women to volunteer to help a Republican, when such effort might cost one his job or business; the Democrats played hardball. If word got around that you were helping Republicans, you could lose your job in some West Virginia towns, even a private sector job. Plus, with all the state and local county employees, the Democrats had an automatic campaign organization, all with pocketbook reasons to keep their party in full control. "When you're a party out of power, you don't have much to work with," Loy told a reporter.[12]

His staff and scores of enthusiastic volunteers gave Arch incredibly dedicated service. "But Shelley was working just as hard," Yost added. The future First Lady put herself at the disposal of the organization, making calls, stuffing envelopes, whatever needed to be done. Of course, much of the time she was accompanying her husband on the campaign trail or looking after their children's interests.

Money was tight and pay was low for Moore's campaign staff. Sometimes the Loy-Yost team would run out of gas and have no cash to refill their tank. Once, speeding through Maryland, behind schedule, they were stopped by police who were going to incarcerate them because they had no funds to pay the ticket. Someone from Moore's congressional office drove over to pay the fine and keep them out of jail. At times, the Congressman would travel with Loy and Yost, which would slow their journey. "Arch knew so many people and he'd yell, 'Stop the car!' and get out and chat with someone he spotted along the way," Yost laughed.

"Our first job was to get name identification established," Yost told *Daily Mail* reporter John Scott, noting Arch wasn't well known outside the First District. "I think we succeeded during our primary campaign. We were up at Blue Creek one day and an old gentleman came up to me and pointed at Arch and said, 'That's March Moore, isn't it?' I knew then we had our problem solved."[13]

For one campaign stop, Arch had mistakenly left the written speech Yost had prepared back in his Washington office. So when they arrived at their venue, Yost wrote it out again, from memory, in long hand and Loy would sneak it, page by page, to the podium and Arch didn't miss a beat.

Some of the forums were less debate format than simply a chance for Underwood and Moore to be given consecutive opportunities to speak to the Republican faithful. Underwood was still very much a crowd pleaser on the rubber chicken dinner circuit, having done that since the Forties. Cecil's pleasant speaking manner and sparkling smile made Congressman Moore somewhat insecure. After each "debate," Arch wanted assurance that he had performed better than his opponent, asking Yost, "How'd I do?" Norm would usually respond, "Oh, 60-40," meaning he'd bested Underwood.

"But one time at a Charleston event, Cecil just gave an outstanding speech. It was beautiful," Yost thought. "When Arch asked my opinion this time, I had to be honest with him. I said, '30-70, Cecil.' Arch got upset with that answer. Noting that both were speaking again the next day at an important event in Beckley, he demanded that I write him an extra-good speech." Yost thought that was a tall order.

"I felt confident that Underwood would give the same speech the next day because it was so well-received," he smiled slyly. "So I decided to have a little fun and give Arch a good speech at the same time. I pretty much copied Cecil's speech, word-for-word, and gave it to Moore who didn't even look at it until he got to the podium. And I made sure the Republican chairman let Arch go first."

As Moore began giving the speech, he realized what Yost had done and kept looking up, glaring at him throughout, as if to ask, "What have you done to me?" Understandably, Cecil sat with arms crossed, seething with anger.

When it was Underwood's turn, Norm was correct—that *was* to have been his Beckley speech. So the former governor walked slowly to the podium, held his temper in check for a moment, smiled, cleared his throat, and told the crowd, "Ladies and gentlemen, I had prepared some remarks for you but, due to the lateness of the hour, I won't deliver them." And as soon as the program ended, he bee-lined through the crowd toward his opponent, storming ahead with clinched fists and flushed face.

"I think he would have beat the hell out of Arch," Norm laughed, "if I hadn't intercepted him. I explained that I was responsible for the prank and got him calmed down."

Just before the Primary Election, *The New York Times* reported that West Virginians seemed poised to throw out the "ins," and that it might be a Republican year in the heavily Democratic state. The paper reported that, based on heavy TV advertising, it was assumed that Arch had "powerful corporate support," but that "in the last two days charges of tax delinquencies and questionable purchases and sales of real estate ... directed against Mr. Moore" might cause him to lose his lead over former Governor Underwood. With its 70,000 union members, the AFL-CIO was supporting union lawyer James Sprouse, "pretty much on the basis of who will be the strongest in the fall," the *Times'* Joseph Loftus wrote. He added that the FBI was investigating Mingo County, where Democrats were accused of "tombstone voting." Loftus quoted the *Daily Mail,* which had observed, "The dead vote and the absentee ballot is exploited—how else does one account for the fact that a precinct with say 200 citizens in residence regularly rolls up a vote in excess of 600?" Statewide, many Democrats were apathetic, mainly because of the Barron scandals, the paper noted.[14]

THE OUTCOME WAS uncertain until the end and many thought it could go either way. But Arch's primary victory was an impressive one. He defeated Underwood for the nomination by 106,299 to 76,659 votes. Arch took thirty-one counties to Cecil's twenty-four. Underwood did well in Cabell, Kanawha and other southern counties, but Moore blew him away in the north, especially in his First District. Arch won 94 percent of the vote in Marion County, 93 percent in Marshall, more than 92 percent in Ohio, 87 percent in Doddridge and 86 percent in Monongalia and Harrison Counties. Underwood suspected fraud by poll workers, especially in Marion County: "There were precincts in that county in which I received no votes at all, and that's hard to imagine, being a former governor." Agreed Oce Smith, of that county: "Hell, there would have been at least a couple of drunks to stumble into one of those polling places to vote the wrong way. But Cecil never contested it. At this point, I felt very sorry for Cecil Underwood."

As a footnote, Peter Beter received a grand total of 1,844 votes statewide. The tuxedo and Arch-bashing didn't work.

Arch would run with a strong ticket that included Charles H. Haden II, a former delegate, school board member and law professor from Morgantown, for attorney general, and a Kanawha County judge, Dennis Knapp, for supreme court.

Bob Mollohan sought to reclaim his former position, now that Arch was out of the way. Surprisingly, he received only 34 percent of the vote. Had there been only one Democratic opponent in the primary, instead of five, he may well have been denied a return to the First District seat. He would hold it until time to turn it over to his son, Alan.

Delegate John D. Rockefeller IV, of Kanawha County, was nominated by the Democrats for secretary of state.[15]

JIM SPROUSE, who won the Democratic primary, would prove to be a formidable candidate, for one reason, because he had never held public office and had no record to defend. A native of Williamson, Mingo County, he was very much a product of the liberal, southern end of the Democratic party. The Sprouse family had been farmers, miners and saloon keepers; his father was a carpenter, painter and wallpaper hanger, when he could find work. (As with Arch Moore's father, Sprouse's dad had periods of unemployment during the Depression. The family had to move in with relatives at a Delbarton coal camp house.) Jim had started working at age eleven, as a part-time school janitor. He had fought in the ring at an early age, too, winning the state Golden Gloves amateur lightweight boxing championship.[16] His supporters wore tiny, gold-colored boxing glove lapel pins. Like Moore, Jim Sprouse had served in the infantry, landing in France after D-Day and had been awarded a Bronze Star. After getting his law degree at Columbia University, he studied in Paris as a Fulbright

Scholar. He may have been the brightest Democratic gubernatorial nominee in a couple generations, at least. Said by a friend to have been fluent in German and French "but in a Mingo County accent," Sprouse had been a CIA agent in Austria for five years before returning to West Virginia to serve as counsel to the AFL-CIO in Charleston. He emersed himself into Democratic politics during the Barron years and became state party chairman in 1965.

Although as party chairman he was very much a Democratic Machine boss, Sprouse successfully marketed himself as an outsider, a reformer, a maverick, someone who wasn't a part of the Statehouse Gang. H. John Rogers, who served as a volunteer driver for the candidate, recalled it being a real uphill battle for the nomination at first. "He was only three percent in the polls, but he had no doubt that he could beat [Attorney General Don] Robertson. He feared Arch Moore, though."

Some thought Jim looked a little like a Kennedy, with a lock of his hair always falling on his brow. (The Kennedys were still god-like among West Virginia Democrats at the time, so Sprouse encouraged the comparison. In fact, he took some front page heat from a Fairmont newspaper for cropping the National Democratic Committeewoman out of the middle of a photo, making it appear in his campaign brochure that he had a private conference with JFK.) Some found his Mingo County accent, which he never fully shook off, to be a bit excessive; at times it sounded as if he was mumbling while his mouth was full. It was a sharp contrast to the northern accent, well-enunciated, almost-TV news anchor man speaking style of Arch Moore.

Any reasonable observer could see that West Virginia had fallen behind its neighboring states in the past two decades, not only economically, but also in education and quality of life. It wasn't simply due to the fact that the state had become a corrupt, one-party entity, although that was clearly a factor that stifled progress. It was also due to the fact that those leaders the machines produced were doing very little to recruit new and different businesses and industries to replace the older, failing ones. They were allowing the rest of the nation to pass them by. It had gone on so long that a permanent pessimism, a lack of confidence, had set in–a belief that the state was doomed to be isolated, poor, and ignorant, forever.

Moore spoke eloquently of the causes of the state's decline in a speech to a group of industrial engineers meeting at Oglebay Park. He noted that West Virginia was the only of the twelve states to have all its counties included in the Appalachian Regional Development Act, and that the study had called the Mountain State "a region apart–geographically and statistically." He blamed that sad situation on a "lack of leadership rather than lack of money."

First, West Virginia had been "outrageously discriminated against in the spending of the defense dollar," he thought. He didn't name them specifically, but likely was thinking of Randolph, Byrd, Kilgore, Neely and others who should have used their clout as had their fellow Southern Democrats in congress, to get their state a military base or two. Except for a few national guard armories, the federal government had yet to "spend one dime for military construction" in West Virginia, Congressman Moore pointed out.

Secondly, the federal government had permitted "cheap imports of foreign oil," which had unfairly competed with coal. Undoubtedly, he was thinking of LBJ's highly-organized efforts on behalf of Big Oil, which had been well-financed by donations funneled to numerous powerful members of Congress. But it wasn't just coal that suffered from unfair competition, he noted. "Cheap foreign steel competes with our made-in-the-Ohio Valley product ... Glass, textile and chemical products made with cheap foreign labor ... damage our domestic industries." The federal government urged those industries to locate in depressed areas like Appalachia, he added, but then takes away the incentive by allowing cheap foreign products to be dumped in the U.S. "West Virginia is in the midst of the most challenging and difficult period in its history," he thought.

Years before others realized it was needed, Moore was telling the audience, "The economic transition from dependence upon a few heavy industries to the wider diversification of light industry must be undertaken with dispatch and vigor. But we are not."As result of the inaction of leadership, Moore noted that there had been an out-migration of 446,700, mainly younger people, in the Fifties and another 162,000 lost to other states from 1960 to 1966. Part of that was due to a labor surplus caused by factory and coal mine modernization, mechanization, he admitted, as well as loss of market of West Virginia products.

But, pointing out that most of the markets—New York, Philadelphia, Baltimore, D.C., Chicago and Detroit—were within a 500 mile radius of the Mountain State, he thought opportunities to market the state were being missed. "We should be the most prosperous, the most industrially oriented, the wealthiest of all states in the union." Instead, he noted, Wheeling had lost Sylvania Electric, Huntington the Ashland refinery, Dunbar lost Gravely Tractor, and the flat glass plants in the Clarksburg and Charleston areas were next. Much of it was too late, he observed. "The glamor industries of electronics, of air and space, of exotic plastics that could have brought prosperity and a more abundant way of life ... bypassed us to locate in already prosperous centers of Houston, Los Angeles and elsewhere. One can only ask: where was the leadership of our state when these decisions as to plant locations were being made by government and industry? Why did West Virginia sit idly by and watch our children follow their hopes and opportunities in the leadership provided by other states?"

West Virginia could not "progress in feudal isolationism," he thought; the state would need to tear the wall down and face reality to have any future. A lack of good roads was a "contributing factor" to that isolationism, he thought. He also called for a reorganized Department of Commerce, one that would be geared to cut red tape and aggressively pursue new business and industry for the state. He wanted a federal tax incentive to make it more attractive for job providers to locate their facilities in depressed areas like West Virginia. Noting that few "successful industries are started any more in someone's garage or back yard," he explained that large amounts of capital are needed to build a new factory, requiring such incentives.

Arch concluded his speech by saying he was "impatient" to get moving on job development. He called on the engineers and similar business leaders and professionals to get involved, create think tanks, telling them that if they pooled their intelligence, experience and resources, "it might give us more answers than all the government studies have given us over the past thirty years."

With Moore's insight and accurate criticism of the Democratic Establishment's ineptitude, Sprouse would have preferred to face Underwood in the general election, for sure. Plus, he would be running against a Republican with a high degree of personal charisma and trust. "He knew that Arch Moore had built a cult of personality [in the First District]," noted Rogers. "It had an enormous effect over the years. Moore had been an ombudsman." Sprouse always thought the Democrats had wrongly "ceded the north" to Arch, Rogers recalled, and now it was going to cause them problems.

BILL LOY RECRUITED a few of the Jaycees presidents with whom he had become friends to work in the Moore campaign. He persuaded Ira "Sandy" Latimer, a geologist working in Morgantown for the West Virginia Geological Survey, to become a full-time campaign organizer, just after the GOP state convention. Sandy had met Arch at a dinner during the primary campaign, at Lakeview. He protested that he was not up to the task. "I was a complete novice when it came to politics," remembered Sandy. "But Bill said, 'It's just organizing, same as the Jaycees.' I took a leave of absence and covered the 2nd Congressional District, which was very large. I did a lot of driving on winding, mountain roads. Dick Coplin of Clarksburg handled the 3rd District and Jack Stafford of Princeton's Jaycees covered the southern counties.

"We met with the county Republican chairmen and committees and tried to get them fired up. We got the word out about the magic numbers— the quota of votes needed from each precinct. Bill Loy was good at looking, not just at the vote, but the margin needed in each county, whether we expected to win or lose it. He would pare things down and know we needed a certain amount of votes from each county, each precinct. One night, coming back in the car, he went over those numbers and it was amazing how close we came [to his projections] in the end," said Latimer.

Loy knew they would lose badly to Sprouse in the latter's southern, very heavily Democratic counties. It would have to be made up elsewhere. "Bill called the Parkersburg-Charleston-Huntington area the 'Iron Triangle,' and that's where we had to do well. Those counties, plus the 2nd District and Eastern Panhandle, [were needed] to offset the loss down south. As it turned out, that's exactly what happened. The fact that Nixon carried the 2nd District helped, too."

Their polls showed the race to be neck-and-neck, with Sprouse occasionally ahead. "We figured it would go right down to the wire," remembered Latimer.

With all those former Jaycees presidents running the show, Moore's campaign usually went pretty smoothly. But occasionally there would be a mishap, Sandy recalled with a laugh. "In Martinsburg, Loy, Arch and Shelley and I were going to a dinner at a hotel. Bill was driving and when he dropped us off, Arch said, 'Get plenty of gas!' But Loy forgot to have the tank filled. He drove up to pick us up, went ten feet, and stopped. The tank was dry. Arch had a fit over that one."

Another time, Sandy had to pick up Mrs. Moore at a GOP Women's meeting in Beckley and ran an hour late. "I drove like a madman to get there. When I arrived there were only five women left. I felt so bad. But, being the lady she is, she was very nice about it and said, 'Oh, these things happen.' She didn't get upset at all."

The hard work and long, tiring hours were paying off. The Moore team was getting good feedback everywhere they went. Sufficient funds for proper advertising started coming in. Momentum was on their side.

For the first time since Ike had departed the White House, it looked good for the national Republican ticket. There was optimism in the Arch Moore camp. This thing was do-able.

Chapter 9 Notes

1. - With widespread speculation that Arch would run for governor in 1960 and 1964 had some thinking he was crying wolf. A Wheeling businessman was heard to remark, "If Moore announces he'll run for governor, there's a 50 percent chance he will."

2. - Just as Loy had picked 1964, a disastrous year for a Republican to run for state senate, and lost, he chose 1974, the Watergate year, to make his unsuccessful bid against Congressman Harley Staggers. When he left in '73, Moore had nominated his friend to become a federal judge but, after cries of political cronyism, Loy withdrew his name.

3. - When Loy died of a stroke while jogging on a Clearwater, Florida beach on April 20, 1985, at age 52 ("He ate a lot of red meat and had a stressful life," Hoy explained), Shingleton had the unpleasant task of informing the family and Gov. Moore, whom he tracked down at the Charleston Civic Center. "There was stunned silence. [Arch] was in shock." Many observers believed that Arch Moore's public relations suffered greatly after Loy left in '73 and even more after he died.

4. - From 1956 through 2000, the names of one or both of these men would be atop every general election statewide ballot.

5. - An example of this was when a Clarksburg newspaper issued numerous articles and editorials critical of Underwood during his first term as governor. Further, they refused to print any of the Underwood Administration's press releases, some of which were important state news. Governor Underwood decided to yank all of the State's legal advertising from it and no longer put all the state's local money deposits in the Clarksburg bank partially owned by the paper's publisher, Cecil Highland. "Highland called me and asked what was wrong," Underwood remembered. "Once we re-started some of the deposits and ads, they started treating me a little better."

6. - *Gazette*, Feb. 23, 1968, referring to Oct. 1967 comments.

7. - Toler, now Audrey Pennington, would be employed by Moore until he went to prison in 1990. No one would be more loyal to him.

8. - Soon after taking office, Moore would talk to the State Health Director, Dr. N. H. Dyer about his desire to create free dental clinics for poor children. "Dr. Dyer said, 'I've been praying for this for years,'" Moore recalled. Together, they set up a few such clinics through county health departments. "These were precious children," Moore said, tenderly. When asked in the final interview for this book what his greatest disappointment was, what he'd like to have done but didn't, Moore said, without hesitating, "I wanted to establish mobile dental facilities," to travel around to low income schools, to provide free dental care. He also wanted to improve diets of school age children, "but we never did get to implement that. They were eating too much candy and junk food. I asked the Health Department to test cholesterol in West Virginia school children and the report was devastating, it was completely out of the sky. And I had hoped to do more to improve water quality." Here, Arch was not giving himself enough credit–his administration may have funded more public water systems than any in the state's history.

9. - Morgan, Ibid.

10. - He stayed with Arch for six months in 1977 after the first two terms as governor, "trying to decide where to go from here," before finishing his career in a non-writing job, with an oil and gas company.

11. - Once Shelley Moore called Norm prior to an important family trip, to ask his advice. Hairstyles for young men were very long at the time, a sore subject with parents in many households, who viewed it as rebellious, for hippies, or feminine. Arch had prohibited their son Kim (Arch III) from accompanying the family unless he got a haircut and Kim refused to have it cut short. Norm asked Mrs. Moore, "What did Arch say, exactly? He said, 'get it cut,' right? He didn't say how short." So Kim got a trim and everyone was happy.

12. - *Daily Mail,* Nov. 8, 1968.
13. - *Daily Mail,* Nov. 8, 1968.
14. - *The New York Times,* May 12, 1968.
15. - *The New York Times* later confirmed that, after Senator Robert Kennedy was assassinated in June, New York Governor Nelson Rockefeller offered the vacancy to his nephew, if he would switch back to Republican. Although Jay had this early opportunity to become a U.S. Senator, and from his home state at that, he declined his uncle's offer, opting to remain in West Virginia.
16. - Sprouse apparently kept his fighting ability into middle age. According to a witness in the room at the time, once when Spouse was on the state supreme court, he disagreed so strongly with something Justice Richard Neely said at a court meeting that he walked over and "decked him." After that incident, Neely reportedly flinched any time Justice Sprouse came near him.

Chapter Ten
The Arch March

"William Wallace Barron, a former governor of West Virginia, and five other men, three of them state officials, were charged today with conspiring to obtain bribes in return for state contracts," announced *The Washington Evening Star* in its Valentine's Day edition, 1968. Along with Barron, the Justice Department announced the indictment of Burl Sawyers, Barron's and Smith's highways commissioner; Vincent Johnkowski, their deputy highways commissioner; Truman Gore, the Finance & Administration commissioner; Bonn Brown, an Elkins attorney and Barron's money man, and Al Shroath, a Clarksburg auto dealer and Democratic operative.

Barron proclaimed his innocence, the *Star* reported: "Since 1963, my political enemies have plotted and attempted to use the IRS and other investigative bodies to discredit my administration."[1] The feds alleged that Shroath set up dummy corporations owned by the Barron gang, in Boca Raton, Florida and Tuppers Plains, Ohio, to which vendor companies were required to make payments in exchange for state contracts which were let without competitive bid.

Despite the blossoming scandal, Attorney General Don Robertson, a Barron-Smith ally, had been almost a sure bet to be the next governor. Shelley Moore thought he would be the nominee. "It had been the normal progression to move up from attorney general to governor. We were gearing up for a race against Robertson." Naturally, many of the organization Democrats, who had previously elected Barron and Smith, supported him. Before the primary, Robertson "had looked unbeatable," agreed Pete Thaw. "But Bob McDonough (who had managed JFK's campaign in West Virginia in 1960 and had served as state party chairman) came to me early on and said we have this guy Jim Sprouse who can beat Arch Moore. He was asking some of us [Democrat operatives] to work for him," remembered Thaw. "About the same time, Arch saw me on the street in Sistersville and said, 'I want to talk to you.' Had Sprouse lost, as I expected he would, I had actually planned to work for Arch in '68. [Moore] was a very, very dynamic guy.

"The Sprouse and [Robert] Kennedy campaigns were very intertwined [in the 1968 primary]," noted Thaw, who worked both, in the latter as Bobby Kennedy's West Virginia campaign manager. Kennedy had announced for president too late to get onto the West Virginia ballot, so he was looking for other means to pick up the state's delegates to the convention. "The Kennedy campaign put about $200,000 into Sprouse's campaign, thinking he would help Kennedy pick up all of our delegates, once he won the gubernatorial nomination." Senator Kennedy had visited the state on April 13, speaking to large crowds in Princeton, Logan and elsewhere along the way. It was the same enthusiastic rock star mob scene Bobby experienced in other states, with thousands crushing in, pushing, screaming, trying just to touch him, as if he was the new Messiah. "We lost four sets of [his] cuff links that day," Thaw recalled. Raamie Barker, the Young Democrat who helped coordinate the Logan visit, and slowly led him through a heavy crowd there, remembered RFK's hands shaking as he spoke. "He was afraid he would be shot." The Municipal Auditorium was filled to capacity for RFK's visit to the state capital that evening.

For the primary, Thaw had been instructed to install three hundred phones and a lot of tables for the Kennedy for President headquarters on Hale Street, "but we never made a call. It was for the illusion that we were organized." Seven pro-RFK delegates ended up winning in May; the rest went to Hubert Humphrey. Kennedy had planned to meet West Virginia delegates at the Greenbrier to woo all of them, but what happened in California ended all that. Thaw worked Bobby's funeral in Washington as a final payment of respect.

The Kennedy people in West Virginia fell back to earth following his assassination, their dreams of great things for themselves dying with the young senator. They were hopeful, with the Sprouse upset, however, that the "reform" branch of the party might actually take over the Statehouse. "We were all surprised by [Sprouse's] win," recalled Thaw. "Even Arch Moore was surprised, I think."

"The press had given Robertson the nomination," agreed Arch Moore. "He had been running for governor since the day he became attorney general." Thaw thought it was troubling to Moore that he would not have a "Statehouse opponent" like Robertson, to whom he could try to tie the Barron-Smith era scandals. But Sprouse, although proclaimed to be clean himself, was an insider in the world of Democratic politics, one who long had represented their chief ally, the unions, and who had served as state party chairman. Those he had served and represented certainly were not always "clean." Despite his protests, many viewed Sprouse as a "Machine Candidate."[2] And with no record to attack, that's how Arch would try to frame his opponent. He would try to tie him to the politics of the past, as he called it.

But, ironically, it was Moore who seemed to be allying himself with the party faction Sprouse had just defeated. Always playing the cards he was dealt, within days of his and Sprouse's primary victories, Arch immediately began wooing powerful Democrats who had supported Robertson. He needed at least thirty percent of the majority party, plus all of the Republicans, and as much financial support as possible from both, to win a statewide race. Robertson and Moore had been in law school together and remained friendly over the years. "When Arch brought Clarence Elmore [Barron's liquor commissioner and executive secretary of the statewide Young Dems] down here, I was concerned [for Sprouse's chances]," recalled Thaw. "Wherever Clarence Elmore was, there was always lots of money."

At the same time, Moore made it clear that he intended to clean up the Statehouse, a promise which he would keep. (He would end up being the governor who stopped the flower funds, once and for all.) Arch also called for reforms to prevent a repeat of the bribery that had occurred during the recent past, at all levels. In a press release, he said he would restore integrity to state government by establishing a non-political board of accounting and purchasing, a uniform accounting system for all departments to "assure honesty among both appointed and elected officials." He scoffed at the ability of the majority party to conduct its own housecleaning. When Democratic legislators also began talking about statutory reforms to counter the Barron-Smith era corruption, Moore declared, "Somehow I feel that this is like locking the stable door after the horse had been led away." He also called for all department heads to be required to file a copy of their federal income tax returns with the governor's office.

Sprouse also had his work cut out for him, even with the huge party registration advantage. He went to work trying to reunite and cement his fractured Democratic party. "Sprouse had one of the best, toughest teams ever assembled," thought Thaw. "He had Rudy DiTrapano, Jim McIntyre, Tom McHugh (all excellent Charleston lawyers) and Bob McDonough." He added, "But Moore had a great team, too, in Loy, Chuck Haden, Ron Pearson, and others. And, of course, Moore didn't really need a campaign manager; he could run his own quite well. Both sides were well funded and well run."

The Democrat nominee had his shortcuts to save time and aggravation as he campaigned. For example, according to long-time Democrat politico Jim "Tiger" Morton, when Sprouse would come into a town he would purposely return phone calls (that he didn't particularly want) during the noon hour, trusting that the individual would be out to lunch. But he'd find out that he couldn't continue to get away with these tricks. He could not be all things to all people. They say all politics is local and trying to keep all competing Democratic factions happy with him has always been difficult for nominees. Each party faction wants the patronage and power and also wants the candidate to promise to deny it to the competing faction(s).

The Abraham-(Tom) Godby faction of the Logan County Democrats had supported Robertson. After his primary victory, Sprouse asked for a meeting with them to try to get things patched up, to get them on his team, to see what they wanted in return. The faction leaders sat at the Logan Memorial Field House for three hours past the two p.m. appointment, and began to stew when Sprouse didn't arrive, late even for him. When someone tipped them off that the nominee was tied up in a secret meeting at "Red" Hager's house, the Abraham-Godby faction's rival, and was making a separate deal for future patronage jobs, Sheriff Abraham arose, growling, "By gawd, we're going for Arch Moore!"

And they did; Arch had the Abraham-Godby faction with him for the General Election.[3] Similar stories were heard around the state—the Democrats were deeply split and Moore, who had gladly worked with Democrat factions up north, was more than happy to pick up pieces, dissenters and the dissatisfied, wherever he could do so, in order to form a winning coalition. In many of these situations, one Democratic faction would have the governor's ear if Sprouse won; the county's competing faction had it if Moore was the victor.

Oce Smith remembered that his "acquaintances from down South of Route 60" previously had scoffed when he warned them to watch out for Congressman Arch Moore. "With an egotistical chuckle they'd say something like, 'Well, you folks can have him up there where he can't do much damage. But if he ever comes down here to try anything, we'll take care of him!'" Oce added, "However, not only did they not take care of him, but he soon owned them, too!"

With the backdrop of the criminal trial of former Governor Barron being conducted during the summer months of the campaign, Candidate Moore continued to make Statehouse corruption an issue. (In fact, the very word "Statehouse" was falling into disfavor—it conjured up images of flower funds and purchasers accepting bribes in the hallways.) Moore predicted that voters were going to rebel against the "excesses and abuses of state government by past administrations." The problems of the people "have been swept under the rug, and the rug bulges as each succeeding administration has tried to cover its own dirt," he charged. "But it can't. So it's time for a cleanup and a clean out."

At the state Republican convention on July 14, Moore shouted, "I serve notice on you [Democrats] here and now, that we are ready to do combat with you up and down this great state of ours." Speaking of the Barron scandals, Arch told the delegates, "We haven't been saying anything about the guys in the Statehouse but he [Sprouse] hasn't been seen for the past two and one-half months since he resigned as state party chairman." He blamed the majority party for an exodus of young people from the state during the Barron-Smith years. "It would be no help to elect an administration that would continue the programs of the past," he warned. "If West Virginians want new leadership" they would not get it from Sprouse, he predicted. Instead, "They will have to follow our cause."

In a press conference after the Charleston convention, Arch expressed his sorrow for the families of the Barron gang, who were attending their trials. He also pointed out that the national press coverage the trials were receiving was bad for the state's image. He added, "The Republican Party offers the people a choice to change that arrogance, cynicism, immorality and dishonesty in their state government which, in the absence of [adequate] state government has caused the Democrat-controlled federal government to seek and obtain indictments against the leaders of present and past Democrat state administrations."[4] Yet, Moore added that no one who was doing his or her job in state government had anything to fear from him and that "the game's over" when it came to obtaining state jobs for political favors.

When Jim Sprouse said, "I believe that the flower fund has been stopped," in the Statehouse, Moore scoffed. "I am reliably informed that there never has been a day that the flower fund hasn't been collected," he said. He ridiculed Sprouse's slogan of "Progress Not Politics." Arch declared that the former Democrat state chairman had been "born and bred at the breast of the Statehouse machine."

Lawyer H. John Rogers met Sprouse in 1966 when the latter had a farm in Beverly, near Elkins, where Rogers was clerking for federal Judge Robert Maxwell. Rogers thought Sprouse was the finest candidate to ever run for governor. "For me it was love at first sight," he wrote in *Graffiti* years later. "Sprouse was the product of a hard scrabble life, but he never forgot he was a native son of Mingo County and not Charleston's South Hills...he was the real thing... Also, along the way, Sprouse had read a few novels and some poetry. Most importantly, Spouse enjoyed talking about intellectual matters–up to a point...His wife, June, was raised on a Native American reservation out west. She was the perfect 'helpmate.'"[5]

Added Rogers, "Sprouse asked me to be his bagman [to gather cash].

I guess he perceived that I was honest and wasn't going to take my ten percent off the top. I agreed to do it, but he never followed up."

Why did/do political candidates use cash on election day, sometimes to pay for legitimate election work, sometimes to buy votes and why do local poll workers demand cash?

Rogers' opinion: "This is West Virginia. They don't *want* checks. It's going to get declared on their income ... [or perhaps] they're on disability. Some places call [cash payments for employment] 'spot wages.' Cash was not used in elections so much in the north, just mainly in the southern counties. Hancock County was the exception, which can be pretty bad for a lot of reasons, mainly because of the gambling enterprises up there. [Gamblers] like to be able to fix drunk driving tickets or keep whores out of jail." Rogers continued, "You had to use cash [on election day] in Logan County and those counties, *or you're not going to win.*"[6]

Wally Barron hated Sprouse for some reason, perhaps because the latter was trying to distance himself from the Barron-Smith era. Or perhaps the former governor thought Sprouse, as the former party chairman, was being a hypocrite. For whatever reason, Barron called a news conference and endorsed Arch Moore. "We were stunned. I couldn't believe it happened," Rudy DiTrapano (who had become state Democratic chairman in June, 1968) would later remark.[7] DiTrapano thought Barron's actions were pro-Moore, rather than anti-Sprouse. Four years later, Cecil Underwood would allege that Moore and Barron had cut some type of deal. But it may have been, plainly and simply, that Barron admired Arch; the two had worked together on several projects for the betterment of the state, including the planning of I-79. In any event, it was an endorsement Moore didn't want because he was running as the reform, clean-the-rascals-out candidate that year.

Organized labor wanted to hedge its bets on the race. Business leader Howard Corcoran brought AFL-CIO director Miles Stanley out to Moore's Maryland residence one summer evening where they chatted on the screened-in porch. Arch reminded Stanley that he once had been a union factory worker himself; had been a friend to working men and women; and that he had even voted favorably on most union legislation during the past eleven years, despite his membership in the "party of Big Business." Naturally, Stanley was not about to give Moore his organization's endorsement over someone who had been their lawyer and the nominee of the political party they then owned, lock, stock and barrel. But he let Arch know that they wouldn't be entirely upset if he prevailed, and that they hoped they could have a working relationship with him if elected. As the two guests parted, Arch said something to the effect of, "Well, just go easy on me."[8]

Arch wanted to reassure, not only unions, but also state employees, and their large extended families—a huge block of votes that could either elect or defeat him, that he was not the boogyman. He was not going to throw them all out of their jobs, as Barron had done to the Republican holdovers from the Underwood Administration in 1961. It was a new era, Moore assured them. Most state government workers in Charleston and throughout the fifty-four other counties, in Welfare, Highways, Unemployment and other offices, had received their jobs during Democratic administrations and because they were loyal Democrats themselves. But party affiliation alone would not be cause for discharge, Arch promised them. He did not want them all going out and supporting Sprouse just to save their jobs. In a speech at Newell, Rep. Moore again sought to ease their greatest fear—that he would replace them with Republicans. Then his opponents produced a tape of a speech he'd given in Parsons during the primary campaign in which Arch had said something to the contrary: "I want to clean them out from top to bottom." The Republican faithful, who wanted some of those state jobs after eight years of being out, were hoping the latter promise reflected Arch's true intentions.

Arch also began to push an optimistic, if controversial, proposal to provide pay raises for school teachers. He promised a thousand dollar raise in 1969 and another $500 in 1970, a huge increase given their current rate of pay. The controversy was in his pledge that it could be done "without raising a dime's worth of taxes." The pay raise was just part of a far-reaching, comprehensive proposal for bringing the Mountain State's educational program—public schools and colleges—up to national standards academically and financially. If the state could not get up to speed in providing an adequate education system–which meant attracting and retaining good teachers–then there was no hope of improving the economy long term, Moore believed. As it was, in the 1960s and into the 1970s, young West Virginians were scoffing at their teachers' admonition that they study hard and get a good education. They knew that, even without completing high school, they could go to the mines, to oil and gas work, power company jobs, or into construction and easily double the salary public school teachers were receiving. Not only was that attitude demeaning to the teachers, who had received four to six years of college, but the teachers also knew that such blue collar jobs were unsteady and uncertain, as the national economy was changing.

Someone yelled out in an audience, "Mr. Moore, just how do you know so much about the problems of education?" Arch thought for a moment and fired back, "Because a member of the teachers' lobby lives at my house!" It was true: Shelley Moore had taught a year in Pennsylvania in the 1950s and more recently at St. Maurice School for Teachable Retarded Children in Potomac, Maryland, part-time, until the campaign began. Similar to a quote later attributed to Hillary Clinton, Mrs. Moore told the press that she was "not standing behind [her] husband," but rather was standing beside him. "I just can't stand on the sidelines," she told a reporter. "I feel as Arch does, a love for the state. In a state which has been at, or near the bottom of the list in education, roads and agriculture, I feel every West Virginian should be concerned. That's why I'm involved so deeply." As to what she'd do if Arch was successful, Mrs. Moore said, "I would like to say I am going to relax for a while and take it easy. But I am married to Arch Moore and I know we will be just as busy as we are now."

The *Charleston Gazette* invited Moore and Sprouse to a debate, co-sponsored by WCHS in Charleston. After being burned so badly in the Republican Primary by the paper, Moore responded, "This is to advise you that I will not participate ... My feelings toward the *Charleston Gazette* have been expressed publicly previous to this time and for me to cooperate or participate with the *Gazette* or its editor in any manner would be pure hypocrisy. I regard the *Charleston Gazette* as I have said before, as biased, unfair and whose almost every day outpourings are devoted to yellow journalism of the worst type."

In what came close to being a debate, Sprouse and Moore took some verbal swings at each other in a 100-minute joint appearance before the Kanawha Valley Technical Society. Both agreed that the $350 million dollar road bond amendment and the Modern Budget Amendment should be passed. But Moore qualified that there was "some question in [his] mind" about whether the bond money would be properly spent by a Sprouse administration. During the course of the exchange, Moore was criticized for talking too long. He jabbed, "You gotta get in your licks where you can!"

He would remind Northern West Virginia audiences that it had been seventy one years since one of theirs had been elected governor, suggesting it was time for someone from that end of the state, who understood their problems and needs. With regionalism strong, it tapped into anti-Southern feelings, that any politician from Charleston southward was part of the corrupt Statehouse machine.[9] Sprouse was quietly doing the same on his end of the state, provoking regional prejudices and pride. Some Democrats were suggesting, in fact, that any officeholder from the Northern Panhandle was surely tied to organized crime.

Try as he may, Sprouse just could not shake loose the "Arch Moore Democrats" of the northern end of the state, who remained loyal to their young Republican congressman. "DiTrapano begged those Italian friends of his to support Sprouse," remembered Rogers. "But they would refuse, saying, 'Arch has always been good to us.'"

Throughout September and October, excitement was being built for Arch by his delightful, catchy campaign jingle that filled the airwaves in every town. West Virginians who had no intention of voting for the Republican candidate nevertheless found themselves smiling when they heard it, whistling or singing along. The song, commonly known as "The Arch March," was written by the talented team at the Robert Goodman Agency of Baltimore, who handled Moore's advertising. It was recognized by the national public relations community as a political advertising masterpiece. There certainly has been nothing like it in any prior or subsequent West Virginia campaign.[10] It is difficult to explain the value of the jingle now, or how it added so much sparkle to the campaign, even majesty and celebrity mystique to Candidate Moore. It made him a recognizable "product," and likely gave him thousands of votes. Sprouse had nothing like it; by comparison, his PR was very dull. There was a version of the "March" for pop music stations (in a vigorous, John Philip Sousa march style) and another (quartet style) for country stations:

Arch Moore is moving through the state of West Virginia,
Talkin' to the folks about the state of West Virginia,
How it's gonna be a better state of West Virginia;
When Arch Moore is governor, he'll move the state along!

Lift up your head and look him squarely in the eye, sir,
Deep down inside you're gonna feel a world of pride, sir,
West Virginia's brighter day is standing by your side, sir;
When Arch Moore is governor, he'll move the state along![11]

"It was really a high energy campaign, especially with that song," recalled Shelley Moore Capito, who was fourteen that year. "And the people they ran with—John Callebs, Dennis Knapp and Chuck Haden and others—were all very enthusiastic campaigners." There had been nothing so full of energy, so electric in West Virginia politics since JFK won the 1960

Democratic primary, and the radio jingle had much to do with the enthusiasm. The song became identified with Arch forever; it was almost like his "Hail to the Chief."

The Moore children—Kim was just sixteen and Lucy eleven—saw little of their parents in 1968; much of the time Mom and Dad were on the campaign trail. "Our grandparents watched us previously when they'd be gone," recalled Shelley Moore Capito, but this time period was too much to expect of the elderly Moores, so Shelley, Sr. hired a full-time sitter.

Occasionally the children would accompany Arch and Shelley to a campaign event. One such trip stuck in Capito's mind. "They took us to the WVU Homecoming parade and, afterwards, we all went to Communtzi's Restaurant to eat. Mr. Communtzi had an area chained off in the back for several of us." Her future husband, Charlie Capito, was among the group. Later, she didn't remember meeting him, but he reminded her of the event and even recalled the dress she was wearing. "I only had about two dresses back then," she laughed.

LATE INTO the campaign, Loy and Yost took a story to the *Daily Mail*, the state's largest and most influential Republican-leaning paper. It inferred that Jim Sprouse and others had bought up real estate near Seneca Rocks, which was being turned into a park, trying to make a quick and questionable profit. As it turned out, nothing criminal or even unethical was uncovered, but it was a sensational story and had an odor to it that Sprouse could have done without, especially in the wake of the Barron scandals.

To counter, the Democratic nominee called a press conference at the Charleston House to offer his financial holdings to a "bi-partisan panel," consisting of failed gubernatorial candidates Underwood and Paul Kaufman, and invited Moore to do the same. When the Congressman failed to appear for this stunt, Sprouse pointed out that Moore's "income tax records and other financial data never have been made available for public scrutiny during the entire campaign," and contended that this should be "proof conclusive as to which candidate is being honest and frank with the people of West Virginia."

Arch countered that he had already disclosed his records to an accounting firm during the primary. He said Sprouse was "seeking to beat a dead horse to divert attention" from the Pendleton County land deal.[12]

Sprouse began calling Moore, "Chicken Arch" because he would not engage in a full-fledged debate with him. Arch replied, "Chicken is better than being a dead political duck," inferring that the latter described his opponent. Moore supporters, noting the on-going Barron scandals, liked to recite: "Old Statehouse politicians never die; they just return to Charleston to testify."

Arch had his 1968 campaign speech down to a fine art by now. It was polished, smooth and easily delivered, time and again. A rally held by Republicans at the National Guard Armory in Fairmont was typical. Comedians and singers, and a color guard saluting the flag, would warm up the audience and a few quick speeches by local political leaders would fire them up a bit more. Then the arena went dark and a spotlight followed Congressman Moore to the podium, with the crowd standing, clapping, stomping and cheering, "Arch! Arch! Arch!" like he was a champion prize-fighter going into the ring. Once he began, his speech would range from quiet and calm to loud and angry; humble statements, then proud ones.

He was a masterful stump speaker in his prime; his speeches were entertaining and exciting, even if they went on a few minutes too long. He dazzled audiences with his humor, wit, sarcasm and the broad spectrum of his knowledge. He seemed to almost speak without notes. Then, after about thirty or so minutes of it, he would end the speeches quietly, and dramatically, "Ladies and gentlemen, you are looking at the next governor of West Virginia." As the crowd gave him another standing ovation, he waved and responded to their "V for victory" hand signals. Then he would wade into the crowd like a Kennedy, shaking hands, putting his arm around friends and supporters, thanking and encouraging them, remembering details about their lives and reminding them of some past shared experience. He would fix his eyes intently upon the object of his conversation, making him or her feel like the most important person in the room or arena.

"Arch Moore was only about five feet, seven inches tall," noted then-TV news anchor man Charles Ryan, who is about the same height. "But he had such a presence that he dominated the room. There was a magnetism about him. Everyone knew he was there. He was the tallest man in the room. He had tremendous energy, one of the largest personalities I've ever known."

Ryan also recalled *The Arch Moore Handshake*. "As he shook your hand, he would very subtly and gently pull you toward him." Why did he do that? "It does all sorts of things: it shows who's in control, it demonstrated his dynamic personality, and it was a friendly gesture, all rolled into one. You're pleased with it," observed Ryan.

Like most others who knew Arch, Ryan was impressed with the Congressman's amazing ability to remember names. "His memory was phenomenal." But there might be times when Moore would recognize the face but not be sure of the man or woman's name, so he had a routine to deal with that. "He'd immediately put his hand out and say, 'Moore's the name.' Well, of course they knew who he was and they'd usually they'd say theirs or give him a hint in the conversation as to who they were. That's something I learned from him [in Ryan's later public relations business]—always initiate the conversation if you don't know who someone is." (M. M. Neely had another method, Ryan added: "Neely knew names too, but if he didn't, he'd ask, 'How's that back of yours?' He knew most people had some kind of back problem, and that would get the conversation going.")

Dr. Tom McCoy, a Charleston urologist who became a self-described Arch loyalist during the campaign, had his exposure to the amazing Moore Memory. "I took him to a Kanawha Medical Society meeting at Berry Hills [Country Club] and introduced him to everyone. The next time I took him there, Arch took me around. He had some personal vignette about everyone in the room. He was telling me something about their family or college days. It was absolutely incredible!"[13]

Judge Dennis R. Knapp,[14] who was running for supreme court, accompanied Moore on his campaign stops in the last week of the campaign. In the last few days, the two Republicans shook thousands of hands and spoke in Parkersburg, St. Mary's, Jackson's Mill, and rode in WVU's Homecoming Parade, before going to Summersville. On Sunday, they went to Hamlin by chartered helicopter, planning to land on a football field for a political rally before heading back to Charleston for more campaigning.

But it didn't go as planned.

A witness in Lincoln County that day observed: "They didn't see the power lines over the field until they were almost on top of them. The pilot had flown right into a trap. He was between the goal post and the flag pole and the wires. As he backed up from the wires, the helicopter hit the flag pole and broke [the helicopter] in two."[15] The aircraft fell thirty feet, on top of a Volkswagen Beetle, which had just been exited by its owner. Another witness continued: "That crash tore everything all to pieces. The helicopter was demolished and it was a miracle anyone inside was alive. When I got to the door, Arch was slumped across the front seat, the pilot had already gotten out, but I smashed the windshield to help Mr. Moore out. That man sure has a world of stamina."

They laid him on a football bench but, within fifteen minutes, Moore insisted on arising to speak for about ten minutes so as not to disappoint the crowd of three hundred (reminiscent to history buffs of the incident in which Teddy Roosevelt gave a political speech after being shot in the chest). "I had to show them I was all right," he later explained to reporters. "When a candidate sees a crowd, he can't just lie there," he joked.

"Ladies and gentlemen," Arch began, shaken, but still with his sense of humor intact, "I'd like to turn around but the seat of my pants is out." (Relieved laughter.) "However, I can't tell you how happy I am to stand in front of you today." He defended the pilot's error, told the crowd he wanted to assure them that they were all right, and then added, "Now I have to go to the hospital for a physical examination."

Moore and Knapp were taken by ambulance to Charleston General. Moore was met there by his old friend, Dr. Carl Roncaglione, the orthopedic surgeon.[16] He recalled, "Arch's injuries were severe enough that I hospitalized him. He had some broken ribs, severe contusions to his right leg and a ruptured muscle in his left leg." Knapp's injuries were worse; he had two fractured vertebrae, a broken collarbone and injuries to his ankles. The pilot needed no treatment.

Charles Ryan remembered that Moore "played it to the hilt" when they brought him back from Hamlin. "He was prepared for the cameras, as they brought him into the hospital. He looked shaken, but firmly in control."

"They brought me to the Charleston hospital by ambulance so there was time for the news media to gather," recalled Arch. "When I arrived, we had a little, impromptu press conference. I think it was Bob Mellace who asked, 'Congressman, what impact will this have on your campaign?' I replied that I wasn't sure how badly I was hurt, but that I hoped it didn't indicate that there would be incompacities." Then he added, "I'm not sure how it will go on Tuesday but we're confident. The Lord voted for me today and I hope West Virginians will follow His advice."

Moore laughed, "I was told that, when he read that quote, Ned Chilton threw the paper into the air and shouted, 'Only one guy could come within an inch of losing his life and make a political statement out of it!'"

Daughter Shelley Moore Capito remembered when her mother got the phone call. "You instantly knew by the tone of her voice that something was wrong.

"The TV clips had him on the stretcher giving the 'V' for victory sign, but when he got home, he let his guard down—he could barely breathe, he was in so much pain from the fractured ribs."

Jim Sprouse knew instinctively that all this last-minute publicity for

Arch could hurt the Democrats' chances. "Sprouse told me that when he heard the news of Moore's crash on the radio, he was driving fast on a windy, mountainous road with hairpin turns, rushing to get to the next campaign stop," recalled Ryan. "Sprouse said that his first inclination was to veer off the road, over the mountain, so he could get some of the sympathy vote, too."

The next day, reporters gathered into the room, around Moore's hospital bed. He told them, "When we got out of that helicopter I had a sneaking suspicion there would be no more campaigning." He smiled, "I wanted to get out this morning and shake some hands at a plant entrance but the nurses wouldn't let me." He assured them that he felt great despite being "awful sore."

But when Nixon's running mate, Maryland Governor Spiro Agnew, made a campaign stop in Charleston on that afternoon, Moore could tolerate bed rest no longer. He surprised a partisan crowd at the Civic Center by appearing in a wheelchair to introduce the future vice president. Former Governor Underwood, now supporting Moore and the GOP ticket, also appeared at the rally.[17] Joe Loftus of *The New York Times* reported that West Virginia Democrats were despondent about their chances of carrying the state for Humphrey, because they feared that inroads made by Alabama Governor George Wallace were going to deliver the state to Nixon. "In the race for governor, the professionals on both sides admit they don't have a precinct to spare," he wrote. "Some competent observers [Loftus was referring to the *Gazette's* Harry Hoffman] who prefer ... James M. Sprouse ... have a hunch he will come in a close second." Loftus continued, "The Democratic fabric is straining against a Republican with a spectacular record for raiding his opponents' natural habitats." He mentioned that the Barron scandal had hurt the Democrats, but, "As a partial offset [they] have questioned Mr. Moore's unusual delay, as counsel for an estate, in transferring funds to a fraternal organization. The money was transferred last week." The article continued, "A valuable ally of Mr. Sprouse is the West Virginia [AFL-CIO], headed by Miles Stanley, whose organizational knowledge and facilities are credited with pulling Mr. Sprouse through a tough three-way primary race last spring. The United Mine Workers, at the national level, has endorsed Mr. Humphrey, but the union has avoided endorsements for governor."[18]

Many Democrats would always contend that it was the helicopter crash that made Moore the victor over Sprouse in that election. But that was not necessarily correct. According to tracking polls, Sprouse had held a lead over Arch until about ten days before the election, when the race tightened. "Sprouse just peaked too soon," campaign manager Bill Loy would later explain.[19] The more the voters saw and heard of both candidates, the more they preferred Moore. He would be able to overcome even the mighty public state employees' organization and its flower funds.

After the Agnew rally, the Moore family flew home to Glen Dale, and awaited the returns. Surprisingly, the voter turnout was under the 75 percent of 1964 which, with the unbalanced registration, meant that more Democrats stayed at home. (The $350 million road bond amendment and the Modern Budget Amendment passed overwhelmingly.)

Normally, the Moore family gathered in his office in Moundsville but this year, because of Arch's painful injuries, the tradition was interrupted—they stayed at their Glen Dale residence. "He couldn't get up and down those stairs" in the office building, daughter Shelley Moore Capito explained. "He sat with his legal pads and pencils, calculating as the phone calls came in from Loy and others back in Charleston. It was a party atmosphere in the house. But it was nip and tuck, we couldn't tell who was going to win." Recalled her mother, "We had at least two hundred people in and out during the evening. Most of them stayed with us until victory seemed assured. Most were friends we've seen down through the years."

Finally, late into the night, with most of the returns coming in from around the sprawling state, it was apparent Moore had won, in the closest gubernatorial election since 1916. A grateful Moore told Herb Little of the Associated Press, "My family and I shall in every way possible do our best to construct a new West Virginia."

THE OFFICIAL VOTE had Arch with 50.8 percent of the vote, Sprouse with 49.2-percent, a mere 12,785 votes separating victor from vanquished. Sprouse carried most of the southern, solid-Democratic counties as expected, but not by margins as large as he had needed. Throughout the evening, as early returns came in, it looked like a big Sprouse win. But then the northern vote began to be reported. As expected, Arch got a big boost from the eleven counties of his congressional district, with more than 37,000 votes to spare. In Ohio County, it was almost two-to-one. Arch also carried fourteen of the twenty counties of the 2nd Congressional District. Despite the closeness of the race, it was quite an accomplishment, given that there were 639,064 registered Democrats to 345,932 Republicans in West Virginia that year. Hubert Humphrey had won 49.6 percent of the vote, to Nixon's 40.77-percent and Wallace's 9.63 percent, so there were no presidential coattails for a Republican candidate to grab that year, as had been the case in 1956 with Eisenhower at the head of the ticket.[20] And the majority party's nominee had run an energetic, nearly flawless, campaign.

The Moore family had stayed up until six that Wednesday morning. Said Mrs. Moore, "We then retired for about three hours of sleep. Then Arch and I were up again to meet the press at about 9:30 a.m."

Soon thereafter, "children from the nearby grade school came to our front yard and sang 'God Bless America,'" Shelley Moore Capito recalled. The Governor-elect told people that this unexpected expression of congratulations and support—the realization that it was for these young ones that he would be building a better future—made him more fully appreciate his new responsibilities. The impact of what had happened sunk in. As in the battle in Germany, there were people depending on him.

About her husband's condition, following the helicopter crash, Shelley told a reporter, "Arch is feeling 100 percent better, inwardly and outwardly than he was yesterday morning." His soreness was resolving, she said. "The first thing we want to do now is get some rest. There's quite a bit to do in wrapping up a congressional office." She added, "I have the utmost faith in my husband's ability as a leader and feel that if he is given the opportunity, he definitely has the ability and courage to guide West Virginia to brighter days."[21]

The battle had been bitter and the Democrats were not gracious in defeat, even though they had won every congressional and state race except for governor.[22] Unable to accept that his candidate had actually lost, Democratic Chairman DiTrapano growled that "something was rotten" about the First District's vote. Sprouse began a recount effort in those northern counties, where Arch had done so well, refusing to concede the election. When that recount effort began adding votes to Moore's column, however, he quickly backed off and admitted defeat. (It might have been interesting, even surprising, to see how many votes would have been added to Moore's column by an honest statewide recount.)

Sprouse would not give up his $5 million libel action against *The Charleston Daily Mail,* its political editor Bob Mellace and Arch Moore, though, announcing to reporters on Nov. 7 that he would pursue that law suit. Mellace had noted in a Nov. 1 column that Republican candidates for governor had been sued for libel in the past three general elections. Usually the suits were dropped, however. But Sprouse said he was doing it for his children. The courts were controlled mainly by Democrats, so it was a good gamble.

The Clay family, the generous philanthropists who then owned the *Daily Mail,* retained the Jackson Kelly law firm and fought back. Their attorneys got the first suit thrown out by Judge Frank Taylor. DiTrapano stepped in as Sprouse's new attorney (when his first was killed in a duck hunting accident), getting the Supreme Court to reinstate the suit, even though a landmark U.S. Supreme Court case, *New York Times vs. Sullivan,* had made it virtually impossible for a public figure to successfully sue a publication for libel. This time, DiTrapano wisely initiated the suit in Fayette, instead of Kanawha County, where there were more Democratic judges and jurors and Sprouse had a better chance.

The suit alleged that the Pulitzer Prize-winning Mellace had knowingly published false stories which had been fed to him by Loy and Yost. In the weeks leading up to the election, the political writer had given it to the Democrats with both barrels. He claimed, in a Nov. 4 column, that a member of the purchasing division of the Department of Finance and Administration (F&A, as it was called) had set up a motel room in which state vendors were shaken down for political contributions to Sprouse, an allegation that never appears to have been rebutted. *The Daily Mail,* on the Friday before the election, published questions posed by Moore's campaign chairman, Wade Ballard. Why didn't Sprouse "disclose income from his Pendleton County land deal?" Ballard asked. He also questioned whether Sprouse had received non-taxable income, a 1964 Chevy, and a trip around the world from the Statehouse "flower fund." He also asserted that Sprouse was part owner of a company that sold gravel and stone to the State while he was Democratic chairman. Ballard said his questions were in response to "one of the most vile, unethical and unfair personal smears ever perpetuated upon a public official (Arch Moore)" in the state's history. He added, "This smear campaign has been planned and executed by the *Charleston Gazette,* which is well known for its yellow journalism and by Rudolph DiTrapano, chief spokesman and hatchet-man for the statehouse machine."

The basis for Sprouse's suit, however, revolved around the Pendleton County land transaction story. The stories had implied that he had used insider information acquired through his chairmanship of the Democratic Party to make money on land near Seneca Rocks when the federal government planned to establish it as a national park, raising land values. He asserted that inflammatory *Daily Mail* headlines ("Dummy Firm Seen Proving Corruption," "Seneca Rocks Tourist Project Property Enriching Candidate Sprouse," "Moore Asks Federal Probe Into Sprouse's Pendleton Land Grab," and "Where Governor Candidate 'Cleans Up'") libeled him and that it lost him the election.

In the trial in Fayette County, Mellace conceded that nothing Sprouse had done was of a criminal nature and that much was public knowledge regarding the land deals around Seneca Rocks. The jury found for Sprouse and awarded him $250,000 plus $500,000 in punitive damages.[22]

The Clay family appealed to the supreme court, which was dominated by Democrats. When it issued its order on Feb. 4, 1975,[23] the court (in a decision written by Judge Neely) strained and struggled to uphold the verdict, trying to contrast theirs with the *New York Times* decision, although it did throw out the punitive damages.

Sprouse would later win a seat on the state supreme court, resigned in 1976 to make another failed attempt to become governor, and was then appointed federal appeals judge by Pres. Jimmy Carter, both positions with strong backing of the state's labor unions.[24]

POST-ELECTION WOULD be as busy as ever; there was precious little time for rest and relaxation for the Moore team.

On November 20, 1968, came horrifying news from the First District. Consolidation Coal Co. No. 9 Mine near Farmington, West Virginia had exploded, killing seventy-eight coal miners. Many of them were young men, with wives and children. It was yet another in a long history of mine explosions over the decades; the worst had been in another Marion County town, Monongah, earlier in the century. The company had to seal the No. 9 mine to stop the fire, after they realized there was no hope of rescuing any additional miners. The Governor-elect and Norm Yost made several trips to the area for fact-finding and to comfort the families. Moore, still on the mend from the chopper crash, arrived in the coal mining town, in his wheelchair, like Franklin Roosevelt. The miners' families gathered around him in appreciation and affection, as he offered teary, heart-felt condolences. The disaster would be a catalyst for health and safety reforms for the miners in the short term and for years to come.

On December 18, the Governor-elect spoke to the state legislature for the first time in a brief address, reminding them that he too was "a creature of the legislative process," and that he was eager to work with them to handle the "tremendous challenge" ahead. Noting that a columnist had written that his narrow margin of victory in the election had not given him a "clear mandate," he assured the lawmakers that he did "not accept this interpretation." Noting that the voters had, by passage of the road bond amendment, "chosen to give [his] administration the largest single sum of money for road construction in the history of the state," he announced his intention to provide "rapid and visible progress" in new highway construction in the next few years.

"Neither political party...has all the answers," he said, adding, "Credit does not matter–it is the solutions that count." He made them a promise he would keep. "These years will be constructive years. These years will be exciting years. With your help, these will be good years for all West Virginians. I ask for your help and support."[24]

That month, Moore also spent a couple of days with twenty-five potential department heads at a Terra Alta resort, Alpine Lake. Most were men and women he had known from WVU days—fraternity brothers, also a few who had helped in the campaign. It had the feeling of a retreat or summer camp and, of course, the glow of the recent victory was still bright; there was a lot of excitement about the future. Moore wanted the group to get to know each other. "I told them it was a get-together of individuals for whom I had respect and friendship, from WVU and congressional days," he said. But it had a more significant purpose than mere socializing.

Arch went around the room, making suggestions as to which department he wanted each to head, so they could give it some thought in the coming weeks. The choices shocked some, like Brooke County lawyer Edwin Flowers, who was told he'd be the likely pick to head the Welfare Department ("I knew almost nothing about welfare," he confessed). "It is going to take someone who's willing to bore in," Arch told Flowers, and he thought Ed was up to the task. "Arch also gave his philosophy of state government," Sandy Latimer recalled. "As usual, he was full of enthusiasm about what he wanted the new administration to accomplish."

The capitol press, excluded from the confab, had a great time predicting who would staff the Moore Administration but "they missed every one of them," Arch recalled, with pleasure. "When we met up there on the mountain, Bill Loy was about to lose his mind" trying to find out who Moore had chosen, "but I didn't share it with anybody." Nine of the individuals he chose were fraternity brothers (Betas), Moore noted.

Arch was building a unified, strong, loyal team for the challenge that lay ahead.

Chapter 10 Notes

1. - Barron never explained who those enemies were. Actually, he had been a fairly popular governor and ruled his party without much opposition. He brought his 1960 primary opponent, Hullett Smith, into his cabinet. "Tiger" Morton, who knew Barron, said he was one who used people up and then conveniently forgot them when they were no longer useful to him, however. "Barron would later pretend that he didn't even recognize men who had worked very hard for his election," Morton recalled. They would come to his office and he'd ask, "What's the name?"

2. - Thaw invited the press to observe when he threw Alex Dandy, a former Barron operative, out of the Sprouse headquarters in Charleston. "[Dandy] was a nefarious person, really bad," he

frowned, "and Curt Trent the same."

3. - Source: Raamie Barker, 2003. Arch would get 6,754 votes in Logan County, nearly half, in a county more than five-to-one Democrat.

4. - *Bluefield Daily Telegram,* July 15, 1968.

5. - *Graffiti,* article by H. John Rogers.

6. - Rogers, June 29, 2005.

7. - *Point Pleasant Register,* Oct. 27, 1988.

8. - Moore, June 7, 2005.

9. - Not another governor from the northern end of the state would be elected after Moore until Joe Manchin of Marion County was elected in 2004. Rockefeller, Caperton and Wise were from Charleston and Underwood had moved to Huntington.

10. - Recalled writer Alexa Smith, "Our high school [near Cumberland, Maryland] even used it for marching band season, it was so great."

11. - Copyright 1968, by The Robert Goodman Agency.

12. - John G. Morgan, *West Virginia Governors,* Copyright 1980, Charleston Newspapers.

13. - Dr. McCoy, as president of the West Virginia State Medical Association, went to Governor Moore after the latter had taken office, to discuss the state's inability to retain young doctors. "We found a correlation to them staying in an area where they'd done their internship and residency." So Moore devised a plan wherein the State would reimburse hospitals for part of their overhead for sponsoring interns and residents, in areas where physicians were needed. The plan worked to help resolve the crisis, noted McCoy. "But what I was really impressed by, was Arch's grasp of the whole subject matter. When I went into his office, I found he knew more about the topic than I did, and had already begun working on a solution." McCoy, Aug. 11, 2005.

14. - Knapp would be defeated in 1968 by Democrat Fred Caplan, but in December 1970, upon Moore's recommendation, he was appointed by President Nixon to the federal bench in the Southern District, where he eventually served as chief judge.

15. - *Charleston Daily Mail,* Nov. 4, 1968.

16. - The physician's wife had been Mrs. Moore's sorority sister at WVU and the Moores had been in their wedding. They were overnight guests at the Moore home in Glen Dale and he was a frequent golfing partner of Moore's at Berry Hills and the Greenbrier.

17. - Despite his late support of Arch, Cecil would essentially be persona non grata during Moore's three terms, with virtually no clout; too much ugliness had occurred in the primary election for there to ever be full reconciliation. Arch resented Underwood attacking his character—a first in all his campaigns.

18. - *The New York Times,* p. 82, October 20, 1968.

19. - *Daily Mail,* Nov. 1968.

20. - 1969 *West Virginia Blue Book.*

21. - *Daily Mail,* Nov. 7, 1968.

22. - Vice Pres. Hubert Humphrey captured West Virginia's seven electoral votes, by 374,091 to Nixon's 307,555 and Gov. George Wallace's 72,560 votes. Nationally, Nixon's huge lead had dwindled, particularly with the inevitable "October surprise," when Humphrey pledged to get out of Vietnam, and the Republican won by a "squeaker," not much bigger than JFK's 1960 victory over him.

22. - "[It is] still the largest libel award favoring a public figure, not an elected one," DiTrapano told an interviewer in 1988. "We proved that the Republican campaign committee flew *Daily Mail* people to Randolph County in a private plane and later took the prepared story and released it statewide on a date that Sprouse could not respond to the charges." *Point Pleasant Register* Oct. 27, 1988.

23. - By then, Sprouse was on that court, but recused himself, as did Moore's protege, Judge Haden.

24. - Charles Haden, a Republican who would serve on the state supreme court with Sprouse, thought the latter had a "fine judicial mind." Moore and Sprouse became friendly enough that, in 1977, they briefly considered going into the practice of law together. "I told him he could handle the [Democratic] side and I could handle the other," Arch recalled. In his third term, Governor Moore even appointed Tracy Sprouse Ferguson, Jim's daughter, and a Republican (!) to the Workers'

Compensation Appeal Board.

24. - *Eight Years, Official Statements & Papers, The Honorable Arch A. Moore, Jr.,* Carl M. Frasure and Leonard Davis, West Virginia University, editors.

Chapter Eleven
1969

Nineteen Sixty-nine provided an appropriate conclusion, a crescendo to what had been an extraordinary, even revolutionary and often violent, bloody decade.

On January 20, 1969, the nation would inaugurate its thirty-seventh president, Richard M. Nixon, who promised to "bring us together." (He succeeded instead to polarize the country as much as did his predecessor. Like LBJ, he brought a lot of people together—*who hated him.*)

That year, the violent, radical Left would still dominate headlines: the "Chicago Seven" trial was held and twenty-one members of the Black Panthers were indicted for murdering a policeman. Eras ended: Dwight D. Eisenhower and Ho Chi Mihn died and, after a "reign" that had extended since World War II, Charles DeGaulle resigned as the leader of France.

In August, Neil Armstrong's would become the first human foot on the moon, fulfilling President Kennedy's earlier pledge of landing a man there before the end of the decade. Just days before the moon landing, his brother, Sen. Edward Kennedy, would destroy his status as heir-apparent to the presidency by abandoning one of his late brother Robert's young campaign workers, Mary Jo Kopechne, to drown in his Oldsmobile which he had driven off a bridge into waters near Chappaquiddick, Massachusetts. (Teddy and his entourage waited until the next day to even report the situation to police, but he would receive a mere two-month suspended sentence for his crime.)

The "Stonewall Riots" in New York City marked the beginning of the gay rights movement. The first Internet (ARPA) went on-line. The PBS children's show, *Sesame Street*, debuted. A Vietnamese village called Mylai became the center of world furor as hundreds of civilians were massacred by American soldiers there, strengthening the argument of the many protestors who wanted the U.S. to exit that war. It would be the Beatles' last year as a group. And one and a half million young people gathered at a farm near Woodstock, New York, for "three days of peace and music" (and lots of marijuana-smoking) in August, receiving for their eighteen dollar ticket performances by Jimi Hendrix, Joan Baez, the Grateful Dead and other great acts of that decade.

And West Virginia had a new governor. The state was about to enter one of its most dynamic, contentious, progressive and interesting periods of history.

As was traditional, Arch Moore's inauguration as the twenty-eighth governor was held on the steps of the capitol on Monday, January 13. On his walk to the inaugural stand, he was stopped by an individual from a lower station of life, asking him for advice and help. Most politicians would have allowed their security people to brush the poorly-dressed man away. But that was not Moore's way. He stopped and gently, patiently talked to him until the individual was satisfied, as if he had nothing more important to do or anyone more important with whom to talk. It was classic Arch Moore.

The oath was administered by the venerable Supreme Court Judge Frank Haymond, who called the Governor-elect "one of my law school boys." A helicopter hovered near the capitol dome for some reason, understandably worrying Moore, who remembered what happened two months earlier. In fact, Arch was still taking pills to ease the pain left by that November 3rd crash. The pills left his mouth dry but, as he reached for a glass of water to begin his speech, he found it frozen solid (the temperature was thirty degrees or lower).

The 45-year-old newly-sworn Governor Arch Moore began his inaugural address with familiar themes, by promising West Virginians good government, calling for integrity and honesty, and promising "the energetic leadership that West Virginia needs." He promised development of technical schools, observing that West Virginia could no longer be "tied to a one-or-two industry economy." Noting that West Virginians had "overwhelmingly indicated their willingness to pay" for good roads by passing the road bond amendment, Moore pledged to the crowd of five thousand, "We shall immediately set about providing the highest, most efficient and most honest use of those funds for the implementation of a massive road building program." Mental health reform, long neglected, "urgently demands our interest and attention," he warned.

He decried the adverse national publicity West Virginia had been receiving: "Too frequently we make headlines in a negative way," the new Governor told the crowd, calling it an irony that a state "abundantly endowed with natural wealth and individual talent should be cast in the role of a poor relative" among neighboring, richer states. Change for the better was entirely possible, he assured his listeners. The state could catch up to its neighbors, he insisted, noting that all that was "lacking is aggressive leadership and a spirit of progress."

He denounced the helpless, negative attitude of so many West Virginians. Too many in the state "have the erroneous assumption that the great influences in their lives are beyond their control," he thought. But the new administration would move the state and "its people from the doldrums of dead center into the mainstream of progress," he promised. He predicted that the term would be "constructive years" and told them that he had "gathered good people and the best minds" to work in his administration. Appalachia would no longer be West Virginia's symbol, he pledged. Instead, all Americans would soon realize that "good things are happening in West Virginia." Arch received applause when he said, "West Virginians deserve honorable government and I will demand it."

He asked for the Almighty's blessing upon his new administration. "With God's guidance, I shall lead; With God's help, we shall have a new beginning; With God's will, we shall succeed."

The speech had been classic Arch Moore: forceful, optimistic, forward-looking. "He was a commanding speaker,"thought Fred Donohoe, who would end up being his state police guard and never was bored in hearing hundreds of the Governor's speeches over the years. "He had a wonderful command of the English language. He could speak to a crowd in a language they understood. I loved to listen to him and never got tired of hearing him speak." (Others would always accuse Arch of being all flash and little substance, however, something akin to the Wizard of Oz. H. John Rogers, from the left, a reluctant admirer of Moore's ["He was the only Republican I ever voted for"], made an observation heard by many who heard the Governor's speeches. "Arch Moore had a lot of charisma. I'd listen to his speeches and be thinking, this is the most brilliant person I've ever heard. But then I'd walk away and ask myself, 'What did he say?'")

Howitzers from the 201st artillery of the West Virginia National Guard fired a 19-gun salute to the 28th governor. The first unit of the two-hour inaugural parade, the 110-member WVU Marching Band, stopped before the review stand on Kanawha Boulevard to play "The Arch March," much to the Moores' and the crowd's delight.

Following the inaugural festivities, the young Moore family settled into the Mansion next to the Capitol and tried to lead a semblance of a normal family life along with public duties. Arch took to his new role with the greatest enthusiasm. "There wasn't a day when I was governor that I wouldn't leave the residence with all the vigor in the world," he'd later note.

He and his staff then began setting up and decorating his new office (from which Gov. Smith had removed nearly all furnishings). The governor's office is located at the front, western corner of Cass Gilbert's architectural masterpiece, a beautiful capitol building constructed during the depths of the Great Depression.

Just a floor below the state senate, the suite of offices reserved for the state's chief executive is somewhat oddly shaped—a long, rather narrow corridor of offices—and is small, considering the power that generates from it and that departments which answer to him have entire buildings to themselves.

A large reception room greets guests. (One of Moore's trademarks, incidentally, was that he always staffed the outer public room with exceptionally attractive, gracious receptionists. At least a few of the several who worked there during his twelve years were ex-airline stewardesses, as they called them those days, and even a couple of former Miss West Virginias. The presence of these ladies "helped make visitors, who were mainly male—particularly male legislators—preoccupied and off guard," noted Kevin Sikora, who would serve in Arch's last term of office. "A few of them were Playboy material." Some powerful men have "trophy wives," but Arch had "trophy receptionists.")

THE TRANSITION TEAM had included Loy, Yost, Stafford, Latimer, Elaine Davidson and a few others. Naturally, Loy was chief of staff and for six years would essentially serve as Moore's "assistant governor" throughout his five years in the governor's office. Yost was the administrative assistant, primarily handling public relations and the news media, but also had a few departments answering to him. Latimer became "special assistant" and Davidson the Governor's executive secretary.

As soon as the election was over "we realized we had to go up to the capitol and do something," Latimer realized. "We knew there would be a lot of correspondence to get out right away, but we had no idea how much it would be." They were greeted by an incredible eight thousand pieces of mail in the first week, some of which were congratulatory, but most of which were from job seekers. His reputation for prompt response at stake, "Arch was very concerned. He wanted each one answered quickly." Each member of the staff took briefcases full of the letters home with them, dictating responses.

"It just overwhelmed me that so many people expected jobs," recalled Latimer. "Every Republican in the state thought he should get a state job, it seemed. The Republican chairmen quickly became upset that Democrats were still in state jobs in the counties. We had to meet with them and explain that you don't fire people just to be firing them. We were able, with those meetings, to settle the troops down until we could get things squared away."

Oce Smith told the story from his perspective. Many Republican and

Democratic supporters had been invited to Moore's inauguration, he remembered, and "they were so very proud of those invitations. But they didn't seem to realize that about 25,000 others received invitations just like them. Consequently, when these old line, stalwart followers of the Grand Old Party couldn't even get a call or letter into the chief executive, they were stunned." Smith remembered that many of them then came to the Civil Service Commission and the Workers' Compensation Appeal Board looking for jobs, and "one man [wanted] to sell a load of advertising novelties to the state and one old fellow wanted to put aluminum awnings on all the state buildings." One Republican wanted to be appointed assistant to the House doorkeeper. When Oce explained to him that the Democrats who still controlled the House and Senate, not Arch, made that one, he exclaimed, "[Expletive], what was the use to have won the [expletive] election? I can't even get back the three hundred dollars it cost me to go to the inauguration ... and I had to stand a half mile back in the crowd!"

"Arch Moore had become too popular. Everybody felt they knew him so well, so personally, that all they had to do was pick up Ma Bell and get just about anything for which they asked. There was no way, though, that he could have taken care of all these constituents, even if he had so desired." But Moore's GOP supporters "stuck with him because he was all they had," noted Smith. "And second, he always knew them, called them by name, and sent them Christmas cards."

To try to manage state government and respond to these thousands of increasingly disgruntled favor-seekers, the small staff Arch brought with him began working from seven a.m. until ten p.m., six days a week. Almost all of Moore's people were green horns, trying to find their way around and trying to manage a bureaucracy that was almost entirely Democratic leftovers from the Barron-Smith era, some of whom were quite hostile and resistant to this new Republican who'd moved in. "I was the only guy in the group who had ever worked for state government," remembered Latimer, "so I was able to help with organizational matters quite a bit."

Eventually, after they got settled in, "we had a system of charting mail," recalled Moore. "[My secretaries] had to track a request when it came in. There were nine desks just outside my office, in that hallway, each handling a set of state agencies. I'd stop at one of those desks from time to time and say, 'Let me look at your mail sheet. You've had this letter for two weeks. What's the difficulty?' They'd give me an answer. They knew there was a time when I'd ask for it." He tried to keep them on their toes in answering constituent inquiries, just as he had done as a congressman.

He would also put in a toll-free, 800 number, which was a new concept then (and would be copied by other states' governors). "It was the first one in the country," Moore noted. "*Parade Magazine* thought it was tremendous. People go put a letter in the mailbox to you and the next day they look for an answer. The theory was, get back to them as soon as possible. They could pick up the phone and call without spending money to mail a letter. It worked well. Soon each agency had its own toll-free phone number." Noted Jim Snoderly of Berkeley Springs, "That toll free number made Arch Moore a lot of friends, especially in the Eastern Panhandle where they feel isolated from Charleston and neglected. People would have a road problem and call the governor's office and, before they knew it, the Highways crews were out there. It was really impressive, the speed at which problems were being handled."

THE NEW GOVERNOR immediately ordered a freeze on spending, hiring, pay raises and purchases (for months, those had to be approved by the governor's office), "to make a complete inventory of our assets and to be in a position to give the people of West Virginia a complete report and accounting of where we stand as a State." Naturally, that caused a howl of protest among state employees and college administrators, but it let them know there was a new boss in town, and it did give some measure of the government's financial status. If allowed to flow unimpeded, it is difficult for any governor to get a good read on how much money is available, and how much is being spent. To slow the cash flow with such a freeze allows not only control, but a better financial snapshot to be made. (It would be a tactic Moore would repeat when he returned to office in 1985.) "There was a question of whether I'd be able to run the agencies of government," Arch reflected, thirty six years later, because "they were being run by people [appointees of Barron and Smith] who didn't support me."

The Modern Budget Amendment had given West Virginia the "strong governor system" it had long needed. Moore would have powers no prior governor had enjoyed. Prior to its adoption, the state budget and, consequently, most of the government's policy and programs, were hammered out by the "Board of Public Works" (the state auditor, treasurer, secretary of state, agriculture commissioner, attorney general and governor). Before its adoption, as Cecil Underwood had discovered, the "buck stopped" with the governor. He received the blame by the public when things went sour, but his control over the government was dependent on a legislature and Board of Public Works that (in Underwood's case) could be quite obstructionist. It had been government by committee. With the reorganization the amendment afforded, the person occupying the governor's office became more important and powerful than ever. It created a strong chief executive.

Passage of the 1968 amendment came along at just the right time, and not just because government was becoming bigger. Perhaps the most important power it provided the chief executive was the line-item veto, which Moore was not afraid to use, or threaten to use, to get the programs he needed and to exclude the fat, the pork-barreling for home districts, of which legislators are so fond. Arch Moore opted to push the envelope, to maximize his rights; he did not shy away from exercising the powers and authority it provided. "The people gave me the tools to be a strong leader and I decided to exercise that power," Moore later reflected. On many occasions, the Democratic legislative leaders would test in the courts the new budget-making powers that were given to the governor's office under this new amendment. Sometimes the supreme court would slap Moore's wrists and rule that he had gone too far in encroaching into the legislature's territory; other times, it would give its approval.

Knowing the "honeymoon" with the Democratic opposition would be very brief, he almost immediately gave the Legislature his "wish list," most of which was adopted. The Roads Development Amendment had granted legislative power to authorize the sale of road bonds up to $350 million. He asked for issuance of $70 million of that, plus $20 million from a prior bond authority; he was serious about quickly building some new highways and fixing old ones. He asked for $1.1 million for improvements to the Colin Anderson Center for mentally challenged children. He wanted $9 million to add buildings to the state capitol complex, to house a growing government. Five million dollars were requested for the Department of Natural Resources (DNR) and $20 million to improve the mental hospital system. It was immediately clear–this was no conservative Republican; Governor Moore was in step with the times, which called for more government help, more involvement, more spending. Richard Nixon was also following in the steps of his Democratic predecessors in expanding the role of the federal government.

The transition to a strong governor, with respect to budget-making, was not an entirely smooth one, however. The legislative leadership had been used to getting their way. With the governor being just one vote of many on the Board of Public Works under the old system, if he was not cooperating, the legislature simply obtained votes from the others on that Board. When he prepared his 1969 budget, Moore said, "I took the offensive, on welfare, mental health, on highways. I handed them a budget, but

I didn't put all the money we had into that budget, so they had no money to waste.

"[Speaker] Ivor Boiarsky was stern and self-assured about everything. He came to me and said, 'Arch, I think you're going to be a helluva governor, but...' And the 'but' was, 'You don't understand the legislature.' I said, 'Ivor, I'm a child of the legislature; I've served for years in the House of Delegates and the Congress. Why do you say that?' And he responded, 'You haven't made arrangements for us [the legislators] to spend money.' I said, 'We don't have money to throw away.' I had funded the state agencies such that they couldn't pare anything out. But I asked, 'Just out of curiosity, what are you talking about?' Ivor said, 'We need $60 million.' I was shocked, and said, 'We don't have an extra sixty cents! I've got fifty-five counties to take care of, this state's going pell-mell in the wrong direction and I have to turn it around.' But Ivor just kept saying, 'You don't understand us.'

"Toward the end of the session, Ivor came back to my office. The budget wasn't approved, as usual. He said, 'We can't get along without $40 million.' I said, 'Well, we've got a problem, then. That's pork barrel. There's no way. I'm willing to put together some money, but I can't go $40 million!'

"Ivor said, 'What will you give us?' When I said, 'Nine million,' he quickly replied, 'I'll take it!'" The compromise ended the impasse, but they began to understand who was going to control the budget from now on.

Within a month of taking office, Arch faced one of his first challenges as governor. Drawing upon public support and sympathy following Farmington's Consol No. 9 mine explosion in December 1968, the UMWA struck, with about 45,000 miners demanding benefits for "black lung disease," or occupational pneumoconiosis. On February 26, two thousand miners marched on the capitol. Congressman Hechler, Drs. I.E. Buff, Donald L. Rasmussen and Hawey Wells, and state Senator Paul Kaufman spoke to them at the Charleston Municipal Auditorium.

Most of the crowd were strong Democrats and had supported Sprouse. When Governor Moore came to speak to them, promising support for Senator William Brotherton's, Robert Holliday's and Delegate Robert Nelson's black lung bills, reminding them that he was on record for supporting the legislation, he was received with only a smattering of applause and even a few jeers. When Moore told them it would be the first order of business in a July special session of the legislature, the miners began shouting, "No!" and "We want it now!" Then they began chanting, "No law, no work!"[1] They were impatient, unwilling to wait and wanted to take advantage of the momentum.

The miners got their bill passed in the regular 1969 legislative session. It made the pneumoconiosis compensable through workers' compensation and Moore signed it into law. It would eventually cost billions of dollars to coal companies (Buff, seen as the father of the black lung movement, joked that the coal operators had a headstone made of coal ready for him). The miners returned to work with a major victory but began realizing that this Republican governor was not their enemy, as their unions had preached to them. West Virginia became one of three states in the nation to allow benefits[2] for just having x-ray evidence of OP, without even proving any breathing impairment. Coal miners (and any worker who alleged dust exposure at work) could get up to a full, life award under this generous system, depending on physicians' opinions regarding their lung impairment. Widows and children began receiving life awards if autopsy interpretations suggested that their husbands' deaths had been caused in part by dust exposure. The legislation also provided for black lung clinics where the miners could be examined and get their claims started.

Upon Moore's urging, Pres. Nixon would also approve federal black lung benefits for the first time. Those would pay hundreds of millions of dollars from the coal industry to the pockets of miners and their families over the next three decades, a major transference of wealth in the Appalachian region which also trickled down to businesses that depended on mining communities. Senator Jennings Randolph had done much to get the bill through the congress, and it passed with votes to spare.

But the UMWA had worked hard for Humphrey and there were fears that an industry-friendly Nixon might veto the Federal Mine Health and Safety Act. For obvious reasons, it was not popular among coal companies. Two coal mining area congressmen traveled from Pennsylvania to Moore's office to request his support of the federal bill, knowing a Republican governor might enjoy the President's confidence. Nixon tracked down the Governor while he was in a New York hotel, preparing for a presentation regarding the state's bond sales. The President warned Moore he was disinclined to sign it. After the lengthy phone conversation, Arch convinced him that the coal industry could afford it, that it would not kill the sale of U.S. coal, that it was the right thing to do for the victims of the disease, and that it simply was good politics. Arch suggested that there were some mining family votes the two Republicans could peel away from their Democratic opponents in 1972. Reluctantly, the President was persuaded by the West Virginia governor. "Federal black lung legislation was dead until I convinced President Nixon to sign it into law," Moore bluntly stated.[3]

The black lung bill aside, the Moore Administration had few dealings with their federal counterpart, the Nixon Administration, although the Governor would see the President from time to time and their relationship was cordial and polite. But "we weren't bosom buddies with the Nixon Administration," Elaine Davidson recalled. Why not? "I don't know, we just weren't."

In less contentious settings, the new Governor asked the legislature for nearly two million dollars to improve state parks. He asked that drugs be exempted from sales tax, but that other exemptions be removed for one year, which he contended would raise $37 million to fund the new expenditures he wanted.

Without asking the legislature, the Governor set up a Management Task Force, a blue ribbon panel comprised of CPAs, business people, educational leaders, architects and others, to determine how state government could be run more efficiently. It resulted in resounding success. "The general revenue budget was then about $795 million," Arch recalled. "The task force showed how to save $200 million and, when I began to implement those reforms, we began to have budget surpluses."

Together, Moore and the legislature was able to provide West Virginia with its first kindergarten system. Although not fully funded at first, it was a popular move and brought the state into line with the national trend of starting education at age five. Typical was a letter Moore received from a Wellsburg teacher that year. "I was so happy [to read about the new kindergarten system] that I had to write and thank you ... I had hoped and dreamed [of it] for years ... If [my child] could have gone to kindergarten this year he would have been better prepared to enter first grade. Attending church and Sunday School isn't enough..." Another writer commended him for it, adding, "You are the best that has happened to the state in forty years."

ONE THING that legislators, members of the news media and others noticed about this new governor was that he put his remarkable memory and comprehension of the massive state government to work immediately. "He was a master of details and a master of politics," noted Ken Hechler. "He had a tremendous memory for details. When he held a news conference, Arch didn't have to turn to an aide for the answer, like Jay Rockefeller [later would do as governor]. He immediately knew the answer, even if the question was about some obscure subject. And he was always so great at being able to stroke the right people. I joined him for a bill-signing and commended him for the legislation. Arch waved around at the legislative leadership there and gave them credit for it."

Pete Thaw, the veteran Democratic operative, agreed. "I've met about every modern politician—President Kennedy, Bobby Kennedy, President Johnson, Adlai Stevenson, many others—and Arch Moore could play with any of them. He's as good as anybody I met. Governor Moore totally understands politics, human nature, how to express himself, how to interact with people, how to make you want to work for him. He never forgot a name or a face. He didn't need to compartmentalize; he is self-contained. He was Politics 101."

Former Justice John McCuskey, who would serve as a delegate from Harrison County and state Republican chairman in the 1970s, and as Moore's finance commissioner in the 1980s, concurred. "Arch Moore was the most brilliant politician and administrator I've ever known. He was in a league with Roosevelt and Churchill in political ability. His greatest personal quality was the ability to use people to their maximum and motivate them to do the best they were capable of being. He also had a skill for finding the best place to utilize their talents."

Tom Tinder, who served in different capacities in all three of Moore's terms as governor, noted that the Governor "had a photographic memory. He was in charge: he was in control of the facts, he was knowledgeable about every aspect of the state and its government. I'd go to meetings with him as prepared as I could be, with my list, and I'd start with two or three things, and then he would pull out figures and start adding things that would just blow my mind. He knew everything about welfare, highways, taxes, etc. And he really had a commitment—he was a true public servant, whether as a soldier, a congressman or governor. He always worked hard in terms of putting in the hours. He was good about keeping things in proper perspective, especially good at handling crisis situations. He was a hands-on guy."

Fred Donohoe, who headed Moore's security detail for most of the first two terms, also became amazed at his ability to recall detailed facts. "He had amazing capabilities. We'd be flying in his helicopter and he'd say, 'You know where we are right now? We're over Johnson Creek. There's a guy down there—and he'd name him—who got me seventy five percent of the vote in his precinct.'" Donohoe was also impressed by his boss's work ethic. "He would routinely work until midnight or 1 a.m. He knew more about state government than any governor up until Joe Manchin. He was the greatest individual I've had privilege to work around or for."

The legislators, for the most part, also were impressed by this dynamic new Governor. It might be said that he took Charleston by storm. His strong leadership style, his take-charge attitude, attention to the most minute detail, was like unto none they had ever seen. But his presentation—the forceful and eloquent way he spoke to group settings, his persuasive one-on-one—was unmatched. They found it difficult to resist his requests. And Moore's feelings toward the Democratic leadership, including House Speaker Ivor Boiarsky and Senate President Lloyd Jackson, Senator Hans McCourt (and others to come, such as William Brotherton and Lewis McManus), were reciprocal. "I was privileged to serve at a time when the legislative leadership was of very high caliber, perhaps the greatest the state ever enjoyed," Arch would later acknowledge. Although there was the usual partisan bickering and power struggles, most of it was conducted at a higher, more statesman-like and intelligent manner, than would occur later in Moore's years of service.

It became well-known that the new Governor was into details. Arch seemed to know, hear, see, and govern everything in state government—often before the department heads or "experts," certainly before the media or public knew about the matter. (Even to date, the former governor loves to gather and process intelligence on a myriad of topics.) Some saw that as a terrible fault. "He was the master of the micro-management style," complained Oce Smith, who alleged that Moore "even chose the brand of coffee the hired help would make." Critics like Oce thought a governor should be tending to more important matters, and delegate the trivial matters to underlings. Others saw Moore's almost-obsessive style as an attribute—they liked the thought that this seemingly all-knowing CEO was minding the store. They believed, as apparently Moore did, that if one took care of the details, often the big items would fall into place much easier. And sometimes the thought—or fear—that the Governor was watching, that he knew what one was doing (whether or not he actually was), could be a good thing.

People also began noticing what a hard worker Bill Loy was. If one could not get into see the Governor, seeing Bill Loy was easily the next best thing—maybe even better. He became highly respected by the movers and shakers for his work ethic and dedication to the state and governor he served. But his controlling behavior also had its downside. "He would get so focused on something that he wouldn't even know what was going on," recalled Elaine Davidson, the Governor's secretary. "One time, I called into him, 'Clark Clifford [the most influential lawyer in Washington at the time] is on the phone for you.' He asked me to have him hold, that he was busy with something. A few minutes later, I reminded him, 'Clark Clifford is holding for you.' He shouted in surprise, 'Clark Clifford's on the phone?!' He had been so focused on what he was doing, he hadn't even heard me earlier."

UNLIKE MOST other governors, Moore did not immediately place his appointees, either in his first or third administrations.[4] He had brought in his skeleton-crew governor's staff, Latimer, Loy, Yost and the other, but waited a few weeks to announce his department heads. Most of those chosen had been present at the secret meeting in Terra Alta in December, but they didn't get the official call until a day or two before the presentation of his cabinet in late January and early February. As always, Arch liked to keep the press guessing.

It wasn't immediately apparent, but these people he chose to lead the government actually were the "best and the brightest," as Arch had promised the public. There may have never been a better state cabinet assembled. Several, including even his second tier appointments in that first term, were very capable innovators, leaders and organizers.

He gave them a key instruction. "I don't want to run your department, but you've got to let me know what you're doing," he told his new cabinet. "Don't come to me for help if you've had a crash landing, if you didn't include me on the takeoff."[5]

For the most part, they were young people. Arch would tell a Youth and Government Model Legislature, "I would venture to guess that my administration is probably the youngest in contemporary history...[We] have put young minds to work." (He mentioned that Alexander Hamilton became involved in the American Revolution and government at age eighteen, Jefferson and John Marshall their involvement in government at age twenty.)

Most, but not all, were people with whom he had attended West Virginia University, many from his fraternity house. "We had the same dreams," Arch later explained. Most, but not all, had worked hard to elect him governor. Many of these men and women would have other, even greater personal accomplishments after the administration ended. Most came to Charleston at great personal sacrifice—they were surrendering secure, often better-paying jobs and leaving their homes to take the risk of what might be only a four-year job and which promised a lot of grief, criticism and extraordinarily long hours of work.

As expected, Charles H. "Chuck" Haden II, a Morgantown lawyer, former delegate, school board member and most recently the GOP nominee for attorney general, was chosen as tax commissioner. William S. "Bill" Ritchie, Jr., a businessman from Ravenswood, would head Highways. Lysander Dudley, a former WVU classmate of Loy's, would be his Commerce Commissioner. State Sen. Jack Miller of Parkersburg was selected to be his first commissioner of the Dept. of Finance & Administration (F&A) which, next to governor, arguably is the most important center of state government activity. Dr. Mildred Bateman, an African-American, continued as the Mental Health director. John Ashcraft became director of the Dept. of Mines. John Gates, from Appalachian Power, became Motor Vehicles commissioner. R.L. Bonar was appointed superintendent of the Dept. of Public Safety (state police). Moore put lawyer Elizabeth Hallanan, a liberal from a powerful Republican family, on the Public Service Commission. Hancock County lawyer Edwin Flowers went to Welfare. Jack Blair was named Adjutant General. Fred Davis, a Parkersburg lawyer, would be his first Workers' Compensation commissioner.

Most of his cabinet members, interestingly, came from the moderately liberal wing of the GOP. As noted, Arch sought a larger, more active, aggressive government, not less programs and spending, and their philosophies meshed with that goal. (The conservative wing of the party had largely supported Underwood, although he also was a progressive governor in both of his terms.)

Dr. B. L. Coffindaffer of Morgantown was chosen as director of the Office of Federal-State Relations, and Democrat politico Jack Whiting of Roane Co., Moore's adversary in the Bailey campaign, was to head his Appalachian Development Office. Sam Weese would be the Insurance Commissioner.

Moore was proud of the star quality of his cabinet. "Sam Weese, Chuck Haden, Elizabeth Hallanan, Ed Flowers and Bill Ritchie all went on to become presidents of their national organizations," he noted. Flowers and Haden would both end up on the state supreme court and they and Hallanan would be appointed to federal judgeships.

THE OPPOSITION had assured that the *entire* "Arch Moore team," at the second and third tier, would never be installed, however. Few of those he needed from around the state to complete his administration would get a chance to serve. In one of those "midnight hour" orders governors commonly issue just before leaving office, Governor Hulett Smith had covered two thousand state employees with civil service protection. This meant that all those Barron-Smith appointees could not be replaced by ones loyal to Arch Moore. The new Governor challenged Smith's actions in court but it was ultimately upheld by the Democratic supreme court.

Although this "dirty trick" by Smith was not totally unexpected (Governor Underwood had put some of his Republican appointees under civil service before leaving in 1961), the magnitude of it was great and made running the government a more difficult proposition for the new, Republican governor. Moore told people close to him that he had a deal with Governor Smith in which the latter agreed that he would not put employees under civil service (in exchange for what, Arch did not say), but Smith had reneged. Many, but not all, of these holdovers were not fond of Arch Moore nor did they care about his goals; they would just as soon see him fail.

One governor's "highly qualified public servant" may be viewed by the next as a "political hack." But once that worker has civil service protection, it almost requires dynamite to blast them from their job, no matter how unqualified, incompetent or uncooperative they may be. A four-step grievance process awaits any administrator who tries to discipline or remove them. Some governors, like Rockefeller, would simply order the objectionable employee to be "put in a corner," with nothing to do, hoping they would leave voluntarily out of frustration. But Moore was left with far too many of Barron-Smith's people to keep them idle.

Consequently, his department heads were quickly frustrated by being "stuck" with offices full of employees loyal to the Democrat Statehouse Machine, who were just biding their time until Moore could be replaced in four years. No wholesale firing was intended, but they did want to bring in some of their own people for key positions. The department heads saw the holdovers to be an obstacle to progress, to the programs they wanted to put into place quickly. These statehouse workers would often smile and agree to directives, but then take their time in executing the orders, an unofficial "slow down strike," cooperating just enough to prevent an enforceable termination.

Moore actually was benevolent toward the holdovers. Regarding the Barron-Smith holdovers, "If anyone was within six months of a pension, I told my department heads that I didn't want them touched. And if they do their work and take politics out of the agency, they'll always have a friend in me." But there were some they wanted to replace.

The Civil Service Commission, which regulated state job classifications, salaries, transfers, promotions, and other personnel matters was itself controlled by Barron-Smith appointees. In late January, 1969, Moore would get to appoint one of the three members to that commission. He chose a Jackson Kelly lawyer, Robert L. Elkins, a courtly, Southern-styled gentleman originally from Logan, but a Republican who showed fierce independence.

"Moore's people—Loy, Haden, Flowers and others–were always trying creative ways to shuffle the bureaucracy and get their own people in place," recalled Elkins. "They wanted to reclassify people loyal to the administration and upgrade salaries of people they brought in, by creating new job classifications." But Elkins would rarely go along with it.

And, of course, the two holdovers on the commission were not going to cut Moore any slack. "The member from Fairmont [Donald G. Ryder] was a union glassworker and he always voted against Moore," Elkins recalled. Even when the commission ruled favorably for the Moore Administration, it was often reversed by the state supreme court, all five Democrats. In fact, the commission was represented by Democrat Attorney General Chauncey Browning's appointed assistants, who would often "concede the case," Elkins remembered, angrily.

Gov. Moore and his department heads would get so upset with Elkins' perceived betrayal that he would frequently be "called in" to explain his actions. "They would call me on the carpet [to the governor's office] where various personnel outrages were discussed," he recalled. "I offered [Moore] my resignation several times, but he refused to accept it."

One time the resentment against the Civil Service Commission by the Moore department heads became so intense that it "boiled over," said Elkins. "Civil Service obtained its payroll from an assessment on all other departments' payrolls. Moore's people decided to 'teach us a lesson' by cutting off our department's income."

What they forgot was that, by statute, the Commission had to certify their payrolls. So Elkins and the two Democratic commissioners decided to retaliate by withholding that certification. No one in state government including Arch Moore, then drawing a $25,000 salary, could be paid.

"It wasn't long before Bill Loy and the others called a meeting. After fussing at us some more, they backed down." They released the Civil Service's money and state payrolls were certified and paid.

On another occasion, Commissioner Haden wrote a long letter of complaint to the Commission, threatening to take them to the supreme court. "After discussing our response, I was delegated to write the reply," chuckled Elkins. "I discovered that the secretary couldn't take dictation and I couldn't figure out how to use the Dictaphone, so I simply wrote: 'Dear Chuck, God speed. Sincerely, Robert Elkins.' We never heard from him again."

Eventually, Moore was able to appoint replacements for the two Civil Service holdover commissioners and the battles (which had filled the headlines of newspapers) died down. Elkins, disillusioned, resigned at the end of Moore's first term. "I'd accepted the appointment to make friends for my firm, but instead I made enemies."

ONE OF THE PROMISES Candidate Moore had made in his race the year before was to provide a thousand dollar pay raise for all teacher and school personnel, including bus drivers, cooks, administrators and maintenance. With the average West Virginia teacher making $7,650 at the time, "It was a big piece of change," as Moore would later characterize the pay raise proposal. Important to all, it would draw and retain better people to the profession.

During the campaign, Jim Sprouse had scoffed at the audacious proposal; it would require an unacceptably huge tax increase, he warned. Arch, always promising first, and later finding a way to deliver, assured voters it could be done without more taxes. Moreover, the teachers had elected Moore; he would not disappoint them.

A few weeks after the '68 election, Ron Pearson[6] bounded across a Morgantown street to ask Chuck Haden the question everyone was wondering. "How are you going to get $100 million without raising taxes?" Pearson could tell by the anguished look on his face that this was a responsibility Moore had dumped into Haden's lap—to discover a method to provide the big pay raise without a real tax increase—seemingly an impossibility. "I'd hit a raw nerve," Pearson remembered. But, as West Virginians would find out in this first term, there was little that was impossible with Arch Moore when he wanted to make it happen.

As it turned out, the Governor, Haden and Jim Sakert, the Tax Department's chief lawyer, sat down and did carve out a creative, workable plan. They temporarily—for one year—closed enough sales tax exemptions, or loopholes, to cover the pay raises. The three percent tax would now apply to goods and services used in manufacturing, contracting, transportation and in mining, oil and gas production.

Then, in 1970, Moore would double the business and occupation tax on coal, "which caused a real blood-letting," according to Pearson. "Arch Moore raised taxes on coal two or three times, from about 85 cents to $3.85 per $100. It was really gutsy thing to do, since those guys were responsible for electing and re-electing him. But we needed the money!" Moore, however, was able to say he did not raise taxes, that he was merely closing tax loopholes.

The Democrats, with an "Ah-hah!" were quick to label it a tax increase, no matter what Moore's people chose to call it. Huffed Senate President Lloyd Jackson, "I can't see any difference in removing exemptions and adding taxes."[7] But the opposition wasn't going to stand in the way of the pay raise; it was politically popular.

ONE OF THE first visitors the new governor had received upon taking office came as a surprise. In retrospect, it was one of the most significant meetings Arch Moore would ever have. At 10:30, on a wintry January morning, his receptionist phoned to tell Moore that *Gazette* Publisher Ned Chilton had dropped in without an appointment, and expected to be seen immediately. Arch had a fleeting thought that Chilton, after the nastiness of the recent campaign, might be wanting to mend fences. But for whatever reason he came to call, Moore was inclined to interrupt his business of the moment to see his guest. After all, the wealthy Chilton was an owner of the largest and most influential news outlet in the state.

Arch bounced out to greet him and ushered him into his inner office. "What can I do for you, Ned?" he asked after some polite small talk and a cup of coffee.

Chilton then pulled out a "laundry list" of his agenda for the Moore Administration to follow during the next four years. He started going through it, item by item, demanding, "I want ____ done; I want ____ done," outlining his expectations.

Arch, still stinging from the allegations made against him by the paper in the '68 campaign, interrupted him by the time he got to the fourth demand. "I want to ask you a question, Ned. Do you do this to every newly-elected governor?"

Without apology, Chilton replied, "Hell, yes!"

Getting a bit steamed at his visitor's audacity by now, the Governor told the partisan publisher, "If you want those things done, you'll have to get yourself elected governor."

Chilton arose from his chair, stomping out, snarling, "You'll regret this every day of your life!"

And from that day forward, Moore's coverage in the *Gazette* went from bad to worse—much worse.[8]

CHILTON'S FIRST opportunity to go after Moore came early in the term. On a snowy March 11, State Road maintenance workers went on strike. They were demanding union recognition and apparently had misguided thoughts that Moore would give in to their demands. Naturally, the *Gazette* supported them wholeheartedly, encouraging them, putting their complaints and threats on the front pages.

But the Highways employees had just made a major, dumb mistake. They gave Arch Moore a valid reason to clean them out, as he really preferred to do, anyway. They were almost all Democrats, holdovers of the Barron-Smith era, did not have a good reputation for industriousness, and there were thousands of Arch Moore supporters of both parties out there, eager to take their place.

Noting that the roads were in perilous condition from ice and snow, Arch pronounced the strike illegal, a danger to the public's safety and intolerable. As then-Massachusetts Governor Calvin Coolidge had done five decades before, Moore warned that the workers were neglecting their duty and would be fired "in the interest of the personal health and safety of those who pay for their services." The law didn't allow him to recognize their union, in any event, he claimed.[9] After waiting a couple days, the Governor fired 3,600 of the strikers (later reduced to 2,627 because some came back to work). "It was not an easy thing for me to do," Arch reflected in 2005. "Everyone had families. But I gave them three days to come back and told them, if they did, they had nothing to fear."

His action was extremely popular with the electorate who didn't enjoy driving on slick roads. Fairly or not, State Road workers as a whole had been viewed by the public as lazy, political appointees, leaning on shovels. But it didn't stop the strikers from marching on Moore's office, calling him a "fink" (a popular epithet at the time), throwing snuff on troopers guarding the office, and releasing some type of irritating gas which brought tears to the eyes of statehouse workers. They even had an AFL-CIO sponsored rally on April 7, their "March on Arch" day, complete with folk singers and clashes with state police. But Moore's firings were eventually upheld by the courts. The Governor replaced the strikers with 1,164 new highway workers of his administration's choosing. It couldn't have worked out much better from his perspective. Additionally, by bringing in his own people, Moore fired a warning shot: others were given the message that this governor was not to be messed with and that he would risk public opinion to do what was right, safe and expedient.

His handling of the strike demonstrated that a new kind of leader was at the helm. It got people's attention, even die-hard partisans on the other side, like Oce Smith. "For some unfathomable reason, Democrats as a whole appear to stand overly frightened of the media or public opinion or the shape of one strident issue," he observed. "They often seem to agree wholeheartedly of the necessity of a project ... but they are scared to death of how the media or the public might react. They are likely to pull in their horns and discuss it for years on end, eventually getting nothing done.

"Arch, however, was more the type of *'Damn the torpedoes, full speed ahead!'* If he once made up his mind that a project was what was needed ... he seemed entirely fearless of the press, the media, the politicians and the public. He knew very well that the entire power of the state government workers and organized labor would be coming down on him when he fired all those state road workers ... However, *he never seemed to care*. If he decided that he should do something, he did it, and that was all there was to the question. We [Democratic leaders] liked that feature, even if we didn't approve of whatever it was that he was doing."

THE GOVERNOR also shot an early volley at newly-elected Secretary of State Jay Rockefeller, in what would be a four-year feud and struggle for power. This, too, failed to endear Moore to liberals like Chilton, who saw the young New Yorker as a future president, a savior of West Virginia and an ivy league aristocrat to whom other ivy leaguers, such as himself, could relate in this backwater, culturally deprived state. In turn, Rockefeller stepped up his attacks on Moore, bashing his programs at almost every opportunity, to the point of absurdity in some cases.

Before leaving the House of Delegates where he had served a term, former VISTA worker Jay got his fellow Democrats to propose a Peace Corps-like program for West Virginia. But Governor Moore, smart enough to see that such a program could be used as a platform for Rockefeller in 1972 should they be opponents in a senate or gubernatorial race, wanted nothing of it. Moreover, Arch had always felt such programs put the state in a negative light, providing fodder for the tongue-cluckers in the New York and D.C. media, with their "poor Appalachia" stories.

Moore said the program, dubbed the West Virginia Service Corps, was politically motivated and vowed that all volunteers for it would be in-state college students and would be operated out of the Federal-State Relations Office, an arm of the governor's office. When Jay charged that Moore's actions were also politically motivated, Arch responded, "He's terribly oversensitive and a degree of immaturity probably controlled his statement."[10] As might be expected, Rockefeller's hoped-for showcase project was dead on arrival. The immaturity theme would become a staple of Moore's approach to his potential rival.

For his part, the Governor tried to give the same individualized attention to the people he served as he had always been able to do as a congressman. As he would often remind his former constituents in the First District, however, he no longer had just a few counties to handle. "I've got fifty-five counties," he'd tell them, "so keep in mind that I'm spread a little thinner." He kept an incredible memory of every town and hamlet of the state, every bridge and highway, and as he would ride along in a car, could recite who lived in which house, all along many routes. His memory bank was like an elephant's; he never seemed to forget anything or anybody.

Pete Thaw, Jay's deputy secretary of state, frequently would be in Moore's office to deliver or pick up state papers. "He'd always have a large stack of phone messages on his desk. I asked him, 'Governor, what do you do with those?' He assured me that, after dinner each evening, he would return from the Mansion to his office at seven p.m., and return every single one of them. That was just amazing, but he did it!"

Moore also continued a tedious, time-consuming practice of signing every letter and photo that went out, often adding personalized notes by hand, a practice he would continue long after he left office. Secretary Audrey Toler recalled that, almost every evening, Arch would often have a stack of correspondence "four or five feet tall," at least 500 photos, letters and documents, to review, sign, and to which he added personal notes. The Governor liked having his staff "close," she said and, "if he had a question, he'd go out into the hallway and talk to the caseworker" about some problem or document.

"He wore out enough blue tip felt pens that he went through dozens a month, signing documents," confirmed Fred Donohoe, who would carry boxes full of correspondence to the Mansion each evening, Moore would work on it, and Donohoe returned it to the governor's office the next morning. "If he agreed with how the letter was written, he'd sign it, but if not, he'd write 'No' in the corner. Often the [preparer of the letter] would have no idea why he did not approve it and would have to ask around for advice on a re-write." Moore also controlled his own schedule, Toler added. The aides and staff would give him lists of speaking invitations, for example, and he'd mark each with a note to accept or send regrets.

"He would come into the office each morning with a, 'Good morning, fellow taxpayers,'" remembered author Dolly Withrow, who worked as one of his letter-writers. (Toler noted that Dee Brown, who was director of the mail room and correspondence, was an invaluable assistant to the Governor. Arch mentioned Nancy Corey as someone he relied upon in his third term.)

Not satisfied with the programs he'd been able to get through the regular session, Moore began what would be a tradition for him. He called the legislature back for a special session in July of 1969, to focus their attention on projects he wanted. He presented a tax investment credit program as an offset against the B&O tax to spur industrial development. Potential investment of $750 million and 15,000 new jobs depended on such an incentive, he said. He asked for civil service coverage for several thousands of state workers, including state highways workers and liquor store clerks. Also requested was revenue bond authority of $150 million to build elementary and secondary school buildings. Health insurance was needed for state employees, he said, and it would cost $2.23 million a year. About three-fourths of state employees were expected to participate, he estimated.

He wanted their permission to sell $70 million worth of bonds (of the $350 million authority by the amendment) to start building interstate highways. He asked for $20 million to build new mental hospitals, to replace the aging Weston State Hospital, and funds to construct a "modern museum and archives building" for the state capitol (to replace what was jammed into the basement) and other improvements to the capitol complex, costing $9 million. The list went on, including a request for authority for the state police to clean up junked vehicles along highways. He wanted amendments on the next ballot to allow governors to have more than one term of office (they'd been limited to one, four year term, since the 1800s), to create the office of lieutenant governor, and for all state offices except attorney general and auditor to be appointed by the governor. There was a mixed bag of results. Some improvements for the capitol were funded; no bill to allow appointment of Board of Public Works offices came to his desk; there was no second term amendment; no new mental hospital; no new archives building; no junked cars bill; but a large portion of highways funds were allowed.

One of the things Commerce did that had a long-lasting, positive effect on the state's image and tourist industry was to help seed the budding whitewater rafting industry on the New and, later, the Gauley River. "Jon Dragon came to me asking for money from the state and we were able to help," recalled Lysander Dudley with pleasure. "It got started in Thurman, West Virginia first. Jon named [one of the rapids on the New River] 'Dudley's Dip.'"[11] The whitewater industry would eventually be third only to hunting-fishing and skiing as a tourist draw, with as many as 225,000 brave souls entering the water. It would also fit nicely into the "Wild, Wonderful West Virginia" image that Moore and Dudley were painting for the state to lure potential out-of-state visitors; it showcased the state's unique and natural beauty.

Commented whitewater businessman Dave Arnold, of Class VI: "Arch Moore and Lysander Dudley were the architects of the whitewater industry in West Virginia. They put the industry on track. Governors Rockefeller and Caperton were great ambassadors for us, they even took trips down the river, but it was Arch who put things in motion."

Arnold continued: "I think, strategically, Moore was the smartest leader we've had. He would take a complex problem and in a matter of minutes understood the issue and come up with a strategy to resolve it. He understood tourism and solved a lot of our problems. He's someone who listened well, assimilated the information and came up with a solution."

The toll-free, 800 number for out-of-state tourists to use, which Moore put into place, would be a no-brainer today, Arnold added. "Everyone's got one now, but in those days, it was radical. It really helped the tourist industry tremendously."[12]

ON JULY 1, Moore got to announce his appointees to the newly-created Board of Regents, a commission established to govern all state colleges and Marshall and West Virginia Universities. It was a particular pleasure for Arch to appoint former Gov. Okey Patteson, by then seventy years old. The former governor had impressed student Arch Moore by his handling of the WVU medical school selection process. His youngest appointee to the Board was John Hoblitzell, the twenty-one-year-old grandson of the late U.S. senator.[13] Having all nine members beholding to him for their appointments, and generally loyal to his points of view, provided the Governor unprecedented power over the institutions of higher learning during the next seven years, with a few exceptions.

Later that month, the Governor's Management Task Force produced a 770-page volume that contained 778 recommendations for reform of the governmental structure, which they claimed would save the state $50 million annually. The task force had been composed of forty-seven business men and women who worked with a Chicago consultant.

Among those recommendations was the proposal of a constitutional amendment allowing governors second terms, which Moore heartily endorsed, and had requested in the special session in July. Four years were not enough to accomplish positive change, he contended. "Programs in one administration often become lost as the result of too frequent changes in leadership." He even offered to remove himself as a possible candidate if the voters would approve it.

He happily announced that the state's unemployment rate had dropped to 4.4 percent and was continuing to decline, as opposed to the national rate of 4 percent, which was rising.

All was not good news, however. Controversies from his lawyering days resurfaced once again. The Moundsville story, which had risen during the 1968 Primary, reared its ugly head once again.

The president of an Odd Fellows lodge in Marshall County charged that Lawyer Moore had overpaid himself by taking $14,500 in fees for handling a $137,000 estate, the proceeds of which were to go to the lodge. He wanted Moore removed as the executor, charging that he had been "extremely negligent and careless in his manner of handling the estate," delaying settlement while he was distracted by congressional and political duties. The local county court upheld Moore's appointment as executor, however, noting that most of the proceeds of the estate had been transferred to the Odd Fellows. Moore was sued for $99,500 and it was a big enough deal that he spent a grueling day in the court in November 1969, explaining the difficulties he had experienced with the IRS, delays in getting tax-exempt status for a non-profit corporation, calling himself a victim of circumstances. The complaint was not immediately resolved.

H. John Rogers was co-counsel to Rudy DiTrapano in that suit against the Governor. "Here I was, cross-examining the sitting governor of the state, really raking him over the coals, insinuating he'd been incompetent for delaying settlement of the estate for eight years. But, to my surprise, he was unflappable. In fact, during a break, he comes running down the hall toward me with a trooper close behind him. He puts his hand on my shoulder and says, 'John, I watched you run at WVU. You were the best runner there since Carl Hatfield!' Here, I'd had given him my best shot, and it didn't even faze him!" Rogers was learning that Arch could be magnanimous to his adversaries, even when it was personal. The Governor was letting Rogers know that he recognized that he was just doing his job, as the plaintiff's attorney. And, undoubtedly, he was using his charm to try to defuse him a bit.

But such a reaction from Moore was not atypical. Another lawyer had sued Moore and made some truly ugly public statements about the Governor. Rogers was talking to that lawyer one day about a great job his son had just landed (in the chemical industry). "I asked him how his son had found such a great job, just right out of school. He answered casually, 'Oh, Arch Moore got it for him.'" Rogers added, "It was almost like a Biblical thing, how Arch seemed to be able to forgive people so easily." [13]

All-in-all, the year ended positively, though, with these stories being minor footnotes, largely ignored by the public. Instead, there was a general satisfied feeling among West Virginians that good government may finally have arrived. Whether or not one agreed with all Arch Moore had done in the past eleven months, none could deny that it had been an exciting, action-packed year for the new executive. West Virginians had been accustomed to observing their governors from their peripheral vision, if at all; in past decades, many probably couldn't tell you the current governor's name. But this new Governor was getting noticed–almost everyone knew he was in charge. You never knew what he was going to do next; he was worth watching.

And Arch was just getting started. This was not going to be an average, ho-hum administration.

Chapter 11 Notes

1. - *Charleston Gazette*, Feb. 27, 1969.

2. - Union lawyer Pat Maroney, later Democratic state chairman, and business lawyer John McClaugherty, of the Jackson Kelly firm, ironed out a compromise in which claimants would get a thousand dollar award (which later evolved into a five percent permanent partial disability award worth $10,000), if they just had a chest x-ray a physician thought showed the lung disease. Sometimes, the true cause of their breathing problems was cigarette smoking, but they normally received their award, anyway. The generous benefit would end in 2003, as result of reforms instituted during the Wise Administration.

3. - Nixon, at a 1972 Huntington campaign stop, would acknowledge that it was Arch who convinced him to sign the bill. Moore prized a photo of himself with a group of supporters of the black lung laws at a 35th anniversary of their victory at the state capitol, in 2004. Expensive for coal companies, often too generous, the state and federal black lung awards nevertheless were a godsend to many mining families and widows and kept them from poverty. As Kanawha County Commissioner David Hardy (who as a lawyer had represented both claimants and employers in black lung litigation) noted, "It spread a lot of wealth into the coalfield communities." By 1972, the Federal Mine Health and Safety Act had benefitted more than 50,776 miners, widows and dependents, who were receiving $6.28 million in federal black lung benefits each year from the coal companies. According to the Social Security Administration, there were then 16,580 miners with pneumoconiosis, who had signed up within those two years. In 1972, Moore lobbied Nixon to approve a bill which liberalized the benefits even more.

4. - Most of Caperton's cabinet, by contrast, would take control of their offices within an hour of him being sworn in.

5. - In a 2005 interview, Moore claimed he only fired one department head in his twelve years as governor, an F&A commissioner who didn't follow his rule, he said.

6. - Pearson was a bright, energetic young lawyer, constantly in a hurry, dashing in long strides from meeting to meeting as if walking was a waste of time. Importantly, he was always full of ideas. The Fairmont native would eventually finish his career as the distinguished U.S. Bankruptcy Court judge for the Southern District of West Virginia. Pearson was brought in as the assistant tax commissioner in April of 1969, and would become one of Moore's most creative minds. Many observers believe that Pearson was the most able administrator Moore ever hired, and that he would have made an ideal governor himself.

7. - *West Virginia Governors* by John G. Morgan, Copyright 1980 by the Charleston Newspapers.

8. - Said Edgar "Hike" Heiskell, "When I first arrived in Charleston in July, 1971, to go to

work in Governor Moore's first administration, I knew nothing of Ned Chilton. Having lived in Morgantown virtually all my life, I hadn't had much exposure to the *Gazette*; I knew nothing of its powerful role in the state's politics; and [I] was oblivious to Ned Chilton's visceral distrust and palpable dislike–hatred–of Arch Moore." Heiskell got to know Chilton on the tennis courts of Edgewood Country Club and their wives became friends. "When [Chilton] heard that I was going to work for the Governor, he launched into a tirade filled with expletives and called Arch a 'crook' at least ten times. I don't think I had ever seen such an outburst by an adult, and I was astonished by Ned's foul language and his level of animosity towards Arch." He continued, "He never missed an opportunity to attack Arch Moore," despite his friendship with Heiskell and support of his work as workers' compensation commissioner and secretary of state. "I came to believe that ...he did it just to raise hell, since he knew I respected the Governor and would defend him." Where did it come from? "I have never understood the origins of Ned's animosity toward Arch but I think, as he saw the Governor becoming larger than life, in the context of the state's political history, Ned felt the need to turn up his own volume in exposing what he thought were the shortcomings and perceived wrongdoing on the part of the Governor. And with the resources of the *Gazette* at his disposal, that volume could be very, very formidable." Heiskell, August 10, 2005.

9. - This same pattern occurred again in 1981 when air traffic controllers struck and President Ronald Reagan fired them all, for public safety reasons.

10. - *Sunday-Gazette* Mail, Dec. 31, 1972.

11. - Lysander Dudley, Feb. 26, 2005. There were several legends as to why it was named that, the most credible one being that Lysander was dumped into the water at that particular rapid. One of the more amusing, but less credible, explanations was that he nearly choked there on a "dip" of snuff, but it's one a few of the raft guides tell the tourists.

12. - Dave Arnold, July 21, 2005.

13. - The state senate later refused to confirm Hoblitzell, saying he wasn't old enough to vote when appointed.

13. - People were shocked when Jess Shumate, Moore's labor commissioner during his third term, made numerous hostile comments about his boss in the newspapers. The public fully expected his employment would be promptly terminated–most governors would not have tolerated such behavior–but Arch just seemed to ignore him, and refrained from firing him. Herb Rogers was correct: although not always, Moore sometimes had a quality the New Testament writer calls "longsuffering."

Chapter Twelve
Life in the Mansion

Although the Governor often worked six to seven long days a week, he also took some time off to play. A favorite activity was golfing at the Greenbrier and, at least once a year, the family would get away for a few days' vacation out-of-state.

Although Arch had literally thousands of acquaintances, it appears that there were only about four men, including his brother, with whom he could relax, who would be classified as close friends. While the Moores rarely socialized with members of their administration, an enduring friendship developed between the Moores and Jo Ann and Lysander Dudley, his Commerce commissioner. "We played a lot of bridge at the Mansion by the big fire," remembered Dudley of those days, with fondness. "If it was a tight game, we might play most of the night." With his bald head, dark complexion and dark rimmed glasses, and almost always a wide grin, Lysander had been a WVU classmate of Bill Loy's, who introduced him to Arch. They both enjoyed a laugh and, no doubt, "Dud's" wit and humor kept the First Couple entertained. Explained Dudley, "We just liked each other and he liked what we were doing in Commerce. He was a wonderful governor to promote the state–he really wanted to turn it around."

For decades, the Dudleys, Moores and Lawson Hamiltons normally would sit together (near the 40 yard line) at WVU games. "Arch Moore is a real Mountaineer fan," noted Dudley, echoing what most who knew the Governor observed. "We would review the games play-by-play on Monday mornings. If they had won, we were ecstatic; if they lost, we were mad," he laughed.

It was the Moores' first time to live in "public housing." But this public housing, the Governor's Mansion, had a large chef, a staff and a director, and a five-member security detail from the State Police, who lived with them on the premises.[1]

The family had to adjust to having a large staff serving them, but it was for the most part very welcome. The Moores' chef, Van Buren Henderson, said that he enjoyed his service to the First Family. "Arch Moore is just a West Virginia country boy who likes corn on the cob and meatloaf with gravy," told a reporter. "And many days he heads for the refrigerator to snack on cheese and crackers between a political meeting and a state function."[2]

Mrs. Moore tried to keep a normal, family atmosphere for her children and husband, in addition to performing all the duties expected from the state's First Lady. By all accounts, she was a truly modern woman who was able to do both quite well.

She also brought a warmth to the capital that few First Ladies could do. Said one who was near the scene, "Shelley Moore made everyone, no matter who they were, feel welcome and comfortable. She was as comfortable as an old shoe. Before too many minutes of talking to her, you felt as if you'd known her all your life." Indeed, "gracious" was the word most often used before her title in describing Arch Moore's partner. She complimented her husband in every way. But she also involved herself in state and local activities as she had always done, in addition to hosting events at the Mansion.

As the Manchins would do when they took office, Shelley began a remodeling and renovation program of the Mansion, which had been in decline. With the help of decorator Mary Ann Winters, who eventually was hired on as Mansion Director, she began re-doing each of the lower level, public-function rooms in pastel colors which rivaled the White House in beauty. The West Virginia Republican Women helped, designing pillow cushions with Mountain State themes. "I consider the Executive Mansion a home that belongs to all West Virginians," Shelley Moore told a reporter.

"We would like to open it up for as many occasions as possible. It is beautiful and should be enjoyed as often as possible by the people to whom it belongs." Friends of Mrs. Moore served as volunteer tour guides of the Mansion each Friday, allowing members of the public, who might never be invited to a function there, to see their Chief Executive's residence. The tours were very popular among school children and others.

"We had a wonderful staff at the Mansion," Mrs. Moore believed. "We were very close to Mary Ann Winter and to Phyllis Yost, the secretary of the Mansion." The First Lady and her staff gave the governor's residence the look and feel of a gracious Southern mansion.

Mrs. Moore told the *Daily Mail* of the family's plans as they moved into the Mansion. "Lucy, who [is] twelve, will come to Charleston with us. There's a possibility that Shelley may finish out her year at Holton-Arms School in Bethesda."[3] Kim Moore decided to live with their friends and neighbors at Potomac Falls, the Grahams, to finish out his senior year at Harker Preparatory School. "Their son, Dave Graham, was his best friend," Shelley explained.

"Lucy took it pretty hard," moving from Potomac Falls to Charleston, recalled her father. "We brought her horse to Davis Creek, where we boarded horses for many years thereafter." Before they finally left the house in which she'd lived since 1959, Lucy wrote on a wall, "I hope you find the same love and happiness we did in this house," the new owners reported.

Recalled Lucy, "When we lived in Maryland, I was in horse country and had gone fox hunting. The barn where my horse was kept was just over the hill, within walking distance. It was a culture shock for me and my horse, going from lush, level land, to the steep hills of Davis Creek." She continued, "I spent most of my free time at Charlie Jones' barn at Davis Creek. His daughter, Jennifer, and I were best friends and we rode every day. I was either riding my horse or showing it, all the time." Her only other activity was playing basketball for St. Mark's Methodist Church.

An animal lover, Lucy had a couple famous cats during the Moores' tenure. One, whom she named Charlie Taylor (thinking it was male), to their surprise, had kittens. The story was publicized in the Charleston papers and as a result, all of the cat's offspring were adopted ("One lady named hers Arch"). Another of Lucy's kittens had to have a bell attached to its collar because it was sneaking up on, and killing, the grey squirrels on the capitol grounds. Additionally, she kept a beagle named Muffin in her five years at the Mansion.

Noted Lucy, "I didn't attend many school functions—I spent my time riding horses. I probably went to only one or two basketball and football games [throughout high school]. I never had a date in high school, never went to a school dance." The social pressures were tough on the Moores' youngest. "It was so hard to be thrown into that role–everybody knew who I was but I didn't know that many people. I think guys were afraid to ask me out, because I was the Governor's daughter."

Lucy went from attending seventh grade in an elite, predominately white, private Maryland girls' school to eighth grade in "inner city schools" of the West Side of Charleston: to Thomas Jefferson Jr. High and Roosevelt Jr. High (heavily populated by lower-income and African-American students). It was another culture shock for Lucy, but made her a well-rounded person, she said (and it was in the West Side schools that she met her future husband, John Durbin).

"The superintendent [of Kanawha County Schools] would not allow me to attend South Hills schools, where many of my friends attended. And on my first day of school, I'm driven [to junior high school] by Arthur, the chauffeur, in the Governor's limo. Talk about making it hard to make friends!" She was fast-tracked in math, which eventually allowed her to transfer to John Adams Jr. High, in the more affluent South Hills section of Charleston. But even there, she often would be embarrassed by being the Governor's daughter. "The troopers would tease me, by blowing the siren or flashing their lights when they came to pick me up," causing her unwanted attention. Like most at that age, Lucy just wanted badly to blend in.

A few students would even give her a hard time about being Arch Moore's daughter. "It wasn't vicious, just verbal. Politics was in the forefront in those times. And they would think you're the wealthiest person in the world. Back then, unlike now, the Governor's Mansion was the biggest house in Charleston." But she added, laughing, "I used to egg people on. If they didn't know who I was, I'd see what they thought of Dad. If they'd blast him, I'd say, 'Oh, that's my dad!'"

She usually took the insults without getting upset, but one stuck in her memory. At George Washington High School, a speaker from Exxon "went off on [her] dad," inappropriately attacking the Governor, on and on, because he was lighting the Mansion for Christmas during a so-called oil shortage. (As Moore would tell the press, it was an oil shortage, not a coal shortage, and the electricity used to light the Mansion was produced by burning West Virginia coal.) "I'm sitting there with seven hundred people who knew who I was; even the principal was cringing. I went home that day and told my dad what all he'd said. He called that guy and set his ass straight!"

As result of "trying to fit in, but be a normal person," Lucy became somewhat of a rebel. "I was a product of the times," she noted. "In 1969, and thereafter, it wasn't cool to be part of the Establishment. All that stuff was brewing with the [Vietnam] war. So I was always trying to get away with crap," she laughed. "In high school, we'd try to get into the Anchor [a Kanawha City bar-pizza den]. I'd hang out on Mt. Alpha and drink beer like the others." Lucy "decided she had an impossible task to measure up to her sister [Shelley]," opined Fred Donohoe, who got to know all three Moore children, and she became a fun-seeker, more interested in partying, he thought.

Lucy also was less interested in her parents' public activities, remembered Mrs. Moore. "She was always asking, 'Do we have to do this?' when there was something the family had to attend.

Lucy was "one of a kind, bless her heart," laughed her mother, affectionately. "She's told me the kids in seventh grade were so mean to her. They teased her a lot because she was the Governor's daughter. They threatened her and even beat her up after school. She required a lot of calming down." No doubt a lot of it had to do with the fact that Lucy was the only one of the three Moore children to be raised in the fish bowl, since the older two were away at school. She welcomed the times when her older sister would come home from boarding school.

"Mom was strict. She kept everybody on schedule," Shelley Moore Capito recalled. When in West Virginia, Shelley, Jr. spent time riding horses with little sister. "Lucy had a tough time," she agreed. "It's not like you can make a lot of friends living in the Governor's Mansion at that age. And she had neither her brother nor her sister there with her, no sibling support." Lucy repaid her sister for her kindness: she was the one who set Shelley up on a blind date with her future husband, Charles Capito. "I thought he was too tall for me," laughed Lucy, "but then my husband was just as tall!"

Lucy would often skip school to work as a page in the legislature, House Sgt. at Arms Oce Smith recalled with a smile. "Her mother would phone me and ask, 'Oce, do you have an extra girl over there?' and I'd send her home."

Before being separated from their parents, all three Moore children had found demands on themselves, with dad and mom being in politics. "We were a team," said Arch. "We had a code. If the children were told 'This is a CP,' they had to abide—'CP' meant 'command performance' and they had to attend a particular function with us. But if it was 'YC,' or 'your choice,' then they could decide whether they wanted to go."[4]

All who worked for the First Lady seem to have been proud and happy to have done so, pouring the compliments upon her. "Shelley was kind and the most considerate person you'd ever want to be around," Fred Donohoe recalled fondly. He remembered, for example, a weekend when her elderly father was visiting and wanted to see Pipestem State Park. Rather than just demand a state trooper for the duty, Donohoe said Mrs. Moore wanted to make sure she wasn't taking someone away from his family on a day off to drive her and Mr. Riley to the park. "She called and gently asked, 'Can I impose on you for some information about your weekend staffing?'"

Noted Mrs. Winter, "The troopers were super, so supportive; there was good rapport–we could talk to each other like family." And they were fond of Winter because she spruced up their residence, providing them with decent beds, curtains and other amenities they'd lacked.

Donohoe, who as a State Police colonel would become superintendent of the department during Moore's third term, recalled that the security detail had a lot of difficulty getting Mrs. Moore "to utilize our services at all." She would drive herself to get her hair done, for example, when the state troopers guarding the family preferred to take her to and from such personal appointments. "She just hated to bother us," the Colonel remembered. "She did not want to inconvenience anybody."

He remembered that Shelley, Sr., as some would call her, was a "white knuckle flyer." Donohoe recalled a time when she and the Governor had flown to Clarksburg in "rough weather." The Governor was giving a speech at the Sheraton Hotel there and "it was a rainy, windy, nasty night. When she got there, she just refused to fly back." Donohoe took the Governor's Lincoln up as fast as he could and drove them both back, getting there five minutes before the speech was completed.

Moore had inherited huge "eight-door Cadillac" limousines when he became the state's chief executive in 1969. A bit too ostentatious for his tastes, he replaced them with dark blue Lincoln sedans (extremely long and wide by today's standards, but smaller than the Cadillacs) which the state leased on an annual basis from the Ford Motor Company as part of a lease program to the nation's governors.[5]

Upon assuming their new role, the Moores sold their Beechcraft, which had been used extensively in the '68 campaign, and asked their pilot to come with them to Charleston to become head of the state's aeronautics division of F&A. "I brought a young kid named Mel with me," remembered Arch. "He had enjoyed hanging around hangers and he always was washing my plane." Mel would become the Governor's new pilot.

Mrs. Moore remembered liking just about everything in their new Charleston home, except "what does my husband call it? ... The Morning Sick Call?" She added, "We'd never had any newspaper that constantly attacked us like it did. But, by the second term, I pretty much got used to it," she smiled. Except for having to tolerate the viciousness of the *Gazette*, "Mansion life was wonderful," overall, she said. "We had a lot of outstanding guests while we lived there. Jimmy Stewart[6] stayed overnight, which was a real highlight. Every day was a new experience." Mrs. Moore would keep a busy schedule, "mainly speaking to women's groups, which I thoroughly enjoyed." One of her annual speaking engagements was at Mother's Day, when she was in great demand. "I passed on one Mother's Day," she added, "because my mom had just died and I couldn't bear to do it."

Those who worked for the First Couple quickly learned how close, even dependent, the two were on each other. "The minute Shelley left town, we knew it," recalled executive secretary Elaine Davidson, who explained that Mrs. Moore was often away, tending to her ailing mother in her last months. "Arch Moore's personality would change when Shelley was gone. He would be hard to get along with. I could tell the moment she was gone. They were, and are, so close."

With all the controversies he must face, a governor's security was taken seriously. After all, several national political leaders–the Kennedys, King and Malcolm X—had been killed in recent years. The main threat to a governor was harassment or interruption, however. The state police guards traveled with him everywhere, guarded the mansion and one sat at the reception room desk any time the Governor was in. One would even accompany him on the short walk between the Mansion and the capitol, since the public knew this was a path often taken by the chief executive. There were no significant incidences during Moore's twelve years in office, however. Usually, a personal confrontation was defused when Moore would take a few minutes and listen to the grievant. The guards were mainly there as a deterrent.

So often in the spotlight and occasionally wearied by public demands, the Moores liked to disappear occasionally, perhaps to in-laws in Georgia, to Florida, or even to the Caribbean, without police protection. For several reasons, Arch guarded such "disappearances" fiercely; for personal and political reasons he did not want people to know when he was gone. Mischief can occur when it's known the chief executive is absent. Moore came into the office one day, demanding to know who had leaked word that they were going out of town. "Chief, it wasn't me," replied secretary Elaine Davidson. "Well, how did the state police find out where we are going?" he snapped. It had Davidson concerned that someone inside might be talking when they shouldn't. "It turned out Lucy had told one of the state troopers, in the cruiser on the way to school," she was relieved to discover.

Two weeks after the Moores came to Charleston, their Glen Dale home was burglarized (and their neighbors, the Yohos, soon thereafter). After that, they generally stationed one or more state policeman in their personal residence in an apartment they prepared especially for them. "They liked staying at my house," said Arch. Their home was never bothered again.

Some of their "burglaries" were not so bad, though. When the First Family returned to the Mansion one weekend after being away for a few days, Mrs. Moore phoned the director. "Mrs. Winter, has anyone been staying in the living quarters? There are candy papers everywhere!" Winter denied it, and called in a maintenance man, George Lewis, to investigate. "George discovered that it was a squirrel who'd come through the third story and dragged the candy dish all over the floor. He caught him with his hands, back in a corner."

The troopers assigned to security grew to love and admire Arch as a man of patience, camaraderie, good humor, who was fun and exciting to be around; it was a duty many of them greatly enjoyed and in which they took pride. Arch would often go out and play some basketball with them behind the Mansion. He was interested in their families, as individuals, and showed courtesy, not treating them as servants or annoyances. "When I traveled with the Moores, I was treated as one of the family," remembered retired State Policeman Larry Nelson. "I ate at the table with them at restaurants and slept in adjoining hotel rooms. It was always a pleasure to be with them." There would be no complaints or disgust as some of the security detail would have with some of the other governors for various reasons (including having to "look the other way" during sexual misconduct or drunkenness); most of the troopers who guarded the Moore family became their loyal, lifetime, respectful friends. "I refused to let the state police separate themselves from us," agreed Arch. "I insisted that they sat with us, at whatever function it was. In the past, the security people had been kept 'someplace else.' But I just considered them members of my family. And we didn't want them to feel there was something about us that we couldn't conduct a private conversation [unless] outside their presence."

Sometimes even the Governor's patience would wear thin, however. He did have a temper which could flare if pushed too far. "One time the troopers were loading the family's luggage from a state police station wagon to the plane on the runway of the airstrip, as they were leaving the Greenbrier Hotel," Donohoe remembered. "In his haste, one of them backed the vehicle over the suitcase in which Mrs. Moore had packed their dirty laundry. The plane's propellers were running and, when that suitcase burst open, their clothing blew all over the place! We were running around, gathering it up, as fast as we could." The trooper who ran over it was devastated and sat as far back in the plane as he could. Through clinched teeth, Governor Moore snarled, "They say you should count to three when you're angry. *I'm at one hundred fifty three!*"[7]

Arch Moore's patience could be almost saintly other times, however, especially when he knew an employee was trying hard to please. The longsuffering side of the Governor was illustrated in his tolerance of mishaps by a new, young trooper, Jimmy Diller.[8]

Trooper Diller was assigned to drive the Governor around in his golf cart at the Greenbrier, during a speaking engagement there. Trouble was, Jimmy had never been on any golf course, much less that one. He drove right up on the green of the first tee and then when the Governor yelled, "Officer, get this off here!" he spun the wheels of the cart in reverse. "It caused the Governor great embarrassment," remembered Donohoe.

But what happened at the fourth hole was even worse. "The Governor was slightly near-sighted, so we had to watch where his golf ball went," said Donohoe. "So I instructed Trooper Diller of that and also warned him not to stop the cart too quickly or it might throw [Moore] out." When the Governor teed off at the fourth hole, Diller drove the cart down over a steep embankment, tumble bumble, and "they were bouncing all over the place, clubs flew everywhere and the Governor was thrown into the windshield of the cart," laughed Donohoe. "After that, Jimmy ran over his ball and buried it. The Governor finally said, 'Officer, you go ahead without me. The Commissioner [Ritchie, who was playing with him] and I have some things we need to discuss.'"

But the slapstick comedy wasn't limited to that incident alone. On another occasion, Donohoe was driving the Governor to a speaking event at the Daniel Boone Hotel in downtown Charleston during the Christmas rush. "It was pouring rain. The Governor always sat up front, 'shotgun,' and Trooper Diller was sitting in back, behind him. The plan was, I unlock the power locks, Jimmy was to get out, open the Governor's [front] door and hold an umbrella for him. But he tried to open it just as I pushed the unlock button and every time I would push it again, he was trying to open it [thereby remaining locked in]. So the Governor, who was out of the limo by now, reached in and manually unlocked Jimmy's door, opened it, and curtsied to him.

"The Governor then started through a revolving door but Jimmy and the umbrella got in at the same time. He got the umbrella jammed and locked up the revolving doors, slamming the Governor's face against the glass. Arch was pushing forward and Jimmy was pushing backward, trying to unjam the umbrella. I knew I was going to get my ass chewed out later, but I just couldn't stop laughing," said Donohoe. Other times, Jimmy would stop and answer questions from passers-by when he supposed to be sticking with Moore. "Arch would move fast through a crowd sometimes, and he was short enough he'd disappear into the crowd and Jimmy would lose him."

But even with all that, Arch still didn't want to "s–t can" Trooper Diller, Donohoe recalled; he didn't want to hurt his feelings or cause him hardship even though Donohoe had recommended they remove the young policeman from the security detail. "The Governor asked me, finally, 'Where would he go if you transferred him?' He didn't want him fired or his family moved too far away. He'd say, 'He tries so hard.' When I suggested that Jimmy really wanted to be an instructor, the Governor asked, 'Can we do that?'" So Trooper Diller was transferred to the State Police Academy in Dunbar where he happily taught recruits the remainder of his career and Moore found himself safer without that particular guard.

Moore could be demanding of Donohoe. He was someone he relied upon, even to help with correspondence and non-police type duties, because he trusted him fully to do the job properly.

In 1975, for example, the Moores were having a legislative reception at the Mansion and a group called "The Gentlemen Five" were supposed to start playing music thirty minutes prior to it, for early guests. About fifteen minutes before the event was to begin, Arch phoned Donohoe, asking, "Why am I not hearing music?" Donohoe protested that the Mansion director handled the entertainment, that it was not exactly his responsibility.

"The mansion director is not here!" thundered Moore. When Fred ascertained that the organ the group had rented had not yet arrived, delaying their performance, Moore demanded, "I want an organ and I want it now!"

Donohoe thought to himself, "What am I, the organ grinder?" And where was he to get an organ on fifteen minutes' notice? But Fred prided himself on obeying orders and solving a problem. Thinking quickly, he phoned the owner of the nearby Clemente's Restaurant, "a guy I had raided for illegal whiskey sales before clubs were allowed to sell alcohol," and told him (not asking him), "Clem, I'm sending a truck and a state trooper up to borrow your organ." Donohoe had it escorted back to the Mansion with a cruiser, blue lights flashing and siren wailing, just in time.

Moore was not hesitant to use state police on another occasion, when it was Governor's Day at the State Fair near Lewisburg and the music attraction, George Jones (aka No-Show Jones), had once again failed to make it on time for the main stage show. When the Governor learned that Jones was across the border in a Virginia bar, getting drunk again, he sent West Virginia state police over to "arrest" the country superstar and bring him to the fair. "We're not going to have these people disappointed!" Arch shouted. The show went on as scheduled.

Donohoe enjoyed each of the three Moore offspring, noting each had a unique personality.

The second child was most like her parents, many observers thought. "Shelly, Jr." or "Sis," the future Mrs. Capito, "was just a perfect young lady," Donohoe recalled. "She was much, much more mature and advanced than you would expect a teenager to be. She had a lot of the Arch Moore charisma and her mother's humility and consideration for others. She continued to develop both of those personality traits as she became a congresswoman. She just showed a tremendous respect for people and a determination to succeed in life." The future congresswoman was dating her future husband, Charles Capito of Charleston, during her father's second term as governor. "She always had a great group of friends," Col. Donohoe remarked. Her mother was more specific: "She was serious, but she loved the boys and had a ball finding the right one. She and Charlie met the year she was graduating from Duke [they would marry in 1976]. Even when she was in the spotlight, Shelley didn't complain."

Arch A. Moore, III (Kim) was "a quiet young man—meditative—but he delves into people's personalities and is very friendly," described his mother. Kim seemed to go through a period of "finding himself" during the Moores' first two gubernatorial terms. "If I was the family rebel, my brother was a close second," insisted Lucy Moore Durbin. A student at WVU, he was having difficulty living up to his father's reputation on that campus and elsewhere; expectations were high, and he was not a clone of the Governor, any more than Arch, Jr. had been of his own father. Kim was also paying for who he was, hearing a lot of catty comments about being the First Son. For every person who thought Arch Moore walked on water, there was another who passionately hated him, usually because of the simple fact that he was a Republican. The Morgantown campus then, as now, was heavily populated by students and faculty who were partisan Democrats, some of whom could say some pretty mean things to Kim about perceived (but false) assumptions that he was getting some type of special treatment, or just plain didn't like his father.

While he was a very polite, easy-mannered young man, in 1973, one WVU student pushed him too far with his bad-mouthing of Kim's dad, prompting a fight. He felt he had to defend his father's honor. "Kim whipped the s–t out of the SOB," was how Col. Donohoe bluntly put it. Kim couldn't remember details but admitted, "I have a flash anger. I can go to a point and then, 'That's it!' I was easy going about a lot of it," he insisted. He recalled one WVU teacher asking about his relationship to Arch Moore, with a negative tone to the inquiry. "I said, 'He's my father. I'll tell him you asked about him.' That shut him up."

"We had lived in Washington where everybody's dad was somebody," said a sympathetic Shelley Moore Capito. "But in Morgantown, it was hard for my brother. I mean, he had the same name as Dad [Arch A. Moore III].

"That was a volatile time, the Sixties and Seventies," continued Capito. "There was an underlying negative tone. My brother graduated [from high school] in 1969. There was a lot of friction between my brother and dad. My dad was obsessed with [the length of] his hair. The newspapers would be saying 'his hair was flowing.' It wasn't flowing, but it was long. But what a thing to argue about! Now my brother [in his early fifties] doesn't even have much hair," she laughed.

"People were growing their hair longer and I wanted to do the same," agreed Kim Moore. "It was never short enough for Dad and never long enough for me, no matter how often I had it cut. But I did get it cut [shorter] for a couple pictures here and there," he laughed. "My dad would often say to me, 'I don't understand how I can run a state so well but I can't handle my own son!'

"I struggled in school," Kim Moore admitted. "I was not taking [WVU] too seriously, for whatever reason. I'd tell my dad I was going to drop out and go work at Myrtle Beach. He'd say, 'So that's what you want to do, huh?' And then he'd warn me that he'd have state police at the border to prevent me from leaving," Kim laughed.

In the summer of 1973, daughter Shelley and a couple girlfriends decided they'd like to get a summer job somewhere adventurous. "How about Lake Tahoe?" one of the girls suggested. Shelley went to her dad with the plan. "He had friends everywhere. So he had this guy from Wheeling, Sig Front, who worked in Vegas and Dad called him and Sig said, 'Yeah, I'll help 'em.' We were only nineteen and the legal age to work in casinos was twenty-one.

"My parents asked, 'How are you getting out there?' I said, 'I'll take my car,' but they said, 'No, you're not.' My brother had dropped out of school at this point and he said, 'I'll take them!' So off we went and we had a blast." They piled into Kim's Chevy Malibu convertible ("All those bags made it a little tight," he recalled) and it took them five days to get to the Sahara at Lake Tahoe. Shelley and her two companions worked as bus girls that summer. Kim had planned to drive back as soon as he got them situated, but when the casino manager learned he was twenty-one, he offered him the job of bar tender. "He added, enticingly, 'You get to work with cocktail waitresses,' so I said, 'I'll take that job!'"

When it came time to leave Lake Tahoe, Kim Moore told his sister, "I'm staying." He drove the girls to San Francisco where they caught a flight back to West Virginia. "He'd changed majors," Capito explained. "He was wandering. He needed to get away, put some distance between [himself and West Virginia]. He really wasn't motivated in school. So he ended up staying there for four years, found his future wife and they moved to (her home-area) San Diego. His wife [Cathy] gave him a lot of focus and he ended up getting back into school and has had a great career in banking."

According to Donohoe, as a bartender, Kim made friends with several show girls/dancers (before he settled down and got married) and loved living in Tahoe. "I don't think his parents knew what all went on out there," Donohoe laughed. The young Moore would often phone Fred if he had a question or problem. "He'd ask, 'Can you help me with this? And don't bother my mom or dad about it.'" But Kim had "good relations with his parents," Donohoe insisted, "even though he was not pursuing life the way they preferred." Kim Moore "had the same determination genes" as his father, Donohoe thought, and was strong-willed about pursuing life in his own style and pace.

The Governor was "not pleased" that his son had dropped out of college to tend bar in Nevada, but eventually "he liked me out there," Kim said. "because he knew I was getting out on my own." There was another reason Moore rather enjoyed his son working at a casino for a time: "He's a helluva blackjack player; he can count cards. So he liked coming out by himself. And that would give us time to talk candidly." When two or three years had passed, though, and Kim had not resumed his education, his father would send him postcards reading, "Time is running out. Love, Dad." Kim would send his father a card with a beautiful scene from Tahoe reading, "Wish you were here. Love, Kim."

Their son did accompany his parents on one official trip during his Tahoe days. On their trip to the Orient, he enjoyed his time with the state trooper security detail, Lt. Donohoe and Trooper Guthrie. "They were good to me wherever we were," Kim added. "They became my hangin' out buddies." As soon as his parents would turn in, "We'd hit the night. In Hong Kong, we took off on a ferry boat. We went into a restaurant where you had to take off your shoes and the table was about a foot and a half off the floor. They served us deep-fried goldfish and Donohoe said, 'I need some steak!' Then, when we were on the streets, we said, 'Why don't we try the rickshaws out!' We decided to have a race in the rickshaws. I was about 140 pounds and Donohoe was probably 225, so I won!"

It would not be until 1978 that Kim would return to WVU, after marrying Cathy, and living in San Diego for a while. But he would get his

Master's of Business Administration degree and move on to become vice president of a Northern Virginia bank. There, far enough away from his well-known father, Kim began asking people to call him "Arch Moore."

In addition to their three children, the Moores enjoyed their extended family, the staff who worked with them on a daily basis. Some of them, like secretary Audrey Toler, "adopted" them as their honorary parents.

Audrey noted that "Christmas was Governor Moore's favorite time of the year. We always had a live Christmas tree in the governor's office reception room, fully decorated, and played Christmas carols." The Moores always made a big production of the outdoor, capitol Christmas tree lighting ceremony, a night time event, with lots of candles in which state employees would participate as a caroling choir. Arch "loved the decorations. He was very sentimental about Christmas; it was a special time, partly because it involved being with your family." His staff always had to work his schedule around family time, Toler added. And Christmas cards were big with the Moores; they sent out 5000 each year, for which, in pre-computer days, would take months for the secretaries to prepare addresses; they would begin preparing them in early autumn.

His staff would surprise Arch with birthday parties. "He loved to clown around," recalled Audrey. "He would often wear wild-looking, brightly colored, or plaid pants, in particular when he played golf. He'd put on oversized sunglasses so we could take photos."

As for the Governor and First Lady, they spent most of their spare time with friends like Dr. Tom and Maggie McCoy. Shelley and Maggie would go shopping, go to fairs together in the summer and take needlepoint classes in the winter months. Remembered Mrs. McCoy, "I was her buddy. Their family is our family and vice versa." Maggie would serve as one of the weekly Mansion tour guides on a volunteer basis. Like the Dudleys, "We started playing bridge with Arch and Shelley in 1969," she recalled. The McCoys were amazed that Arch could play bridge, work a crossword puzzle, converse with them and take phone calls, all at the same time. "I was the official gubernatorial tomato supplier," added Dr. McCoy. "I'd go down to the Mansion in my gardening clothes. The [security] state troopers always welcomed me–they were just part of the family." The four friends would sit around the Mansion in the evenings, enjoy conversation, and maybe even sing some songs. "I never remember Arch cursing, taking the Lord's name in vain, or using barracks language once when I was around him," recalled Tom. "We might sing a humorous, raunchy college song, but nothing bad." As to drinking, Arch might have one "Seven and Seven," a "nice Canadian blend," but never more than that, as he recalled. "I never saw Arch once with too much to drink. It was always measured, discreet. He would never get risque."[9]

McCoy and Moore would play golf at the Greenbrier "when he could get loose," and "they'd just lay that place out for him." The two never talked business or politics when on the golf course, he added. "One time we were on the twelfth tee of the Old White course and Arch'd had a good round. I said, 'By the way, Governor, about the med school ...' His ball veered off course. He stopped and said, 'Thomas, we've never talked business on the golf course.' I promised I'd never do it again. We were just two good ole boys having fun." According to Dr. Yoho, Moore's other best friend, the Moores would usually stay at the Top Notch cottage at the Greenbrier, "the same one Nixon used."

The Moores and McCoys would go off to New York once a year to conduct a little business—"Arch would go off to the World Trade Center"— and also to buy Christmas gifts for family and friends. "They'd go to Macy's and Saks and get all their shopping done at once." By blending business with their shopping trip, they could take a much-needed tax deduction as an expense, laughed McCoy.

Maggie McCoy summed up their lifelong friendship: "We have the comfort level friends have when they're not trying to impress each other." Arch and Shelley would need such trustworthy friends for the rocky days ahead during the next two decades.

Chapter 12 Notes

1. - The security force would increase to twenty-one troopers under Rockefeller.

2. - Morgan, Ibid.

3. - *Charleston Daily Mail,* Nov. 7, 1968.

4. - Years later when the roles reversed, and Congresswoman Shelley Moore Capito would need her father to cover for her at a dinner or event, she would phone and say, 'Dad, it's a CP.'" Arch Moore, April 22, 2005.

5. - After he left office in 1977, friends chipped in and bought the 1976 Lincoln from Ford and gave it to the Moores as a present. It has been parked in their Glen Dale residence's downstairs garage ever since, rarely in use, its interior leather still smelling new. "Our grandson took it to the prom a few years ago," smiled Mrs. Moore, noting that the tags expired in 2000. Moore also bought a desk he'd used as governor, which is his main office desk in Moundsville, to date.

6. - The movie legend had been in the Northern Panhandle, starring in the film "Fool's Paradise," which had been written by a West Virginian. The motion picture was premiered on June 17, 1971, at the Court Theater in Wheeling and Governor Moore made some opening remarks there.

7. - Col. William Fred Donohoe, April 5, 2005.

8. - A fictitious name used to protect the guilty.

9. - Although he socialized and vacationed with people like Lawson Hamilton at times, Dr. Tom McCoy, brother Harry Moore and Dr. David Yoho appear to have been Arch Moore's three truly intimate friends in his adulthood. Dr. Yoho agreed that Arch almost never had more than one drink. "He liked a good bourbon, something like V.O., on the rocks, with Seven Up on the side," he noted. Moore was rarely observed drinking any alcohol in public, though.

Chapter Thirteen
Arch, the Road Builder

Roads had been a problem since pre-historic times in that rugged, twenty-four thousand square mile patch of terrain known as West Virginia. The difficulty in moving through a territory with steep mountains that drop into narrow valleys was a reason that most of the area remained a largely uninhabited hunting reserve for most of the indigenous peoples. The few settlements of the Native Americans were restricted primarily to the rare level land near rivers and creeks. The few roads existing when the European settlers moved across the mountains were buffalo and deer trails that followed the contours of the mountains, as the herds moved to salt licks, pasture areas or to escape predators.[1] As those pioneers pushed westward, they generally went around this mountainous area, rather than through it, when at all possible, meaning that states with flatter terrains like Ohio and Illinois were more quickly and densely settled.

Until motor vehicles came along, forcing changes in the 1920s, most roads outside major West Virginia towns were unimproved. They were mainly dirt, which meant mud in the winter and spring months. Ashes, rock, gravel, were all that was available to keep them passable. Residents would pitch in with their shovels and mattocks to fill in the potholes, clear out mudslides, often using teams of mules to pull someone out of rut or to "work the road."

The National Road had been a dream of George Washington, completed from Cumberland, Maryland, through Western Pennsylvania, into Wheeling in 1819 (now U.S. Route 40). But decent roads through West Virginia were rare; the area remained isolated and heavily dependent on railways.

The Republican majority in the legislature pushed through the Good Roads Amendment of 1920, authorizing the issuance of a huge amount–$50 million in bonds–to pay for highway construction, and the first two-lane, paved roads began to make ground travel a little easier. The federal government helped finance roads that were used to deliver mail. In 1932, the Depression caused voters to approve amendments limiting the amount of money that could be raised from local property taxes, prompting the legislature to relieve counties of the responsibility of maintaining roads. Consequently, West Virginia is one of only four states in which there is no county ownership of highways.[2]

As millions of Americans bought cars and trucks and the vehicles' horsepower increased, many urban areas began constructing four-lane freeways to ease and speed traffic flow. Copying the autobahns he'd traveled in Germany, President Eisenhower began a network of these roads, which came to be known as the Interstate Highway System. It was initially promoted as a military, rather than transportation, expenditure in a time when it was easy to imagine having to evacuate cities because of a nuclear attack. The Appalachian Regional Commission, created in 1965, would open other opportunities for four lane road building in the multi-state region which included West Virginia.

Thus far, the new superhighways had largely passed West Virginia by. Construction of a two and three lane, somewhat dangerous West Virginia Turnpike, a toll road from Charleston to Princeton, had begun in 1954. However, only a few miles of I-77 between Ripley and Charleston, and a stretch of I-64 between Huntington and Dunbar were available to travelers when Arch Moore was elected governor in 1968. I-79, the highway expected to reduce that arduous, eight-hours-plus drive between Morgantown and Charleston, was still on the drawing board. There had been a lot of talk, meetings and planning by state officials since the Barron years, but very little concrete poured for the Interstate highway system in the Mountain State. Whether correct or not, there was a deep-seated perception among West Virginia's business community that the lack of four-lane highways was stunting the state's economic growth. They reasoned that new business and industry would not locate in a state in which it was so difficult to move products to the market.

There was also concern about existing roads and bridges, especially after the Silver Bridge Disaster. Old, fragile bridges would need the urgent attention of the new administration. (There would be no more fatalities from bridge collapses, thanks in no small part to the efforts of the Moore Administration.) Road issues would dominate, as they always had in the Mountain State for decades.

GETTING A LARGE portion of interstate highway built during the first years of his administration, in addition to better maintenance of existing highways and bridges, certainly seemed to be Arch Moore's chief goal when he took office in 1969. "I remember riding with my dad when we were campaigning in 1968," said Kim Moore. "We were on one of those very short spans of existing four-lane highway in the state, about five miles long, and he exclaimed, 'I'm gonna build roads, by god!'"

Quickly catching up with other states was critical, in Moore's view. He would not tolerate the inertia of the past eight years, time he felt was wasted by Barron and Smith. Some of it was altruistic, but much of his motive was purely political, he admitted. "I knew we had just three years to show what we could do," said Moore. "My plan had been to serve four years and do a great job as governor and then run for the U.S. Senate in 1972." The highways would have to be built at a frantic pace to meet his goal, something to which the existing bureaucracy, mainly political appointees of his two predecessors, would have difficulty adjusting.

The opportunity to fire striking road workers in the winter that he took office gave the new governor a chance to show he was tough, that he meant business about providing good, safe roads to the state. Arch also used some theatrics (one could never be sure whether his tantrums were genuine or staged for effect) to get his point across—that this was going to be a new era, and that he was expecting results. He told his highway commissioner, Bill Ritchie, to start making visible, noticeable changes. "Move the entrance door of your office, do whatever you need to do to show that someone new is in charge, that a new era has begun," he instructed Ritchie. He wanted to shake things up, as Kennedy had done in Washington, not simply settle for the status quo or even a slow pace of action.

Soon after taking office, Moore asked Ritchie to call a meeting of the State Road Commission (as it was then known) administrators and walked over to their office to speak to them. An astonished elevator operator asked him, "Are you who I think you are? I've worked here for decades and you're the first one of you [a governor] to ever come into this building!"

When he arrived in the lobby of the Highways office, the first thing Moore noticed was a "flow chart," what Arch called "a legend," on the walls of the waiting area, titled "How to Build a Mile of Road in West Virginia," illustrating the slow pace of new highway construction: six months for planning, then six months for a survey, six months for land acquisition and title work, and so forth. "I'm reading this, and when I got to the fourth year, we'd completed a mile of highway. I only had four years! I didn't have that kind of time!" Arch recalled. It was way too slow to suit this impatient, ambitious governor. He had Ritchie to climb up on a step ladder and tear it all down in front of the administrators, as a "visual," to illustrate to them that it wasn't going to be business as usual during the next four years. But he wasn't done with the theatrical; he wanted to get his point across, strongly, that a new and dynamic era had arrived in road building. He wanted to put the fear of Arch, if not God, in them.

Moore jumped up on a table, to better be seen and heard, and to be able to look down on his audience. He told the department holdovers, "I don't care if you're a Democrat or Republican, I just want to get this job done." According to Hoy Shingleton, Moore's appointed road supervisor in Hampshire County, Arch got red in the face as he shouted to those county leaders in another such meeting. "Governor Moore really got in those guys' faces," Hoy, Jr. remembered his dad telling. "He told them, 'But this is not going to be the politics of the past. You will either perform or you will not stay here!'" Whether feigned emotion or not, Arch got the point across. Most of the administrators were scared to death of the "Little White Haired Guy," as state employees would sometimes call him. That was fine by Arch Moore, who wanted to keep them guessing, keep them on their toes. This effort was to be conducted with urgency, like a war. "Arch succeeded in getting highways built by kicking do-less bureaucrats in the butt," as Richard Neely put it, bluntly. "He succeeded better than anyone."

Even Bill Ritchie, the historical figure who oversaw the building of most of the state's Interstate highway system, was not immune to "the Arch Moore treatment." The Governor would often get impatient with Commissioner Ritchie's excuses, for his defense of the bureaucratic delays or legal fine points. Behind the doors of the governor's office, the two argued constantly, sometimes in a very heated, loud, profane manner. "Bill resigned many, many times," recalled Audrey Toler, who served as a secretary to Moore for years. "He'd call and say, 'I'm coming over to give him my letter of resignation.' But then they would cool off, patch it up and go on."Observed Sandy Latimer, "Bill and Arch both had very strong wills, so they clashed a lot."[3]

Ritchie agreed, telling *The Charleston Daily Mail,* "I quit several times and he fired me several times. We sometimes wouldn't speak for days. I would write a letter of resignation and give it to my secretary. She just put it in her drawer and waited a day or so for me to cool off. Then the governor would get mad and fire me. His secretary would put my dismissal letter in her desk and wait for the Governor to reconsider. We both were both wanting the same thing. But there was a lot of pressure building the interstates. It was big money and a lot of people had ideas as to how we should do it."[4] When asked about the noisy bickering, Moore shrugged it off. "Every now and then, we'd get some good ideas," he said, simply, before going on to another topic.

Moore remembered one such conversation with Ritchie, though. "I discovered that smaller municipalities, like Cameron, for example, couldn't afford to pave roads going through their towns." He asked Ritchie why the State couldn't do it for them. "Because they're not in the system, that's why," Bill replied. When the Governor insisted that the Administration help some of these towns, Ritchie replied, "That's a little off the path!" Moore remembered.

"So I told Bill, what we'll do is take them into the [state highway] system on Sunday, pave it on Monday, and give it back to them on Tuesday." And that's what they did, for several small municipalities.[5] Again, Arch was thinking outside the box—before anyone called it that. The two–Moore and Ritchie—had been friends since WVU days, when both were on intramural teams, both Betas, married and lived a block apart. They ended up being dependent on each other, and were both extremely knowledgeable, capable and dedicated when it came to creating new and better West Virginia highways. They knew each other's minds; they ultimately held the same goals; they both had huge egos and strong wills.

Few thought Ritchie could be persuaded to return for a third term in 1985 (and take a pay cut from his private sector job) after all the grief and pressure his former boss had given him. But Moore turned on the charm and appealed to his patriotism. "Will you walk with me one more time and get this job done?" he asked his friend. Ritchie, who still had some aspirations of being governor himself, and who enjoyed being a father of the West Virginia interstate highway system, could not resist. Although Ritchie had little to say about his comrade after Moore went to prison, Arch had nothing but good things to say about Ritchie, and seemed genuinely concerned about his health and well-being and sympathized with his loss of a son.

Call it luck, serendipity, playing the cards dealt you, God's will, right-place-at-the-right-time, or whatever: Arch Moore was very fortunate to take office in 1969, weeks after the state's voters had just approved the largest road bond issue ever. The Roads Development Amendment, passed by 366,958 to 159,971 votes in November 1968, had authorized the borrowing of $350 million. Calling it "the highest priority," Arch immediately asked the Legislature to approve the issuance of $70 million along with another $20 million from a prior bond amendment. He was going to leverage this money to get started on highway construction, getting as much as 90 percent federal matching funds, in many cases. The funds, from the ARC[6] and federal highways funds, were available, awaiting claim. Within five months, the state went from last to first place in road construction in the nation, ending his first year with almost $200 million to be spent on highways, as he noted, "far surpassing any previous twelve-month period in the history of our state." (That employment was the highest and unemployment the lowest in state history that year added to a sense of excitement, satisfaction that West Virginia indeed "was moving along," as his campaign jingle had promised.) "A lot of our time was initially spent on planning, design and financing," Arch said. "We viewed our methods as 'pre-financing,' assuming that federal money would come in, and we would gain three years." (Road construction was experiencing inflation like everything else. That mile of four lane, that had cost the prior Underwood Administration a million dollars per mile, now cost several million dollars per mile to build. Time was of the essence, as they say.)

One of many controversies Moore and Ritchie faced was choosing the path of I-64 as it passed through or near the state's capital. While one faction wanted it to go through Charleston, another argued that it go around, as a beltway. A few weeks of dealing with the city's traffic jams, the fact the town needed more bridges to handle heavy trucks, and that 70 percent of motorists then using the Interstate wanted to go to Charleston anyway, convinced Ritchie a through-route was the best choice. But the *Gazette* fought a downtown route, tooth and nail. ("Their opposition delayed it for years and cost us $40 million more to build it," Moore charged.)

"I finally told [the opponents to a downtown path], 'Sorry, we're not using your suggestions,' and said, 'I'm not waiting,'" Moore recalled about the project. He began building an elevated highway for much of its path, through the business district of Charleston, as had been done in larger cities, "and we destroyed nothing underneath." Five badly-needed new bridges for the capital city resulted from it taking a downtown path. Another unintended, but welcome result occurred. Scores of run-down houses had to be removed to make way for the highway, providing some urban renewal as a side benefit. (That the I-64 bridge crossing the Kanawha River—with its two on-ramps, two off-ramps—would become too busy and often the most dangerous place in the state for motorists, was also an unintended and unforseen result.) Moore recalled that, when the ribbon was cut for I-64 to open through the city, former Charleston Mayor John Shanklin "cried like a baby." As he shook Moore's hand, he said, "I never thought I'd live long enough to see it become reality."

Perhaps because of his war-time engineering school background, Governor Moore took a personal interest in the minutest details of every road project. He was meticulous about, not only getting the projects done, but also getting them done right. "I think he knew the torsion on every bolt on every bridge his administration built," laughed Fred Donohoe. "He demanded excellence in everything. He was a nuts-and-bolts guy."

He remembered that Moore had demanded that the four lane which eventually would become I-68 be built in more durable, stable and visible concrete, rather than asphalt. "We were flying back from the White House and the weather was degenerating badly. We were bouncing, getting beaten around, when we were near the West Virginia-Maryland line. The Governor was looking out the window at the construction of the road when he saw a black strip below. He asked me, 'Lieutenant, do you see asphalt down there?' and I replied, 'Yes, sir.' He asked again, 'That's on the West Virginia side, isn't it?' When I agreed, he had me tell the pilot to make another pass over it. The pilot was pissed off to have to do that in such bad weather, so he did a sharp bank and u-turn, taking us in really low; everyone was hanging on.

"When we got over it again, Arch said, 'That *is* asphalt!' and he demanded that Bill Ritchie come see him immediately when we got back." Donohoe phoned Ritchie at home in Ravenswood that night to let him know he'd been summoned. Ritchie had to get dressed to come to the Mansion, all the time protesting that whatever it was could surely wait until morning. He made some phone calls once he got to the kitchen area of the governor's residence, ascertaining that the road indeed was asphalt, but that it was a haul road, not the final, four-lane highway. He assured the Governor that the road he was building was concrete.

By the time Moore had finished his first two terms, most of I-79 would be finished. Perhaps more than any other, that highway—cutting through the center of the state, connecting from Erie, Pennsylvania, through Pittsburgh, then the Morgantown-Fairmont-Clarksburg corridor before ending in Charleston—transformed, opened up West Virginia more than any other. While some, like humorist and *West Virginia Hillbilly* editor Jim Comstock, bemoaned the fact that the superhighways by-passed (and helped dry-up some locally owned, mom and pop businesses in) the small towns along the way, most motorists greatly appreciated the convenience and time-savings. "Getting I-79 finished was a wonderful thing," said Lysander Dudley. "Before it was finished, it was at least a four-to-five hour drive to a WVU game [from Charleston]. You'd get up early, drive up there in the fog, usually to watch the Mountaineers get the sh—t kicked out of them, and then take the long drive back." The highway would shorten that drive almost in half. "I would ride with the Governor in his helicopter to games, and I can remember how exciting it was to watch [from the air] the construction of I-79."

At the end of Moore's second term, John Morgan would write about the remarkable record:

> Many highway construction records were broken dur-

> ing the eight years under Moore. The sights and sounds of heavy road-building equipment became increasingly familiar along the main highway arteries during this period. Great concrete pillars, elevated roadways, high retention walls, new Kanawha and Elk River bridges and complex interchange systems appeared in the Charleston area as construction neared completion of three interstate highways within the city. It was all a part of the process of opening up West Virginia, the heart of Appalachia. As Moore prepared to leave office [in 1976], the main statistics were: 184 miles opened to traffic and 52 still under construction in the Interstate system, 206 opened and 42 under construction in the Appalachian [Corridor] system, an additional 1,364 miles built and 7,647 improved [in secondary highways], all at a cost of $1.8 billion. Moore's highway construction achievements were aided tremendously by road bond amendments approved by the people in 1964, 1968, and 1973 in amounts totaling more than $1 billion. About $700 million of this money was made available for Moore to spend or obligate under contract.[7]

And then, by the end of his third term, all of I-64 would be finished, from Wayne County to the Virginia line, helping make it one of the nation's main arteries. Only a few stretches of those roads were built under other administrations, beginning with Cecil Underwood's first term. Much of I-68 and other Interstate highways were also built and completed under Moore's terms.

At the outset of Moore's tenure, the West Virginia Turnpike (started in 1954, but still a dangerous two- and three-lane road)[8] was burdened by bonded indebtedness and, because its ends had not yet been connected to other Interstate highways, was essentially useless to all but local traffic. One of Arch's first memories as governor was *Gazette* reporter Don Marsh, sitting on a crate outside his office, shouting out, "On what date do you expect the Turnpike to go bankrupt?" In usual fashion, the new Governor responded, "Mr. Marsh, it will never go bankrupt on my watch." Arch made adjustments to the tolls and had to fight Transportation Secretary John Volpe to even keep them on. "When I reminded Volpe that Jacksonville, Florida and Dayton, Ohio then had toll portions of Interstate highway and that he'd have to ban those, too, he backed down, and we were able to keep the Turnpike under tolls and solvent." (Before leaving office, Moore would reduce the number of tolls to three on the highway, turn the road into a much safer four- to six-lane highway, and keep it in the black. "Now, it's a cash cow," Moore remarked in 2004.)[9]

In 1986, Moore was able to cut the ribbon, re-opening the Turnpike as a four-lane, Interstate highway, I-77. And while Senator Byrd was properly accredited with turning U.S. Route 19 between I-79 and Beckley into a superhighway, Moore first made it possible by building the New River arch bridge. Although never the boon to drawing additional jobs, business and industry, as had been hoped and expected, the new roads changed life as West Virginians had known it and helped unite the state's people. These modern highways would have signs bearing other names: Underwood, Randolph, Byrd and Smith, all of whom were important in planning the routes and keeping the road-building dollars coming. The efforts of Presidents Eisenhower and Kennedy cannot be overlooked, as well. But most of these superhighways were constructed during the Moore-Ritchie tenure by aggressive and creative use of federal dollars and those who were "in the know" (even Jennings Randolph) acknowledged that.

At the end of the day, it was the Arch Moore team that made it happen. More than any other individual, Arch and Bill Ritchie were the "fathers" of the four-lane highway system in the Mountain State. Because of Moore's ultimate disgrace in 1990, however, his adversaries were able to erase his name from that great accomplishment.

Much, in fact, was accomplished with regard to road construction just in Moore's first three years of office. The new roads, safety and convenience they created, the feeling that progress had come, helped get him re-elected in 1972.[10] Without Moore's push-push-push, there is no question that the projects would have been delayed for many years, would have cost much more, and in some cases, may not have been built at all. As the corridor highways are largely Robert Byrd's monuments, the remainder—the majority of the West Virginia four-lanes—are concrete (and asphalt) reminders of what Arch did for his state—the most lasting and permanent of his accomplishments. Moore's constant pushing the bureaucracy, sometimes seemingly unrelenting agitation to "get it done," his leadership on highway construction, changed life for West Virginians more than any other project in memory. About 504 miles of Interstate and Appalachian highways were built during Moore's three terms, moving more than a billion cubic yards of dirt at a cost of $2.6 billion.[11]

But, again, there would be no public acknowledgment of the fact that

Moore built the highways; no sign, no monument documents that for future generations. Only a bridge on a four-lane in Jackson County would be named for Bill Ritchie. But those who lived in West Virginia in the 1970s knew the truth.

Quite a few of the routes for the Interstate highways had already been chosen before Moore took office, however. In a 2004 interview, Moore confirmed prevailing rumors that many such route choices were aimed primarily at making local Democratic leaders wealthy, by crossing land they owned. "When the Democrats built a new road, the first thing they looked at was who owned the land." He admitted that in Marion County, for example, much of the land for I-79's eastern, circuitous route around Fairmont had been owned by two powerful Democratic judges, who added to their personal wealth by the state's purchase of their hills and fields. (The route, several miles from the city, may have hastened downtown Fairmont's business decline.) "My policy was, 'the hell with that,'" remembered Moore. "I said, 'Let's just build the road.'"[12]

Speaking of benefits, Moore's campaign coffers also benefitted from the massive road building campaign. Especially during the 1972 re-election effort, hundreds of thousands were donated by the contractors–the engineers, excavators, suppliers, trucking companies, gravel and concrete companies, and others. The Governor reportedly told them, "If you want to keep building these roads, you've got to keep us in office." Ethics were far laxer in those days and it was not considered unusual to invite such contractors to fund raising events and give them a hard sales pitch, as Ritchie reportedly did on a Kanawha River cruise. It was an advantage of incumbency, as Moore's Democratic predecessors had learned in the past. A lot of money was being made and the recipients were expected to pay up, to share some of it, specifically, to reward the one who was making it possible.

Secondary roads were not being neglected during this great undertaking. During Moore's terms, 12,816 miles of road were resurfaced at a cost of about $842 million. He rebuilt or repaired 746 bridges.[13] Moreover, he did not forget about air transportation, building or expanding eleven airports during his tenure.

In the course of such massive road-building, many large and beautiful bridges were constructed, in accordance with Arch's plans. He loved the details of how they would look, as well as the purpose they served. The New River Bridge, for years the longest span of its kind in the world (and featured on the West Virginia quarter), was an Arch Moore design (called an "arch" bridge, pun, no doubt, intended). He had some fun with his opponents as he announced that design at an Oak Hill meeting. He drew a rough sketch for the crowd and then playfully drew an "A" and "M" as support beams beneath it. Taking him seriously, state Sen. Pat Hamilton, a Democrat, ran out of the room, yelling at a reporter, "My god, he's going to put his initials under the bridge!" (So high is this beauty that it is the site of "Bridge Day" each October, when BASE jumpers parachute from it to the New River banks below.) Ironically, the span originally was intended to be a suspension bridge and was 90 percent along in the planning stages, when Ritchie realized it could not support the load because of coal mines on both sides of the gorge. "That's when we came up with the arch design." Engineers came from all over the world to study and copy it. The magnificent structure would be opened sixty days after Moore left office in 1977.

Moore was proud that he put at least thirteen large new bridges across the Ohio River alone.[14] One of those was a cable-stayed span at 31st Street in Huntington, which would be known as the East End Bridge. As often would happen, Moore had difficulty getting the community to agree upon where it should be located. The city fathers fought and fussed over the subject and gave him no clear consensus of what was wanted. So he had some fun with that one, too. He called a press conference to announce the location. "I've decided where we will place it," he told the eagerly-awaiting crowd. "I'm going to build it on a barge in Pt. Pleasant and then move it here when you've decided where you want to place it." Another similar structure was built across the Ohio in Weirton and Moore was quick to have an "opening" before he left office in 1988, although it would not actually be ready for traffic until his successor took over.

Progress on these projects was neither smooth nor easy, as two bridge incidences in the Weirton area illustrate.

Governor Moore had pushed to get the Weirton bridge built quickly, so he could take credit for it, while still in office. When Ritchie questioned how in the world he could meet Moore's requirement that it be built twice as fast as normal, the Governor had a solution: two construction companies would begin portions of the project on the Ohio and West Virginia sides, and meet in the middle. Ritchie thought it just might work, and bids were let for two builders, for portions of one job, and that's the way it and others were done.

A few months into the two-contractor project, he rushed into the Governor's office one afternoon, all in a dither. "We've got a big problem," Ritchie announced. Perspiring, the road commissioner told his boss that the engineer had surveyed it and projected that the two ends were not going to meet in the middle of the span. When completed, one end was going to end up about six feet higher than the opposing end. They were going to be the laughingstock of the state, if not the entire nation.

First thing an alarmed Moore whispered to Ritchie was: "Who all knows about this?"

When assured just the three knew–Moore, Ritchie and the engineer—the Governor offered the solution. "You will have the side that has progressed the least, partially torn down and started again at the correct angle." It was quietly and quickly accomplished and neither the news media nor the public, ever found out about it.

In another such Weirton bridge project, it is fortunate that several of the participants did not go to jail. But it was another example of Moore's common-sense ingenuity, solving what could have been a big problem with a simple solution.

The Veterans Memorial Bridge, a span across the Ohio River from Weirton to Steubenville, had the green light except for one small problem: there was a small, historical building directly in its path on the Ohio side and that state was not interested in moving it to allow the bridge project to begin. Subject of the controversy was a log structure that had served as the first land office of the Northwest Territory. It wasn't even on its original location, so the land on which it sat was not of special significance. Nevertheless, because of its historic significance, it was considered a "4F project," protected by all sorts of governmental regulations and requiring months, if not years, of federal bureaucratic study, public hearings, comment periods and so forth, a delay that was intolerable to the impatient Arch Moore.

Some advocated re-routing the new bridge around the structure, but by the time it was realized that this would be a problem, surveys had been made, land purchased, factions on both sides appeased as to the route choice, and it would present another unacceptable delay of many months to start again from scratch. "When Jim Rhodes was governor of Ohio, I could pick up the phone and get a quick resolution on a problem like this," Moore noted. "But by now it was Gov. Gilligan and, although we'd served in Congress together, I didn't enjoy the same type of relationship with him." (Rhodes was Republican and Gilligan a Democrat, he might have added.)

State Senator Sam Kusic came up with an audacious solution: that the small log building simply be moved out of the way. It was just outrageous enough to capture Moore's attention and consent.

Soon after Sam's proposal, the Governor called Col. Bonar and Fred

Donohoe of the Dept. of Public Safety to his office to review a plan. The state policemen were instructed to report at precisely two a.m. to a particular parking lot in Steubenville, where they would receive further instructions. No more information was given to them at that point, because of the secrecy of the mission.

There they discovered their role in the clandestine expedition. As pre-arranged, an Ohio crane operator met the two men. They quickly belted the log structure to the crane and it was gently and carefully removed, unharmed, into a nearby field, outside the path of the proposed bridge.

A day or two later, a puzzled Bill Ritchie reported to Moore's office. "Governor, the damndest thing has happened. That building we talked about, that was holding up the Weirton bridge, has mysteriously disappeared!" The bridge went on as planned, with no further controversy.

Some of the road innovations Arch Moore wanted to make did not survive, due to lack of money or failure of his successors to follow up. An example was his interest in installing heating elements in Interstate bridges to use in ice and snow. "A study in Vancouver, British Columbia, proved that it saves money because you don't have to use salt [which necessitates costly repairs to the structure]," noted Henry Payne. "If the bridges have enough slope, it melts the snow and it drains off. It would especially be cost-effective in West Virginia where electricity generated from coal is relatively cheap." Payne's engineering company had installed a test unit at Milepost 29 on I-64, which did not escape Governor Moore's eye. The former engineering student phoned Payne and, telling him that he notice the bridge because of "a slight ripple" asked whether he could provide a quote on installing heating elements in the Nitro bridges. But, alas, Gov. Caperton did not follow up with Moore's proposal. Payne noted that the DOH obtained enough money to heat one bridge, at Pliny, West Virginia, but it was too flat to drain properly. Who knows how many lives, cars and bridges would have been saved had Moore's dream of heating bridges been fulfilled?

But at the end of their three terms, Ritchie was very proud of what they, along with hundreds of dedicated Highways employees, had accomplished over twelve years. "I keep thinking to myself," he told a *Daily Mail* reporter, "how many lives have been saved by those four-lane roads?"

When asked, in 2005, what he thought his greatest accomplishment in public life had been, Arch Moore answered without hesitation: roads. "Before we came into office, the attitude had been, 'When we get the money in the bank, we'll let contracts on the [new] highways.' That was their creed. But I only had four years. I was not going to wait. If you know the federal dollars were coming, you sell bonds now and let the contracts on the roads and bridges. We built 95 percent of the four lane highways in eight years."

Norm Roush, who had been deputy commissioner of Highways since 1965, summed it up in an interview with the *Daily Mail* upon his retirement forty years later. When he began in the department, "we had 50 to 60 miles of four-lanes in the whole state. It took five and a half hours to drive [from Charleston] to Fairmont. Now you can make it to Martinsburg in less time than that."[15]

The better highways have not yet made West Virginia an industrial center but did make the state a far more pleasant and safer place in which to live, work and travel. In large part, today's motorist can thank Arch Moore and Bill Ritchie for that convenience.

Chapter 13 Notes

1. - According to lore, a large portion of the dirt road that became U.S. Route 19 began as a winding buffalo trail.

2. - George Hohmann, *Charleston Daily Mail*, June 16, 1999.

3. - Toler thought that Ritchie's "frustration level [at least, in Moore's third term] was because of funding issues," primarily. She noted that, four years in a row, Ritchie had sought an extra nickel tax on a gallon of gas, but the Democratic legislature would not approve it until Caperton took office. "We had no matching state monies" to qualify for federal road funds, as had been possible in Moore's first two terms. "And, of course, Governor Moore would want [Ritchie] to come up with money to pave everywhere," but it couldn't be done in that third term.

4. - *The Charleston Daily Mail*, Dec. 2, 1988.

5. - Moore, Aug. 19, 2005.

6. - Gov. Marvin Mandel of Maryland and Sen. Robert F. Kennedy of New York actually got more highways funded through the ARC than other Appalachian states, although their states were among the wealthiest in the nation; it had little semblance to the stated goal of fighting Appalachian poverty, but just a slightly-disguised pork barrel project.

7. - Morgan, Ibid.

8. - At one point, while accompanied by Speaker Lew McManus in Beckley, Governor Moore announced that he was going to convert the entire Turnpike into a six-lane highway. "McManus left the meeting, called [Senator] Jennings Randolph, and my plan was [thwarted]," Moore remembered.

9. - It eventually had so much excess revenue that his successor, Gaston Caperton, was able to use Turnpike funds to build the arts and crafts center, Tamarack, which he allowed to be named for himself. Caperton kept the tolls on the Turnpike, even though studies showed they could be reduced, if not eliminated.

10. - The voters passed an amendment in 1970, allowing a governor two terms, and Randolph ran for re-election to the Senate, so Arch opted to seek re-election, which will be discussed later.

11. - *Charleston Daily Mail*, Dec. 2, 1988.

12. - Moore stated that it was rare for a special road to be built to please a particular office-holder but that he did build a mile of highway in Braxton County once to fulfill a request by Senate President Hans McCourt, whom Arch admired. "When they criticized me on that, I responded, 'Every highway benefits someone!"

13. - The *Charleston Daily Mail*, Dec. 2, 1988

14. - Moore interview, March 26, 2004.
15. - Feb. 17, 2005 interview by George Hohmann, *Charleston Daily Mail.*

Chapter Fourteen
"He Knew How to Fleece the Federal Government!"

While campaigning in 1968, Moore's eyes were for the first time fully opened to the plight of West Virginians in the lowest economic stations of life. He became compassionate about helping them. His dream was to offer medical care to the poor, either at low or no cost.

Unfortunately, the only mechanism with which he had to work as governor, the State Department of Health, was staffed by elderly and less adventurous people, some of whom were Director N. H. Dyer's (himself in his nineties) relatives, and they were not accustomed to the rapid pace at which Moore hoped to introduce improvements in health care. There was bureaucratic resistance to his proposals. So Moore allowed six of the board members' terms expire without removing them. The move essentially made Dr. Dyer a "will and pleasure" director since, at any time, the Governor could appoint a new board who could remove him. "Arch was always two steps ahead of everyone else" in planning such strategies, noted one who followed his strategies of management. It got Dr. Dyer's attention, and the department became more cooperative.

Since at least the 1930s, coal company physicians had serviced the primary care needs of many West Virginia families. By the time Moore took office, however, many of the companies no longer offered that service. Others company doctors had retired, died, or gone elsewhere. There was a crisis and need to replenish family physicians was not being met by the state's lone medical school at West Virginia University.[1] Occasionally, a high-caliber physician would come to rural West Virginia to practice family medicine, for altruistic reasons, or to try out a new method of treatment. But that was rare. More often, rural and coal camp residents were unable to find nearby physicians to set broken bones, deliver babies, give them antibiotics, and treat grandma's high blood pressure.

Governor Smith had established a regional public health care/emergency services/health education project in a nine-county region of Southern West Virginia to respond to the crisis. "There were all these idealistic people who came in from California to run it. Plus, the director's son, Allen Dyer, was overseeing the project," explained one who was involved, noting that the project was controversial and without widespread support, as result.

Moore decided to use newly-available federal funds from the Appalachian Regional Commission to set up what would eventually provide thirty-five primary health care clinics throughout the state, a few of which survive to this day. Moore's staff had initially sought funding from Health, Education and Welfare. But that federal department wanted to spend three times more than what was needed, to establish hospital-type facilities, which would not exactly fit the real world need. To get around HEW's rigid bureaucratic restrictions for such grants, Moore's people would order pre-fabricated buildings delivered by trucks, which allowed them to be called "mobile units," even though they were placed on permanent foundations and used as clinics. "Governor Moore was real creative about how he spent federal dollars,"recalled Beth High, who as a member of his administration, oversaw the creation of the clinics. "We adopted his unspoken attitude about the feds: 'Screw 'em when you can!' Get what you can from the federal government and give back as little as possible."

Tom Tinder, who served Moore in all three terms, agreed. As a compliment to his former boss Tinder said, "He knew how to fleece the federal government!" As chairman of the Appalachian Regional Governor's Conference, Moore had added clout with the controllers of the ARC purse-strings and in other such federal agencies, as well.

High recalled that the directors of the regional medical program at WVU's medical school did everything they could to sabotage Moore's health clinic plan, apparently viewing it as unwanted competition for funding, or purely as part of a turf battle. "But many from WVU: the pharmacists, former agriculture extension people, and others–got in under the radar screen and unofficially helped us a lot. They were good community development people who helped make the clinics work."

Moore's staff was unable to create a "showcase system," said High. "We could only get enough money initially to set up four clinics. We told them we would get government assistance for only one year and then they were on their own; they had to become self-sufficient." Some would survive, but some did not. The UMWA health and retirement fund put many of the clinics on retainer and "it kept them going month after month," said High. "Soon we were delivering basic family health care to areas that didn't have it before. The feds eventually patterned their system in other states based on what we did in West Virginia." These clinics, initially started with ARC money, "remain the basis for West Virginia's primary health care system today," High pointed out. "We probably have more of those than any state in the union."

Physicians were recruited. "Some came from the National Health

Service Corp," she recalled. "They were people who had gone to med school on scholarships that required they practice for a period on an Indian reservation or in a poor, rural area. Some were even from Harvard's med school, physicians who had ideas about how a health system should be run."

MOORE'S STAFF WAS persistent in pursuing ARC grants for these and other projects. Beth High made numerous trips in the state plane to the ARC office in DuPont Circle, at the nation's capital, carrying box loads of grant applications, especially toward the end of their fiscal year, when such agencies are more apt to dispose of unused funds, so they can qualify for more. "We utilized combined data bases [from different state agencies] to obtain statistics and got 100% of our applications approved, even if we had to rewrite the applications occasionally."

Brenda Nichols-Harper soon found herself working with High, Ben Green, Carl Bradford and others in the Governor's office to obtain as many federal grants as possible for the Mountain State. "Having been in Congress, Governor Moore was still well-connected to what was going on in Washington," she said. "So if he heard that some federal agency had been authorized to provide grants, before the President's ink was dry on the bill, he'd say, 'Let's put a grant together for West Virginia!'" They would have more success that they ever expected, in getting federal dollars into the state for worthwhile projects. "I became aware of how powerful the governor's office is in West Virginia," Nichols-Harper said.

As would be true in all three of Moore's terms, younger people such as Brenda were common; the under-thirty crowd was heavily represented, as was the under-forty. "Governor Moore attracted young people to government like none other," Nichols-Harper thought. "He thought our best and brightest were here. And you look around and see what [scores of people who began their careers working for Arch Moore] are now doing with their lives and you see that he made good choices. I'm humbled by the company." He chose his administration well, she thought; what they did during his terms, and subsequent to serving him, proved that Arch rarely made poor personnel choices.

Tom Tinder agreed. "I've heard criticism, especially about the third term, that Governor Moore just brought in young people to work for him because he could mesmerize them with his strong personality. But they were good people and had a strong desire to get things done for the state." Plus, Tinder correctly observed, aggressive state government is a younger man or woman's job; they have more stamina, energy, creativity, willingness to work long hours, which more than compensates for lack of experience in most situations. People into their fifties and sixties lose some of that drive, the enthusiasm of youth and their ability to look at a problem afresh and try new solutions.

It wasn't a glamourous life for these young grant writers, even though the results of their work was so important, affecting so many lives in a positive manner. Nichols-Harper remembered that the young group worked in cubicles in the cubby-hole offices near the capitol rotunda (now occupied by the legislature). "We were state of the art," she laughed. "Xerox machines were just coming out, so we didn't have to make copies [the slow and awkward way] with onion skin paper and carbon, like many offices were still doing." And in a pre-computerized word processing era, they had "mag cards" which allowed hundreds of pages of boilerplate to be added to each grant application. "We'd crank out [two or three inches thick] of the same documents for each one, outlining West Virginia's demographics, its needs." Being able to include such voluminous documentation in each grant request, a common practice today, increased their rate of success in obtaining approval.

Economic Development Administration grants would allow small towns to provide comprehensive training to potential employees, Brenda recalled. "It would allow local governments to teach unemployed people how to be policemen, maintenance workers, whatever they needed."

One program they were able to initiate, by getting federal grants, particularly stuck in her memory as worthwhile. "We were able to set up a network of respiratory disease centers for victims of black lung, working through existing hospitals. We discovered that there were only three pulmonary physicians—Drs. Rasmussen, Gaziano and Jim Walker—in the entire state, but they agreed to serve on an advisory panel [which satisfied a federal requirement]. You take what you have in West Virginia and maximize it. We had a lot of advisory panels in those days, which was a new thing for state government then, although there are lots of them today." Part of what they did was educate the miners and their spouses on how to deal with the effects of the black lung. "They were able to teach them how to make it easier day-to-day by using loafers, pull-over shirts, the importance of staying hydrated, and how to do respiratory percussion to relieve the phlegm."

Moore would also use millions of available Appalachian Regional Commission dollars to help local communities build water systems, sewer projects and vocational centers. "ARC was a relatively new entity," continued Nichols-Harper. "Federal funds for highways were maximized by the Governor through ARC, but most of the other state agencies hadn't come to the grant-providing solution" until Moore's federal-state grant-seeking group worked the system aggressively.

"The funding formula was usually half federal money and the other half state and local," said High. "But we'd get ARC to kick in thirty percent, so the state or local government [applicant] would only have to match twenty percent [to come up with their half]."

"The ARC was a great program for governors to play politics with," thought Ron Pearson, who served as Moore's assistant tax commissioner, F&A commissioner and as State Treasurer. "Many of the southern governors would not spend all their allocated ARC money—I don't know what was going on with those people!" Moore, on the other hand, would spend his own, then obtain unused ARC funds from other states, Pearson recalled. "And he would never pay it back! What were they going to do to him?" Plus, Pearson noted, while the ARC might not like the "creative" ways Moore used their money, they needed his support to stay in business and get the same level of funding the next year. "He was one of their best advocates. He would always go to Congress and testify on behalf of more ARC funding." While the ARC staffers did not love Arch Moore, they definitely respected him, said Pearson. "He convinced them that they couldn't go to Congress next year, without spending all their money the previous year."

A young director of ARC for the Philadelphia region finally got tired of Moore's "creativity" in drawing more ARC funds than most states and using them for practical projects, ones Washington bureaucrats hadn't thought up. He shouted, "Your governor doesn't know what's going on," recalled High. He was going to explain to Moore "how it was going to be." When he demanded to meet with Moore in order to read him the riot act, High and fellow staffers were quick to let the Governor know he was coming and that he had an agenda. "That guy could never get on the Governor's calendar for months," she laughed. "When he finally did get in to see him, the Governor told *him* how it was going to be! All he could do is sit there and say, 'Yes, sir, Yes, sir.'"

Jennings Randolph was also one the ARC wanted to keep happy, since he was a senior U.S. Senator with a lot of control over the federal purse strings–and he had been the father of the Appalachian Regional Commission more than anyone else. Randolph would often join his efforts with Moore's staff to find ways to deliver needed services to the Mountain State. One of the many endeavors on which they cooperated was the creation of the Marshall University medical school, which partnered with the Veterans Administration hospital near Huntington. Moore announced the creation of that school during his second term and included funding for it in his budget (although it would not become reality until 1977).

In his usual fashion, Governor Moore had discussed his Marshall med school proposal with no one before his dramatic announcement. "Even those of us who worked for him never knew anything; we had to read about it in the papers," chuckled Ron Pearson. As expected, the directors of the existing school at WVU "went ballistic," remembered Pearson. "They claimed the state could not have two medical schools, even though Marshall was going to focus on rural health." Opposition in the legislature to the Marshall project was fierce, Pearson recalled, especially from Kanawha County members. (Dr. Tom McCoy was one of Arch's closest personal friends. But as president of the West Virginia State Medical Association, he opposed it publicly. Dr. McCoy contended that "the state could not adequately fund one med school, let alone two.")

And, without consulting the Governor, a defiant Board of Regents Chancellor Ben Morton simply failed to include the Marshall medical school in the higher education budget he sent to the legislature. Moore called a press conference the next day, stating that he had fired Morton and that, until further notice, college and university matters would be overseen by F&A Commissioner Pearson. The Commissioner had all the outstanding state college invoices boxed up and placed in his office for dramatic effect and newspaper photographers captured what a significant matter it was.

"Morton didn't know that Moore had no authority to fire him," Pearson laughed. "He came to my office, teeth chattering in fear." Morton's power and office was eventually restored and he "got with the program." Arch's point had been made. In the Governor's view, the Board of Regents was to carry out the policy established by the governor and legislature, not create its own agenda.

And Moore would not stop with two medical schools. Said Beth High, "Two old osteopathic physicians, who'd been practicing by the seat of their pants, bought the former Greenbrier Military School in Lewisburg[2] and wanted to start a school there. I went to look at the facility and never thought it could be turned into a medical school."

They called it The Greenbrier College of Osteopathic Medicine and accepted thirty-six students when the doors opened in 1974. High continued, "With federal grants it just got turned around. Arch Moore made it happen. He knew how to get federal funding, having been a congressman for twelve years." With Moore pushing it through, the school became a public institution in January of 1976, and was renamed The West Virginia

School of Osteopathic Medicine. The first D.O.s would graduate from there in June of 1978. Many would go into family practices, others obtaining advanced credentials in orthopedic surgery, even psychiatry, doing everything M.D.s could do.

The competition produced by these two new medical schools caused WVU's school to be more attentive to the needs of the state, High believed; they no longer saw themselves as simply a research institution. They finally began trying to keep their students in-state after graduation.

Another result of getting the federal money into the state was the initiation of regional government. With fifty-five independent counties, all jealously protecting their turf, and many too small to qualify for grants, Moore knew that it was time to consolidate efforts and get them to work together toward common goals and needs.

"State law allowed Regional Planning and Development Councils," said Nichols-Harper. "What the Governor was trying to do was prepare and plan for what they were doing, where they were going. It was the first regional plan" for the state, she noted. Putting these eleven Regional Planning and Development Councils together in 1971 educated the county and municipal leaders as to what was available from the state and federal government, allowed them to coordinate and pool their intelligence, experience, efforts and resources and, in the end, get far more for their communities than they otherwise could have done. Eventually, the communities were looking at emergency services, transportation, mental health facilities, infrastructures, and other issues on a multi-county, multicity, regional basis, which made far more sense.

Before Habitat for Humanity was popularized by Jimmy Carter, Arch Moore's people built more than two hundred homes for low income West Virginians, using six panelization factories set up around West Virginia through the state's OEO. Through another grant, the medical examiner program was established and criminal justice programs were started at Marshall, Parkersburg Community College and the West Virginia Northern Community College. In 1973, the Governor started the Comprehensive Employment and Training Act (CETA) program to begin retraining the unemployed for new jobs, serving 75,000 men and women with $100 million from various sources. He began a Fuel and Energy office during the Seventies oil crisis, to help residents winterize their homes and to encourage them to buy home heating oil in the summer months when prices were lower and supplies more abundant. What the Moore Administration did to utilize federal funds and plans in the Seventies could fill a book in and of themselves–the projects were almost as abundant as FDR's New Deal.

"A lot of what Arch Moore did," Brenda Nichols-Harper concluded, "was to help them develop strategies. He believed, 'West Virginia is good–it could be better–we need to get there!'"

Chapter 14 Notes

1. - For example, in 1974, about $54 million in tax dollars had gone to the WVU med school, but only two graduates opted to stay in state to practice. The Morgantown school had been largely formed by physicians from Minnesota, and they were not interested in altering their program to accommodate poor, rural West Virginia; WVU graduates were oriented to more lucrative big city practices. Neither WVU President James Harlow nor the Board of Regents showed any sign of a willingness to help.

2. - The military academy had existed since 1812.

Chapter Fifteen
Welfare Reform

After a couple years in the Air Force and settling into a small law practice in New Cumberland, West Virginia, Edwin Flowers and his wife enjoyed volunteering in Arch Moore's congressional campaigns. "Without Arch's knowledge, Ellie and I distributed his literature, put up his signs and told friends about him. By 1958, he realized we were getting him some votes, but I never asked him for anything. We just supported him because he was an outstanding leader."

Flowers was another friend who had urged Moore not to get into the 1968 gubernatorial race. "On a plane from Washington to Pittsburgh, I told him, 'I don't think you should do that.' It wasn't the answer he wanted to hear. But Arch was the ranking minority member of the House Judiciary Committee, was helping to write the nation's criminal laws. As a lawyer, he was making a great contribution in the Congress. Besides, I thought West Virginia was beyond repair and he would just be wasting his talents [as governor]."

But when Moore announced his candidacy for governor, Ed sent him a note, promising to help in any way possible. "I didn't realize until later how literally he would take that offer." Moore included him in the Terra Alta summit and there asked him to be his Welfare Commissioner. Flowers had already taken a lot of time from his small practice to help in the 1968 campaign, and was reluctant to accept the offer, "although I thought we all owed some obligation for public service."

He thought welfare was a hopeless morass and wasn't eager to get involved. Plus, he knew nothing about welfare, and felt unqualified. "I made a smart-aleck statement, 'If I'd known you were going to [put me at Welfare], I'd have voted for your opponent.' My colleagues told me there was no future there. But Arch asked me to talk to Ellie about it and finally I agreed to do it, but for no longer than two years."

Flowers recalled that there was "great skepticism and doubt about this firebrand from the North [Arch Moore]. Plus, Arch had no demonstrated administrative experience. And some had trouble with his huge ego. But it was my feeling that anyone in public office needed [a strong ego] because there will be enough people who have ill-regard for you."

When Flowers and the others finally assumed their positions, a few weeks after the January inauguration, he had to have someone tell him where the commissioner's office was. He was replacing a commissioner,

L.L. Vincent of Fairmont, a career social worker who thought Moore might keep him. "He was stunned when I showed up," recalled Ed.

At first, Flowers, who had a mortgage on his home and a practice to which he'd planned to return in two years, shared a room at the Daniel Boone Hotel with two other Moore appointees, Bill Loy and Bill Coffindaffer, returning home on the weekends. "We worked long, hard days, and then returned to the hotel room to watch the eleven o'clock news, to see 'what we'd done wrong that day.'"

During his first six months, he visited the county Welfare office almost constantly, getting to know the department's 3,100 employees and their needs in the communities they served. He rode around with the caseworkers ("I may have been the first commissioner they'd ever seen") and "learned an awful lot. Soon, I had more knowledge about what was going on than their administrators, and it also helped me know how to change the rules [and reform the department]."

The Welfare Department employees (all were holdovers from Barron-Smith except one "exempt" slot Flowers got to fill with his own choice) had the misguided thought "it was going to be a political thing and these Republicans wanted to starve people and take them off the [welfare] rolls." But Flowers and Arch Moore surprised even them.

Flowers began to learn quickly that there were many in West Virginia who desperately needed help with their lives, not just a handout. On one visit, the new commissioner accompanied a caseworker back into the hills and hollows of Mingo County, driving through a creek to get to one "client's" house. "She had a whole houseful of kids," he recalled. "She later told the caseworker, in private, that she guessed the 'sassafras tea wasn't working' as a birth control device."

So the new commissioner inititated the policy of social agencies providing birth control advice and got the State to pay for pills and birth prevention devices. "It stirred up a hornet's nest with the conservatives [who didn't think the State should be into the birth control business], but the medical community was all for it."

Flowers, with Moore's approval, made many other reforms. After a "listening tour" in which he asked welfare mothers, "What can I do to help you?" the Commissioner received similar responses from most: "Get me a job," and "Hang the old man." He could help with the first, at least, if not the second request.

"Not all women are good mothers and homemakers," he learned. So he set up programs in which social workers trained such women to obtain jobs, worked with them to improve their personal hygiene and got them ready for job interviews. For those who were more homebound or afraid of going out into the workforce, he set them up as day care providers. In their homes or elsewhere, they could look after as many as six children whose welfare mothers were seeking work outside their homes—sort of a communal setup. "So it was a win-win situation," was Flowers' view. "We let those who wanted out of the house to pursue outside work, and those who didn't could do day care." Using IRS records, Flowers' department also started going after "deadbeat dads." These were revolutionary concepts for West Virginia at the time. But all these reforms sounded like Eleanor Roosevelt had returned, and Flowers had as many sceptics and critics on the right as he did on the left.

According to an Oct. 1, 1973, *U.S. News & World Report* article, the reforms worked. "Until 1971, West Virginia was typical of most of the nation, with relief rolls climbing regularly–even in times of relative prosperity," the magazine noted. "In a recent two-year span, however, this state led the nation in reducing the number of families receiving aid to dependent children–the critical problem area in welfare everywhere in the U.S." The article pointed out that, when Moore began his reforms, there were 5,376 fathers "on relief," but that, in 1973, it had dropped to 945, with a goal of getting them all into jobs by Christmas. Family welfare rolls had dropped from 23,518 cases to 18,713.

Arch recalled that several things had to be accomplished to reform the Welfare Department. "The case workers were socialistic–they thought everyone who came in was eligible for benefits," so that had to change. "I told Ed Flowers to solicit anonymous letters [from within the department] to tell us how to improve what we're doing." That brought in many helpful suggestions, he said. "And then we got the Welfare workers' salaries up by boosting their Civil Service classifications," Moore added.

Moore's friend, Dr. David Yoho, attended a National Governor's Conference with him in Sun Valley, Utah and recalled California Governor Ronald Reagan quizzing Moore on the welfare reforms made in West Virginia. "Reagan said West Virginia had the best welfare program of any state. He wanted details." The future president later phoned Moore and asked, "Can I send a couple of my people to West Virginia [to study its welfare reforms] for a few weeks?" He sent two assistants, one of whom was Caspar Weinberger (a future cabinet secretary), to observe and learn. Soon Reagan would be implementing many of those in the Golden State, and getting high compliments from conservative columnists. Reagan would talk frequently of those reforms when he ran for president in later years and would adopt much of the West Virginia model of reform in the

1980s for the federal government.[1]

According to records of the U.S. Dept. of Health, Education and Welfare, West Virginia was one of only three states in the nation to have fewer family assistance cases at the end of the 1970 to 1974 period than at the beginning. By 1974, unemployed fathers receiving welfare dropped from 7,200 in 1969 to an all-time low of 384 by 1974 even though average family benefits rose from $138 to $249 during that period.

"Critics said it was slavery. I responded, 'We're freeing them from welfare!'" Flowers remembered, with emotion.

The system had been mired in the worst form of politics for decades and, in some cases, needy people who were registered Republican were unfairly cut from benefits and low income, government-sponsored jobs, just the opposite of what happened in the 1920s when Republicans were in charge. And, sadly, thousands of West Virginia families had been on the dole for three generations, with no effort by the Democratic Establishment to get them off. "Support our slate, and we'll keep your checks coming," was the unspoken policy. And in West Virginia, with its outhouses, abundant firewood and coal to heat, and cheap, hillside land, one could live cheaply, even on a small welfare check. Thus, many able-bodied people were content to do that. They would readily vote straight Democratic in exchange for the opportunity to live off the taxpayers.

The Moore Administration chose to change all that, to de-politicize the system and to modernize it. They computerized and moved Welfare records to a central office in Charleston. Moore eliminated county control of the welfare system, making it a state network instead. They consolidated fifty-five county Welfare offices to twenty-seven, with thinly staffed satellite offices where there were none. They initiated public service radio programs to educate the public, particularly in high welfare usage counties. The goal was to give the truly needy *more* assistance, and get the indolent off the welfare rolls completely. And in doing so, the recipient's politics would play no role, whatsoever.

Remarked Flowers: "What we did wasn't brilliant, but I just learned from listening. I had no agenda or philosophy, except to be 'my brother's keeper.' It was nothing fancier than that."

For those who could not immediately get back to work, the Moore Administration wanted to offer more generous, meaningful benefits, not just a bare subsistence, but more fitting to their needs. In fact, welfare benefits would be increased *six times* during Moore's first two terms. Says Flowers, "We offered goal-oriented assistance. They'd get six months on welfare, good care, medical care, but it was considered a time in which to get ready for a job. We were looking at the end from the beginning, try to get them off welfare rolls faster."

West Virginia was the first state to experiment with, and adopt, the use of food stamps for those who could not afford to feed their families. Because many recipients were older, frail, blind, handicapped and/or without easy transportation, Moore initiated mail distribution of food stamps, the first in the nation. They no longer would need to find someone to drive them to the office for a long and humiliating wait to pick up their food stamps. Welfare application periods—how long it took to get checks started—were shortened from six weeks to one week in most cases. According to the *U.S. News* article, they established foster care arrangements, home repair plans, provided subsidized bus rides, plus the day care and family planning. For children, there was an early screening and diagnostic system aimed at spotting and promptly correcting health problems. Welfare children began receiving a thirty dollar grant for back-to-school clothing and ten dollars extra for winter clothing, a first, and an amount that bought a lot at that time, if used prudently (it was later raised to fifty dollars per student under Moore and is a couple hundred dollars per student today).

Although it was a small amount, the clothing allowance generated scores of thank-you letters to Moore from grateful recipients. One teacher thanked the Governor for her several pay raises and added that the clothing allowances had helped a family in her school whose father had abandoned them. "The look on their faces as they listed the items they planned to buy was a good sight to see. I don't often see them looking really happy." Typical of the many letters was from a welfare mother who wrote to him, "It would have been impossible to have gotten any school clothes at all without [it because I'm receiving] only $182.00 a month and ...pay $54 [out of that] for food stamps. We sure did appreciate it." Another was a mother who said it "was impossible" to "stretch $159 [to] clothe my three school children." They now had "shoes and underclothes" thanks to the grant, she added. She thanked him, too, for letting her get an education to become a nurse under the "WIN program."

"I still get choked up when I think about meeting with Flowers and Governor Moore when they were about to announce [the clothing voucher program]," said former Secretary of State "Hike" Heiskell (then workers' compensation commissioner, later Republican state chairman), who thought it defined Moore's compassion for the poor. "That was a golden moment for me. I was so pleased, realizing what that would mean to hundreds of thousands of children. As I sat across from the Governor, I was thinking of those little children in coal mining camps, or the impoverished neighborhoods of Charleston and Wheeling, the children from broken homes or with sick or disabled parents. So many of them would dread the first day of school as the more privileged children looked with disbelief or scorn at their tattered shoes and soiled shirts and jeans. The Governor's program would ensure that each child would be spared such embarrassment. As I thought of all this, I could not suppress my tears of joy; tears of happiness streamed down my cheeks. I was so proud of Arch Moore, so proud to be a part of his administration."

The food stamp concept worked so well that, in his second term, Moore decided to extend it to public transportation needs. He established the TRIP program, which provided low income people with TRIP tickets for use on buses—often their only source of getting to work, to physicians, or to shop.[2] Then Moore obtained available federal funds to buy rural communities small buses and large vans, which suited their needs and "are still in use today," Flowers' assistant and successor, Tom Tinder noted. "The TRIP program was so successful that bus systems bigger cities like Huntington and Charleston began accepting the tickets." A new Medically Needy and Catastrophic Illness program was started, plus the country's first comprehensive Legal Services Plan for the poor.

Governor Moore personally "cared about" welfare recipients, Flowers noted. The Governor met with Welfare Department employees fairly often and gave them "pep talks," to spur interest in the reform the Administration was making. But often it was more direct. "The phone number for the Kanawha City office that distributed food stamps was close to that of the Governor's Mansion," Flowers laughed. "They'd get the Governor by mistake at his residence and he'd talk to [food stamps recipients] when they'd call about a problem. He would call me the next day, to get it fixed."

The fact that the Moore Administration was trying to get welfare recipients off the rolls and back to work was a relatively new concept in America at the time and not a universally popular one. It ran counter to the "welfare state" culture that was growing, not just in the Mountain State, but nationally, in the 1960s and 70s. Flowers and his staff ran into an unexpected adversary, however, as they tried to make much-needed reforms: the federal government, upon which the states are heavily dependent for welfare funds. Several local sectors also had a vested interest in protecting the status quo.

The Kennedy and Johnson Administrations made increased welfare spending, "social justice," and redistribution of wealth a high priority in the "Great Society." They had the strong backing of the academic and news media elite who then naively believed that, if the government would just spend more on the poor, all of society's ills—racism, the break-up of families, drug and alcohol abuse, teenage pregnancies, riots in the cities, and such—would disappear. Many of the proponents of the welfare state were Marxist, but others were not; they believed capitalism was strengthened by a richer, stronger, more stable lower income class. But with holdovers from the Kennedy and Johnson Administrations and their allies, there was also an ulterior, political motive: a large percentage of African-Americans were poor, and the Democrats wanted to keep them in their column as they voted in ever-increasing numbers, liberated by civil rights laws (which, ironically, had long been suppressed by Southern Democrats). Plus, JFK and his brother Robert were genuinely touched by the poverty they saw during the 1960 West Virginia presidential primary; they wanted to help Appalachia recover.

One of LBJ's "War on Poverty" programs was the Office of Economic Opportunity. Part of its goal was to get poor people involved in "community action," including the organization of opposition to the local power structure. It soon became apparent that taxpayers were subsidizing a program that was stirring up a lot of agitation. Even Pres. Johnson himself told people he thought virtually everyone at OEO was disloyal and a troublemaker. JFK's brother-in-law, Sargent Shriver, who was its director, had to constantly assure LBJ that OEO employees were not instigating the riots that were burning down parts of American cities in the 1960s. Nicholas Lemann wrote in *The Atlantic Monthly* that the OEO was supporting "strategies of political confrontation instead of accommodation," and in one case even funded Chicago youth gangs.[3]

These big government welfare and "anti-Establishment" programs came into full blossom under the presidency of Richard Nixon, who was greatly influenced in particular by one advisor, Daniel Patrick Moynihan, later the Democratic U.S. Senator from New York. Wrote Lemann:

> Presidencies are shaped by their times, far more than they shape their times. Nixon's first term took place in the ideological shadow of the Sixties. The consensus ... was more liberal than it had ever been before and than it has been since. Among the people advising Nixon on domestic affairs, those we would now think of as conservative Republicans were distinctly in the minority...Nixon [increased] welfare, food stamps,

> social security, and disability pensions, and partly as a result, government transfer payments to individuals rose much more during Nixon's presidency than they had under Johnson's.[4]

Moynihan advocated a "guaranteed annual wage" philosophy, Flowers recalled. "They thought people would work out of pride, not loaf. But they were making loafing the thing to do." Nixon, "who didn't pay much attention to welfare," according to Flowers, twice proposed the Family Assistance Plan (derisively referred to as "FAP,") which would have given every American a guaranteed minimum income.

So, for a period of time, what the Moore Administration was doing to force welfare recipients back into the workforce, off the government dole, was contrary to what the liberal national establishment and even those in the Nixon Administration were advocating. Flowers had to "bend," and even break, some federal guidelines to accomplish what was needed to succeed. "The OEO got an HEW administrator to say 'West Virginia is not going to get away with it,'" Flowers recalls. "The headlines read that the Welfare Commissioner had been chastised."A battle between the West Virginia reformers and the Washington bureaucrats escalated. They nit-picked and fussed at every new thing the Moore reformers tried to do, even when they clearly made good sense. The feds insisted upon showing their authority, having their way over the state.

The feud got so bad with the federal government that Flowers finally had enough of it. "I said [to the feds], 'You're not a good partner, so I'm ceasing relations with the federal government.' I began cutting off reports they required monthly. So the feds said, 'We're cutting off your money!' I responded, 'Good. That will get us a congressional hearing. Bring it on; we'll see who is right and wrong.'"

But that was the last thing the feds wanted. They wanted no light shown upon their bureaucratic pettiness or incompetent, unworkable policies. "So they threatened, 'We'll send our auditors!' And I responded, 'No, you're not–they won't be authorized to talk to anyone working for me.' They just didn't know what to do about it, so they kept sending the money," Flowers chuckled. "Arch was tickled by it all." In the meantime, Flowers' staffers continued preparing the financial reports for the feds, knowing they'd have to send them eventually ("They were knee deep"). "We had a Cold War with the federal government; they were stymied," Flowers reflects.

In addition to dealing with constant confrontation with the federal bureaucracy and its conflicting views about how taxpayers' money should be redistributed to the poor, Flowers was the target of numerous lawsuits, often filed by OEO lawyer Larry Starcher of Morgantown. Starcher would go into federal court every time a new policy was adopted that he didn't like and usually get a federal judge to agree with him. A lot of the department's time and resources were wasted on these court battles and, of course, The *Gazette* enjoyed reporting all the setbacks. Readjustments were constantly made, but Flowers was not deterred in continuing with his overall reforms.

Likely organized by the OEO, welfare recipients, some of whom were Sixties-style "hippies" or "career college students," would stage noisy "sit-ins" at Flowers' office. Sometimes he would have to sneak out a side window, down a fire escape, and be escorted by a state trooper out of his building, to assure his personal safety. The Flowers family lived in Charleston by now, their children attending George Washington High School. There were constant, personal threats against them. Flowers was not overreacting to the threats; these were potentially dangerous "mobs." It was a volatile period of time and such "demonstrations," as they called them, were getting people hurt elsewhere in the nation.

Once a long-haired, angry mob of several dozen people marched on the Welfare office on Hale Street in Charleston and it promised to be an ugly affair. What was their demand? "They expected one hundred percent of their needs to be covered by welfare, as the feds were (unrealistically) discussing," Flowers explained. But just as they came marching down, "a big storm, with hail, wind and rain, drove them away," he chuckled. "My deputy commissioner remarked, 'People said Arch Moore could walk on water–now even I believe in him!'"

Eventually, Gorham Black, an HEW administrator, came to Flowers' office and resolved the standoff. "He told the federal government to 'back off' and 'gave us some slack.'"And the West Virginia Welfare Department resumed submission of the financial records the feds required.

Eventually, under Nixon's subsequent HEW Secretary Caspar Wineberger, the Moore Administration's reforms were not only accepted, but even copied, and eventually adopted into federal law and policy. "Other states, even other nations, came to West Virginia and studied what we were doing," Flowers recalls proudly. In the 1973 article cheering Moore's accomplishments in welfare reform, *U.S. News* reported, "Federal officials say what is going on [in West Virginia] is an example of a trend they hope will catch on across the nation."

Respect for Flower would rise to the point that, during the Ford

Administration, he was considered a serious candidate for HEW Secretary. Had Jimmy Carter not prevailed, it might have happened. Instead, the controversial commissioner would be appointed to the West Virginia Supreme Court of Appeals by Governor Moore. He failed, however, as a Republican to retain the seat in the 1976 election, being "excused by the people of West Virginia" in the big Democratic sweep of the state that year, as he phrased it. (He would finish his career in two more roles: as a respected federal bankruptcy judge, then as vice president of West Virginia University.)

"Arch Moore had very progressive ideas about social services that made West Virginia a leader among the states," summarized Tom Tinder. "For a Republican in a conservative state like West Virginia, his ideas were not what you'd expect."

Chapter 15 Notes

1. - Moore noted that Georgia Governor Jimmy Carter also sent people to Charleston, to study his state government reorganization. Another national figure who admired Moore's work, he noted, was New York Governor Nelson Rockefeller. "When I led the charge on Revenue Sharing, Nelson Rockefeller came up to me after a meeting and said, 'You just balanced my budget, Arch.'" The federal money Moore had succeeded in helping extract for the states (as chairman of the National Governors) represented $600 to $700 million extra for New York. "He never forget that," said Arch, noting that, in 1972, even though Nelson's nephew Jay was then opposing Moore, "he came to an association meeting being held at the Greenbrier and spoke to a business group on my behalf. He was so grateful."

2. - "He brought Grace Strain out of retirement to run the TRIP program," remembered Tom Tinder. "She had run the food stamp program so well that the Governor wanted her to manage this new, but similar program."

3. - *The Atlantic Monthly,* January 1989. See previous chapter, regarding Shriver's letter to Moore.

4. - *The Atlantic Monthly,* January 1989.

Chapter Sixteen
Environment Takes Center Stage

The results of the 1970 U. S. Census confirmed what West Virginians had suspected: the last decade had been a time of further exodus of thousands of job-seekers to other states. The trend—which began in the 1950s, when the coal mines began automating and miners went to Cleveland and Akron for job— had continued. There had been a net loss of 157,710 in population, dropping to 1.7 million. Only ten counties had seen growth. Charleston, which had lost Union Carbide jobs, an Owens-Illinois glass factory and an FMC ordinance plant, experienced an 18 percent decline in its population.

Governor Moore told *The New York Times* that out-migration had reversed in 1967, according to DMV records, and the state was now growing. But Jay Rockefeller, recovering in a New York hospital from a "slipped disc," told the paper it was "just silly" to say the state was not continuing to lose people and that graduates would continue to flee to other states unless more job opportunities were made available. Arch noted that coal was experiencing an upturn and that West Virginia was now exporting it to Japan. Sales tax revenues were increasing, Charleston Mayor Elmer Dotson confirmed. However, State School Superintendent Daniel Taylor said the school population had dropped, from 423,850 in 1967 to 403,900 that year, and called the out-migration of young people "overwhelming," especially in southern coal and central mountain counties, where there were no jobs. Nevertheless, there had been $1.7 billion in industrial investment in the past year, so there was "tremendous growth potential," Moore told the reporter.[1]

The Governor said he wanted to "do everything to protect the number of seats we have" in the U.S. House of Representatives following the census results, but that seemed unlikely, given that other states were growing in population. West Virginia would lose another seat.

MOORE INCLUDED 187 items on his call for the thirty-day regular session of the legislature as it opened on January 14, 1970. Consistent with the mood of the times—growing state and national governments—he asked for more tax increases to fund more government services, proposals designed to raise an additional $38 million each year. Part of his program called for an "adjusted gross receipts tax," to move the state away from an unpopular business & occupation tax, on which gross receipts of a business (regardless of whether there was any net profit) were taxed. He also proposed raising the consumers sales tax from three to five percent, but to exempt food purchases. Cigarette and gasoline taxes would increase (by twelve cents a pack and one cent per gallon), but corporate net income tax would be reduced from six to two percent. He asked that real and personal property taxes be boosted enough to give counties a 20 percent increase in revenue.

Half of what he was trying to raise would fully fund the newly created kindergarten system, allowing all of the state's five-year-olds to attend. He also wanted funds to set up "seven demonstration centers for the purpose of training the teaching personnel who will provide the reservoir of expertise needed to put this program on line." An additional $427,000 was needed to qualify for a $1.1 million federal match.

He thanked and congratulated the lawmakers for the teachers' pay raise given the previous year and asked them for another five hundred dollar raise. He requested that they consider establishing an Elementary and Secondary Public School Building Authority (which they had rejected in the July 1969 special session). He wanted $100 million from the 1968 road building bond authority and another $20 million from the 1964 bonds and recommended a program that would share responsibility for maintenance of primary and secondary roads. He wanted to start a Criminal Investigation Bureau in the state police and requested enough money to hire fifty more troopers.

He asked the legislators to approve a million dollar increase in welfare assistance, "which would result in a considerable increase of federal matching funds," and another $6 million for medical needs of the "ill, disabled and unfortunate." He wanted coal mine safety laws brought up to federal standards. He proposed an airport development program to build twenty new airports for "nonaccessible" areas of the state, an expansion of what he started in 1969. He renewed his request for a "new central modern mental health facility," to replace the aging Weston hospital.

To access more federal funds and avoid duplication in the multiple counties, Moore proposed regional planning and development districts, which the legislature approved in 1970, and which were proving to be so successful. He asked for liberalization of unemployment benefits and a lowering of employers' premiums when the fund had a surplus in excess of $100 million.

The Democrats controlling the legislature had some different ideas about tax increases/reductions and funding, however, and Moore would receive only some of what he wanted that year.

MUCH TO Governor Moore's surprise, Secretary of State Jay Rockefeller, widely speculated to be the Democratic nominee for governor next time, began supporting the Governor's Succession Amendment that the Governor's task force had recommended. The Secretary instructed his deputy, Pete Thaw, to join Bill Loy in lobbying legislators to adopt the amendment and send it to the voters for approval. Jay was so confident he would be elected governor in 1972 that he was willing to seek passage of the amendment while a Republican governor was in office. Jay already was being considered the Democrats' heir apparent and, without his strong support, the amendment likely would have died an early death in a legislative committee.

"Loy thought we were either crazy or playing games with them," laughed Thaw. "The Speaker of the House berated Jay for supporting it–he said it was a terrible, terrible political mistake. The Speaker cautioned him, 'Wait until you get in and then pass it.' But Jay retorted that it would look opportunistic to wait until he was governor. 'I don't want to do that,'" he responded firmly to the seasoned legislator. "Arch Moore thought there was some other agenda on our part [because we supported the amendment], but there wasn't."

Rockefeller simply shared Moore's belief that the possibility of a second term was a good thing for government, that there were sound reasons why most other states allowed it. One term was not sufficient time in which to get one's programs accomplished. Under the one-term system, a governor was a lame duck as soon as he was sworn in. Furthermore, the West Virginia governor's office had been a dead end for most men. A rich, ambitious young New Yorker certainly did not desire that result. No modern era governor except M. M. Neely had been able to succeed politically after his four years (he served in the U.S. Senate before and after his term); most retired or disappeared into private sector employment.

The amendment would pass both houses and go to the voters in November. They would pass it overwhelmingly and Arch would be permitted to be the first governor to seek a second consecutive four-year term. None of the Rockefeller people, including Jay himself, saw it as a blunder at the time, insisted Thaw. "Because of the money [Arch's lack of it and Jay's unlimited supply], none of us thought Arch could beat Jay if the two ran against each other."

That assumption may have been true until a huge, controversial issue changed that equation and made it possible for Moore to raise campaign contributions more easily from the state's key industry.

On a Saturday morning early in 1970, the thirty two-year-old Jay

Rockefeller assembled his political wise men at the Secretary of State's office to discuss a major issue he wanted to raise in his anticipated run for governor two years hence. The attendees included Don McClure of his personal staff, plus James "Tiger" Morton, Tom Winner, lawyer Charlie McElwee, environmentalist Bill Schecter, state elections director Mike McClister and Thaw.

Jay wanted a theme for his race, a crusade, but it wasn't offered in exactly those terms. If the group approved, the young Secretary informed them, he would hold a press conference in which he would call for a ban of surface coal mining in West Virginia "completely and forever," as he put it.

"I'll confess that I was all for it," admitted Thaw about the plan to ban surface mining. "Jay would often explain that, every time he looked at a strip-mined mountain, it was like someone had slashed a beautiful painting. We believed it in." Indeed, the majority of his advisers were wildly enthusiastic, Thaw remembered. Jay would have an issue and it would be a noble and popular one. The nation was prosperous and largely self-contained; oil crises were yet three years away; any thought of coal jobs or market loss, or disastrous tax revenue repercussions was tossed aside. West Virginia was finally prosperous enough that consideration could be given to terminating an entire industry, they thought. Besides, the responsible deep mining industry would absorb all the demand, they naively argued. Their vision of ridding the state of this environmental and unsightly plight was a grand one. Gone would be the days when coal companies could come in, recklessly remove the coal and leave the mountain eaten away like an apple core, with dangerous and ugly high walls, slag and mud slides and polluted or filled streams below, with little or no reclamation. Besides, everyone knew that the state didn't enforce reclamation laws, at least not strictly enough.

Such a ban would be in keeping with the times. The Western world was becoming more sensitive to the damage caused by industrialization. Earth Day was first celebrated that year. "The Vietnam War was starting to wind down," noted Thaw, "and the hippies needed somewhere to go, somewhere to take their Volkswagen buses and do a protest march." Environmentalism was very much "in," especially on college campuses and among "progressive thinking" people who supported Jay and other perceived reformers. There were no opinion polls that prompted Jay to call for the ban, as some had suspected, Thaw insisted. "This was just something he believed in his heart. He said it and he meant it." Jay had not adopted the issue just to get elected, he was certain. "It would have been easier to finesse [the strip mining ban issue] and deal with it later. But he was very idealistic then. He wanted to do it, and do it now." Part of Rockefeller's motive, wrote Richard Grimes, was to lead a movement. He had missed out on civil rights, and in West Virginia he had let other politicians like Moore and Hechler take the lead in providing black lung benefits. Missing out on the latter crusade really bothered him; Jay would have loved to have lead that one, Grimes recalled. Rockefeller saw himself as a savior, a liberal reformer, a new Bobby Kennedy or Martin Luther King. This issue was it! He couldn't miss!

Only Winner and, to a lesser extent, McElwee, understood that the issue might have a downside, that there might be negative political fallout. "Tom was apoplectic," Thaw admitted. Importantly, as they would later learn, was that "we gave Arch Moore what he didn't have–unlimited amounts of money. We made some real shrewd moves [by supporting a governor's succession amendment and calling for a surface mining ban]," Jay's former deputy noted sarcastically. "Tom Winner correctly argued that the issue would stir them all [coal operators] up and get the Tracy Hyltons against us. Up until then, there was no good reason [for the coal industry] to oppose Jay. [After Rockefeller came out for a strip mining ban] Arch got all the money he needed."

While the environmentalist movement was strong among the liberal wing of the Democratic Party and even with some Republicans,[2] the coal industry was stronger with the group that mattered most: the legislators. King Coal was still on his throne. Wrote the *Gazette,* "Ken Coghill ... described the disguised bribery—especially a 'coal suite' that stayed open 24 hours a day in the former Daniel Boone Hotel. It was a hideaway where lawmakers drank free booze, ate free food, played card games and lounged like pampered guests. When a coal issue came up for a vote in the Legislature, Coghill wrote, the average coal suite regular was as predictable as 'a son of the Prophet joining a jihad.'"[3] Reportedly, a legislator could get almost anything he desired, including female company, in the first half of the Twentieth Century at the coal industry suite. (The Daniel Boone, which hosted JFK and Elvis, among others over the years, was the center of legislative activities when away from the capitol, not just coal lobbying.)

Governor Moore had kept Theodore Roosevelt "Pete" Samsell, Governor Smith's commissioner, as head of the Department of Natural Resources. But the two clashed and, in January 1970, Samsell resigned. Moore tabbed Sandy Latimer to become DNR commissioner.[4]

"The job looked good, with the parks, hunting and fishing under my jurisdiction," chuckled Latimer. (And while in office, he oversaw the completion of Pipestem and Canaan Valley State Parks, among others, getting the state voted into the Top Five for best state park systems in the nation.) "But I soon found out that those pleasant topics would not command most of my attention."

Although much was accomplished in outdoor sports,[5] "I found out that most of the focal points would be water and strip mine pollution, since I had the Reclamation and Water Resources Divisions under me."

The newly-formed "Citizens to Abolish Strip Mining" directed most of its attention to the legislature and would march in the rotunda area, making lots of noise. They would sit in the legislative galleries when key votes were being debated. "They got very emotional," remembered Latimer. "They always picketed any time the surface miners were in town for a meeting."

When the bill to abolish strip mining eventually came to a vote, state Senator William Brotherton, at Jay's request, offered a successful amendment when it was clear the proposed ban would not succeed. It put much stricter guidelines on what strip miners could and could not do. It banned surface mining in a few counties, like Pocahontas and Berkeley, where there was none.

Actually, the compromise bill was a very good start to fixing the strip mining problem, which had been long neglected. The coal companies were forced to do better at reclamation after they had extracted the coal and no jobs were lost. The results of Jay's crusade and the way the DNR enforced the new reclamation law birthed the practice of mountaintop mining, "which was not controversial then," said Latimer. "[Mountaintop mining] provided an orderly way to dispose of the spoil. Before that, the old way, the materials just lay there or were dumped into the streams and there was no way to fix it later on. [After the reclamation law was passed] I announced at a surface mining operator's dinner, 'Any material you dump over the sides, you have to bring it back up. If you dump it over the wall, you will be fined.' There was a lot of grumbling, but it lead to the mountaintop removal method, where the refuse is disposed of in a designated area–I think it worked out for the good."

Citizens Against Strip Mining, and other similar environmentalist groups, were at Latimer's door each week, making demands that he clean up this or that, or to enforce pollution laws. They were generally hostile to the Moore Administration, assuming it was in the pocket of its business supporters. But, much to their surprise, they found the new commissioner to be very cooperative and hospitable to their sentiments. Moore's chief environmental control officer did not fit their stereotype. Perhaps they forgot that he had just recently been a WVU geologist. "There was more awareness by the public of pollution, and more demand for results," he remembered. "The reclamation act made a lot of changes. It didn't make the [coal] industry happy at first, but they got adjusted to it, as they usually do." Importantly, Latimer doubled the amount of surface mining inspectors and there was a higher number of conservation officers hired (135) than almost any time in history.

Moore's DNR also began enforcing existing pollution laws against chemical plants, to clean up the Kanawha River. "Before we did that, you wouldn't have wanted to stick a toe in it," said Latimer, "it was that bad. But later, people started fishing out of it again."

DESPITE THE President's attempt to "Vietnamize" the war and pull American troops out, the process did not move along quickly enough to suit many of its opponents. The war continued to polarize the nation in 1970, especially when Nixon began bombing the Ho Chi Mihn Trail in Cambodia. Generally, older Americans supported remaining in the war, believing our troops could be gracefully withdrawn or that we might even defeat the Communists. Others saw it as a civil war, or a war of national liberation in which the U.S. had no business whatsoever, and decried the loss of American blood; they strongly supported a complete withdrawal of U.S. military, no matter the cost.

Nowhere was the latter sentiment stronger than on college campuses and, with the Cambodian intrusion, demonstrations were again growing stronger and more militant. In some cases, students were being encouraged to oppose the war by left-leaning faculty. University presidents' offices were being seized by anti-war protestors and entire universities were being shut down across the nation. It was a time of great rebellion against authority, against The Establishment, a confrontation which coincided with and was strengthened by a growing drug culture. Marijuana was for the first time very common on campuses and often not the only drug of choice. The music, the movies, the hippy-influenced clothing and hair styles of the younger generation, all reflected "The Movement." To many of them, the military, the flag, the government, even the olive green of the military, became hated icons of U.S. oppression and imperialism. There was a Marxist tone to much of it–when students talked or sang about "The Revolution," they meant a Fidel Castro-Che Guevara type overthrow, not George Washington and Tom Jefferson. Yet, the majority of the anti-war demonstrators were not anti-American or pro-Communist—

they just didn't want to die for a questionable cause. Many sought college deferrals, joined the National Guard, or even fled to Canada (Neil Young sang, "Think I'll go out to Alberta") to avoid the draft. Some burned their draft cards. Conservatives (Nixon called them his Great Silent Majority) feared the movement. To them, it seemed like insurrection, almost civil war. From the 1930s through the early 1960s, Americans feared the Soviets; now they feared their own kids more.

The Right began to fight back, retaking college and university campuses, led by the likes of California Governor Ronald Reagan. Ohio's Governor Jim Rhodes was one of those who began to crack down on college protestors. But, when Ohio National Guardsmen fired into a crowd of rock-throwing Kent State students on May 4, 1970, and killed four of them (including one coed who was just a passerby), it set off a firestorm that could not easily be quelled. It sparked sympathy protests on campuses that until then had remained relatively quiet, including West Virginia University's. On May 8, one hundred fifty students marched on the administration building (President James Harlow's office)[6] and Woodburn Hall where they smashed windows and tore up ROTC pamphlets. When the crowd grew to 2500, Governor Moore took action to protect what he called "my University." A hundred state troopers in riot gear skirmished back and forth with the students and used tear gas a few times. The riot was largely contained with only a few injuries and a few hundred dollars of damage. The containment effort was largely successful, considering that scores of other campuses were closed due to the antiwar demonstrations. Harlow wanted the ring leaders prosecuted, but Monongalia County Prosecutor Joe Laurita,[7] a Republican, refused, as did the U.S. Attorney's office.

As result of the incident, Governor Moore lost some support from West Virginia liberals, anti-war students and newspapers that supported their cause. It was seen by them as another right wing overreaction, a stifling of free speech. His tough response, and the fact that nothing like Kent State occurred, won him friends among the more moderate and conservative, however. It was not a good time for weak or wavering leadership but, with such an unpopular war still killing dozens of Americans each week, even keeping campus peace and order had its costs. It was impossible to please all sides.

In a rare comment on national issues, the Governor gave the Memorial Day address at Grafton on May 30, 1970, urging the audience to be patient with President Nixon as he went into Cambodia "to buy time in order for Vietnamization to take over and bring our men home." He mentioned that he had just returned from a governors' conference at the White House in which Nixon had assured them that troops would be in Cambodia and Vietnam only another year or so before coming home. He admitted he'd been skeptical about the move into Cambodia but the President had convinced him of its need. Moore asked that dissent be expressed peacefully. "Those dissatisfied, who turn to violence to show their disapproval of the Vietnam conflict, are not only hindering the cause of peace, they are by their actions practicing hypocrisy as well."

He cautioned a Veterans of Foreign Wars convention the next month not to lump all protesters together, however. "It is extremely important to distinguish that those caught up in student unrest are not one and the same group as the mob and rabble-rousers." Those committing violence in war protests were only a "small number," he assured them. He expressed gratitude that West Virginia campuses were not "beset with large numbers of violence-prone militants."

Moore also used that convention to vent against the Democratic legislature, who had gone home without passing his ambitious agenda in a special session. They had a "don't give a damn attitude," he charged, only marching to orders of their leadership, "the same way they have for the past twenty years." They had decided that children were "not relevant to them" because they had declined to give him money to match $1.1 million in federal funding for pre-school centers, he said. They had ignored his plea to substitute other taxes, rather than their 75 increase in income tax rates. "They closed their ears to the pleas of the poor," by not properly funding Medicaid and had ignored the needs of the mentally ill by not giving him the new mental health complex he had requested. They had not even given "a bit of consideration" to his request for another $500 teachers' pay raise.

JAY ROCKEFELLER effectively had begun his 1972 campaign for governor four year ahead, in 1968. "If they thought we began organizing early for [John F.] Kennedy, they hadn't seen anything," laughed Thaw. With national aspirations from the outset,[8] Rockefeller did not want to be constrained by the limited personnel budget of his elected office. In addition to state appointees, Jay hired dozens of good people and put them on his own, private payroll. For six months before becoming Jay's deputy secretary of state, beginning December 1968, Pete Thaw had been one of those. "Rockefeller had an old house on Virginia Street [Charleston] where he kept his private staff, including economic development people. We were paid from a [Rockefeller family company] on 47 Broadway. I was paid $16,000, which was good money back then. We were all well paid."[9]

In retrospect, Jay's courageous, if politically risky, crusade to rid the state of surface mining, may have been his all-time greatest achievement. He not only got a reclamation act on a statewide basis, but brought reforms from the federal government, slowly but surely, by his interviews with the national TV networks and news magazines, spotlighting the blight on Appalachia from the unreclaimed mines. And, although Moore was associated with the coal industry at the time, Latimer's DNR enforced old and new laws, more than any prior administration. But the short term political fallout of the movement and the reforms hurt Rockefeller more than it did Moore.

The effects of the call for a ban on strip mining—taken very seriously by the state news media—did not immediately become apparent from a campaign fund perspective. That would not become apparent until early 1972, when coal operators would begin unlimited check-writing to the Moore re-election campaign. What was first noticed was that Rockefeller could go almost nowhere in the state without being heckled, even harassed, by coal miners, their families and others dependent on the coal industry. Those people would be rude to him, confrontational. He hadn't counted on that, especially from deep coalmine workers. Prior to his advocacy of a strip mining ban, Jay had enjoyed an extremely polite reception from West Virginians, whether Democrat, Republican, blue collar, business, rich or poor. But even deep miners felt threatened and suddenly this carpetbagger from New York was feeling major hostility. For the first time, harsh, mean things were being said and written about him. True, he was building a strong base among college students, professors and other environmental-friendly types, but in most areas they were outnumbered by the "real" people, those who knew they depended on coal to feed their families.

These hostile West Virginians would get in his face like never before, challenging, questioning, taunting and ridiculing the Secretary of State; paying no deference to him or his office. United Mine Workers leaders began talking about how Jay's great-grandfather had run roughshod over the disadvantaged, and they vividly suggested that the same would be repeated by this anti-coal stance. Griff Jarrell, of UMW District 17, told an angry group of miners at Bald Knob, "We feel Jay Rockefeller is attempting to shackle and destroy a great number of jobs which are now dependent upon surface mining. It would appear that Mr. Rockefeller is attempting to get more West Virginians on the rolls of the Department of Welfare so he will be able to dominate a greater number of people."[10]

How did Jay react privately to this outright hatred from people he wanted to serve as governor? "It was tough out there, but he took it better than most would do," recalled Thaw, who could never recall hearing Rockefeller complain about the pickets and confrontation. "It gives you strength when you really believe and Jay was a true believer," he reiterated.

"If you believe in something strongly, you go out and fight for it; it doesn't matter what they say about you, you don't turn away from it, you don't get upset." According to M. Blane Michael, who would later be associated with Rockefeller, Jay worked hard to win these opponents over, and subsequently succeeded in many cases. He liked to be liked. He did not want enemies, not just because it cost votes, but because he wanted public approval and affection.

Thaw came as close as anyone could do in "explaining" Jay Rockefeller. "He's different than you and me. If you're raised in that environment that he was, you react differently than those of us who fought and scrapped to get where we are. You develop a certain serenity—you're above it all. It's not a bad thing, it's just the way it is for him." But, he noted, "Rockefeller is not an alley fighter and if you're not, you sometimes get yourself killed."

From day one, Governor Moore enjoyed making the young secretary of state look foolish, by demonstrating at meetings and public events that Jay was clueless and immature. At every opportunity, especially in front of other leaders and news reporters, the Governor would pointedly ask Rockefeller questions that he knew he couldn't possibly answer, designed to show that Moore was in command, knowledgeable, and that Jay was not. More often than not, a red-faced Rockefeller would reply politely or turn to an assistant for help. At one Building Commission meeting, the Governor asked Jay, "How many employees does the Building Commission have?" As Rockefeller fumbled through his notes for a response, Thaw spoke up, "Twenty-eight, Governor." Moore fired back, "I didn't ask YOU. I wanted HIM to answer." The audience broke into laughter.[11] Arch would belittle, scoff at his every proposal until he began realizing he didn't need to do that–with issues like the strip mining ban proposal, Jay was digging himself deeply into trouble without any help.

Eventually, the Secretary of State quit attending time-consuming governmental meetings, such as the Building Commission, at which Moore might make him look stupid; he would send Thaw or others to cover for him. "He didn't like to mix it up with Governor Moore," recalled Thaw. "Who would? It would be like going into a fight against Mike Tyson at his peak." Confessed Thaw, "I suspect Jay actually respected Governor Moore." In any event, he insisted that he never heard Rockefeller privately say an unpleasant word about Arch at any time. Michael agreed. "Rockefeller had a respect for Governor Moore's abilities."

BUT OTHERS WERE saying unpleasant things, mainly his old adversary the *Gazette* and a UPI reporter, Fanny Seiler. When Moore banned Seiler from future press conferences due to what he thought were inaccuracies and unfair attacks, Ned Chilton decided Fanny was his gal! The Moore-hating publisher hired her away to the *Gazette* where she would report on Statehouse activities and do a twice-weekly political gossips column for more than three decades. But even Ned Chilton could not protect Seiler from the Governor's charms. "Arch and I eventually buried the hatchet and became friends," Fanny explained. "It was an amazing turnaround," agreed another reporter of the era. "Arch and Fanny came to terms. He'd confide in her. She had access to Governor Moore and became quite fond of him."

With the exception of that newspaper and a few other partisan Democrat editors around the state, Moore's media coverage as a congressman had been positive. But, as governor, his confrontational style rubbed some of the press corp the wrong way. Arch sometimes did not like the way they treated him, his programs and the way they often mangled or distorted the message he wanted to convey. Like all successful politicians, he wanted to control the message. So, as he did with Jay, he would often belittle reporters in press conferences, slashing them with his wit and sarcasm. But he seemed to forget that they controlled what was reported, and Moore was sometimes the loser in that battle (especially in his third term). Some reporters began to portray the Governor as a cranky egomaniac. A few women, like TV reporter Jackie Wilcox, thought he was a bit sexist and arrogant in his style. Other reporters developed an intense hatred for the man which they never shed.

He was not without friends in the Fourth Estate, however. Herb Little of the Associated Press, one of the best to ever cover the capitol for many decades, often said Moore was his favorite governor, as did Richard Grimes, Adam Kelly, Bob Mellace and many great West Virginia journalists.[12] Charles Ryan, news director for WCHS in Charleston from 1969 to 1974, initially an antagonist and critic of the Governor's, later came to be a great admirer and a friend for life. "Governor Moore looked forward to penetrating, probing, well-researched questions. He was very sharp-witted and coverage of him, whether in a press conference or out on the hustings, was always exciting," thought Ryan. "We both appreciated humor.

"I only saw him lose his cool a couple times; he was not a guy to lose his temper. But he felt he had the right to retaliate [against a hostile question from a reporter]; he was not going to take unfair criticism. He felt, [reporters] can criticize without 'being in the ring' and having to 'fight the fight.' And that ticked him off more than anything else." Ryan had covered governors from Barron through Rockefeller and thought "Arch Moore understood the media better than any of them. He loved the give and take, the dialogue. And he knew the public loved (his confrontations with the media)."

Ryan, who later started the state's most successful public relations agency, remembered an incident in which Bob Brunner of WSAZ ambushed the Governor on his way out of a Board of Public Works meeting, asking, "Governor, why won't you answer our questions?" Moore growled, "Ah, grow up Bob!" Said Ryan, "All of us [in the press corp] took delight in that. Al Sahley would use it as a frequent sound bite on his morning radio show, played it over and over."

Ryan's Atlanta-based employer had "crunched [his] budget" and instead of the normal 10,000 feet of film per month, he was allocated a mere one thousand feet, so he had to use it sparingly. "Governor Moore was typically verbose [in the press conferences] so, to save film I'd ask the question and give a thumbs-up to my camera man, who'd start filming. I'd give him a signal to cut in about 30 seconds. But that wasn't enough for Arch and he heard the whir of the camera cease before he was done with his answer. He asked, 'What's the matter, Mr. Ryan, won't they give you enough money for your film?' So we turned it back on and gave him another two minutes," Ryan laughed.

"The power center of government was clearly evident in Moore's relationship with the news media," wrote John Morgan. "Virtually all major announcements involving the executive branch of government, especially those bearing good tidings, were made by Moore or under his name. Press conferences, with Moore presiding under the television lights in the governor's conference room, were the scenes of most major news breaks. The Governor normally opened the conferences for questions on general subjects ranging beyond his announcements. He fielded all questions with professional skill and knowledge, almost without exception.

But "there were times when the Governor's enthusiasm for his subject exceeded the apparent facts of the case," Morgan wrote, gently and generously, "when [Arch Moore] perhaps said more than he intended to say. As a consequence, there sometimes existed an overstatement and credibility gap between the Governor and the press."[13]

Some of Arch's antagonism toward the media was just part of the era. Investigative reporting, which would reach its height in the Watergate story, was becoming more popular and the "gotcha" mentality among news and opinion writers was growing. Vice President Spiro Agnew had flamed the fires of this press-government battle, going after the liberal news media (he called them "radiclibs") in speeches around the nation.[14]

Moore's increasing dislike of the media was displayed in January of 1970 when he attacked their coverage of the shocking, sensational news that two WVU coeds had been decapitated[15] and the fact he had kept the names private for a day or two. "Some of the ridiculous things that appeared in print were not the best hour of the Fourth Estate," he charged. "I thought it absolutely incumbent upon me to inform the parents before they heard it on the news media. That's my sole reason for handling the situation the way I did." Wire service reporters and local press had vilified Moore for censorship of the news, with regard to state police investigation.[16]

It was not always a hostile situation for Moore and the media, however. They enjoyed some lighthearted jabbing at each other, especially in less intense times. The press corp took time each year to lampoon the politicians they covered daily at the capitol in a skit in which they took a lot of time, effort and pride, called "Third House." In one of those, held in the House chamber, members of the news media played different figures, including Speaker Boiarsky. But Arch, who often used the royal "We" when speaking of himself, was the choice target.

"I powdered my hair white and played Arch Moore," Charlie Ryan remembered with a laugh. "I wore a crown, a robe and had a commode plunger as my scepter and others carried me in on a litter, like royalty. I kept beating [the reporter playing] Bobby Nelson with my 'scepter.'" The actors took "Arch Moore" to the Speaker's podium where he spoke from the dais. "I pointed to the galleries and winked at people, just like Moore always did," chuckled Ryan. "About fifty times through my speech, I'd repeat the phrase, 'And I say that in every sense of the word.' Governor Moore quit using that [overused] phrase after that. I finished my speech by singing, 'If I Ruled the World.' The Governor, who was sitting two rows back, loved it!"

And, even though many in the press corp absolutely detested Moore, none could honestly question his superior intellect or ability to communicate. "Later, when Lew McManus was Speaker, I heard Governor Moore speak to a joint session of the legislature for an hour," remembered Ryan.

"He was discussing some arcane subject which I've now forgotten. Arch spoke without any notes, citing statistics at length and historical information about the topic. It was just a masterful performance and they gave him a standing ovation when he sat down."

Ryan became one of the few in the daily press corp that Moore truly liked being around. No doubt, much of that was because Ryan often wrote flattering things about the Governor in his column which was carried by several West Virginia weeklies. "We had a running thing about the 'snow button,'" Ryan recalled. "When Arch was congressman and his kids were still in school, he would watch the weather forecast. If a winter storm was coming in he would (tease them by telling them) he hit the 'snow button' and school would be called off the next day. So his children were always asking him to hit that snow button, so they could stay home. I wrote a column on that one time, which likened his ability to get things done in the state to 'hitting the snow button.' He got a kick out of that one."

The hostility of the *Gazette* stemmed, of course, from its publisher, Ned Chilton. It was unceasing; there was something negative written about the Governor several times per week. Undiscerning *Gazette* readers quickly came to view Arch as some type of crooked, dictatorial ogre, for that was primarily the way he was portrayed on the paper's pages and that was Chilton's obvious goal. But Moore fought back. "He found ways to make Ned pay a price," noted "Hike" Heiskell, who was friendly to both men, "not the least of which was the Governor's timing of news conferences and major announcements so that his friends at the afternoon paper, the *Daily Mail*, could break the story and assure that, by the time it appeared in the *Gazette*, it was day-old news. Over an eight-year span, I believe Arch actually boosted sales of the *Daily Mail* at the expense of the *Gazette*. Even if Arch's maneuvering didn't cost the *Gazette* in terms of circulation, it must've driven Ned and his editors crazy. No love lost, as they say."

MORE THAN WAR and environmentalism dominated the news in 1970. Acting U.S. Attorney Warren Upton obtained 107 indictments from a federal grand jury on January 6, including former Governor W.W. "Wally" Barron, who now was charged with bribery and conspiracy in pursuit of state business.[17] Most of the crimes covered in the indictments covered acts between 1961 and 1969, the Barron-Smith era. The Democrat state supreme court would interfere in mid-year, nullifying the bulk of the indictments.

Nineteen Seventy saw more vote buying exposed in southern West

Virginia. State Senator Bernard Smith of Logan, the county's sheriff, Earl Tomblin and three other Democrats were convicted of vote fraud and sent to prison. Smith would lose his license to practice law, as result, but that right was later restored by the state supreme court.

THE TAX REFORMS Moore had proposed in his January, 1970, State of the State Address were not readily adopted by the legislature. Senate Finance Chairman Hans McCourt charged that the Governor had presented a "budget balanced on the edge of a razor blade" and a "hodgepodge of programs put before the people as glittering promises, without the cold, hard cash to do the job." He shouted, "The Governor is not responsible! The legislature is responsible. It intends to lead."[18] The Democrats passed a value added tax and a 75 percent increase on the personal income tax, contrary to Moore's wishes. They cut the Governor's budget by $1.5 million explaining, "It's cutting him back to size."

As he'd promised, Arch vetoed it. The legislature overrode his veto and made the personal income tax increase law, and put additional tax on fuel and cigarettes. Contributions to their retirement were doubled, but no pay increase for working teachers that year. In a move apparently designed to show the taxpayers what the Democrats had done to them, Arch planned to raise the income tax 150 percent for the remaining six months of 1970, which produced screams from the legislative leadership that it wasn't what they intended.

Moore cut the budgets of his office, the secretary of state's and attorney general's but insisted, "There will be a tightening of the belt to be sure, but this state is in pretty good shape." In April, he called state finances downright "rosy."

"Governor Moore liked to play games with the budget estimates, for lack of a better way to put it," recalled Judge Ronald G. Pearson, who was serving as the assistant tax commissioner at the time. "He would adjust the estimates to get the money he needed for his programs, and [Tax Commissioner] Chuck Haden wouldn't always go along with it. His numbers would not match those the Governor wanted to send to the legislature." One time, Pearson and Haden were in the back of the Governor's limousine and Moore was up front with the trooper/driver. "The argument between them got really hot over the budget estimates. He was angry at what Haden had told a legislative committee, the estimate he had given them. Finally, Arch turned around in his seat, pushing the button that raised the window between us [that separated the front and rear sections of the car]. He didn't speak to Chuck for months after that, he was so mad at him!" Pearson laughed.

Moore admitted this was a true story, and that he nearly fired his Tax Commissioner, but he justified his anger at Haden. "It was a matter of who was gathering the material for whom," he explained.[19]

When the Democratic legislature failed to give him what he needed, Moore called them back into a special session on June 16, 1970, requiring them to review twenty-three items on his agenda. He again asked for money to start seven centers to train kindergarten teachers. He repeated the request for a five hundred dollar pay raise for teachers. Again, he wanted a new state mental health complex. He asked for legislation changing definitions of slot machines and multi-coin pinball machines. He renewed his request for authority to transfer items within the budget (without specific legislative authority) to quickly qualify for federal matching funds, especially regarding welfare. He again proposed a constitutional amendment to provide a homestead exemption for those "living on fixed incomes."

Taking a swipe at the state supreme court (all five justices were Democrats) for wiping out many of the indictments against the Barron gang, Arch complained that the latest chapter of "failings of the past" was by the court. Its ruling, effectively, had held that the state had no bribery statute. So the Governor called another special session on July 28, to rewrite the statute concerning bribery, since the high court had denied there was one. His bill, he told them, would close the "loopholes in our bribery and conspiracy laws that prevent appropriate prosecution of those who would commit criminal acts against the people of the state and its government." One bill would "apply felony penalties to state employees who demand or accept bribes in relation to their public duties and responsibilities." The second bill corrected the small technicality upon which the court recently had thrown out several of the Barron gang convictions.

The honeymoon between the legislature and the Governor was over (if ever one existed). They were in no mood to pass his entire agenda. They recessed themselves until August, but did pass Moore's bill to make bribery illegal.

AS GOVERNOR, Moore continued to make frequent use of aircraft to save time get more accomplished. Even though he was no longer using his own, small plane, he found air travel to be just as adventurous. One scary flight in 1970 included three aborted takeoffs from the Kanawha Airport, another when the engine wouldn't start, yet another when the electrical equipment failed and the tower had to talk the pilot in. On one trip, the

Governor was disturbed to see a trooper get on his knees and pray, as the plane was being buffeted by a bad storm.[20] He wanted a new, safer plane but there wasn't yet money for it.

That year brought finality to the controversy surrounding the Taylor estate he'd settled as a private attorney. Moore was awarded $7500 in fees by the court which settled it, but was denied an executor's fee in the same amount. In any event, that story was finally put to bed.

Arch used his lawyer skills to personally argue a case before the supreme court, in which the attorney general's office had challenged a $2 million cut of the budget. Assistant Attorney General Vic Barone contended that Moore's cuts were void and that his only recourse had been to veto the budget. Moore countered that the Modern Budget Amendment allowed him to cut as necessary. The court ruled against him, as expected, so he called a special session and told the Legislature that the decision would cause a $2.7 million deficit. A revised personal income tax was obtained from the session. But, after returning from a trip to Japan, the Governor announced a six percent cut in spending to prevent an imbalance in the state's budget. He also decried Nixon's announced hold- back of $900 million in highway trust funds, of which $29 million was designated for West Virginia.

In his second year in office Moore directed Commissioner Haden to develop a coal valuation program. By the time he left office in 1976, it had resulted in actual collections statewide on an annual basis of at least $27 million. While extracting more revenue from the state's main industry, he provided some relief to families by exempting household furniture and fixtures from real property tax. Moore would also set up regional tax offices throughout the state and developed a new procedure to expedite taxpayers' petitions for reassessment. He also created a research division of the Tax Department to provide reliable revenue estimates.

As secretary of the State Building Commission, Jay Rockefeller asked that it terminate Moore's plan to demolish private residences surrounding the capitol, for his planned expansion of the capitol campus. Jay thought the building project should be delayed due to the financial pinch. The Commission proceeded as planned, despite his opposition. It was another Moore-Rockefeller confrontation. The Governor would go forward with building the three new office buildings and the science and cultural center.[21]

The Governor took a forty-five-member delegation to New York in May to promote the state's business opportunities. He credited his administration with creating "a thrust that in one year has transformed West

Virginia from the old stereotype of a weak and backward state to one of dynamic aggressiveness and high national prestige in vital sectors that reflect the well-being of a state."[22] At a Republican Leadership Conference in the Charleston Civic Center, Moore said, "There is no question in my mind that the sands of time are running out on those who retard the growth of our state." He said the state was No. 2 in Interstate highway contracts and first place in the development of Appalachian highway projects. About his many accomplishments in the past year, Arch repeated over and over, "They said it couldn't be done!" As to programs the Democrats had rejected, he said, "They didn't let it be done."

AT THE 150th ANNIVERSARY of his home church, Simpson United Methodist in Moundsville, the Governor revealed some of his inner beliefs. He called for "a return to the basic truths and moral values that have held us in strong stead throughout the turmoil, social and economic unrest." He continued, "Small wonder that our youth feel lost, that they have no sense of guidance or direction when expression of belief in God is prohibited in our schools, when acknowledgment of God is considered synonymous with official adoption or establishment of a sect of religion." He called the U.S. Supreme Court's ban on school prayer "a complete denial of the opportunity to share in our nation's spiritual heritage."

JUXTAPOSITIONED to that Arch Moore sermon, political gossip columnist Jack Anderson, successor to Drew Pearson, wasn't making any kind and gentle comments about the West Virginia governor, however. In July of 1970, Anderson began a series of investigative articles, alleging that Moore had federal income tax problems. Jim Batten of the *Charlotte Observer* also had written in March that the White House was considering prosecuting Moore for under-reporting his income but Nixon's aides denied the story. Anderson charged that Arch had under-reported his income by $131,000 from 1962 to 1967, had "paid personal bills out of his campaign collections," had pocketed $80,000 from contributors, and had "been living like a millionaire," buying a "home in the fashionable Potomac hunt country of Maryland where he kept horses and threw lavish parties." He even accused him of putting his "pilot [Floyd Graham] on the public payroll," and charging his printing expenses to the government.

After ignoring the charges for a while, the Governor read a statement to reporters on July 24, calling Anderson a "muckraking liar." He said that it was a "deliberately calculated campaign to equate your Governor and his administration with [the Barron-Smith era crooks]." He blamed the accusations on his Democratic opponents. "You are witnessing an attempt to destroy by innuendo and lies–to tear down one who would seek to clean up this state." He thought that his "efforts to clean up their playhouses are uncomfortable to certain members of the opposition. I have destroyed too many playgrounds. That's what this is all about."

Anderson, in a day when newspapers were more heavily circulated and read, was widely followed across the nation and, despite the fact that his allegations were sometimes far-fetched and unsubstantiated, had a degree of credibility. He went on a radio talk show to insist that his information on Moore was accurate and added that he expected Arch to overpay his tax so he could obtain a "refund check and wave it around West Virginia as evidence that he has overpaid rather than underpaid his tax."

On October 2, the Moore-friendly *Daily Mail* added credence to the story, quoting a Justice Department spokesman as saying, "Governor Moore has an income tax problem of some magnitude and that it has been transferred from the Internal Revenue Service for possible criminal prosecution." But the story quoted the spokesman as adding, "Don't convict him." Moreover, the White House confirmed that an appointment of the West Virginia governor to the President's Advisory Committee on Civil Defense was withdrawn by Nixon because possible income tax violation charges were pending.

But, late in October, Justice Department attorneys were rejecting criminal prosecution (upon the instructions of Attorney General John Mitchell) and, reportedly negotiated a reduction of the amount in dispute to a mere $10,000 that the Moores owed the tax man. That didn't stop Anderson's crusade against Moore. He kept threatening, even in a Parkersburg speech, to make public some unidentified papers he possessed, proving his charges[23]

The *Intelligencer* chided Moore for denying his tax problems. He "would have been wiser to have admitted from the outset that certain of his tax returns [covering several years while he was a member of Congress] were being investigated. Certainly there is nothing reprehensible in such an experience. Thousands of honest men have found themselves in the same boat," the Wheeling editorial stated. The episode had put his administration "under a cloud," they wrote, and would "leave a tarnish on West Virginia's image beyond our borders and to some extent at least hamstring a good Governor in serving his state." Nevertheless, the paper called Moore "the best the state has had in modern times," noting that he had whipped a "rebellious Road Department into shape," and had rooted out many statehouse incompetents, as well as improving state services and giving personal attention to local problems all over the state. It classified the Governor's tax problems as "minor."[24]

If the White House did intervene, it may have saved Arch's political career. A criminal tax charge, even if acquitted, would have been disastrous at this point. He had much work left to do and didn't need the distraction of such personal difficulties. But he would later discover that future presidents would not be as helpful as his friend Richard Nixon apparently had been in the tax case.

The public actually seemed unperturbed by all the fuss. The tax story did not seem to harm the Governor or his party at the time. In November of 1970, the Republicans did better than usual in picking up legislative seats. Giving another signal that Moore's job approval rating was high, the voters overwhelmingly approved the Governor's Succession Amendment, which was seen as a great personal affirmation, since he would be the first governor to be able to seek a second four year term. Suggesting they were also pleased with the progress made by the legislature, they approved a legislative pay raise and an amendment allowing session extensions, as well.

A report issued by consultants to the Governor's Management Task Force identified savings of $7.2 million during the first year after recommendations were effected.[25]

Arch went to the locker room at half time in his first term with satisfaction, with several points on the board, not too many fouls and the crowd remained enthused.

Chapter 16 Notes

1. - *The New York Times*, Aug. 3, 1970.

2. - A few Republicans, including Fairmont's Paul Prunty, would be elected to the legislature in 1972, primarily by running on an anti-strip mining platform.

3. - *Charleston Gazette*, Jan. 26, 2005, quoting from *The Lawmaking process in West Virginia: A Study in Legislative Ethics*, 1970 by lawyer Ken Coghill.

4. - "Two feet of snow had fallen the night before (the announcement) and I couldn't get out of my driveway in South Hills or even catch a bus down to the capitol," Latimer laughingly recalled.

5. - For example, Latimer's DNR imported wild boars for hunting in southern counties because deer were scarce and did much elsewhere in the state to increase deer, bear, turkey and fish stocking and relocation. His department would aid outdoorsmen by presenting "Hunter's Hotline and Fisherman's Forecast," broadcast on 45 West Virginia radio stations. Pipestem State Park was built under Latimer's term. The DNR's magazine would increase in circulation to 70,000.

6. - WVU President James Harlow was the brother of Nixon's counsel, Bryce Harlow, which added to the distrust the Left had for him. Harlow was a cold, stand-offish president, unsuited for the times.

7. - Laurita, who was more aggressive than most in going after gamblers and drug dealers, had his car bombed that year, leaving him with permanent physical impairment and making him a Buford Pusser-type statewide celebrity for a few years. He would run unsuccessful races for attorney general (although he defeated liberal Charles Haden in the 1972 GOP primary) and congress in the

1st and 2nd Districts.

8. - Jay had told close friends that he expected to be elected President in 1980.

9. - There was no co-mingling of Jay's private staff funds and the employees of the secretary of state's office, Thaw noted. "[Lawyer] Charlie McElwee, who is squeaky clean, made sure of that. If you did something wrong, you hoped the police would get to you before Charlie did."

10. - *Jay Rockefeller: Old Money, New Politics*, copyright 1984 by Richard Grimes, p. 101.

11. - Grimes, p. 79

12. - Former TV man Bob Brunner said, "I told Arch Moore that he was the toughest governor for a reporter to work with, but he was the best governor we had."

13. - Morgan, Ibid. The term "credibility gap" had first been used as a euphemism to describe Lyndon Johnson's misleading the public about the Vietnam War and other issues.

14. - Agnew, who like Moore, would be disgraced for crimes, used alliteration for humor, calling the press "nattering nabobs of negativism," and "effete corps of impudent snobs," both lines written for him by speechwriter William Safire and "pusillanimous pussyfoots" and "hopeless, hysterical, hypochondriacs of history," lines written by speechwriter Pat Buchanan. Agnew became the darling of conservatives who were tired of a liberal-dominated media, telling the nation how to think.

15. - Nineteen-year-olds Mared Malarik of New Jersey and Karen Ferrell of Greenbrier County had been hitchhiking from a movie back to their dorm, a practice then common. It was not until April 16, 1970, that the girls' headless bodies were found. Police were unable to solve the crime. Eugene Paul Clawson, in a Camden, N.J. jail for a sex crime, babbled in his sleep in January, 1976, about the murders. Testimony of a cell mate got him convicted in a second trial and he was sentenced to life in prison.

16. - The incident began a rocky relationship for Arch Moore with a Morgantown newspaper, *The Dominion News*, which was owned by Agnes Greer. Her grandson, John Raese, would, eighteen years later, challenge Moore in a re-election bid. The Democrat paper would run endless political cartoons and editorials putting Arch Moore in the worst possible light.

17. - Said Steve Goode, "Someone would come to Governor Barron with a proposal and he would listen to them. On the way out of his office, he'd put his arm around their shoulder and ask, 'So what's in it for ole Wally?"

18. - *Sunday Gazette Mail*

19. - In a final letter to Moore on June 23, 2003, then-Judge Haden remembered the incident with amusement. "I also thank you for your confidence [in me], even though I can also recall at least one occasion and probably several more, where I exasperated you through such antics as persisting in my views as to proper revenue projections for the State of West Virginia. At the time, I really did think that was my job until you, Bud Seibert, Chet Hubbard and others disabused me of the notion. Six months later I recall your wife and my wife reintroduced us and we resumed our relationship as if there had not been even a brief break. I do recall, however, it was coupled with the admonition, 'Charles, never do that again.'" Haden ended the letter with, "Thinking back on all of that and where we are today, I can only say thank you, thank you, thank you for the wonderful experience. It has been quite a ride."

20. - *Gazette Mail*

21. - Jay's deputy, Pete Thaw, accompanied Moore as they inspected the houses that needed demolishing. A tour bus unloaded "and we couldn't move," recalled Thaw. "They all wanted to shake Moore's hand and talk to him. He was a real celebrity at the time."

22. - *Sunday Gazette-Mail.*

23. - *Gazette-Mail, State Magazine,* December 31, 1972. Certainly, this incident was Arch's "get out of jail free" card and he should have taken note that future encounters with the IRS would come and the outcome not be so easy. Moore would later assert that he had been audited only one time by the IRS; presumably he was referring to this 1970 incident. In reviewing tax records Governor Moore made available to this author, the "one time" appears to have been for an extended period of several years, beginning in 1961.

24. - The *Intelligencer*, Nov. 2, 1970. 25. - *Sunday Gazette Mail*, Ibid.

Chapter Seventeen
Almost Heaven, West Virginia

Moore's third year as governor began with a renewal of his proposal for a $25 million state mental health complex. In a meeting before a special legislative subcommittee, he drew a wheel on the map of the state. It illustrated his plan to have a central facility with multiple, comprehensive mental health centers in communities in the far reaches of West Virginia. Other, old mental health facilities would be converted into homes for the aged or infirm who were in reasonably good mental health, he offered.

The proposal had flopped in the 1970 regular and special sessions, but the Governor found more interest in it among legislators, especially when he suggested that half of the system could be federally-funded. The solons knew by now that Moore wasn't joking when he promised federal dollars; he had delivered time and again. This plan would not be accomplished overnight, in part because the West Virginia Association for Mental Health opposed Moore's plan, calling the single, central facility concept "archaic, ill-conceived and outdated." The misguided theory du jour was that all of the mentally ill could be treated on an out-patient basis in community clinics. Despite Moore's urgent call for one, a new state mental health hospital in Weston would not be up and running until he returned to office in the 1980s.

In his January 14, 1971, State of the State Address,[1] the Governor also asked the legislature for $50 million for education, for kindergartens through college and university levels. He offered no new tax source, but promised to work with the Democratic leadership "in this very sensitive area" to come up with revenue. To their surprise and disappointment, the attorney general advised the state senate that the governor was not obligated to present a balanced budget to them, and Arch had thus won a key, ongoing battle, because it helped him put them into a box. The legislature did get the kindergarten system funded and even provided a 7.5 percent pay hike for all teachers. The 159 percent increase in severance tax, previously mentioned, was imposed on coal and other business and industry taxes were raised by ten percent.

Moore again ask the legislature to establish an Elementary and Secondary Public School Building Authority with bonding authority of $150 million, the same request he had made in 1969. He also asked for another five hundred dollar teachers' pay raise. Twelve million additional dollars was requested for colleges and universities.

He announced that $90 million in road bonds would be sold that year and asked for approval for sale of $110 million to finance the Interstate and Appalachian highway construction. Seven and a half million was requested for welfare assistance for children. He wanted a revised mine safety law. He wanted laws to extend and increase unemployment benefits and to reduce tax for those benefits for new employers to encourage "development of new jobs." He announced that all state insurance policies were being consolidated, which would save a half million dollars per year. He proposed consolidating all agencies with "environmental control responsibilities," about seven in all, under one roof, which he wanted to call the Department of Environmental Conservation, patterned after the federal EPA. The proposal was dead on arrival. As in previous years, he had mixed success with his agenda.

After the legislature adjourned, however, Moore used his powers to cut out $8 million from the budget act, including $7 million for highways, one million from legislative accounts and a quarter million from the attorney general.

Early that year, President Nixon announced plans to kill the Appalachian Regional Commission. He wanted to get rid of such regional federal programs and substitute his revenue sharing plan for the entire nation. His proposal to kill off the ARC was met with howls of protest from the several states it served, especially West Virginia, however. Senator Jennings Randolph, among other powerful legislators, would block Nixon's move. He chaired the Senate Public Works Committee which, at his direction, approved a four year extension of the program on March 2. Senator Byrd, whose power in the Senate was increasing but not yet at Randolph's level, also fought for its life.

In his memoirs, Byrd acknowledged another's role in the fight, as well: "West Virginia Governor Arch Moore, co-chairman of the commission, and host of the conference at the posh Greenbrier resort, said he supported the concept of revenue sharing. But, he added, 'the priority must be with the ARC.' Other governors echoed Moore's feelings, saying they favored revenue sharing but could see no reason why they should give up the ARC's concept of regionalism."[2] Nixon and the Congress decided one program was not exclusive of the other, that the country could afford both, which would prove to be a blessing to the Mountain State. Moore would make excellent use of both the ARC and federal revenue sharing funds.

Revenue sharing proved to be highly popular at the state and local levels. Nixon's plan poured tens of millions into West Virginia, sometimes more than the government knew what to do with. It was like hitting the lottery. "We were getting two hundred thousand dollars a year for Williamson," remembered long-time Mayor Sam Kapourales. "It was great! Like finding money on the street!" (But like a drug, revenue sharing funds would become addictive and it was difficult for governments to withdraw from the effects, once those days of federal largesse ended.) But, in the 1970s, governments would enjoy it while they could. Again, it was a redistribution of wealth, but this time from wealthier states to needier ones.

ON ARCH'S forty-eighth birthday, April 16, he threw out the first ball at a Charleston Charlies game[3] and then returned to the front steps of the capitol building where a small crowd was gathered to observe the first lighting of the complex with 65,000 watts of mercury vapor lights. He called the majestic building a "beautiful, beautiful sight," adding that the "capitol speaks to you."[4]

Emboldened by successes of the previous year, environmentalists pushed several, unsuccessful bills which would ban all types of surface coal mining in the state. Secretary of State Rockefeller again came out in favor of complete abolition of strip mining. Moore, eager to throw a punch at his likely rival, said he could not understand why Jay would want to ban the industry in West Virginia, but let coal be stripped from the mountains of other states. He accused Rockefeller of failing to take a stand on federal legislation which have abolished strip mining nationally, not just in the Mountain State. It is difficult now to appreciate how polarizing the issue was; it was as controversial in West Virginia as the Vietnam War was on the national stage.

Generally, 1971 was one of progress and which progressives would later look back upon with nostalgia. Left-leaning WVU history professor John Williams tried to explain the reason for the shift leftward, without giving any credit to the leadership of the Republican governor. "[Since] Moore's occupation of the statehouse had sharply curtailed the amount of patronage available to county Democratic organizations, liberal, issue-oriented Democrats had been correspondingly strengthened. Headed by House Speaker Ivor Boiarsky of Charleston, a leader widely admired for both competence and integrity, the liberals were in a stronger position than at any time in recent decades," he opined.[5] Williams continued:

> In these circumstances, the 1971 session emerged as one of the most productive of the twentieth century. Its output contained something for everyone: a labor-

> relations act of the type that organized labor had sought since 1941; a civil-rights act that banned housing and job discrimination; more money for roads, schools, legislators, and teachers; measures that reformed the state's drug laws and lowered the voting age to 18; extensions of the civil service; and new regulations governing mine safety and air pollution...[A] moratorium on [surface mining] in twenty-two counties was adopted along with stiffer regulations governing the reclamation of strip-mined land.

The legislature called itself into special session on April 27, 1971. The Governor announced that he had started two training centers for kindergarten teachers, using federal money, but he wanted state funding for five more. Additional money was again requested for mental health facilities. Two hundred thousand was wanted for ISSD, which was coordinating the information services of a "multitude of agencies and departments," he said. Moore again asked them for line item transfer authority in the budget process, noting he was the only governor without such authorization, and that it was needed as federal moneys came in. He urged ratification of the amendment to the U.S. Constitution (sponsored by Senator Jennings Randolph) to allow eighteen-year-olds to vote.

Moore asked for "stop-gap" funding for the State Penitentiary in Moundsville, after a convict knifed a fellow prisoner to death (a situation which would become more common until the facility was closed in the 1980s). With federal matching funds, a half million dollars would be available to improve it, he said. Again, there were opponents who contended that strengthening the maximum security prison was not the answer; as with the community mental health advocates, they argued for multiple, smaller prisons. The Governor just knew that the Moundsville facility needed replaced, noting that there was a question of whether the old facility in his home town had "outlived its usefulness."

The right place at the right time, perhaps, but the Moore Administration more than any other brought state government into the modern computer age. Arch issued Executive Order No. 3-71 in 1971, requiring all state computerization to come under ISSD (the Information System Services Division of the Dept. of Finance & Administration). By the next year, there were 270 different programs in use and a $1.5 million annual savings were being realized. The state payroll system was computerized for the first time, and the police traffic record system and treasury system were so state of the art that other states began modeling their programs after West Virginia's.

With regard to prisons, former Governor Wally Barron entered a guilty plea on March 29 in federal court, to the charges of conspiracy, bribery and obstruction of justice (related to the jury tampering from his previous charge). He was immediately sentenced to 25 years in prison with the possibility of parole. Charges also were brought against Barron's law associate, Bonn Brown, who was convicted in federal court in Virginia and his former lawyer, Robert Perry, who was tried and acquitted in Charleston. Later that year, another prominent Democrat, state Sen. W. Bernard Smith of Logan (formerly Barron's welfare commissioner), was convicted in a Huntington federal court for vote fraud. The trials and pleas made national news, further embarrassing the state.

Overall, the state was experiencing an era of good feeling, however. There was optimism in the air, a feeling that things were getting better for the Mountain State. Historian Williams gave the Moore Era a reluctant, backhanded compliment—again, without mentioning the Governor's name:

> West Virginia was not yet a leader among the states. It was still a follower, struggling to catch up with the others. The most that could be said in 1971 was that this struggle had become somewhat less desperate than before. By almost any standard of measurement, West Virginia had drawn perceptibly closer to national norms, and this was important. For fifty years, even longer if one looked all the way back to the start of the mine wars, West Virginians had repeatedly found their state being examined in the national limelight as some place different, a bad example, a backward, unprosperous, violent island in the rich and placid current of American life. Most West Virginians were tired of the limelight that showed only blemishes; even those who were most critical of the state's continuing deficiencies sometimes longed to be thought of as typical, ordinary, normal Americans. In 1971 these feelings did not seem so unrealistic as they had in earlier years. For most people it was a time of satisfaction and optimism, a well-deserved and long-awaited moment.[6]

And on cue, almost as if to celebrate this new-found optimism and era of good feeling in the Mountain State, came what would become the state's unofficial anthem. In the autumn of 1971, West Virginians were thrilled to hear their state being sung about on national airwaves, in idyllic, picturesque, if sentimental terms. "Take Me Home, Country Roads," was a ballad written by Bill Danoff, Taffy Nivert and Seventies superstar John Denver, who barely knew anything about the state (the Shenandoah River and Blue Ridge Mountains it mentions cross the state's eastern panhandle for just a few miles), only what they'd heard about this "Mountain Mama" from Bill's artist friend. (Some even thought they might actually have meant, "western Virginia," instead.) The simple, clear, country-style song made it to Number 8 on the charts that year and spent about six months on the "hit parade,"[7] well into 1972, dovetailing perfectly with Governor Moore's re-election effort and his long-time campaign to get West Virginians (and outsiders) to think positively about the state. Moore and Lysander Dudley even changed the motto on license plates and tourist advertising to "Almost Heaven," to capitalize on the positive feelings the song had generated, literally around the globe. For decades to come, "County Roads" would be a standard, and the first thing associated with West Virginia by those who had never been to the state.[8]

"I was driving down the Turnpike when I first heard the song," recalled Dudley, laughing at himself. "I thought to myself, 'What local yokel wrote this?'" But he soon learned what a big hit it had become and invited Denver to the state capitol for a free concert. It would have been a good place for him to be, with an election coming up, but "Governor Moore was at the Greenbrier playing golf–he didn't dream that the song would be so popular. I took the state plane up to get Denver. Twelve thousand people showed up for the concert. Women were screaming, trying to touch him. Denver had never seen anything like that." It was John Denver Mania in West Virginia! He had put the state on the map with an excellent song and they appreciated it.

Edgar F. "Hike" Heiskell (who had been acting prosecuting attorney of Monongalia County after the attempted assassination of Joe Laurita, whose car was bombed) had just become Moore's second workers' compensation commissioner. He and his wife were in the crowd. "It was an uplifting, shining, unforgettable experience. It was an electric moment. Before, people in the Morgantown area hadn't paid much attention to state government or what was going on in Charleston. But Arch Moore was resonating with the people. He was showing West Virginians what they could do, what they were capable of." About Denver's capitol concert, Heiskell continued: "Under the brilliant sun, it seemed that the people from all of the disparate regions of the state were, on this day at least, finally united. The glow stayed with us a long, long time."

Even though he missed the concert, Governor Moore came to love it enough to adopt it as his official State theme song. "He would have the band cued at a public function," Fred Donohoe recalled. Upon Fred's suggestion, Arch "would end his talk by saying, 'If the Governor had any authority whatsoever, we could probably have the band play Country Roads now!' And on the word 'now,' they would start the song, which always amazed the crowd."

Dudley also got a lot of personal mileage out of "Country Roads." Louise Palumbo asked him to participate in a style show, a fundraiser for the Charleston Symphony (later, West Virginia Symphony) to be held at the Little Theater of the Civic Center. "Dud" appeared on the stage in a robe with angel wings and, on wires, was lifted into the heavens to the strains of "Almost heaven, West Virginia..." much to the crowd's delight. "I tried to have a lot of fun while I was [head of Commerce]," Dudley acknowledged.

Not everyone would find Lysander Dudley so amusing, however. A few months later, there were probably those who wanted to kill him. An Arch Moore campaign fundraiser was held on the P.A. Denny, as it cruised the Kanawha, with many high profile road contractors and others aboard. Moore's people, including Bill Ritchie, explained to the attendees that they expected to be up against one of the best-funded opponents ever to run for office in the United States in 1972. Rockefeller's was virtually a bottomless chest of money. Cash was desperately needed, they also explained. The Democratic local leaders who would help re-elect Moore would most certainly not be caught with checks in hand; it could be political suicide for them, plus they had never operated any other way. They reminded the invitees of the amazing job the administration was doing, and how another four year term was needed to complete the job. It was like preaching to the faithful at a revival meeting. They took the call seriously. Cash reportedly poured in from these prominent businessmen, many of whom were doing business with the state.

Unfortunately for all involved, Dudley kept a little black book with a list of those who'd been on the river cruise. Word leaks out about such affairs. The *Gazette* somehow found out about it and ran to the federal prosecutor with their allegations and he had Dudley's records subpoenaed. Most of those listed were summoned before a grand jury and questioned about what had transpired, who gave what, and in what form. As to Dudley's list, "It was like having your photo taken at a stag party," said one who remembered the event.[9] It was not appreciated by the participants, as one might imagine. And it would spark unwanted attention to the "underground campaign," as Arch would later characterize his campaigns' efforts to get onto Democratic slates using cash donations (playing the same game as most successful statewide Democratic candidates).

And there was a sudden demand for lots of cash for the 1972 campaign. Several Democratic county chairman, mainly in the southern counties, were fearful of Jay Rockefeller because he had talked a lot about election reform, making specific, negative comments about a few "players" such as Mingo County's Democratic County Chairman Noah Floyd. Indeed, Jay had put his money and clout on the line by trying to defeat Floyd, Lloyd Jackson and a few other Southern Democrats in the 1970 primary. They didn't know what to expect if Jay was elected governor. He might put them out of business. (After 1972, Rockefeller would make his peace with many of these players and his huge checks would bring them into his camp, but not yet–he remained a threat to them.) Normally, only Democratic candidates could buy onto their slates, but this year was different.

Several of these individuals let Arch Moore know (probably through Dick Barber) that their slates were up for grabs that year and, of course, they only accepted cash on the barrel head–no checks, no credit cards. It had always been cash. Things had not changed since JFK bought the state in 1960. Floyd wanted $50,000 for the Mingo County vote. For that amount, a candidate was added to his slate and guaranteed to win the majority of the county's vote or very close to it–the outcome was just that locked down. It was being offered on a platter. With these political machines controlling thousands of votes, it would have been a difficult proposition to decline for someone like Governor Moore, who needed a second term to finish his goals, was up against Rockefeller millions, and staring at a five-to-one party registration imbalance against him in most of those counties. Victory over his likely opponent was far from a sure thing at this point; in fact, most astute observers thought Rockefeller would defeat Moore in 1972 because of the money and party registration advantage. Before one judges him too harshly, he needs to consider the dilemma Moore then faced. Those votes were going to be delivered to Arch or to his opponent—it was his choice.

And the Moore people strongly believed, correctly or not, that Jay already was making arrangement to funnel tons of cash into those counties that were for sale. Said Heiskell, Rockefeller's successor as secretary of state, "We were always pretty sure that Rockefeller cash came down into those eight southern counties. That was just the way it was always done. They had learned from Kennedy's [1960] campaign." As it would turn out, Arch would even "use Jay's cash against him" in some instances, Heiskell noted, getting some of the Democratic bosses who took Rockefeller cash to sponsor Moore on their 1972 slates; they double-crossed their party's candidate.

Sam Kusic, formerly a state senator from Weirton, said there was "no question" that both parties used cash in the 1972 race. "In fact," he recalled, laughing, "there was one incident in which Bill Loy—God rest his soul—was in one stall of a men's room dealing in cash and one of Rockefeller's people [who remains in public office, to date] was in the stall next to it, doing the same."

Rockefeller was "insulated by a layer" or two in the campaign organization, Heiskell thought, which gave him deniability regarding the dirty work. "Jay didn't have his hands on the distribution of cash. He wouldn't personally authorize unlawful use of cash. But he let his representatives do what was customary in those counties, which involves vote-buying. They knew he needed to spend cash on election day. I assume his people said, we need money in this account or that account, for election day expenses." And Rockefeller "made sure there was lots of money in those election day accounts," thought Heiskell (who remains a personal friend of Senator Rockefeller, to date).[10] In other words, Jay turned a blind eye to it all, having been warned by his own advisers that if he didn't play the game, if he was too "clean," he was sure to lose. (Ideally, Moore and Rockefeller would have made a compact for both to refrain from using any cash, but they did not trust each other enough to do that; each was trying to get an advantage over the other.)

Richard Neely admitted that, in the 1972 Democratic Primary, he personally put about ten thousand dollars, in five and ten dollar bills (raised by his "Eastern Establishment" friends in the Northeast, he said), into Democratic machines in Kanawha, Mingo and Mercer Counties for election day use.[11] But Rockefeller would spend enough, Neely laughed, "to pay every West Virginian to take every other West Virginian to the polls," he said. "He'd pay a person $200 to haul voters on election day. You'd ask, 'Who am I supposed to haul?' and the answer would be, 'Yourself and maybe your wife and mother.' There were legal and illegal ways; we didn't actually pay people for votes. But everybody got the cash in there in different ways."

Rumors would circulate, during the years Moore was governor, that he was "on the take." A typical story would have a favor-seeker–perhaps a coal operator wanting a haul road paved, or someone seeking a lucrative contract or license–bringing Arch an envelope containing cash, to prompt some type of state government service. After all, such activity had been common in the years preceding his administration. Some thought there was too much smoke for there not to be some fire. Richard Neely, who served as a Democratic member of the House of Delegates before becoming a supreme court justice, discounted those rumors, however. "In all my years of politics, I never heard one credible story of Arch Moore doing anything illegal," he said in a 2005 interview. "And I was in a position to hear it. When people would say he's a liar, or a crooked SOB, no one could ever give me an example."[12]

Money issues aside, there were signals that Moore's re-election might not be as difficult as his election had been in '68. Letters by the dozens poured into Moore's office daily, thanking him for this bridge, that road, telling him how much easier and quicker it was to travel through the state with the new four-lane highways he'd built. Constituents were thanking him for teachers' pay raises, improved retirement checks for retirees and widows of miners who had been killed on the job, for improvements in education and mental health facilities. A 46-year-old Charleston Democrat wrote to him, "I ... never realized that progress was possible to the extent which you have demonstrated during your short tenure." One wrote that she'd planned to vote for Rockefeller in '72 but had changed her mind: "Since your term, there seems to be more of a feeling of optimism about the state and politics. I believe people are thinking more now and are not as apathetic as they were." The staff at Bartley Elementary wrote, thanking him for the clothing vouchers for the poor students, writing that their appearance had improved and "they are coming to school much cleaner and attending more regular." An 89-year-old Spencer resident wrote that Arch was "the best Governor that West Virginia [ever] had," a compliment Moore must have heard thousands of times during those years.

ALWAYS ON vigilant defense of his beloved state's image, Governor Moore warned presidential candidates that they were not going to come into "his" state and bad-mouth it in the 1972 primary like some had done in the past. He wrote letters to eight potential Democrat candidates and two Republicans, threatening to retaliate if they overexposed the state's problems. They could "just pack their bags and do their whistle-stopping in their home states," if they had that in mind, he told a Charleston Lions

Club. In another letter to the city's chamber of commerce, he responded to Eureka, California's claim to be "The Rhododendron Capital of the World" by informing them that "we have more rhododendrons growing on one mountainside than you have growing in your city."[13] Such protective parochial puffery was popular among the voters, as A. James Manchin had already discovered. In a Parkersburg speech, Moore proposed a novel means of dealing with national politicians "who use West Virginia as a backdrop of poverty and neglect." They should be forced to pay a $10,000 or $20,000 fee for coming into the state, he said, facetiously.

President Nixon was seeking to pull the Supreme Court to the right after the Warren Court had issued one radical decision after the other, acting as a super legislature. In 1971, his two nominees, Clement Haynesworth and G. Harold Carswell, southern conservatives, were rejected by a liberal Democratic Senate, however. As a strategic measure, he briefly considered appointing one of their own, West Virginia Senator Robert Byrd (who then was still considered a conservative). *The New York Times,* among others, predicted that Byrd would "be Nixon's first choice and easy confirmation is predicted." Even left-leaning senators like George McGovern announced they would support a Byrd nomination. Henry "Scoop" Jackson said he would overlook Byrd's Ku Klux Klan past to vote for him.

Trouble was, Byrd had gone to night school for ten years (while serving in the Senate) to get his law degree, was never admitted to any state bar, had never been a judge or even practiced law and, fairly or not, was considered an intellectual lightweight. Although the law does not require that a member of the high court even be a lawyer, nearly all have been. Traditionally, nominees have come from the better law schools, have clerked for appeals courts and have served on a federal court of appeals. Arch candidly advised the President that he did not think Byrd was qualified. For some reason, Nixon conducted this exchange with Governor Moore in utmost secrecy, perhaps so as not to unnecessarily offend Byrd. On four occasions, not by phone or U.S. Mail, but through Secret Service couriers, their correspondence was delivered through Bryce Harlow, Nixon's counsel (and WVU President James Harlow's brother).

How much Arch's opinion influenced the President's decision will never be known, but Nixon eventually accepted that appointing Byrd, to whom he referred as "that little rooster," would be a serious mistake. Instead, he appointed William Rehnquist, who would prove to be a conservative stalwart among more liberal Nixon appointees and served until his death in 2005. Arch stressed that he never "vetoed" the Byrd nomination. "The President never asked me 'yes or no,' but did ask generally my view on the subject. And I gave it."

Opposing Byrd's nomination to the Supreme Court actually was an unselfish, patriotic move on Arch Moore's part. He could have appointed himself to fill a Senate vacancy, if Byrd had gone to the Supreme Court, and service in the Senate was Arch's dream.

Moore continued with serious fund raising efforts for his 1972 campaign (uncertain yet whether it would be for re-election or the U.S. Senate seat held by Jennings Randolph). Two thousand very enthusiastic supporters attended a spectacular "Salute to Gov. Moore" dinner in Charleston on June 16. It was attended by former Michigan Governor George Romney, then Nixon's HUD secretary. Governors Richard Ogilvie of Illinois and Edgar Whitcomb of Indiana, who admired Arch from their association with him in the National Governors Conference, also sat at the head table. Legendary film star Jimmy Stewart served as toastmaster, introducing Moore as the "author, producer, director and leading star of Wild and Wonderful West Virginia." In a short, emotional speech, Arch turned the praise on the audience but undoubtedly was talking about his own administration: "You have made it possible to turn this freight train around on a single set of tracks."

Later that month, he announced that 595,400 West Virginians were employed, the highest in two decades, and the unemployment rate was just six per cent, under the national average of 6.3 per cent. It demonstrated the "resiliency of the economy of West Virginia," he proclaimed.

Arch was also honored on September 14 of that year by being elected chairman of the National Governors Conference, which was held that year in San Juan, Puerto Rico.[14] *The New York Times* reported that Moore had defeated Washington Governor Daniel J. Evans for the position, on a secret ballot. It was an office he was very proud of; no other West Virginian had ever been elected to the post; and no subsequent West Virginia governor ever had that honor. He would work very diligently at being Chairman, taking its duties seriously. He met with President Nixon at the White House before returning to an "Arch Moore No. 1 Day," his staff had arranged. Among other things, Arch used the role to lobby on behalf of the states for additional revenue sharing funds, which were increasingly popular.

AMERICAN UNIONS were still strong in numbers and a more dominant force in the early 1970s. The United Mine Workers of America traditionally conducted a long and angry contract strike about every three years, with unpredictable, issue-oriented wildcat strikes in between. Such was the case when the union struck the Bituminous Coal Operators Association on Oct. 1, 1971. It idled 100,000 miners, 80,000 of whom were union members and 40,000 of whom were West Virginians, the hardest hit of the twenty coal mining states. It caused related layoffs in the railroad industry, threatened coal supplies to the electric companies and other industries, greatly harmed needed cash flow from tax revenues, and made it difficult for small business who supplied and serviced the mines.

This strike was made more difficult, perhaps, by the fact that a corrupt W.A. "Tony" Boyle was being challenged by insurgents within the union, reformers led by "Jock" Yablonski (whom Boyle's gang would eventually have assassinated in his Western Pennsylvania home). There was civil war within the miners' union. Boyle felt in danger of losing his job as head of the UMW, and was under great pressure to produce a good contract for his membership.

Another complication entering the formula was President Nixon's misguided belief that wage and price controls would bring down inflation. His national pay board had set a 5.5 percent annual pay increase limit. Retailers, even supermarkets, could not raise prices based on supply and demand or fluctuating seasonal price differences, as a free economy requires. It was the most control the federal government had exerted over the economy since FDR and the Depression and war years.

The contentious strike would go on for forty-five days, costing the state's economy about a half-billion dollars and putting 15,000 West Virginia miners on food stamps.

Not so surprisingly, given his growing national reputation, the opposing parties turned to one man to resolve the situation. The union leaders and coal companies, spread across the nation, asked for one chief negotiator: Governor Arch Moore. It was tacit acknowledgment, perhaps, that both sides trusted Arch to be fair, balanced and trustworthy. It also illustrated his reputation as one who got the job done.

Despite failing to receive their union's endorsement in the 1968 race, the UMW had endorsed Arch in his last two congressional races and many, if not most, of the rank-and-file had quietly supported him, even when leadership had not. And the coal industry, despite the additional taxes he had imposed upon them, trusted Moore as a dependable friend, one who understood that "Coal IS West Virginia," as their association's radio ads then proclaimed. Arch knew that both sides could come out winners and made that his goal.

Moore had offered to host both sides in his office in October, when it became apparent that the strike was hurting the economy and negotiations were going nowhere fast. Naturally, the Left was suspicious and began its usual barrage of scurrilous attacks on Arch. Dr. I.E. Buff, for example, made the ludicrous allegation that Moore had promised the coal companies no state taxes if they would just let him negotiate the strike in his office. When, on October 22, Moore announced that "we have ninety per cent of this coal contract in our pocket, essentially," the *Gazette's* Harry Hoffman scoffed, "Zilch for 'Mr. Action,'" as he sarcastically called the Governor in a November 2, 1971, column. Whining that "there is no indication a settlement is near," Hoffman wrote, "Gov. Arch Alfred Moore's much heralded and dearly beloved magic evidently lacks the quality of black magic," whatever that meant.

But Moore was sincerely and diligently working on the problem behind the scenes, as the end result would reveal. In November, he presided over three days of tough, heated negotiations between a nine-member union, nine-member management team, at the Roosevelt Hotel in New York City.

Moore was observing the body language, as much as what was being said, in the closed meetings. At about ten minutes before midnight on Nov. 12, Tony Boyle put his hands on his chair's arms and began to slide away from the table, indicating that he was giving up on a final resolution, at least for another day. Moore snapped at him. "Don't move that chair another inch! We have lots of people depending on us [to get this resolved]. Stay here!"

By midnight it was settled.

When the terms of the new contract were announced (Arch held a press conference upon return to the Kanawha Airport), both Moore and Boyle suddenly were heros, champions to the miners. It was the best contract in union history, by far. Average pay went from $37 to $50 per day and industry contributions to the miners' welfare fund were doubled, from 40 to 80 cents per ton of coal, providing $382.5 million to it. Sick pay provisions were included and clauses provided more care for disabled miners and miners' widows and children. "It sounds almost too good to be true," Richard Wayt, of UMW Local 1635 in Moundsville was quoted as saying.

But it was true. And some locals even paid out strike benefits, as icing on the cake. "Governor Moore has played a role no other governor ever has," in settling a national coal strike, verified Tony Boyle. The industry spokesman, John Corcoran, president of Consolidation Coal Company, agreed: "The one person most responsible for this agreement is Governor

Moore."

But it wasn't over. Additional effort was required by Moore, Boyle and others to get the contract past Nixon's pay board and Cost of Living Council, because the contract represented a 39 per cent increase, far in excess of the 5.5 allowed at the time. But that was accomplished within a week or so, perhaps through some phone calls from Arch to the President, and it was overwhelmingly ratified by the miners and unanimously approved by the companies.

Arch Moore had, indeed, worked some more of his increasingly legendary "magic," despite Harry Hoffman's petulant, partisan scoffing. There were no *Gazette* accolades for the Republican governor, as usual, no apologies for the mean-spirited editorials, columns and political cartoons which viciously attacked Moore during the lengthy ordeal.

NIXON WAS NOT so helpful to Moore in a situation which immediately followed the long strike, however. Arch had proposed John T. Copenhaver, Jr., son of the former Charleston mayor and a bankruptcy referee, for a vacancy on the federal district court in the Southern District. Copenhaver had been cleared by the American Bar Association as "well qualified," and had even been recommended by Nixon's Justice Department for the bench.

But to the surprise of many, and the disgust of state Republicans, Nixon accepted Sen. Robert Byrd's nominee of a Democrat, a Social Security administrative law judge, former circuit judge for Lincoln and Boone Counties, K. K. Hall. Byrd normally was a guest in Judge Hall's home when he ran for congress and thereafter, and it was pay-back time, even though, according to one lawyer who practiced in his courtroom, Hall was a "country lawyer who mangled the king's English." The Senator had arranged for Hall's administrative law judge appointment, in fact. The President, who had built a coalition of Republican and conservative Southern Democrats, apparently felt he needed Byrd's vote in the Senate more than the allegiance of the West Virginia GOP, Arch Moore included.[14]

Hall would prove to be a competent federal judge, despite the origin of his appointment.

During the ordeal with the miner's strike, the Kanawha Valley was suffering from another one that disrupted its daily routine and commerce far more. Bus drivers went on a strike that last nearly two months. Again, Governor Moore stepped in and, with the help of area lawyers and business leaders, also negotiated an end to it, which he announced at a press conference on October 23, 1971. The Kanawha Valley Regional

Transportation Authority was started as a result of those terms. Although it had little impact outside the region and meant nothing to the rest of the state, Moore's actions were hailed in the Charleston metropolitan area, where thousands of workers are dependant on the public transportation system to get to the capitol complex, to downtown offices and retail outlets.

Even the *Gazette* buried the hatchet for a brief time, to salute Arch's near-miraculous achievement. Columnist and political cartoonist Jim Dent of that paper did one of his usual "King Arch" cartoons, showing him having knocked out the Democrat donkey in the boxing ring. Dent, a friend and reluctant admirer from WVU days, also did a humorous *Gazeteer* column paying homage to the Governor in Biblical-style prose, accompanied by a caricature sketch of Moore as Michelangelo's Sistine Chapel depiction of the Almighty.[15] (And then they later puzzled at why Arch began believing his own myth!)

As the accolades continued to be rained upon Governor Moore, as his achievements stacked up, there was pressure to name buildings and other structures after him. It is a common technique of favor-seekers to buy support of governors and senators of their pet projects, by promising to name the facility after them.[16]

But, long before his disgrace in 1990, Moore always resisted that. He felt that the roads, bridges, courthouses and others belonged to the people of the state, that they were purchased by the taxpayers. He considered himself the facilitator. Moreover, he undoubtedly remembered the saying of schoolteachers everywhere: "Fools names and fools faces, are often seen in public places." He wasn't going to disgrace himself by plastering his name all around West Virginia; it wasn't seemly. His parents and pastors had taught him better than that.[17]

In November, Moore announced that monthly checks to the aged, blind and disabled welfare recipients would be increased from 52 percent of their need to 100 percent, a goal welfare advocacy groups had sought. He also overruled Ed Flowers and announced that 27,000 striking miners could receive food stamps through December 15. Both groups would have a happier Christmas as result of Moore's end-of-the-year liberality.

Chapter 17 Notes

1. - Moore wrote all twelve of his State of the State addresses out in long hand, on legal pads, the night before the address was to be given (your author noted that they were in his usual perfect penmanship, page after page, with almost no changes). "Most governors work on theirs for weeks, but he had to be in the right frame of mind," explained secretary Audrey Toler. (Likely, Arch had

been composing it in his head for a few weeks.) Norm Yost would often assign different portions of the speech to separate secretaries to type out, for secrecy sake, so none would have the full text and leak it out. Unlike most governors, Moore did not release the text to the press or the legislators the night of the speech. He didn't want them reading along and flipping pages while he spoke but, rather, to actually listen to what he was proposing and reporting. "We didn't have computer in the first two terms so everything had to be typed error-free on electric typewriters," recalled Toler. One night, she was typing into the wee hours and the streets outside the capitol were so slick the state troopers had to deliver her home for a few hours of sleep and then she was back at it very early in the morning.

2. - Byrd, Ibid.

3. - The baseball team, then a farm team for the Cincinnati Reds, was later renamed the Wheelers, then the Alley Cats, and most recently, West Virginia Power.

4. - Morgan, Ibid.

5. - *West Virginia: a History,* by John Alexander Williams, copyright 2001 by West Virginia University Press.

6. - Williams, Ibid.

7. - *The top ten,* copyright 1982 by Gary Theroux and Bob Gilbert.

8. - The author's son was amused, in 2005, to find the song on a karaoke version in China, where most locals knew it. However, "For the video version, it depicted a pickup truck driving through the palm trees of Hawaii," he added.

9. - Robert Elkins, Feb. 26, 2005.

10. - Heiskell, Aug. 8, 2005 interview.

11. - Neely, Aug. 26, 2005. Richard Neely was a Dartmouth and Yale University law graduate and formerly clerked for New York lawyer Richard M. Nixon. His education and early employment gave him powerful, wealthy Northeastern connections and they were the ones who pushed him to run his brief, quixotic campaign against Senator Randolph in 1972, he explained.

12. - Neely, Aug. 26, 2005.

13. - John Morgan, *Sunday Gazette*-Mail, Dec. 31, 1972

14. - The Moores took their friends, the Yohos, with them on that trip and made a beach holiday out of it.

15. - The humorous column ran at the very top of Page One of the October 28, 1971 issue of the *Gazette*. Dent's Gazeteer was titled, "The Earth did Tremble, and the Buses Runneth." He began, "Here beginneth the Book of Transportation. Harken now unto the word. There was in those times a darkness upon the face of the land and the people wept, for their buses had been taken from them ... And the people spake among themselves, saying, is there not among us one who can restore the buses?...And then there was a trembling felt in the earth and the people clutched themselves, one unto the other, and cried, what calamity comes upon us now?...And the people fell down and worshiped for it was Arch their awesome lord and He said unto them, fear not, be of good cheer. For I have heard your lamentations and from this day shall your buses be restored unto you. Once more ye shall ride from one end of the valley to another...Here endeth the Book of Transportation. Read it, oh ye Democratic candidates, and weepeth."

16. - Reportedly, Sen. Robert Byrd's staff have always made that stipulation a requirement before Byrd would agree to lend his support to any project; it must be named for him.

17. - At the time of his guilty plea, only a vocational school and a state government building in Fairmont (the name of which had been arranged by the Manchin family) bore his name. Both were promptly renamed although, in Marion County, there were buildings and at least one business that bore the names of politicians who had mysteriously become quite wealthy while drawing a small public paycheck.

Chapter Eighteen
Buffalo Creek

An active coal mine produces a lot of waste. For every four tons of coal extracted from the ground, something has to be done to dispose of about a ton of "slag" or "gob," that mixture of shale, dust, lay, low-grade coal and other impurities. In the old days of mining, coal companies simply dumped all that wet, oily, black, nasty stuff, along with junked roof bolts, timbers and crib blocks, wherever it was convenient. That usually meant, over the side of the mountain, into a creek or into the nearest hollow.

Stricter laws eventually forced them into finding other ways and the companies began constructing crude settling ponds by blocking streams with such slag piles. The theory, at least, was that most of the solids and impurities would drift to the bottom of the man-made "lakes" that these slag pile dams would create, and that the water would seep and filter through the gob pile, cleaner on the other side as it drained into the creek.

In 1947, the Lorado Coal Company built such a gob pile on Middle Fork, one of the three streams that feed Buffalo Creek, in Logan County, West Virginia "Building" might be an inaccurate term, because there was no engineering to speak of. There was no clay core in the middle, no rebar of any sort to stabilize it; nothing to compact it except the weight of the coal trucks and bulldozers that worked and rolled over it each day. It was just a huge pile of mine refuse.

Buffalo Mining Company bought Lorado in the 1950s and The Pittston Company then purchased Buffalo in June 1970, inheriting the dam, or "impoundment," at Middle Fork and many others like it. A second pile had been constructed 600 feet upstream in 1960, and a third above it in 1968. With the three dams and ponds, the company thought it would be fail-proof, that it could not overflow and pollute Buffalo Creek. By 1972, they were dumping about a thousand tons of slag per day, the refuse from five underground mines, two auger mines and a strip mine.[1] By then the slag heap was huge–it trapped over 132 million gallons of water, a lake twenty acres in size and forty feet deep at the edge of the impoundment.

Coal was booming in Logan County in the early 1970s, providing nearly full employment to the area. Pittston, the nation's fourth-largest coal producer at the time, did $500 million in business per year, had $400 million in assets and netted $43 million in profits in 1971, very good for that era.

IN LATE FEBRUARY 1972, one of those rainy-snowy weather patterns that seem to stall over West Virginia's mountains was causing the mine's "lake" to rise dangerously to the edge of its banks. By Friday the 25th, some of the Buffalo Creek residents were moving to higher ground out of caution. They had been apprehensive about the potential danger looming above their homes for quite some time. Indeed, their fears had started in 1967, when they wrote to Gov. Smith after a partial break in Dam No. 2 had caused a flood fierce enough to rip out a highway, a set of railroad tracks and fill several basements. Smith sent the DNR to investigate but, beyond a recommendation that Logan County prosecute the company for lack of a permit, nothing else was done.

During the night, company employees had been measuring the water levels with concern. Steve Dasovich, the most senior Buffalo Mining employee on site, called his superior in Virginia in the wee hours of the morning, seeking permission to install a drain-off pipe, a spillway, to relieve the growing water pressure. Many such slag pile dams already had such drains in place.

Buffalo's strip mine superintendent, Jack Kent, was worried enough to warn some residents that "it may go before daybreak" and they should seek higher ground.[2] Kent, with his 24 years in the colliery business, had a gut feeling that something was amiss. Likewise, heavy equipment operator Denny Gibson noted that the structure was getting soft, "real soggy...it was just mush. I had a funny feeling. I just wanted to get off of it."[3] Gibson rushed to move his family that morning, also blowing his horn to warn passers-by.

As rumors flew all night, at least one resident tried to call the local unit of the National Guard. No luck there, she phoned Sheriff Ralph Grimmett at home. He dispatched two deputies to see if an evacuation was needed. The deputies would later testify that they met Dasovich around 6:30 on the morning of Feb. 26th at the Smoke House diner in Man. He reportedly gave them a friendly assurance that all was taken care of. "We've dug a ditch. We're channeling around that thing and the problem's all taken care of. You can go on home now, boys, there's nothing to worry about," they quoted him saying. The deputies went on to Doty's Shake and Burger for some breakfast while Dasovich stopped at the Island Creek Coal Co. store to buy raincoats for his men, who would soon be starting on the overflow project. They would not act quickly enough.

ALL HELL BROKE loose at eight a.m. The dam collapsed! It did not wait for Dasovich's overflow project to begin. It gave no further warning, no mercy, to those below.

All 132 million gallons contained behind the dam gushed through the hole within a matter of minutes. Witnesses would describe it as a "wave," or "a black ocean," or "rolling lava." Its roar could be heard for miles away. When the cold water broke through and splashed onto the hot, burning embers deep inside the slag, it caused a loud explosion. It blew boulders all around, belching smoke and steam like a pressure cooker blowing its lid. Successive explosions occurred as the mess took out electrical lines in its path.

Some heroes, like miner and National Guardsman Billy Aldridge, did what they could to save the unsuspecting residents from destruction, some of whom were still sleeping. Afar off, he saw the black water coming as he was driving his truck toward the dam to investigate. As fast as he could, he raced like Paul Revere through the Buffalo Creek valley, blaring his horn, flashing his lights, shouting warnings, never ceasing his efforts until he had to escape from its path for his own safety.

Sue Browning was sixteen at the time. Her family was sitting down to a breakfast of sausage, eggs and biscuits when a man banged on their door, warning them to get out. When they resisted, he yelled, "Get out or I'm packing you out!" He had heard on his CB radio that the water was coming quickly. "We got to high ground just in time," said Sue. "When we returned, the house had been destroyed, knocked off its foundation, slammed into another house, but breakfast was still on the table as we'd left it."[4]

Surprisingly, it took a while for the water and debris to pass through the little communities of Three Forks, Pardee, Lorado, Craneco, Lundale, Stowe Bottom, Crites, Latrobe, Robinette, Proctor Bottom, Saunders, Amherstdale, Braeholm, Accoville, Crown, Becco and Kistler. The community of Saunders, among others, was flattened. The waters carried away houses, vehicles, and a church, scraping the ground as if plowed by many bulldozers. After the smoke and water cleared, "We couldn't see nary a thing, not a living thing, nothing standing," recounted one witness.

Rushing through the fifteen mile valley, the wave of sludge would get trapped temporarily by a bridge, then burst out again in rage, smashing through its barricade. It had an uncanny mind of its own, this black wave, wiping out houses on one side of its path but leaving others with barely a splash. By 10 a.m., the first of the sludgy water and debris had begun dumping from Buffalo Creek into the Guyandotte River at Man. By eleven a.m., it was exhausted, fully spent.

BY FINAL COUNT, 125 were killed and a thousand more injured. According to the U.S. Dept. of Interior, the flood caused $50 million in loss, destroying 507 houses, causing major damage to 273 more and causing minor damage to 663 homes. Phone, sewer, power and water systems were destroyed. Ten highway and railroad bridges were taken out. Six hundred vehicles and 30 businesses were destroyed. A C&O Railroad line was ripped out.

Four thousand of Buffalo Creek's inhabitants were suddenly homeless in the middle of winter. Bodies had to be dug out of the silt piles. Others were washed up on creek banks. Some were even unidentifiable, a few headless or so mangled they were buried in unmarked graves. The landscape was a mess. It was an absolute, real life horror, an utter catastrophe.

Logan radio disc jockey Marty Backus recalled, "The look on their faces was unreal, they looked as if they were in a shell-shocked state. Just staring, with blank looks on their faces. One person said, 'The water took my family.'" When he rushed up to see the aftermath, Backus found homes lifted from their foundations, turned in every direction, cars twisted into bizarre shapes, bodies everywhere, covered with thick black sludge. "I just shivered. My heart actually ached for those people." He found one young person's body, unrecognizable, with a Man High School ring on his/her finger.

There were thousands of similar stories. One boy had a two-by-four plank bludgeon through his body but, fortunately, after surgery, he lost only his spleen. One couple tried to outrun the flood in their pickup but was snatched up by it. When the truck was dumped on the porch of a house, the woman realized that her husband had been thrown from the vehicle. The flood passed, she walked downstream, frantically searching for his body, praying intensely as she stumbled along. After walking several miles down the valley, she looked up and here he came, all beaten up, but she didn't care. She was just thrilled that he was still alive. Appropriately, her name is "Grace."

Sue Browning remembered three children who screamed and jumped around every time it rained after the flood. They could never get rid of the image of their mother clinging to a tree, before the flood waters had pulled her away to her death.

As for Dasovich, "They found him walking around in a daze in the hollow," remembered Sheriff's Deputy Otto Mutter, who remained convinced that Dasovich didn't mean to place the communities in any danger. Said another close to the scene, "Dasovich was very hurt, very remorseful over that deal."

THE MOORE ADMINISTRATION sprang into action immediately. National Guardsmen were ordered onto the scene by mid-day, sealing off the area and opening an access road. By Sunday morning, the Guardsmen were combing the area for bodies. Governor Moore also sent in the state police and highways workers for emergency management. In fact, the full force of state government was sent into action.

A temporary morgue was set up in a Man elementary school. Soon the Red Cross and the Salvation Army arrived and began providing emergency relief. Local schools were set up as shelters. Local hospitals evacuated the injured for treatment, some by Civil Defense helicopters. Other coal companies brought in heavy equipment to help with rescue and recovery.

Moore appeared at the scene numerous times, talking to victims, to workers, to see what more could be done, showing his compassion for them. His "ambassador for disasters," Norm Yost, appeared daily for two months, "as a sign of respect as much as anything," according to Yost. Recalled Raamie Barker, who covered the disaster for several TV stations and CBS, "Governor Moore provided the kind of strong emotional leadership that Mayor Rudy Giuliani did in the wake of 9-11 in New York. It may have been his finest hour. And I was a Rockefeller supporter at the time. The people of Logan County appreciated Governor Moore."

Continued Barker, "I remember going to the graveyard near Chapmanville where many of the victims were buried. The crowd would gather at one grave then move on to another, and the next, and so on. Most of those at the grave sides were on crutches, bandaged, bruised and their extremities were cut. It was literally a hell of a sight."

BY PHONE, THE Governor reached President Nixon (who was making his historic trip to China, to reopen relations with the U.S.). From Shanghai, the President ordered $20 million in emergency relief for Logan County victims and ordered the Office of Emergency Preparedness and the U.S. Army Corps of Engineers in to help. There was no mention of charging West Virginia taxpayers for the services of the Corps.

Nixon also required the Department of Housing and Urban Development to provide mobile homes for the survivors, rent-free, for a year. Thirteen HUD trailer parks housed 2500 refugees in 700 government trailers. Most grumbled about the cheap quality of the mobile homes, but others were grateful to have a roof over their heads, as humble as the trailers were. The fact was, many of the residences that were destroyed were old company houses, some of which had no indoor plumbing. "We stayed with neighbors for three weeks until the trailers came in," recalled Sue Browning. "We were fortunate to get a new one, which was pretty nice." The darkness of the flooded area in the aftermath was what she remembered most, an eerie effect with no electricity to light it.

Moore sent in the State Department of Health, Employment Office, the Southern West Virginia Regional Health Council and dozens of other state agencies to offer their assistance. He exhausted all resources to help these people. The Governor even sent lawyers to offer free legal services, including bankruptcy filings, to those who wanted it.[5] The Governor announced plans to build a superhighway through the area. Eventually, they settled for a new two lane; Moore could not obtain federal matching funds.

The Legislature had appropriated one million dollars in emergency relief funds during the regular 1972 session and Moore asked for another $1.2 million when he called them into special session on April 19. Further, he requested financial assistance "to drain and inspect every impoundment of similar nature" in the state. Moore already had ordered that all similar impoundments be drained to "zero" and promised "they will never hold another drop of water as long as I'm governor."

THE BLAME game soon began. A religious area, many Logan Countians tried not to blame God. Their anger toward the coal company was another matter. It intensified after a Pittston spokesman in New York allegedly told a *Gazette* reporter that the disaster "was caused by the flood which we believe, of course, was an act of God." She quoted him as saying there was nothing wrong with the gob pile except that it was "incapable of holding the water God poured into it."[6]

The callous statement was a terrible blunder, creating a long-term public relations disaster for Pittston and the entire coal industry for many years to come. It fit the stereotype West Virginians had about coal companies in general. The comment became a focal point for all the pent-up anger and resentment toward the coal company; it caused a firestorm. Typical of the responses of residents were, "God didn't pile that slate up in the hollow–men did," or, "Did you ever see God riding a bulldozer?" and, "The big shots told a lie on God and they shouldn't have done that."[7]

Some of his adversaries, including union officials, tried to stir up the community against Governor Moore, too. They tried to blame him for the disaster. Don Bryant, for example, chairman of a local black lung association, called Nixon a "thief" and threatened to "throw Arch Moore out of office." Despite the fact Arch had taken steps to prevent similar situations, Bryant bellowed to his audience, "They must decide that they aren't going to be dominated by coal operators any more; that they aren't going to sit around waiting for the next disaster."[8]

The Governor was probably not surprised by those comments, in a county that was twelve-to-one Democrat, sometimes violently pro-union, and hostile to anyone who supported business interests. What he didn't anticipate was that Buffalo Mining would join the chorus. Moore was infuriated by a company's comment to a Kentucky newspaper in which West Virginia's anti-pollution laws were blamed for the flood. Superintendent Ben Tudor was quoted as saying, "[The DNR was] too concerned about the trout downstream," and had denied Buffalo Mining permission to drain off its massive impoundment."[9]

Arch was even more angry at the national news media, however. It had taken yet another opportunity for cheap shots at West Virginia, portraying the state as a bunch of poor, dumb hillbillies. For about a week, until outraged cries of censorship forced him to back down, Moore closed the area off to the media. In the heat of the moment he, too, made a terrible blunder, a statement he probably regretted as soon as it left his mouth. With hyperbole, he complained that the negative press the state was receiving was worse than the disaster itself. The Left never let him live that one down; they wave the statement, as evidence of Moore's alleged disregard for the victims, on the Internet even today.

At the outset of what promised to be a difficult re-election campaign, Moore was not going to accept the criticism lying down. Moreover, it was not a disaster for which he was going to take responsibility, any more than would be expected of previous governors, prosecutors or federal inspectors. He did what politicians do in such situations: he appointed an investigative committee.

An investigation would not simply be a frivolous, blame-shifting maneuver, however. There were some important issues to discover and resolve. The PSC had required a permit for the construction of any barrier of water higher than ten feet and there was no record that Buffalo Mining (Pittston) had ever sought a permit. Second, the Federal Coal Mine and Safety Act of 1969 had required hazardous water impoundments to be inspected weekly by the owner. No inspection report on the "Three Forks Dam" which had exploded was ever filed with the Bureau of Mines. Although not required by law, the company had also failed to devise a warning system of any kind to alert the residents below the dam, such as sirens, in case of a breach of the reservoir.

SO, ON MARCH 2, 1972, Moore formed a special, nine-member "Governor's Ad Hoc Commission of Inquiry into the Buffalo Creek Flood and Disaster." It included the dean of the WVU School of Mines; Charlie Hylton of *The Logan Banner*; directors of the DNR, the Dept. of Mines and the PSC; the state geologist; and two members of the U.S. Dept. of Interior. Critics noted that it didn't include any miners or Buffalo Creek survivors.

The commission first met in April. At one of the hearings, Wayne Brady Hatfield, who had lost his wife and daughter, burst in and threatened to fist fight the panel. He screamed that he was "looking for Steve Dasovich," and "let them send me to the penitentiary if they want to." He charged that the dam broke because Dasovich "cut that ditch through there and dynamited it."[10]

The more sensible evidence gathered was tough enough on the company. After the earlier, 1967 incident, Joe Holly of the DNR testified, he had warned the company's management of danger "numerous times," because of a lack of a spillway."[11]

Ultimately, the commission blamed the coal company for the disaster, declaring, "No evidence of an Act of God was found..." Instead, they concluded that Buffalo Mining had shown "flagrant disregard for the safety of residents of Buffalo Creek."[12] The panel hinted that some of the witnesses had lied. But with no power to prosecute, they urged that a grand jury be convened to conduct a criminal investigation.[13] Nevertheless, Moore's critics would not relent; they called his commission a "whitewash." It is difficult to know what would have pleased them.

A Senate labor subcommittee held simultaneous hearings on the tragedy. The Dept. of Interior recommended speedy passage of Pres. Nixon's "Mined Area Protection Bill," complaining that Congress had not previously given the department sufficient authority to make such dams safe.

BY THE FALL OF 1972, Pittston had paid off hundreds of claims to individuals through temporary insurance claims offices. Incredible as it now sounds, West Virginia's statute then limited "wrongful death" awards to $10,000 per person, and most who had lost family members accepted that. Negotiations were hammered out by lawyers for property loss damages. Reimbursement for loss to businesses and state liquor stores were paid. A total of $25 million was paid to victims.

Phillip Gaujot resigned as assistant attorney general and sued for psychiatric damage to about 1200 plaintiffs, many of whom were children. The suit, styled *Justice vs. The Pittston Co.,* was settled in 1978 for $4.8 million. Another 625 victims refused to settle. A Charleston legal aid lawyer, state Sen. Paul Kaufman, brought in a high-powered Washington D.C. law firm, Arnold & Porter, which demanded $64 million. That case, styled *Prince vs. The Pittston Co. and Buffalo Mining,* was settled for $13.5 million after months of wrangling and depositions before U.S. District Judge K.K. Hall.

Arnold & Porter's lead attorney, Gerald Stern, was so proud of the settlement that he wrote a nationally-sold book about the law suit, boasting that his clients were elated to receive so much money (only $13,000 each after Stern took his fee). In reality, this hotshot had been outfoxed by Buffalo Mining's legendary, backwoods country trial lawyer, smooth-talking Zane Grey Staker of Kermit.

Had Stern taken the case to trial he may have done much better. Even in those days of lower verdicts, a jury just might have given his clients the $64 million. As it was, they received little or no more than those who settled early, without a lawyer. Many had bought their company houses for as little as $2000, some having outdoor toilets and poor wiring, so they were well-compensated for their property loss. As for Pittston, the price of coal had risen from about $30 a ton at the time of the disaster, to almost $100 per ton by settlement time, making it less burdensome to pay. Plus, it was all a tax write-off.

BUT THE LITIGATION continued. Although the victims' financial loss had been compensated, the Legislature instructed Attorney Gen. Chauncey Browning to sue Pittston on behalf of the state government. He retained a top Charleston trial lawyer, Stanley Preiser, to file the suit. He asked for $100 million for loss of bridges, highways, state liquor stores, damage to schools, plus overtime costs for the state police and National Guard.

At some point, F&A Commissioner John Gates allegedly signed an agreement for the State to reimburse the U.S. Army Corp of Engineers $3.7 million it supposedly spent to help clean up the mess. If Gates ever signed such a document, no one could seem to find a copy of it. And, if he signed it, it was without the Governor's knowledge or approval, without lawful authority. When Gates was elected State Auditor in 1972, Ron Pearson was appointed to fill the F&A slot.

"About once a year I would get a silly, one-page letter from the Corps of Engineers demanding that this bill be paid," Pearson recalled. "I always responded by writing that we didn't know of any such obligation and had no ability to consider reimbursing such a 'contribution." I refused to call it anything else." He continued, "I always asked them for further details, but the Corps never provided any itemization of what they had done, a copy of the contract or anything. Just the same demand letter each year. I assumed it was from some [federal] bureaucrat needing to paper his file. So Arch Moore was really unaware of any outstanding debt [when the State's lawsuit against Pittston was being negotiated]." A state statute required a dual signature for such indebtedness, Pearson would explain in his letters to the Corps, and Attorney General Browning had not signed the agreement to reimburse them, even if Gates had done so. Thus, there was no valid contract and, without supply of any justification documentation from the Corps, Pearson refused to pay what he considered a bogus invoice. Most who had given it any thought believed the Corps had simply performed a duty paid by federal tax dollars, just as a fire or police department would do. No bill to the State was expected.

But there has been ongoing controversy about the settlement of the suit the State filed. At every opportunity, the *Gazette* continued to suggest that Arch Moore, perhaps even Browning, had taken some type of bribe to "let Pittston off" for a mere one million dollars, just before Moore left office, in some sort of secret deal. The accusation was repeated so often that it came to be accepted as fact, even by those who should have been more skeptical.

The accusation is without merit, according to a lawyer who was very close to the settlement process.[14] The Governor was largely removed from the settlement negotiations, in fact. Our source was one of many who has long been incensed by the endless attacks upon Moore regarding the settlement, because the rumors were baseless.

The reason for the timing and size of the settlement had everything to do with rulings by then Kanawha County Circuit Judge Thomas McHugh, he explained.[15] As defense lawyers are paid to do in such litigation, motions were filed to dismiss all or portions of what Preiser was seeking. Judge McHugh delayed ruling on those "motions for summary judgment" until early December 1976, just a few weeks before Moore was to leave office. When his ruling was made, "it gutted the case," as our source puts it. "The value of the case was reduced immensely." Some of the damages had already been settled–such losses as liquor store inventory and damage to school buildings. But McHugh ruled that "certain other portions were 'non-recoverable.'" For example, the judge ruled that the State was not entitled to damages for the expense of deploying the National Guard or state police; it was for such emergency services that Pittston paid taxes.

Recalled the lawyer who was involved in the case, "I had an argument with James Haught (of the *Gazette*) about this subject in 1977. I asked him, 'Mr. Haught, if you poured gasoline on your hot lawn mower and it caught your garage on fire, should you be required to reimburse the City of Charleston for putting out the fire caused by your negligence?'

"When he replied, 'Of course not, that's what I pay taxes for!' I replied, 'Well, that's exactly what the judge ruled!' He hung up on me."

Haught, not to be confused by the facts, continued to write editorials and stories criticizing the settlement, making inferences and accusations for years thereafter. Interestingly, he never seemed to mention McHugh's ruling and barely acknowledged it was Browning's suit; he just continued slamming Arch Moore. Arch had sold the state out, he tried to convince his readers.

After Judge McHugh gutted the suit, the parties were then forced to settle, and there wasn't much left to settle. Heated discussions between Staker and Preiser continued through December 1976. Finally with Prieser demanding $2 million and Pittston offering $700,000 to the state, Prieser said, "I wouldn't settle for less than a million." Staker replied, "Done!" and it was over with.

The settlement documents were signed in January 1977, not long before Arch would turn over the keys to his successor. Moore had not even been involved in the negotiations and almost missed the acceptance of the check. Just days before Arch left office, Alvin Hunt stepped in to handle the finalities on behalf of Preiser, who was in Florida. Apparently, there was nothing sinister about the timing–the last delay was because of Preiser's unavailability.

"[Moore's critics] claimed this all happened in secret," noted this book's source. "But the check was handed to Governor Moore and Chauncey Browning in the governor's press conference room, in the presence of Herb Little of the Associated Press, with lawyers from Jackson Kelly (who had handled the settlement documents), secretaries and others present. There are photos of them holding the check. It was very public."

But the Democrats, spurred on by the *Gazette*, would not let it die, especially after the U.S. Corps of Engineers continued to demand reimbursement after Moore left office. Moore's rival and successor, Jay Rockefeller, would see the bill as an opportunity to embarrass Moore. But "Jay was dumb enough to pay what wasn't even a binding contract on West Virginia," in Pearson's view. " I don't think it was an enforceable contract. If Arch had known about it, I think he would have got it waived."[16]

Warren McGraw, then a state senator with statewide ambitions, began an "investigation" of the settlement in the 1980s. The hearings, always held on Sunday afternoons, subpoenaed few who knew anything about the settlement; they were just forums for people like then-state Sen. Bob Wise to rant and rave. Nothing came of it. "McGraw was just hoping to find some dirt," our source said. The Democrats were trying to create a scandal where none existed, with James Haught egging them on.

When asked whether it was possible that Moore and/or Browning took a bribe to settle for one million dollars, our anonymous source responded emphatically, even angrily, "No way! Neither Zane Grey Staker, nor any Pittston official I knew, would ever have considered giving a bribe to anyone!" He continued, "Staker was an honorable gentleman; he wouldn't have stood for such a thing. None of the several lawyers involved would have risked his career to be involved in something like that." Instead, our source insisted, the settlement was simply the best deal Preiser could obtain, after McHugh's ruling on the motion wiped out most of the suit. Moreover, he reiterated, the settlement wasn't Moore's to settle, for all practical purposes.

Nevertheless, there will always be those who perpetuate the unsubstantiated assertion that Moore sold out the taxpayers, or that he even contributed to the cause of the disaster. An unfair aspect of the false stories is that, by every reasonable, objective measure, the Governor and his administration handled themselves with extreme skill, efficiency, dedication, hard work, emotion, compassion and honor, in the recovery effort. Despite some disappointments—such as failure to get a community center built—its performance was highly commendable. But that part seems to be forgotten by all but a few.

A footnote to the saga was added in 1977. Dasovich had retired from Pittston soon after the flood and began consulting work for other coal companies. He was taking off from Yolyn airstrip, near Man, West Virginia, in a small plane bound for a Pittsburgh hospital to have his ill, ten-year-old son treated there. The pilot had flown in and out of that airport hundreds of times. But he crashed that day, killing them all. The pilot's daughter always wondered if someone with a deer rifle shot the plane down, perhaps someone who harbored bitterness toward the former coal company official.

A year after the disaster, Raamie Barker covered the Buffalo Creek memorial dedication, as a reporter for WCHS-TV. He was surprised to see Governor Moore enter the gymnasium with House Speaker Lew McManus and Senate President Brotherton, all of very solemn demeanor.

"I was standing next to a state trooper who was with Moore, whom I knew. I remarked that it was an unusual sight to see a Republican and Democratic leaders so closely together at any event. He very thoughtfully reminded me that, unless they work together, nothing gets done and that, if they aren't successful, then we, the average citizens, are not successful." Said Barker, "That sort of changed my political view when I learned that lesson–that there is something much larger than political gamesmanship, as fun as it is. I realized that our state and our nation has to have men and women of good will and good intentions if we are to achieve our potential."

About the recovery effort, Barker said, "Buffalo Creek was the local equivalent of Hurricane Katrina [in 2005]; scale-to-scale, Buffalo Creek was as disastrous as New Orleans." The State wound up paying for most of it and nobody whined and complained about 'Where is the help?'

As he would do again in 1985 [when a huge flood struck the eastern counties of West Virginia], Arch Moore took personal control of everything. He had in his mind's eye protecting the families. He put a lid on the reporters and TV people coming up and down the hollow.

"But when he got done, Buffalo Creek became a model for rural development—new roads, sewage and schools." Then president of the Logan County Young Democrats, Barker was nevertheless impressed by his candidate's opponent, this guy Arch Moore.

Chapter 18 Notes

1. - *Everything in Its Path,* Kai T. Erikson, 1976, Simon and Schuster.
2. - *Death at Buffalo Creek,* Tom Nugent, 1973, W.W. Norton.
3. - Governor's Ad Hoc Comm. Vol. I, p. 189.
4. - Sue Browning, July 15, 2004 interview.
5. - One of those began his first lawyering job, leaving restauranteur Danny Jones where he'd been a waiter, to become an Appalachian Research and Defense Fund (APPALRED) attorney. His name was Bob Wise. Recalled Barker about that future governor, "[Wise] seemed to me to be a long-haired, hippy-type at the time. But those lawyers didn't have much to do. Surprisingly, none of the Buffalo Creek victims filed bankruptcy. Creditors like Sears forgave their debt."
6. - Nugent, p. 156
7. - *Everything in its Path,* ibid.
8. - Nugent, p. 12
9. - Nugent, p. 154
10. - Nugent, p. 179
11. - Dasovich had built such a spillway days before the disaster, at the Elk Lick Hollow site.
12. - Nugent, p. 180
13. - Logan County Circuit Judge Harvey Oakley did just that, appointing WVU College of Law Dean Willard Lorenson and former Cabell County Prosecutor Lafe Chafin as special prosecutors. The grand jury met in November of 1972, but returned zero indictments. According to Lorenson, the grand jurors, in a close vote, refused to fix all of the blame on Dasovich alone and, since they couldn't indict other Pittston officers, they decided to indict no one. *The Buffalo Creek Disaster,* copyright 1976

by Gerald M. Stern. *The Grafton Sentinel* (Nov. 16, 1972) quoted Lorenson as saying about the experience, "It has been a noble exercise in American justice."

14. - The source was extremely reliable and credible, and not a fan of Arch Moore's. He was a corporate lawyer, a West Virginian who was heavily involved in the settlement, but who wished to remain anonymous for professional reasons.

15. - McHugh would serve with distinction as a Democrat justice of the West Virginia Supreme Court of Appeals and as a member of the State Ethics Commission.

16. - The Corps eventually sued the State in federal court and in 1987, when Moore was in his third term, won a $13.7 million judgment, $10 million of which was interest. Atty. Gen. Charlie Brown negotiated it down to $9.5 million.

Chapter Nineteen
Arch the Giant Killer

Moore had long sought health insurance for state employees and, in 1972, he was able to get the legislature to provide such a program for the first time. It afforded nearly full coverage for all major medical expenses, with almost no deductibles—an added incentive to work for state government, worth as much as a salary to some.

The West Virginia Public Employees Insurance Board, or PEIA, as it would be known, was actually started the previous year, but funded in the special session to begin coverage in 1972. Partly funded, that is. The legislative leadership didn't want Moore to look good during an election year, so they provided only half of what he needed, anticipating that he would be gone by January 1973, when they could then properly fund it for his successor, whom they confidently presumed would be Jay Rockefeller. Arch outsmarted them again, however. "I waited until mid-year to begin the program and so was able to fully funded it for the last six months of 1972," he remembered, laughing. His maneuver gave employees what they needed and forced the legislature to come up with the rest, or let the program collapse. He knew they would not want to take the heat for taking away a benefit to so many thousands of people, once given.

"Arch sold the legislature on starting the PEIA by convincing them it was cheaper than giving state employees a five percent pay raise," remembered Richard Neely. "Health care was far less costly then, without MRIs and other expensive technologies. Arch realized that, by giving people health insurance, he was taking care of them on a long-term basis; it was more beneficial than a pay raise."

Neely continued, "Arch Moore didn't just play politics. He didn't come into office having any racial, ethnic, class or political bias. He didn't come in with, 'We've got to take care of labor, business, women's issues,' or whatever. He looked as each issue without ideology." He added, "Arch's approach was always, 'Can government do this efficiently?'"

The Governor also continued his fight for mental health care reform, as he had done in the past three legislative sessions. He told the legislators that there was a $46 million surplus in the budget from which he proposed spending $17.4 on mental health—$7.9 million to upgrade existing facilities, $7.5 for a central mental hospital, and $2 million for community mental health centers. But the trouble, as before, was there was no strong lobby for such actions, no pressure on the legislators to do anything about the growing crisis. They did allocate $6 million, but insisted that no central facility be built, only community centers—a position advocated by mental health (so-called) experts of the day.

In addition to providing health insurance for the first time, he had asked the legislature to increase state employees' salaries by five and a half percent and to establish a minimum $4000 salary for all. Regarding education, he wanted "plans for a comprehensive community college education program" for the state and, to overcome a lack of physicians, a program of "intern and residency support of community hospitals," costing $300,000.

Moore told them he had directed the Board of Regents to "undertake building the necessary foundation for the establishment of a medical school at Marshall University." There would be more than $46 million in budget surplus that year, he predicted, and he had a list of projects—vocational rehabilitation, park improvements, water and sewage projects, libraries, airports, FFA-FHA camp, state police expansion, School for the Deaf and Blind, and agricultural improvements—that needed the excess funds, he said.

The Governor proposed an elections reform bill, that would limit expenditures by candidates for governor and other state offices (just in time for a likely race against you-know-who), require strict reporting of campaign contributions (which would someday be used against him) and making buying or selling a vote a felony.

Three state hospitals—Fairmont Emergency, Hopemont and Denmar—had undergone improvements, he announced. Huttonsville prison inmates were undergoing vocational and other educational training. Improvements had been made in numerous state-run facilities, on which he elaborated. Coal mine fatalities had dropped from 63 to 41 in the past year, making 1971 "the best record ever in the history of West Virginia," but he added that "we must never be satisfied until the fatalities are diminished to zero" (a goal he would reach in a subsequent year as governor).

As might be expected, Arch had an amazing report to make regarding road construction. Nineteen seventy one had been the greatest in terms of highway construction and repair, he told them, with $388 million having been spent. A thousand miles of road had been resurfaced, 63 miles of new four-lane highways had been opened and 14 miles of new two-lane had been opened to traffic. A final contract had been awarded for 140 miles of I-79 from the Pennsylvania line to the Kanawha County line—40 miles having been finished and another 38.5 miles to be opened shortly, meaning it would be half-way complete before the end of 1972. The new road "will open vast sections of the center of West Virginia that have heretofore been deprived of development potential," he said. What he called "Corridor E," now I-68, was under contract from I-79 to the Maryland border, with the exception of the long bridge across Cheat Lake. The 63-mile four-lane (Route 50) from Clarksburg to Parkersburg, which he called Corridor D, was now finished, connecting to I-77. He announced that contracts would be let for numerous single projects, including one for the New River bridge, "which will be the third highest bridge in the nation and the most expensive highway contract ever in the state's history."

An "expensive, complex undertaking" was being started to widen and improve the West Virginia Turnpike (taking it from a dangerous three-lane to a straighter, four- and six-lane highway, a project that would still be in the works when Arch returned to office in the Eighties). "Corridor L," from near Sutton to Beckley, "is progressing rapidly," he told them. Initial contracts for a Wheeling bypass for I-70 would occur that year, with a new bridge across the Ohio River, costing $50 million. Corridor G, Route 119, was being built from Charleston to Williamson, and 19.5 miles was under construction. Corridor Q (Route 460), a four-lane expressway in Mercer County, was under construction. Altogether, 3,500 miles of roads had been built or "greatly improved by the highway department," he said, to applause. The "five year $1.5 billion program of highway construction goal which we set for ourselves in 1969, will be exceeded by the end of 1972," concluded Moore on that subject. "All of our state is benefitting and all of our citizens are traveling on better roads than ever before." To build these new highways had required the purchase of 2200 parcels of private land, costing the state $23 million alone.

In his January 12, 1972, State of the State address, the Governor had requested authority to sell an additional $120 million in road bonds from the 1964 and 1968 issues. He told them, "I don't need, nor does the state of West Virginia need, additional road user taxes to support road bond debt service [as the news media had suggested] even after we sell all the bonds." But Moore's proposal to issue additional millions in road bond money was blocked by state Senator Alan Susman, a Democrat from Beckley, and six other "Young Turks" in the senate, who contended that he already had $135 million available.

Moore strongly disagreed and put the item on the agenda for a special, April session of the legislature (in which he asked for $100 million road bond authority). In it he asked for authority to begin construction on fourteen community mental health centers and one central mental health facility plus eight mental retardation centers. Public employees health insurance was on his list, and he wanted authority for deep-earth oil and gas exploration. He also wanted enough money to fund kindergartens everywhere in the state, not just in limited locations, noting the likelihood of a successful lawsuit due to "unequal educational opportunities" if no action was taken to provide enough funds for kindergartens in all counties. "It's unfair when 10,000 youngsters can go to kindergarten and 20,000 can't," he declared.

This time, the legislature granted authority for the use of $100 million in road bonds, providing $20 million more than would have been given Moore in the bill it rejected in the regular session.

When not enough funds were available for all his programs, Moore cut $20.8 million from the budget again, primarily from donations to the teachers' and public employee retirement funds. (Due to his and subsequent governors' cuts, those funds would become seriously underfunded by the 1990s.)

THE MOST INTERESTING story of the year, however, was the battle everyone had been anticipating for four years, in which the 35-year-old Secretary of State would challenge the 49-year-old Governor for his position. The money was, literally and figuratively, on the ex-New Yorker to send Arch Moore packing. Not only his wealth, but intense national media attention, had given John Davison Rockefeller IV a mystique in West Virginia, and even in some other quarters, similar to that given to the Kennedys or to a crown prince. This was the Rockefeller who would be president some day, according to *Look* and some of the other national magazines of the day.

But all would not go as conventional wisdom had expected. Those national writers may have been engaged in wishful thinking, but they did not know West Virginians as well as they thought they did. While Jay had money and mystique, he was yet to be an individual of substance. Without the name and money, it is unlikely he would have risen above House of Delegates or have been noticed outside Kanawha County. On the other hand, Arch entered the race with a longer list of accomplishments, perhaps, than any political leader in the state's history, to that point. Even in a two-to-one Democratic state, that meant something. But Rockefeller's people were confident enough that they were already picking out what department of government they wanted to head. Some were already thinking about "beyond '72," and a possible race for the White House in 1980.

With those expectations, Jay and Sharon flew from town to town on January 25, 1972, to formally announce his candidacy for governor in multiple locations, for maximum exposure.

Richard Grimes noted one incident that first day, that would pretty much set the tone for the entire campaign season. "An elderly man on crutches, wearing an Arch Moore button, stepped in front of a crowded elevator and demanded an audience with Jay, which he got. He proceeded to give Rockefeller a tongue-lashing for being a carpetbagger." Grimes continued, "Meanwhile, an aide feverishly tapped the elevator operator on the shoulder trying to get him to shut the elevator door. Unfortunately for Rockefeller, the elevator operator was a Moore supporter and loved every minute of it." He added, "This was typical of the kinds of situations Jay would encounter week after week in his [1972] campaign."[1]

If Jay thought Moore would be easy to defeat, due to the party registration imbalance and controversies with which the Governor had dealt, he was in for a rude awakening. Jay, more than Arch, became the issue, to the surprise of many. Rockefeller had not yet convinced West Virginians that he was in the state to stay, or that he was "one of them." To many, he still appeared to be an opportunist, who was using the state merely as an easy launching pad for a presidential bid or, at the least, a Senate seat that might be easier to win than in his home state of New York. Most West Virginians fully expected him to return there if he lost an election. "He's just using us," was often heard.

His enormous wealth and family background were not the assets that he and others expected them to be in that election cycle; they may have even caused distrust and suspicion. And perhaps most importantly, although he would break records, he would not spend the obscene tens of millions on this race as in subsequent campaigns; there would be no "scorched earth" Rockefeller campaign in 1972, in which every possible "election worker" would be purchased with a portion of his vast inheritance.

ON FEBRUARY 2, 1972, the Governor entered his press conference room, made a few announcements and then was joined by Mrs. Moore and their three children. A hush fell over the crowd of staffers and media reps. Until now, he had kept mum his political intentions. There had been some speculation that he would challenge Jennings Randolph for the U.S. Senate; that was where he wanted to land eventually. But Arch announced that it was his decision, along with the "people of my party," to seek "re-election as governor," noting that there were calls and letters which advocated both races. The news media was delighted that the Jay-Arch bout had now been confirmed.

Arch was proud to run on his record of the past three years. Employment had increased by over 52,000 jobs in those thirty-six months. Per capita income growth was the fourth highest in the nation. Workers' and unemployment compensation benefits had been raised, there were far more occupational safety laws on the books, fewer occupational fatalities, a kindergarten program had been launched successfully, teachers' salaries had raised from 44th in the nation to 20th place. A community college program was in the works. Federal funds were seeding twenty vocational schools. Thousands of miles of highway had been constructed or repaired. Eight new medical clinics had been built by the Moore Administration. The results of computerization, more honest and efficient bidding procedures, and government reorganization could not be underestimated–they had saved state government millions. A third budget surplus was announced that year. The elderly, blind, disabled, the mentally ill and those on welfare were getting better assistance. Junk was being cleaned up, surface mine violations were being prosecuted, 2500 young people were cleaning up litter in the summers and the air quality standards had greatly improved during Moore's term. State government was cleaner than it had ever been; the flower funds were gone. While there would always be political considerations, politics no longer dominated every decision the way it had done in past administrations. People were being hired and retained, contracts were being granted, choices were being made based on merit, a business-like basis, which was a refreshing change.

Both men would sail through their primaries with token opposition, carrying every county. Jay would mistakenly interpret his landslide Primary Election victory to be an affirmation of his call for an abolition of surface coal mining. There was a "strong demand that certain wrongs can be righted," he told a crowd and it confirmed to him that there were "strong abolition feelings." Moore said he didn't see the primary wins as a mandate on anything.

Moore decided to base his re-election bid, not on any promise for the future or special issue, but simply upon his record as governor. He again retained the Robert Goodman Agency of Baltimore to do his advertising, remembering their classic performance of 1968.[2] Goodman recommended several alternative slogans, including, "He made us proud again!" "A great beginning deserves Moore!" "We'd Rather Do it Ourselves!" (a phrase Moore used to end most of his campaign speeches, to remind voters that Jay was from New York), "We're Doing Just Fine, Thank You!" "Arch Moore IS West Virginia!" and "Doing Great–Doing it Ourselves!"

Moore's people settled on, "Re-elect a Good Governor," as his campaign theme. Attractive white political buttons, posters and billboards carried that theme. The buttons and ads often did not even mention Arch by name; everyone seemed to know who the "good governor" was.

Goodman wrote a theme song that was played publicly for the first time at the Republican State Convention in Charleston in the summer of '72. It was designed to play as a ballad accompanied by guitar and banjo. Like the slogan, it didn't once mention Moore by name. Goodman felt it was unnecessary to do so. The song, in a low-keyed fashion, reminded voters how Moore's efforts had changed the state for the better, while emphasizing traditional mountaineer pride and independence. It had a John Denver flavor to it, similar to "Country Roads."

> Hear what they're saying 'bout West Virginia
> Kinda get the feeling we're on our way;
> Skip to the hollers, bow to the mountains,
> Got us a bright new day.
> West Virginia, our time has come
> The hammers are swingin' and the truck wheels hum
> The road that wasn't is the road that is
> And it leads to a life we've a right to live!
> West Virginia our time has come![3]

Again, the Democrats had nothing like the colorful and musical campaign Moore's was playing on the airwaves. What they did have was a glamorous young candidate and wife (Sharon Percy Rockefeller was a daughter of liberal Republican Charles Percy, a wealthy U.S. Senator from Illinois). At first, Jay campaigned confidently, as if it was all over but the counting. He would even make self-depreciating jokes. "I'm just a tall, cool glass of milk," he would tell audiences in his then somewhat awkward, goofy style.

Governor and Mrs. Moore hit the campaign trail in their usual high-energy, action-packed, fast-moving style. It was a fun campaign for them this time, however, running as popular incumbents and statewide celebrities for the first time. It may have been their happiest race ever. Most of their appearances were at party dinners or at civic organization events,[4] where the First Couple would be welcomed as heroes. Arch would give his usual speech, highlighting his administration's accomplishments and ending with a quiet, dramatic, "My fellow West Virginians, we can do it ourselves!" and roaring, standing ovation. Moore supporters were fired up more than they ever had been, or ever would be again. Arch was successful in making them feel "it is us against them," the "them" being outsiders, liberals, people who simply didn't understand West Virginians or their needs, their way of life.

Lucy Moore was a student at George Washington High School that year. "The Worley boys' dad was working for Rockefeller, so we joked back and forth" throughout the campaign season, she remembered. What she didn't know was that the same rivalry, give-and-take, was happening on high school and college campuses around the state. With eighteen-year-olds voting for the first time, younger people were interested in the gubernatorial race, as much as the presidential battle. (Like a football rivalry, both sides loved to show their colors. Interestingly, it was not unusual to see a student wearing both a McGovern and an Arch Moore political button. The strip mining issue rallied a lot of college and university students to Jay's cause as the environmentalist movement grew.)

Goodman capitalized on the "carpetbagger issue" with a series of TV ads that were later recognized by the political advertising industry as classics. Released by "Democrats for Moore," so the regular re-election campaign would not have to "go negative," the best one showed a man-on-the-street interviewer asking residents of New York City whether they would like to have a West Virginian running their city. The respondents' negative responses to such a preposterous proposal, in their heavy Bronx and Brooklyn accents, made the point perfectly and with great humor. They were highly successful in emphasizing the "outsider" image. Better yet, they got people talking.

In addition to all the color, advertising and charges and counter-charges in the campaign, there was a realization that there was a fundamental difference in philosophy between Rockefeller and Moore. Not necessarily that one was good and the other evil, or the one fully right and the other wrong, but they were quite different in the way they viewed the role of government and their own personal responsibility as leaders. It would become even clearer when Rockefeller later became a U.S. Senator, but even in the 1960s and 1970s he had developed the belief that government's role, primarily, was to help, to subsidize the poorer elements of society, to tax business and wage earners to pay for programs that would provide those less fortunate ones and the elderly with medical care, housing, food and funds on which to live. In that regard, he had a lot in common with the European socialists. It helped, of course, that the lower income strata, and the government employees and academics who supported them, voted very heavily Democratic; this was a primary constituency and dependable vote. It also fit into the West Virginia culture which was similar to big city political machines and had existed since the New Deal, the quid pro quo which held, "You keep voting us into office and we will make sure you have all the benefits and programs you want at someone else's expense."

Arch Moore proved through his actions that he also was sympathetic to those in need and did much to alleviate their burden, their needs (after all, he'd once been poor, unlike his Democratic opponent), and he'd raised his share of taxes. But serving the less fortunate was only part of his program. He envisioned a state in which business and industry thrived and jobs were readily available. He geared much of the efforts of his three terms as governor to accomplish that. In his view, only with the economic opportunities that earning good wages offered could all citizens prosper. And if more people were working, more government services could be made available to all. He believed in a "hand up, not a hand out," as Lyndon Johnson would sometimes phrase it. During the Reagan era, critics would call this "trickle down economics," but to Moore and other like-minded Republicans, it was just common sense, a continuation of the capitalist, free enterprise system that had made America strong and the lack of which made other nations weak, ignorant and poor.

Restoring pride and confidence in the state—among its own people and outsiders who might invest—was also part of what Moore tried to do. He had preached it incessantly, since his days in Congress—that West Virginia could be as good, as great as any state; it was his theme. Those efforts weren't simply cheerleading or provincialism; they were designed to boost the economy and to offer a better future. As a young man, Arch observed the good Franklin Roosevelt was able to accomplish simply by restoring hope and optimism to the American people; FDR gave them vision and confidence in a way that was self-fulfilling. Arch wanted to infect his fellow West Virginians with the same optimism he had about the state; he hoped it would be contagious.

And, although Arch did not believe "L'etat c'moi," as some of his critics suspected, he did see himself as one who had the state's best interests always in mind. He quietly shared the strong suspicion of many West Virginians that Rockefeller was simply wanting to use the governor's office as a springboard to a U.S. Senate seat or even the presidency, that the position was not an end in itself. Jay's national career, in his mind, was more important than the state's future, in other words. As Arch would say about himself and other candidates, "The people can look into your eyes and tell very quickly whether you are sincere." He and many others weren't sure Jay was sincere.

In the Spring of 1972, the project Arch had helped initiate nearly three decades earlier, to erect a Mountaineer statue at West Virginia University, reached its goal. A graduating law student, Tom Tinder, was Arch's successor as Summit of the Mountain organization that year. He invited the Governor to do the unveiling of the statue at the WVU Mountainlair. Tom would write to Welfare Commissioner Edwin Flowers soon after meeting Moore for the first time that day, asking if he needed any lawyers. Flowers replied negatively, because the State then had no lawyers in state agencies; they all worked for the attorney general, housed in his offices. But he did have an administrative assistant position; Tinder eagerly agreed to take it.

Within a few weeks, however, Bill Loy asked Tinder to take a leave of absence to go manage the Governor's campaign headquarters on Quarrier Street in Charleston. "I did real important things like make sure there were enough brochures and coordinated volunteers' activities," Tinder laughed. Except for the days when the Governor's daughters, Lucy and Shelley, would join the team doing mailings, it was pretty routine, mundane duty.

"I had grown up in Pittsburgh and had no political connections," Tinder noted. "My law school friends told me I'd made a terrible mistake. They said, 'Jay is going to win and you'll be out of a job in six months!' We didn't do constant polling like they do now, but there was the feeling that, here's the fair-haired representative of the Democratic Party, this big, tall Jay Rockefeller with a lot of charisma, who's come down here to help West Virginia, gave his time to Emmons, has an overwhelming [party registration] majority. A lot of people thought Jay was going to win." Agreed Richard Neely, who was on the statewide Democratic ticket that year: "We all thought Jay was going to win."

Loy and many others who worked in the administration would put in a full day of work at the capitol and then join Tinder at the headquarters at five or six and work late hours there, meeting with people like T.K. Killen, a Logan County Republican politico, who arrived late one night with a handgun strapped to his belt, Tinder recalled. Campaign field workers like Tom Craig, Dalyn Curry and Rod Clay, would come in at ten or eleven to pick up posters and materials for the next day's work.

Tinder got to work up close with Bill Loy, whom he considered "a political guru" and came to admire his total dedication to Arch. "He was one of a kind. He was the prototypical right-hand-man. He was the Governor's biggest supporter. The lieutenant governor.

"[Loy] was not very tall, maybe five-seven or five-eight and very friendly; he could really work a room. He and the Governor were both good for each other. The Governor relied on Bill but Bill understood who the Governor was–it wasn't that the Governor was the boss and Bill the underling or that Bill was pulling the strings in some Machiavellian way; it was a partnership; they worked together." Tinder believed that Loy brought with him from the mountains of Romney a strong work ethic and desire to make the state a better place. Loy's only obvious fault, Tinder recalled, was that, unlike his boss, he was always chronically late. "I don't mean a few minutes, but always at least a half hour or an hour late."[5]

GOVERNOR MOORE had always felt that the capital, the most populous center of the state, deserved to have a training facility for physicians. The WVU Medical Center had won out in the bid to become the state's sole medical school during Governor Patteson's administration and Morgantown remained the only place in the state providing a medical education. In the summer of 1972, he found a solution. Two million dollars was made available by the Sarah and Pauline Maier Scholarship Foundation to create an area health education unit at Charleston Area Medical Center, which would be matched by state funds, the Governor announced, a $6 million project that has succeeded to this day.

On Sunday, June 4, Moore lead a group of governors—Mandel of Maryland, Milliken of Michigan, Anderson of Minnesota, Sargent of Massachusetts and Smith of Texas—on an *NBC Meet the Press* interview by Lawrence Spivak which originated from Houston where the National Governors were meeting. Governor Moore spoke forcefully for Nixon's revenue sharing plan, $3.5 billion for cities and $1.5 billion for the states. He added that it "would be a real concrete contribution to the tremendous burden [the states] carry if the federal government would take over 100 percent [of] the present welfare burden," explaining that he thought it only fair, since the federal government and its federal judges were telling the states how to spend their welfare dollars.

When asked whether former Texas Governor John Connally should replace Vice President Spiro Agnew on the GOP ticket, as Nixon was considering, Arch conceded that Connally had done a "commendable ... outstanding ... job as Treasurer," and would be "as legitimate to be considered as any" should Agnew be dumped. Spivak asked him if the recent shooting of Governor George Wallace caused him to support gun control. He said no, that Congress could not legislate safety. Outlawing hand guns would not bring "stability or tranquility," he told the national audience. But he added that any gun control would have to be initiated on a federal, not state, level. He voiced opposition to Nixon's national sales tax proposal.

In response to Spivak's question of whether the concerns of environmentalists could be reconciled with the need to extract coal, Moore reminded him that "it's our prime basic industry," but also pointed out that West Virginia had adopted its "first effective means of controlling strip mining" in 1971. He told Spivak that in his three years, 57,000 more West Virginians had become employed and he was "not in the position of wanting to immediately unemploy 20,000 people who are identified with a productive energy industry." When another interviewer asked, "Aren't you putting short range goals ahead of long range goals?" Moore responded, "I don't think so, because we have very effectively moved, under the authority we have now, to control the reclamation process of strip mining."

HIS TERM was ending that year as chairman of the National Governors. Moore pledged at his last press conference while in Houston that he would "put all [his] efforts toward passage of the revenue sharing act," Nixon's program which eventually would pour tens of millions into states like West Virginia.

In the meantime, he continued to defend his administration from the challenger, Jay Rockefeller, who continued to turn up the heat on the strip mining issue. Moore denied that he was in the pocket of the coal producers, pointing out that his campaign contributions were coming from diverse interests across the state. Until this point, Arch had not emphatically taken a position one way or the other regarding "Jay's issue." But when pressed by a student to state his position on the abolition issue, the Governor replied, "I am against the abolition of strip mining. That is the best English I can give you."

Arch continued to warn crowds that the state was not ready for the young, New York import. "I happen not to believe it's time to turn this state over to inexperienced, unsure, immature hands. We need strong leadership in the state. West Virginians are going to ring up the biggest 'not for sale' sign on November 7 that you've ever seen. I think this whole [Rockefeller] campaign is directed at trying to destroy the coal miner, whether above the ground or down under. If you destroy the American marketplace for West Virginia [coal], you destroy West Virginia. Coal is our way of life, and I am concerned that our way of life has been challenged." Moore would call Jay an "economic royalist" and "the most ruthless man in America." He was sent here to "destroy the coal miner and his family," the Governor would charge, toward the end of the campaign, turning up the heat of his rhetoric. "You're not going to sell your birthright to some stranger who's here to destroy us."[6]

In the last couple weeks of the campaign, Arch and Shelley would board the campaign motor home (leased by the campaign, but dubbed "The Mobile Governor's Office") and visit one small town after the other. They were generally daytime visits when most were in school or at work, but an enthusiastic, small crowd would be waiting at almost each stop. Seeming to draw excitement and enthusiasm from those greeting him, Arch would wade in, shaking every hand, with a different but similar phrase to each one in his deep voice, "Good to see ya ... Nice to say Hi ... Hello, I'm Arch Moore ... It's been a long time ... Good to say Hi ... Nice to say hello!" While shaking each hand and looking each one directly in the eye (it helped that he was about the same height as most in his crowds), he would energetically and quickly work his way down the line to an impromptu lectern or table, where he'd give a short, off-the-cuff speech, about the last three years' accomplishments and plans for the next four years, before dashing off to another town.

Shelley would return to the bus, a calm refuge from the chaos, where she would get in a relaxing smoke between stops. The couple, always a team, was clearly having a good time. This was fun. The respect and affection they felt increased their confidence as they went along. Local fans would join them on the bus and drop off before they departed to another county. (Arch's mother had accompanied her son to appearances in Northern West Virginia, such as the Mannington Fair in 1970 but, getting up in years, pretty much sat this one out.) The couple was no longer just "Arch and Shelley" to some—they were treated with awe by those who respected how Arch had turned the state around in so many ways, so quickly. He was becoming legendary.

Although confident, they kept a hectic pace, as if they were running far behind Jay. "I enjoyed the campaigning when we would get into it," said Shelley Moore. "It was a fast life. But then we'd come back to Glen Dale to get away from it for a while, or we'd have the family come to Charleston to be with us."

He had heard it so often from his allies that Jay was convinced that his opponent was corrupt. He believed that, if he could just expose some evidence of it, he could do much to defuse Arch Moore. He announced to his advisers in a closed meeting that he had come up with a solution. "I've got two of the best lawyers in the state working on it," he told the group. "Charlie McElwee and John McClaugherty are going to investigate Arch Moore!" Tiger Morton was not impressed and, with his sarcastic wit blurted out, "Oh, good! Put those two together and maybe they'll have an IQ equal to Arch Moore's!" Jay was not amused. He ordered Tiger from the room.

It wasn't just Rockefeller who suspected Moore's ethics, however. Even his friends and allies heard the rumors buzzing around the state, from time to time, and wondered if they were true. "It's almost like they didn't care," however, noted Larry Swann, then a Republican Delegate from Doddridge County and Moore supporter, who thought the public apathy shown on that subject was "because they appreciated his enormous leadership capabilities." (Years later, even after his legal problems sent him to jail, Arch still could not fathom why there were suspicions that he had used the governor's office for private gain. For one thing, he simply hadn't the time to pursue corrupt activities, he contended.) As people close to him would acknowledge, his long, action-packed days as governor were spent improving the state. "He, Bill Loy and Dick Frum were in there, almost seven days a week, working late into the evenings, burning the midnight oil," Swann admitted. "They really worked hard for the state, especially in that first term."[7]

Arch's GOP adversary of two decades, former Governor Cecil Underwood, popped up again in the 1972 campaign, apparently still licking his wounds. In June, the former Republican governor had alleged to the *Gazette* that former Governor Wally Barron had offered (Underwood) an industrial job in New York, if he would endorse Arch Moore in 1968, but that he had refused, calling it a bribe. He said he was then convinced that Barron's and Moore's organizations had been cooperating with each other four years earlier. It was unclear as to whether Cecil or the Democratic newspaper was responsible for conveniently "waiting" until the middle of Arch's 1972 battle with Rockefeller to reveal this alleged deal. It was not corroborated by other evidence.

Moore's only response to the charge was to quote a caller, "If the former governor [Barron] did anything to help your election, it was probably the most constructive thing he ever did for the state." The situation further strained relations between the Moore and Underwood. Looking back on it, Arch asked, "Why would I have even wanted Barron's support? I won [Democratic votes] by meeting people one-on-one." Besides, Barron had his legal problems in 1968, had been out of office for four years, and his endorsement would have been essentially worthless in that election in any event, Moore pointed out. Trying to imagine why someone would even have such a suspicion, Arch remembered, "I once had Bonn Brown [Barron's associate] in my office. But I'd see anyone, whoever they were, if they asked to see me. It didn't matter if they wore bib overalls or a tux, I'd see them."[8] But Underwood's guilt-by-association allegation won some long-term admiration from the *Gazette* and even from Rockefeller. It was as if their common dislike of Arch Moore caused them to bond. Not even their own battle in the 1976 race would erase that bond. (As governor, Rockefeller would recommend Craig Underwood, the former governor's son and a WVU student body president, for a Rhodes Scholarship to Oxford, for example.)

Carrying some more of Jay's water, the *Gazette* trotted out an old incident, inferring that Moore had taken a bribe during his congressional years, pointing out that he had received campaign contributions ranging from $100 to $1000 from six people in his district who were not yet citizens, for whom he had sponsored a private immigration bill. State Democrat Chairman William Watson called it "a conflict of interest," but GOP Chairman Tom Potter said it was a "cheap political shot in the characteristic Democratic campaign to this point." Potter said Moore's "noble effort to bring medical services to the people of West Virginia is being made something sordid and dirty by half truths and innuendoes."

The Charleston paper continued attacking Moore relentlessly throughout the campaign. "Ned Chilton was close friends with Jay. And I think Ned originally was upset about the charges that he'd taken advantage [as a lawyer] of an incompetent," explained newsman Charlie Ryan. Arch, who called his opponent "High Pockets" continued to use his favorite name for the *Gazette*, always a big hit among his fans: "The Morning Sick Call." He never referred to it by name; it was always, "The Sick Call," or "that paper."

In dramatic fashion, the Governor once said to the capitol press corp, "If I, Arch Moore, crossed the Kanawha River in a canoe and a child was drowning and I, Arch Moore, walked on water to rescue that child and deposited him safely onto the shore, the headline in the *Charleston Gazette* the next morning would be, 'Arch Moore Can't Swim!'" *Gazette* columnist and humorist Jim Dent did a political cartoon or two thereafter which depicted Moore walking on water. His favorite and recurring version was Arch with a robe, crown and scepter, however, Little King Arch. "I think that's how Ned always perceived the Governor," thought Ryan. "Dent was probably drawing those at Ned's request."[9]

The political stories by the *Gazette*, whether regarding Arch or other subjects, were always agenda-driven, advocacy journalism; they were as unbiased as a lawyer's brief. But it could never be accused of being dull. Its attacks on the Governor and his responses just made readers buy more copies to see what each would say next; maybe that explained the colorful, if sometimes bitter, feud better than anything else. The *Gazette* "always set the pace for the press," thought Ryan. "They always had an agenda, an editorial stance, always wanting to seek a change, whether good or bad. Other papers were not as strong in that regard." It had success, too, "because it was the morning newspaper in the state capital. It circulates widely throughout the state and the *Sunday Gazette-Mail* has an even wider, more dramatic impact." *The Daily Mail,* which then matched the *Gazette* in circulation and remained Republican, business-leaning, "was widely read by the legislators and throughout Kanawha County" because it was the capital's evening paper, Ryan observed.[10]

And the harsher the attacks, the more Arch's friends wanted to rescue him. Money was extremely easy to raise, recalled Moore friend Tom McCoy. "It was wonderful–people would call me to find out how they could donate to Arch's campaign. It was so easy to get money that year," thought Dr. McCoy who believed Moore "was the best damn governor we ever had!"

The polls from the Rockefeller side were fairly close through mid-year, but "started looking bad" in October, remembered Pete Thaw. "But we still thought we were going to win." For his part, Governor Moore was confidently, quietly assuring his supporters "we're just where we want to be," in the polls, without revealing how far ahead he was.

Thaw believed the campaign to have been clean on both sides. There was perhaps one small exception. Some of Moore's volunteers, almost certainly without his knowledge or consent, would go into one of Jay's many headquarters, pretend to be supporters, and ask for boxes of his materials, which were plentiful to the extreme. After dark, they would promptly dump them into a nearby river. "If fish could vote, Jay would have been elected," laughed Tom Hopkins, who volunteered in the Moore campaign toward the end.[11] On one occasion, Jay couldn't understand why he had such a small crowd at a Martinsburg rally. It was later discovered that someone, presumably Moore supporters, "had deliberately advertised his appearance at the wrong hotel to make Jay's supporters think they'd been stood up," wrote Grimes. "To some extent, it worked."

Thaw thought the national Democratic race to be a "disaster," noting that Senator George McGovern had not been an attractive candidate, and pretty well ended his chances when he dumped Senator Thomas Eggleton as his running mate, after the latter admitted he had undergone shock therapy for severe depression. "Nixon's landslide [the President would be the first Republican since Eisenhower to carry West Virginia] was just

At left, Cadet Moore, left, at Lafayette College. Photo at right, Cadet Moore, right, stands with colleague. —*Photos courtesy of Arch A. Moore, Jr.*

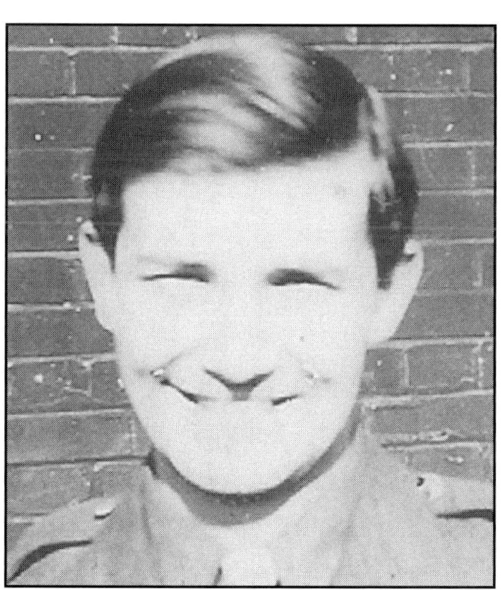

Above, Sgt. Moore, before his near-fatal wounds put him out of action. —*Photos courtesy of Arch A. Moore, Jr.*

Above, Arch gives his first speech, as a junior at Moundsville High School. At right, Arch's Moundsville High School senior photo. —*Senior photo by Photo Crafters, both photos courtesy of Arch A. Moore, Jr.*

Governors Cecil Underwood, Ronald Reagan and Arch Moore, 1978, Morgantown, W.Va. —*Photo by Brad Crouser.*

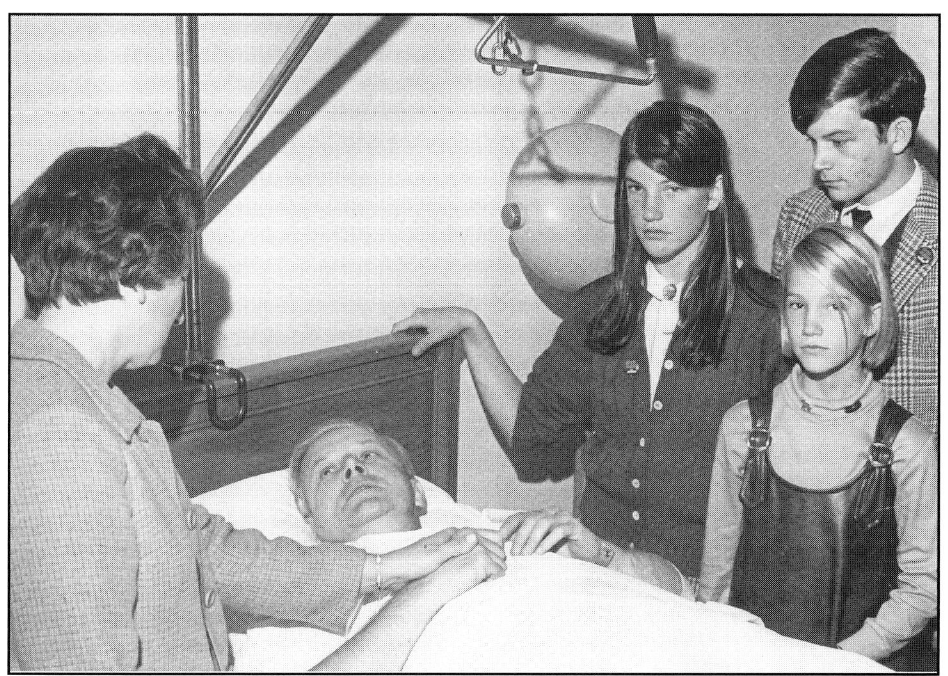

With his family at Charleston General Hospital, following the November 1968 helicopter crash. —*Photo by Earl Benson.*

Some believed a sympathy vote regarding Moore's helicopter crash in Hamlin made a difference in the tight 1968 gubernatorial race. —*Photo courtesy of the W.Va. Division of Culture and History.*

Dr. Carl Roncaglione, Norm Yost and Sandy Latimer ease Congressman Moore's wheelchair down the steps of CAMC General, following his 1968 helicopter crash. Mrs. Moore and their children follow. —*Photo by Earl Benton.*

Congressman Moore's CIA helicopter was shot down on one of his several visits to Vietnam during the war. —*Photo courtesy of Arch A. Moore, Jr.*

F.T. and Eldora Moore, Arch's paternal grandparents. F.T. made and lost a fortune. —*Photo courtesy of Arch A. Moore, Jr.*

The future Congresswoman with Dad on her wedding day in 1976. Shelley and Charlie had their wedding at the newly-opened Cultural Center. —*Photos by William Hubbard, courtesy of Shelley Moore Capito.*

EVERETT F. MOORE, (R), of Moundsville, was born April 29, 1885, at Beeler Station, Marshall County, son of F. T. and Eldora (Redd) Moore; educated in the public schools, at Wheeling Business College, University of Virginia and West Virginia University, graduating in law from the latter institution; married April 15, 1914, to Gertrude M. Redd, of Denver, Colorado, who died April 21, 1938; Methodist; Elk; Knights of Pythias; actively engaged in the practice of law since 1906, practicing in the courts of West Virginia, Ohio, Pennsylvania and Illinois; member of the Bar of the Supreme Court of the United States since 1912; member of American Bar and West Virginia Bar Associations; city attorney at Moundsville, 1913-1925; serving his sixth term as a member of the House of Delegates from Marshall County, having been elected in 1908, 1910, 1918, 1920, 1922 and 1938, and serving as Minority Leader at the sessions in 1911 and 1923, and as Chairman of the Judiciary Committee in 1919.

Everett F. Moore, Moundsville lawyer and politician, was Arch's uncle and mentor. "He was the smartest man I ever knew," said his nephew. —*Photo credit: West Virginia Blue Book, 1939.*

After Bill Loy departed, observers noted a marked change in Arch Moore's success. —*Photo courtesy of The Charleston Gazette.*

Arch with his parents, Genevieve "Sis" and Arch, Sr., January 1969. —*Photo courtesy of Arch A. Moore, Jr.*

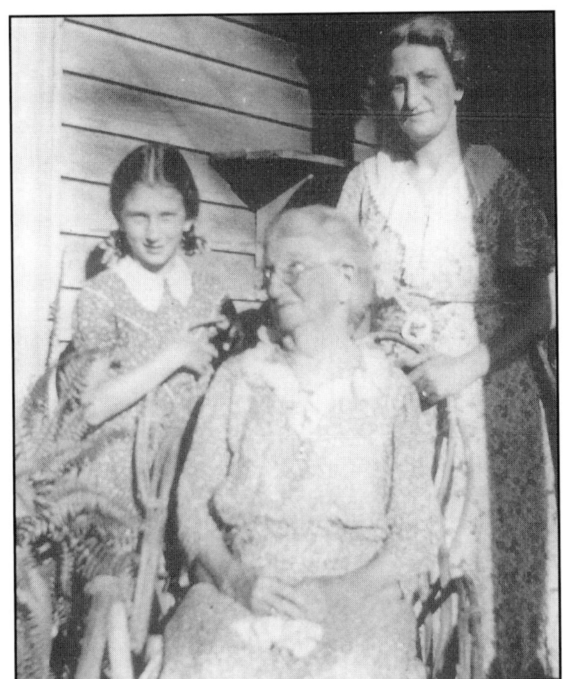

At left, the future First Lady with her grandmother, Anne Wellons and mother, Sadie Shelley Riley. *—Photo courtesy Mrs. Arch (Shelley) Moore, Jr.* At right, the future governor of West Virginia at age three. *—Photo courtesy Arch A. Moore, Jr.*

Arch is sworn in as governor, January 1969. *—Photo courtesy of The Charleston Gazette.*

1969: Governor Moore announces what was possibly the best cabinet ever assembled in West Virginia. —*Photo courtesy of The Charleston Gazette.* At right, friends of Moore donated this bust to the Cultural Center. Governor Rockefeller tried to have it removed, only to find it had been anchored into the foundation. Governor Caperton simply had it boarded up. —*Photo by Earl Benton.*

Jay Rockefeller signed this one, "To Johnny Owens, Looking at 1980 and beyond!" —*Photo courtesy Johnny Owens.*

Attorney General Robert F. Kennedy praised Congressman Moore for his authorship of federal crime bills.

With President Lyndon Johnson on Air Force One. In background, John Slack and Ken Hechler. —*Photo courtesy of the Lyndon B. Johnson Library.*

A jubilant Governor Moore talks to the news media, following his acquittal in 1976. Beside him, Mrs. Moore and daughter Shelley. In the background, Col. Donohoe, Stanley Preiser and Charlie Capito. —*Photo courtesy of The Charleston Gazette*. Below, there were more than twenty Arch Moore for President organizations across the nation in 1976.

Above, Arch and Shelley hosted an annual picnic for his Congressional staff and summer student interns. Susan Hardesty sits between Arch and Shelley Moore in this 1967 photo. The Moore daughters are to the left, standing, and Kim Moore is second from the right, standing. David Hardesty is fourth from left and Bill Loy is third from the left, standing. In the photo below, the Moore family pose for this portrait at the Governor's Mansion. —*Photos courtesy of Arch A. Moore, Jr.*

The Moore family—The Governor, Shelley, Kim, Lucy and the First Lady, circa 1969. —*Photo courtesy of Arch A. Moore, Jr.*

Arch has been a lifelong fan of the WVU Mountaineers. —*Photo courtesy of Audrey Toler Pennington.*

Governor and Mrs. Moore at the January 14, 1985 Inaugural Ball. —*Photo by Sue Ogrocki, United Press International.*

Above, with Justice James Sprouse, right. —*Photo courtesy Audrey Toler Pennington.* At right, Governor Moore and his faithful friend, Col. Fred Donohoe. —*Photo by Earl Benton.*

Governor and Mrs. Moore share a laugh with Bill Loy. —*Photo by Steve Ladish, courtesy of Audrey Toler Pennington.*

With two unidentified congressmen on the Capitol baseball team. —*Photo courtesy of Arch A. Moore, Jr.*

The Moores wade through the crowd at the 1968 W.Va. Republican Convention, at the Charleston Civic Center. —*Photo by Earl Benton.*

Above left, Moore's official Congressional photo, late 1960s. At right, Congressman Moore, circa 1967. —*Photos by Fabian Bachrach, courtesy of Arch A. Moore, Jr.*

Arch served one term in the W.Va. House of Delegates. —*Courtesy of Arch A. Moore, Jr.*

Candidate Moore with his former commander, Dwight D. Eisenhower, 1954. —*Photo courtesy of Arch A. Moore, Jr.*

The Arch Moore for Congress Bandwagon, 1956 campaign. —*Photo courtesy of Arch A. Moore, Jr.*

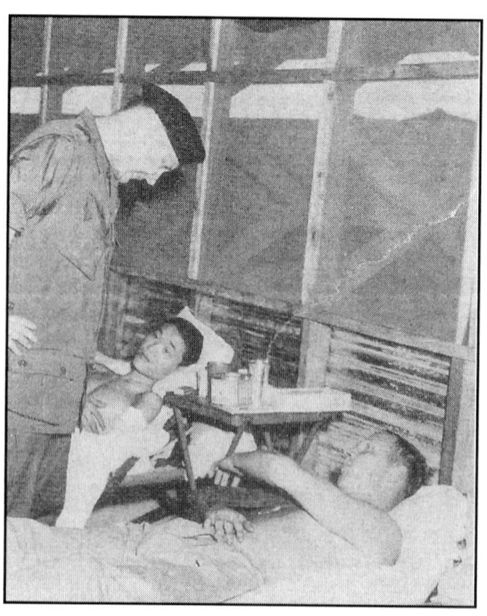

Congressman Moore visits the wounded in Vietnam. —*Photo courtesy of Arch A. Moore, Jr.*

Arch's mother, Genevieve "Sis" Moore spent her career as a pianist for a Moundsville dance studio. Photo circa Christmastime 1980. —*Photo courtesy of Arch A. Moore, Jr.*

A change of less than one vote per precinct would have made Moore a U.S. Senator in 1979. *—Photo courtesy of Arch Moore, Jr.*

The Moores meet Pope Paul VI. *Photo from the Vatican, courtesy of Arch Moore, Jr.*

Governor and Mrs. Moore, circa 1988. *—Photo courtesy of Arch Moore, Jr.*

Arch found private funds to re-gild the capitol dome, after Rockefeller sold the gold he'd set aside for that purpose. *—Photo courtesy State of West Virginia.*

President Reagan's conservative policies shut off the tap of federal funds to West Virginia when Arch needed them the most. —*Photo courtesy of the Ronald Reagan Presidential Library.*

Moore, who trained to become an engineer before the war interrupted that career, learned construction techniques, such as this stayed girder bridge, from the Germans. *—Photo by Earl Benton.*

The Moore Family on the Inaugural parade stand, January 1973.
—Photo by Jay Wildt, courtesy of Arch A. Moore, Jr.

The win over Jay Rockefeller in 1972 was the apex of Moore's career. —*Photo by Earl Benton.*

The Moore family celebrates at the 1973 Inaugural after defeating Jay Rockefeller. —*Photo by Earl Benton.*

Rep. Moore makes a point to LBJ and Defense Secretary McNamara. For some reason, Johnson called Arch "Judge." —*Photo courtesy Lyndon B. Johnson Presidential Library.*

Below, Actor Jimmy Stewart's overnight stay was a highlight of their years in the Mansion, said Mrs. Moore. —*Photo courtesy Arch A. Moore, Jr.*

With then-Vice President George Bush, 1987. —*Photo courtesy of the George H. W. Bush Presidential Library.*

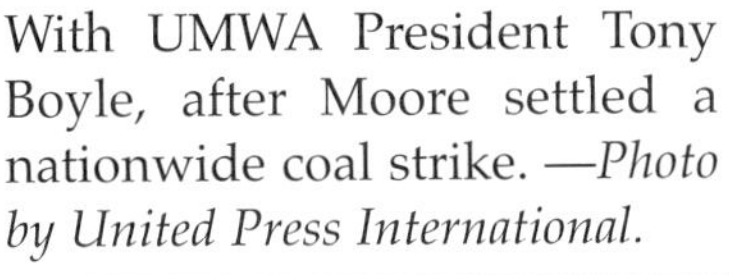

With UMWA President Tony Boyle, after Moore settled a nationwide coal strike. —*Photo by United Press International.*

Governor Moore and Senator Byrd discuss the Appalachian Regional Commission. —*Photo by Ronald Thomas, UPI. Courtesy of The Charleston Gazette.*

With Arnold Palmer at the Greenbrier. —*Photo courtesy Arch A. Moore, Jr.*

Above, his friend, President Gerald Ford, hands Governor Moore a pen with which he signed a federal highways act, 1976. —*Photo courtesy of the Gerald R. Ford Presidential Library*. Photo below, Arch "Rosie" Moore, Sr., (Arch A. Moore, Jr.'s father) gave up football at Bethany College to marry sweetheart, Genevieve Jones. He's fifth from the left in front row. —*Photo courtesy Arch A. Moore, Jr.*

Congressman Cleve Bailey and his campaign manager, Jack Whiting. — *Photo courtesy of Frances Whiting.*

Governor Moore joins General Charles E. "Chuck" Yeager, as Kanawha County's airport is renamed for the West Virginia pilot who first broke the sound barrier and inspired "The Right Stuff." Yeager took Moore for a wild jet ride after the ceremony. —*Photo by Audrey Toler Pennington.*

Arch's maternal grandparents, Zebedee and Lucy St. Clair Jones.
—*Photos courtesy of Arch A. Moore, Jr.*

Euan, Cherie and Tony Blair with Governor Moore, 1986. —*Photo courtesy of the State of West Virginia.*

Old friends Moore and Randolph let others sling the mud in their 1978 U.S. Senate race. —*Cartoon by Brad Crouser, Better Times Weekly*

Congressmen Arch Moore, John Slack, Ken Hechler and Harley Staggers, Senators Jennings Randolph and Robert Byrd, and Governor Wally Barron join President John F. Kennedy at the White House to kick off West Virginia's Centennial, May 20, 1963. —*Photo by Cecil Stoughton, courtesy of The John F. Kennedy Library.*

Governor Moore signs into law the state black lung bill and ends a three-week strike by 42,000 coal miners. —*AP photo, courtesy of The Charleston Gazette.*

With *Daily Mail* editor Bob Mellace, Governors Underwood and Smith. —*Photo courtesy The Charleston Gazette.*

Governor Moore escorts another inmate from Moundsville Penitentiary after peacefully ending another prison riot there in January 1986. *—Photo courtesy The Charleston Gazette.*

From his Moundsville law office, surrounded by family, Arch concedes the 1988 gubernatorial race, ending his political career. —*Photo courtesy The Charleston Gazette.*

Governor Moore cheers as West Virginia's votes put President Gerald Ford over the top to defeat Ronald Reagan in the 1976 GOP Convention. —*Photo courtesy The Charleston Gazette.*

Arch and A. James Manchin coach a friendly basketball game between the Democrats and Republicans. —*Photo courtesy The Charleston Gazette.*

Chief Judge Frank Haymond, preparing to administer the oath of office in January 1969, to "one of my law school boys." —*Photo by Jay Wildt, courtesy of Arch A. Moore, Jr.*

When not sleeping, Arch always kept his mind occupied. Here, playing Solitaire on the state plane. —*Photo by Jay Wildt, courtesy of Arch A. Moore, Jr.*

The A Team, 1987. Front row: Ben Bailey, Hoppy Shores, John McCuskey, Governor Moore, John Scott and Nelson Robinson. Standing: Richie Robb, John Leaberry, Ken Faerber, John Durbin, Charlie Capito, Kevin Sikora and Mike Roark. —*Photo copyright 1987 by Steve Ladish, courtesy of Kevin Sikora.*

At left, a Taylor Jones caricature, 1980. At right, cartoon by James Dent. —*Courtesy The Charleston Gazette.*

A somber Arch and Shelley leave the federal courthouse on May 8, 1990 after formally entering a guilty plea on five felony counts. —*AP wirephoto by Dale Ferrell, courtesy The Charleston Gazette.*

Brother Harry "Moo" Moore said that when he dropped Arch off at the prison in Alabama, it was the saddest day of his life. —*AP photo, courtesy of The Charleston Gazette.*

The extended Moore family at their annual vacation at Sea Island, Georgia, 1996. —*Photo courtesy Arch A. Moore, Jr.*

Audrey Toler Pennington with the Moores in 2004. Audrey was de facto "Assistant Governor" in Arch's third term and a long-time, loyal secretary. —*Photo courtesy Arch A. Moore, Jr.*

Charlie and Congresswoman Shelley Moore Capito, with her parents, Christmas 2004. —*Photo courtesy of Arch A. Moore, Jr.*

Cartoon by James Dent. —*Courtesy The Charleston Gazette.*

Arch and Shelley Moore, 2005. —*Photo courtesy Arch A. Moore, Jr.*

another nail in [Jay's] coffin." (There were some who urged Jay to disavow McGovern, but he ended up endorsing him and even joining the South Dakota senator when he made a campaign stop in Logan, squatting by a stream to complain about pollution. At his Logan County stop, McGovern tried to take the anti-poverty mantle of Robert Kennedy by announcing that, as president, he would give every poor family a thousand dollars, sort of a reverse income tax, and a lot of money for the time. The proposal went over like a lead balloon and caused more than a few to call McGovern a Communist.)

Raamie Barker was an inside precinct worker in Logan, where the Democrats had a seven-to-one advantage. Yet, as they streamed in to vote, many asking for assistance from inside election workers, voters would say, "I just don't want to vote for that 'Govern," and Barker and others would have to show them how to split their ticket, voting for Nixon at the top. Ticket-splitting was a new concept to many. McGovern, lumped in with the anti-war protesters and dopers, fairly or not, would take only 33 percent of West Virginia's vote, and carry only Logan County. Recalled Barker, "People I knew to normally be straight Democratic voters would actually come in and say, "I want to vote straight Republican." Himself a Rockefeller Democrat that year, Barker would coax them, "Are you sure you want to do that?" But the Logan Democratic voters would assure him that was exactly their intention: "'Yes, I'm afraid I'll lose my vote if I don't.' So they'd pull the lever for the entire Republican ticket." They had been frightened off, he thought. "Republicans had been calling those who supported the Democratic ticket that year 'pinkos.'"

Barker actually thought that Arch did not really need to spend the money he reportedly dumped into the southern counties that year. "He would have won those anyway," he thought. "The strip miners and all those who depended on them for their livelihood went out to vote against Jay because of his position on abolishing surface mining."

The other problem was that "Jay never took the rubberband off his bank roll," thought Thaw. "He spent only $2 to $3 million in 1972. He learned his "lesson." By contrast, he spent over $20 million [against a much weaker candidate, Cecil Underwood] in 1976." With the strip mining coal money available to him, Moore had been able to stay in the game at that level. Thaw added wryly, "The night we lost [the 1972 election] Bob McDonough said, 'We did something tonight. We made the next person who works for Jay Rockefeller a lot of money.'"

Fumbles had followed the Rockefeller campaign throughout the year. At the national Democratic convention, for example, then-CBS reporter

Roger Mudd stuck a microphone in Jay's face on live, national television, telling him that someone had slipped him a note, saying that Jay had something important to say to the nation. "What was it?" asked Mudd. "Nothing," mumbled an embarrassed Rockefeller, who was taken by surprise. Someone had set him up, or perhaps Mudd was just having some fun.[12]

He would make careless blunders, from time to time. For example, he decided that, with Moore's sterling record for road building, he would try to divert attention from the subject by pointing out that secondary roads had too many potholes. So Jay and a film crew went out into Kanawha County to make a TV commercial in a particularly pocked road. They had to stop when it was pointed out that the City of Charleston (with a Democratic mayor and council at the time) had the responsibility for that stretch of highway, not the State.

Far worse were the hostile crowds that greeted him in coal country, presumably put up to it by the surface mine operators, but in some cases simply as result of genuine anger at an outsider whom they believed disrespected and wanted to eliminate their source of subsistence, their livelihood.

"To say that Jay Rockefeller was harassed ... would be an understatement," Richard Grimes wrote. "It was closer to a violent reaction." Dozens of miners would follow Jay around, from town to town, terrorizing him and his entourage as he campaigned. They would even threaten shop keepers to lock their doors as he made his rounds. They would taunt, interrupt and shout him down as he spoke. In Boone County, protesters poured beer in his gas tank. In October, his bus tires were flattened in Lumberport. At an intersection, one miner blocked Jay's campaign van with his Cadillac, refusing to move until forced to do so by police. His campaign staff had several scares; they were convinced someone was going to take a shot at him. Many times, they wanted him to stay in the van. Other times, they would stuff his large frame in to a decoy Volkswagen to divert the tag-along protesters so he could make an appearance in peace.

Lesser men would have given up, but Jay was courageous; he kept a stiff upper lip and stood tall, through it all. His bravery and poise was amazing. The Secretary of State appeared almost fearless, going in among the hostile crowds without guards. He would just smile, maybe blush a bit, patiently waiting for their yelling to cease. At most, he would politely call to the protesters, "Ok, boys. You can go home now. You've been paid and done your thing."[13]

Rockefeller later "actually became friends with those people," thought Blane Michael, who eventually would work for him. "He brought a lot of them around." Michael added, "He's dedicated, smart and charming. He's genuine, because he's kept at it."[14]

In addition to hostility from surface miners, the state's hunters (there were at least 100,000 in West Virginia at the time) and adherents to Second Amendment rights became distrustful of the Democratic candidate when Sharon Rockefeller came out for gun control. She told a national magazine that she favored restrictions of gun rights because her sister had been murdered and because the Kennedys and Martin Luther King had been killed with guns.

Likewise, it did not help his chances when GOP State Chairman Tom Potter pointed out that the Rockefellers had taken opposing stances on the abortion issue, one which had suddenly heated up when the U.S. Supreme Court chose to act as a Super-legislature by issuing *Roe v. Wade* that year.

Republicans also circulated leaflets that pointed out that Jay had sought college deferment to avoid the military, not popular in a state with more veterans per capita than any other.

Jay continued, as he would in subsequent campaigns, to promise to produce 50,000 new jobs in West Virginia. Governor Moore called it "the depth of mediocrity and a fertile nothing," much to reporters' delight.[15]

In Logan, where Moore was greeted by a crowd of more than a thousand, he charged that $95,000 (cash) had been sent by the Democrats into twelve southern counties, $14,000 into Logan, to buy the election for Jay. "It's time he's removed as chief elections officer," Arch told them. He called Rockefeller "the most ruthless man in America," at one rally. (Much of Moore's hyperbole originated from comments made by a Washington atomic energy consultant, who thought the Rockefeller financial empire, including Chase Manhattan Bank, was trying to shut down the coal industry to benefit their financial investment in worldwide nuclear energy.)

Before leaving Logan County, Arch went over to Buffalo Creek, where he broke ground for a new housing development to replace many of the homes that had been destroyed. In Braxton County, he opened another section of I-79 and announced a grant allowing the grass airstrip there would be paved. The Clay County High School Band and two hundred fifty enthusiastic supporters greeted him at the courthouse there. He said, "I'll tell you, there's only one special interest in this state. It begins with an 'R,' and ends with an 'r,' and it's in here to use us."[16] Moore made a sweep up through his First District counties, in the campaign motor home. Large, warm crowds welcomed him in Bridgeport, Clarksburg, Shinnston, Mannington, Rivesville, Grafton and elsewhere. Joe and John

Manchin accompanied him on some of the tour, the latter sporting a Moore button. A. James Manchin was on hand to welcome him to the Farmington town hall but, wore only a McGovern button. Everywhere were Democrats, openly proclaiming their alliance to Arch, an almost unprecedented phenomenon.

The Governor slammed Rockefeller for questioning the integrity of the supreme court, with regard to a ruling it had issued the previous week regarding election officials in Mingo County. "It is typical of his reckless irresponsibility and immaturity, and should raise serious questions about the qualifications and objectivity of this individual," he said. (But Jay was probably right about that one.)

The *Gazette* tried to create an "October Surprise," by running on the front page a very old story, the Marion County prosecutor's criticism of Moore for pardoning a convicted felon whom Arch had represented as a lawyer, years earlier. The Governor's spokesman justified the pardon, saying the early release had been due to medical reasons, based on advice of a physician. (The story may have caused Arch to lose Marion County, but seemed to do him no damage elsewhere.)

Despite the heaviest spending in the state's history on political TV ads, Rockefeller was not gaining traction. He knew things were bad when Senator Robert Byrd would not give him a strong endorsement. When pressed to state his position regarding his party's gubernatorial candidate, Byrd would only tell reporters, "Let's just say that Bob Byrd supports Democrats." Byrd even stood Jay up, failing to show for a McDowell County rally at which he'd promised to play his fiddle for a Rockefeller rally. His lack of support understandably irritated Jay. His friend, Senator Edward Kennedy, did help out, though. Teddy appeared for a torch light parade in Clarksburg and elsewhere.[17] When Teddy spoke at a heavily-attended Rockefeller rally in Logan, however, there were far more Arch Moore posters in the audience than ones favoring Jay. Kennedy said with a smile, "I'm glad to have you Arch Moore supporters here, since you don't have a rally of your own to go to." Said Raamie Barker, who was on the platform, "That eased the political tension. Before he said that, I was afraid a fight was going to break out."

A *New York Times* writer claimed that Jay had problems even with the environmentalist liberals. He was "no god to the tiny band of liberation activists in the state," the article alleged, because "they claim he bungled the fight in recent legislatures for abolishing strip mining, and was reluctant to fight for a black-lung law when miners were striking in 1969." The paper added, "Some West Virginians think [Rockefeller] hopes to use the elections in his adopted state as a springboard to national office—perhaps a shot at the vice presidency in 1976. Hence, he is frequently labeled a carpet-bagger." Despite a three-to-two edge Nixon had in the polls in West Virginia, they thought the gubernatorial race "was very close."[18]

As late as October 31, however, the *Gazette,* with Jay's friend Ned Chilton pushing hard for him, ran a front page poll which alleged that Rockefeller held a ten-point lead over Moore. "It is highly significant," the paper's Harry Hoffman crowed, that their poll allegedly showed Jay beating Moore in Kanawha County, since it normally went Republican for governor. It "should be most encouraging for Jay Rockefeller," Hoffman wrote. Arch beamed with confidence throughout the campaign, however. He knew what his polls showed.

Moore joined Secretary of Transportation John Volpe, First Daughter Tricia Nixon Cox, Senators Randolph and Byrd and Congressman Harley Staggers in Morgantown on October 24 to open the Public Rapid Transit system for WVU. Boeing had designed the PRT as a prototype, hoping that it would be used in cities like Los Angeles, to cut back on smog and crowded highways. It proved to be a white elephant over the coming decades, however. (Some said that the government could have purchased every student a car for the millions that went into building, maintaining and operating the PRT. It certainly proved to be no better than the previous bus system, which remains on campus to supplement it, more than three decades later.) According to Byrd, "about 150 protesters ... some dressed hippie-style, shouted 'stop the war' and other slogans."[19]

The President made a campaign stop in Huntington on October 26, landing there in a Convair rather than the full-sized Air Force One, explaining, "this airstrip was a little bit short." Nixon acknowledged that Governor Moore had influenced him on important issues during the past years. "I had a decision to make about the black lung," he told the wildly enthusiastic crowd. "It was a difficult decision...I will never forget, however, the day Arch Moore came to the White House. He sat there in the Oval Office. You know, he doesn't pound the table. He doesn't shout. But, boy, does he come across. So I signed the bill and, Arch Moore, we thank you for coming in for that."[20]

Arch ended his campaign the same place he had in 1968: Hamlin, Lincoln County. This time about two thousand people showed up at the field where the Moore's helicopter had crashed four years earlier. During the speech, Arch looked over and said, "Boy, oh boy, every time I look at that flagpole..." He ended by confidently assuring the crowd, "I've checked time again and, ladies and gentlemen, we aren't going to give them one area of this state. It will be the most resounding victory any man in public life has had in West Virginia."

It was boasting a bit, but not too far off. When the votes were all counted, no Democratic candidate for governor in West Virginia had ever lost so badly to a Republican—Arch won by a 73,355 margin—423,817 to Jay's 350,462, with 54.7 percent of the vote. What's more, 30,000 more people showed up at the polls than had voted in the tight race of 1968, giving Arch 45,000 more votes than he received that year. Moore won forty of the fifty-five counties. He called it his "greatest victory, considering the identity we were running against, the resources available and obvious numbers in the state," which was Archmoorespeak for: "We did fantastically, considering we were running against a Rockefeller with millions to spend and nearly a three-to-one Democratic registration disadvantage." By putting money into Democratic organizations, Moore also assured that his votes were actually counted that year.

His staff put a sign over the entrance door of his office, "You proved it. West Virginia is not for sale. You're the greatest!" As he entered, shaking hands and accepting congratulations, the campaign song played in the background, "Hear what they're sayin' about West Virginia, kinda get the feelin' we're on our way..."

Even the *Gazette* gave a nod, with a Jim Dent cartoon depicting Moore as Clark Kent, ripping off his suit to reveal, "SUPERARCH!"

The size of the Moore victory was a shock to Democratic leaders. "I truly thought Rockefeller was going to beat him," admitted former Justice Richard Neely, who ran on the same ticket, albeit against token opposition. "It was one of the biggest political upsets in West Virginia history," thought Tom Tinder, (who then returned to his former job as Ed Flowers' assistant at Welfare). "Here, Jay had the name, the Democratic [nomination], he spent the money, and it wasn't even that close!" Tinder thought the fact that it was the first time a governor had been able to run to succeed himself for a four-year term had been a factor. "But it mainly was because West Virginians thought Arch Moore was doing a good job."

Ironically, despite his emotional crusade for a ban of surface mining "completely and forever," Jay nevertheless won many of the coal producing counties, including Boone, Logan, Marion, Monongalia, Lincoln and McDowell, if more narrowly than a Democrat normally did. The money pumped into those counties had kept them from going totally into the Moore column. "It wasn't the strippers who beat us," Tiger Morton told Richard Grimes. "It really was the people like grocers and merchants who had strip miners as their customers. They told [Democrat] party chairmen in their counties, 'Sorry, I'm going to have to sit this one out.' And they did."[21] West Virginians, since the Great Depression, would elect the Democrat every time, unless and only unless the Republican opponent gave a good reason why they should not do so. In 1972, Moore had provided positive reasons to re-elect himself. But he also gave the voters—at least those who realized the state's economy and tax base depended heavily on coal, and always would—a reason not to elect the Democrat nominee.

But the Moore organization (due to the efforts of those like Dick Barber) had cut into the vote of many of those counties, not winning them outright, but obtaining a bigger chunk of their vote than any Republican since before the Great Depression.[22] Statewide, the Democrats were worried and upset that Arch had been able to buy onto so many of their local slates, in some cases slates that Rockefeller supposedly had nailed down with his "donations." Moore had beaten them at their own game–he was laughing, but they were furious.

Jay was just one of their losses that year. Nixon had won a landslide victory over McGovern, even winning West Virginia by 484,964 to 277,435. The President and Governor Moore had coattails for a change, helping sweep fellow Republicans into a majority of statewide offices, the best year for the GOP since Calvin Coolidge's day and a victory not duplicated since 1972. The majority of voters split their tickets for a change, and agreed that it liked Arch Moore, and the people he had chosen to serve in his administration. Moore's workers' compensation commissioner, Edgar "Hike" Heiskell of Morgantown, won the secretary of state's office by three thousand votes over Jay's protege, Tom Winner. John Gates, Moore's DMV and F&A commissioner, defeated a dead Denzil Gainer by seven thousand votes to become State Auditor. Charles Haden won a state supreme court seat by a wide margin.[23] The Morgantown prosecutor who defeated Haden in the primary, Joe Laurita, came within less than two thousand votes of upsetting Attorney General Chauncey Browning.[24] The legislature would have a greater percentage of Republicans than any time since the 1920s, and many Democratic incumbent legislators were nearly defeated. Republicans were rejoicing; for a time (until Watergate changed their fortunes in the next election) they had delusions that the state might be transforming into a healthy, two-party system.

Phones of Democrats who made their living from public office were ringing off their hooks as the disastrous results sunk in. The Democratic leadership—Byrd, Randolph, Rockefeller, and others—agreed that this fiasco must never happen again. A viable Republican party could not be tolerated in the Mountain State; their futures could all be in jeopardy, otherwise. Office holders must be chosen within the Democratic primary, as had been the case for decades. In subsequent elections, straight ticket voting in general elections would be demanded and enforced. They had to make the lopsided registration figures work for them. Too much was at stake. Money—whatever amount it took—would be spent in future races to defeat Moore and his minions. Threats would have to be made to wayward Democrats. And this Arch Moore guy just had to be stopped; he was dangerous to their comfortable and lucrative way of life. Whatever it takes.

But for the moment, Arch had made believers of the state's Democratic leaders; he was not some accident or fluke as they'd viewed Cecil Underwood. At least for a time, they backed off and started treating him more respectfully. Some made their amends, tried to mend relationships damaged by his four year battle with Jay when some Democrats had opposed Moore for purely partisan reasons. Then-Delegate Larry Tucker, for one, went to Moore's office soon after the election, shook hands and then took off his belt, laying it on the Governor's desk. "I'm ready for my whipping," he told Moore. "Arch loved that!" remember Charlie Ryan.

At the end of 1972, even Ned Chilton had to recognize that the people of West Virginia really had "re-elected a good Governor." His Sunday paper named Moore their West Virginian of the Year, an honor they had bestowed upon the likes of Pearl Buck, Cyrus Vance, the Rev. Leon Sullivan, Senator Randolph, Senator Brotherton, Sam Huff and Jerry West, Chuck Yeager, Mike Benedum, and others. They summarized some of the accomplishments of his first four, exciting years in office:

- Monthly welfare benefits increased to 100 percent of basic needs;
- Clothing vouchers were given to 44,000 poor children;
- Pay increases of $1500 were given to school teachers and other school personnel;
- Medical insurance was provided to 122,000 state government and education employees;
- He settled a national coal strike, putting 39,000 West Virginia miners back to work;
- He restored bus service to the Kanawha Valley, affecting 13,000 commuters;
- He started a kindergarten program for 30,000 five-year-olds;
- Workers' compensation benefits were increased 75 percent and unemployment 59 percent;
- Information and assistance was made available to military veterans; and
- State employees received five percent pay raises three of the four years.

The lengthy article noted that Moore was the first West Virginia governor to be re-elected in a hundred years and that he was the first in history to serve as Chairman of the National Governors Conference. It also mentioned that highway construction contracts reached a record-breaking $1 billion during Moore's first term. John G. Morgan, a historian who wrote the *Gazette-Mail* article, tried to explain Arch Moore to the few who did not know about him by now:

> The Governor thrived on adversity and applied an uncanny sense of timing to his big moves in government and politics. He was decisive and dramatic throughout his first term, generally speaking. Rather than sit on the horns of a dilemma, he was inclined to take the bull by the horns. He displayed a knack [for] turning political disaster into an advantageous situation. His speeches reflected an obsession to "turn this state around" from its poverty-stricken and corruption-ridden image to one of beauty, progress and governmental integrity.
>
> As a public speaker, Moore ranked among the best of the West Virginia governors. The volume came on strong, the language and accent suggested an adequate measure of sophistication for the job, and the gestures and hesitations generated enthusiasm and applause. A keen memory of names, faces, figures and facts, an extremely uncommon understanding of people and politics, as unexpected sense of humor and relentless industry on the job added to Moore's personal image as a successful Governor. His usual working day began about 10 a.m. and ended about 11 p.m. with a final reading of the mail in the Governor's Mansion. Aides said the Governor personally signed all of the outgoing mail.
>
> An egocentric style of government, with almost everything revolving around the Governor, characterized the first Moore administration. This method of running state affairs, featuring the strong ego as the hub, fits neatly into the modern expert concept of government, with executive power concentrated in the

> Governor. During peak periods of Moore popularity, the stories about his governmental feats grew from the remarkable to the legendary and–with the help of satirists–to the supernatural. A cartoonist [*Gazetteer* Jim Dent] regularly pictured him as "King Arch," complete with crown and various subjects sitting around. And there were those among the multitudes who said in jest that Moore could walk on water.[25]

AFTER THE grueling campaign had ended successfully, the Moores rewarded themselves with a seven-nation European tour, taking the Yohos with them. "We started in Rome, then on to Athens, then Yugoslavia, where we had to watch what we said," remembered Dr. Yoho. "Then we went to Belgrade, to Austria, Switzerland, Paris, and ended up in London before we returned to New York." He and Arch's daughter Lucy remembered the stops being pulled out for her birthday in Greece. "They had a big party. It was great!" She also enjoyed their stay at a seaside resort in Dubrovnik on the Adriatic coast. Yoho added, "We stayed in a hotel in Athens where I saw some of the wealthiest people in the world. One owned the Greeks' oil company."

ONCE AGAIN, Arch caught the attention of the national news media. His defeat of the rich young ruler *The New York Times* called "Prince Charming," was recognized. In a front page story, Jay's hometown paper hailed Moore's "four year record as the tough and canny head of one of the most successful state administrations in recent history." It conceded that Jay's call for banning surface mining "brought him political grief." Even environmentalists became disappointed with Rockefeller, the writer thought, "after the legislative defeat." That Moore had beaten him meant Jay's chances of being on the national ticket in 1976, as they had earlier predicted, were gone, the writer admitted.[26]

Chapter 19 Notes

1. - Grimes, Ibid.

2. - Goodman had also waged a very good radio campaign for the Coal Association, "Coal Is West Virginia," that played on Mountaineer football and basketball games, until anti-coal industry liberals at WVU and in the UMW (both whom benefitted financially from the money coal extraction generated) caused the network to cease airing the coal industry ads.

3. - Copyright 1972, Robert Goodman Agency. After the campaign ended, commented the

writer of the ballad, "It started as a campaign song, but soon became apparent that there was so much more involved. The music, the words–released for West Virginia, is the spirit and pride they had earned for themselves during the four-year period of totally new and progressive state government. It was a time to take stock of our new situation and to realize that an administration devoted entirely to the betterment of West Virginia could make a vast difference in our lives and in our standing as a state. West Virginia had come alive and was putting its detractors to shame. The best of our resources–human resources–was combining with the spirit of the mountaineer to build a state that was becoming the ideal of the nation. Most states could not match us in increased road building, improved educational standards and bettering of our individual standard of living. Experts from Washington and from other states realized that they weren't so expert that they couldn't learn from West Virginia. We were pioneers, innovators of social programs that worked, administrative systems that saved money. We were doing more things for more West Virginians and earning consecutive state surpluses at the same time. No new taxes were asked for, and unemployment had reached an all-time high. All of it was a promise made good by a former West Virginia congressman from Moundsville who said that there was more he could accomplish on the banks of the Kanawha than he could on the banks of the Potomac. In his first inaugural address, on January 13, 1969, he said, 'The task of making West Virginia a better state is not merely an exercise in politics, but it involves each of us.' West Virginians understood and accepted the challenge. On Nov. 7, 1972, West Virginia convincingly decided that they wanted that challenge to remain alive. We were doing it ourselves and we wanted to keep it that way. Only a few people had noted that the lyrics don't mention Governor Moore by name. It wasn't necessary. In voting to continue his remarkable administration in office, West Virginians have voted to continue a much bigger idea of which we are all a vital contributor. We were voting for ourselves and what we're building in West Virginia. And that's a mark of a great leader."

4. - Occasionally on these campaign stops, Arch would noticeably slip into a side room where, behind closed doors, he would have private discussions with local Democratic machine leaders.

5. - Tinder, June 23, 2005.

6. - Morgan, Ibid.

7. - Swann, Sept. 14, 2005. (Arch agreed that he had been too busy to have been involved in corrupt activity. In response those who said he was a crook, that he used his office for private gain, Moore exploded in anger, with an example of his diligence, which he believed countered those rumors: "I built eleven airports and five hospitals, for goodness sake! They asked what I did?" Answering his own question, he said, "He worked his ass off, that's what he did!") Moore, June 7, 2005).

8. - You will recall that Pete Thaw indicated Barron's money man came over to Moore's side after Sprouse defeated Robertson in the Democratic Primary of '68, however, a development which may have convinced Underwood that Barron and Moore were in cahoots.

9. - Ryan, March 9, 2005.

10. - Compared to today, far more people got their news in print form in those days, and the two Charleston papers would have circulations each sometimes exceeding 55,000. When the two joined their efforts to create one Sunday paper, reportedly it was decided on a coin toss that the *Gazette* would get to publish it. "The *Daily Mail* staff actually thought they won the toss, though, because they didn't have to work weekends," Ryan laughed.

11. - Hopkins later served as Virginia Governor Allen's cabinet officer for environmental issues before his premature death at age 47.

12. - Grimes, Ibid.

13. - Grimes, Ibid.

14. - Michael explained, "There were those who thought Rockefeller would go to Washington [as U.S. Senator in 1985] and never come back. But he's back in West Virginia almost once a week."

15. - Grimes, Ibid. When Jay would eventually get to be governor, the state would lose about 160,000 manufacturing jobs and the unemployment rate would rise to Depression-levels.

16. - *Charleston Gazette*, Nov. 1, 1972.

17. - Jay would not reciprocate when Kennedy needed him, however. When Ted asked him for his support for the Democrat nomination for president in 1980, a Governor Rockefeller refused, sticking with President Jimmy Carter.

18. - *New York Times*, Nov. 5, 1972.

19. - Byrd, Ibid.

20. - Transcript, Oct. 26, 1972, The Richard Nixon Presidential Library.

21. - Grimes, Ibid.

22. - In Logan, for example, the vote was Jay 11,688 to Arch's 8,687; Boone 6485 Jay, 5031 Arch; Webster 2505 to 1731, Braxton 3134 to 2864, Marion 14,715 to 13,506, McDowell, 8490 to 7,681,and others were similarly close. Moore actually won Mingo, Monroe, Brooke, Hancock, Wyoming, Nicholas, Summers, and lost Lincoln by only eight votes. Money had been judicially invested into Democratic slates in those counties by the Moore organization, and it made a difference. Ticket-splitting was an unknown, new concept to many of these Democratic voters, some of whom had sworn to Depression-era parents that they would never vote for a candidate of Herbert Hoover's party. In addition to the fact that Arch's name was on dozens of Democratic slates, making it "safe" for them to vote for him, many of those Southern and Northern Panhandle West Virginians just couldn't stomach what the presidential candidate the liberals had foisted upon them that year.

23. - Moore's 1968 opponent, Jim Sprouse, won a supreme court seat, as did Delegate Richard Neely. It would prove to be one of the most colorful courts in history.

24. - Had Joe Laurita not lost his home county, Monongalia, by six thousand votes, he definitely would have won. He lost it mainly due to a muckraking series of articles by *The Dominion News,* a partisan Democratic paper owned by Agnes Greer.

25. - STATE MAGAZINE, The *Sunday Gazette-Mail,* December 31, 1972.

26. - *New York Times,* Nov. 8, 1972.

Chapter Twenty
Working With "The Dirty Dozen"

On January 16, 1973, Arch Alfred Moore, Jr. became the first governor of West Virginia to be sworn in for a second four-year term, and the first to succeed himself in more than a century. With no outgoing governor to do it, he was introduced in the ceremony by Senate President William Brotherton. Supreme Court Judge Charles Haden administered the oath of office to his former boss, as daughter Lucy Moore held a 113-year-old Bible (which had been used by six prior governors) on which the Governor placed his hand.

The Governor told the gathered crowd that his first inaugural address could have been summarized in one sentence: "I truly believe the people of West Virginia *expect more* of this administration than they have of any administration in recent history." It had *delivered*, he reminded them: "We have said what we would do and we have done what we said we would do. We have never been satisfied to be told that something is impossible of accomplishment."

Injecting into the speech some indications that he was eyeing a future White House bid, the Governor suggested to his audience that state governments were on the rise, in relation to the federal government, and that there was "a new quality of leadership in a vast number of our state governments." State governments could be more innovative, more quickly and effective in responding to problems, and were becoming more important. He offered his opinion that "what our nation needs in its Presidency in the future is a governor."

In a note of generosity and a plea for a more cooperative second term, and in the spirit of "let bygones be bygones," he commended his Democratic opponents for the progress their partnership with him had allowed, calling it "excellent cooperation," and boasted that "no governor of any state in this union has stronger legislative leadership available to help than evidenced in West Virginia by [Brotherton and House Speaker Lewis McManus] and [House Minority Leader George "Bud" Seibert]." But he did take a shot at the opposition press, stating, "However, our greatest obstacle to even greater cooperation in order to produce the most good for the most of our people is a little narrow band of self-proclaimed oracles who seek to pit us, one against the other, without concern or regard for the state or its citizens as a whole."

Working together, the governor and legislature could "even yet write a finer chapter in the history of our state," he proposed. "While it has been suggested by some that the last four years were great years for the State of West Virginia and its citizens, we are constantly challenged to go well beyond our present progress, and to meet our even greater rising expectations, and to improve further every area of the life of the state for which we have the responsibility. The goals we have set, and to which I am personally committed, will far exceed our efforts of the last four years."

Arch received some rare accolades from three prominent Democrats in attendance. Senator Byrd pronounced the speech "excellent," and even Jay Rockefeller called it "energetic" and "appropriate." Former Governor Smith commented, "I think he has done a good job." Governor Meldrim Thompson, Jr. of New Hampshire came to hear Moore and study his welfare reforms, which were still getting national recognition.[1]

Seventy five bands paraded down Kanawha Boulevard for the inaugural parade and The Rose City Cafeteria provided over 15,000 box lunches for the attendees.

As can be imagined, the Governor's supporters pulled out the stops for an inaugural gala. There was a huge victory, as well as the last four years of unprecedented success, to celebrate. And, hey—they hadn't got there by defeating just anyone—it was a Rockefeller they'd beaten to get there! Savoring the victory was as intoxicating as any beverage served that night. The crowd at one inaugural ball especially loved it when Duke Ellington's big band (Lionel Hampton substituted as the orchestra's leader for "Sir Duke," who had the flu) played "Sunny Side of the Street," and the crooner emphasized the line, "... rich like Rockefeller."

This may have been the apex of the Moores' public life.

As more than hinted in his inaugural address, Arch began to dream aloud about a possible White House bid in 1976. "Very frankly, I am satisfied that what our nation needs, to undertake the challenge of our times in its presidency of the future, is a governor from one of the states," he told teh press. When asked whether he had anyone in mind, Arch replied, "There's nothing frightening [about the presidency] that makes me think I couldn't handle the job."[2]

And no one laugh when a "President Moore" was suggested; most could visualize him handling the job quite nicely. Arch thought a governor in the White House might be the answer to the nation's problems; he wanted someone closer to the action, more in touch with everyday people and challenges. "I really feel the federal government has failed in responses to finding the answers to the problems that its people have." Sam Hindman would write in the *Daily Mail*, two days after the inauguration, that "many party dignitaries wore red, white and blue campaign buttons which read: 'Moore for President - 1976'" at a GOP dinner at the Charleston Civic Center. He mentioned that Governors Winfield Dunn of Tennessee and Linwood Holton of Virginia had been "highly complimentary" of Moore in a reception they had attended and mentioned him as presidential timber. Hindman speculated that Arch was really running for the nation's second highest post, but that Moore had responded, "I think everyone knows that no one runs for the position of vice president and that certainly applies to me." Hindman noted that "Governor Moore has worked closely with President Nixon and has been considered by many political analysts as one of the more respected Republican governors in the nation."

Soon the parties were forgotten and dreams of higher office shelved, and it was back to the tough task of running a state in which there was always some type of new crisis demanding the chief executive's attention. And try as he might, it would be difficult to top what he'd accomplished in his first term. It was hard to do an encore as thrilling as the first performance.

"It was like starting again," remembered Tom Tinder about the beginning of Moore's second term. "It was the first time a governor had been able to run for re-election so it was different. There was not so much a feeling of continuity, but rather like we were walking in on the first day in office, like a new administration."

By now, a cultural change was felt in the nation. Among the young people, the hippies, the sit-ins, the marches, the radical, militant behavior, the intense anger that had built up in the late Sixties, were all surrendering to a more mellow time of colorful polyester leisure suits, bellbottom jeans and love songs and the beginnings of disco music. Nixon was withdrawing American troops from Southeast Asia and there was still optimism that his "Vietnamization" might actually work. The Cold War with the Soviets seemed to be easing. Energy crises and problems in the Middle East would take center stage, nationally. Overall, however, the country seemed to be calming down a bit.

Many new faces were seen in the legislature in 1973. In his State of the State, Moore offered congratulations and assured them their work was important as, together, they would seek to pursue "progress and [an] unrelenting attack on generations-old problem areas." With forty-two Republicans now in the House of Delegates, a greater bipartisan balance than any time since the 1920s, Moore had enough friendly Democrats lined up for his coalition that he could have elected his mentor and ally,

Minority Leader George Seibert, as Speaker. (Seibert declined: "I'm flattered by the offer, Governor, but that wouldn't be right.")

"Governor Moore outdid Machiavelli himself in wrestling moderate and disaffected Democratic state senators and delegates away from control of their leaders and then using a divide-and-conquer strategy to get his initiatives passed," noted "Hike" Heiskell, who was now observing these machinations from the secretary of state's office across the hall. "The Governor's ability to put together such a coalition was an exercise of power that impressed even his most virulent critics."

"They called them 'The Dirty Dozen,'" laughed Larry Swann, a Republican in the House who admitted he received a better political science education watching Moore, than he had in his preceding college years. Twelve Democrats in the House of Delegates, including Larry Tucker, Gino Columbo, Donnie Kopp, Adam Toney, Harry Pauley, Dan Tonkovich, Kim Carey, Bob Reed, Ronnie McKenzie and Joe Wayne Hatfield, along with a couple others in the Noah Floyd faction, almost always voted with the Republicans.

As reward for their membership in the Arch Moore Coalition, "The Dirty Dozen" were able to get all sorts of projects approved for their districts, "reaping the spoils," as one legislator put it. Kopp and Columbo, for example, got approval of a U.S. Route 50 bypass for Clarksburg, money for a state park and a senior center for Harrison County. Freshmen Republicans were shocked to find they could get projects in their districts approved, too. "A lot of dramatic things were accomplished those two years," recalled Paul Prunty, who represented Marion County in the House for the first of his twenty-two years in that session. "We were able to get money to complete Valley Falls State Park and Pricketts Fort, Fairmont Emergency Hospital, the Feaster Center for Fairmont State, a new bridge for downtown Fairmont and other projects. That was an exciting time to serve. Because the parties were so evenly matched, it was always a fight and every vote counted. Governor Moore would sometimes send state troopers out to round up legislators for close votes. I was shocked to see one of them brought in on a cot one day, for a vote."

At every opportunity, House Finance Chairman Billy Burke tried to punish "The Dirty Dozen" for their defection. When he cut $3,000 from a Clay County festival, "it was the straw that broke the camel's back," said Swann and, with the Republicans' help, they pulled a coup; they put one of their own in his place. They wielded power like a small third party in a parliament's coalition government. Tucker and Tonkovich would go on to become leaders in the Senate, in no small part due to their accomplishments for their districts in that session. Kopp would become Speaker of the House.

With a working majority, Governor Moore tried to maintain discipline among his troops. Prunty (then a Republican, later Democrat) recalled how he and other legislators opposed the Governor on his requirement that counties bond themselves eighty percent to qualify for grants from the Better Schools Amendment. "I knew Marion County would never vote themselves a bond issue like that and, if they didn't, they would get nothing under the Governor's proposed bill." But he found, when he and others came out against the plan, "It wasn't easy to buck Arch Moore." Yost and Loy, Prunty recalled, "twisted our arms and threatened everyone. The Republican leaders—Seibert, Potter and Judy Herndon—got all upset when we [freshmen] wouldn't got along with the Governor on such plans. They all made life tough for us. But, in the end, he couldn't get enough votes and backed down." Money was available to counties without passing large bonds. "That's how we got the new North Marion High School," he noted. "And Arch eventually forgave us; he didn't hold a grudge."[3]

One incident with Delegate Hatfield demonstrated how Arch thought about five steps ahead as he mapped out long-term strategy, and wasn't afraid to use power to get what he needed.

In 1973, the Governor had about $18 million in revenue sharing funds that he wanted the legislature to authorize him to match with other federal money, in order to replace twelve bridges which were in dangerous disrepair. One, in Swann's district (Middlebourne), was of particular interest to him. "The school buses had to have the kids get off, cross the bridge, and then get back on, because it wasn't safe. It could collapse." But Speaker McManus and President Brotherton did not want to give Arch the $18 million, said Swann. "They wanted to put it in the bank." But each time the leadership would propose adjourning and going home, they could not get the fifty-one votes necessary in the House; "The Dirty Dozen" were voting with the GOP to stay in session until the bridge funds could be authorized. Arch wanted to keep them in town until it was done.

Finally, Lew McManus called Delegate Hatfield into his office and gave him a party loyalty lecture, "about FDR and Kennedy and all that stuff," according to Swann, and Hatfield reluctantly gave the Speaker his word that he would vote with his fellow Democrats to adjourn and to deprive this Republican governor of another feather in his cap. The Republicans got word of Hatfield's "defection" (he would draw enough of his allies to give the McManus fifty-one votes) and ran to the Governor.

Arch called Hatfield to his office later that day. After exchanging pleasantries ("How ya doin', Joe?"), Moore told the Mingo County delegate, "I need you to stick with Mr. Seibert so we can get these bridges built." Hatfield excused himself off, telling the Governor about giving his word to McManus and sticking with his own party on adjournment. "Ok, that's fine," Arch told him, as he led him into the Eagle Room, a small conference area off from the governor's chambers. "Here are some people who've come up to see you," Moore said, and he left the room. Sitting at the table was the Liquor Commissioner, Dickie Barber, who had with him several of Hatfield's relatives–a niece, some cousins, nephews—all Democrats whom the Moore Administration had placed in patronage jobs at Hatfield's request, to run the state liquor stores in Mingo County. Less astute politicians would have appointed Republicans to those non-civil service jobs, but Arch had them there for times like these—leverage to be used. The Democratic leadership was playing hardball and Moore would reciprocate. Scared to death, Hatfield's relatives warned him, "Joe, you vote against the Governor and we're all gonna lose our jobs."

Within the hour, Hatfield was back in McManus's office, literally in tears. "Mr. Speaker, you know I'm a man of my word," he sobbed, "but I'm going to have to stick with the Governor." Forced to back down, McManus and Brotherton conceded, giving Arch the money he needed and the bridges were quickly replaced with new ones. The schoolchildren could ride across in safety.

IN ADDITION to the bridges, Moore sought approval of another constitutional amendment to provide $450 million in additional bond sales to "build, as rapidly as possible, our modern transportation arteries throughout the state." Road building in the next four years, he predicted, would continue to break records.

With regard to the public school building program the voters had approved in a constitutional amendment in November, Moore wanted legislators to approve a separate board to administer the funds, adopt a formula for their disbursal and set a "Decision Day for Education," a date for elections in which each county would vote on acceptance of school building dollars.[4] He wanted free textbooks for every student in the state, improvements in vocational education, maximum funding for school lunches, all of which he'd put in his budget, he assured them. He wanted a $500 raise for school teachers and a minimum salary of $4000 set for school service personnel. He declared the Teachers Retirement System "sound" and asked for approval for higher benefits for those who had retired prior to July 1, 1970. He proposed the creation of a medical school at Marshall University, to be connected with the Veterans Hospital in Huntington. He wanted more tuition support for state college and university students' tuition.

He proposed dividing the state's federal revenue sharing funds with local governments on a 50-50 basis for construction of streets, sidewalks, people-oriented programs and recreation. He also proposed state assistance for water programs, using federal matching funds. He wanted a single environmental protection agency "wherein the right hand knows what the left hand is doing," and proposed a small tax on appliances and tires to help fund REAP (more about that later). A continuation of the ban on strip mining in twenty counties and a $100,000 mine drainage fund were requested for the Department of Mines. Moore wanted authority to use two million dollars from revenue sharing for land development by the West Virginia Housing Development Fund. He proposed a constitutional amendment for provide a homestead exemption on property tax for those 65 or older. The Governor recommended a partial removal of the sales tax on food, instituting capital punishment for murder (a perennial favorite of state Sen. "Bud" Harman), lifetime sentences for "hard drug" sellers, improvement of the state park system, establishment of a public defender system, increasing the number of state police, and improvements in public institutions, libraries, the state capitol, airports and the arts and humanities. He wanted a Vietnam War bonus for those who had served in that conflict, as well as the survivors of those killed there. (It would be passed by voters as a constitutional amendment later that year.)

Moore's friend Tom McCoy proudly summed it up, "With a Democratic and Republican coalition in the House, he got a lot of things done those two years." Although not in the majority, GOP legislative leaders like George "Bud" Seibert, Judy Herndon and Tom Potter continued to find themselves influential power-brokers during that '73-74 term, working in tandem with the Moore agenda. It wouldn't last beyond that two-year term but it provided West Virginia with a rare exhibit of what a true two-party system could do to enhance progress. The results even made Brotherton and McManus look good, they began to realize.

While it was a more productive legislature, it was just as sleazy as any before it. As had been true for decades in the past, the legislature was "wide open" those years, Paul Prunty noted. "Back then, the State controlled all the liquor sales. The liquor companies would donate cases of their product for promotion and [Liquor Commissioner] Dickie Barber would donate it to the legislature, to keep them happy. I was shocked to find that the Speaker's walk-in safe was full of it! Legislators of both parties would return home on the weekends with trunks so full of liquor that their cars sagged." State-owned farms, established to provide food for prisons and other institutions, would supply the legislators with free meat. All the colleges and universities gave them free football tickets. "There was nothing ethical about any of it," Prunty said. "And in the closing days of the session, the Mafia was in [the legislature] in their three-piece suits, with an open bar in the women's lounge of the House, breaking all the rules. They were trying to get some gambling legislation approved."

THAT YEAR, the Governor announced the creation of a program that would still be running strong when he returned to office in the 1980s. TRIP (Transportation Remuneration Incentive Program) would provide millions of dollars (mainly federal funds) to local transportation systems, senior citizens programs and others needing vans and buses. He also announced the creation of the West Virginia Legal Services Plan, funded by OEO grants, that would provide free legal services to low income residents.

THREE MONTHS into Arch's second term, on March 20, 1973, inmates staged a riot at the West Virginia Penitentiary in Moundsville. It was one of several riots to erupt during the last years of the facility's existence, which had been built in 1867 (as part of a legislative compromise: Weston got the insane asylum and Morgantown the state's only university). Inmates demanded better living conditions and treatment.

A helicopter flew over the prison where two hundred inmates held five guards hostage. A prisoner had overpowered a guard with a knife and then got control of others, who were forced to unlock doors. There was no sending of professionals—the Corrections department head, or the superintendent of state police—inside to negotiate with the rioters. Governor Moore personally went into the prison and handled it himself. He bravely, calmly, but firmly negotiated the guards' release the next day.[4]

He and other prison officials agreed to twenty of the demands made by the inmates. He explained what occurred during this tense time:

"I told them, I'm not here to give you anything. But I will help you. Bring the hostages in here while we converse. They met for fifteen to twenty minutes among themselves and agreed to bring out the hostages. We met for an hour or so. [Mainly] they wanted better food and treatment."
The Governor also agreed to meet with a larger group of rebellious inmates out in the yard ("The State Police were having fits when I agreed to do that," he recalled. "I was surrounded by a large crowd of inmates.")

Moore told them, "I've listened to what you have to say. My father was postmaster here and I used to come in here as a little boy. I'm not gonna let you tear this place up. You list your injustices. Let the hostages remain here when the guards take you back. Surrender the institution back to the guards. If you can't do that, I can't do anything for you." He warned them, "If I have to use pressure or force to take [the prison] back, some of you are not going to be here tomorrow. I'm not going to let anyone abuse you—regardless of what part you played in this, there will be no personal punishment. But the guards will run this institution."

To his surprise, the men applauded him.

The hostages were released and Moore had skillfully prevented further bloodshed. The uprising ended within twenty-six hours. One inmate had been killed in the riot and two others stabbed. The dead prisoner, Willie Hale, had been killed "because he was the warden's rat," a UPI story said. A prison guard had been killed in October and three of the inmates had been indicted for his murder.

But it all could have been much worse. Other states had put down prison riots in a violent fashion which had caused the death of dozens of prison personnel as well as prisoners. Arch had kept that from happening in West Virginia, using little more than the forcefulness of his personality and some sympathy for what was a miserable daily life for most of those inmates.[5]

"We're moving fast in our rehabilitation program and straightening out the problems that were generated by the riots," he told reporters when he went outside the walls, near the huge Native American mound for which the town was named.[6]

Despite the kudos he gave them in his inaugural address, the Governor found himself in a continual battle with Democrats in the legislature and the supreme court. Arch won and lost some of the skirmishes, but it seemed there was constant contention, a struggle for how the state would be run. He found his partisan opponents as equally strong-willed and confident as himself.

Moore would call twelve special sessions altogether, which would work about 106 days. His vetoes totaled 159 in his first two terms and the legislature would override those vetoes sixty-four times. Opponents would take him to the supreme court fifteen times but, even in there, he would often lose the battle but win the war, gaining some new legal ground that was ultimately beneficial. Richard Neely, who was on the court at the time, noted that he often voted in favor of the legislature because that was his background but Justices Sprouse and Haden, who always wanted to be governor themselves, often sided with the power of the chief executive. "Arch would use the Modern Budget Amendment to cut things the legislature had put in the budget against his will. There were three cases, styled *Brotherton v. Blankenship,* filed by the legislature for the purpose of seeking mandamus to reinstate items Governor Moore had stricken. I wrote dissenting opinions in the first two and on the third one we overruled [Moore] and restored the line item."

Reporter and historian John Morgan added to the story:

> In his game of budgetary intrigue with the Legislature, the Governor put more emphasis on revenue estimates during his second term. By deliberate underestimates, he gained more control of the budget through creation of surpluses that might be appropriated to his liking. The Legislature tried desperately to adjust to Moore's various strategies, and often took long recesses to cope with his expected changes to the budget bill and vetoes of other measures [so they could come back and override the vetoes]. For its convenience, the Legislature frequently chose to recess until just after an election.[7]

Brenda Nichols-Harper had been out of law school only a brief time ("I was just a puppy") and was working for Tax Commissioner Dick Dailey during that period. When Dailey took her along for a meeting with the Governor one day, Moore's first impression of Brenda was favorable enough that he asked her to represent two of his commissioners before a joint committee on government and finance, which was meeting momentarily. "It was one of those times when the legislature was out to hang the Governor on his micro-management style," she explained. The issue was his plan to have motor vehicle license plates manufactured more cheaply and with better quality than was being produced by prison industries and Brotherton and others objected; they wanted the plates made by convicts, as had been the case since the 1920s. When Brenda protested that she didn't have sufficient time to research the issue and was unfamiliar with it, Moore replied, "Well, you have an hour!"

"It was my baptism by fire," she laughed, noting that, in that quick hour of research, she discovered that, under certain circumstances, a governor did have the right to opt out of using convicts to make the plates. Nervously, she advised the two commissioners, from Corrections and

DMV, to refrain from answering any of the legislators' questions until they checked with her. "They opened by asking him to state his name and he turned to me and asked, 'Can I answer that?'

"But we got through it, and interestingly—and this was before we had all these electronic monitors—we went immediately to report to the Governor and he already knew what happened. I do not know how he knew such things. But he looked at me and said, 'Brenda, you went up there and did a better job than any man. You busted their balls!' This was a great compliment to me, since women were rare in the legal profession then."

Generally, Moore was a tough coach and, unless one was inexperienced or showed good intentions but just messed up, they could expect to get chewed out by him if they dropped the ball. But his exasperation with the offender usually blew over quickly and he rarely held a grudge against any subordinate.

Whether for public relations reasons or because he had high standards or both, Arch didn't permit personal scandal among his administration members. It was a day when a couple living together out of wedlock was still frowned upon. Once, when word reached Moore that a top department head was living with his secretary he asked him, "So when's the wedding?" The individual replied, "There's no wedding planned." Moore followed up, "Well, if there's not going to be a wedding, then you don't have a job." The couple soon married.[8]

As governor, Arch could also be downright miserly with the taxpayers' money when it came to salaries of his appointed staff and cabinet heads. He would be generous with pay raises for lower paid civil servants and school teachers but, when it came to department heads, he squeezed every penny like Scrooge. Moore resisted pay levels that would draw attention or cause complaints from the public or news media.

School teachers received another five percent pay raise during a May, 1973, special session of the legislature called by Moore. He twice vetoed a consumer protection bill that arose from that session and the senate missed, by two votes, overriding his veto.

During his second term, Arch re-entered the national political scene as chairman of the Education Commission on States and as chairman of the National Republican Governors Association. As such, he took official trips to Japan, China and Russia. In his role as chairman of the Republican governors and in the National Governor's Conference, he frequently spoke on behalf of the nation's governors at special events, just as he once had done for the freshman class in Congress.

He recalled one dinner party at the Vice President's residence. Spiro Agnew, Nixon's liaison to the governors, arose to toast those present. Moore, in turn, returned the toast, with his usual flowery oratory, saying complimentary things about his host and his hospitality. Frank Sinatra, at the table as Vice President Agnew's friend, had heard many a toast in his lifetime. But Frank was so impressed that he walked over to Moore's seat, gushing, "I've never heard a toast like that! I think we need to toast this governor!" And they did.

The new road bond amendment, which passed in 1973 by an amazing vote of 199,588 to 36,929, was allowing the momentum to continue as the state continued its frenzied pace of constructing new four lane highways. It was a tremendous vote of confidence in the progress Moore's administration had made. The bond amendment gave him $500 million more with which to finish the job. It had provided that $120 million be spent on bridges, $130 million to continue the Appalachian corridor highway system, $100 million for secondary roads and $50 million each for West Virginia Route 2 and U.S. Route 52 upgrades.

Always thinking of ways to draw visitors to the state, Moore proposed the building of a National Track and Field Hall of Fame, similar to the football museum in Canton, Ohio (it would not succeed, despite his strong efforts). The Governor even broke ground for the facility, in Putnam County. He also committed $34 million for the arch bridge across the New River near Fayetteville. The Governor had succeeded in getting two much-needed office complexes built on the capitol complex.

Now he proposed a science and cultural center to be built during his second term, prompting critics to say he had developed an "edifice complex." The contract for the Cultural Center was let to an Ohio construction firm in September, 1973. The state's leading architect, Howard Johe, was selected to design the library/museum/theater. (Johe had designed most of West Virginia's greatest structures during the last half of the Twentieth Century, including the WVU Coliseum, Mountainlair and Medical Center, plus prisons, civic centers, court houses, libraries and several college campuses.)

The "edifice," which would cost $14 million and be finished toward the end of his second term, brought controversy and criticism (difficult to imagine today, given the Cultural Center's subsequent popularity). The modern architecture, low-profiled structure (Arch didn't want it to distract from the beauty of the nearby capitol) which the Governor designed was often derided as "Arch's Bunker," a play on the then-popular TV sitcom character's name. Throughout the years of building the Cultural Center, the capitol press, especially the *Gazette,* howled continuously about its construction for that reason. The same papers that later would write nothing negative about the hundreds of millions of tax dollars spent on opulent palaces named after Robert C. Byrd, accused Moore of building a monument to himself. A leading paper would write that Moore's "critics complain rather peevishly," but they were mistaken: "Arch Moore's monument is eight years of the kind of government West Virginians have always deserved, often voted for and, more often than not, done without."[9]

As he would do on other occasions, Moore toyed with his critics, while giving a humorous nod to his own reputed big ego. The inscription, etched in large gold letters on the facade of the building, would include the words: "ARCHIVES - HISTORY - LIBRARY - MUSEUM - THEATER." For fun, the Governor had the workers carve only the first four letters, "ARCH" and left it at that for a few days.

"The opposition was frantic," he laughed, recalling the prank. "They were certain that I was going to name it 'Arch Moore Complex.' When a state senator saw 'ARCH,' he raced onto the senate floor while they were in session. I think Bill Brotherton was at the podium. 'He's named the Cultural Center after himself!' this guy shouted. I think they adjourned to go see for themselves."

He wouldn't name it for himself, but eighty of his supporters did pay to have a realistic, majestic, Caesar-like bust of the Governor placed in the new center ("I knew nothing about that; I was never asked," insisted Moore). His successor, determined that there would be no monuments to the man who once defeated him, would order it removed as soon as he replaced Arch. But his workers would discover that it had been heavily anchored by steel cable into the concrete foundation and gave up in frustration—tearing it out would cause expensive, major damage to the building. Those who placed it there anticipated what would happen and had secured it so that Rockefeller couldn't tear it out. (His second successor, Gaston Caperton, would have it boarded up to hide it from public view.)

The Cultural Center would become a tourist, entertainment, educational and research center showcasing the Mountain State and enjoyed by thousands each year. It quickly blended into the campus and was enthusiastically accepted as one of the state's finest government structures.

Unfortunately for Moore, all was not about building, celebration and accomplishment. Questions continued to arise in his second term about his personal tax situation. In 1973, *The Washington Post* and *The New York Times* both ran articles that claimed Arch's battle with the IRS was still ongoing. They reported that Moore had retained Washington lawyer William G.

Hundley (a former Justice Department lawyer who was representing Attorney General John Mitchell in a criminal charge related to the Watergate break-in and coverup). Stories in those papers alleged that Moore had owed the IRS $170,000, which included $38,000 in interest and $44,000 in penalties, in an audit which extended back to 1964.[10] It was also charged that he had misused $80,000 or more in campaign contributions.

Hundley was respected by Democrats and Republicans alike (he'd worked for Eisenhower and John and Robert Kennedy) as a lawyer of high personal integrity. He downplayed the stories about Moore, calling the case against his client a "turkey." Despite allegations by the press that Arch had received special treatment and that most similar cases were prosecuted criminally, Hundley insisted the tax case was "peanuts...no good...It should never have been brought. What happened, I think, was that Moore didn't pay much attention to the money. He throws himself into a campaign violently, going eight different directions at a time. He was that way every time I was down there to see him ... It was all reviewed by four or five career attorneys in the division and they all agreed there was no criminal case. It was the worst criminal tax case I ever saw. We had it thrown out." He denied a report that Moore had settled the tax liability. "I told him, don't pay anything," Hundley told a reporter.[11]

AS DID PREVIOUS governors, Arch had realized that West Virginians had a particularly bad habit that needed attention. It wasn't unique to the Mountain State, but it seemed to be worse there than in any other state. It was a reason people sneered when they said "Appalachia." Big cities had their urban blight, but West Virginia had its eye pollution, mainly in the rural areas. Detracting from the natural beauty of the state, making them look like a bunch of backward hillbillies to the rest of the nation, and impairing outside economic development, was the fact that many junked up their or others' land with old, rusty cars and trucks, refrigerators and assorted trash. Often such junk would be thrown over a hill, down into a hollow or creek, along a highway, but just as commonly was left near their houses, which might also be in disrepair and in need of paint. This problem, perhaps more than any other, contributed to the negative stereotypes of West Virginia and Arch knew it. Moreover, the junk often posed a health hazard. Something had to be done and it had to be more extensive than anyone had tried in the past. He needed to find someone with talent and enthusiasm to lead a war on junk and this was a bigger project than any existing department of state, such as the DNR, could handle. The Governor thought he knew who to get to do this important, but seemingly unglamourous, job.

Arch and Shelley Moore had known A. James Manchin since their common days at WVU, as did nearly everyone else on campus, because "Tony," as he was then known, made sure everyone knew him. He was perhaps the most colorful character on the West Virginia political stage in a century; he was almost a caricature from a comedy. Increasingly rotund, always with a fedora covering his thick, wavy black hair, a bright kerchief in his pocket of his wide-lapeled coat, highly theatrical and willing to make a fool of himself, he was a relic of an earlier era. "Jimmy," as he would later be known, was gregarious, friendly, loud, flamboyant; he loved to give long speeches in the tradition of his Marion County mentor, M.M. Neely, with frequent patriotic and Biblical references.

Once, to dedicate a sewer plant, Manchin was accompanied by twelve trumpeters. "He made that sewage plant seem like the biggest thing in the world," Ken Hechler laughed. Rules that applied to others were routinely ignored by A. James. He normally would plant a tree at any ceremony to which he was invited. An aide remembered an instance in which the sapling had been forgotten. Undeterred, Manchin had him pull the car over to a random spot where they dug up someone's small pine tree, and proceeded to the event. Moore later remembered a groundbreaking ceremony at which Manchin spoke. "He pulled a pistol out of his pocket, fired into the air, and proclaimed, 'Let the bulldozers roll!'"

A. James was "on," seven long days a week, as if constantly in a frantic campaign for office—on the phone, on the road, going from town to town, shaking hands, chatting with people, doing favors for any and all, handing out ribbons, medals, certificates, giving flowery speeches, making common people feel special—no matter what office he might hold (or be seeking) at the time. Manchin clearly loved people, almost as much as he loved himself; he, too, had a huge ego and strong will. And generally, people loved him back, they didn't see it as buffoonery; he had thousands of fans. He was entertaining! One knew if A. James was present that it would be a memorable, colorful event.

His humorous and gregarious style had delighted the Kennedys, especially Ted, with whom he would remain a friend until his death; no doubt A. James reminded them of an Irish Boston pol. President Kennedy rewarded his service in the presidential campaign with an appointment to state director of the Farmers Home Administration. A. James turned what had been a low-keyed bureaucratic position into a high profile job, getting his photo in newspapers constantly, opening a water system, or breaking ground for this or that. Humorist Jim Comstock wrote that Manchin's foot seemed to have a shovel permanently attached to it.

He survived the Johnson years. But the Nixon Administration had recently chosen their own director and Manchin was out of a job. He and brother John Manchin asked Arch if he had anything for him. After all, John had helped Moore win Democratic votes in the northern end of the state for several election cycles. Moore had the perfect spot for his old friend, something that would utilize his people skills.

He announced that A. James would direct a newly-created agency, REAP (Rehabilitation Environment Action Program), to clean up the state's junk. The first target was an estimated half million junked motor vehicles. In the interview for the job, Arch asked A. James if he could spell "environmental." A. James replied, "Do I have to do it right now?"[12]

Manchin became an even closer friend of Moore's, often dining with him in the Mansion, and calling him at all hours of the day and night about some project. (He would always begin his conversations with Arch, *"Your Excellency ..."*) He attacked the trash problem in his usual enthusiastic, colorful style. He skirmished with a few property owners who thought their junk should not be hauled off, and was threatened many times, physically and with lawsuits, but for the most part, REAP was an enormous success and solidified the Farmington Democrat's position as perhaps the best-known figure in the state. A poster of A. James, atop a mound of junk, became a collector's item.

Fond of alliteration, Manchin would call upon West Virginians to "purge our proud peaks of these jumbled jungles of junkery." He succeeded during Moore's second term in ridding the countryside of 100,000 junked vehicles, in an environmental improvement program that is yet to this day unmatched.[13] The REAP program earned a "Keep America Beautiful" award and was publicized widely through the national press.

It was noted to the Governor, on numerous occasions, that Manchin was getting more publicity than he was. "I don't care what he does as long as he gets headlines," he would tell some of them. He was proud that Manchin was cleaning up the state and was pleased that the project was getting recognition.

ON OCTOBER 10, 1973, Vice President Spiro Agnew suddenly resigned, as part of a plea bargain with prosecutors who had developed enough evidence to convict him of taking bribes while governor of Maryland. Agnew, who had been a darling of conservatives for his attacks on the liberal news media and on anti-war demonstrators, quickly disappeared into obscurity, lucky not to have gone to prison. Under new constitutional powers, Nixon (who was in trouble himself, due to his participation in the cover-up of the Watergate break-in a year earlier) had an opportunity to choose a new vice president. With the real possibility that he might not be allowed to finish his term, the nomination was a critical one; the individual chosen might soon occupy the White House.

With his sparkling record as a productive, progressive governor of a challenging state, Arch Moore was one of at least four candidates Nixon considered (George Bush and Sen. Mark Hatfield reportedly were other possibilities). Undoubtedly, the West Virginia governor's recent tax problems precluded serious consideration at a time when ethics were on the front burner of American politics; he may have been unable to pass an FBI background test and the scrutiny of congressional hearings. Nevertheless, Nixon gave Moore a courtesy call to advise that he would not make the final cut. "Mr. President, in that case I'd like to see you choose my old friend Jerry Ford," Arch suggested to him. Ford seemed to be popular with everyone Nixon polled, in fact. And House Minority Leader Ford it was, and easily and quickly confirmed by the Senate.

THE AUTUMN of 1973 ushered in an ominous, sometimes frightening era. A controversy over content of school text books in Kanawha County became violent, drawing national attention and requiring police protection. For the most part, Governor Moore was able to stay out of that fray.

But a national issue drew more attention. The gasoline which fueled our gas-guzzling V-8 engines had been cheap, plentiful, and taken for granted by American consumers. But late that fall, the oil producing nations of the Middle East and, undoubtedly the U.S. oil companies eager to run prices up, cut supplies. Americans suddenly felt vulnerable and frustrated. Prices were almost doubled and shortages caused vehicles to line up a block long to buy gas at "filling stations" where it was still available. To conserve, Nixon ordered speed limits lowered to 55 miles an hour ("double nickels," the truckers called it) nationwide. Motorists who had to travel sometimes hoarded gas in fifty-gallon drums. Car pooling became popular again for the first time since 1945. Governor Moore set up a rationing system, to avoid the panic buying and long lines. A motorist could buy fuel only on certain days, based on his license plate number and in some cases only certain amounts of fuel per purchase.

With chaos at the gas pumps and shortages of fuel, tractor-trailer drivers began a violent protest. On January 25, Arch warned truckers to end the strike or that the state police would arrest them. He said that "lawlessness and violence would not be tolerated...I am advised that...several drivers were attacked, some were beaten and considerable damage was done to vehicles whose drivers wanted to operate on the highways of our state." The situation was "acute," he said, in the Morgantown-Fairmont-Clarksburg corridor. The Governor called a press conference from the Mansion (he was suffering from a flu bug) on February 5, 1974, declaring a state emergency and activating the National Guard to assure safe delivery of gasoline and home heating fuel. He issued an executive order on February 20, 1974, which extended a rule he had imposed on five northern counties earlier. It prevented gas station owners (few were then self-service) from selling gasoline to a motorist whose vehicle still had more than a quarter tank of fuel. Moore also asked the legislature for $5 million to deal with the trucker strike, which ebbed that month (they gave him a half million, instead). Truckers or companies that refused to haul freight and gasoline would have their license pulled by the Public Service Commission, Arch warned.

The United Mine Workers of America were still in the mode of striking for almost any and all reasons, and the gas shortage also caused 20,000 miners in southern West Virginia to begin a protest over the gas shortages and Moore's rule. On March 13, three mine pickets were shot by snipers. Under pressure, the Governor backed off and provided exemptions for those traveling more than 250 miles per week. Incited by negative comments of their president, Arnold Miller, they remained unsatisfied by the concession and a crowd of them marched on the capitol and stormed loudly into Moore's reception area. "It was a scary situation," said daughter Lucy, who remembered the mob surrounding the family's residence. "They were yelling bad things about Dad. I wasn't allowed to go out."

Against advice of his state police security, the Governor calmly walked out into the reception room to meet them. Arch showed the same calmness and authority he exhibited when he went into Moundsville Penitentiary. He slowly moved through this crowd of rough and rowdy men, shaking a few hands, calling several by name, and soon their leader was shushing them so he could speak. They sat down on the plush chairs and carpet and politely listened to him as he explained the crisis and his predicament as a leader. "If I don't somehow space this gasoline, we're going to go dry by the end of the month," he warned. He assured them the situation would soon improve and they seemed to accept his promise. In fact, they laughed when Arch told them, "If we can't have one hundred percent of the miners' needs within two weeks, then I'll come out with you." But then he quickly added that if he joined the strike it might be a mistake: "If I went out, a lot of people might say, by God, that's the best thing that's happened to the state in a long time!"

Six days after the confrontation, the Governor suspended his rule for thirty days and did not thereafter re-impose it. Miners returned to digging coal. Besides, having obtained their price hike, OPEC began easing oil supplies and the crisis largely subsided for several months. The "oil shortage" magically disappeared as prices rose. Oil barges, which the oil companies had held back in the Baltimore harbor, were allowed to unload. The price was nearly doubled for a gallon of gasoline, from thirty-some cents to sixty-plus.

With conservation of energy the watchword, however, Arch had caught flack from the opposition press and from conservationists for refusing to turn off the floodlights that showcased the state capitol. He countered that there was a supposed oil crisis, not a coal shortage, and that it was West Virginia's own coal that produced the electricity needed to keep the grand structure lit at night.

That same winter, Arch suffered his first real public relations disaster. Some began wondering what had happened to him–whether the absence of Bill Loy (who departed to practice law in Martinsburg, and make some money) was causing him to blunder, that he'd become a bit arrogant as result of the '72 win and all the accolades that accompanied that victory, that he'd lost his well-established connection with the common people, or whether it was simply the Governor doing the right thing for the state, unconcerned about the bad publicity.

In a period sandwiched between the former use of tire chains and today's era of all-season tires, front-wheel and all-wheel drive traction, motorists depended on studded winter tread tires to get their cars and trucks across icy and snowy mountain roads. Trouble was, the Highways engineers were warning Bill Ritchie and the Governor that the studs were causing expensive, serious pockmarks to the pavement of thousands of miles of state highways. The studs were especially destructive to patched potholes. Moore summarily banned the use of studded tires.

Again, coal miners protested, contending they needed the tires to get to work in wintry conditions. Even Republican delegates such as Paul Prunty circulated petitions to rescind the ban, drawing tens of thousands of signatures.[14] Facing another possible strike in the coalfields, growing hostility from the citizenry in general, and a possible mutiny from the legislature, the Governor backed down again, removing the ban on October 30.

In the 1974 legislative session, the Governor had asked for authority to sell $150 million in road bonds, declaring the progress on the construction effort so far to be "tremendous."A five percent raise for teachers and support personnel was requested. He wanted to sell $50 million of the newly-authorized school bonds and again asked for higher benefits for teachers who had retired prior to July 1, 1970, to bring them in line with other retirees. He wanted four million dollars to fund scholarships for West Virginia students attending in-state private institutions. Moore wanted to fund regional health facilities under the Department of Health. He called for continued efforts to upgrade correctional facilities, more money for the Department of Commerce to lure new industries into the state, higher workers' compensation benefits, and more money for REAP to rid the landscape of "visual pollution."

He announced creation of the Commission of Minority Affairs in the governor's office and an Office of Minority Business Enterprises to aid African-Americans and other minorities in starting their own businesses.

The energy crisis which had caused long gas lines and an almost-doubling of gasoline prices in the past several months provided a "golden opportunity" for coal, he told the legislators. He had created the Governor's Commission on Energy, Economy and the Environment, comprised of department heads from agencies related to coal, he said. It would study coal supplies in the state, identify sources of demand for coal, and initiate research and development efforts through the Bureau of Coal Research at WVU. He was also trying to arrange a conference of the governors from the sixteen coal producing states, he announced.

An April special session would contain thirty five items. One asked for the takeover by the state of Morris Harvey College (now University of Charleston). He wanted legislation to help "crippled children"; to require competitive bidding for school board projects; fire protection rules for mobile homes, which were becoming so prevalent in the state; authorization for municipal courts; requiring railroads to obtain PSC permission to abandon lines; authorization for sale of Vietnam Veterans' Bonus Amendment bonds and from the Better Highways Amendment the voters had approved in 1973; funds for reclamation of abandoned strip mines; amendments to bring state water pollution laws in compliance with federal requirements; authority for the DMV to create a new license plate; and creation of a West Virginia Energy, Economy and Environmental Commission and a state Environmental Protection Agency, as well as the Interagency Council for Child Development Services. Most of the remainder of the items pertained to budget changes or a repeat of other items he had included in his January legislative agenda.

During that first legislative special session, in May of 1974, the Moores visited China with five other governors for two weeks, on a fact-finding mission. Such an official visit by American officials to China was still a rare occurrence. "I saw more poverty than any place in the world," he told reporters upon return. "But with all that I saw a happy people." He also felt his Cold War animosities fading. "I came away with the feeling I was not so afraid of them militarily as I had previously conceived."[15]

A front page *New York Times* story told of the nation's first "transportation stamp" program, which began in Charleston on June 13, 1974. Patterned after the food stamp program, which had begun in the Mountain State thirteen years before, it was aimed at 135,000 low income people who were over sixty, or had some type of handicap. According to the Federal Highway Administration director, it was a pilot project which was expected to be used nationally. It had a double purpose: to increase the spending power of those receiving the stamps, and to keep public transportation systems alive, the article said. A retired physician, Dr. Eldon Tucker, had proposed the idea to Governor Moore, the writer explained. The state expected to contribute $6 million and the OEO $4 million to the project. The remainder of its $23 million price tag was going to be picked up by ARC, Departments of Transportation and HEW funds. "People have asked me, can they be used for airplane trips?" Governor Moore was quoted as saying. "I say, yes, although they'll have to accumulate quite a few of the stamps." Until the 1970s, a West Virginian living anywhere along a major route could catch a Greyhound, Blue Ridge or other bus almost every hour. But buses were disappearing like street cars had in the early 1950s. Welfare Commissioner Ed Flowers, noting that the state had been losing three of those bus lines per year, most of them in the rural areas where they were most needed, said a fleet of ten-passenger minibuses were being purchased by community groups that would accept the stamps. A Keystone widow, who had no car to get her to the hospital or stores, bought a booklet of eight dollars worth of the tickets, pronouncing the plan "wonderful."[16]

Upon return from China, the Governor had called another, June 1974, special session. In that call, he asked for a five to 7.5 percent increase in pay for teachers and school service personnel, because the legislature had declined his request for a raise in January. He wanted to take over the entire premium for state employees' health insurance (they had been paying thirty percent). He again asked for expansion of the Child Development Program, into all counties, pronouncing it a great success in the limited area it existed. He sought authority to share $20 million of federal revenue sharing funds to counties, cities and towns. He wanted a Rehabilitation Environmental Action program with the Department of Highways to obtain certain ARC funds which were soon to expire. The budget he submitted in 1975 was $27.5 less than the previous one, he noted, but still met needs. He was raising revenue estimates for 74-75 by $29.5 million. He succeeded in getting the 7.5 percent pay raise for the teachers. A battle ensued when he cut portions of various budget bills, however, and again the Democratic legislature took him to court. The supreme court upheld Moore's budget powers on eight of ten litigated points, however.

Moore's popularity may have been at its peak at this time. A June, 1974 poll showed him with an 80 percent approval rate. This contrasted to Nixon's 30 percent (the besieged President would resign soon), a dismal 21 percent for the Democratic Congress that was attacking the President, and even a 53 percent positive rating for the governor of Ohio.

Psychologists or political scientists would probably have a lot to say about the fact that Arch Moore was always in a battle with someone or some entity, his entire life. He was known as a fighter, a feisty scrapper; he seemed to actually thrive on conflict and movement, he almost seemed to need that to succeed. In early days, it was his personal battle against poverty and to restore his family's station in life. Thereafter, he literally battled the Germans and later he fought on in the courts as a lawyer. Then it was the Democratic Establishment as he won congressional races. Later, it would be battles against the *Gazette* and other hostile news media, then against wealthy Democratic opponents, and later still against federal investigators, prosecutors, and in his golden years, against his daughter's foes. But during the twelve years he served as the state's chief executive, it was his constant battles with the Democratic leadership in the legislature that seemed to propel him. The struggles certainly kept the capitol press corp with plenty to write and discuss.

Clashing with the legislature "was sometimes a strong point for me," Moore acknowledged. "But I always got the question, 'Why is Arch always fighting with those guys?' They would say, 'Arch Moore enjoys fighting!' But I always thought it was the governor's responsibility to lead, to build progress. I wouldn't let them waste money. I would tell [the complaining constituent], 'You gotta understand, friend, that I'm the only representative you've got down there.' I tried to get them to understand that it is not Eastern West Virginia, Southern West Virginia, the Northern Panhandle or North-central West Virginia. What was good for Bluefield—if we put a plant in there for example—was good for Wheeling. We were four states when I became governor. It was my challenge to make it one state." While the legislators represented the interests of their respective constituencies, Arch saw himself as the guardian of the interests of the state as a whole. He wanted West Virginians to understand that when he fought with the legislature, he was fighting on their behalf.

Increasingly, Moore warred with Senate President William T. Brotherton of Kanawha County, whom he nicknamed "Senator Bothersome," as if he could casually brush him off. Both men were bright lawyers, were overachievers, had best intentions for the state, but often held different ideas as to how to achieve their goals which, when combined with partisan one-upmanship, caused numerous clashes. But throughout the battles, which became bitter and quite public at times, each seemed to respect the other's abilities. "I could best describe their relationship as 'adversarially respectful,'" said Brotherton's son. "They were like two heavyweight boxers who took punches at each other."

Continued Will Brotherton, "Daddy liked Arch personally, but he enjoyed getting his goat, enjoyed being a well-intentioned antagonist. His staff was fearful of the governor's office when something was up. He'd get a command, 'The Governor wants you down here.' But Daddy enjoyed it–he knew he'd have another chance to stick a spear in Arch. They had a professional camaraderie. I think part of it was that he was a little envious of Arch, he always wanted to be governor himself, some day.[17] So he never abused the relationship, because he understood what Arch was doing.

"[Brotherton] actually greatly admired Governor Moore's abilities and thought he was the finest governor we ever had," his son admitted. "People would say to him, 'I don't know how you can stand to serve with Arch Moore!' and I'm sure others said the same to Moore. But there was such a high level of ability, desire to do what was best, to make government function better, that it was a pleasure for him to go to work during those years. It was a challenge and honor for him to work with Moore; he said that after Arch Moore left, it was never as much fun. He enjoyed the fray.

"When you have two people in an adversarial role and when it's not about personal animosity, you get positive results. These were the state's most creative, productive years," the younger Brotherton added.

"And they weren't breaking the rules, they both went by the book. But they used every opportunity to use 'the book' in their favor. Both men were very learned in what their offices were capable of doing. The constitution provides checks and balances and both used the checks and balances to their end. When the system worked well, it produced good results. They were two talented guys."

But there were times when there was a lot of "tit-for-tat" occurring between the Senate President and the Governor. "They would sometimes act like little kids." As an example, Will Brotherton said that the elevator which goes from the governor's office to the senate upstairs was commonly called "The Governor's Elevator," because of its location and because, generally, he was the only one to use it. "But my dad used it. He said it was the 'people's elevator.' He walked in there and used it whenever he pleased." But when "Senator Bothersome" and the Governor had been having a tiff about something and had been arguing through newspaper stories to retaliate, Moore shut off the elevator. "He could give as well as he got," laughed Will.

He recalled another incident in which it was late March (near the end of the session) and Brotherton was publicly complaining that he hadn't yet received the Governor's budget proposal. "So finally an impressive package arrived from the governor's office with all the official governor accouterments, labeled Budget Recommendations. When they opened it up, it was empty! They found a note in it, 'April Fool!'

"That was Arch Moore's way of saying, 'Push me and this is what you get!' But my dad was upset, he went nuclear. 'That's not the way you do it in government!' he yelled. "But Arch was defensive of the executive branch and my dad was defensive of the legislative branch. They definitely were proud of their branches of government."

He fully realized it had never been a personal feud, Will added, when the former senate president and justice died in 1997. Justice Brotherton had not talked to Moore for a couple decades at that point. "A large crowd was packed into St. Matthew's Episcopal Church for the funeral," remembered Will Brotherton. "I turned around and saw Arch Moore walking through the door. The whole family took note of that, notwithstanding how hard they had fought against each other, Arch thought enough of him to come to Charleston and to the church."[18]

"No one has ever been better with the legislature than Arch Moore," thought Richard Neely, a Democrat who was elected to the House of Delegates from Marion County in 1970. "He could come to a legislative dinner and be spontaneously witty and funny, saying something about everyone in the room. I thought he was always easy to work with. He knew most of what was going on. He was always hands-on." Neely thought Moore was an "intellectual–he'd listen to underlying research" on such issues as the debate over whether the State should build a new central mental health hospital vs. many local, community centers where the mentally ill could be treated on an out-patient basis.[19]

But, according to Oce Smith, Moore's people were capable of literally strong-arming legislators into doing his will. "I was personally aware of one legislator heading to Charleston in his Lincoln for a vote in which the Governor was particularly interested in, and which he had good reason to believe that [the legislator] was not in his camp." Smith recalled that the lawmaker was stopped at least twice by state troopers on his way to the capital, and finally evaded the police by outrunning them. (Inference being, Moore was trying to slow or prevent his arrival for the vote by siccing the patrolmen on him.)

In another vote, as Oce recalled it, the Moore administration was trying to keep Republican delegates on board for legislation of special interest. Ed Flowers and "another Moore appointee" actually "manhandled the legislators," and "hustled [them] into a bare room where it was succinctly and quickly explained to them just how they were supposed to vote on the issue and what could happen to them politically and perhaps personally if they didn't. They demanded that he push his button just exactly and precisely upon the call of the Governor. And that type of activity went on for years. That disturbed me terribly."

By now, the "Arch Moore style" was very much a part of the political landscape of the state. A big part of that style involved playing his cards close to his chest, using the element of suspense and surprise to outwit and outmaneuver his opponents. Again and again, he demonstrated that he was a skilled card player. "Governor Moore knew the value of keeping his thoughts to himself until the optimum time for announcing his answer to the problem," observed "Hike" Heiskell. "This, of course, kept the competing interests, the media and the people of the state in general focused on their governor, everyone asking, 'What's Arch going to do?' Occasionally, he'd drop a hint that would create a frenzy of media speculation and would then watch with interest as his comments drew others out on the subject." Heiskell continued, "Trying to predict what Arch was going to do became a favorite pastime for the state's politicians and news media and they often looked foolish as he would finally come forward to announce his decision. Arch Moore was always a step ahead of everyone else."

ONE OF THE highlights of 1974 was the unveiling of the bronze statue, "Lincoln Walks at Night," which was and is located to the front of the state capitol, facing the Kanawha River. Fred Torrey of Fairmont had carved the original, honoring the Republican president who signed West Virginia into being in 1863. It had been funded by school children, who raised the $40,000 to make it possible. On the state's June 20th birthday, Governor Moore said, "We hope that we have lived up to the measure of faith and confidence that [Lincoln] gave to us and sustain the legacy from which the state was born."

On October 14, 1973, in a speech the Governor gave at a Ravenswood United Methodist Church, he urged laymen in the church to make "moral choices and decisions in the market place," to "live the implications of worship" in their day-to-day world. Avoidance of "padding expense accounts, special privileges, shoddy workmanship" allowed a Christian to "declare his faith by moral choices," Moore told the crowd. By so living, "There will come a sense of integrity and wholeness to your life." He ended by saying, "For we are the people of God, living out our faith, with all of its implications in His world, a world He loved enough to send His Son to save."[20]

In November, the *Gazette* published a poll it took in Kanawha County, asking respondents to identify their most admired West Virginian. Senate Majority Whip Robert Byrd was No. 1, of course, but Arch Moore ranked second. Randolph, Rockefeller, basketball great Jerry West and Arnold Miller (president of the UMW) and even an honorary West Virginian, John Denver, were other choices.

The Moore Administration continued its efforts to automate state government at every opportunity. Punch card systems and paper records were being rapidly replaced by large, mainframe computers. As the computers became affordable, faster and more powerful, Harold Casali helped bring state government into the modern era with the work of the Information Systems Services Division of F&A (ISSD). Millions of records, from various state agencies, were now stored and accessed within seconds or minutes throughout the state on state-of-the-art computerized systems as a result of ISSD's work. What is now taken for granted was revolutionary and exciting progress at the time. It allowed the police, welfare case workers, the Tax Department, the DMV and other state employees to provide services more efficiently and far more quickly. Again, because of talented people Moore had put into place at ISSD, the state was in the forefront of electronic information management and their innovations were copied by other government entities.

THERE WERE new opportunities to improve higher education during the second term. In the summer of 1974, Marshall University's acting president, Robert Hayes, with Dr. Albert Esposito, a Republican delegate from Huntington, visited Governor Moore to determine if he was serious about starting a medical school there. Hayes asked Arch, "Is this just politics or is there a need for a medical school in this area?" Moore replied, "There is a need and I will help you any way I can. Let me know what you need." The Board of Regents was opposed to the creation of a second state med school, though, and was set to vote it down. Major arm-twisting from someone to whom the Regents would respond was desperately needed. Moore appeared in person before the vote was taken. "He told them, 'The medical school is in my program, and if you can't support it, you can resign,'" Hayes recalled. "That's about the time Regent John Amos, who had strenuously opposed the school] quit. The Governor was so emphatic. That was his procedure." Later that day, the Regents approved the resolution creating the school, by an eight-to-zip vote, with Amos abstaining. Hayes started the very difficult part–finding funding, from private and government sources. They came to a point where the need for money was desperate, so Hayes and the Regents' chancellor, Ben Morton, went to see the Governor. Moore asked Hayes what he needed. "I gave him some figure like $300,000—it may have been less. 'Ok, Chancellor Morton,' Moore said, 'I have half of it. Can you match it?'" Morton couldn't say no to the governor, and Hayes had enough funding to hire his first dean. Senator Randolph arranged for millions to be made available by the Veterans Administration and, before long, Hayes had his med school up and running.[21] Hayes wanted to name the school for Arch Moore, but the Governor would not hear of it. He believed it was disgraceful for a public official, using taxpayers' money to build edifices, to put his own name on them.

Representatives from the Northwestern University Medical School came to West Virginia to determine whether Marshall's school would be accredited. Without their approval, the project unlikely would have got off the ground. It would not have found adequate funding, for one thing. "There were Ph.Ds, chairmen of departments, neurosurgeons and the like among the delegation," remembered Larry Swann, a delegate who was close to Esposito. "They met with Governor Moore in his office for two hours to discuss the plan for the medical school. I'm sure he'd studied it for hours. It was impressive, because he was a lawyer, not a doctor. But Arch convinced them, and when they came out of that meeting, I was in the reception room, hearing one of them say, 'I've met with lots of leaders but I never met one who knew so much about medicine.'

"Delegate Esposito, an ophthalmologist who ran for the legislature every two years, just to push the Marshall med school, and spoke for it at every opportunity, was really the father of that school, but Arch Moore was also its father. The Governor's acumen made it happen. Esposito said it was the turning point; his ability to convince them was ultimately responsible to get Marshall a medical school," attested Swann.

Creation of Marshall Medical School had not been uniformly popular outside Cabell County. "WVU fought it all the way," Swann noted. Ironically, one of the chief opponents of the new school was Moore's close friend, Tom McCoy, who that year was president of the state medical association. "I just didn't think we needed more than one med school and said so publicly," recalled Dr. McCoy. "I still don't think we need three medical schools–we're just educating a lot of people from Pennsylvania and Ohio at the expense of West Virginia taxpayers." Soon after his comment to the press, McCoy was interrupted at a meeting by state troopers. "They said the Governor was on the phone, wanting to talk to me–he was in Hawaii. He yelled at me, 'Stay out of this!' I explained my feelings, but he said, 'It's a political thing, not a medical thing.' He didn't want to offend the voters in the Huntington area."

Swann noted that Moore's expertise on numerous subjects always baffled and amazed the experts. "He had an ability to understand an issue no matter how arcane it was," said Larry. "He could understand architectural drawings or engineering concepts. They would go away in awe of this leader."

A FEW PERSONNEL changes of significance occurred in the middle of Moore's second term. First, the colorful Commerce commissioner, Lysander Dudley, left the administration to become director of the WVU Foundation, where he would serve for a decade. He was replaced by the captain of Air Force One, Ralph Albertazzie of Martinsburg, who retired after Nixon resigned.

Edwin Flowers, the successful welfare commissioner, was appointed by Moore to a supreme court vacancy.[22] Tom Tinder, Flowers' twenty-seven-year-old assistant, was pleasantly surprised to be asked by Moore to succeed his boss as welfare commissioner. "Ed was a wonderful person to work for; he taught me so much," remembered Tinder, who hit the ground running. "I visited all fifty five counties' field offices, went out and made house calls with them, and discovered that some of Welfare's employees had been working for the department longer than I'd been on the face of the earth."

In a major shock to political observers, the handsome, popular young Secretary of State Edgar F. "Hike" Heiskell, the Republicans' "crown prince," suddenly resigned, citing financial stress, and returned with his growing family to Morgantown to practice law. "My third child was on the way and I couldn't live on the $22,500 salary," he recalled. The tall, blonde, ex-fighter pilot was well-liked, even by the *Gazette's* Ned Chilton, with whom he played tennis. Republicans were pushing "Hike" to be their gubernatorial nominee in 1976, but he realized it would be an extremely uphill battle against the presumed Democratic nominee, Jay Rockefeller, and resisted their overtures.[23]

Moore replaced Heiskell with Consol's public relations man, James McCartney, also of Morgantown. Although as short as Governor Moore, Jim McCartney was a former WVU basketball player. He had run unsuccessfully, the previous year, for state senate. McCartney would run for the office in 1976, only to be defeated by Democrat A. James Manchin, who resigned as REAP director to run. During his tenure, McCartney, a close friend of Senator Byrd's, would push unsuccessfully for the creation of an office of lieutenant governor.

Soon thereafter, State Treasurer John Kelly, a Charleston Democrat who had served in that position since 1961, pleaded guilty to extortion, bribery and mail fraud and received a fine and prison term. The Governor replaced Kelly[24] with perhaps the finest treasurer to ever serve the state, Ronald Pearson of Fairmont, who had been Moore's deputy tax commissioner and, more recently, his Finance & Administration commissioner. Pearson, who had initiated multiple reforms at F&A and was an "idea man" for Moore, plunged into the job with his usual energy, vigor and enthusiasm and quickly restructured the investment of state deposits, causing taxpayers to earn millions in interest over the next several years. (Pearson would be rewarded by voters for his excellent job by being defeated in 1976 by a relatively unknown Democrat, an individual Moore had handily defeated in a congressional race years earlier.) Greenbrier County millionaire Cleve Benedict, who would later serve a term as congressman, as agriculture commissioner and would be the GOP nominee for governor, replaced Pearson as F&A commissioner.

The Republicans' fortune in West Virginia and elsewhere would be adversely affected by events in Washington. Nixon's Committee to Re-Elect the President had been engaged in covert operations, lead by G. Gordon Liddy, a former FBI agent. *Washington Post* reporters began disclosing the story piece by piece, as given to them by several sources including Mark Felt, whom the President had passed over in appointing a successor to FBI Director J. Edgar Hoover. When Nixon, Attorney General John Mitchell and others took steps to cover up their involvement in a burglary of the their Watergate Hotel headquarters, Democrats in both the House and Senate began extensive investigations that dominated day time TV and the evening news. The Justice Department began prosecuting members of Nixon's administration, including Attorney General John Mitchell, and legal counsel Chuck Colson, with the U.S. District judge "Maximum John" Sirica giving defendants long, exceptionally harsh sentences.

As tapes later revealed, Nixon frequently made wild, sometimes illegal demands of his staff, asking them to punish enemies and spy on them, calling into question his mental stability at the time. When it appeared inevitable that he would be impeached, Nixon resigned on August 9, 1974. Arch's long-time friend Jerry Ford was sworn in as president. Governor Moore had liked Nixon, had shared some experiences with him. (To this day, he keeps a large certificate signed by Nixon on the waiting room to his Moundsville office.) Like others, he admired some of Nixon's accomplishments. The Governor made a Lincolnesque statement about the resignation of the President, "I feel strongly and prayerfully that America must now unite for a better tomorrow, without malice, without hatred, without rancor. With great courage, America has proved that it is capable of absorbing a severe shock."

But the resignation changed the chemistry of the next election in which Nixon had been widely expected to push former Democratic Texas governor and Johnson bagman, now Treasury Secretary John Connally, for the GOP presidential nomination. Governor Moore quietly let the new President know that he was available for the vice presidency, and again mentioned to the press that he might run for president himself in 1976. Ford chose Jay's Uncle Nelson Rockefeller, the liberal New York governor, instead.[25]

Ford started well, enjoyed some initial popularity with his laid-back, pipe-smoking style, but then pardoned Nixon (and offered an amnesty program to those who evaded the draft during the Vietnam War) for any crimes he may have committed, which proved to be a very unpopular move. As result of the political turmoil in the United States, South Vietnam collapsed to the Communists and Americans were forced to evacuate. The long, ugly war was lost, at least from America's perspective, with nearly 60,000 Americans in the prime of their lives now dead with even more wounded and psychologically scarred, and seemingly nothing to show for the terrible loss.

For these and other reasons (an oil shortage imposed by the Middle East suppliers had thrown the country into a period of inflation and unemployment), and in contrast to the Nixon landslide just two years earlier, the GOP took a terrible beating in 1974. In West Virginia, Democrats gained 25 seats in the House of Delegates, changing the ratio to 82 Democrats to 18 Republicans. They added two in the Senate, for a 26-8 ratio. The next day, Arch commented, "A freight train came through here last night ... If Santa Claus had been running on the Republican ticket, he would have been defeated."[26] The most bipartisan, arguably most productive and progressive legislature since the 1920s, abruptly ended.

THE GOVERNOR continued his efforts to bring new business and industry into the Mountain State, through the end of his second term. For example, in the mid-1970s, Moore tried to help Henry Payne and a group of partners start an airplane manufacturing facility. Several Union Carbiders and "twenty five coal barons" had invested a half million dollars to build a prototype aircraft called the Bellanca Skyrocket. They needed to transport it to the Huntington airport on a Lowboy, so Moore had I-64 westbound closed for traffic by state police on New Years Day 1975, so they could accomplish that. "CB radios were big then," laughed Payne, "and we heard a trucker in the eastbound lane say, 'Boys, these West Virginia cops are tough–they have an airplane pulled over at mile-marker 42.'"

The Bellanca Skyrocket, a modernized version of a classic plane from the 1930s, "set five world speed records" when tested in Huntington, said Payne, who obtained his degree in aeronautical engineering. When he heard of their progress, Moore said to Payne, "Young man, I want to see that in production in West Virginia."

Payne said the investors had 200 orders for the new plane but needed a hanger at the Kanawha Airport. Moore's term had expired by the time they were to that stage and, even though Payne's next-door neighbor was Miles Dean of Rockefeller's administration, he could not get their cooperation in the six years he tried. "If Arch Moore had still been governor, he'd have got it done," Payne thought. "So the stockholders voted to sell the plane out of state." West Virginia's opportunity to have an airplane manufacturer in the Kanawha Valley went down the tubes due to failure of state and local government to help them get it up and running.

IN HIS 1975 State of the State, Moore noted that state revenues continued to climb, allowing a surplus for the fifth year in a row. With optimism, he told the legislators that "West Virginia today is strong–strong in its leadership at all levels, strong in its economy, strong in its finances, strong in its governmental integrity, strong in its hopes that our rising expectations will continue to be met."

He cited progress in the REAP, TRIP, early childhood education, the Governor's Council on Coal and Energy, increasing employment in the state, and success of other programs. The message "abounded in a feeling of optimism," wrote Professor Carl Frasure.

Moore announced his desire to "pre-finance" the building of new highways immediately, rather than waiting thirteen to eighteen years for federal matching funds. He wanted to build the four lane highways at 1975 rates, as opposed to tomorrow's inflated ones. To do that, though, he would need $300 million more in road bonds, he said. The legislature would not go along; the state's indebtedness was already too high, many thought. In retrospect, it would have been cost-effective over the next three decades to have agreed to his proposal. As usual, Arch had foresight but too few others shared his vision, his ability to see the big picture, much to the state's detriment.

He renewed his request for removal of the sales tax on food, contending the state could afford the $28 million it would cost each year. He wanted their approval to consolidate all health and welfare services under one agency. Moore asked for authority to give local governments $20 million. He announced a decrease in the welfare budget by $3.5 million but increased benefits for those eligible for welfare benefits. It had been the best year in the state's history for mine fatalities, he announced. He also called for a variety of items to be approved for the state's participation in the national Bicentennial celebration the following year.

Nichols-Harper was called in to help Dick Frum, Moore's assistant general counsel, with the legislative agenda in the 1975 session. "Governor Moore had us to put together information on any bill that came out of committee," she recalled. "His ability to stay on top of a multitude of issues was an amazing skill. And he made me feel very valuable in that experience." Moore was supremely gifted in making everyone feel like they were part of a team, on an exciting quest to make a better state.

Nichols-Harper began noticing, as others did, that Arch Moore treated *all* state employees with dignity and appreciation, no matter their station. He had not forgotten his own roots. "My secretary's husband was a grounds keeper. He treated them with such respect. He would have [the grounds keeping crews] come in and have a Coke with him," a practice which would not continue under subsequent governors. "To Arch Moore, there were no greater or lesser jobs in state government. Such humanism was way ahead of his time. By his actions, Governor Moore empowered employees who never felt connected to the executive officer of government. It's not someone's words, but his actions that teach. I'm glad I got to see that. Every place I worked thereafter, I realized I was just part of a team."

In 1975, Arch requested that the legislature allow a special election to approve a $300 million bond issue to finish the Interstate highway system. They refused, contending the Governor kept them in the dark too much about his plans.

That year, the School of Osteopathic Medicine in Lewisburg, and the Marshall University Medical School, for which Moore had pushed so hard in the past two years, were funded by the legislature, $1.2 million for the former and $871,915 for the latter. In his usual fashion, Arch had announced the creation (state takeover, in the case of the Osteopathic school) of these med schools and boxed the legislature in, forcing them to fund them or face local backlash from supporters.

The state takeover of the Osteopathic School was not without an ugly battle, however; it was delivered in great travail. Board of Regents Chancellor Dr. Ben Morton was cool to the idea and the Board itself was unenthused; they could not foresee the benefits it would bring to a state which desperately needed the additional family practitioners the med school would provide. Democratic Attorney General Chauncey Browning issued an opinion agreeing that the Board was within its right to decline the new medical school, but Morton realized he was in a major battle with the Governor and began backing down.

The issue became moot when the legislature mandated that the Board take over the school. Moore signed Senate Bill 155 on March 6, 1975, officially bringing the medical school into the state system. The size of the student body at the Lewisburg facility would continue to grow, as did its prestige as a training grounds for future physicians. And Arch Moore's assistance in making it a reality would not soon be forgotten by those who managed the college.

Dog racing was legalized on a county option basis, setting the stage for the huge gambling facilities that would eventually be built in Cross Lanes and Wheeling, drawing hundreds of thousands and providing hundreds of well paying local jobs to the economy.

The legislators gave themselves nearly a fifty percent pay raise and the bill came to Moore's desk faster than any piece of legislation he had received since he took office. He vetoed the unpopular bill, which caused an outcry among the lawmakers, and a quick override of his veto. Brotherton accused Moore of "strictly grandstanding and pulling the heartstrings of the public," and said it was always, "I, Arch A. Moore, Jr."

They battled in the supreme court again over the budget. As a strategic measure, the Democrats began passing a "bare bones" budget and then passed individual supplemental bills, to be able to respond more easily to Moore's frequent vetoes, under the powers given to him by the 1968 amendment. He took them to court, but it was almost a total victory for the legislature.

Despite the numerous and generous pay raises of recent years, about eight thousand school teachers marched on the capitol, resulting in a five hundred dollar pay raise in the regular session and another seven hundred dollar raise in a special session. Moore said the money was available, when legislators questioned it. West Virginia Education Association President Charles Moses was prompted to call Arch "one of the greatest politicians this state has ever known."

State Banking Commissioner George Jordan and former Labor Commissioner Robert McConnell were indicted in 1974, for falsifying expense accounts. Jordan was acquitted by Ohio County Circuit Judge George Spiller and McConnell entered a no-contest plea in Kanawha County.[27]

With the oil crisis in mind, the U.S. Department of Interior had contracted with a consortium of corporations, including Union Carbide, to build a huge coal hydrocarbonization plant known as Coalcon. The Moore Administration made a gallant effort to land the $237 million plant, which was expected to produce hundreds of jobs and provide a market for high sulphur coal, converting it into clean fuels and chemicals. Moore took his team to New York to make a sales pitch, and offered up to $35 million in tax and other incentives, but Illinois outbid West Virginia and sealed the deal for that state. "Very simply, the State of Illinois bought Coalcon," complained Moore. But a lesson was learned.

In May, 1975, Arch had represented President Ford at the opening of the Franklin-Jefferson Bicentennial Exhibit in Warsaw, even speaking from a text prepared for the President. "I took Shelley and Lucy with me. We went in there in a Polish plane and were scared to death–we landed in fog up to your garter belt and with no runway lights!" Then, also at Ford's request, he flew from Poland on to the Soviet Union for a scheduled meeting with six other governors and a tour of Moscow, other Russians cities, a theater and a collective farm. Mrs. Moore visited some Russian schools. The Governor found the Soviets to be twenty years behind the Americans, which was an improvement from when he visited there as congressman in 1964, when they were fifty years behind the U.S.

Ford appeared at the Forest Festival in Elkins to crown the queen in October of 1975 (as Nixon had done in 1971 and Carter would do in 1978), and took the opportunity to say nice things about Moore. But the Governor was not present. Instead, he was watching his Mountaineers defeat Southern Methodist in Dallas.

Moore did join the President at a Republican dinner at the Charleston Civic Center that year, however. After the Governor introduced the President with glowing compliments and references to their long-time personal friendship, the eighteen thousand men and women in attendance heard Ford return the compliment by calling him "without a doubt one of the greatest governors in the history of West Virginia." The Governor had good reason to strengthen the bonds of friendship with the man now in the White House, as would become clear in the coming months.

Ford agreed with Moore's recommendation of his protege, Charles Haden, for nomination as federal judge. Haden had been appointed by the Governor to the West Virginia Supreme Court of Appeals in 1972, to fill a vacancy, had won election although then registered Republican, and had been re-elected to a full term. Haden was friendly with Rockefeller and even had constant support of the *Gazette.* He was well-liked by Democrats and Senators Randolph and Byrd presented him to the Senate Committee for confirmation. At 38, he would, in December of 1975, be the youngest member of the federal judiciary.[28]

AS HE ENTERED his final year of his two terms, Moore already had accomplished more than any governor in history, without question. In addition to creating the Board of Regents and a new Department of Highways, his administration had replaced an antiquated Department of Civil Defense Mobilization with a new and more efficient Office of Emergency Services. He had restructured Welfare and the Department of Mental Health, much for the better. He had established programs for the elderly, created public service districts for water and sewage service which continues to provide benefits to regions of the state to date. He signed into law a bill which provided for open meetings and required disclosure of campaign contributions and expenditures by political candidates. The roads on which West Virginians now traversed were light years ahead of anything they'd known, pre-Arch Moore. Miners and factory workers were receiving compensation for pneumoconiosis.

A bonus for Vietnam veterans was made possible by a constitutional amendment. Another amendment reorganized the state's judicial system and, once and for all, rid the state of a corrupt and backward justice of the peace system. Sheriffs and governors were allowed a second term, as a result of other amendments. Federal funds had been obtained by the hundreds of millions—not to build unneeded, expensive Taj Mahal buildings or monuments to Arch Moore–but rather to provide health clinics, four lane highways, education and other services which were of use to the general public, which enriched their lives, making their existence easier and more enjoyable. Teachers, in public schools and in higher education, were receiving the best pay checks by far they'd ever received. Public employees were being paid much better and now had health insurance. Senior citizens were enjoying centers Moore had arranged to be built with federal dollars. He had abolished sales tax on drugs. He had established the TRIP program and passed a Homestead Exception tax act.

If education reform was all that Moore had accomplished in his first two terms, that alone would have made him one of the state's greatest governors. As he would recount in a 1986 speech to the West Virginia Roundtable, "In only five years we moved from virtually no state-supported public kindergarten programs to a program for all five-year-old children. We made great progress in providing equal education opportunities for the exceptional child. We lowered the pupil-teacher ratio. And we experienced unprecedented school construction." He added, "We initiated vocational educational programs which targeted the skills required by the changing job market... and we encouraged the growth of associate degrees and continuing education programs."[29] It is impossible to quantify what those education improvements meant to that generation of West Virginians, but it obviously meant being better prepared for jobs and enjoyment of life. When he told audiences, as he often did, "Education is on the move in West Virginia!" it wasn't just campaign rhetoric—it was reality during his tenure.

In an action that received almost no attention at the time, but would prove to be quite important as medical costs escalated in the coming decades, Moore established a Council of Pharmaceuticals, an advisory council geared to promote the use of cheaper, generic drugs by all medical suppliers to the state. Soon, they would also become available to the general public.

His administration spruced up the state capitol, fitting the doors with attractive brass fixtures, and installing its first central air conditioning and computer-based fire alarm system.

The Public Service Commission he installed saved the public more than $100 million in power, gas and phone bills by regulating rates of the utilities.

Moore added dozens of state police and built them a new training campus at Institute.

In past administrations, motor vehicle license plates were reissued each summer. Moore changed that to a staggered five year pattern, eliminating the need for 150 jobs and saving the taxpayers hundreds of thousands each year. He signed legislation and put into effect several programs to combat drunken driving.

He built dozens of libraries around the state and at the end of his two terms had extended them into 65 communities, getting tapes, films and videos into communities. His administration also got media into the hands of the blind and deaf.

And the list of accomplishments just went on and on.[30]

Although the second term was not as glamorous or exciting as his first, even his critics had to admit that Arch Moore had been a governor who "got things done." He became widely regarded–to this day, by many—as *the most effective public servant ever to hold office in West Virginia, barring none*. There was increasing talk of him seeking national office in 1976, not just among his West Virginia supporters, but elsewhere in the nation. At Republican gatherings in Washington and elsewhere, his name continued to be mentioned as someone who was up-and-coming, ready to hit the national stage. Maybe vice president? Daresay, president?

But as he would find out within a few months, merely being a great, popular, efficient public servant did not insulate him from investigation and prosecution. The attention from what would come in 1976 would forever dash his hopes of any national office. Within months, he would go from being a serious national contender to someone fighting to stay out of prison.

Chapter 20 Notes

1. - *Daily Mail*, Jan. 16, 1973.

2. - Morgan, Ibid. Moore was correct–it would be a year for a governor to win the White House, but it would arguably be one less competent one, certainly one with a lesser state record than himself, Jimmy Carter of Georgia.

3. - Prunty, Sept. 16, 2005.

4. - "Governor Moore's 'Decision Day for Education' was copied successfully in the 1990s by Governor Gaston Caperton," noted Raamie Barker, the senate president's assistant. At Attica Prison, New York in 1971, prison officials had rushed in, causing 43 inmates and ten hostages to be killed. Governor Nelson Rockefeller was blamed for mishandling the situation. Governor Moore was determined not to allow "another Attica" even if it meant risking his own personal safety to prevent such bloodshed.

5. - Ironically, seventeen years later, Arch Moore was on the other end of the situation; he would be a prisoner desiring humane treatment.

6. - The old prison was eventually closed by the state supreme court, with the excuse that it was overcrowded. It was later turned into a museum for tours and haunted house activities. In 1995, a new maximum facility was opened at Mt. Olive in Fayette County.

7. - Morgan, Ibid.

8. - John Davidson, August 12, 2005.

9. - *Charleston Daily Mail*, January 10, 1977.

10. - For decades, the *Gazette* would repeat its mantra: "As a lawyer, Moore pocketed 900 shares of Exxon stock from the estate of a dead hermit."

11. - Morgan, Ibid.

12. - *Charleston Gazette*.

13. - His nephew, Governor Joe Manchin, announced the re-establishment of the REAP program in 2005, in honor of his uncle. It was time for another crusade against the blight of junk.

14. - Prunty said he presented the Governor with his set of petitions as he came out of the Mountainlair on a WVU game day. "It was about eight inches thick. His face turned beet-red and he literally threw it at Bill Ritchie who was with him. It really made him smoke!" Prunty said that Moore was actually looking out for the state's best interest in banning the studded tires. "They had told him federal matching funds were jeopardized if we continued to use studs. It turned out that was not correct; there was no penalty."

15. - Morgan, Ibid.

16. - *The New York Times*, June 14, 1974.

17. - Brotherton would be defeated for his senate seat by Bob Wise, and then was later elected to the supreme court; he never ran for governor, but many thought the moderately conservative Charlestonian would have been just the right governor the state needed in the 1990's.

18. - Will Brotherton, June 17, 2005.

19. - Neely recalled that experts from an excellent Psychology Department at WVU had advocated shifting all state mental health care to community, out-patient centers, but Moore had reservations about whether they severely ill would be served by that system. "It turns out that Arch was right about that one," Neely observed. "What do you do with the unfortunate people who bang their heads against the wall or walk around [masturbating]? What is [an out-patient mental health facility] going to do with someone like that?" Neely, in retrospect, agreed with Moore that some of them need institutional care for their protection and that of the communities in which they live.

20 . - Vol. III, *Eight Years.* An Episcopalian, Dr. Tom McCoy admitted that, in all the hours they'd spent together over the years, his Methodist friend, Arch Moore, never discussed his religious faith. He just knew that the Moores attended church faithfully.

21. - *Herald-Dispatch,* April 25, 2005.

22. - "Flowers had so much respect for Governor Moore and his office that he would put on his suit jacket to receive a phone call from him," noted Larry Swann.

23. - Heiskell had a standing tennis game with Rockefeller every Monday. "He told me as he left the secretary of state's office and I moved into it, 'Hike, I am running for governor again in 1976 and will spend whatever it takes.' I think he was giving me a friendly warning not to run against him. They told me he was keeping an eye on me; he respected that I might have a chance against him. He repeated the warning in '75. Jay was very friendly to me." So friendly, in fact, that Bill Loy had called Heiskell in to his office when "Hike" was Moore's workers' compensation commissioner. "You think [playing tennis with Rockefeller] is a good idea?" Loy asked Heiskell. "It might be perceived as spying or being unfaithful," he told the young commissioner. "I took it as a warning from Bill," said "Hike," who claimed, nevertheless, to find the conversation "amusing."

24. - "Arch never engaged in 'pile on' when someone was down," observed Richard Neely. "When Kelly was indicted, Arch said nothing, even though Kelly had once sued him in a case styled *Kelly v. Moore*. Governor Moore never attacked or disparaged someone who was indicted. He didn't even say anything about it when Bernard Smith or Truman Chafin were indicted." To Neely, this showed that Arch was a gentleman and played the game of politics with dignity. "I'm happy to be an aggressive political player, but I'm not happy with someone coming up on your porch and blowing you away with a shotgun," added Neely. "That's what is done when they use the indictment process against someone in office. It's a political tool, and it discourages good people from entering politics," he thought.

25. - Appointing Nelson Rockefeller was one of several poor personnel choices made by the new President. Gerald Ford apparently attributed his fast ascension, from congressman to president, to the elite, international business establishment, to those who are educated in the top-tier universities, who controls banking, trade, the news media and most of the world's economy. Ford, like Jimmy Carter

thereafter, staffed his administration heavily from members of the Trilateral Commission and Council on Foreign Relation. Interestingly, these people were closely affiliated with Jay's uncle, David Rockefeller, and other world aristocrats who promoted globalization of the economy to increase their profits (and which ultimately lost millions of American manufacturing jobs to East Asia, Mexico and elsewhere). Reagan, the Bushes and Clinton would appoint many of these establishment proteges to high positions, but not quite to the extent that Ford and Carter did, perhaps demonstrating the lack of confidence and malleability of those two weak presidents. The Trilateral Commission types would get both Carter and Ford in trouble on several fronts; their economic goals were not always in America's best interests, which the unions and other sectors recognized.

26. - Morgan, Ibid.

27. - Morgan, Ibid. Moore's Democratic opponent in 1984 would cite these two crimes as proof of Arch Moore's "corruption."

28. - Haden would rise to chief judge of the Southern District and died of cancer in March 2004. In his latter years, he switched from Republican to Independent and became a hero to environmentalists for his court orders which attempted to shut down mountaintop coal mining, a method particularly offensive to them.

29. - *Third Term*, Ibid.

30. - Serious students of the Moore era can read more about the accomplishments of his first two terms in his three volume set of official papers, "Eight Years," and the third term is documented in volumes appropriately named "Third Term."

Chapter Twenty One
Indicted!

In addition to celebrating America's 200th anniversary of its independence, 1976 provided a highly contested, interesting presidential race between an incumbent who'd never been elected to anything greater than a Michigan congressional seat, pitted against a peanut farmer, whose one term as Georgia governor was unexceptional. It was a year of hope and optimism that the Cold War was thawing and that the oil crisis may be resolving. The nation was feeling good about itself again, with the memories of Watergate and Vietnam fading.

But for our subject, 1976 wasn't his best year.

Four years earlier, Warren Upton, then an Assistant U.S. Attorney who had sent the Barron Gang to jail, had been walking through the federal courthouse in Charleston when he spotted a state trooper guarding a door to the office of an Internal Revenue Service auditor. The surprised Upton learned "it was Governor Moore inside." Following the 1972 campaign fund-raiser on the Kanawha River, [1] the *Gazette* and Democratic leaders had lobbied the government to begin an investigation of Moore and his campaign.

Others knew about the audit; Charleston is a small town in which it is impossible to keep secrets, even those guarded by federal law. The town was buzzing with rumors of an investigation of the Governor. Soon *Gazette* investigative writer James A. Haught was driving his Volkswagen out to the residence of IRS investigator John Weaver to try to get him to talk. "I refused to say a word to him about it [because of confidentiality laws]," Weaver insisted, "but I guess he could see something in the expression on my face." That was enough for Haught to write a front-page article announcing that Moore was under investigation for tax problems. Within a day or two, the IRS Inspector General's investigators "were all over the place," recalled Weaver, trying to find out who had disclosed to the news media what purportedly was transpiring behind closed IRS doors.

Cecil Underwood speculated that the tax investigation of Moore actually began when the ethics charges were made in the 1968 Primary by Peter Beter and others. "I think they probably continued investigating Arch from that time forward," he said.[2] One reliable, but unconfirmed, story was that Moore's original personal tax debt after the 1972 audit was about $450,000 (although it was reportedly reduced to $10,000, thanks to his lawyer's negotiations).[3] Moore noted that, when the crisis arose (there was talk of prosecution), Bill Loy did some intensive advocacy on his behalf at the White House, which may have made Hundley's job easier. A problem with campaign cash being raised and spent without records is that the candidate gets "stuck" with it as personal income if the Tax Man finds out about it and its disbursal cannot be accounted for. When IRS agents hear from several people that they have donated cash to a campaign, then that candidate can either deny the allegation and possibly get his donors in hot water, or be prepared to account for where the money went. If unable to do so, then he can be in trouble for not reporting it as personal income. Naturally, it was impossible to obtain a written receipt for cash from a Lincoln, Mingo or Logan County Democratic chairman, particularly one who has just added a Republican candidate to his slate. They would have laughed him to scorn, had his committee asked for a receipt. This may have been the scenario with which Moore was dealing in the 1972 tax audit. He may have been unable to account for cash that had been funneled through his 1972 campaign and the government expected him to pay personal income tax on it. Such audits, of course, are confidential and he never chose to reveal its precise nature.[4]

From all indications, the feds were investigating cash raised and spent in the 1972 gubernatorial campaign during the three years thereafter. Whether the Nixon White House intervened to prevent prosecutions will probably always remain a mystery, but it was widely speculated that it did.

It remained almost impossible for a statewide candidate, especially a Republican, to succeed without bending at least some of the rules. One either raised cash and spent it to get onto those heavily-Democratic county slates, or he did not win those elections, it was as simple as that. Moreover, it wasn't nickel-and-dime stuff after 1960; John F. Kennedy with his suitcases full of cash had raised the expectations of West Virginia's cash-only Democratic chairmen. If a candidate wanted the bloc of votes he controlled, he or his minions better bring cash and lots of it or else the party chairmen would just as easily sell out to his opponent.

There were news accounts of Moore, State Republican Chairman Tom Potter, Harry Moore (who was a lobbyist for Ashland Oil), Senate President Bill Brotherton, Moore's executive secretary and two aides being summoned before a federal grand jury.[5] The Governor reportedly declined to respond to the subpoena to testify before the grand jury, but offered to meet with the feds informally.

With the *Gazette* continually discussing the Taylor estate story, then the 1972 Kanawha River fund-raiser controversy, plus Moore's personal tax audit, Robert Elkins remembered that the newspaper and Democratic leaders had stirred up public sentiment against Moore, especially in the capital city. "They had created a foul political air," thought Elkins. "There were whispers of scandal." The feds felt pressured to heed their complaints, he noted.

Soon the feds thought they had their vehicle to use against the Governor.

Powerful bankers throughout the state, especially in Charleston, were highly upset that a corrupt savings and loan company, Diversified Mountaineer Corporation (DMC) was acting in excess of its regulatory rights and, most of all, that it was heavily cutting into their business. Theodore Price, its CEO, "had built quite an empire but had overstepped the statutory provisions for his company," said Moore. "The bankers got the feds on him."

It hadn't been but a few months since several Huntington and Charleston bankers, along with State Treasurer John Kelly, a Democrat, and his assistant had been convicted of making and accepting bribes. Now the U.S. Attorney brought a thirty-count indictment against Price. Among other things, DMC was accused of juggling funds from profitable offices to cash-starved ones, to make it appear that they were all financially sound.

Facing a maximum of 180 years in prison got Price's attention and, as often occurs, he offered to cut a deal. In exchange for leniency, Price agreed to testify that Governor Moore and his chief of staff, Bill Loy, took $25,000, between May of 1972 and March 1973, for their help in getting the West Virginia Banking Commission to approve DMC's application for a bank charter. The fact that the Banking Commission had actually denied the request did not deter the U.S. Attorney. He accepted Price's offer and allowed him to plead guilty to a single count of securities and mail fraud.

Interestingly, the new Southern District U.S. Attorney, John A. "Jack" Field III, had received his job in no small part due to the intervention of Arch Moore. Field was a lowly assistant prosecutor in an Eastern Shore county of Virginia in 1972 when the federal prosecutor Nixon had appointed, Wade "Jim" Ballard, decided to return to Monroe County. (A federal judge had appointed Warren Upton, a Democrat, as interim U.S. Attorney.) U.S. District Judge John Field, Jr. had asked Moore to recommend that Nixon appoint Jack Field, his son, to fill the vacancy. "He wanted to bring him home," explained Moore. "It was an easy decision to make because I respected the Judge." Arch complied and Jack Field replaced Upton (who then went to Jackson Kelly).

However, Field did not "dance with who brung him." He continued the investigation against Moore that Upton's team had started. He was also rather ruthless about it all. "Jack Field could be very arrogant and rude, unlike his father," noted Robert Elkins. In the grand jury's investigation of the 1972 Moore fund-raiser, "Jack Field had mistreated honorable people," Elkins felt. When he had "one very honest state senator" on the stand, for example, Field asked him, "So, how much money did *you* get?" Said Elkins, angrily, "If he'd asked me such a question, I'd have come after him [physically], federal prosecutor or not!"

For some reason, Field was unable to get much traction on the campaign cash spending issue and did not bring an indictment. But, with Price's cooperation, he would pursue the alleged DMC connection.

THUS, IT MADE sensational, national news when, on December 18, 1975, Field announced that Moore and former aide Bill Loy, by now a Martinsburg lawyer, had been indicted for extortion.[6]

Arch was in the White House at the time the indictments were announced, sitting across the table from President Ford, chairing a "State of the States" conference. He immediately flew back to Charleston upon receiving the call.

Adopting the maxim that the best defense is a good offense, Moore called a press conference the next day to announce that he would be running for a third term as governor in 1976 (more about that later). In a very feisty and defiant mood, Arch accused the prosecutor of having a "bitter personal hatred of him" and said that Field was trying to "engineer and conduct a vicious political vendetta."[7] Moore demanded that the proceedings begin immediately, so he could clear his name. Field "doesn't have a case. He knows it. The people of West Virginia know it," charged the Governor. "I'm not yielding one inch to this inquisitor or any other ambition-fired zealot. I'm going to fight, and I'm going to ferret out and lay bare the abuses and excesses employed by this United States Attorney's office in subverting the grand jury process. I know they have heaped abuse on good and law-abiding citizens who have appeared before the grand jury; have called them liars when they were telling the truth; have irresponsibly and frivolously threatened some with indictment; and have demeaned and misled the grand jury for their own private purposes."

Moore spun the story, portraying the situation as if the feds were trying to prevent him from being elected to a third term. "I believe the people of the state of West Virginia want a true and honest choice when they go to the polls to cast ballots for their next governor. I do not believe that the people will tolerate or sanction dirty tricks manifested by the action of today to hand-pick for them the next governor of West Virginia," he told reporters, to loud applause from staff and cabinet members in the room. "I have an abiding faith in American justice, I have an abiding faith in our courts. I firmly believe that the truth will prevail. The disposition of this matter will prove me right and innocent and will condemn the U.S. Attorney's office of this city." He then he wished all a Merry Christmas and departed the press conference room without taking questions.[8]

Gazette reporter John Morgan observed, "However, Washington sources later made it clear that the U.S. Department of Justice, not Field, made the final decision to indict Moore. Also, the Department's insiders said President Ford knew in advance about the indictment. In view of that information, Moore was asked how he could justify his attack on Field. The Governor had no comment."[9]

The day after the indictment was announced, Moore was fingerprinted and a mugshot was taken by the U.S. Marshals. Federal Judge K. K. Hall asked, "Are you Arch A. Moore, Jr.? Are the governor of the state?"

"I am, sir," replied Moore.

"How do you wish to plea?"

"I am not guilty, sir."

The trial was set for April 20, 1976 and U.S. District Judge Joseph H. Young of Baltimore was assigned to preside over it. "It was historic, dramatic, pathetic," wrote John Morgan. Jim Sprouse, Jay Rockefeller and Senate President William Brotherton complained publicly about the embarrassment the indictment brought to the state, but the latter two also wisely cautioned about the presumption of innocence until proven guilty.

Faced with up to a $10,000 fine and twenty years in prison if convicted, Governor Moore retained Stanley Preiser of Charleston, arguably the state's best trial lawyer. Each day, Arch would make the humiliating trip from the Governor's Mansion to the courthouse downtown in the dark blue Lincoln Town Car, with state trooper security and Mrs. Moore at his side, walk past the gauntlet of reporters and photographers into the courthouse, and sit for most of the day listening to sensational testimony which was reported in detail by the state media.

"I was with Arch in the courtroom through it all," recalled Mrs. Moore, sadly. "We are a team. We don't hesitate to hold each other's hand." They were encouraged by their supporters through the ordeal, she recalled. "The number of friends who stood by him was unbelievable, from a cadre of young people, to those our age." Those friends who showed their support by being in the courtroom included urologist Dr. Tom McCoy, who cancelled his patients that week to be there. John Manchin drove down from Farmington to be with his friend Arch Moore, telling those who asked, "He was there for me when I was in trouble."

The Moore children were anxiously awaiting their father's fate from their respective locations–Shelley Jr. at Duke University in North Carolina and Kim out West. "I was at WVU by then," remembered daughter Lucy Moore Durbin. "Dad wasn't good about clueing us in. I'd phone Mom each day, back and forth, to check on developments."

In the past half century, only Maryland's Marvin Mandel had shared the disgrace of being an indicted sitting governor. It was a humiliating and irritating, nine-day ordeal for the one who'd been dubbed King Arch. In the evenings, the Governor would be spotted by passers-by, pacing around the grounds of the Governor's Mansion, his head bowed, arms clasped behind him, deep in thought. A fairly good courtroom lawyer himself, perhaps he was planning strategy. Or perhaps he was contemplating what a conviction, even an acquittal, would mean to his future.

A seven-woman, five-man jury was impaneled, including a homemaker, aluminum plant inspector, welder, machinist, auditor, bank teller, nurse's aide, high school teacher, piano teacher, medical technician, housewife, and employee of the Department of Employment Security.[10]

The trial itself was ugly–testimony of witnesses and information disclosed to the judge by Preiser would become fodder for pundits and opponents of Moore to use against him for the rest of his life. There was talk about a five thousand-dollar blank check in the Governor's top desk drawer, written by a John Greene of Milton and endorsed on the back by "Amos Jones." Further, it was disclosed that Clyde Webb, a vice president for Ashland Oil, delivered twenty thousand dollars in cash to Moore (presumably for his 1972 campaign). Commerce Commissioner Lysander Dudley was identified as the handler of a fund-raiser at which surface mining operators gave Moore's campaign aboard the 1972 riverboat fund-raiser. A statement that Moore received $400,000, of which $120,000 was cash, did not coincide with 1972 campaign finance reports. Christmas gifts from well wishers to the Governor, as large as five thousand dollars each, were disclosed by Moore's lawyer to Judge Joseph Young.

The New York Times reported that there was testimony in the ten-day trial "that the Governor had received $6,000 in other covert gifts, money he reportedly converted into traveler's checks. But Judge Young...ruled that the prosecution would have to limit its case to the narrower matters alleged in the indictment," and even ordered that the U.S. Attorney's statements about those not be reported in the news media. "The trial offered insights into politics in this corruption-ridden state," the *Times* reported.[11] In fairness, Moore never had an opportunity to explain all of those disclosures. But it was not positive publicity, to say the least.

The government's chief witness, Price, testified for five hours. He claimed that Nolan B. Hamric, a member of the State Banking Commission and a Gassaway banker (a co-conspirator in the case), told him that if he wanted a bank charter then he needed to "take the money and get down to the governor's office." Price claimed he then made three deliveries of the money in the autumn of 1972, two envelopes containing ten grand and another with five thousand dollars in it. Hamric testified that he set up a meeting between Price and Moore and told the Governor that DMC had some interest in contributing $25,000 to his re-election campaign that year.

But when he was cross-examined, Hamric deleted a phrase from a statement prepared for him by the U.S. Attorney that linked the contribution to the bank charter. Banking Commissioner Jordan, another co-conspirator, testified that the Governor was sympathetic to the charter being granted but he never pressured him to support it and, after it was denied on a three-to-two vote, the Governor never spoke to him about it further.

When it came time for Moore to tell his story, the direction of the trial changed. Arch turned his chair around and calmly looked each juror in the eye as he spoke directly to them. In his deep and commanding voice, he began telling them, step-by-step, his version of the events and convincing them of his innocence. Even the *Gazette* conceded that the Governor "assisted his defense through firm, unflappable ... confident .... testimony." Historian John Morgan, who watched the trial, agreed. "For all practical purposes, the Governor was the ideal witness for himself. His denials were almost total. He spoke in the manner of a trained expert witness, and he appealed to the jury with the skills of a seasoned lawyer. He kept his voice low, firm, even. With appropriate timing and minimum motion, he used his hands to emphasize points." Dressed in a navy suit, white shirt and striped tie, the 53-year-old chief executive "played to the jury with the skill of a seasoned orator," the *Gazette* wrote. He "never lost his composure," even when Field posed sarcastic questions. Moore stuck with the summary of his position: "I've never had a thing from Mr. Price in my life." He could not help but inject "Archmoorespeak," words and phrases the news media reps were accustomed to hearing from him, including, "identity," "on stream," and "come on board."[12]

Preiser, in his pinned-striped, finely tailored Italian suits with kerchiefs in the breast pockets, showcased his skill in what was possibly the highest profile trial he handled in his career. He warned the jury that the government would not be able to prove its allegations against the Governor. At the beginning of his cross-examination of the government's key witness, he bolted up from his table and, with a contemptuous tone sneered, "Is it not a fact that your real name is not Theodore R. Price?" (Price's name had been legally changed at age thirteen, an irrelevant piece of trivia, but the question planted seeds of suspicion among the jurors.) In his opening statement, Preiser claimed Price had "bought himself out of 180 years in prison" by agreeing to implicate Governor Moore.

Times were different than they would be in the 1980s, and the Governor had the good fortune, perhaps, of enjoying a friendly and sympathetic jury, who may have viewed his administration favorably during the past seven years. That, plus a healthy economy, possibly caused them to give him the benefit of the doubt. A jury must like a defendant to acquit him. Then again, they may just not have been willing to accept the story of a convicted felon (Price) who was testifying in exchange for leniency.

In his closing statement, Preiser called Price "the biggest liar this state has ever seen." The lawyer said the biggest proof that Moore didn't receive a bribe was that DMC did not get the bank charter they had sought. He argued that, because Moore was such a strong governor, if he had wanted them to have the charter, it would have been granted. He called Price a "phantom" because no one in the governor's office could ever remember having seen him around there, nor was there any record of his visit(s).

On May 5, 1976, after deliberating for seven hours, the jury came back into the courtroom. After a pause their verdict, which was unanimous, was read: "Not guilty" for both Moore and Loy.

The New York Times' Ben A. Franklin reported, "The verdict brought a roar of approval from partisans of Governor Moore who had packed the courtroom." The Governor had remained seated and stared forward as the verdict was read. Mrs. Loy sobbed loudly. Arch hugged and kissed members of his family who were with him. Mrs. Moore exclaimed, "I'm just so relieved and happy!" to which her husband said, "What you've gotta do is take a deep breath." He shook hands with and thanked each of the jurors.

"We didn't actually hear any proof of guilt," a juror explained to reporters about their acquittal. Juror Clara Mae Kinder of St. Albans said the jury just "didn't get the concrete evidence" they had expected. "It restores my faith in humanity," commented one person who left the courtroom. "Amen," agreed his companion.[13]

"A great apology is due the citizens of this state," thundered a triumphant and relieved Arch Moore to reporters outside the courtroom.

With his chest puffed out and half a smile returned to his face, the Governor said, "My fellow West Virginians, this should never have happened to you," to a crowd of applauding well wishers. Then, with tears and in a choking voice, he thanked those who had stuck with him through the ordeal. About the wait, the suspense of the outcome, Arch added, "It helps a heck of a lot if, in past experience, you've been through cliff hanger elections." He hugged Mrs. Moore, who had remained at his side from the outset. Standing proudly and loyally next to her father was his eldest daughter in from Duke University—Shelley, and her soon-to-be spouse, Charles Capito, who stood in the background.

Franklin wrote that Moore "denounced the investigation of his affairs and indictment as a political vendetta by a prosecutor allied with an anti-Moore Republican faction," whatever than meant. Despite the acquittal, the Governor's "political future is in doubt," he wrote, adding that, prior to the indictment, Arch had been considered a viable contender to challenge Robert Byrd for his Senate seat.[14]

Price was led away to a Florida prison to begin serving his three-year sentence.

There were no winners. The 44-year-old Bill Loy's hopes for a congressional seat in the 2nd District or a federal judgeship were forever dashed. And despite the acquittal, Arch Moore's reputation with the voters would never be the same. He was tarnished, as he would learn during the next four election cycles. The reputation of the U.S. Attorney also suffered. *The Martinsburg Journal* called for Field's resignation, writing that, at worst, "he showed himself malicious and at best he proved himself incompetent." *The Kanawha Valley Leader* demanded an investigation into the reasons for presenting a "cheap indictment" against the Governor in an election year. The Democratic *Wheeling News-Register* was "amazed that the Justice Department ... approved this case for prosecution on the basis of the evidence at hand." *The Charleston Daily Mail* wrote, "No competent person we know, Democrat or Republican, believed the government had a case [against Moore and Loy]." In their eagerness to "get" Moore after his tax problems disappeared in 1972, did the feds trump up charges against him? Or were they just poorly prepared and should have convicted him, as some thought? Or was Field counting on the evidence the judge did not allow into the record? Whatever the reason(s), it did not reflect well on the Justice Department.

Moore's friends and supporters hoped that his acquittal would be a wake-up call for him, however. They expressed hope that the Moore organization would forsake dangerous and illegal fund raising activities.

Moreover, they feared that the federal investigators in the IRS and Justice Department would not go away. Lt. Fred Donohoe, Moore's chief of security, drove him to and from the trial each day. He was among those convinced that the not-guilty verdict only made the feds want Arch all the more. "He walked out of that courthouse with a big red target on his back, which he wore every day."

The feds now had an intensified desire to prove themselves correct, to reverse this embarrassment. "Frank Jolliffe[15] was angry to have lost that trial," recalled former state Senator Larry Tucker. "They believed that Bill Ritchie was accepting cash for Arch [Moore's campaign] from contractors and other businessmen–they thought that was where the 'money in the desk drawer' was from. But they could never prove it." Tucker continued, "Those guys [in the U.S. Attorney's office] never give up when they want you."[16] The feds would await another opportunity, scrutinizing his every move. Would Arch give them a second chance to "get him" in the future?

Interestingly, years later, Jack Field would end up in big trouble himself, after becoming director of enforcement for the U.S. Commodities Futures Trading Commission. When he saw how much money was being made by those he investigated, how gullible and greedy their victims were, he decided to jump into the criminal activity himself. But he proved to be no more competent a crook than he had been as a prosecutor in the Moore debacle. In 1998, he would plead guilty to conspiracy charges in a Newark, New Jersey U.S. District Court for his role in a series of boiler-room investment scams that cheated victims out of $200 million. Two weeks earlier, Field had pled guilty in a New Hampshire court to racketeering and money laundering. He agreed to cooperate with investigators in nabbing others of these con-artists, but was sentenced in February of 2001 to two years in prison. After his father the federal judge died, Field had inherited an estimated three to four million dollars; his grandfather had been part-owner of several of Charleston's most prominent buildings, including ones housing Montgomery Ward, the Diamond Department Store, several banks, and The Daniel Boone Hotel. But that apparently had not been enough wealth to satisfy him.

The day after the not guilty verdict sunk in, reporters pelted the Governor with questions such as, "Who is Amos Jones?" But Arch refused to respond, referring them to the jury's verdict and contending it settled all issues.

MOORE ALWAYS had an amazing ability to compartmentalize his life. Bombs could be dropping around him and he would calmly continue with the task at hand. Through all his tribulations of 1976, he continued governing as if nothing was distracting him.

In his January 14, 1976, State of the State, he had proposed a tax rebate system to help low income families pay their skyrocketing fuel costs. He proposed an education energy resource center for West Virginia University, where research could be conducted. "Desulphurization, coal gasification and liquefaction should be expanded in all of their many ramifications." The center would be funded by a ten cents per ton tax on coal.

He refuted allegations that state employees were not being paid enough, noting they had received a fifty percent increase in pay from 1972 through 1975, but he did ask for a $1040 increase in starting pay for new hires. To respond to the problem of out-of-state medical malpractice insurance, he proposed setting up a state-run insurance mutual for doctors and hospitals. He wanted physicians' premiums to be no more than $2000 per year and to set that rate for ten years!

Noting that the population of the state mental hospitals had been reduced by half, he asked for $5.3 million in federal revenue sharing funds to complete three more comprehensive mental health centers in different regions, plus one "mental retardation center." In that address and in subsequent special sessions that year, he continued to call for $600,000 for a "full body scanner" for WVU Medical Center. (When it would again be denied, Moore paid for it before he left office, out of the Governor's Contingency Fund.)

With urgency, he begged the legislature once again to permit voters to approve a $300 million bond to finish the Interstate highway system, locking in costs, "pre-financing" and attracting federal matching funds, because inflation was making it more expensive, the longer they waited. "Let me give you an example of what will happen if you further delay," he warned them. "Two years ago we were ready to close the I-79 link from Big Chimney to ... Charleston. Then, we estimated the cost to be $35 million. A two-year delay was forced upon us by federal legislation." Now it was going to cost $65.7 million, he said, nearly twice as expensive due to inflation in construction costs. Finishing I-470 in Wheeling was another example he cited–$6.5 million two years ago, but the price tag in 1976 was $11.5 million. "Should we not move as rapidly as possible? You can make it happen if you will just help me in this regard!" (But they would not; apparently the legislators felt there was already too much bonded indebtedness; they could not see the long-term benefits and caused taxpayers to pay dearly for not following Moore's advice; inflation was in double digits in the late 1970s and early 1980s.)[17] Arch also asked them to sell $100 million of the 1973 highway amendment's improvement bonds for other road-work.

The Governor called a special session on June 21, to require that the legislature address his need for supplemental appropriations in thirty-five categories, mainly highways. Another one was called on July 26 to address other needs, including a $1200 pay raise for teachers and school personnel, scholarship funds, money for WWVU-TV, a Public Library Support Amendment, the Marshall University Medical School, DNR and State Health Department projects, vocational schools, TRIP, the Rehabilitation Center, increases for retired teachers, child development, welfare medical programs, and funding for various programs. He renewed the request to remove the sales tax on food. He asked for a few million to complete construction at Fairmont Emergency and Welch Emergency Hospitals, and Canaan Valley State Park. Legislation permitting voters present at the 7:30 closing of polls to vote (before that was passed, the voting stopped, no matter how many remained in line at closing time) was sought. He renewed his request to spend $100 million from the 1973 highway bonds. Altogether there were seventy-one items in his call, many of which were rejected by the Democratic-controlled legislature. Arch was becoming a lame duck.

THE REMAINING sand was quickly slipping through the hourglass of his two terms. Never out of office since the 1950s, he was trying to decide what next to do with his life, given that he remained a relatively young man and had great reserves of energy. In the months prior to his 1976 trial, there had been some scattered discussion in the out-of-state press of Moore running for president. They talked of the near-miraculous reforms the state had made, the roads he had built, the strikes he had settled, and thought he would be a good administrator for the nation.

Indeed, Arch's administrative skills, his ability to work with a cantankerous Congress and hostile foreign leaders, probably exceeded President Ford's, Jimmy Carter's, and others of that era. But such articles did little more than flatter the recipient. Despite the fact that there were Moore for President organizations in more than twenty states, and many of his fellow governors looked favorably on such a candidacy, Arch's party already had a sitting president and some thought Ford should receive the nomination unopposed. The Republicans also had a prominent challenger, former Governor Ronald Reagan, with a reform record in much-larger California that surpassed West Virginia's. Arch could not be a serious candidate for the nation's highest office, nor could he raise the millions such an effort required. So, when it got down to making a decision about whether to enter any primaries, as much as he would have enjoyed trying, Moore knew not to waste his time on such an effort. The highly publicized legal problems closed any thought of doing that–he was fighting for his very survival. Coming from a small Democratic state, Moore had little to offer a ticket even as a vice presidential candidate.

So Moore's eyes briefly turned to the prize he'd long coveted: the United States Senate. Trouble was, the seat up for grabs in 1976 was held by a very popular politician, Robert Carlyle Byrd, who had been winning impressive victories over token opponents for two decades. Recent polls run in the *Gazette* that pitted him against Byrd had always shown Moore well behind and barely ahead of the Senator even among Republican voters, who still (incorrectly) perceived the Senator to be a conservative.

Sen. Byrd was then morphing from the Southern-styled conservative[18] he had always been—to the partisan, more liberal Democrat he would later become, in part to accommodate his rise in Senate leadership positions. Moreover, he was not yet the one who brought home the federal bacon to West Virginia; that was still the role of Sen. Jennings Randolph. But Byrd was nevertheless the most popular political leader in the state. Like Moore, he had an uncanny ability to remember names and details about thousands of his constituents. Byrd and his fiddle were welcomed at dinners and luncheons around the state. He'd held his seat since 1959 and would be difficult for anyone, including a successful two-term governor, to beat.

Nevertheless, Byrd never in his career was forced to run against a tough candidate and didn't want to start now; he had more important things to do—he wanted to become the Senate's majority leader and even aspired to chair the Appropriations Committee. Arch Moore was also very popular and had been the unexpected victor over Jay Rockefeller. At the very least, a challenge to Byrd by Governor Moore would be expensive. Anything could happen. Byrd would have to call in favors to get popular national Democrats to help him, like Cleve Bailey did. Such a race back home would distract him from important senate business for at least eight or nine months. Arguably smarter, better-educated and definitely more articulate, Arch could probably tear him up in a debate. And, as the last two gubernatorial campaigns had proven, Bob Goodman surely knew how to produce some good advertising for Moore; they'd have people singing along to some damn jingle! Even if he beat back a challenge from Arch, which most would expect, he could still come out badly bruised. Bob Byrd had an incentive to keep it as it had always been—no more than token Republican opposition.

A few months before the 1976 primary election, Sen. Jennings Randolph called a highly secretive meeting in the bowels of the U.S. Capitol Building, in a small room near what some called "The Tomb,"[18] at which Moore, Senators Randolph and Byrd, like Mafia dons, sat around a table and tried to arrange a "peace treaty" among the three, to avoid unnecessary bloodletting.

Randolph started, "Arch, I know you are considering running for the U.S. Senate. If you will wait a couple of years, I am going to retire and you can have mine. You don't want to run against Senator Byrd, when you can soon have my seat." Perhaps other assurances were made to Moore, as well. Randolph added that he did not "want someone like Ken Hechler to get my seat."[19]

The three shook hands, entering into a gentlemen's agreement that Arch would have an open seat in 1978. Randolph, who'd long been a friend of Moore's, even indicated that he would support him in that later race. That was fine with Moore; he knew it would be very uphill struggle to go against the legendary Byrd. Besides, an open seat is always preferable for a West Virginia Republican; that's how he was elected to his congressional seat (and how his daughter would get hers). It is almost impossible to defeat an incumbent Democrat in the Mountain State, especially a popular one. Arch thanked them (and kept the agreement confidential until this book was written). But he would later find out, these were not true gentlemen, men of complete honor; they did not keep their word. They were merely politicians, making a promise they would not keep.[20] As he promised Randolph and Byrd, Moore announced he would stay out of the Senate race because Byrd had a chance to become Senate majority leader. He told the news media, "All West Virginians, Democrats and Republicans alike, have much to gain if Byrd is elected."[21]

Many times, Arch wondered "what if" he had responded positively to Nixon's proposal to appoint Byrd to the Supreme Court in 1971. As Governor, he could have appointed himself to fill the vacancy and likely could have remained a U.S. Senator for the remainder of his life. (As with rescuing the *Gazette* back in his congressional days, it was one of those episodes of his career in which he would have appreciated the opportunity for a "do over.")

So with the possibility of a Senate race gone and the criminal trial behind him, the Governor quickly turned his attention to the possibility of running for a third term as governor. Defiantly announcing his candidacy when he was indicted in December of 1975, he followed up by paying the fee and filing his candidacy papers with Secretary of State McCartney. He had projects he wanted to complete, not the least of which was the Interstate highway system.

His legal and logical argument for a third term was simple, if inventive. Because he was already serving a term as governor in November of 1970 when voters ratified the Governors Succession Amendment (which allowed two consecutive terms), he contended that his first term did not count and that he was entitled to serve two more if the voters agreed. In other words, he argued that, in order for the amendment to cover to him, it would have to be applied retroactively, which the law and the Supreme Court normally would ban. The *Gazette's* Harry Hoffman scoffed at that, noting that the amendment specifically stated that the governor sitting at the time of its adoption would not be prevented from serving another "term"—singular, not plural. Hoffman complained that Moore's announcement for a third term was bogus and put the GOP "in a strait-jacket for building up a viable gubernatorial candidate."

Beneath his partisan veneer, Chief Justice Richard Neely secretly admired Moore, although he frequently criticized him publicly, even calling him the "greatest liar since Ananias." He saw that Arch was much like his grandfather, Governor and Senator M.M. Neely, in style (in fact, the Ananias comparison was a line stolen from his colorful grandfather). The question of Governor Moore's third term eligibility was challenged by a marginal Republican candidate, Melton Maloney of Dunbar, a 71-year-old retired fire engine salesman (likely "put up to it" by the Democrats), who took the issue to Neely's state supreme court in a mandamus action.

On April 6, 1976, little more than a month before the nominees were to be chosen in the primary election, the Supreme Court issued its decision.[22] The governor's lawyers had argued that voters who wanted him to serve a third term were being denied equal protection under the law and, secondly, that the state's limitation on succession was "patently and latently ambiguous." In writing the decision, Neely did not dismiss Moore's arguments outright; he treated them respectfully, as "scholarly and sophisticated arguments in defense of his eligibility to a third term."

Predictably, Democrat Justices Fred Caplan and Thornton Berry joined Neely in holding that Moore could not seek a third consecutive term and blocked his filing with McCartney. As predictably, Justices Edwin Flowers and Donald Wilson, Republicans appointed by Moore to vacancies on the court, dissented. Flowers wrote, "The people can be trusted to make, they have the right to make, and they cannot constitutionally be restrained from making the choice as to their public officials. A majority of this Court today takes away the ballot of thousands of West Virginians."

Moore would appeal to the U.S. Supreme Court, retaining former U.S. Solicitor General Erwin Griswold, a former Harvard Law School dean, as his appellate counsel. The high court refused the appeal and his name was stricken from the May 11 primary ballot. Suddenly, for the first election since 1952, Arch Moore was not in the middle of a term or seeking public office. Come January, he would be a private citizen.

So it was on to Plan B, finding an acceptable successor who might have a chance to defeat Jay Rockefeller in November. (He didn't want Governor Underwood as his party's nominee.) Although it was late in the game, Moore put his seal of approval on his last Commerce commissioner, Col. Ralph D. Albertazzie, a Martinsburg businessman, author and former pilot of Air Force One, who had some national recognition but had never held office. In the May Republican Primary, Albertazzie would be buried by Cecil Underwood, in the latter's fourth try for governor, in a 64% to 29% landslide in which he won all but Taylor County. (Maloney received only 3408 votes.)

"A lot of people thought it was crazy for [Governor Moore to have pursued the third term issue]," recalled Tom Tinder. "They thought it was detrimental to whoever the Republican candidate for governor was going to be." Was Moore serious about it, or was he just yanking Rockefeller's chain? "Probably both," Tinder speculated, with a laugh. But the venture once again illustrated Moore's style, thought Tinder. "He'd have big ideas. He would always look at things creatively. Always thinking outside the box. He would spring these [unexpected] ideas on you, and your eyes would get big. But after hearing the details, you'd say, 'That's do-able!'" What seemed like a far-fetched, off-the-wall idea didn't seem so outlandish, once one listened to Moore's reasoning.

While the third term idea was one of those few fantasy concepts that never materialized, some wonder what the outcome of a Moore-Rockefeller rematch would have been in 1976. The next time they met in battle, Jay would be the incumbent and with the upper hand.

THE YEAR was not only about trials, politics and the Bicentennial, however. Moore had another year in which to be the state's chief executive. One of the year's highlights, indeed a highlight of the entire eight years, occurred on May 11, when the newly-completed Cultural Center was formally opened. John Morgan recalled the day:

> A festival atmosphere prevailed in the 92-degree

> weather that day. Free ice cream, sodas. And balloons were offered to the thousands getting their first glimpse of the large, square new facility with an exterior of Indiana buff limestone similar to that on the Capitol. In the Cultural Center area, people wandered along winding paths, across the reshaped landscape, with its transplanted sweet gums, evergreens and other trees. They admired the flowers and shrubbery near the building in the sunken gardens. They entered the Great Hall with its high walls of marble and granite floor. They saw the panorama of history in the museum, the theater, the art exhibits, the libraries of old and new books. They heard music from symphony to dulcimer to bluegrass and jazz.
>
> Moore, in an extremely good mood, found happiness in mingling with the crowd, shaking hands and posing with babies. In a brief dedicatory address to an overflow audience in the theater, he said [that the] Center will "encourage and foster what can be described as the spirit of West Virginia...It is a historical, scientific and cultural tapestry of a mountain people which will afford the opportunity to understand ourselves as better West Virginians."[23]

He concluded by saying, "I'm proud to be a West Virginian." He received a heartfelt, standing ovation. As Morgan noted, "It was a time of ecstasy after the courtroom agony of the recent past." Along with the arch bridge that crosses the New River, the Cultural Center symbolized the Arch Moore Period, his massive building projects and the new and modern era he helped usher in. They were done in a First Rate manner, with beauty, class and style, as well as to serve a utilitarian purpose.

The Cultural Center would be the site of his daughter Shelley's 1976 wedding to Charleston broker Charles Capito. "We had no idea where [else] to go," recalled Mary Ann Winter. "It was beautiful, fabulous, a wonderful event. We had to rent everything, such as the tables. But it was relaxed, just great." The *Gazette* would strongly object to it being used for that purpose. "I remember a newspaper interviewing the groom, Charlie," said family friend Tom McCoy. "They asked him about the controversy and he said simply, 'That's not my ball of wax.' He's an outstanding fellow."

His infamous battles with the Democrat legislature did not end during his eighth year in office; if anything, they intensified because he had "a long way to go and a short time to get there," as went a popular trucker song of the day. In the regular session, however, the lawmakers passed the fewest bills ever in its history. They refused Moore's request for $46 million for highways and $42 for the rebate system for utility bills.

The Governor called a special session to consider roads only. He explained, "I've found you can't divert the legislature. If you give them two subjects, it's hard for them to handle." They gave him half of what he asked for, $28.6 million and authorized spending $349.4 million in federal road money and highway bond funds.

Shorted of what he wanted, he instructed Commissioner Ritchie to spend "every dollar" of available highway maintenance money before the road construction season ended in November, leaving the remaining seven months of the 76-77 fiscal year unfunded. Coming up with the other half of what was needed would be his successor's problem. "I don't need the legislature anymore," Arch explained, somewhat bitterly. "I'm going to fix the roads myself, if it's my last great act."

The legislature did give yet another thousand dollar pay raise to school teachers and $100 per month raises for all other school personnel, short of what Arch had requested, but better than nothing.

Because it was becoming increasingly difficult to sell Northern West Virginia's high sulfur coal in a more pollution-conscious nation, mining jobs were being lost and some mines closed. To combat that economic problem, Moore issued an executive order relaxing standards of sulfur dioxide emissions in electric power plants, which was approved by the Air Pollution Control Commission in October and by a legislative rule making committee, effective December 10. It put the burden on the EPA to raise the standards again, which it eventually did. Moore's action was unpopular among environmentalists, but appreciated by the UMW and the coal industry.

IN THE AUTUMN of 1976, Governor Moore would bury the hatchet with Underwood for the first time since their bitter primary battle in 1968. His staff gave the former governor some advice and assistance, and Moore went out on the trail, giving campaign speeches on his behalf. But there was still bad blood between them which was illustrated by an incident recalled by Charleston lawyer John Hoblitzell who was, for all purposes, Underwood's campaign manager that year. "Governor Underwood and I showed up at the appointed time at the governor's office to meet with

Moore about scheduling joint appearances and so forth. We waited a long time and he didn't appear. Finally, we went over to the Governor's Mansion and rang the door bell. He came out and, with a state trooper, accompanied us back to the governor's office for our discussion."

Among other things, Underwood asked Moore what he saw as the key to defeating Rockefeller, what had worked for Arch in 1972? "Show that he's immature," suggested Moore. "And put him on the defense. We know he doesn't screw cattle, but make him prove it!"[24]

The two did six fund-raising dinners honoring "The Governors." At the one attended by 800 contributors in Charleston, Moore charged that Rockefeller didn't have sufficient talent to serve as governor, adding that it wasn't a question of whether he was "too rich to steal" (a phrase often heard from West Virginians regarding Jay). Into his 1972 warrior mode, Arch charged that the Secretary of State "can't even read a road map and in West Virginia, that's tragic!"

Surprisingly, Jay Rockefeller had not been widely accepted as the inevitable candidate for governor in the Democratic Primary, although he'd kept his network intact during his four years as president of West Virginia Wesleyan College in Buchannon. Jim Sprouse, Congressman Ken Hechler, Charleston Mayor John Hutchinson and populist New Martinsville lawyer H. John Rogers, all decided to challenge Jay for the nomination for governor. In the end, it was 49.6% Jay, 28.5% Sprouse, and 12.6% Hechler.[25]

That spring and summer saw the Republicans' most recent, true intra-party contest for president. Former California Governor Ronald Reagan lost West Virginia's primary to President Ford by 56.8% to 43.2%, despite three West Virginia campaign appearances—Parkersburg, Morgantown, and at the state GOP convention at the Charleston Civic Center, accompanied by his vice presidential designee, Sen. Richard Schweiker.

Pipe-smoking, laid back, plaid sport jacket-wearing, slow-talking Ford, a former football star,[26] was at first considered a breath of fresh air to the American public, following the imperious, moody, gloomy, scheming Nixon. With his unsophisticated style and manner of speaking, he was sometimes compared to Harry Truman. He told reporters, "I'm a Ford, not a Lincoln." Even his family was unlike the proper, buttoned-down Nixons. Jack Ford brought the likes of George Harrison, Billy Preston, Bianca Jagger and Andy Warhol to the White House to meet dad. But some thought Ford was not quite up to the task ("All I ever aspired to become was Speaker of the House," he told friends). He relied heavily on pros like Henry Kissinger and his newly appointed vice president, Nelson

Rockefeller. He was also dependent on two former congressmen, Dick Cheney and Donald Rumsfeld, both relatively young and inexperienced, if brilliant, men. And when the new president pardoned Nixon and offered conditional amnesty to Vietnam War draft dodgers, the Republicans would take a beating in the 1974 congressional elections. Ford himself became very vulnerable. Reagan, a true conservative, was attractive to many in the GOP. "[The late Wheeling Delegate] Judy Herndon and [former Monongalia County Prosecutor] Joe Laurita were pressuring me to support Reagan," remembered Arch. "Reagan called me a few times, asking for my support."

The fight by Reagan and Ford for the GOP nomination would go right down to the wire. Each was pulling out the stops to pick up every possible convention delegate. Laurita came home to find his son on the phone one evening, chatting away to Ronald Reagan, who wanted his dad's vote. The phone call paid off, he received Laurita's convention vote. Reagan was then still viewed by many as a dangerous, unelectable right-winger (and still a Hollywood cowboy). Arch was fully aware that a generous federal purse was vital to West Virginia's future and Reagan was known as a budget-cutter. While Moore knew Reagan through the National Governor's Conference, they were not, nor would they ever become friends like he and Ford had been.[27]

President Ford told an interesting story in his autobiography, about when he phoned Arch Moore in pursuit of West Virginia's convention votes. It revealed an Arch Moore, trying to horse trade something he wanted for something the President needed, quid pro quo. Wrote Ford:

> [West Virginia] had 28 delegates and I needed every one of them. The leader of the delegation was Governor Arch A. Moore, Jr., a long-time personal friend. We had served together in the House; he had helped me when I became Minority Leader and I had campaigned for him in West Virginia. Theoretically, he should have been behind me all the way. But it wasn't as simple as that. The United States Attorney for the Southern District of West Virginia was a tough Democratic (sic) prosecutor named John A. Field III. He had been conducting an investigation of political corruption in the state, and had persuaded a federal grand jury to indict the governor on extortion charges. Moore had proclaimed his innocence all along; indeed,

a federal court jury later acquitted him. But even before the verdict was in–and acting upon the recommendation of Attorney General Levi—I had announced my intention to nominate Field for another four-year term and Moore was mighty unhappy about this departmental decision.

On the afternoon of May 9, after his own acquittal and just two days after his state's primary, Moore telephoned me at the White House and we talked for nearly an hour. He insisted that he had been the victim of a U.S. Attorney who had been waging a vendetta against him. Now, through my Attorney General, I was rewarding that U.S. Attorney by reappointing him. "What's a Republican Administration trying to do to me?" he asked.

"When Attorney General Levi accepted the job," I replied, "he got an assurance from me that I would not get involved in criminal matters. Any mention of this matter by me to Levi would be way out of line. You can't ask me—and I know you haven't asked me—to call the Attorney General and have him recommend someone else."

Arch completely agreed with that. And he also admitted that if Levi had not pushed for Field's reappointment after the grand jury had handed down its indictment, that would have looked bad too. The press would have charged that the Administration was engaged in a cover-up. Arch never threatened me. He never said that if the Administration reappointed Field, he'd have to withhold the delegates he controlled. But he sure wanted to get some things off his chest.

"Arch, you've got to look at the bigger picture," I said. "Do you want Reagan to win the nomination?"

"Absolutely not. You're my friend and I want to help you."

"But, Arch, we could lose the nomination if West Virginia doesn't help, doesn't support us."

"I know that," he answered.

He had made his point and I had made mine.

> Neither of us was about to make a "deal," so there was nothing more to say. On May 11, when West Virginia Republicans cast their ballots, I won 57 percent of the vote. What mattered most, of course, was the number of delegates, and all but a handful of them were uncommitted. Moore told our people that he could probably deliver about 20 of the 28, but he didn't want to be more specific than that. This was disappointing, because we needed those delegates desperately. [28]

Moore delivered for Ford, even though the President refused to replace Field with a U.S. Attorney more acceptable to him. At the Republican convention in Kansas City, on August 19, 1976, Ford won on the first ballot by a narrow margin, 1187 delegates to Reagan's 1070. Without Arch Moore's controlled West Virginia votes and a couple other swing states, the fight would have gone to a second ballot and likely the momentum would have shifted to the former California governor.

As it turned out–coincidence or not–Gov. Moore got to put Ford over the top with the announcement of West Virginia's vote. The next morning, newspapers across the country carried photos of Arch, with arms raised in glee, beaming from ear to ear, after casting the state's vote and making the appointed President his party's nominee.

After Ford's victory at the convention was clear, Gov. Reagan came to the platform, moved to make the vote unanimous, then gave his classic "Shining City on the Hill" speech, almost without notes. It was a good thing for Ford that it was heard after the nomination vote, because after hearing what was possibly Reagan's finest oratory, many in the hall and in the TV audience looked at each other with dropped jaws, agreeing, "We've nominated the wrong man!" The former movie star and California governor was absolutely brilliant, and that night kept alive the possibility of another day, despite his advancing age.

Ford would trail Jimmy Carter by a wide margin, but the gap narrowed as the election drew nearer. Had it been a little later, Ford may have pulled it off.[29] With Ford's defeat (he was too hoarse and too sad to even give a concession speech) the chances of a federal appointment for Arch ended forever.[30]

Despite Moore's lukewarm help, Cecil Underwood was buried by Jay Rockefeller in the 1976 election, with a record-breaking margin of 242,207 votes. "That year was probably the nadir for the Republicans in West Virginia," thought John Hoblitzell.

According to H. John Rogers, his friend and former classmate Gene Hoyer was paid fifty thousand dollars (big money then) to be Rockefeller's campaign manager that year. Hoyer admitted to Rogers privately that they had secretly spent a lot of cash in that election. "Hoyer told me, the only way [Jay] can be defeated is if someone knocks out those Election Day expenditures."[30] Rogers, who had filed an unsuccessful suit trying to limit campaign spending by people like Rockefeller, quoted Hoyer as saying cash had to be spent to win the southern counties. "It's just a given that Sprouse, Rockefeller" and other statewide candidates spent cash in elections, Rogers believed. Moore's campaign most certainly would not be the only to have done that, he insisted. Arch "was just beating them at their own game" when he did it, Rogers laughed.

The Rockefeller team would have preferred to have beaten Arch instead of Underwood. Said Jack Canfield, who would serve in Jay's cabinet: "We couldn't get Moore off our minds the entire campaign, even though he wasn't running that year. And when it was over and we had won, it was Moore from whom we really wanted to hear. I guess it was a personal thing. But he never gave us the privilege." He continued, "Underwood was very nice about it after the election and we expected he would be. But Moore never called. It bugged us. It's like it wasn't enough that we had won. We wanted it to be Moore we had beaten, but knew we hadn't." Canfield added, "You're kind of happy and sad the same time. I remember that two weeks after the 1976 general election Jay wrote Moore a really nice personal letter, saying that the staffs should work together. Moore never answered. We did a slow burn."[31] Moore's aide Tom Craig did work with Jay's Don Richardson, however, to smooth the transition.

In 1969, Moore's people had been upset with the fact that outgoing Governor Smith had put thousands of his Democrat appointees under civil service protection and the Democrat courts had upheld it. In 1976, Arch did the same thing. He locked in 7500 jobs under civil service–from the Departments of Highways, Public Safety, Mines, the Adjutant General's office, Federal-State Relations, Sinking Fund, the Building Commission, the Aeronautics Commission, and Archives and History.

Just before Christmas, he formally opened the stretch of I-77/I-64 from the Greenbrier Street Exit to the West Virginia Turnpike, completing the monumental four-lane highway construction project through Charleston.

He announced that a contract had been awarded to restore and gild the capitol dome, a project which would cost about a million dollars. The gold was purchased and in State Treasurer Pearson's vault, to be applied in thin sheets, requiring only three pounds of the precious metal for the entire structure. The gilding would restore the glory of the original Cass Gilbert masterpiece, he explained. It was fully anticipated that his successor would go through with this project, restoring the majesty of the seat of government, to be admired by passing travelers, a source of pride to state residents.

Arch would leave the state and its government in far better shape than he had found it in 1969. To begin with, he was leaving his successor a whopping $234 million budget surplus, having ended each of his eight years with multi-million dollar surpluses. Although there was always room for improvement, the economy was perking along.

But it was much more than money. Moore had built libraries in sixty-five communities, under the strong leadership of Commissioner Fred Glazer. He had built forty-one vocational-technical schools, with nine more in planning stages. There were 134,968 West Virginians–students and adults–in the voc-tech program by Moore's final year in office, learning skills that would provide them with lifetime incomes. He had started the kindergarten program. He had built the roads. Airports had been improved and expanded. Help for low-income families, for the blind, aged and disabled, had taken a giant leap forward. People were no longer going hungry. Clothing vouchers were available for low-income school children. Using ARC money, thirty-two primary health care facilities had been built. Sixteen public health centers were established. Thirteen additional community mental health centers were added during his tenure. Three medical schools had been added (counting WVU's in Charleston). Veterans of Vietnam had received benefits. Pay raises had been generous to state employees and schoolteachers. Strikes had been settled and buses were running, as result of Arch's personal efforts. His administration as a whole had been a clean one; the flower fund was history and political firings were rare. The government had been run as an efficient business for eight years, which was a remarkable change for West Virginia.

It was an astounding record by any measure. Most of all, he had restored a sense of pride to a state which much needed a jolt of self-confidence and hope for the future. There would never be another eight years of West Virginia government that would even come close in comparison.

Chapter 21 Notes

1. - The 1972 fund-raiser for Moore's campaign was held on the P.A. Denny, a tugboat-turned-party-boat then owned by Lawson Hamilton. On the "cruise," road contractors and others donated

cash and checks to the campaign. Lysander Dudley's "black book" recorded who gave what. When the book was discovered by the feds, they subpoenaed it and called many of those listed before the federal grand jury.

2. - An IRS operative, Chuck Little, reportedly hounded Moore for decades, not satisfied until he pleaded guilty to charges in 1990. Little then sought appointment as U.S. Marshal, but another man he'd helped put in jail, Bill Ellis, claimed he had Little's appointment blocked by his powerful brother-in-law, Fred Haddad, much to Ellis' satisfaction.

3. - After reviewing these figures, Moore wrote, "Not so," in the margins, indicating he disagreed with those rumors. He did not reveal what he considered accurate figures, however.

4. - Records indicated that the audit may have gone back to early congressional days.

5. - According to *The New York Times* and other sources, Ashland disclosed that it had given Moore (or, perhaps, his campaign committee) twenty thousand dollars in cash.

6. - Moore had persuaded Nixon to appoint Loy to a federal judgeship, but Loy withdrew his name, perhaps because of the pending investigation.

7. - Fanny Seiler, the *Charleston Gazette*, Dec. 19, 1975.

8. - *Gazette*, Dec. 19, 1975

9. - Morgan, Ibid.

10. - Morgan, Ibid.

11. - *The New York Times*, May 6, 1976.

12. - Morgan, Ibid.

13. - *Gazette*, May 6, 1976

14. - *The New York Times*, May 6, 1976.

15. - Jolliffe was then an Assistant U.S. Attorney and has later served as a respected Democratic circuit judge in Lewisburg.

16. - Tucker and others would be caught in the net when prosecutors "got" Arch Moore in 1990.

17. - Governor Cecil Underwood had also tried without success to get the legislators to accept that argument. In the 1950s, during his first term, four lane highways could have been built at little over a million dollars a mile! It would have been a huge bargain to have financed as much as possible then and in the 1970's.

18 - Byrd was born Cornelius Sale, Jr., in North Wilkesboro, North Carolina in 1917, and never seemed to give up his Southern Klan roots. He claimed he quit the anti-black, anti-Catholic, anti-Jewish organization after one year but almost always voted with the segregationists in his first couple decades in Washington. In a March 4, 2001, interview with Fox News' Tony Snow, Byrd used the inflammatory term "n-word" on two occasions, raising eyebrows across the nation. He played a Confederate general in the 2003 movie, *Gods and Generals.* Upon the death of Strom Thurmond, Byrd would become the longest-serving member of the Senate.

18. - In which George Washington's body originally had been planned to be entombed.

19. - Sen. Byrd, by correspondence of June 25, 2004, refused an interview to discuss topics in this book, contending he was too busy for such things.

20. - As we know, Randolph broke the agreement in 1978. In the attic of an exclusive Washington gentlemen's club, with tears in his eyes, the elderly Senator told Moore, "Arch, my old friend, I'm sorry but I can't keep the agreement we made. I know what I promised, but my party has been very good to me over the years and they want me to run one more time." A shocked and disappointed Arch would respond, "Well, Senator, then I guess we'll do battle."

21. - Morgan, Ibid.

22. - *State ex rel. Maloney v. McCartney*

23. - Morgan, Ibid.

24. - Cecil Underwood, 2004.

25. - That race would be Sprouse's last; he would be appointed to the Fourth District Appeals Court with support of the unions. Hechler would later serve as secretary of state. He was defeated by Betty Ireland, a Republican, when he sought to return to that office in 2004, at age 89, having spent a million dollars of his own fortune in the unsuccessful comeback attempt.

26. - Lyndon Johnson said Ford played too much football with his helmet off.

27. - Interestingly, Governors Moore and Reagan were the featured speakers at the 1973 National Young Republican Conference in Washington. Reagan, in his black suit and crisp white shirt,

rapidly read a speech to the young people, almost impersonally, with nothing of the likable, relaxed style he would later develop. He waved to the crowd and quickly departed without socializing with his future potential supporters.

28. - *A Time to Heal,* Copyright 1979 by Gerald R. Ford, Harper & Row, Publishers, Inc., pp. 382-384. Arch denied to your author that the conversation with Ford ever occurred "I never asked a president for any such favor," he insisted and wrote, "Not so!" over Ford's quotes when reviewing the manuscript of this book for errors. However, the reader may note that Presidents normally have very well documented, and even tape-recorded, conversations which allow them to be accurate in their recollections. Moreover, it is difficult to imagine why Ford would have fabricated such an authentic-sounding story.

29. - Nearing 90 years old at the time, Pres. Ford joked to this author, "I peaked a week too late. We did all we could, but we just came up a bit short."

30. - Rogers, June 29, 2005.

31. - Grimes, Ibid.

Chapter Twenty Two
Almost Senator Moore

Before he left office in January, 1977, Arch gave a final State of the State address to the legislature, a rather meaningless tradition all governors follow, issuing a wish list of items they would liked to have accomplished, if they had been given just one more year in office. (They also present their budget, which is usually discarded by the new governor. The legislators listen and applaud politely, but await the "real" budget from the newly elected governor.) Among those "wish list" requests Governor Moore made was $20 million to rebuild WVU's Mountaineer Field, either on its existing location on the downtown campus, or elsewhere in Morgantown. Significantly, in his twenty eight minute address, Moore told the legislature that he was leaving them and the incoming governor with a $234 million surplus. There was enough money to take the sales tax off food, he insisted.

The stadium proposal was a personal wish on Moore's part; he would have loved to have added that one to his long list of accomplishments. As congressman and governor, Arch had rarely missed a WVU football game; he followed his Mounties through thick and thin, just as he did the Washington Redskins, his favorite NFL team. As his son mentioned, "He died for the Mountaineers!" As governor, he had enjoyed coming to the president's box at Mountaineer Stadium a bit late, testing his popularity with the crowd. "By that time all the people were there and they would give us a loud ovation or hiss at us. I am happy to say most of it was cheering," he told John Morgan. "Arch was always very supportive of the Mountaineer program," remembered legendary Coach Bobby Bowden. "He was always there, cheering us on. He'd often be up in his usual seat, with Lysander Dudley, another WVU alumni. He would occasionally visit the locker room and give our boys a pep talk."[1]

He outgoing governor began his speech by mentioning, with tongue in cheek, that it "could only happen in the administration of Arch Alfred Moore, Jr., that William Brotherton would be unanimously elected president of the state senate of West Virginia!" He told the Democratic leadership in both houses that he had "respected the tenaciousness of [their] leadership, the honesty of purpose of [their] leadership, and the political problems that any legislative leader has ..." He insisted that they could never once say that he faulted them. "Push them, yes! Shove them, yes! Urge them, yes! But never once did I fault them for maintaining the independence of a legislative body."

Arch also said that all "West Virginians wish the new Governor [Rockefeller] well." He urged continued spending on education and warned that the Department of Highways had now [because of his instructions] spent itself "down to practically the last dollar," and it would need a $27.5 million supplement it that year and at least $97 million for each following year. He noted that, with federal revenue sharing funds, the state budget had grown to almost one billion dollars a year.

The outgoing Governor mentioned that they lived in an age of cynicism wherein "everybody had a measure of dislike for everybody else," not just "disrespect for public officials," but also "the clergy, the doctor, the lawyer, the laboring man, to every area of our society today." He warned them that no "matter how high your goals, or how high your ambitions, and how much desire you might have to fulfill your personal commitment in this your public life, a lot of your actions will be suspect." He added that God "tests our strength, our physical being, our mental attitude, our honesty and our ability to determine whether or not we are worth our salt." He told them they weren't worth their salt "if we don't keep our eyes fixed firmly on the goals in front of us." He urged them to conduct their service in such a way that they could some day say, "I made it a better West Virginia." Moore said that he had "never apologized to anyone for my deep love and affection for our state. I have felt so very much, as you have in growing up in it, that it took some pretty unfair cracks and was hit from the blind side more than once as a state." Some of the state's problems were due to its terrain, which "makes us susceptible to disasters; our terrain inhibits us in some of our growth."

He ended by telling them that he'd been proud to be their governor, that his family was proud to have served as the First Family, and that his "hard working parents" were "distinctly proud." He finished by saying, "Thank you for that opportunity."

Almost all of the state newspapers had nice things to say about the outgoing governor. The *Daily Mail* headlined an editorial, "Much As He Promised, He Turned it Around," and summarized, "Arch Moore is quite simply the best governor West Virginia has had in this century, at least." Writing about his handling of striking highways workers, "Arch Moore could say no and mean it." They noted his grand improvements in education and welfare. *The Martinsburg Journal* agreed: "We can truthfully say that West Virginia has never had a more dynamic governor or one who was able to get things going than Arch Moore." They cited the success of the task force Arch had established to make government more efficient.

They noted he'd been "a little rough and tumble and maybe even a little abrasive," but had to "contend with a Democratic legislature whose principal intent seemed to be to embarrass and harass the Republican governor whenever possible." The editor added, "Moore took all of this in stride and, in fact, appeared to enjoy the combat because if we ever had a fighting governor, it has been Arch Moore." They saluted his highway building, and help for upgrading education, including vocational and handicapped training, higher teachers' pay and mental health programs. Moore was leaving with "governmental integrity" and "financial soundness." The Journal concluded, "He will be a hard act to follow."

The Parkersburg Sentinel saluted Moore's role in starting the Marshall University and Osteopathic medical schools, and the fact he was leaving Rockefeller with a $234 million budget surplus. Their January 15 editorial mentioned that he had a record 159 vetoes of which sixty-four were overridden, and a record number of special sessions (twelve). "His personal style was often criticized but no one can challenge the gains of the past eight years," they wrote. The *Republican Delta* of Buchannon thanked him for cleaning up the welfare system, "eliminating the chiselers and increasing the payments to the deserving." Who else had the record Moore had established as congressman and governor, they asked? "I'll tell you: Nobody." The *Bluefield Daily Telegraph*: "Arch Moore was a phenomenally good governor." Huntington's *Herald-Dispatch*: "[We] suspect that future citizens of the Mountain State, looking back at his years in office, will consider him one of the best chief executives the state ever has had." The normally critical, Democratic *Wheeling News-Register* noted that, "despite constant and open warfare with a Democratic legislature," Moore "was able to achieve considerable progress in almost all fields ... He was an unusually gifted leader, wildly inventive, always unpredictable and with a certain touch of ruthlessness about him ... For the most part state government under Governor Moore has been clean." They touted the New River Gorge bridge and the Cultural Center as symbols of his achievements, and noted that teachers' salaries had literally been doubled under his reign. All the papers gushed about the hundreds of miles of four lane highway his administration had quickly built. The Wheeling editorial concluded that, "regardless of political party affiliation," all West Virginians would remember Arch Moore as "a good governor."

Some of the accolades would be dispensed privately, even begrudgingly. Bill Hart, the highly partisan Democrat who edited Morgantown's *Dominion News* for years and who was a chronic Moore critic, was asked privately whom he would choose as the greatest politician in state history.

Would it be M.M. Neely, Byrd, Randolph or some other? After pondering the question a while, Hart conceded that it would have to be Arch Moore, because "he did everything Matt Neely did and he was a [expletive] Republican too!" Moore had performed as well as the best of the Democrats and with the disadvantage of achieving it all as a member of the minority party. H. John Rogers, who heard Hart make this statement, noted that by being at least as effective as the Democrats had been, yet a Republican, Moore was "like Ginger Rogers who danced as well as Fred Astaire, only backwards and in heels."

Each departing West Virginia governor has an oil portrait made so it can be displayed along with all the others, first in the governor's reception room and then out into the main hallway of the capitol. When Arch unveiled his to family members for a preview, his brother-in-law bluntly commented, "Well, that's a nice painting, but who is it?" Arch and Shelley had to admit, it just didn't look like his face. They had the face redone by another artist, "But then we couldn't use it," Shelley noted. The revised one hangs in their home, looking a lot like Arch Moore, circa 1977. Another was later commissioned for the capitol display but it, too, does not quite capture Moore's face–it makes his features look too bony and thin and doesn't quite capture his expression. (A beautiful Shelley Moore painting, circa 1970, looking regal in a gown, was commissioned by her husband as a gift and hangs in a room of their Glen Dale home.)[2]

THOSE WHO PREDICTED it would be a cold day in hell before a Rockefeller became governor of West Virginia were not too far off. The temperatures on that Inauguration Monday in January, 1977, had dropped to six below, so cold that the bands could not get their horns to work. Many of the invitees who had gathered to see Jay sworn in were upset to be locked out in the cold, unable to get into the warm capitol corridors because of heavy security for Jay's uncle, outgoing Vice President Nelson Rockefeller. Secret Service snipers guarded the roof.

The Governor-elect's father, John D. Rockefeller III, went to the Governor's Mansion for the traditional reception that is hosted by the outgoing governor. Arch Moore met the wealthy man at the door and showed him into the residence which, because of the frigid temperatures, had blazing fires in the fireplaces. Mr. Rockefeller, apparently thinking he was in some terribly backward place, asked Moore if the Mansion was kept warm with the fireplaces or if it had central heat. Arch assured him that it had a modern heating system "and air conditioning, too!" Laughed Moore at the comment, years later, "I think he believed he was in one of the original thirteen colonies!"

Little did Jay's parents know what had to be accomplished to get ready for that reception for the new governor and his family. The night before, a Secret Service agent had allowed his cigarette to catch a sofa on fire, filling the Governor's Mansion with smoke. After the burning couch was removed from the building, Mary Ann Winter and the staff opened the windows, fanning the smoke out by flapping towels. It was so cold outside that it froze all the fresh-cut flowers, requiring them to be replaced. Mrs. Winter replaced the sofa with one from her father's Nitro furniture store temporarily.[3]

In his last act as the state's first eight-year governor, Arch Moore announced his 39-year-old successor to the crowd in his usual commanding voice, "It is my high privilege and great honor to present to you the Governor-elect of West Virginia, the Honorable John Davison Rockefeller the Fourth!" Then the tall, handsome young man from New York was sworn in as West Virginia's twenty-ninth governor.

For the first time in two full decades, Arch and Shelley Moore were private citizens. It seemed as strange to them as it did to the public. After the swearing in ceremony, they left the capitol and returned to Glen Dale, having moved their belongings back home in the weeks before. The Moores had state police drivers for the past eight years and it felt odd to take the wheel. "It took me fifteen minutes to find the light [switch] on the dashboard," Arch joked.

Jay, who had been sworn in the night before at his Burberry Lane, Charleston, residence out of an abundance of caution, found his new office space pretty much bare. It had been stripped of pencils, pens, scratch pads and files. Moore's people had even disconnected the phone system, forcing the new Governor to walk out his door each time he needed a secretary, or to communicate anything. Jay complained to reporters that his long legs would not fit under the desk a shorter Arch Moore had left him. One explained to Rockefeller that, by turning the chair to the left, it would go down and he was able to fit his knees under the desk well. "Most of that furniture had belonged to Governor Moore and he took it with him," noted Tom Tinder. "It was several weeks before Governor Rockefeller had his office fully furnished."

Perhaps because of the perceived slights and pranks after the election and the gnawing suspicion that they might someday face each other again in an election battle, the new Governor quickly began criticizing his predecessor. "[He] set out to unravel as many things as he could that Moore had done," wrote Richard Grimes. "He repeatedly tried to sell the public the idea that Moore had made one mistake after the other. He became so obsessed with Moore's ghost in his closet that it interfered with Rockefeller getting anything of his own started. He was fighting the 1972 election all over again."[4]

He even cancelled the capitol dome gilding project Moore had readied, but had not accomplished upon his departure. The gold leaf that Governor Moore had stored in a vault, to restore and beautify the tarnished and tattered dome, was sold upon orders of Governor Rockefeller. If it was an Arch Moore project, it couldn't be a good one. Profits of the sale were used to buy Preston County a new snow plow/blower, which had been requested by the House minority leader from that northern, mountainous snow belt county, Jim Teets. Rockefeller didn't understand the significance of gilding the dome, what it could do for state pride. He just knew it was a "Moore project" and he was going to kill it.

Sharon Rockefeller had the red velvet wallpaper stripped from the capitol corridors, telling friends it made the capitol look like "a whore house."[5] The Governor had crews try to remove Arch Moore's bust from the Cultural Center. The frustrated workers reported that Arch, apparently having anticipated Jay's move, had heavily cabled it into the floor, making it impossible to take out without a lot of damage and expense. Toppling it would have to wait.

Of greater significance, Rockefeller would ruthlessly fire hundreds of state employees who had been hired during Moore's eight years, without regard to competency or necessity. Those he feared might sue in federal court due to the political firings (where there were a couple judges appointed by Republican presidents), he "put in a corner." One Highways Department administrator was given a desk with absolutely nothing to do, day after day, until he finally quit out of sheer boredom. Most prospective new state employees were screened by local Democratic county party bosses. Jay issued an executive order, revoking civil service coverage Moore had extended to 8,000 highway workers.

Due to reorganization, Rockefeller appointed a completely new Civil Service Commission, with two Democrats, one of whom had been a labor lawyer, and Tom Tinder as his Republican member.[6] The Democratic Senate, angry that the Civil Service Commission was refusing to approve the wholesale replacement of Moore's people with their Democratic appointees, refused to confirm Tinder, however.

Sadly, Rockefeller axed a new, $20 million mental health facility Moore had planned to build just north of Charleston in the coming months. He did away with the Department of Mental Health, making it a division of the Health Department.

John Lennon had a line, "Instant karma's gonna get you." Jay was cursed, in his first two years in office, with two of the worst winters to ever hit West Virginia. Nineteen Seventy seven and 1978 had long stretches of extreme, prolonged sub-zero cold, with heavy snows, which caused water and gas lines to burst everywhere and schools to close for weeks. There was such a demand that it was difficult to pump adequate natural gas supplies to homes. The heavy and frequent salting of highways and streets caused potholes like no one had ever known. Some mountainous counties, like Preston, were so inundated with snow that the National Guard had to bring in bulldozers to tunnel passage-ways through the streets of the towns. It was an especially burdensome two winters for the Highways crews. "God must be a Republican!" Jay reportedly muttered.

In one of his very first acts, Governor Rockefeller overreacted to reports of a heavy snowstorm coming through the state. He personally went on the Emergency Broadcast System, normally reserved for war or extreme disasters, warning West Virginians to go home. He closed schools, including colleges and universities (then, almost unheard of) and government, sending everyone into a panic. When the storm passed with little precipitation, he temporarily became the laughingstock of the state. "Jay's Blizzard," they called it, and it was an embarrassing start for the young governor, who had little management and no military experience and simply panicked.[7]

Rockefeller's mishaps gave Arch Moore plenty of speech material during the next eight years, as he continued to speak at Lincoln Day and other dinners and functions, keeping himself before the public. There was the inevitable fun-poking, and reminding audiences how he had done it all differently–and with much better results. As always, Moore would rarely mention Rockefeller's name, instead referring to him as "high pockets" or "that tall fellow." Regarding "Jay's Blizzard" that fizzled, Moore would tell laughing audiences, "If Arch Moore had said there was going to be a blizzard, then by golly, there would have been a blizzard!"

For those who thought a Rockefeller Administration would cause sweeping reform in the way business was conducted in West Virginia, they were sorely disappointed. As H. John Rogers astutely observed, there is a "Permanent Government" that really runs West Virginia, no matter who sits in the governor's chair: "It's the money players." No matter whether the governor is named Moore, Underwood, Wise, Rockefeller, Caperton or Manchin, the same network influence and control much of what goes on in state and local governments.

"For a time, that 'permanent government' was coal. But now, while coal is still a big part of it, that's changed. It's the guys who have the most money in the game," Rogers continued. "There is nothing nefarious about it; they have it on the national scene, too." He thought such big "players" in recent decades would include the likes of Buck Harless, Don Blankenship, Lawson Hamilton, Ted Arceneaux, Bernard Folio, Ogden Nutting, Al Summers, John McClaugherty and Sam Kapourales, to name just a few. But more often, it would be lesser-known names. In many towns, no matter who was in office as governor, the same businessmen and women would continue to lease buildings or have other contracts with the state. And it was simply business. They had no special ideology or even personal or party loyalty; many would often would contribute to both candidates if it looked too close to call, or as with Clarksburg's D'Annunzios, one family member would donate to the Republican and the other to the Democrat, to keep access no matter who won. It was always said about Jay, "He's too rich to steal," but he continued to cater to this loose network of business leaders. This "permanent government" continued to rule behind the scenes throughout Jay's eight years, just as they'd always done and always would do. "It was even worse under Rockefeller," opined Rogers, "because he got into a bidding war with those crooks in the southern counties."

AS ARCH adjusted to private life for the first time since the mid-1950s, he kept law offices in Moundsville and another on the seventh floor of the One Valley Square (now BB&T Building) in Charleston, with a view of the capitol he'd left behind. "He never stopped campaigning," though, according to Charles Ryan. "He'd be in the elevator, going to or from his office and someone would get on. He'd put his hand out and say, 'Arch Moore.'" A third office was located at 1710 Pennsylvania Avenue in Washington ("as close as I could get to 1600," Moore would say), under the firm name of Conner, Moore & Corber.

Wrote John G. Morgan, "Politically speaking, Moore kept a low profile most of 1977, but he gradually emerged and moved once again to the center of the old and familiar arena. In June, he said at a Marshall University seminar that he didn't want to be [the] 'house critic' of the Rockefeller Administration." He added, however, that Arch didn't have many good things to say about his successor's performance. He continued, "In August he accused the administration of eroding public confidence. He said the main ingredient to qualify for public office was to 'have done nothing for forty years of your life.' The comment was made two months after Rockefeller became forty."[8]

Moore declined an offer, in April of 1977, to take the presidency of Morris Harvey College (now University of Charleston).

By late into 1977, he had made a final decision about his future. Arch was ready to "get the campaign bus on the road," as wife Shelley would put it. Not content with the practice of law, in which he continued to make big bucks putting deals together and using his thousands of good connections to help clients, he felt the sirens of the political life calling him back to their shores.

REMEMBERING THE "DEAL" he had with Senators Byrd and Randolph in 1976, Arch thought he had a straight, open shot at the prize he had coveted for years, the U.S. Senate.

When Randolph reneged, contending that his party called for him to run for re-election one more time, it was clear who the "party" was in this case. It wasn't Democrats in general; most had expected the elderly senator to retire. It was two parties, actually, who wanted Randolph to run for reelection–Sen. Byrd, who did not want a Republican, especially one who could overshadow him, as the junior senator from West Virginia–and Governor Rockefeller, who wanted Randolph to keep the seat warm for him until 1984. Both prevailed upon Jennings to go one more time, even though a bloody battle likely awaited.

Arch had been double-crossed and he would never forget it. What could have been an easy walk into the nation's most exclusive club of one hundred would be an uphill challenge. But he was going to do it, regardless. He wanted to serve West Virginia in the U.S. Senate.

Moore announced his candidacy for the Senate on December 12, 1977, at the Charleston Civic Center, with a thousand supporters cheering the announcement. He said that he'd been urged to wait and run for governor in two years, but "waiting is a luxury neither I nor any West Virginians can afford." Even though he was running against Randolph, he could not resist a swipe at Governor Rockefeller: "We left them $234 million surplus in the bank and gold in the vault for the dome. Now the gold is gone and the cupboard is bare!"[9]

David Garth & Associates, a Manhattan public relations firm catering to Democratic candidates, was retained by Randolph to do his advertising for the 1978 campaign. Garth did his usual excellent job, albeit not as colorful as the campaigns of Bob Goodman. With input from pros like "Tiger" Morton, he discovered Randolph's selling points and then just repeated them over and over to the electorate. He emphasized the good job the senator had been doing for years, the pork he had brought home in the form of highways and other federal projects.

For his part, Moore trumpeted that it was he who built the interstate highways in West Virginia, noting that virtually nothing was done with regard to federal, four-lane highway construction during the eight years his Democratic predecessors held office. Before he became governor, Arch reminded voters, the state was 49th among states in rank of receipt of federal funds, per capita, but had risen to 36th place under his eight years in office. He could do more to bring home the bacon, he promised. Moore also decried the growing dependence on foreign oil (which hurt coal sales and jobs, he argued). He called for a stronger dollar to fight the high inflation rate,[10] and for curbing federal spending, which continued to grow.

Randolph relied on the New Deal Democratic machine, as he had every election since 1932–the labor unions, the older straight-ticket Democrat voters, and the thousands who were dependent on the state's Democratic organization. A unified majority party was all it would take to defeat Moore, he knew. Governor Rockefeller had quietly put his organization, which had grown by now to include hundreds of state government workers, at Randolph's disposal. He had going for him the fact that his party controlled the presidency and both houses of Congress. It was a good year to be a Democrat. The voters had not yet become sick of Jimmy Carter, as they would by the autumn of 1980. He argued, quite convincingly, and at length (Randolph normally spoke for at least an hour, without notes, and if interviewed would even filibuster news reporters, not allowing difficult questions), that West Virginians still needed him in Washington. He reminded voters that he had been serving them for five long decades, since 1933, and could recall with clarity his days in the Oval Office, when FDR signed New Deal legislation for which he had voted as a congressman. Named for three-time presidential nominee William Jennings Bryan, a friend of his father's, Randolph had also worked with Eleanor Roosevelt to bring federal, socialist projects into his congressional district like the one at Arthurdale. Voters–unions, more specifically—had thrown him out of office in 1948 to punish him for his support of the Taft-Hartley Act, but he had been a loyal Democrat despite that one "blot" on his otherwise liberal record.

Like Moore, Randolph had made thousands of families happy with him personally by serving as their ombudsman at the Capitol. "If you needed something from the federal government, Jennings Randolph was always the go-to guy," remembered lawyer Robert Elkins. The Senator was very attentive to individual needs of his constituents. He would often give his private, direct number to a West Virginian or provide the "code" for getting a letter directly to him, and add, "Please call me if I can be of help," and he meant it. The Salem native was much more approachable, personal, accessible and connected to the average man and woman than either Senators Byrd or Rockefeller would be. He seemed to genuinely love people, even toward the end of his term. He showed appreciation to those who were kind to him. In short, he was the Democratic version of Arch Moore and that was a big reason he was such a difficult opponent.

Although he was well past his prime and his last term would not be nearly as fruitful, Randolph had accomplished much. Senator Randolph had been widely acknowledged as the "father" of the Appalachian Regional Commission in 1965, which had funneled so many millions of dollars into the state. As chairman of the Public Works Committee, he had shepherded planning and funding for I-79 and other major projects. He was also the father of the constitutional amendment to allow 18-year-olds to vote. The blind and handicapped had their greatest friend in the Senate with Jennings Randolph; he had done much to provide funding and help for them.

He could be proud of himself and his accomplishments, but he never demanded that his name be tacked onto projects he sponsored. Moreover, Randolph lacked ostentation. He would pull his brown, beat-up 1967 Chevy up to the U.S. Capitol and put a cardboard poster on the dashboard, on which his crayon handwriting scrawled, "This is Senator Randolph's car." (No capitol policeman bothered it.)[11] The only time he was known to "pull rank" was when he'd get stuck on a Washington runway when he was in a hurry to get somewhere. The Senator would call a flight attendant and have her tell the pilot to advise the tower that Senator Randolph was aboard. The plane would be cleared to go immediately (Randolph was chairman of the committee that oversaw the FAA. In fact, he had brought in millions of dollars to upgrade West Virginia airports).

If he had a fault, it was that he went too long–he would give an hour-long speech when ten minutes would have been more appropriate. He had the old style of Nineteenth Century political orators in that regard, much like the man for whom he was named. But like a relic, he didn't seem to realize that the era had passed and people's attention spans were much shorter, less tolerant of his incessant "hot air." Wrote James E. Casto of the *Herald-Dispatch* when the Senator died, "Dignified. Extremely courteous. Forceful. Concerned. Randolph was all these and more. And yes, he loved to talk. How he loved to talk." Casto continued, "Congressional colleagues often held their breath at committee meetings when he proposed to 'say a few words' on the subject."

Importantly, Randolph was very likeable; he was down to earth, despite his blowhard oratorical style. Even Republicans could not resist his down-to-earth charm.

Neither candidate had any real negatives at the time, the 1976 indictment of Arch being the exception (and perhaps a deciding factor for some voters). Both remained very popular figures. Neither had a large army of potential job-seekers working for him, as Arch had enjoyed when he ran for governor. They relied instead on a media battle and it was not a particularly exciting one.

Norm Yost was the titular manager of Moore's senate campaign but, reportedly, was not aggressive, and Arch was de facto chairman. "[Yost] rarely even put out a press release," said one who was active in the campaign. Moore's longtime Moundsville secretary, Mary Louise Lipsky, served as campaign treasurer. Noted Audrey Toler, his Charleston law office secretary at the time, "We had a beautiful headquarters, and lots and lots of supporters. But he should have had someone like Bill Loy to run the campaign. He [Moore] tried to run it himself. He even drove himself everywhere he went. You can't run your own campaign like that and succeed." Another problem, said Toler, was that Moore "didn't have a finance committee like he did in other campaigns. We didn't organize, we didn't have meetings. If it had been organized like the 1984 campaign, with committees out in the counties, he'd have won."

"He ran that campaign by himself," agreed Tom Tinder. "There was no organization to speak of, no field coordinators, people weren't called. There were few fund raising activities. It was a stealth campaign. I had people say, after it was over, 'Geez, if he'd only asked, I'd have helped!" Tinder, a lobbyist and lawyer by now, noted that he personally had offered the former governor his assistance that year, but never received the anticipated phone call.

"We badly needed a field operation," admitted Sandy Latimer, who helped with the organization toward the end of the 1978 campaign. "We needed (paid) people out in the counties like we had in other campaigns, at least three or four people moving around the state, coordinating and working on the vote, and it may have turned around. Loy and I tried to get some of the old troops lined up, but it was tough–very tough." Most of the labor for Arch was volunteer and not well-coordinated or supplied. Importantly, there was no new, dynamic radio ads as had made the 1968 and 1972 campaigns for Moore so colorful and fired up potential voters. Even the campaign buttons were nearly identical to the ones used in

1968—dark blue background with red letters.

In an exception to an otherwise mundane campaign, fifty dollars bought one a ticket to the February 8, 1978, Lincoln Day dinner at Lakeview Inn in Morgantown, hosted by Governors Moore and Underwood, who were joined by former California Governor Ronald Reagan, who flew into Hart Field in a rickety two-propeller airplane. It was the future president's first visit to the Mountain State since his unsuccessful 1976 bid to wrestle the party's nomination away from President Ford.

Loy would get involved in the final weeks of the match. Money was tight; Moore did not have political action committees pouring money into his campaign; the national GOP and Democratic organizations didn't help then as they do now with millions pumped into such a race. The special interest groups hadn't yet started their practice of putting millions into challengers' races; mainly, they stuck with incumbents. So Moore relied on common, everyday West Virginia donors, the usual physicians, lawyers, business people, Chamber of Commerce types, loyalists he'd accumulated over the years, few of whom had a strong interest in who their senator would be. There was almost no patronage for a U.S. senator to offer as a potential governor has; few people saw any personal stake in the race.

Mudslinging was left to subordinates. For example, State Republican Chairman John McCuskey and Randolph's chairman, former Justice Thornton Berry, engaged in verbal fisticuffs, with the latter calling Arch Moore a liar and Delegate McCuskey labeling Berry a "political hack."

Political action committee money and other special interest money, plus that made available from the Rockefeller connections (Randolph was close to Jay and Nelson Rockefeller), gave Randolph a spending advantage.

Moore and Randolph were so civil to each other (after all, they'd worked on multi-million dollar projects for the state for many years and both loved West Virginia), that they actually agreed on something that election year. At the request of West Virginia housewife Marian Lucille Herndon McQuade, who had started her quest in 1970, then-Governor Moore, in 1973, had proclaimed the first Grandparents Day. She and her team then turned their efforts onto the Congress and, in 1978, Senator Randolph obtained passage of his resolution to recognize the first Sunday after Labor Day as National Grandparents Day. It was signed by President Carter (and later became a focal point for grandparents' visitation right of grandchildren in divorced situations).

During this campaign, Arch sometimes would be asked about what he thought about Jimmy Carter, whose abilities and competence to handle a national economy, on-going oil crisis, and as the leader of the Free World (as they called it then) were starting to be questioned. He rarely responded directly, but would make his point in his usual jovial fashion, "Well, you know, I assigned him a task [when Arch was chairman of the National Governors Conference and Carter was Georgia's governor] and he has yet to report back on it!" The President appeared with Randolph and Rockefeller at the Forest Festival weeks before the election, landing in Elkins in his Marine One helicopter. (Nixon had done the same for Arch in 1972.)

One of the few controversies of the season revolved around the Panama Canal giveaway. Carter, upon the urging of his internationalist backers in David Rockefeller's Trilateral Commission and the Council on Foreign Relations, decided to return the huge, profitable canal the U.S. owned in Panama to the local government. Its proponents could give no real good reason for the giveaway of such a valuable, treasured asset except to say it would create good will for the U.S. among Latin America (it did not). It seemed to be the result of some secretive deal the internationalists had with other nations, for a purpose never disclosed to the American public. But they had their man in the White House and this was a favor they absolutely demanded from a willing Jimmy Carter.

Former California Governor Ronald Reagan who, unlike other politicians of the era, remained unattached to the internationalists, decried the act, noting, "We paid for it, we built it, and we should keep it!"[12] The canal had been built by Theodore Roosevelt, with loss of life and expenditure of billions of dollars (in today's funds), and was considered a strategic holding of the United States. The giveaway (to a corrupt Panamanian government) was not at all popular with West Virginians, at least those who paid attention to the controversy. An increasingly ambitious (and, accordingly, partisan) Senator Robert Byrd had shepherded the President's canal giveaway treaty through the Senate. Senator Randolph wanted to vote with his Democratic colleagues on the issue, but didn't want to hand his opponent an issue.

Moore had agreed with Governor Reagan's position, that the canal was an American product, belonged to the U.S. and was a military and commercial strategic asset. "We're not going to defend the canal by surrendering it," Arch said. He called Carter's canal surrender treaty a violation of the American conscience and history. Randolph wavered back and forth, holding his vote on the treaties until he was sure the Democrats had enough votes to ratify in April of 1978, then voted against them.[13] For some reason, however, Arch was never able to make the political hay out of the controversy as one would have expected. It was too far away, too abstract, for most West Virginians to see that it was an unwise concession, a potential danger in time of war or crisis.

Randolph's advancing years, wrote John Morgan, " was an obvious issue from the beginning. But the 76-year-old, overweight senator put forth such a sustained demonstration of energy and endurance that age and vigor became subdued issues."

The 55-year-old Moore "often used old-fashioned oratory as he would build emotions, stir up enthusiasm, bring on the applause," Morgan continued. "At a high point in Williamson one night, he shook his head and quivered his jowls in imitation of Randolph's larger jowls flapping in the act of speaking." He swiped at the increasingly vulnerable Jimmy Carter, saying, "Our state already has a senator [Byrd] who speaks for the White House. I want to speak for West Virginia."[14]

"He never referred to Randolph's age," though, Arch's friend Tom McCoy noted, "or to his obvious infirmities. Senator Randolph was almost incompetent" by that time, Dr. McCoy believed.

But Moore charged that the senator was waging a "campaign of announcements," and, indeed, Randolph was using his office to make announcements, left and right, of pork he had brought to the Mountain State. Said Morgan, "With master strokes of satire, Moore dreamed up a mock Randolph advertisement in which the Egyptian pyramids, the Empire State Building and Eiffel Tower were shown with the claim that Randolph built them." Undoubtedly, Arch wished he had some announcements of his own to make.

Randolph brought up the matter of the $180,000 allegedly kept in Moore's gubernatorial desk drawer. Arch countered that the opposition was taking the campaign into the gutter, because they saw that their defeat was at hand.

For the first time, Arch had to fully reveal his personal assets because this was a federal, not a state race and the filing statements were more demanding. He stated that his Glen Dale home was worth $100,000 to $250,000. Another Moundsville residence, in which his mother was living, was listed in the $15,000 to $50,000 range. His stocks, including Exxon he'd acquired in 1957 from the Taylor estate, were listed in value as $175,000 to $445,000. He claimed $100,000 in debts, including loans from a Clarksburg bank and on his life insurance.[15]

It was a neck-and-neck horse race all the way. "We were scared to death," remembered "Tiger" Morton, who helped his friend Jennings

Randolph as much as he could, although he also got along well with Moore. "Our polls showed us behind right up to Election Day. Garth was fine-tuning [the advertising campaign] up until the end." But Randolph's people underestimated the still-very strong Democratic organization and, especially, the labor union get-out-the-vote effort. Arch's grass roots Election Day organization ranged from very weak to non-existent in most counties. He was counting on the allegiance of grateful voters who remembered all he'd accomplished as governor from 1969 through 1976. But would it be enough? Would they remain loyal to him or to the old, loveable Senator who had also served his state very well?

Arch visited all fifty-five counties in the six months before the election. The day before the November 7th election, he moved quietly through Lewis, Doddridge, Ritchie and Barbour Counties, telling them, "There will be a new voice in the Senate ... Again pride will come back and West Virginia will be on the move again."[16]

His devoted friend, Dr. Tom McCoy, took time off from his busy urology practice (as he'd also done during the 1976 trial) to travel with Candidate Moore. "I drove him in that big Lincoln [the Governor's limousine that had been purchased and given to Moore after his term ended] to Welch for an oyster dinner. My worried mother called, asking, 'I understand you're now Arch Moore's driver?' She thought I'd quit being a doctor. That car had an oversized, fifty five- or sixty-gallon tank. I remember a Summersville gas station attendant filling it up and when he got past thirty gallons, he went around to see where the gas was pouring out!"

McCoy said the two would sing along with Statler Brothers eight-track tapes ("Whatever Happened to Randolph Scott?") as they traveled together, to Parkersburg, Morgantown, White Sulphur Springs and elsewhere during the campaign. "What *did* happen to Randolph Scott?" Arch would ask, apropos of nothing, in one of his speeches along the way.

During the weekend before the final face-off between the two legendary candidates, Bill Loy made calls around the state, handicapping the race. He concluded that Moore would win, but only by about 2000 to 3000 votes. "He was just a political genius," reiterated Loy's protege, Hoy Shingleton, Jr. "He really knew West Virginia politics." But Bill was wrong this time, for reasons beyond his control. Loy had been involved in the final few weeks in all but four of the fifty-five counties for Arch's campaign. Those counties–Ohio, Brooke, Hancock and Marshall–were in Moore's backyard, part of his old congressional district. Those were "hands-off," Arch handled those himself, and Loy did not have a feel for what kind of vote they would produce. Normally, they were solid counties for Moore. As it turned out, Loy obtained the margin he needed in the remaining fifty-one counties to produce a victory. "Arch's counties," however, fell short of the goal. Had they produced what was expected and needed, he would have had that margin Loy predicted. There may have been a good reason why Moore thought he was in better shape in those counties than it turned out. "We heard that the Randolph people dumped a lot of cash into the Northern Panhandle three days before the election," remembered the soft-spoken Audrey Toler. "We couldn't prove it, but we heard it from so many sources that it had to be true." She was not certain whether the cash came from Randolph's organization, the Democratic Party, or the labor unions, but was confident that it was spent on Election Day 1978, in large quantities, to defeat Moore.

Latimer blamed the close loss to the lack of a field operation, having no workers out in the counties, shaking the trees for votes, firing up the faithful. "That was a tough one to lose," Sandy said. "It was really a shame. It was winnable." It was the first time Arch had lost a race since 1954. "I think it kind of took the wind out of his sails forever, to have lost that one," said Larry Swann.

The lopsided registration figures–around 700,000 Democrats to about 350,000 registered Republicans–and Randolph's ability to maintain relatively good party unity—made the difference, probably more than any other factor. "In my party, nothing is a cake walk," Moore once told writer John Morgan. "The problem is always one of numbers. I always swim upstream. It's the only position I've known in my political life."[17]

Money had not been as critical to Arch's defeat this time; it was the least lopsided of the modern spending campaigns against Moore. It helped that Randolph did not have a personal fortune in which to dip and that the special interest political action committees were not yet at full steam. Officially, Randolph's campaign spent $664,907 to Moore's $450,614.[18]

Ironically, Arch's old habit of "working with the Democrats" (as Mrs. Moore called it) may have cost him this one. In Kanawha County, Moore gave $10,000 to Democratic kingpin Bill Allen to spend on his behalf on election day. "We [Republicans] only had $2500 to spend on election day," remembered John Charnock, who helped manage the Republican effort in that largest county. "We had a big victory, with Mike Roark winning prosecuting attorney by 16,000 votes, and Peggy Miller, Hoppy Shores and Bobby Silverstein also won by similarly large margins. We elected three or four new Republican legislators." But Arch Moore had not thrown his lot in with the victorious Kanawha County GOP and won that county only by a 5000-plus margin. "If his majority had been as great as the least of our county Republican candidates, he'd have been the U.S. Senator," observed Charnock.

The Moore-Randolph battle was an example of every single vote making a difference in the outcome, just like the Florida presidential vote in the year 2000. Statewide, with about three thousand precincts voting, Arch needed to shift less than one vote per precinct from Randolph's column to his own, for it to go the other way and he would have been sworn in as a U.S. Senator in January of 1979; it was one of the closest elections in history. The final tally was 249,034 for Randolph, 244,317 for Moore, only a 4717 margin. One vote more per precinct and they would have been calling Arch "Senator Moore."

With Byrd and Moore, the state could have had a powerful advocacy team in the Senate for decades, no matter which political party was in the majority. Randolph's power and stamina were waning; he would accomplish little in his final term. On the other hand, Moore was still full of vitality and could have been building seniority had he been the victor. There is little doubt that the voters did themselves a major disservice by failing to make him their new Senator. "He was talking to me privately seven years after that one," recalled Larry Swann. "The Republicans had retaken the Senate. He'd figured out that, by then, he likely would have been the chairman of the Commerce or Energy Committee," and highly valuable to the Mountain State.

But Moore's dreams of representing his state in that august, powerful body were forever dashed.[19] While it was possible, given the state's notoriety for ballot mischief, that Arch could have picked up enough votes in a recount to win, he did not request one.

The supreme irony of the '78 race was that Arch's own success as governor may have backfired on him. There were thousands of well-intentioned voters, enough to make a difference in the outcome, who thought Moore had been such a good governor that they didn't want him to go to Washington; they wanted to "save" him for governor again. "I heard a lot of people say, 'I don't want him for senator, I want him again for governor,'" Audrey Toler said. Arch had been well aware of this flattering, if misguided, sentiment throughout the campaign, but there was little he could do about it. In retrospect, he may have changed those people's minds had he firmly ruled out another run for governor, but that was not his style. He did not want to play games by making a promise he might later need to retract; he did not want to close that door. So it was a backhanded compliment that some voted for Randolph, who wanted Moore as governor.

Arch told Morgan that he had by no means "run to lose," and thought his twelve years as a congressman and eight years as governor would have made him a valuable senator. He told him he couldn't have run harder than he did. He suggested that some unpopular choices he had to make in the past had hurt him. "As governor I had to solve problems. But a congressman [or senator like Randolph] can serve 25 years and never have to say yes or no."[20] He also blamed the loss to Randolph on lack of funds. "I'm a man of modest means," he told Morgan. "I couldn't run a deficit campaign. I had to be careful in terms of finances." He was pleased to have ended nine hundred dollars in the black.

WITH SUCH A close election result, there was no way Arch was going to retire from politics.[21] He had too much invested. It was apparent that, despite the 1976 troubles, he still had a lot of friends. So he returned to his office in Moundsville (where he "practiced law by phone," as Ron Pearson laughingly put it—getting problems solved largely by calling upon contacts in Charleston and Washington, and putting business deals together, rather than doing courtroom work, where his skills had grown rusty). He continued to manage his growing financial portfolio; he had become a comfortably wealthy over the past decades of wise investments and proceeds from his law practice.

The Moores traveled the world together and enjoyed their Florida residence. They were empty-nesters. Shelley, Jr. had obtained her bachelor's degree from Duke and a master's from the University of Virginia. Kim Moore was working on a master's degree in finance at WVU. Lucy had finished her degree at WVU and was working for Bell Atlantic.

Some news painful and even harmful to Arch would hit the front pages in 1979. It involved his loyal soldier, J. Richard "Dickie" Barber, who had done so much to bring in Democratic slate votes for Arch in Southern West Virginia in the 1968 and 1972 campaigns and had served as his liquor commissioner from 1970 until 1976. The Justice Department was now under a Democratic administration and the feds had gone after Barber, charging that he had used his office to obtain about $11,000 in cash and 1800 cases of liquor, worth about $80,000. Barber admitted to the court that he collected contributions from the liquor industry for Moore's re-election campaign and Bill Loy's 1974 2nd District congressional race. There was also testimony alleging that liquor had been withdrawn from the state's inventory[23] to supply the Governor's Mansion, members of the legislature and for various social and political events. "The whiskey river was there," said the U.S. Attorney, referring to the popular Willie Nelson song of the day. On August 30, 1979, Dick Barber was convicted on twenty counts and sentenced on October 2 to three years in federal prison.[24] Throughout the trial, Barber refused to implicate Arch Moore, although he probably could have plea-bargained away any jail time, had he done so. He took the bullet.

About the free-liquor-for-state-parties situation, Kevin Sikora (who would serve in the third Moore term) said about Barber, "He was a victim. What he did was no different than what the Democrats had done for years. When cases of liquor were unloaded at the warehouse and a bottle broke, the whole case had to be returned. However, for years, successive administrations would simply store the salvage product and use it at events at the Governor's Mansion, and give it to legislators." But practicing the ethics of the past had been risky, and Barber paid the penalty.

None of the Democrat legislators, some of whom were observed bringing home trunk loads of liquor after the sessions, was prosecuted. The timing of Jimmy Carter's Justice Department 18-month probe of Moore's commissioner was also suspicious, given that Arch was running against Randolph and expected to run against Rockefeller if he failed. Certainly, the Democrats resented that one of their own (Barber) had done Moore so much good in signing up Democrat slates for Arch; they wanted to disable him. If it was such a priority to put Barber in jail, they said, then why wasn't the investigation and trial conducted during the time Moore had held office, rather than at this later date when Arch was seeking office again? Would the feds have bothered Barber, had Moore retired from politics in 1976 or had they obtained a conviction of Arch that year?

Of course, the *Gazette* used the opportunity to write that Moore "should have been on trial right along with Barber." When Moore defended Barber, calling him a good commissioner, even his friends at the *Daily Mail* chided him.[25]

DESPITE THE SETBACKS, there had little doubt about Arch's next step. There would be no political retirement for him; he was still relatively young and energetic and felt that he had a lot to offer the state. Besides, friends and supporters around the state were pressuring him hard to return to the state capitol.[26] He would seek to expel the current occupant of the Governor's Mansion.

There would be a rematch and both Rockefeller and Moore looked forward to it.

Rockefeller was running one of the most honest administrations ever, but some believed Jay was showing the same fumbling incompetence at governing as Jimmy Carter was doing in Washington. In Arch's view, Jay was making a mess of things, allowing the economy to go down the tubes, and the news media and business community were letting him get away with it. He believed that the 1978 prolonged coal strike, which he thought Gov. Rockefeller had done little to end quickly (in contrast to Moore, who had brought such strikes to a swift end by doing arm-twisting, personal arbitration), had just ruined the state's economy–not only people and businesses dependent upon coal, but government coffers as well. For years, Moore would say that the strike, which finally ended on March 25, 1977, after 111 days of violence, had started an economic decline from which the state never fully recovered.[27] Jay had learned his lesson about messing with West Virginia's foremost source of income in the early Seventies. Consequently, beginning in the 1976 campaign, and increasingly as the 1980 re-election approached, Governor Rockefeller talked coal, coal, coal, so much that one might think he was the industry's public relations officer. Reporter Andy Gallagher called him "The Man from Coal" in a column, which Jay liked. During the on-going oil crises and call by President Carter for clean, additional uses of American coal, Jay completely jumped on the bandwagon. He even promised that fifty new mines would open in West Virginia, which did not occur; to the contrary, many of the mines, especially in the high-sulphur veins of the northern counties, were closing.

While secretary of state, Rockefeller had been full of naivete and idealism. He was a crusader, a reformer almost without caution. A lot of people loved him for that; they admired his courage, especially liberals and college students. But it had cost him the 1972 race, he was certain. Moreover, he realized he wasn't going to change the state, not overnight, anyway. He earlier had thought he could put corrupt southern Democratic bosses out of business and clean up elections, for example, but he underestimated their tenacity. And he watched as Moore's forces preyed upon the party division he'd caused, picking up some of those factions for Arch in that race. Jay vowed that would never happen again. By 1980, the Governor had unified his Democratic party; they were almost all with him this time. He would not rock their boats. He had learned to work with even those corrupt political bosses he previously had opposed. He would feed them money, lots of it, and they would help each other, the old fashioned way Democratic politics had always been practiced in West Virginia. He had learned how to play their patronage game, to scratch their backs when they itched. From idealistic dreamer to Machiavellian pragmatist, the transformation of John D. Rockefeller IV was complete.

Nothing, nor anyone, would get in his way this time.

Arch knew all this, that the tables were turned 180 degrees from 1972, but he could not help himself—he felt lured to come back. In his mind, the state had gone down a slippery slope since he left office in January 1977. He needed to rescue it. West Virginia needed him. He would run for a third term as governor, he announced on a stage at the Charleston Civic Center on March 25, 1980, again to a cheering, supportive crowd of about a thousand people.

This time Rockefeller would be ready for his nemesis. He would have kryptonite in his pocket, awaiting the short Superman from Glen Dale. He hired the Garth agency and turned them loose.

In 1979, he had already met with Democratic chairmen and executive committees around the state, making sure the local people were behind him. It was also a not-so-subtle way of reminding them from whence their patronage came, and that it might dry up if Moore unseated him.

As Bob McDonough had predicted in 1972, Jay would make some people rich next time he had a real contest. Rockefeller opened his enormous family wealth to the campaign, paying for most of it himself; the state would never see anything like it. At Garth's recommendation, the Governor moved a bright young lawyer who had served as his counsel in the Governor's Office, M. Blane Michael, to become the campaign manager.[28] Jay had chosen Garth because he had been so successful with the Randolph campaign and "because it was the general consensus that he was the best Democratic consultant around," explained Judge Michael, who denied Richard Grimes' allegation that the PR firm was actually calling the shots on state government policy decisions.

The Governor decided that there would be no "personal politics" and no negative ads were made against Moore, Michael noted. "We made that judgment early on," he said. "We were simply going to make the case that Governor Rockefeller had been a good governor." Around him for several decades, Blane said he could never recall Jay ever saying anything bad about Moore. "I think it was his upbringing. It was Governor Rockefeller's nature not to be uncharitable toward people, including Arch Moore. He understood there was nothing to be gained by that. Being governor is a hard job–there is no time for that stuff."

And, again, Jay had his party united behind him this time, so it was unnecessary to attack his adversary; he could remain above the fray in that regard. "[The Democratic Party] tends to rally around an incumbent governor," noted Michael.

"Plus, Jay Rockefeller is a very likeable fellow. People like him," he continued. "He's a good campaigner, too. He would get up early in the morning and go until late at night, campaigning. He never turned down any suggestion that he go to an event or go see somebody–he was always willing to do it." Additionally, the Governor was working hard as usual in his government "day job," according to Michael. "He took two briefcases of work home with him every evening."

SANDY LATIMER, then doing business development and consultation for a Washington, D.C. engineering firm, would become Moore's manager, by default. "Bill Loy was too involved in his Martinsburg law practice; he would not come on board until the last few weeks. Tom Craig was Arch's first choice, but he was studying for the state bar exam at the time. Arch just called me and asked, 'How about handling this thing?'"

The goal of the Moore campaign was to raise a million dollars, said Latimer. "Tom Potter raised most of the million, with Gold Eagle (thousand dollar donors) and Silver Eagle (five hundred dollar donors) dinners and receptions. Tom did a really good job." As was the case in Moore's last four campaigns, Potter was assisted by John "Slim" Wells and Bob Hooten, and the campaign treasurer was Moore's Charleston law office's secretary, Audrey Toler. With Jay's emphasis on coal, he had dried up Arch's chief source of campaign money of 1972, however. The coal operators saw little reason to buck the incumbent governor, "although we tried to remind them of what Jay had tried to do to coal earlier," Latimer smiled. "The main source of our money in 1980, was small businessmen and the Republican faithful. We used some mailing lists given to us from the Republican National Committee."

But they were facing endless Rockefeller money—a bottomless, very, very deep pocket like none had ever witnessed, not even in the Kennedy campaign in 1960, a virtual cornucopia of cash originating from one of the wealthiest empires of New York—of the world, actually. This time, in response to the question frequently asked, Jay would continually and, without shame, vow to "spend whatever it takes." He wouldn't even set a limit. Governor Rockefeller spent at least twelve million dollars, mostly from his own purse, the most spent per capita in any race in the nation's history at that time. Although one of the nation's smallest states, his spending dwarfed what statewide candidates spent in California, New York and Texas. It was an astonishing amount to spend at the time and drew some national attention. "You just can't fight twelve million dollars," thought Toler. The press presented the Arch-Jay rivalry as if it was being played on a level field. But it was "not much of a rivalry when you have

72 percent of the vote registered your way and Fort Knox," Arch Moore said about Rockefeller's advantage.[29]

The New York Times reported that almost all of that money came from the $19.7 million Rockefeller had inherited. Moore had spent only $814,335, as of October 31, it said. It quoted the director of the Citizens' Research Foundation at the University of Southern California as condemning Rockefeller's spending for being "the most expensive gubernatorial campaigns ever waged" in U.S. history.[30] Apparently that's what Jay thought it took to defeat Arch Moore. Rockefeller had "taken the rubber band off his wad of money," as "Pete" Thaw put it.

As a result, Rockefeller's campaign kept trumping Moore's at every juncture. "If we did a few billboards, he would do hundreds of them, all over the state," noted Latimer. (The billboards would each make a boast of some sort with the same tag line: "Just another part of Jay's record for West Virginia," which would be remembered with irony in the second term, when the economy went south.) "If we put out a brochure, Jay would send a better one to every household in the state. He was always outdoing us, big time." Rockefeller's reelection campaign bought so much TV and radio advertising that little was left for other candidates; they had to ask him to release some time to them. He ran so many commercials on Pittsburgh and Washington, D.C. stations in order to reach the northern and eastern counties, that many residents in neighboring states thought he was running for governor there.

That the Governor was spending so much was, in fact, a backhanded compliment to Arch Moore; it showed how seriously Jay viewed the challenge. "We had a healthy respect for Arch Moore," admits Judge Michael. "Everyone [in the Rockefeller organization] recognized that Moore had been a popular governor and a good campaigner so we thought it would be a hard fought race."

Some were not so sure that what was reported was all that Jay spent to beat Arch Moore in 1980. Grimes quoted one Rockefeller associate: "Jay pays out a lot of what is called up front money. It's not the money that directly goes into an election, or the money that is reported. But it has an effect on the outcome. It goes to organize outlying areas. We used to sit around and calculate that Rockefeller probably reported about 70 cents on the dollar. He couldn't really report the other 30 percent. It was ground money. There was always a buffer."[31] There were heavily circulated rumors of cash flowing freely in Jay's campaign (whether converted from checks or not, was unclear), with some of his supporters buying vehicles and even homes with the proceeds in some cases—it allegedly wasn't all getting to poll workers. With so much money out there, it undoubtedly would have been impossible to track. It was as if the state Democrat Machine had hit a big lottery. It was a gleeful, party atmosphere for workers out in the counties; they'd never seen anything like it. "A few of my neighbors were working for the Democrats on election day, hired to haul voters to the polls," recounted one Marion County resident, "and they'd show me their checks for twenty five dollars, to which a crisp, one hundred dollar bill was attached."[32] Added Toler, "We [in the Moore camp] always heard that Rockefeller brought in cash. They would write legitimate checks, which complied with campaign laws. We heard that they'd generate checks for one thousand dollars each and then [at the county level] they'd cash them. Just because they were in a check form doesn't mean that cash wasn't flowing. I think that was the norm but, again, I couldn't prove that."[33]

On November 3, *The Williamson Daily News* reported that Kanawha County Prosecutor James "Mike" Roark was presenting to a grand jury in that county evidence of cash use by the Rockefeller organization, which would have been a violation of state election laws. Roark was investigating charges that, among other things, four Mingo County Democratic leaders met with Jay's people in Charleston at which time cash use was discussed and planned. Rockefeller's campaign manager, Blane Michael, was quoted as saying, "We are absolutely not dealing in cash ... We are violating no laws ... It's our money and we can designate an agent in the counties to spend it for us if we choose." (And there was never any evidence that Michael, personally, was authorizing use of cash for the Governor's re-election.)

As there had been in 1972, bumper stickers shouted, "Make him spend it all, Arch!" Some—including, it was reported, Rockefeller family members—thought Jay might actually do that. The family didn't like the image that one of theirs was buying a West Virginia election; it wasn't seemly.

Moore kept a gallows sense of humor about it. With regard to the shameful amount of money Rockefeller was throwing against him, Arch talked of seeing the light at the end of the tunnel and realizing it was a train coming at him. Certainly, none of Moore's contributors could or would match that kind of money. Further, Arch had never spent his own money to win his elections and wasn't going to start now in this uphill battle.

The Moore campaign set up a headquarters in an empty music store building on Quarrier Street in Charleston. Audrey Toler, Tom Tinder, Bob Plantz, John Cain, Latimer and later, Loy and Craig, were joined by two national Republican PR consultants, Eddie Mahe and Don Ring. Moore Administration veterans Mike Hoback, Rod Clay and Mary Ann Winter helped out. "Tom Craig found about ten young people, including Dave Tyson and Jim Kline, to work as field people out in the counties," said Latimer. "They really put in a lot of work." The strategy was to repeat the success of the 1968 campaign, by "pushing to get the Republican chairman to get out the vote for Moore, keeping everyone pumped up, setting quotas of votes needed in each county." But all of them were no match for David Garth's New York limitless PR machine and the money Jay would spend on Election Day.

Nevertheless, Arch "had a loyal following, a good cross-section of people," pulling for him, Latimer remembered. "There was a wide spectrum of people who would come into the headquarters to meet with him, from a delegation up in a hollow somewhere, to top businessmen. As always, both Democrats and Republicans were with him." But Latimer noted that Jay just overwhelmed them with the money he spent. "The [southern counties] were his base. He definitely put a lot of money into organizations down there, put lots of people to work." As former Justice Neely only half-jokingly put it, Rockefeller "paid every West Virginian to haul every other West Virginian to the polls."

According to a Huntington newspaper, Rockefeller paid some election day workers as much as one thousand dollars. "In 1980, Rockefeller paid several people, including former Mason County legislator Charles Damron, $1000 each," it reported." In Huntington, three members of the same family were paid $252, $50 and $50 for their services, and many of the 400 people [Jay] hired in Cabell County were paid more than $100."[34] (Eventually, H. John Rogers would file suit in an effort to seek an end to the practice, and in July of 1986, by a 3-2 margin, the state supreme court agreed that it was tantamount to vote buying. "Obviously, payment of $200 to a voter for distribution of ten leaflets on a street corner or for transportation of a voter and his or her spouse to the polls is not proper, reasonable or fairly commensurate with the services rendered," wrote Justice Darrell McGraw for the majority in that 1986 opinion. "It is pure and simple vote-buying.")

Blane Michael flatly and firmly denied that any hanky panky had occurred with Jay's campaign funds. If there was cash spent on Jay's behalf at the precinct level, neither he nor the Governor was made aware of, or officially approved it, he insisted. "First, the bulk [of the $12 million] was spent on advertising. The money that went to the precincts was disbursed in small amounts–$50 to $75 per person–and they had to report back how it was spent. Any claim that someone got enough to buy a car or house is ridiculous." He added, "Our contributions to committees were limited by law to a thousand dollars each." Judge Michael remembered one critic complaining about some individual in Logan County, a Mr. Queen, to whom the Rockefeller campaign had given about $1500, noting such a large payment violated the law. "We searched the records, and the payment was made to 'Dairy Queen,'" Michael laughed. "It was for hot dogs and other picnic supplies."

Jay did spend enough money on election day to make a big difference, however. For example, he reported spending $176,435 in the six southern counties of Mingo, Logan, McDowell, Wayne, Lincoln and Wyoming. Rockefeller's organization wrote a check for $32,500 to Johnie Owens, Jay's dispensing agent in Mingo County. Eight years later, Owens would be sentenced to fourteen years in federal prison for election law violations. "In my opinion, what we did then wasn't wrong and it still could be done today," Michael told the Beckley *Register-Herald* on May 20, 1988. (As Jay had learned in 1972, Arch would re-learn a lesson from this debacle—that it took money and lots of it to get elected these days, especially to "win" the votes of Southern West Virginia where slates were still the only way. Trouble was, he knew that Democrats such as Owens no way, no how, would accept a check from a Republican that might "incriminate" them, provide proof they were working with the other party.)

Owens, among other southern Democratic chairmen, denied taking cash from Rockefeller campaigns, admitting only to accepting very large ($37,000 or more) checks for "election day workers," which was legal. Others were skeptical, however. They didn't doubt that Blane Michael or Rockefeller himself was removed from the dirty business of cash use, but they found it incredible that no one in the organization authorized or dealt in non-check expenditures. "Blane would never have seen the money if it was cash," opined H. John Rogers. "He would never have been near it." And, to Rogers' knowledge, "North of Parkersburg there was no need to spend cash;" it was a southern phenomena. But there was no question, whatever, that the money—whether checks, cash or both—was what gave Rockefeller the huge advantage. "Gene Hoyer always said that, unless you knock out that election day expenditure, no one will ever beat Jay Rockefeller," Rogers reiterated.

In addition to breaking all spending records, Jay also made several audacious promises to the voters in 1980, none of which materialized. He pledged, over and over, in every town and in dozens of advertisements, that he would deliver a $1.5 billion coal liquefaction plant in

Morgantown—a joint venture by three nations, and the biggest building project in West Virginia. In September, he called a press conference to announce that his Japanese connection had paid off and Chiyoda Steel Corporation was investing $19 million in a steel plant near Parkersburg. In October, he would promise a $2 billion coal gasification plant in Point Pleasant that would produce 3500 additional mining jobs and 1500 plant jobs. He talked about his "clout" incessantly and promised a "Decade of Destiny."[35] People believed their governor; they thought the jobs were coming, that a new day was dawning for the poor Mountain State. None of these ever became reality, however.[36] It is unclear as to whether they were ever really more than a pipe dream. In any event, neither the news media nor the public ever seemed to hold Jay accountable for these false promises.

Judge Michael defended the failure of the coal conversion plant in Morgantown to materialize. "That was tied into President Carter's national energy plan and would have been built, had Carter been re-elected. It was killed by President Reagan, not Governor Rockefeller." He noted that Moore had supported the project, too.

The two candidates debated, at the Chamber of Commerce convention at the Greenbrier in August, and later in the fall, on public TV out of Huntington. Governor Rockefeller's staff had practice sessions in which they would pepper him with tricky questions. "One of his strengths was that he prepared" for such events, said Michael. "He had an amazing ability to remember what he read and what you told him." Governor Rockefeller's attention to detail had vastly improved over his early years as secretary of state, when observers said he was easily bored by the mundane and had an attention span of about 15 minutes; he had matured. Jay was not apprehensive about tangling with the sharp wit of Arch Moore, Michael insisted, noting that they had debated in 1972. "It was just a given that they would debate; he knew that going in."

"Tiger" Morton claimed that Jay never trailed Moore once in the entire 1980 campaign and, in fact, lead as much as eighteen points in the early months. Latimer agreed. "We [Moore] were never ahead."

Rockefeller's manager said his side was never ashamed of the more than twelve-to-one spending advantage over Moore. "I don't think you ever feel there's overkill if a campaign is going well, and it was going well," said Judge Michael. "No one was embarrassed by it."

Moore's key to success had always been to retain at least 90 percent of the Republicans and convert 30 percent of the Democrats. "He couldn't get the Democrats," lamented Latimer. "And he probably lost some

Republicans, too, because of the 'Jay mystique' and because Rockefeller was the seated governor." Plus, Latimer added, "the state's economy was still in fairly good shape" in 1980. It was not until after 1980, in Jay's second term, that things really started dropping off for the West Virginia economy. In Jay's first term, the federal dollars were still coming in somewhat and he was also living off programs and successes we had started [during Moore's eight years]."

The struggle to raise one-twelfth of Jay's money, a million dollars,[37] plus the fact they could not draw close to him in the polls, took a toll not only on the morale of the top staffers but, more importantly, on the candidate himself. Arch was not his usual, upbeat, buoyant self out on the campaign trail. Moore's affect was often flat, subdued, like he was tired. "He just didn't have the spark," conceded Latimer. "The continual bad polls were worrisome and the fund-raising was a 24-hour job, always a problem. It took a toll on him. It was much different from 1968 when it was go, go, go."

With constant bad news, tempers occasionally would flare. Remembered Latimer, "One of the TV stations, Channel 3 or 13, wouldn't run one of our commercials because it didn't have a disclaimer to suit them. It was a good one—two regular guys in a store saying, 'We need Arch Moore back again to solve our problems.' Bill Loy was just jumping up and down, screaming." Loy thought there was a constitutional right to get the commercial aired. "I laughed [at how upset he was] and that just made him madder. He ended up going to [Charleston attorney] Paul Bowles, wanting him to do something [to the stations]. Paul just told him to change the disclaimer to suit them." Generally, though, Loy kept things fun and provided a welcomed sense of humor in all the Moore campaigns, Latimer added.

There was a battle for the teachers' endorsement, the WVEA. Despite all the great things Arch had done for teachers during his eight years, nearly doubling their pay and providing health insurance, they turned their backs on him and went with the incumbent. (Jay would deliver by getting them a pay raise in 1981, but none during the last three years of his administration.) It helped that one of Jay's staffers had been a former employee of the union.

For his part, Moore just hammered away at the "standard issues," as Latimer put it: "jobs, education, roads, community development, 'turning the state around,' his usual. There was really no one big issue." Thought reporter Richard Grimes, Moore's message in the 1980 campaign focused too much on the past, while Governor Rockefeller talked constantly about the future (even though he ultimately did not deliver).

With Arch's subdued manner, some of Jay's people advocated spreading a rumor that the former governor was sick, that he was going to Johns Hopkins University Medical Center for some terminal condition. Wiser heads prevailed and the strategy was killed. Besides, they didn't need to go dirty; Jay was expecting to win by a 100,000 margin.[38]

Rockefeller desperately wanted to take the large, somewhat sophisticated "WVU vote" away from Moore. To do that, he rushed the construction of the new Mountaineer Field, to get the football stadium on Evansdale opened before the election. He took money from other sources, *a la* Moore, and funded it, placating Marshall fans by building them a new sports facility. Jay discovered that there was no good route into the new football stadium now that it was no longer downtown and that there would be a terrible traffic jam before and after games, so he took much-needed Highways money, to the tune of $20 million, to build a four lane access connecting to the Mileground and to what is now I-68.

It went as planned and the Governor even brought in John Denver, whose "Take Me Home, Country Roads" ballad had become the state's unofficial anthem, to play the song for the opening game. The crowd gathered on that hot, sunny day cheered Denver and his acoustic guitar, standing at the ten yard line. He was still an iconic figure (WVU's marching band plays a version of the song at the start of every football game, to date) and making popular movies (like "Oh, God!").

But when the singer introduced Governor Rockefeller, the Mountaineer fans booed Jay, loudly and long. "Come on. Be nice, be nice," Denver scolded them. For a few minutes, one wondered if the polls could be correct. These people, more than 50,000 of them, strongly and clearly resented that Jay had politicized the event, was bribing them to vote for him. Could it be that Arch was going to prevail after all?

Jay was understandably furious at the reaction of the crowd, for being humiliated in this fashion. It shocked him! He had given the fans, the school, a new stadium, and they were ingrates! (First Lady Sharon Rockefeller was so incensed that she never felt the same about West Virginians again. In her view, her husband had done something wonderful, and this is what they got in return. She began spending more and more time out of the state to the point in which, once Jay was elected to the U.S. Senate, she rarely set foot in the Mountain State at all. Never enamored by West Virginians to begin with, Mrs. Rockefeller was now totally disgusted.)

A September 1980 visit to the state by former President Ford, to help his old friend from congressional days, made an interesting story but did nothing to help Moore's struggling campaign. Likewise, an appearance by Ronald Reagan on November 3rd did little to boost Moore.

While he didn't get his 100,000-vote margin, Jay ended up defeating Arch by 402,725 to 336,469, getting about 54 percent of the vote. As Grimes wrote, "He had finally gotten revenge."

Jay was subdued in victory, however. Perhaps the fact that he had bought an election—lock, stock and barrel—fully sunk in that night. Maybe he was considering how tough the next four years would be, governing a state where the economy was going nowhere fast.

The same could be said for Moore–he was very lowed keyed that evening. The Moores watched the returns with the staff, took phone calls and then the former governor gave a short concession speech from his Charleston headquarters when it was clear he had lost. "He was not angry," recalled Sandy Latimer of the private scene before Arch went before the cameras. "He was downcast, very somber. He said simply, 'This one's over.' We had all seen the handwriting on the wall.

"He was very happy about Reagan's (landslide) win (over President Jimmy Carter).[39] He was very pleased, because he and Reagan had been good friends when they were both governors." Moore didn't console those gathered at the headquarters with him. He did not discuss what his future plans might be. "It was a somber night," was how Latimer remembered it.

Did Latimer want to manage another campaign after that loss? "No, not unless I had $12 million," he laughed.

THERE WAS another note of sadness for Arch in 1980, this a personal one. A lifetime of chain-smoking (which his son called his father's "one severe difficulty") having caught up with him, Arch, Sr. succumbed to lung cancer and emphysema. Moore sat by his father's bedside often in those last days, tenderly nursing him, letting him know how much he loved and appreciated him. "Dad never required attention for himself. He was usually helping someone else." Arch A. Moore was buried near his parents at Beehler's Station Cemetery on Route 250, near Moundsville.

After his second political loss, Moore returned to the practice of law, putting business deals together, and preparing for the next campaign. Often his law practice involved projects that enhanced the state's economy. As often happens in the law profession, a lawyer's contacts and their impression of him/her are often more important than sharp legal skills and arguments. And it doesn't hurt if those you're trying to persuade perceive that you might be in a position to help them in the future.

Such was the case when David Arnold and three others in the whitewater rafting business formed Teays Landing to create a second take-out area on the New River.[40] The late Jon Dragon, a whitewater industry pioneer, then owned the only take-out area on that river and, because of his monopoly, the sky was the limit on what he could charge his competitors for leases. If they refused his price, they had no egress for their customers and were out of business. Moreover, the one take-out area was getting clogged as whitewater rafting and kayaking was becoming more popular. Arnold (owner of Class VI) and his partners wanted CSX to allow them to build a tunnel under their railroad tracks (CSX had tracks on both sides of the river which 28 trains, including the Amtrak Cardinal, used) so they could have a take-out area and not be dependent on Dragon's. The railroad would not allow them to temporarily close and dig up the tracks for the few days necessary to build the tunnel and other means were prohibitively expensive. Further, Dragon and his attorney were fighting their efforts to build another take-out area. What Dragon was shocked to learn, many years later, was that Arnold and his partners had retained the services of a powerful lawyer: one Arch A. Moore, Jr.

Teays Landing was to a make-or-break point in their negotiations with CSX; the young partners had spent hundreds of thousands on the land on both sides of the track and the steel to build the tunnel. They had pooled and risked their money on this attempt to create a new take-out area. If they could not get permission from CSX, they would all go belly-up. So when Arnold was sitting in a Whitewater Commission meeting in DNR Commissioner Ron Potesta's office, and someone handed him a phone message ("CSX has declined your permit"), he went into shock. "I went blank. We had everything on the line on this."

Ten minutes later, as he sat in the same meeting, another note was handed to him. It was a message from John Snow, CEO of CSX[41] which read, "Your plans have been approved."

Arnold asked to take a break and ran to a phone. He asked his partner, "What the hell is going on? I about had a heart attack!"

He later got the story. Attorney Moore had phoned Snow as soon as he received CSX's rejection notice. Arch told the railroad's chief executive, "I understand the score is CSX, One and Arch Moore, Zero. Thank you for your time." And he hung up. A few minutes later, Snow called Moore back, and told the former governor, "That score is very uncomfortable with us and we've decided to give your clients permission to open the trench."

Arnold and his partners closed the track for 96 hours, they dug their trench and quickly had their tunnel open to tourists. The industry was able to expand, serving 225,000 rafters per day at its peak (the third largest tourist industry in West Virginia). Moore had saved their businesses with a phone call. "Arch's friends from Congressional days would ask him about it," Arnold laughed. "They'd say, 'Tell us the zero-to-one story.'"

Chapter 22 Notes

1. - Bowden, one of the nation's all-time legendary college football coaches, spent most of his interview with this book's author talking, not about football, but rather the Southern Baptist church he helped start in the Suncrest section of Morgantown. He taught Sunday School there and was very proud of having helped to get it established. The Bowdens sat on the front pew with their sons, who would go on to their own coaching and TV careers. Perhaps he preferred to forget his less than sterling results at WVU; students once burned Bowden in effigy on campus, before he left for his new position in Florida.

2. - Bill Loy's first choice for artist of the Arch Moore official portrait was the renowned and beloved American illustrator of magazine covers, Norman Rockwell. "Bill asked me to call him and I was surprised when he answered his own phone," recalled Elaine Davidson. But Rockwell "said he mainly did caricatures, and declined." (Rockwell had done Nixon's and Kennedy's portraits.)

3. - Sharon Rockefeller was "chomping at the bit" to get into the Mansion, Winter recalled. The Moores had moved out a week ahead of the '77 inauguration and Mrs. Winter gave Mrs. Rockefeller her first tour. "I said, 'I guess you'll be happy to get into a residence this large,' and Sharon replied, 'Oh, we've had much bigger houses than this one.'" Winter, July 26, 2005.

4. - Grimes, Ibid.

5. - Grimes, Ibid.

6. - Jay had actually considered keeping Tom as his Welfare commissioner, and was grateful for the smooth transition he'd facilitated for his appointee to that job, Leon Ginsberg. Tinder visited Moore in his Charleston law office to see whether he'd object, before accepting Rockefeller's offer to serve on the Commission. "It's your state, you ought to do it!" Moore had urged Tinder. "That was Arch Moore," Tinder said. "He really had a commitment to public service, whether it be as a soldier, congressman or governor. I thought he would oppose it, that he might say, 'You shouldn't be working for that SOB,' but instead he encouraged it."

7. - Your author was a budding political cartoonist at the time and did one that week depicting Chicken Little (Jay's face, glasses), running around the barnyard, screaming, "The sky is falling, the sky is falling!" as a lone flake of snow fell.

8. - Morgan, Ibid.

9. - Morgan, Ibid.

10. - The national inflation rate had ranged from 6.5 percent in 1977 to an astonishing 13.5 percent in 1980. Mortgage rates would rise to the high teens by the early 1980s. The U.S. unemployment rate hovered at 6 to 7.7 percent during that period which, combined with the high inflation rate, made for what was possibly the worst, most dangerous national economic situation since the Great Depression. It caused presidential candidate Ronald Reagan, in 1980, to throw Jimmy Carter's "misery index," which the latter had used against Gerald Ford, back in his face, asking voters, "Are you better off today than you were four years ago?"

11. - Once, when your author was transporting Senator Randolph back to the Morgantown airport, he suddenly yelled out, "Stop the car, I need to take a leak." I responded, "Oh, Senator, there's a restroom just up ahead at a nearby gas station; I'll get you there as quickly as possible." "No, I need to go right now," he insisted. He climbed behind a nearby tree to relieve himself, his rotund frame sticking out on each side. He got back into my Chrysler Cordoba, saying, "Thanks! Let's go!"

12. - Reagan debated conservative writer friend, William F. Buckley, on the issue at the University of South Carolina. It helped endear the Californian to Republicans even more, helping to

launch his 1980 campaign for president.

13. - Morgan, Ibid.

14. - Interestingly, this is the same thing his daughter's Democratic opponents would say about Arch's daughter, Shelley Capito, in the 2004 and 2006 races, regarding her close relationship with President George W. Bush.

15. - Morgan, Ibid

16. - Morgan, Ibid.

17. - Morgan, Ibid.

18. - Source, Federal Election Commission. $91,291 of Randolph's and $59,124 of Moore's money came in contributions less than five hundred dollars. $204,885 of Randolph's were $500 and up, $120,063 of Moore's. Randolph got $119,000 from the unions, Moore none. $71,100 of Randolph's and $62,882 of Moore's was designated "corporation" donations.

19. - Most observers knowledgeable about how the Justice Department operates speculate that it would never have dared conducting the massive investigation, witness brow-beating, and prosecution of a Senator Arch Moore. So by losing to Randolph, he also lost the protection against his former adversaries that he might otherwise have gained by a victory in 1978.

20. - Morgan, Ibid.

21. - Reportedly, Mrs. Moore did not favor another race after Arch went through the 1976 trial; the risk of being prosecuted and humiliated were not worth it to her. But she was a faithful wife and a real trooper, as they used to say; she went along with the program with enthusiasm once the decision was made.

22. - The state controlled the wholesale and retail market in a monopoly until Moore changed that in his third term.

24. - Morgan, Ibid.

25. - Barber would not be silenced forever. He was key, behind the scenes, in getting Moore re-elected in 1984, and then was an informal political adviser during the third term. He was treated respectfully by Moore's administration in the third term and his suggestions regarding hires and strategy were given attention. Certainly, nothing that happened with beer or liquor industry without "checking with Dickie." The powerful and lucrative liquor industry still knew him and worked with him, reportedly into subsequent administrations, even after Moore's third term. Barber, whose political instincts were nearly as good as Bill Loy's, was so in tune with the grass roots that he privately predicted in 1986 that Moore would not be re-elected in 1988.

26. - Charleston Mayor Danny Jones, then a restauranteur, sent a sandwich to Moore's office around this time. In it, he'd slipped a note to the former governor which read, "Danny says run!"

27. - There would be other harmful, often wildcat, strikes during Rockefeller's tenure. One, in 1981, produced a lot of violence, damage and bitterness. On one occasion, pickets stormed a Boone County mine complex and set it afire. Jay's state police would just cruise such scenes and do nothing. Coal mining jobs declined continually throughout Rockefeller's terms; over 19,000 coal mining jobs would be lost from when he took office to 1983. Manufacturing jobs dropped by more than 35,000. This, from one who, in 1976, promised the state 50,000 additional jobs.

28. - Michael, WVU's 1965 student body president, Jay's manager again in 1984, then Senator Byrd's, and a partner at Jackson Kelly, was appointed by President Clinton to the U.S. Court of Appeals for the Fourth Circuit.

29. - *The New York Times* and Associated Press, April 29, 1984.

30. - *The New York Times*, Nov. 1, 1980. Jay's wealth was subsequently acknowledged to be much greater than $19.7 million; four years later the same paper would admit he was worth at least $150 million.

31. - Grimes, Ibid.

32. - Vivian Ashcraft, Aug. 21, 2005.

33. - Toler, Aug. 21, 2005. To this author, there seems to have been far too much smoke for there not to be fire, regarding the Rockefeller cash-spending allegations. The stories came from many parts of the state and were too similar to be all be lies. No one, of course, would admit to it because it was illegal, and there is no indication that the FBI or other federal authorities ever investigated them. But even if the strong rumors were not true, the perception, the strong belief, that Rockefeller's camp was spending hundreds of thousands of dollars in untraceable cash on election days to secure votes,

explains why the Moore camp later believed they needed to do the same, why they needed to "fight fire with fire."

34. - *Herald-Dispatch,* July 13, 1986

35. - Before his administration was over, the unemployment rate would rise to 20 percent and the amount of permanent, well-paying jobs lost would be well into six figures, making a bitter mockery of his pledges in 1980 and his 1976 promise to add 50,000 additional jobs to the state's economy. West Virginia would resume its former 50th place in the U.S. economy.

36. - Rockefeller did deliver at major Toyota plant in Putnam County, however, but did that much later as a senator.

37. - Officially, Moore failed to even reach a million. Records of the West Virginia Secretary of State indicate that Moore's campaign reported $941,705 expenditures and Rockefeller $11,648,091. If both sides used unreported cash, however, then the figures are low.

38. - Grimes, Ibid.

39. - West Virginia was one of only eight states that did not go for the former California governor. With the severe energy and economic problems and the Iran hostage crisis, former peanut farmer Carter had become the most unpopular president since Herbert Hoover and Richard Nixon. But not in West Virginia. The fact that an Iranian mob had held scores of Americans hostage for months had hurt Carter as badly as the disastrous economy and confiscatory tax structure. "I asked Arch what he would do with the hostage situation, if he was president," Dr. Tom McCoy remembered. "He said, 'This wouldn't last long!' And I don't think it would have."

40. - The New River was once known as the Teays.

41. - Snow was later President George W. Bush's Secretary of the Treasury. Everyone else at CSX was afraid to give permission to temporarily close the company's busiest railroad line; the decision had to be made by Snow.

Chapter Twenty Three
Governor Moore to the Rescue

As Rockefeller's two terms as governor concluded in 1984, West Virginians were still suffering from three very tough years. A loss of lower-tech manufacturing jobs to Asian countries, steel to Europe, and the auto industry to Japan, had hit the "rust belt states" particularly hard. Billy Joel had a hit at the time called "Allentown" which lamented the situation. No longer could a young man drop out of high school to make a college professor's salary in the local mill. Another popular song of the time was from the musical "Annie," called "The Sun Will Come Out Tomorrow," which also seemed to fit the mood. The Democrats were eager to blame Ronald Reagan, who had just taken office, but soon it was clear he not only didn't cause it, but he was going to solve it with tax cuts and optimism. So the nation as a whole began recovering from the 1981 recession fairly quickly but, as usual, West Virginia was harder hit and its recovery was much slower.

Particularly throughout the northern part of the state glass plants, steel, coke, and other manufacturing facilities were closing, never to return. As result, tens of thousands of good-paying jobs for those lacking a college education were lost. Sadly, blue collar towns like Fairmont, Clarksburg, Weston and Weirton were drying up, dying and would never return to their former glory days. Their downtown business areas were like ghost towns. Byrd, Randolph and Rockefeller seemed impotent to do a thing about the dire situation. West Virginia's unemployment rate hovered between a shocking 15 to 20 percent during some of those years. Middle-aged men, accustomed to decent factory wages, were grabbing janitorial or fast food jobs, just struggling to make their mortgage payments. As in the late 1950s, there was an exodus to find work, this time not to Ohio, but mainly to North and South Carolina. The terrible job loss had made a mockery of Jay Rockefeller's promise of 50,000 new jobs for the state and all the big plants he'd assured 1980 voters were coming any day. There was no economic development to speak of.

And despite the Governor's constant talk of coal, coal, coal, those jobs too were being lost; coal production had eroded significantly, in the north especially; West Virginia had fallen from first to third among states producing coal. Mining employment was a mere six percent of the workforce as compared to 23 percent in pre-1955 days and even eleven percent when

Moore left office; there were only 38,000 West Virginia miners employed now, versus 138,000 in 1948. Manufacturing, which generally provided higher pay than the service industry jobs that replaced them, dropped from 28 percent of the state's economy in the 1960s, to only 15 percent of it during Jay's second term. The state's overall labor force had dropped from 658,000 in 1979 to 596,000. Economists were saying this was a permanent realignment of the state's economy.[1]

Despite the tremendous loss of jobs and decline of the state's economy, however, the size of state government continued to mushroom under Rockefeller's two terms—the state budget had doubled. As a result, personal income tax was the highest in the nation, at 13.5%. Business was carrying one of the largest tax loads, per capita, of any state. The Employment Security Fund, which paid unemployment checks to the many idled workers, was bankrupt, owing the federal government more than $375 million. Public employee insurance costs had risen from $17 million, when Arch Moore left office in 1977, to a whopping $135 million by 1984. Medicaid owed health care providers $125 million. The Rockefeller Administration's response to these many government crises had essentially been inertia, apathy and an inability to respond. It had not looked so hopeless for the state's economy since the Great Depression. And at no time in the state's 121 years of existence had its government been so nearly bankrupt, with no plan to extract itself.

The state's news media had been extremely lenient with Rockefeller, but the voters were not happy with him. His popularity was at an all-time low, far worse even than when he was calling for an end to the surface mining industry in the early Seventies. For any other candidate with such a disastrous record, it surely would have marked the end of his or her political career. But Jay had a cornucopia of money, millions to spend, as he had proven in 1980.

He announced that he would be a candidate for the U.S. Senate seat being vacated by the retiring Senator Jennings Randolph but no one laughed. They knew the nomination, at least, was pretty much his for the asking, despite his dismal record as governor. Who could beat him?

There were many, nationally and locally, who urged Arch Moore to go for that Senate seat and certainly it was his most attractive option. He had long coveted a Senate seat and knew he could be very productive for the state in that position. It would be a far, far easier job than serving as governor, with less criticism, more opportunities to please, easier to be reelected.

In late 1983, "I had made up my mind that I was going to run for the

U.S. Senate," Moore recalled. Sitting around a table at the Greenbrier Hotel, he polled his wise men, among them Dick Barber, Tom Potter, Cleve Benedict, Tom Craig and Bill Ritchie, to decide who the Republicans should run for governor in '84. After a lengthy discussion, "they decided there was only one candidate," Arch recalled. Because no one else was enough well-known, he was their sole choice, the only Republican they believed could retake the governor's office. "I never felt I had control of my own political destiny," Moore complained. He felt that he merely responded to decisions made by others. He added, "When I was running against Randolph, I had people tell me, 'You got me my job, you're responsible for me being able to support my family—I won't vote for you [for senator] because I want you back as governor.'" And he was absolutely correct; that mentality may have cost him the Senate seat in 1978.

Moreover, Arch knew he could not possibly match the ten or twenty million dollars that Jay would put into the upcoming Senate race. The majority of his mail and phone calls was calling for Arch to come back to Charleston as governor, to clean up the mess his successor had left. That was a less attractive option, but certainly more do-able. In that scenario, he would have thousands of job and favor seekers who would help him.

In his usual fashion, Arch kept his plans completely to himself. He didn't even tell his trusted secretary, Audrey Toler. "I typed up one statement announcing that he was running for U.S. Senate and another for governor. I had so many people calling or stopping by to ask me, he didn't want to put me in a position of lying to his supporters. I could honestly tell them I didn't know,"she laughed. Even at his announcement in Charleston, there was an air of extreme suspense at to whether he would seek the Senate seat or the governor's office. He played with the emotions of the crowd a bit, talking about how the state needed him at the capitol, leading them to believe he was announcing for governor. But then he shifted his talk to the needs in Washington, and how the United States Senate seat made more sense for himself, the state, the nation. He talked about the struggle he and Mrs. Moore had, trying to decide which path to take.

But then he brought it back full circle, ending with a climactic, "We're staying home!" The crowd immediately exploded into a loud cheer. They were clearly happy with the choice. There was a glimmer of hope that the state could be rescued from the crisis in which it found itself. Wrote *The New York Times* reporter who had been at the Civic Center for the announcement, "Mr. Moore promised to bring jobs to the state, where a lingering coal recession has been blamed for a 17 percent unemployment rate as late as January."[2]

With his announcement that he again would run for governor, a young Morgantown businessman, John Raese (pronounced, "racy"), announced that he would challenge Governor Rockefeller for the Senate seat. Unable to get Governor Rockefeller to debate him on issues like right-to-work laws, Raese would debate AFL-CIO President Joe Powell. He presented a clear, conservative alternative to Rockefeller. George "Buffy" Warner, who would later serve a term in the state senate,[3] would manage his campaign. (More about Raese, later.)

A young Weirton Democrat, Kevin Sikora, had worked the First District hard for John McCuskey's race against Alan Mollohan in 1982. McCuskey had lost but, with a friendly, engaging personality, Sikora had secured hundreds of Democratic votes for him in those northern, ethnic counties. His work caught the attention of the former governor, who was then practicing law in Moundsville, and Sikora was hired as Arch Moore's first campaign field worker, covering the area of Tyler through Hancock Counties. "I ran a little Chevy Vega up and down Route 2 so many times I wore the tires off," he laughed.

The first thing that amazed Sikora, in working with Candidate Moore, was his legendary memory for people's faces and names. "On the streets of Wheeling, we ran into a lady about seventy years old, whom he hadn't seen in thirty years. Her appearance must have changed during that time. But she started to introduce herself to Arch, 'I'm from ...' and he finished her sentence, '... Clarksburg! How are you, Shirley?'" Sikora, who would be the first to travel with Moore in 1984, and the last to do so as he finished his course in November of 1988, began to realize that Arch's genius for remembering names was a key factor to his political success, in convincing voters he was a personal friend who did not forget them.

Huntington lawyer Tom Craig—the bright, Yale divinity graduate who had distinguished himself in helping to manage the Buffalo Creek disaster relief effort, and who had served as chief of staff during the last couple years of Moore's second term—would run the campaign. Bill Loy, still practicing law in Martinsburg, would provide behind-the-scenes campaign help. Dick Barber, Pete Thaw, Howard Mullins and other Democrats would quietly but effectively provide advice and contacts to southern Democrats. Mike Fotos, John Leaberry,[4] Rod Rogers, Robert Duvall, Robert Chehi, Nelson Robinson, David Williams, Craig Rothwell, Jim Rardin, Dave Schles, Bart Potter (Tom's son), Glen Stotler, Jacob Reger, Sikora and others would serve as field coordinators. An attractive blonde, Debbie Buzzard, served as Moore's appointments secretary for the campaign. Charleston attorney Tom Potter would again serve as Moore's chief fund-raiser (as he would do again in 1988) and Bob Hooten and "Slim" Wells would pitch in, as well. Audrey Toler would serve as campaign treasurer, one of the most important day-to-day managers of the operation.[5]

"West Virginians Are Coming Back" was the theme in 1984, although it certainly wasn't as catchy as "The Arch March" of 1968 or even "Hear What They're Saying About West Virginia" that Bob Goodman's people wrote in 1972. Despite the double-entendre of his theme song's title (a New York native had been governor the past two terms) Arch would run a positive campaign, rarely mentioning Governor Rockefeller or even his own opponent, Clyde See. That could not be said for the other side, however. They would make every attempt to cause the questions about Moore's 1972 fund-raising and spending to be the issue in 1984 and it almost worked for them.

Attorney General Chauncey Browning, Senate President Warren McGraw and House Speaker Clyde See fought it out for the Democratic nomination for governor. Governor and Mrs. Moore predicted the Attorney General would prevail. But they were wrong again on that one. "The vote broke down to about a third for each of them," observed H. John Rogers. "McGraw was the labor/liberal guy, Chauncey represented the good ole boy politics and See was the conservative, business Democrat." He noted, "That has held as a basic demographic of many West Virginia Democratic primaries–it's about a third each time for each of those factions."

See would prevail, but barely. He would be the party's nominee.

The Speaker grew up in the type of difficult circumstances not unusual for a resident of the West Virginia mountains. His father was a farm hand and his mother, a teacher, died in a bus accident when he was five. Clyde grew up in the outdoors, doing a lot of hunting and fishing. He was no Jim Sprouse, no intellectual. In 1957, See had dropped out of school at age sixteen, when he learned he would fail the ninth grade due to excessive and unexcused absences. "I said to heck with it, waited a couple months and joined the Army," he later recounted. He obtained his GED while stationed in Hawaii but was rejected entry by every college except Concord when he returned to West Virginia after his military discharge. He dropped out again, this time to work for an aircraft parts factory in California before attending WVU and then law school there. He later got elected to the House of Delegates from Moorefield.

In 1979, the witty and sarcastic politician (he called himself "a Don Rickles comedian") became the youngest member to be elected Speaker of the House, and the first from the Eastern Panhandle since 1915. See was, as his successor Joe Albright put it, "from the conservative wing of the [Democratic] party." As Speaker in a part-time legislature, coal companies like Pittston sought him out to be their lawyer. His tenure as Speaker was marked by battles with liberals, especially Senate President Warren McGraw and the UMWA became his bitter foe because he would not cater to their demands. But Democratic businessmen, lawyers, bankers, who might be tempted to support a Republican candidate, could be quite comfortable in supporting See and many of them did.

Moore administration veteran, now lobbyist Tom Tinder rather liked Clyde See. "He was a very colorful, folksy speaker. He would use phrases like, 'Fat possums travel at night.'"

In 1982, when See announced he was running for governor, his name recognition was only one to two percent. But, in May 1984, after campaigning non-stop, he defeated the better-known Attorney General Chauncey Browning and McGraw. He compared campaigns to "selling dog food" and thought "running for governor is like applying for a job at Kroger's–anybody can line up and do it."

HAVING PULLED the rest of the nation out of the recession of 1981, driving inflation down to a tolerable rate, and having succeeded in reducing the federal tax rate (which had reached confiscatory levels under Jimmy Carter), President Ronald Reagan was riding high by 1984. He was on his way to becoming one of America's most popular presidents ever. The grace with which he'd handled the assassination attempt, soon after assuming office, also added to public affection for him. In 1984, he would win one of the largest landslides in history, over Carter's vice president, Walter Mondale.

Mondale would sound the alarm that Democrats trot out every two years to scare the elderly, a large source of straight Democrat votes: "The Republicans are going to take away your social security." Arch Moore had to face that issue, even as a gubernatorial candidate in '84. His method would be to point to the flag (usually there would be one near his podium, wherever he was speaking), and state firmly, "As long as that flag is flying, you will receive your social security check!" to appreciative applause. (In his stump speeches, Arch also liked to mention Mary Lou Retton, the nation's darling gold medal-winning Olympic gymnast from Fairmont, as an example of American and Mountain State tenacity, also guaranteeing applause that year. Mary Lou's Uncle Joe, a popular Fairmont State College coach, was a friend of Moore's.)

His party's Senate candidate would prove to be problematic for Arch Moore, in this election and even more so in the coming years. John Raese was in his early thirties and had never held an office in his life, had done nothing significant except inherited a large estate, a business empire, when his grandmother, Agnes Greer, died. His personal wealth helped him get the GOP nomination for the Senate, defeating former state Senators Sam Kusic and Frank Deem and Fairmont pharmacist Hank Viglianco. Most gave hell's snowballs a better chance, but Raese would nearly upset the very unpopular Governor Rockefeller that year, despite being outspent $13 million-to-one.[6] He would also gain the support of the national Republicans, several Senators and other national figures coming in to campaign for him. (One of the biggest "what-if's" in Arch Moore's career was, what would have happened if he, instead of newcomer Raese, had been Rockefeller's 1984 opponent. Most astute observers thought Arch would have prevailed in that one, with Jay so obviously vulnerable that year.)

For a decade thereafter, Raese insisted to anyone who would listen a theory of which he was convinced: that he would have defeated Rockefeller had he not been sabotaged by Moore. He had vitriolic hatred for both men that spilled onto the pages of *The Dominion Post*, which was among the many Greer assets he and his brothers inherited.

First, he believed Arch hogged most available money from Republican donors for his gubernatorial campaign, which may not have been a far-fetched concept. Raese charged that, if he announced a fund-raiser, Moore would schedule one in the same town, inviting the same people and soaking almost all of it up. Arch had helped hundreds of Republicans in their efforts over the years, but those were always candidates whom he respected, who had come up through the ranks, or who had worked in his campaigns or administrations. But he barely knew John Raese, and distrusted most mavericks like this young candidate who had, in his estimation, failed to pay their dues. Like most, Arch seriously doubted that Raese had any real chance of defeating the well-funded Rockefeller, even with the latter's current unpopularity. Arch would have had no qualms about beating John to the available campaign funds. Like most successful politicians, Moore put his own campaign first; that's the way it had always been and Arch made no apology for it. Being a newcomer to politics, Raese apparently didn't understand that rule.

But Raese's accusations went even a step further. He believed that Rockefeller and Moore made a secret deal in 1984 to avoid running against each other, then to allow each other to win, to refrain from criticizing the other publicly, to stay out of each other's way, and allow the defeat of See and Raese. He would never, ever forgive Arch for this perceived conspiracy. It was an allegation that even some Moore loyalists came to accept, given that Jay and Arch barely mentioned each other in the '84 campaign and were often on the same Democrat slates come election day. But Judge Blane Michael, who was involved like no other in Rockefeller's campaign, insisted that nothing of the sort occurred. "There was no deal" between the two camps, he was certain. "See was a Democrat from a county neighboring my own, and I would not have tolerated [Clyde being sold out]," Michael, a loyal partisan at the time, noted. But, as they say, perception is everything and John Raese believed that Moore had somehow sold him out; he could not accept that he lost the election on his own. He would become one of Arch's most bitter, unforgiving and dangerous enemies of all times.

THE WVU MOUNTAINEERS were having one of their most exciting football seasons in history. They won seven of their first eight games, beat Heisman Trophy winner Doug Flutie of Boston College for the fourth time, and were ranked tenth in the polls. So when President Reagan made a campaign stop at Parkersburg High School on October 29, and put on a West Virginia University ball cap (asking, "How 'bout them 'Eers?"), he received thunderous applause from the crowd packed inside and outside the auditorium. Reagan spoke highly of Senate candidate Raese (who rode with the President in his limousine). About the gubernatorial candidate, the popular President told the crowd, "Greetings to my good friend and your once and your future very great governor, Arch Moore." (More applause.) "I'd like nothing more than to work with Arch so we can see to it that West Virginia shares in the prosperity that is sweeping across America. We were governors together, and I know that he knows that leadership means more than just raising taxes."

For his part, Arch made no big promises in 1984, virtually none at all. He just presented himself as a known, trusted product who had performed in the past. Privately, he would tell friends about the mess in Charleston, "I know how to do it, but I just don't know what's there." He no longer had trusted informants in state government who could provide him an accurate lay of the land, the financial status of the various departments of state, the tax revenue situation, and other data needed to strategize. Moore would also avoid talking to the press, knowing that little good could come from an unexpected or trick question. Instead, he would stick to appearing at GOP dinners, party headquarter openings, receptions, country fairs and other controlled events where he would not be bothered by pesky reporters. When he gave interviews, it usually was to friendly editors. He had learned well from Senators Randolph and Byrd; that was generally their style, to stay above the demands of the news media, to remain aloof from it. But it was more than that. One had the feeling that Arch had set personal parameters for himself, that because he wasn't all that enthused about running for governor a fourth time, and that there was only so much grief and aggravation he was going to tolerate in the campaign. Kissing up to the news media was not on his list, even if it cost him.

The support for Arch, even among Republicans, was not as strong as it had been in previous elections. Part of it, no doubt, was that he was no longer seen as an automatic winner, having lost the last two elections. Jacob "Jake" Reger, who served as a campaign field rep for the Moore campaign that year, remembered a campaign event in Putnam County. "The people on the Republican Executive Committee were upset with him, complaining that they hadn't seen him since the last election. I had a bad feeling about him even coming." But, Reger said, Moore quickly worked his magic on them. "When he got off the helicopter, I started to introduce them to him, but he immediately started greeting each by his or her first name. They were happy as hell!"

Arch had a new substitute to appear on his behalf when he could not make it to a particular campaign event. "Arch could not go to [a Republican dinner] in Calhoun County, so his daughter, Shelley Capito, went and spoke for her dad," recalled Reger. "Her charisma just charmed them."[7] John Raese, who was accompanied to that event by Senator Slade Gordon, also had nice words to say about Arch Moore, remembered Reger. "It had been disclosed that Jay Rockefeller had his picture superimposed in a photo of a crowd at a WVU game," he said. "John Raese told them that he remembered when he'd played baseball for WVU, that no one ever came to those games. But one day he'd looked over into the small crowd, and there sat Governor Moore in the pouring rain, a faithful fan, watching them play." The comparison of Arch the Real Fan to Jay the Pretend Fan went over well with the partisan crowd.

As would later be revealed, Arch raised and spent cash to secure Democratic votes in the 1984 campaign, just as his organization had done in 1972. It was illegal to accept more than fifty dollars in cash from a single donor, but they'd been warned that he could not win without raising and spending lots of cash. He later admitted to raising and spending at least $100,000 in cash. Moore would later testify that manager Tom Craig handed him a three-by-five card which listed four Democratic leaders who demanded cash: Kemp Morton of Kanawha County, a Mr. Beasbaug, Doc Whitley of McDowell County and Johnie Owens of Mingo County. If Arch could raise the needed cash, Craig would distribute it to these Democrats for delivery of the thousands of votes they supposedly controlled. Moore denied being able to remember where most of it came from, perhaps to protect the donors. He would later testify that an Ira Copley gave Vernon Harless $10,000 in cash which came to Moore, which he then passed on to Campaign Manager Tom Craig for use. "I have no knowledge as to what he did with that money," Moore would later insist in a deposition. He recalled another $5000 being donated by Vincent D'Annunzio, a Clarksburg beer distributor, brought to his Charleston law office in an envelope. Vincent's father, Sammy, was supporting Clyde See. They were making sure that, whoever won, they would have access to get favors. This cash being handled by Craig was separate and apart from the "legitimate" fund-raising being conducted by Tom Potter, Moore would explain. He would later insist that he wasn't sure what the law was, pertaining to cash donations and expenditures.[8]

THE TELEVISED debate between See and Moore in the fall was the nastiest Arch ever had tolerated, even worse than when Peter Beter attacked him in the 1968 primary. Clyde See came after him like a rabid pit bull; Arch never before or after had such a vicious opponent. In his candidacy for the presidency that year, former Vice President Walter Mondale had parodied a funny Wendy's commercial of the time, asking President Reagan, "Where's the beef?" Referring to the revelations from the 1976 trial in which Moore was acquitted, and in which there was testimony of cash in Arch's desk drawer, Clyde See kept harassing him with, "Where's the cash?" Moore referred to See as a "high school dropout," unfit to serve as the leader of the state.

Raese's campaign against Rockefeller was getting more attention than the Moore-See battle, though. He would continue to bring in heavy hitters from the national party, including Bob and Elizabeth Dole, to campaign for him. Jay was running scared. He ran a series of full-page newspaper ads that stressed his opponent's inexperience and the fact that he had no record, had done nothing for the state. Raese, in turn, ran ads that begged, "Don't Let Jay Rockefeller fool you again!" They listed the outgoing Governor's record: "80,000 lost jobs; 100,000 [West Virginians] unemployed; the highest unemployment record in the nation; the worst business climate in the nation; and one [West Virginia coal] mine shut down every 43 minutes."

Against that record, how were the Clyde See Democrats to respond, "More of the same?" Even the unions had turned on them this time; several made no endorsement, which was a victory for Arch. With virtually no platform of his own, no real proposals for change, solutions or reform, See's forces made blasting Arch Moore their total, scorched-earth campaign, unlike the positive approach against Arch Moore that Randolph had taken in 1978 and Rockefeller had repeated in 1980. Every allegation and accusation against Moore was rehashed this time. See's ads brought up all the issues of the 1976 trial in which Arch was acquitted. They claimed that Moore's "liquor commissioner went to prison for racketeering" after telling "FBI agents he gave $50,000 to $70,000 to Moore" in the 1972 campaign. The ads accused Arch of allowing "the Pittston Co. to escape a $3.7 million Buffalo Creek cleanup bill and left West Virginia taxpayers stuck with it."

Naturally, the Democrat papers began singing from the same page, a "Greek chorus," as one columnist put it, taking their cues from the See organization. But Arch refused to allow his opponent to establish his ethics as the issue. The *Gazette* editors asked about his "integrity." Moore responded, "I don't consider it an issue." Referring to the results of the 1976 trial, his acquittal by a jury, he told them the questions had been answered "in the American system of justice." When Huntington journalists asked him about the allegation that former Liquor Commissioner Barber had personally delivered envelopes of cash to him (in the '72 campaign), Arch evasively replied, "That's the first time I ever heard that question." When pressed for an answer, he said, "That's my answer."

Arch rather enjoyed toying with them. "There are some who think I talk fast..." he was quoted saying about himself in October of 1984. "...Some who say I don't answer the question. But you know, that takes some artistry." With a chuckle, his supporters shrugged off the glib responses as classic Arch Moore. "He was our Edwards and Huey Long," said a Moore loyalist years later, referring to colorful Louisiana governors known for cutting ethical corners, strong leadership and colorful rhetoric.

But his non-responses to their hounding on behalf of See drove the partisan press up the wall. Even Ken Hechler called Moore "slippery." Just before the November election, a UPI columnist labeled Arch a "Teflon" candidate[9] and asked, "Since when is something not an issue simply because your opponent brought it up?" She continued, "I used to believe, years ago, that the voters' credo in West Virginia was, 'Throw the rascals out.' We may need a new one after Tuesday, 'Throw the rascals in.'"[10]

Clyde See's TV commercials repeated the theme—mostly negative ones, harping over and over again, "Arch, where's the cash?" It began to sound like an annoying parrot. But the numbers showed that the attacks were effective; the ads were running up the former governor's negatives with the electorate. For the first time, average voters were using words like "crook" and "dishonest" in the same sentences in which they discussed Arch Moore, and were openly questioning whether they should vote for him again. Wisely or not, Moore essentially ignored See's attacks on his integrity; he did not respond. As it continued, his huge lead in the polls over the Speaker continued to dwindle. Moore's crowds seemed to shrink a bit and those who did show up seemed less excited to see him; there was a diminution of his former star quality, his "cult of personality," as H. John Rogers put it. Others were puzzled by his passivity in view of the relentless attacks. Were the allegations true? Whatever had happened to the fighting, feisty Arch Moore they'd once known and loved? Why wasn't he defending himself more aggressively?

Nevertheless, *The Charleston Daily Mail* enthusiastically endorsed Moore on October 30, based on his solid record of service in the past. Said its editorial:

> Nothing could be more symbolic of the current state of West Virginia affairs than the condition of the state capitol's dome; neglected, blackened, dulled by the elements. Nearly a decade ago, Governor Arch Moore was ready to restore Cass Gilbert's masterpiece, protecting it from the harsh environment, preserving it as a source of pride for the state. Moore's successor did not have the foresight to complete the project. Perhaps, at the time, he lacked the innate good sense to see the significance of such rich symbolism. Perhaps he did not realize that West Virginians looked to their governor for leadership that is not always political.
>
> This has never been a problem with Moore. It is, in fact, his strength. He has an uncanny sense of what West Virginians want from their state government and their chief executive. And he has demonstrated an ability to transform that intuition into achievement. To gauge Moore on his record of public service is to find him a doer, a battler. He is audacious and there are those who would claim he is confrontational. But in

> his eight years as chief executive, he used that style to the state's advantage. He got the Democratic-dominated legislature to move West Virginia forward. State government under him was positive and aggressive. Moore is not without his skeletons. Agreed. Moore's opponent, Clyde See, is an attractive candidate. Agreed. But we'll let the former governor have the last word here: "It seems that if you had a good governor or great governor in good times, that is what you require in bad times." Agreed. Arch Moore was one of the most effective leaders this state ever had. We recommend him for governor again.

Even the Raeses' Morgantown *Dominion Post* gave Moore a lukewarm endorsement in its November 4 edition, stating that he "looks like a certain winner and we urge approval of his candidacy." Of course, it heartily endorsed John Raese for Senate.

With an "October surprise," the Democrats tried one last-ditch effort to tar Arch badly enough to defeat him. Using an WSAZ-TV reporter as their front man, Charleston lawyer and Democratic leader Rudolph DiTrapano went into federal court, demanding documents that the See forces claimed to prove that Moore exercised his Fifth Amendment rights in refusing to testify before the grand jury in 1975. While not admitting such a letter existed, a Justice Department lawyer came to Charleston to argue that the sealed records should not be released. She noted that Moore had a constitutional right to take the Fifth and, "Just because Mr. Moore is a candidate for governor he does not forfeit his right to privacy." Judge Robert Staker agreed, refusing DiTrapano's motion, in an order which he released the Friday before the election. Staker wrote that the release of such records would be an "unwarranted invasion of privacy." Normally a lawyer respectful of the court system, DiTrapano called the judge's ruling "nuts." But even with the defeat in court, the Democrats had obtained at little cost exactly what they wanted–several front page stories about their "issue." The partisan *Sunday Gazette-Mail* ran a headline for the story, "Letter Exists: Democrats; Moore Accused of Ducking Voters."

ON ELECTION Day 1984, there were tons of cash spent by candidates and their organizations, just as had always occurred since days when Daniel Boone won a seat in the Virginia legislature from Kanawha County. While laws required that all campaign spending be done in traceable, recordable form, old habits were hard to break in a state in which a vote was considered worth at least two dollars or a sampler-size bottle of whiskey.

The $100,000 in cash that Arch raised and Tom Craig distributed to Democrats on his behalf was not reported to the secretary of state on election reporting forms, which would cause them a tremendous amount of grief six years later. But they were not alone in the practice on Election Day 1984, by any stretch of the imagination.

In a subsequent civil trial deposition, Moore would provide a rare comment as to why he used cash in Boone, Logan, McDowell and Mingo Counties, which he termed "that soft underbelly of the State of West Virginia." An "underground campaign," as he called it, was used in 1972 and 1984 "to maintain the integrity of the voting process...of the ballot box...To make sure that the votes that were cast for you were counted for you." When opposing counsel pressed him as to why he had to, essentially, bribe those southern Democrats to count his ballots, Moore provided an exasperated explanation: "People steal votes in West Virginia and, basically, it's the majority party that steals votes because they control the precinct mechanisms. It's as simple as that." He said the cash he spent in those counties, eight in all, "makes people tell the truth." He added that he "lost every one of them by an overwhelming majority," nonetheless.[11]

But it wasn't just the Moore campaign that seemed to be using cash on election day. Recalled Reger, "I was in Mason County that day. Someone pointed to [an outside precinct worker] in a truck and asked, 'See that guy?' It was a Rockefeller worker and it appeared he was handing out cash [to voters who would join him, one-by-one, in his truck]. They [the Rockefeller people] knew the vote totals in every precinct by noon—they had inside information." While Reger could not be certain that anyone was buying votes for Jay, or even that the man in the truck was on Rockefeller's election day payroll, he knew what he saw with his own eyes. And his story was corroborated by others, elsewhere in the state that day.

About Moore's people spending cash on election day, Reger said, "I had no knowledge of it. I never saw any of it." But he conceded that cash transactions occurred for Arch. "I think Tom Craig worked with people he trusted and knew. I assume some of them were given cash." Surprisingly, not only was cash spent by Moore's organization to get onto Democrat slates, but it also was given to local Republican organizations, he recalled. "Not every county received cash. It wasn't like it went to every precinct. Just select precincts." Democrats wanted cash because they didn't want traceable proof that they were helping Republican Moore. But why did

Republican workers need to be funded for election day in cash, not lawfully with checks? "I don't know," confessed Reger, now the Upshur County prosecuting attorney. He had no answer. "In some counties, that was just what was expected."

Ken Hechler, who would be elected secretary of state that year and become responsible for election law enforcement, admitted that there may have been cash spent by the lower levels of the Rockefeller campaign. "You're not going to get anyone in the Rockefeller camp to admit cash was used. When cash is used, it's illegal so other people don't know about it. They're not going to broadcast it. But I know Rockefeller spent a lot of money," Hechler said. "[Rockefeller's campaign] frequently had signed checks that were not made out to specific individuals, they were going out without the names filled in. [Jay] assumed it was being used for legitimate purposes, I guess."

John F. Kennedy, Hechler reminded, "sent several suitcases of money" into West Virginia, "as documented [in Keith Davis'] book, 'West Virginia Tough Boys.'" Obviously referring primarily to Rockefeller, Hechler concluded, "People at the top are to blame [for use of cash in West Virginia campaigns]. The system would dry up if the people at the top would quit making big contributions."[12]

Moore and See knew the race would be close, they just weren't sure how close or how soon the result would be known. Despite the high-profile Senate and presidential races, more West Virginians voted in the governor's race than any other that year. Based on exit polls, CBS's Dan Rather, NBC and CNN projected Moore to win as early as 7:30, right after polls closed. But See would not concede until very late; the early returns were going his way. (Many of the exit polls were showing Raese beating Rockefeller, as well.)

Arch and his family watched and listened from his Moundsville law office and he accepted a congratulatory call from Vice President George Bush. The vote totals from the southern, heavily-Democratic counties were coming in better than he had anticipated. Apparently he wasn't convinced of a win (he'd subsequently tell his well-wishers, "We knew we had it all along!"), however. Recuperating from a nasty cold he had picked up in the waning days of the campaign, Moore delayed, and then cancelled, a flight to Charleston for a victory speech on election night.

Incredibly, the Wednesday morning edition of the *Gazette* called the gubernatorial race "too close to call." They couldn't even seem to admit in their Thursday edition that Arch had won. They hid the story back on Page D-1, under a headline of "See Manages Smile," with a huge photo of the

Democrat's concession speech. It was as if they just couldn't bear to concede that their old adversary was the Governor-elect, that their efforts to defeat Arch had failed. The next Monday, they ran a Jim Dent cartoon of Moore in his "King Arch" robe and a caption, "Ready or not, four Moore years."

MOORE HAD WON thirty-seven of the fifty-five counties and the election by 394,937 to 346,565, a convincing victory, but about eight percentage points under the margin of victory his own polls had predicted. See had narrowed the gap as election day approached, picking up most of the undecideds. There "weren't any coattails" from Reagan's sweep, Moore told the *Daily Mail.* (No other statewide GOP candidates won. Delegate John McCuskey lost his attorney general's race to Charlie Brown, an Ohio native. Former Congressman Ken Hechler was elected secretary of state, as A. James Manchin was elected state treasurer.)

Arch told the media by phone, "We're quite pleased. We accept that we have a great challenge ahead of us and we are more than willing to accept that challenge." He finally spoke out about See's negative strategy, calling it "perhaps the ugliest campaign that was ever run in the history of the state."

He entered his downtown Charleston headquarters for a victory speech on Thursday accompanied by a teary-eyed Mrs. Moore. He signed autographs for the children, kissed elderly ladies, and waved to supporters in the crowd. "It's great to be back," he grinned to the crowd. "We can only repay you by giving you the best and finest government this state's had. You'll have a feeling from the beginning that things are different in West Virginia–that the A-Team is back."

He warned, "We know it's not going to be easy times, but we have to work with the cards that have been dealt to us. It's going to take all of us to put this thing together and measure up to the challenge. It's going to take the best of everything we have."

He expressed his view that Rockefeller had allowed the legislature and the supreme court to take over the government. "When the executive branch has failed to lead," it created a vacuum, causing the courts and the legislature to "come in and usurp the executive's authority," he stated. Amendment 4, which would have provided education funds to comply with the *Recht* decision in 1982,[13] was soundly defeated by the voters, who were in an anti-tax mood. Moore said that the state would have to learn to live within its means and he vowed that he would not be controlled by supreme court orders requiring him to spend certain amounts of money for education (as had been done under Rockefeller). "I am not frightened by court orders. I consider them significant treatises on the optimum in the field of education, but historically, under our system, there have been three branches of government. I don't believe the courts are permitted to raise taxes. I don't intend to be pushed around and I don't intend to let the legislature be pushed around." He said the state could survive without a "judicial fiat." But he did say that he would provide a strong education program and give teachers pay raises, despite the amendment's defeat.

Arch also told the celebration/press conference that he would make his pledge of getting the state out of the liquor business a high priority and would present legislation to that effect in the first session of the legislature (which he did). He said that, if he could get $50 to $65 million in road trust funds that was currently "locked up" in Congress, he intended to get to work on finishing the four-lane highway system he started in the 1970s, and that he would also re-pave primary and secondary roads, which had fallen into disrepair. Regarding the large Democrat majority in the legislature that he faced, Moore said it wasn't much different than in his first two terms and that, "Without a little give-and-take it would be a little dull."

For his part, See made no apologies for the way he ran his campaign, nor would he concede that the constant negativity may have actually backfired on him. "It was obvious that we're weren't going to beat someone with [Arch Moore's] popularity by saying I was a nice guy. Maybe the media will pay a little more attention to [Moore] this time." About the loss, See said, "We came from behind. We said from day one that we could swim upstream and we did. But we couldn't swim up Niagara Falls." As would be repeated in 1988, the defeated Moorefield lawyer did not lose gracefully. He said it was "poetic justice" that Arch Moore was returning to office at a time of high unemployment, decreased government revenues and no school or road bonds, because his previous two terms had been served during good times. "It will be interesting to see how he can do in these tough economic times." He was also bitter toward Governor Rockefeller for not supporting him. When Jay twice phoned his headquarters after the loss, See refused to take the calls. He was burning his bridges.

See blamed his defeat on the fact that Ronald Reagan had swept the state (by 405,483 to Mondale's 328,125). The truth was that voters trusted Arch Moore to restore the bankrupt economy and state government slightly more than they did the Hardy County Democrat. "Arch did it before, can he do it again?" was heard on the lips of many that autumn. They weren't sure it could even be done even by one with the mythical skills of the former governor.

Records from the West Virginia secretary of state indicate that Clyde See spent $1,245,156 to Moore's $1,752,960, perhaps the only time in which Arch outspent his Democratic opponent in a governor's race. It helped Moore, of course, that See was not independently wealthy and able to spend limitless millions from his own pocket. In fact, See was "shell-shocked to find a campaign debt of $188,000" awaiting him. Then, in the flood of 1985, he would suffer severe loss, so much damage to his house that he, his wife and four children would be forced to live in a hunting camp.[14]

Like Clyde See, John Raese did not go away quietly. After his near-defeat of Rockefeller (374,233 to 344,680), despite being outspent 13-to-one, Raese met with an Assistant U.S. Attorney in Charleston on Thursday after the election, contending that he had enough information in hand to launch a formal FBI investigation into voter fraud. "We have over one hundred instances of documented voter fraud, vote buying, machine manipulation, and tabulation irregularities" by the Rockefeller organization, his campaign director said. "We have people coming out of the woodwork saying they saw fraudulent practices and these people are willing to testify in court." Raese claimed the actual vote tally did not correlate with exit polling by the TV networks, confirming his suspicions. The Republican's accusations were almost certainly worth looking into, but the Justice Department refused to investigate the Rockefeller campaign. Jay was now a Senator-elect, after all, and a member of arguably the most powerful family in the world.

Before he died, attorney Bernard Smith, the infamous Democratic operative in Logan County, told several people that Rockefeller was losing to Raese in that county on election day. Smith claimed there wasn't time for them to get names and write checks, so cash was sent into that county to secure the vote. Smith claimed that the last-minute infusion of cash was what turned it around, delivering Logan County to Jay just in time to save him from defeat. If Smith's story was true, the same likely occurred in other counties, as well. But the evidence of Rockefeller using cash is anecdotal; it was officially denied. As Ken Hechler mentioned, it will never be officially admitted, if true, because it would have been illegal activity.[15]

The press was eager to discover with whom Arch Moore would fill his administration, since his team in the first two terms had been so outstanding. This time, there would be no "Terra Alta Summit" as Moore had hosted in December 1968, to let candidates for appointments in his administration know they would be chosen and for what position, or to build teamwork and camaraderie. He would not reveal his choices for staffing, would not even make them, until February of the next year, after he'd been in office a few weeks.

In the meantime, the campaign field workers began to fidget. Some had families and had been subsisting on a very low salary for several months now. They did not know if they even had jobs in the new administration, didn't know whether to return to their home counties to seek private sector employment. Lack of information from the top was causing increased dissension.

Friction had already built up between the field workers and the headquarters, specifically, Campaign Manager Craig and Kathy Bullard, Craig's assistant manager. They felt that they'd been out in the trenches, in the counties, getting the job done, but that no one was giving them any credit or reward. Most were just doing mundane correspondence, waiting and waiting for something to happen. "Everybody respected Tom Craig because they knew he was closest to Arch Moore," noted Jake Reger. "But he was kind of arrogant. Some of them hated him. He would hold things pretty close to his vest, but it was probably because Governor Moore wasn't telling him anything, either." Reger remembered one tense meeting during this period in which a field worker was especially vocal about being kept in the dark about their future. "Tom Craig said, 'I'm going to just mark that off as tension, but if it happens again, you're going to be asked to leave!' It was one of those awkward moments of complete silence." But one of the field workers, John Leaberry, would endear himself to Craig, partially by keeping him informed as to what the others were saying and doing.

Within a couple days of the election, the *Gazette's* Don Marsh was already predicting that Moore would fail in his third term. Pointing out that Human Services social workers were expected to handle 300 to 500 cases a month, that WVU and Marshall Universities had the lowest faculty pay in the nation, that West Virginia was at the bottom in funding secondary education, that "the road system is falling apart," that the state had a "narrow job base," and because there was going to be a "net loss" in tax revenues because the B&O tax was scheduled to phase out, and expenses and interest on loans was increasing, Marsh wrote that the magician Arch Moore "will have a very large rabbit and a very small hat to work with." He thought that the "short term problem that West Virginia faces is not capable of being resolved by Moore or any other person." Marsh wrote that, if a private business had the problems West Virginia was suffering, it would "seek protection from the bankruptcy court." (Interestingly, Marsh made no such comments as long as Governor Rockefeller's election to the Senate was at stake. All his utterances about the dismal economy were fairly positive until then.)

Not everyone was as pessimistic as Marsh, however. Moore "had the ability to squeeze a lot out of a dollar," noted Democrat Delegate Gino Columbo of Clarksburg. "The guy just makes things happen on a little bit of money." Former Senate President William Brotherton conceded that Moore was a great political leader. "He out-dueled us on a number of occasions," he remembered. "He was a formidable adversary. He used all the tricks he could use. He would call my senators down and persuaded them sometimes. What he promised them, I don't know. They didn't tell me." Senator Larry Tucker said he'd often voted for Moore's programs in the past because they were good for his district. "He knew how to trade," he said. Arch's attention to details of government was also noted. "He knew each county highway superintendent–he knew the supervisor of the night shift at Weston State Hospital," said Columbo. Former Speaker Lewis McManus recalled that Moore "was very persuasive on an individual and collective basis. He believes in himself and his information."[16]

IN DECEMBER, Arch's campaign held what is commonly called a "come to Jesus" reception at the Charleston Civic Center, an opportunity for all those who supported his opponent to join his loyalists in retiring his campaign debt. Businessmen from all over, who wanted access to the governor but had put their money on the losing horse, poured in and coughed up contributions. Moore's speech that night was hopeful but not overly optimistic. He repeated his themes that state government and the state's economy was in a mess, and that it would take a while to dig out. Arch continued to try to lower expectations about any miracle-working on his part. This was not the 1970s, when federal dollars were flowing freely, he subtly reminded them. And he pointed out publicly, for the first time, one of the main reasons why West Virginia traditionally had a difficult time luring new business and industry: "this rugged piece of real estate called West Virginia" had few large, flat areas for factories to build and spread out, he admitted. It was a moment of candor, of Moore taking his audience into his confidence.

It would not be an easy upcoming four years, he seemed to be saying, but he would give it his best shot.

Chapter 23 Notes

1. - *The New York Times,* May 8, 1986.

2. - *The New York Times,* March 25, 1984.

3. - Warner's brother Kris would later serve as party chairman and brother Kasey would be appointed by President George W. Bush for a short stint as U.S. Attorney for the Southern District. Dr. James B. Whisker, a West Virginia University political science professor, had been John's father Dyke's first choice for campaign manager. Whisker, who had impressed the elder Raese with conservative columns published in family's Morgantown paper, sat in John Raese's office for a long time, waiting for the candidate to get off the phone and finally walked out in exasperation. "I gave him one piece of advice," recalled Whisker. "I told him that, because he was an unknown, reporters would ask him who he admired. I told him to say, 'Washington, Jefferson and Lincoln,' all safe names. He was asked that and responded, 'Washington, Jefferson and Lincoln...and Jesse Helms.'" [Helms was a right wing North Carolina senator, thought by many to be slightly kooky.] Whisker was glad he did not take a semester's leave of absence to run the Raese campaign.

4. - Leaberry, the 34-year-old son of a top officer in Huntington's International Nickel Company, left his job as a tax lawyer for Ashland Oil Co. and walked in off the street to ask for a job with the Moore campaign.

5. - Arch Moore kept Toler "totally out of" the solicitation and expenditure of cash, she insisted, convincingly. "He never wanted me to be involved in that. People say to me, 'You had to know what was going on,' but I knew nothing about it. In '88, John Leaberry had separate accounts set up to which he was funneling money. I have no idea where the cash came from or where it went. And that's what I told the [federal] grand jury."

6. - Raese won 344,680 votes to Rockefeller's 374,233 and won 30 of 55 counties, including Jay's "home county" of Kanawha and did remarkably well even in heavily Democrat counties. A *New York Times* article of June 2, scoffed at Jay's campaign theme of "Leadership in Tough Times," and quoted the *Gazette,* "generally regarded as pro-Rockefeller," as saying "what Rockefeller is now spending is obscene." If Jay "can't win save by flinging millions on a political organization and at television screens, politics isn't his forte," the *Times* quoted a *Gazette* editorial. "He should take his licking, find another endeavor and leave political adventuring to his wife, Sharon, or the oncoming generation." In an April 29 article, *The New York Times* raised its estimate of Governor Rockefeller's personal fortune to $150 million, a more realistic figure than the $19 million it earlier had reported, but probably still too low. Raese had proposed that he and Rockefeller cap campaign spending that year at $3 million. Jay just laughed; he'd already spent $4 million and was just warming up.

7. - Arch would end up reciprocating when his daughter was a congresswoman; he would often substitute for her at Republican dinners and functions.

8. - Arch Moore's deposition of January 15, 1992, in a civil trial.

9. - The national press had been calling Ronald Reagan "The Teflon President" because he had survived so many accusations, even criminal ones, completely unscathed, remaining popular.

10. - Deborah Baker, *Capitol Window,* Nov. 5, 1984.

11. - Trans., p. 137, deposition of January 15, 1992.

12. - Hechler, July 1, 2005.

13. - An activist state supreme court had appointed Ohio County Circuit Judge Arthur Recht to hear a case in which it was alleged that public schools in certain counties were not being fairly funded. Recht effectively demanded that the state spend more money on education and that the richer counties subsidize the poorer ones, even though taxes were lower for residents in the latter.

14. - *Sunday Gazette-Mail,* March 6, 1988.

15. - Some argued that, while there was a legal difference, there was no difference, morally, between buying an election using cash or checks. When asked in an interview for this book whether Jay's campaign spent cash, Johnie Owens hesitated, looked to former Williamson mayor and Rockefeller friend Sam Kapourales for guidance as to how to answer, and both then said, "Oh, no, Jay always used checks. Never used cash."

16. - *Charleston Gazette,* Nov. 1984.

Chapter Twenty Four
Tax Cuts!

Arch Moore was stepping into a huge mess, an economic hole, when he again took the mantle of chief executive after an eight year absence, and he knew it.

Wrote professor and historian Otis Rice, "When Governor Moore began his third term in January 1985, the economic conditions in West Virginia were reaching a critical state. The unemployment rate stood at fifteen percent, the highest in the nation. The coal industry, historically a mainstay of the state's economy, was sinking at an alarming rate."[1]

Wrote *New York Times* reporter James Barron, "[This] time around, the mood is bleaker and few people are certain what the state government can do to brighten it." West Virginia had a sixteen percent unemployment rate as recently as October, he noted. Coal, steel and glass had lost thousands of jobs. "Our prospects are not good," Prof. Alan Hammock of WVU told Barron. "The trend in the nation is away from so much of what we do here that, unless something dramatic happens, it's going to be difficult around here." Moore admitted, Barron wrote, that the light at the end of the tunnel he had seen upon taking office the first time in 1969, "is exceedingly dim today." One problem was that the price of West Virginia coal was about eight to ten dollars per ton higher than the world market price and there wasn't "anyone who out of the kindness of his heart is going to give you" that extra ten bucks, Arch explained. Moore's lofty goal was to get 100,000 West Virginians back to work; doubling coal exports could provide 25,000 new jobs. He had to find ways state government could help drive down the price of West Virginia coal and he had some ideas.

Barron continued, "Under Mr. Moore, a self-made man with a booming voice and a no-nonsense manner, state government will have a different flavor than it did under Mr. Rockefeller, a Harvard graduate, amateur classical pianist and great-grandson of one of the world's richest men." Arch "tends to paint a big picture of grand design and try to follow through with his charismatic personality," and "a talent for winning compromises from union members and managements whose differences seem irreconcilable." Moore had promised in his 1984 campaign to not raise taxes, the article continued.[2]

He could have added that Jay had left town without mentioning that the state owed a $375 million unemployment debt to the federal government; Rockefeller had kept that disaster very quiet during his campaign for the U.S. Senate. If Moore faced none other, that hole alone would be a tough one from which to dig out. Rockefeller had escaped a burning, exploding disaster, sneaking off to the political safety of Washington, joining that 100-member exclusive club called the U.S. Senate, where there were no longer any risky executive decisions to be made. With some luck, they'd blame the mess he was leaving behind on his successor!

Nevertheless, there was guarded optimism that Arch might be able to once more work his magic and get the state moving again. "Arch Moore's trademark was to move the state," the new attorney general, Charlie Brown, was quoted as saying in *The New York Times* article, "and he'll do that with effectiveness and drama. Even people who don't like him respect him for that."

The optimism was justified; Moore would get the economy back on its feet, but not without great controversy, criticism and even a lack of appreciation from the majority of the electorate at the end of his third term. His image would be so distorted, so tarnished by 1988—by political and media opponents, by his own missteps—that few would ever recognize or acknowledge the good his administration accomplished in three to four short years, during that third and final term of office. His third term would be a success in most objectively-measured ways, but almost no one, friend or foe, accepted that as fact. The four years would be perceived as a failure, not up to traditional Arch Moore standards. Arch's subsequent legal problems would solidify that perception of failure. (In discussing the subject for this book, Moore agreed that, given what he faced in 1985, and how the economy positively turned around in the next four years, *his third term may truly have been his finest effort.* Although highly controversial at times, his administration's efforts likely prevented the state from sinking more deeply into an economic depression.)

GEORGE "BUD" Seibert, who had served in the House of Delegates from 1957 until 1976, minority leader since the early Sixties, and "Mr. Republican" to many in the state, had managed most of Arch Moore's legislation during his first two terms. Through many battles, local and statewide, he and Moore had remained good friends, loyal to each other; Seibert had mentored Arch like none except Uncle Everett Moore. Normally, the chief justice of the supreme court administers the oath to the new governor. In January of 1985, Moore afforded "Bud" Seibert that honor. The distinguished Wheeling attorney would die a year later at age 72.

Moore's third inaugural address did not contain lofty promises.

Instead, he warned that there was "no quick answer or instant solution to the challenges at hand...Patience is asked as we strive to create a new West Virginia. Patience is required because the nature of our problems is indeed awesome." He quoted Lincoln, "We are not permitted to choose the frame of our destiny. But what we put into it is ours. He who wills adventure will experience it ... according to the measure of his courage."

His oft-repeated call for West Virginia pride and confidence rang once again from the capitol steps: "People who view West Virginians as 'just coal miners or hillbillies' miss the side of us that has West Virginians safely handling, processing and making things that the rest of the world needs to eat, sleep, drive and survive."

He also repeated his theme that Rockefeller had allowed the courts take over the government. But he added, "What the judiciary has been trying to do has been suggested to be right. When it said we need better education, it has been suggested it was right. When the court said we have to take care of our mentally retarded, it has been suggested it was right. The shame of it is that the court ever had to say it at all." But he promised that "the creative solutions will originate with this Governor and this government to deal with these human needs."

The new Governor also promised to "revamp our governmental structure so that it rewards investment, entrepreneurial ability and productivity rather than penalizing it." He made clear that he was talking largely about the state's No. 1 industry: "Coal is inextricably tied to our future and our future is most assuredly tied to coal." He noted that the state was blessed by an abundance of coal, oil, gas, water and forests but West Virginia's markets had been "severely diminished while all around us our sister states are enjoying a healthy and stable growth. There is a reason for this. State government in the main contributes to this dilemma more than the sum total of all our difficulties."

Arch ended his speech with his campaign slogan and in FDR's optimistic style: "There will be a new West Virginia and as time and success will be ours, be assured my fellow citizens that *West Virginians are coming back!"*

This necessarily would be a belt-tightening administration, quite unlike Arch's first term in which taxes were often raised and liberal spending had programs and projects popping up everywhere. The mess he had inherited tied his hands. Moreover, the times were different; the public had different expectations. Most significantly, with the new tone in Reagan's Washington, the generosity of the federal government to the states from the Johnson and Nixon era had all but dried up. Revenue sharing was a distant memory and ARC money was much harder to come by. (Reagan was increasing defense spending instead, which would help end the Cold War, but the President was not in the least interested in increasing domestic spending.)

In his official papers, Moore would note, "Our first general budget submitted in 1985, provided for an outlay of $1.482 million ($80 million less than the previous fiscal year budget). For the next three years my administration introduced budgets of approximately $1.462 million. We were the only state in the nation to keep its spending at the same level over a four year period of time." He added that, to keep the same level of spending as had occurred under Rockefeller, $1.562 million, the personal income surtax would have needed to be extended and, "This I refused to do as Governor. The corporate net tax and the surtax was (sic) also particularly burdensome in that these taxes were tripled by 200 percent."[3] The surtax would be allowed to expire on June 30, 1985. "Therefore, by these reductions, the new administration had $125 million less dollars available in general revenue to support its first budget than the previous administration had available to it."

And, yet, there would be additional tax cuts. Arch saw the positive results Reagan's tax cuts had created in 1982, to pull the nation out of a deep recession; President Kennedy had been able to end a national recession with tax cuts in the early 1960s, as well. Arch decided to try the same experiment for heavily-taxed West Virginia. Before long, the Governor would reduce corporate net income tax by $500 million in four years; business and occupation tax by $224 million in his last two years; repeal the state inheritance tax at a cost of $68 million over four years; and cut workers' compensation premiums by at least $90 million over three years. "In this brief four-year history of our state, $882 million in tax relief of one form or the other, was provided to its citizens," Arch would boast in his official papers.

But, unfortunately for him (and the state's vendors and tax payers), all these well-intentioned, economy-stimulating tax cuts eventually would catch up–they would cause cash flow problems, delaying payments and tax refunds. Although the extra money the tax relief put into the private sector served to get business flowing and people working again, it would not leave enough funds in the State's account to keep its books stable—there often would not be enough cash in the bank to pay the bills. So Moore would succeed in getting the state moving again, but would not receive credit for it, because of the cash flow problems. Perception is everything, as they say.

MOORE'S DOZEN or so campaign field workers, plus Ben Bailey, Tom Craig, Kathy Bullard, Audrey Toler and a few others took over the governor's office as soon as Arch was sworn in as the thirtieth governor. For a few weeks, the field coordinators served as liaisons for the various departments, most of which were being run by career administrators, because Jay's cabinet had departed. As he had done in 1969, Moore did not immediately name his cabinet, as most governors do even before taking office, which no one could ever explain. He waited until a day in February, when the snows were deep, to announce all at once in the capitol rotunda.

John "Jack" Redline, president of Weirton Steel, was the biggest "star" to be announced. He would become the new director of the Office of Community and Industrial Development.[4] First term veteran Lysander Dudley was named director of Industrial Development and successful businessman Pat Graney of Beckley would be the financial strategist. Drew Payne was brought in as financial analyst of the office.

To no one's surprise, and despite the fussing that had occurred between him and Arch in the first two terms, Bill Ritchie returned as commissioner of the Department of Highways. Nothing in the private sector had given Ritchie the adrenalin rush that building new four-lane highways had provided; he wanted more of it. Thanks to a slow-down in that effort during the Rockefeller years, there remained hundreds of miles more of new roads to be built. Dave Allen (whose family's company had helped build many of those four lane highways) and Craig Rothwell would be Ritchie's assistants.

Romney native Mike Caryl, a Yale law grad and partner of Bill Loy and Hoy Shingleton in Martinsburg, became State Tax Commissioner. Campaign field worker John Leaberry was named his deputy. A Democrat, former Beckley delegate and State School Board member, Mary Martha Merritt, became Workers' Compensation commissioner with Nelson Robinson as her assistant. Dr. Sharon Lord of Williamson became Human Services commissioner. Lord's deputy was Regina Lipscomb, a pretty, gracious African-American who had served as Moore's receptionist in the first eight years, and who, upon Moore's urging, had finished her college education in the eight year interim. (Lipscomb would succeed Lord as commissioner, later in the term.) Dr. David Heydinger of the Marshall University School of Medicine, would be state health director.

A friendly and likeable WVU professor, Fred Wright, another of Moore's fraternity brothers, was named Insurance Commissioner. Three-term Wood County Sheriff Lee Bechtold was named commissioner of

Motor Vehicles, with campaign field worker Dave Williams as his deputy. Rockefeller's deputy director of the Department of Natural Resources, Ron Potesta, was elevated to director, after Sandy Latimer declined an offer to return to that post. State Police Colonel W.F. Donohoe, Moore's security chief in the first administration, became superintendent of the Department of Public Safety.

Arch named Mike Greer, a Republican delegate from Salem, to the Public Service Commission, along with Kanawha County Delegate Charlotte Lane.

The unsuccessful GOP nominee for attorney general, former Delegate John McCuskey of Bridgeport, was Moore's choice for commissioner of Finance and Administration. Campaign field worker Kevin Sikora was moved from the governor's office to F&A and Rockefeller's deputy finance commissioner, Alan Drescher, was kept on by Moore and was joined by your author as the other deputy. Veteran Budget Director Jim Boggs would also stay.

A.V. Dodrill of Huntington, a federal probation officer who had attended WVU with Moore, was named commissioner of the Department of Corrections. Ad Thomas, who had worked in state and Fairmont governments, became commissioner of the Department of Employment Security. Charleston chemist and developer Ken Faerber was named acting commissioner of the Department of Energy, which was created at Moore's request in an early special session, to allow a one-stop shop for coal permits.[5] George Banker, who owned Pepsi Cola Bottling in Barboursville, would be liquor commissioner. Rockefeller's adjutant general, John Wilson and Norm Fagan, his Culture and History commissioner, were kept on. Bob Trocin, a Huntington businessman, was named Commerce commissioner, with Brenda Nichols-Harper, as Trocin's deputy and Mike Herron as the marketing director for the state. Fred Glazer, Moore's talented and energetic Library Commissioner, had survived the Rockefeller Administration and was retained. Jim Rardin, a campaign field worker, would go to the Labor Department.

Later in the year, Ralph Peters, who had been director of Vermont's lottery, was brought in to head up West Virginia's newly-created Lottery Commission with Fred Haddad, Sam Kusic, Charlie Wendell, Bill Abraham, Susan Dean, Charles Hughes and Jim Foster serving as members.

It was widely assumed that, as the campaign manager, Tom Craig was destined to run the show, to be the "new Bill Loy." But for reasons which were unclear, perhaps due to disputes with the new Governor,

Craig would get frustrated within weeks of beginning his duties as Moore's chief of staff. "I saw him outside the Governor's door, literally beating his head against the wall, mumbling something, and thought, 'Oh, no, we're in trouble!'" recalled Nelson Robinson. Craig would leave the governor's office to return to a Huntington, as soon as the first legislative session ended. He would be named by Moore to the Board of Regents as the thank-you for his services. As documents would later reveal, he was also given a five thousand dollar bonus for management of a winning campaign.

Tom Tinder, another veteran of the first two terms, would be brought in to replace Craig. Tinder thought the reasons for Craig's early departure were financial. "Tom had a young family, had probably been making a ton more money in the practice of law, and had been away from his Huntington firm for a year and a half by now." Tinder noted that Craig's firm had not been happy to give him a leave of absence to begin with, because "he was their fair-haired boy."

Harvard law grad Benjamin Bailey of Parkersburg, who had served as an Assistant U. S. Attorney, would serve as the Governor's assistant. Audrey Toler, who had joined Moore's campaign in 1968, had worked in the Governor's Office beginning in 1969 (at $350 a month), and had served as his campaign treasurer, became the Governor's executive secretary. Many began to view Audrey as the one closest to the throne. With Craig gone, she filled a vacuum—she was the rare employee who would risk the Governor's wrath by making a tough decision or insisting on an answer from the boss. As result, and no doubt because of her intense loyalty, she seemed to enjoy Moore's complete confidence and support. (Moore himself agreed with the characterization that Toler was his "assistant governor." He added, "She was a walking encyclopedia when it came to state government.")

Wheeling radio newsman John Price would become the Press Secretary and would be assisted by Deputy Labor Commissioner Raamie Barker of Chapmanville. The latter, along with Tim Armstead, Mary Cobb, JoAnn Humphreys and Charlotte Roberts, would also work in the press office and write speeches. Campaign field worker Dave Schles would serve as a legislative assistant. Arch's brother-in-law, Bill Sievertson, would serve as director of his northern, Moundsville, office. Mary Ann Winter would return to oversee the Mansion.

Several months into the administration, Moore would reward "Pete" Thaw, Jay's former deputy, with a lucrative appointment to the Racing Commission, much to the consternation of Republicans around the state, who thought such a plum appointment should be reserved for one of their own.[6] Some later charged that the men and women Moore chose to fill his administration were substandard and the cause of the ultimate public relations failure of the third term. There would be criticism, even among Moore's closest supporters, that the people who staffed the third term administration were not of the high caliber and stock of those who had served in the first and second terms.

At least on paper, that was not true; overall, their credentials were much better. "They were every bit as talented," agreed Arch, looking back two decades later. Using a Moore-ism, he added, "The qualitativeness of those in the third term was equal to those who served in the first eight years." He missed Elaine Davidson (who'd remarried and moved to Elkins), he admitted, but Audrey Toler "knew what I wanted in running the governor's office. And they don't get any better than Tom Tinder." But he noted that about sixty percent of the third term administrators had not been veterans of the first two terms and were "younger people. I didn't know them personally," in part because "not that many of them identified with me in my years at WVU."

The age gap between Arch and several of his third term appointees meant that, in many cases, he was old enough to be their father. So they were less likely to confront him, to disagree, to tell him when they thought he was wrong, especially since he was still a living legend at that point. With his great ego, and an inability to know all things at all time (sometimes governors cannot see the forest for the trees) Arch, like all leaders, occasionally needed confrontation from his people. But only Bill Ritchie was able to do that in the third term; he was a veteran and a contemporary of Moore's. The rest of his administration rarely felt comfortable getting in the Governor's face about anything. Another problem was the fact that almost none of Moore's young administration had been personally involved in elective politics and were not up to speed on how to keep the feathers smoothed of political operatives around the state, upon whom Moore was dependent for a fourth term.[7] And times had changed–people were more cynical about what government could do, often didn't trust those in power (Clyde See's campaign attacks didn't help the atmosphere), and there were far less federal funds available to keep communities happy than in Moore's first go-round. Importantly, many in the news media who would cover him had been in high school when he was governor the first time; they had little respect for his accomplishments and reputation as a great leader. Arch Moore was not legendary to them.

Noted Richard Neely, "Arch always tried to appoint good people. He didn't have the glitz of Rockefeller, who was able to attract people from outside the state who knew what they were doing, or to draw people like Dr. George Pickett or Leon Ginsberg (away from his tenured WVU professorship) in-state.[8] Arch Moore attracted good people based sheerly on the force of his personality."

But it wasn't just the people he'd chosen to staff his administration that was different. Those who were close to him in the first two terms said they noticed a change in the 62-year-old Arch Moore's demeanor and attitude. "I noticed a difference in him," offered Judge Ron Pearson, who in the first eight years had enjoyed Moore's confidence in implimenting daring and innovative plans. "Occasionally, I would call him about some great idea, an opportunity to hire someone good or a project that I thought deserved attention, and he just didn't seem interested." Moore's friend and public relations consultant Charles Ryan later said he thought Arch's heart simply was not in it during that third term, because of his preference to be in the U.S. Senate. As Larry Swann noted, the loss in 1978 seemed to have "taken the wind out of his sails" and that his former high work ethic even lagged. Larry alleged that, during most of the third term, Arch would work four-day weeks, not the six and seven of his first two terms. "He would often leave on Thursday evening and go to Florida or somewhere, and fly back Monday morning."

Tinder, who probably spent more time with Arch Moore than anyone except First Lady Shelley Moore from 1985 through 1988, agreed that the tone was different in the third term and part of it was organizational. "My sense was that it was not the same as in the first two terms. With Bill Loy and then Tom Craig [who served after Loy left in the second term] there had definitely been a chief of staff. But, in the third term, the Governor wasn't going to have a single chief of staff." Each of the triumvirate—Tinder, Bailey and Bullard—had their own tasks, he explained, and "often ours were fluid and different. Often it was whomever's office the Governor went into first. Our jobs were task-specific, assignment-specific. Everything flowed through him. Either Governor Moore was not as close to us, or didn't have as much confidence in us, but he never chose one to be his chief of staff."

As a result, sometimes things were confused, if not chaotic. "We never had a staff meeting where you'd sit around a table and discuss things. You'd just get time on his schedule. The left hand didn't know what the right hand was doing, as result. Kathy, Ben and I didn't know what was going on half the time. But that's the way he operated." Such a management style "has to cause problems and puts more burden on staff people." Tinder added that Moore would work with some department heads one-on-one, such as Caryl or McCuskey, for example, but others in smaller departments, such as the Insurance commissioner, "would work through me, Ben or Kathy."

Noted Nichols-Harper (who also had worked through the Rockefeller years and was underwhelmed by Jay's management style) the way the office is set up, the strength of the chief of staff, can make a world of difference. "Working in the governor's office is constant crisis management," she observed. "It's a constant prioritization of the constant crises. It's very frustrating–you can't get everything done to make everyone happy. You have to balance priorities which have the greatest impact on the health, safety and well-being of the highest number of West Virginians."

Despite the fact that Moore acted as his own chief of staff, Tinder heaped praise upon his former boss. "The Governor always worked hard, relative to putting in the hours. He always gave you the attention you needed–there was never a situation that he didn't give you enough time. He was good about keeping things in proper perspective and he was hands-on in crisis situations." Criticism that Moore micro-managed continued, but those critics did not understand that he was fully capable of doing that. It did not deter from his consideration of the "big picture." And, as Tinder noted, he made time for people who needed to see him and read memos from those who didn't make it onto his schedule. "I was available from 4:30 to 6:30 for the President of the Senate or the Speaker," Moore noted, "and my department heads from 6:30 to 7:30."

Often he'd do two or three other chores while talking to them about legislation or problems. Moore could "multi-task" before that was even a catch phrase, Tinder added. "At the end of the day, he would have six to ten blue felt-tip pens lined up on his desk, signing document after document while carrying on a conversation with you, answering your questions. Every once in a while, he'd hold up one of those pens to see if its point was getting too dull—if so, he'd set it aside and grab another," Tinder smiled, remembering the evening routine.

Part of Moore's decision to go without one strong chief of staff may have been related to his obsession about secrecy. He liked the ability to suddenly spring upon—the legislators, the bureaucracy, the business community, the news media—something new, a blitzkrieg of ideas and proposals. Having another with whom to share those bold proposals risked leaks. He almost obsessively played his cards very close to his chest.

Brenda Nichols-Harper helped Tom Craig, Mike Caryl and others with the effort in those first few weeks, pushing through the legislature the

Governor's reorganization plan. (Each new governor seems to think he must reorganize departments, some for purely political reasons, but Moore wanted more efficiency—he wasn't trying to get rid of anyone.) "Among other things, he was trying to create a new Department of Commerce, set up the Lottery, create a new Department of Energy and a Division of Forestry." Nichols-Harper, whom the legislators would call "the Governor's mole," thought "we had a very successful session. All these things got passed. In those days, the legislature would hold a conference meeting anywhere–in the hallway, in the men's room."

THE BOLDNESS of one of his first acts as governor shocked conservatives and business leaders, for it was what one would expect from a liberal Democrat. Moore created two authorities, one to get the State into "the business of gathering and transmission of West Virginia natural gas" and the second which "would allow the state to construct electric power generating facilities which would burn West Virginia coal." The legislation allowing the authorities resulted from Arch's view that industry and investors were not doing enough to get the state's natural resources to national and international markets. It was a bold move, one that seemed quite contrary to his usual deference to the private sector. But his goal was clear: to "provide employment for some 3,500 miners." It allowed for bonds to be issued, to be repaid from revenues received. The plan, which some believed was nothing less than socialism, never came to full fruition, in part because Moore did not have eight years to see it through. Some lesser projects, such as the one in Grant Town, Marion County, which extracted burnable coal from a slag pile, did have some success, however.[9]

"All of you have heard football coaches explain, 'This is a rebuilding year,'" Arch would tell a bankers' association meeting at the Greenbrier in July. "The message they are conveying to the press and the alumni is, 'Hey, you guys, take it easy on us; we don't have the depth this year to win 'em all!' This is a rebuilding year in state government, too, but I'm here to tell you that I'm not asking the media or anyone else to go easy on my Administration while we are in the rebuilding process."[10]

Nichols-Harper recalled that one of the reorganizations of government which received less attention was nonetheless important: making state parks more user-friendly and to draw in more tourist dollars. "The state only had $800,000 with which to market itself then," she noted. "Now the budget is three or four million.

"The Governor had great loyalty to the state park system; his family still vacations at Pipestem," Brenda noted. But her task in getting the bureaucracy to move, to change its way of thinking, was not always easy. "Those park superintendents had never had a female boss," she noted. With the Governor's approval, she began bringing a woman's touch to the state park's ability to please its customers. A large part of what she did was try to change the attitude of the state park workers–from seeing themselves as a police force, guardians of the forest, to a new role. She wanted them to realize they were hosts to tourists, public servants who should give directions and make the visit more pleasant, so they'd want to return to West Virginia in the future. She wanted their facilities to be user-friendly, and the park system itself run more like a tourist business.

Brenda got the park workers into more attractive, durable, quality uniforms, like national park rangers wore ("The polyester uniforms they'd been wearing would 'pick' when they brushed up against something"). Micromanaging some more, Governor Moore also thought the parks should provide lodges and cabins with hotel-quality towels and mattresses, not the institutional, prison-issue, thin, uncomfortable ones. So Brenda took the Purchasing Division agents on an educational shopping trip to Huntington to lie on better mattresses. And she had the parks put amenities—shampoo, toothpaste, mints, etc.—beside guests' beds, just like one would get at a decent motel. Governor Moore quietly insisted that those packets be prepared by the mentally-challenged in workshops set up for similar projects. "It was a side of him a lot of people didn't see," noted Nichols-Harper. "He looked for embracing meaning in people's lives, no matter their station, disability or what their access to opportunities were."

THE IMPRESSION that the past eight years had been bad for the state extended even to the Governor's Mansion, Shelley Moore's domain. "The Rockefellers had left that place in a mess," she said. Sharon and Jay had brought their own personal furnishings into the Mansion and sent all the state-owned furniture down to Surplus Property in Dunbar, to be auctioned to the public. When they went to Washington, they took their furniture with them.

Mansion Director Mary Ann Winter, an interior designer, had a major task ahead to get the governor's residence back into living condition. "Thank goodness, the director of Surplus Property [George Afflerbach] had held onto the [Mansion] furniture and we salvaged what we could, reupholstering what was salvageable after being stored so long in a warehouse." The Rockefellers had "cut maintenance," Mrs. Winter explained, and "it took us a year to put everything in order. It was a mess." Wallpaper was peeling off the walls, hardwood floors were soaked from plugged-up radiator heaters; there were not enough beds; they'd left "the kind of sheets you can read through"; ginger lamps of all colors; and "they'd even taken the light bulbs out." Said Winter, "It was a nightmare."

Water from the heating system had burst in the master bedroom upstairs in the family quarters, shooting a rainbow colored spray into the Governor's bed and soaking through the floor, down through the ceiling into the state dining room. "They had a washtub in the middle of the dining room table to catch the water dripping off the chandelier," Winter recalled. "Needless to say, I could not believe it!" Governor Moore told her, "You know, I like to take a shower in the morning, but I'd like to get out of bed first!"

Said Mrs. Moore, "I decided this shouldn't happen again to future governors' families. I got Mrs. Hulett Smith and Mary Ann Winter involved. We started the West Virginia Mansion Preservation Foundation." The Foundation, established by Charles Ryan and Tom Potter, raised private donations to help refurbish the tattered residence, which hosts dozens of public functions throughout the year and is open for weekly tours. "I'd set it up so there would be staggering terms for its chair, and not a Republican-Democrat thing."[11] The Foundation was patterned after the private fund Nancy Reagan had established to refurbish the White House, after critics had complained she was spending too many tax dollars on the presidential residence.

The Foundation would sponsor fundraisers, including a concert at the Cultural Center by Lou Rawls. Once private funding allowed remodeling, Winter admitted she was "in hog heaven." Carlton Varney, who had redone the Carter White House, Ethel Merman's house and others, volunteered to help her redecorate the Mansion. "We put in new carpets, designed especially for the Mansion by Lacy Champion of Atlanta," said Mrs. Winter. "In the ballroom carpet, the capitol dome was represented. On its corners were the rhododendron, the black bear, the cardinal, and the state tree; there were floors redone in hardwoods from around the state. CSX donated furniture—it was like Christmas when they brought it in!"

ARCH DISCOVERED that, in the eight year interim, Rockefeller had ceded much of the control of the budgetary process back to the legislature. "When I came back in, I found that [the legislature] had this Budget Digest. I asked Jim Boggs [the veteran state budget director], 'What do we have here? Essentially, it's a second budget. Did they change the constitution?' Boggs told me, 'They put this off to the side, they pass the budget and then they earmark it [for pork barrel projects in their respective districts].' I told him, 'Well, this Budget Digest is going into my bottom drawer. I told F&A that not one check was going to be drawn on the Budget Digest. And there wasn't a Budget Digest in that four years, but it came back under Caperton." (The move would not endear him to the legislative leadership.)

Moore realized there was another important change since he left office in 1977. "Hans McCourt, Lew McManus, Bill Brotherton, Ivor Boiarsky—they were statesmen," Arch remembered. "McManus was my friend. When "Bud" Seibert got on his feet [in the House], you could hear a pin drop. But in the eight years I was out of office, the legislature had changed. We didn't have giants running the legislature anymore." It was a very serious problem, dangerous to his agenda, as he would discover in the remaining years of his term.

Some "fixes" did not require legislative action, fortunately. The Moores were able in 1985 to rescue an increasingly popular program being generated from Charleston on public radio, *Mountain Stage*. National Public Radio had ordered twenty-six of their programs, which presented an eclectic array of folk, blues, country, alternative, cajun and popular musical acts. The program was gaining national popularity and putting West Virginia on the map. But their funds had been cut by $20,000, making it impossible to keep the show alive. In the book *20 Years of Mountain Stage*,[12] the author explains how Governor and Mrs. Moore saved the show:

> *But when things looked bleakest, Mountain Stage got a boost from a surprising source. Republican Governor Arch A. Moore, Jr. entered the fray, restoring Culture and History's money and adding $20,000 from the Governor's Contingency Fund. Moore, however, said the credit actually belonged to his wife, First Lady Shelley Moore, who lobbied her husband persuasively on the show's behalf. "With the press banging on one side and my wife banging on the other," Moore joked in a 1986 story in The Charleston Daily Mail, "I figured I better fund it." Mountain Stage staff responded by sending the First Lady roses and [Andy] Ridenour quipped that Moore's pledge might create "a few new Republicans."*

As the Moores reintegrated themselves into Charleston, they

resumed attendance at the Christ Church United Methodist. "We were staying with them in the Mansion one weekend and they asked us to attend church with them," recalled Dr. David Yoho, who had not attended for many years. "The next week the church burned down!"

THE ECONOMIC recovery the rest of the nation was experiencing (but that had largely bypassed the Mountain State) was credited by many to the fact that Reagan had obtained massive tax cuts at the federal level, spurring job growth, investment and consumer spending. "Getting West Virginians to work again was the No. 1 priority when we took office," Arch told an audience later in 1985. As previously noted, Arch Moore thought West Virginia needed jump-started with the same medicine Reagan had given the nation. He began seeking massive tax cuts. The Democratic legislature did not oppose the cuts; they went along with most of them. As it would turn out, they would give him enough rope to hang himself.

One of those cuts was to the inheritance tax. Moore thought that by eliminating that tax, more West Virginia retirees would stay home and spend their money here, rather than to flee to Florida or other tax-friendly states.

But most of all, Moore knew that as long as the Western and neighboring states were selling coal more cheaply than West Virginia mines, there would be continued stagnation. Like it or not, coal was and is the majority of the state's entire economy—it is what pays for its government, paves the roads, funds its public schools and colleges, and fuels much of the retail and service industry. He knew that he absolutely had to get West Virginia coal sales back on track, or there would be continued disaster—it was as simple as that. Wrote Professor Rice, "Moore immediately initiated a program of recovery, which centered around the revitalization of the coal industry and the attraction of new industries to the state. To improve the competitive position of West Virginia coal in national and world markets, he took steps designed to cut its production costs by two dollars on the ton."[13] Moore began to look for creative ways to get other industry back on track, looking for ways government could help the private sector survive and succeed. Looking at how other states treated their job-creators made him realize that the Mountain State had a lot of catching up to do. It would not be easy.

But he also believed that business tax cuts and incentives were crucial if the state had any hope of recruiting new industry and growing companies already in the state. Other states gave tax incentives to business and industry, causing West Virginia to fail time and again to land new manufacturing plants. Wrote Rice:

> In pursuit of the goal of drawing new industries to West Virginia, Moore and the legislature made a special effort to lure a multibillion-dollar Saturn automobile plant that General Motors was planning to build. Well aware that competition for the plant, with its thousands of jobs and other economic benefits, would be extremely keen, the governor and the legislature turned to the idea of a substantial tax incentive to General Motors if the company located the plant in West Virginia. Such incentives were time-honored methods of attracting business and industry and had been used extensively by federal, state and local governments. In 1985, the legislature passed for that specific purpose the Business Investment and Jobs Expansion Act, which Governor Moore promptly signed into law. The act, nevertheless, failed to win for West Virginia the much-desired Saturn plant. The decision to locate the Saturn facility in Tennessee galvanized the West Virginia government into making even greater efforts to expand business investments and job opportunities in the state.[14]

"In 1985, Governor Moore said we needed a spectacular investment incentive in the tax structure to lure in new jobs," remembered Mike Caryl. "We [the Tax Department] drafted a bill and the legislature passed it, commonly called the Super Tax Credit.

"It was an extremely liberal tax incentive that gave a company a fifty percent deduction if it made a capital investment that created at least fifty jobs, and more, if 280 jobs or greater. It was easy to create, but hard to target for the purposes it was intended and to avoid abuses. It only applied to new taxes, not existing ones. It was complicated, but was meant for new companies, not existing ones. It did work–Kentucky hated it because it made West Virginia more competitive."

Years into the incentive, there was a growing perception, Caryl conceded, that the Super Tax Credit, or investment credit, was abused, especially by coal companies already doing business in the state. Rice agreed: "The chief beneficiaries of the super tax credits proved to be coal corporations, which garnered about ninety percent of the total. Unfortunately, the credits to coal companies yielded no immediate benefits to the state."[15]

But overall, Caryl thought the program was a good one—a well-intentioned effort, and would have been salvageable "if they would just audit them to see if they were playing games."[16]

Another huge tax change occurred in the first year of Moore's third term and the results of this one would ultimately help drive him from office. In 1982, a legislative commission on which David Hardesty, Ned Rose and others served, had begun a study to see whether the highly unpopular business and occupation tax which was based on gross, rather than net, income of a business or industry, could be eliminated. A guru from Carnegie Mellon University, Robert Strauss, "was the intellectual driving force" for the Democratic legislature, Caryl said. "He was pushing a franchise tax, like his Pennsylvania had, and wanted to eliminate the B&O."

"They wanted to go with 'ability to pay' rather than paying tax on gross receipts," Caryl noted, which is good for business, but from the State's point of view is less stable. The legislature had begun phasing it out even before he took office and then passed a bill to eliminated the B&O tax, half way through Moore's first session. The plan was to replace it by increasing the corporate income tax from about 6 to 7% to 9.75% and to impose for the first time a 0.75% business franchise tax. Trouble was, no one knew what those changes would produce in income. Moore did not want to repeal the tax, as unpopular as it was, but knew not to oppose it too vocally. He had other tax reforms in mind that he thought would better stimulate the economy, including the Super Tax.

The Governor kept vetoing the bill—three times—based on technical flaws, after it was reviewed by the attorney general's office and his own tax lawyers. Plus, he insisted that the actual changes be deferred for two years so revenue impact could be seen before it went into effect. Finally, Speaker Joseph Albright, House Finance Chairman George Farley and six other leading Democratic legislative leaders called Caryl and Tom Craig into the Speaker's office. "What is your problem with this?" Farley demanded. When Craig started reading a list of constitutional and other objections, Albright "became so frustrated and angry that he got up and left the room, his own office," Caryl recalled.

"We finally got into the time frame, toward the end of the session, in which Arch Moore could veto [the B&O tax abolition] and the legislature couldn't override it," smiled Caryl. "So that's when Arch got the quid pro quo–he would sign it, but there would be a concession of a two year trial period before the repeal became law." So the Tax Department would get time to build data over a 24 month period, to see what the impact of the repeal of the unpopular tax would be, whether the state could actually afford to lose it. The Tax Department began collecting "informational returns" to see what the deficit would be from the tax repeal, if any.

Great controversy stirred when the Moore Administration would not divulge the details of tax settlements struck with large companies, most prominently CSX in Huntington. This was done to prevent long litigation with questionable outcome, to keep the companies and the jobs they offered up and running in the state, and the terms of such agreement had always been confidential, by law. But the *Gazette* screamed loud and long that the "secret deals" should be disclosed, hinting that something improper was going on.

The battle over the tax issues would arise and continue again in the coming years.

DURING THE 1984 campaign, there was nothing Candidate Moore heard from business people more than their complaint about the high cost of workers' compensation. The expenses of that program exceeded by two to four times that which they paid in bordering states, many told him. Horror stories abounded of claimants getting life awards, or being on temporary benefits for years with little wrong with them. Rather than come to West Virginia and pay such high comp costs, most companies were locating in Virginia, the Carolinas—even locating in a third world nation made more economic sense when the potential of union violence in the Mountain State was also factored in. Arch was determined to do something about the problem. It was a must, if the economy was to recover.

No one yet knew that a crisis was looming ahead, including Moore, the legislature, the workers' compensation bureaucracy and certainly not the actuaries who tried to get a grasp on the constantly moving monster called Comp. Audits, from the 1980s until 2005, were all over the board–showing no deficit at all, to as much as a $6.7 *billion* deficit under Wise administration. It had settled to "much less" than a one billion dollar deficit by September of 2005. A June 30, 1984, audit conducted by the outgoing Rockefeller Administration had shown a $179 million deficit in the regular Fund, but there was more than a $200 million surplus left in the Coal Workers' Pneumoconiosis Fund.[17]

West Virginia was one of four remaining states in which the government ran the program; all others had gone to private insurance which was more conservative with employers' money. The state's system had been overly politicized for many decades. It was the "bone" thrown to labor unions and the plaintiffs' attorneys in exchange for their financial and other election support. The old adage, "Those who rob Peter to pay Paul, will always enjoy the support of Paul," was the unspoken motto with regard to workers' compensation. Claimants were dealt with more generously than perhaps in any state in the nation, beginning in the 1960s, and they began viewing the program as an entitlement like social security, a retirement supplement, especially in counties to the south of Kanawha, where the anti-company culture was particularly strong.[18]

Often these claimants would have little impairment, certainly not enough to prevent them from working. Some were even young individuals, in their thirties and forties, but saw it as their right to retire early and "go on comp." Logan lawyer Amos Wilson had begun a huge, lucrative industry by showing others how incredibly easy it was to get rich from West Virginia's comp system. He and a few other lawyers around the state, plus physicians and other experts willing to sell their opinions or treat thousands of comp claimants, were each making several millions of dollars a year from the system. Unscrupulous physicians, chiropractors, vocational consultants and others, got in on the multi-million dollar comp machine and many became very, very wealthy from it. "Getting on comp" became ingrained into the state's culture more than perhaps any other state.[19]

On the other side, companies would refuse to pay their compensation premiums or go out of business owing hundreds of thousands in uncollected comp premiums, and almost nothing could be done to recover the debt. Large employers could afford good lawyers to make back room deals with the commissioner of the Fund, to get their premiums or delinquent fees reduced or erased. A perfectly legal system encouraged employers' and claimants' attorneys to collude in dumping liability for permanent total awards into a Second Injury Fund, one of the chief sources of the multi-billion dollar comp deficit. And there was virtually no scrutiny, no oversight by the news media, and certainly by no governor, until the Fund began running out of money in the late 1990s. It was an ongoing scandal, through numerous gubernatorial administrations, with legislators also lobbying to get their constituents on compensation.

Moore knew that battling the comp "industry" in 1985 was unwinnable and it was a battle he certainly had no time to wage, given the other disasters, such as the unemployment debt he had inherited, that he had to deal with at the moment. At that point in the state's history, it would have been instant political suicide for anyone to have advocated tightening compensation benefits; any hint of cutting costs created screams from unions and claimants' lawyers that were widely trumpeted by the *Gazette* and other liberal media. Moreover, it simply wasn't Arch's style to decrease claimants' benefits any more than it had been his Democratic predecessors.

So, without making any adjustments on the claimants' side of the ledger, Moore simply decided to offer employers a twenty to thirty percent cut in their workers' compensation premiums, beginning July 1, 1985, which would cut employers' costs by $180 million during the following three years. He also cut in half the premiums required for the Coal Workers' Pneumoconiosis Fund, because it was taking in more than needed. "Commissioner Mary Martha Merritt believed that, although there was a deficit, the [twenty percent] cut in premiums could be offset for a few years by the CWP surplus," observed Nelson Robinson, who would become Moore's third commissioner during his third term. "Audits showed that it was balanced between the two funds by mid-1986, but then started going into overall deficit."[20]

Moore believed the compensation premium cut helped him recruit new business and industry. "I would never have been able to get Bruce Hardwood to open a plant here without that cut," he said years later. Just as Kennedy, Reagan and George W. Bush had used tax cuts to stimulate the economy, Moore was using workers' comp cuts to try to shock-treat, jolt back to life West Virginia's industry, which was dead in the water. Actually, no one knows what would have happened had he not cut premiums; the Rockefeller recession may have worsened. It is hard to quantify the entire effect of the cuts.

But the news media, lead by the *Gazette,* for decades would blame Moore's three-year cut of premiums (Caperton restored them and increased premiums by fifty percent soon after taking office) for the eventual huge workers' compensation deficit, refusing to acknowledge any other cause. The unions and claimants' attorneys, opposed to reform, also joined in the cry, "It was Moore's fault!" Any sensible person capable of basic arithmetic could readily see that Moore's cut denied the fund tens of millions, certainly nowhere near a multi-billion-dollar deficit. But the myth—that Arch caused the workers' compensation deficit—took root and even otherwise sensible business papers such as *The State Journal,* union and trade magazines would repeat it for nearly twenty years. For a decade or so, it was easier to blame it on Arch Moore than to concede that benefits to claimants were far to generous, that doctors, lawyers and others were getting rich from the system, and that drastic reforms were necessary. Claimants' attorneys and their allies killed the goose that laid the golden egg, when it came to West Virginia workers' compensation litigation.

"Our workers' comp administrative expenses were $15 million when we left office," Robinson added. "They quadrupled since. There was no question in my mind that [Moore's premium cut] did not cause the deficit. That became apparent as early as 1992–how did it grow $900 million in four years? From liberalized benefits [under Caperton], that's how." Governor Moore agreed: "Caperton greatly liberalized claimants' benefits as a pay-back for labor's support in 1988. That accounts for most of the current workers' compensation deficit. You can readily see that by reviewing the statistics."

Robinson noted that Caperton's first commissioner, Harvard educated Emily Speiler, even fired about a dozen fraud investigators Moore had hired to help stop claimants from abusing the system. "And she moved the compliance division to a warehouse, eliminating many of the collections people." It would not be until 2003 and 2005 sessions that true workers' compensation reform was passed by the legislature.

BILL LOY died in April, collapsing during a jog on a Florida beach. A few partisans complained when the Governor ordered state flags to be flown at half-staff, but he paid them no heed; the gesture was a measure of the regard he had for his old friend and an unspoken acknowledgment that he would not be sitting in that governor's chair without Loy's efforts over the years.[21]

Many would view Loy's death as a turning point in the career and life of Arch Moore. "When Loy was around in the first two terms, we in the legislature could call him and, by god, it was done!" noted Oce Smith, echoing what scores of others said. "Without Loy, Arch didn't seem to know how to handle [the legislature]. He was not the same Arch Moore."

Whether or not Loy's influence was overemphasized, there was no question that Moore appreciated and loved his faithful, former chief of staff. Arch gave the eulogy at the funeral and joked about Loy's only fault: "He lived on the telephone." As a final farewell and thank you, and continuing the humor the two men shared, he slipped a phone into Bill's casket, along with a Moore for Governor campaign button. "He was an extraordinary person," Arch reiterated. "He was deeply embedded in his Methodist Church. He would not hurt a soul. He tried to frame an answer so that it would hurt the fewest people." It would not be the same without Loy.

FEW THINGS pleased Governor Moore more than road and bridge building. He announced a much-delayed (for twenty years, city fathers couldn't agree on where to locate it) East Huntington Bridge on August 8, 1985. It was the first of its kind in the state, with an asymmetrical cable-stayed girder design, which Sgt. Moore had admired in Germany forty years earlier. It would be a half-mile long, with distinctive, 370-foot tall A-shaped towers.

On October 14, 1985, the Kanawha Airport had a name change. It was renamed in honor of Brig. General Charles "Chuck" Yeager, from Lincoln County, the first pilot to break the sound barrier and a legendary pre-space era pioneer. Governor Moore was joined by Senators Byrd and Randolph in the dedication ceremony. Thereafter, Yeager took the Governor on a quick flight in a jet he was trying to sell the state. The crowd was amazed to see the plane shoot almost straight into the air, like a rocket–Chuck was trying to impress Arch with its power and speed. (The state ended up purchasing another aircraft, however; Yeager never got the sales commission.)

Nineteen eighty five had been another exciting year with Arch Moore in the governor's office. But an unexpected event would occur late in the year that would provide a set-back to his efforts to "get the state out of the ditch." It was one that he neither could have anticipated or prepared for. Another "act of God" would strike the Mountain State in November that would stretch its resources and its people, again bringing great tragedy and grief.

Chapter 24 Notes

1. - *West Virginia, A History*, Otis K. Rice and Stephen W. Brown, Second Edition, Copyright 1995, by the University Press of Kentucky.

2. - *The New York Times*, Jan. 15, 1986.

3. - *Third Term, The Official Papers of the Honorable Arch A. Moore, Jr., 30th Governor of West Virginia*, Copyright 2002 by the State of West Virginia.

4. - After the news media complained about his use of the state's aircraft for trips to and from his residence, Redline was indicted by a local Democratic prosecutor and subsequently resigned. He'd obviously been accustomed to such perks as a corporate leader and perhaps had the green light from the Governor to use the planes as part of his agreement to accept the position.

5. - The Democratic legislature would withhold confirmation of Faerber's nomination to be director because–gasp!–he had ties to the coal industry. Environmentalists and unions, who'd become accustomed to department heads bowing to their demands during the Rockefeller years, constantly attacked Faerber for alleged lax enforcement of safety and environmental laws. The *Gazette* would hound Faerber during his entire stint, and a Democratic Kanawha County prosecutor would actually bring criminal charges against him because his children had donated to Moore's campaign. (It was not an unusual practice; Democrat plaintiff lawyers, among others, continually require their staffs to "voluntarily" donate the maximum campaign contributions to sympathetic judges and other candidates, and then assure they are reimbursed at pay raise time, a fact which has always seemed to escape the attention of law enforcement.) Faerber, who would die of cancer in the late 1990s after a long battle,

would be acquitted but political and environmentalist enemies did their best to destroy him until Moore was voted out of office. His and others' investment in a questionable savings and loan, Evergreen, would also receive considerable scrutiny. Faerber would continue finding success in entreprenual endeavors after his four years with Moore ended, even during his long battle with cancer, including the development of one of Charleston's premier and most exclusive neighborhoods, high upon the hills across the river from the capitol.

6. - When asked how he received such a well-paying job from Moore, Thaw smiled knowingly, "I helped him in the 1984 campaign with Democrats." Oce Smith, who also had been a Democratic adversary of Moore's for decades, and had done nothing except try to defeat him, election after election, was surprised at Moore's largess, his forgiving spirit when Oce was down and out. Smith had lost his Fairmont real estate office had only his two-months-per-year work in the House of Delegates, his wife was out of work, and they had a child to support. Right after Arch was acquitted in 1976, Oce asked him for a state job and "he took care of me; I had a job that required inspecting seed houses, for two years." Smith added, "That was the Arch Moore that not many people knew. If he could help, he usually was there." However, the fact that Arch would appoint Democrats who had opposed him in the past, ignoring Republicans job-seekers who had toiled in the vineyards for him election after election, was a source of irritation to those GOP loyalists and may have hurt him in the 1988 Republican Primary.

7. - It was similar to LBJ's complaint about Kennedy's Ivy League crowd: "None of 'em ever ran for sheriff!"

8. - Neely, with characteristic humor, said many people wanted to work for Jay because they "saw Rockefeller as an overgrown tit. If they could get their lips around it, it would give milk indefinitely."

9. - "That project made Joe Manchin a millionaire," Moore claimed. Manchin was brokering coal at the time, and was a partner in the Grant Town project.

10. - *Third Term,* Ibid.

11. - Ned Chilton's widow and Charleston Newspapers owner Betty Chilton would later chair the Foundation for many years.

12. - Copyright 2003 by Friends of West Virginia Public Radio, Inc., p. 22.

13. - Rice, Ibid.

14. - Rice, Ibid.

15. - Rice, Ibid.

16. - Moore's successor, Gaston Caperton, did away with the Super Credit for coal and all natural resources. Wrote Rice: "A study of the super tax credits in 1990 revealed that the number of jobs in coal mining had fallen by 1,300 in spite of an increase of 13.3 percent in coal production." Deputy Tax Commissioner Alan Mierke, Rice noted, had estimated that the tax write offs had amounted to $48 million annually. Several other important coal producing states, including Kentucky, which had no super tax allowance, had actually increased their level of coal production and retained more of their mining jobs than West Virginia with its much-touted tax incentive, Rice wrote.

17. - "The Workers' Compensation Fund in 1989 [when he left office] was solid, with a substantial surplus and without any unfunded liability," Moore insisted in his official papers. "From this point forward, my successor [Gaston Caperton] changed the Fund's direction. New leadership at the Workers' Compensation Fund took over, and a new philosophy was adopted. The Fund went on a financial spending spree, with no concern for the Fund's solvency. The Workers' Compensation Fund, including the $252,478,075 in combined surpluses from the two Funds, went deeply into debt and the unfunded liability skyrocketed." Having worked at the Fund from 1987 to 1988, and defending employers in workers' comp litigation since that date as a lawyer, your author can readily attest that what Arch Moore wrote in that regard is absolute truth. Moore included a bar chart on page 845 of Volume Two of *Third Term,* which graphically illustrates the damage done to workers' compensation by the Caperton Administration, as result of opening the floodgates of awards to their claimants' attorneys and labor union allies through the 1990s, bankrupting the Fund.

18. - Although Moore's successor, Gaston Caperton, would be the first to impose workers' compensation reforms, in 1995, most of the people (except Andy Richardson) he chose to run the Workers' Compensation Commission and the Office of Judges were pulled directly from the claimants' Bar or were union choices. Those appointees changed the rules as to how awards were made, liberalizing the

system even more. One Caperton-Wise appointee, with a rule change, tripled the value of permanent awards overnight. He urged administrative law judges to grant more permanent total awards, although the state was already granting tens times as many as the national average. Their actions contributed heavily to the deficit, although the news media, including the business press, never picked up on that cause. Governor Wise would follow with even more left-wing appointees who continued to unjustly give away employers' money, causing scores of companies to flee the state and those remaining to lose jobs, benefits and profits for their workers. It is doubtful that Wise, Caperton or their supporters ever understood the damage they caused, the increase to the deficit that occurred, as result of the action of their top comp appointees. The collapse of the workers' compensation fund was so severe that, within days of taking office in 2005, Governor Joe Manchin had the legislature to partially privatize a system which had always been a government function.

19. - One somewhat sacrilegious joke that circulated had Jesus going about healing one after another sick and impaired West Virginians. But when he got to one fellow he yelled out, "Don't touch me Jesus, I'm on comp!"

20. - Audits revealed that the workers' comp deficit would grow to $222 million in 1986, $316 million in 1988 (Moore's last year in office), $355 million by 1990, $1.2 billion by 1992, and $1.85 billion by 1995, and $3 to $6.7 billion by the late 1990s, even though Caperton doubled comp premiums charged to employers and all administrations began aggressively pursuing delinquent or non-paying employers. It became very clear during the Caperton years that it was excessively high and generous claimants' benefits that were increasing the deficit, more than any other factor.

21. - Moore was shaken by Bill's death, more than most. After all, he was several years the Governors' junior. But he had taken a lot of stress in his years of service, too much for one man, most agreed. The day after the news of Loy's death, in a fatherly manner, Moore cautioned a group of his young assistants who were gathered in his office, about the necessity of taking care of their health and watching what they eat.

Chapter Twenty Five
Another Disastrous Flood

In mid-October 1985, what remained of Tropical Storm Isabel softly struck the coast of Georgia and then spun back into the Atlantic. Half of what was left of that weather formation joined a large mass of unstable air near the Gulf of Mexico. By October 26, it had created a nastier storm, dubbed Hurricane Juan. Juan lashed his 85-miles-per-hour winds across the South, from Texas to Florida, causing $1.5 billion in damage and the death of twelve people. But the storm refused to die as it blew northward. Juan left enough moisture in the West Virginia atmosphere that, when joined by another weather system, caused four to nearly eleven inches of rain to fall in the northern, eastern and central counties within five days.

Creek and river levels in the eastern, mountainous region had been rather low, almost dry, as is common in the autumn. But with the constant, heavy downpour of rain, the waters of the North Fork, Greenbrier, Cheat, Tygart, Little Kanawha, Shenandoah, South Branch of the Potomac, and other rivers, became stronger and more rapid. Levels were rising quickly and dangerously.

By Monday night, November 4, many West Virginia counties were suffering the worst, most devastating flood in recorded history. The muddy, brown-gray waters escaped their banks with a furious, awesome force that most had never witnessed before or since.

Tremendous damage resulted in a huge portion of the state, from Parkersburg to Morgantown, into the Eastern Panhandle, even down into Marlinton. The mountainous eastern counties, where life was already difficult and average incomes much lower than the national average, took the brunt of it. Preston, Tucker, Pendleton, Hardy and Grant Counties were hardest hit, the "elbow" of the state map.

In all, the flood waters would cause the death of thirty-eight West Virginians, cause ten to be missing and presumed dead, 2,587 to be homeless, and cause a $500 million property loss. One hundred thirty one private businesses were destroyed, twenty-three condemned, with another 800 or so suffering major to minor damage. Many would never reopen. For residential homes, it was 4,389 lost, 762 condemned and almost 5000 with major to minor damage.[1] "This situation has affected more people in the state than any single circumstance of the past," Governor Moore noted at the time. It was the worst natural disaster to ever strike the state since it was settled. It was to West Virginia what Hurricane Katrina would be to

Louisiana and Mississippi, two decades later.

"There was unbelievable devastation," recalled Tom Tinder, Governor Moore's aide, who traveled with him frequently. "The scope of it...the degree of destruction ... half the state was devastated. For some areas it was a hundred-year flood [happening only once in a century] and for others it was a thousand-year flood."

Thousands of families were forced to into shelters, or to family and friends, for lodging. Most lost all their worldly possessions, including clothing, food, motor vehicles and furniture. Not only were mobile homes destroyed, but even large, stone and brick buildings were washed away. Highways and railroad tracks twisted and crumbled by the hundreds of miles, yanked out of place and contorted by the rushing waters. It made ingress and egress from the towns and villages nearly impossible by ground. DNR and State Police helicopters rescued some of the victims during the flood and then continued flying in and out, for weeks thereafter, to help with the recovery. Of course, schools were closed for weeks to come.

Some entire towns were nearly destroyed. Riverton, which had long ago re-routed the North Fork to use the flat valley for development and building homes, was shocked to find Mother Nature putting it back into its original path—right through the middle of town. The town of Hendricks, among others, was completely wiped out, as if hit by a nuclear bomb. Farm land was badly damaged and thousands of heads of cattle lost. A classic, if tragic, photo of the "killing waters" was that of a dead cow carcass stuck in the underpinning of a Tucker County bridge, left by the high waters. Cars and trucks were found miles down river from their original location. The wonderful fishing streams and rivers were left with huge boulders.

The aftermath required removal of the tons of mud, tearing down and hauling away heavily damaged structures, repairing others. Such infrastructures as pipelines and sewers had even been uprooted. There was a stench left from all the mud, dirt and debris.

THE NIGHT THE flood struck, Governor Moore and Tinder rushed down to the basement of the East Wing of the Capitol where the Office of Emergency Services was headquartered, to join others monitoring the grave situation. Unlike so many weaker leaders of today, Arch didn't wait for FEMA or the President to come rescue West Virginia. He jumped right in and immediately assumed strong leadership, without complaint or whining. Dressed in a khaki work uniform, with boots and a cap, he looked like a general leading a battle, which in fact he was. "He was a hands-on leader," noted Tinder. "He was especially good in crises. I mean, this was the guy, when there was a prison riot, he was in there negotiating with the prisoners, not leaving it to others."

Information was sparse that first night, but what was being received was all bad. There was a somber mood among the state workers there, a feeling of helplessness and intense sympathy for the victims. Neither Moore, Col. Donahoe, nor anyone in leadership could even get into the affected area at first, either by air or ground. Not much could be done until the storm passed and the high water levels started to recede.

Through it all, the Governor was cool and calm, methodical and very much in charge. After all, he'd been through a flood disaster or two before; he knew the drill. He'd been in command during many life-threatening situations, beginning in 1944. He knew that, eventually, federal and state governments could be mobilized to provide much-needed aid. You could almost hear him thinking, "I've been elected to lead in times like these."

Long before Bill Clinton was feeling the pain of others, Arch "went up there and lived with them for ten days," noted Tinder. He sloshed around in the stinking mud and debris in his boots and rain gear, not only providing sympathy and moral support, but surveying needs, asking questions, planning a course of action, taking notes, connecting state offices with projects–a total hands-on approach in which few details were missed.

"We flew all over in the helicopter," remembered Tinder. "In Marlinton, the Governor was walking up and down the streets. Mud, crud. People were throwing out their lives onto the streets. A lady came out and collapsed in his arms, like he was all she had–she was relying, trusting in him to put her life back together." He continued, "We'd land the helicopter beside the Mansion at eight a.m. each morning, and tour the flood area all day. But Arch Moore always wanted to be home at night, sleep in his own bed, so we'd return late each evening [to Charleston]."

Within a day or so, Moore had hundreds of National Guardsmen and state troopers into the area to keep order and help with evacuation and relocation. (Fortunately, West Virginians are more honorable than inner city dwellers during disasters; there was almost no report of looting or other crimes in the aftermath.) As soon as was practical, the Governor had DOH equipment into the region, clearing landslides, removing boulders and debris, filling huge holes, hauling in tons of rock and gravel, and doing all that they could to reopen roads and bridges. Naturally, the welfare social workers were trying their best to help with family needs, bending rules and speeding the process to get people fed and clothed quickly. Most families had no flood insurance and regular homeowners insurance often did not cover their loss.

One of the first to get a report from Gov. Moore was President Ronald Reagan, who immediately declared 29 counties federal disaster areas, eligible for assistance from the Federal Emergency Management Agency (FEMA) and other disaster relief agencies. FEMA brought in temporary trailers, as had been done at Buffalo Creek in 1972.

Moore appointed a czar, his trusted state police superintendent, to head up the recovery effort. Fred Donohoe would spend the next year in a duel role, leading the state police and serving as state coordinating officer for the flood recovery. It was "the man with the gun" he chose, Moore said, because he wanted authority and order, foremost, in this relief effort. He wanted someone leading the recovery to whom it was difficult to say no.

Moore's administrators went to work, almost around the clock, pulling in millions of federal dollars for rebuilding damaged roads and bridges, for loans and grants on an unprecedented scale, in such a short time. Partisanship and competition were temporarily set aside. The Democratic legislature and Senators Byrd and Rockefeller tried to outdo each other in helping the Moore Administration get the eastern half of the state back on its feet during those difficult, dark days of despair. True compassion and a sense of teamwork were in abundance. The legislature appropriated emergency flood relief funds for the counties. Byrd assured President Reagan that the damage was "the worst in the history of the state," asking for his cooperation "in expediting approval of the Governor's request for a disaster declaration and in directing the emergency relief assistance for this area as soon as possible..."[2] Moore, who'd brought in hundreds of millions of federal dollars as congressman and governor, met with the senior Senator to coordinate strategy. Each would complement the other's efforts.

According to Moore, Senator Byrd learned valuable lessons in the course of obtaining federal relief for the 1985 flood victims. "Before that, he'd hardly brought a hundred dollars into the state. Prior to helping us with the flood, he'd simply watched the legislation coming through the congress and attached his name to anything he [could take credit for]." But when Governor Moore put together a package of needs from the federal government to help with the flood, "I wanted someone to push it and I raised that with [Senator Byrd]. Bob Byrd never moved, until I moved him in '85. He then found out the value of interfacing with West Virginians" and began bringing millions of dollars worth of projects into the state." In Governor Moore's view, the exercise of getting federal dollars into the state for the flood recovery helped Byrd to "start learning what he could do."[3] The flood was the equivalent of wartime destruction or worse, but as Moore would note, "We'd been through floods before. We knew what to do. We made the best recovery anyone could expect." Two decades later, among the few treasured mementos in Moore's office were plaques given to him by these flooded communities, in appreciation for the efforts of his administration's efforts. "He was tireless, committed," thought Tinder.

The relief effort required a tremendous dedication of his time, energy and emotions. Moore and Tinder would accompany Donohoe in visiting possibly hundreds of flood sites, usually landing in the fields near the towns (or what was left of them) in SP 79, the state police's only twin engine helicopter, a Bell 222-UT. "Sometimes the weather would be so bad, we'd get as close as we could and state troopers would drive us the rest of the way in," remembered Fred. "I would go in uniform and speak on his behalf, but people wanted to see their Governor. He was a very hands-on, ambitious and caring individual as [the relief effort] unfolded. The needs of the people and their communities weighed heavily on his mind. He was always trying to figure out how to take care of the needs that government couldn't touch."

Despite its magnitude, the West Virginia flood did not receive the national news media attention it deserved, nothing like hurricanes and floods in, say, Florida or New Orleans. First, noted Moore's press secretary John Price, a story of a "volcanic eruption in Columbia that killed twenty-some thousand people dwarfed our disaster and replaced it in the news." Additionally, "National coverage of our disaster was muted by the fact that the flooding was so geographically spread out and affected mostly small communities." John arranged for the news photographers and videographers to take a helicopter tour over the ravaged area but "they saw little or no damage" because the National Guard pilots refused to fly low enough through thick cloud cover to "give the news media the pictures they needed." Then, "to add insult to injury, the Guard refused to fly them directly back to Charleston. Instead, they were flown from Clarksburg to Parkersburg where they waited for a relief flight crew and then flown back to Charleston and didn't arrive until well after dark. They could have taken I-79 from Clarksburg in less time."

FEMA SENT Tom Hamner in from Region 9 in California to be Donohoe's federal counterpart. "Before any federal dollars can be spent for disaster relief, they require a federal-state agreement to be signed," explained Donohoe. "Normally, those agreements say the federal government pays 75 percent of a project and the state 25 percent. But the magnitude of our loss was such that requiring even 25 percent would have bankrupted West Virginia for ten years." Hamner was very bureaucratic, as all FEMA people who came to the state during that crisis seemed to be. He was insistent that the usual 25-75 agreement be signed.

"Governor Moore told him that, until a reasonable agreement was available, neither he nor his designated coordinator would sign it," said Donohoe. "Hamner got red-faced. He told us we were spending too much. He insisted that we sign it and could modify it later." Perhaps because he was still stinging from the demands the feds had made after the Buffalo Creek cleanup, Moore refused to budge. "Governor Moore's vast knowledge of how the federal government operates—that absolutes are not absolute if there's valid reason for change—eventually got FEMA to acquiesce to his demand. Which was not unusual for him, I might add," said Donohoe. "In the final analysis, there was a cap put on [how much the state would have to match] for our remuneration to the federal government."

But the battle with Hamner and FEMA was not limited to the operational agreement. He quibbled on everything, Donohoe recalled, always citing verse and chapter of the regulations that prevented him from approving what needed to be done. "The flood had washed huge boulders from the river into the farmed meadow lands along the South Branch of the Potomac, some of them half the size of a car. Hamner agreed with me that the government could pay to remove debris from private property if it was needed to help them continue their livelihood. But it was Hamner's opinion that the boulders were not floating debris, so FEMA couldn't pay to haul them out of the farmers' fields.

Donohoe exploded at Hamner, "The boulders didn't grow here! They weren't dropped in from a plane! This stuff appeared here overnight!" But he was adamant that he would not pay.

Governor Moore told Donohoe that Hamner's was "not an acceptable answer. 'I want that cleaned up!' So after months of anguish and letters back and forth, FEMA could not convince the Governor that the boulders got there anyway but by floating in from the flooded rivers, so they said yes."

Said Tinder, "He used every technique, every tactic, in new and different ways, to get the mobile homes in, get the land cleared, get new sewer and water lines in. He came up with innovative, creative ways to get federal assistance, knowing the state didn't have hundreds of millions of dollars to take care of it. This was where his 'thinking outside the box' helped. He made use of his relationship with President Reagan, with whom he'd served as a governor, to make sure we got everything and more from FEMA. He was hard on FEMA," Tinder agreed. "The flood illustrated what kind of leader Arch Moore was. He used all his experience and expertise. He almost fleeced the federal government," he laughed.

But government can only do so much in a time of such intense tribulation. The true silver lining in the dark cloud of the 1985 flood was the generosity, selflessness, kindness and hard work demonstrated by the people of the region themselves, working night and day to help their friends and neighbors. The recovery effort showcased the mountaineer spirit at its very best, making observers proud and grateful. By the thousands, unsung heroes provided food, shelter, comfort, and spent untold hours wading around in their boots, shoveling, digging and cleaning out the mud, helping restore structures, families, businesses, often with no financial reward, whatever. Volunteer firemen led the way, but were joined by volunteers from the West Virginia Council of Churches, The Salvation Army, The Red Cross, Catholic organizations, the AFL-CIO, and many others. There was almost competition to see who could help the most.

Realizing that many would continue to have unmet need after the government and volunteer workers went home, and hearing from thousands who wanted to help, Gov. Moore ordered that a private source be established to help the flood victims. A non-profit fund (100% of which went to those in need), called The West Virginia Recovery Foundation, was formed[4] to accept and disburse contributions. It was administered on a day-to-day basis by Pam Dukate and led by F&A Commissioner John McCuskey with a board of directors from various sectors of the business, religious and non-profit community, including the Rev. John Price and beer distributor Jack Catalano. National companies, like Coors and Anheuser Busch, would compete to see who could give a larger contribution to it. Olympic gold medalist Mary Lou Retton, originally from Fairmont, flew in from Houston to donate $50,000. Her contribution was matched by Sharon and Jay Rockefeller and a West Virginia timber and paper company. But most were smaller donations, $25, $50, even $5 and one dollar contributions from school children, civic organizations and individuals. About $2 million was eventually raised–not nearly enough to go around, but supplying about $1500 to $3000 per flooded family.

Public Radio's Andy Ridenour and Larry Grose persuaded the 1970s music and film star, John Denver, to come to the Cultural Center for a fundraising telethon during the first week of December. Carried by all fourteen West Virginia TV and some radio stations, the show also featured

Kathy Mattea, George Jones, Chuck Yeager, Richie Havens, The Vandells, Chris Serandon, the WVU Percussion Ensemble (lead by Dave Satterfield), and many more. Yeager summed up the emotions of the affair by saying, "Everybody always pitches in. It's always been that way in West Virginia" Business leaders manned the phones and were joined for a time by Jay and Sharon Rockefeller. Sen. Byrd showed up, to brag about federal money he'd obtained for flood relief. [5] An endless line of donors streamed through to hand their checks to Commissioner McCuskey.

The highlight of the evening was when Denver was joined by co-writers Taffy Nivert and Bill Danoff to sing their *Take Me Home, Country Roads,* the Mountain State's "anthem" and the last time they would perform it together. Denver also sang a poignant, *Hey, It's Good to Be Back Home Again.*

Secretary of State Ken Hechler and Auditor Glen Gainer, the latter often a vocal opponent of Moore's, began investigating where some of the federal flood money went, in their capacity on the Armory Board. They discovered that the National Guard had used some of the money intended for flood relief instead to build plush apartments for their officers, mostly for use before and after WVU football games. "The carpet on those floors seemed to be four inches thick," Hechler remembered. They called for an accounting. After their investigation, "[Adjutant General John] Wilson had a few drinks and called us both traitors to a group of Guardsmen.

"Gainer heard about it and complained to Arch at an Armory Board meeting at which the press was present." The situation was ticklish, and Hechler waited to see how Moore respond to the outrage. "He looked at Gainer and said, 'Yes, I know. And I was going to have you both shot at sunrise but I thought the expense of the bullets would cause the state budget to be unbalanced!" Hechler said the awkward moment was defused, as the members of the media roared in laughter.[6]

Overall, the work of Gov. Moore's people was generally praised, however, for its speed, honesty and thoroughness throughout the long recovery period. In some cases, the post-flood status for some families was actually better than before. Certainly, many roads and bridges in the mountain counties had been improved. The recovery effort may have been the greatest accomplishment of Moore's third term. Agreed his former press secretary, John Price: "The Governor's reaction to that disaster was the shining gem in his third term. I believe that our recovery from it would have been much slower had anyone else been governor of our state."

"I remember we were at a community meeting in a little church in Hardy County a week after the flood," said Tinder. "People were worn out. Some were hopeless, not confident anything would happen [to help them]. Governor Moore was telling them what [all the state and federal relief workers were] doing. At the end of his remarks he asked if there were any questions. One old boy clear in the back stood up, he was a rugged West Virginian. 'Governor, tell 'em we're comin' back!' The place exploded."

Tinder concluded, "In 1986, 87, 88, they'd invited us to flood anniversary commemorations. It was just amazing, the change to the place years later. But today, they take for granted the new roads, the bridges, and raised highways [that were built after the flood]. There had just been unbelievable devastation."

But the flood was also a portent of things to come. Although it would not be apparent for a time, the severe loss would be an impediment to the economic recovery Moore hoped to lead in his four year term. Businesses had suffered loss that could never be recovered completely. Some had lost their entire inventory, and lacked insurance to cover it. Employees, such as those of Kingsford Charcoal, were laid off as plants were temporarily closed due to flood damage.

In his usual, upbeat fashion, the Governor tried to shrug it off, keep a positive attitude and engender optimism. The flood was a set-back, however, there was no way around that fact. God had seemed to smile upon Moore's first eight years; so much had gone right, at the very least he seemed "lucky" during his first two terms. But the 1985 flood was the beginning of another kind of luck for Moore in his third term of office.

Chapter 25 Notes

1. - Governor's Press Office, Nov. 29, 1985
2. - Byrd, Ibid.
3. - Byrd, Ibid.
4. - Established by your author.
5. - "I had phoned Senator Byrd to ask if he would earmark additional money to FEMA to help the state's flood effort," recalled Moore in an August 2004 interview. "He said that he would 'do his best,' and he did. He learned there was value to [his seniority]. It was then that he first used his authority in the Congress to help West Virginia on a regular basis."
6. - Hechler interview, January 29, 2005.

Chapter Twenty Six
Losing Control of the GOP

As if the flood had not been enough, the second year of Moore's third term began with another prison uprising in Moundsville, the worst riot in its violent history. On New Years Day, 1986, inmates took fifteen correctional officers and a food service worker hostage and murdered three fellow inmates they accused of being snitches. They demanded that the prison, which had been built in the late 1860s, be air-conditioned, more evenly heated in the winter, rid of rats and roaches, that more hot meals be served, that more visitation be allowed, and they generally be treated more humanely—fifty demands altogether. They also demanded to talk to the Governor.

The Governor "had dropped out of sight" for a few days, visiting Shelley's brother's family in Georgia and attending the Orange Bowl in Florida. Upon word of the crisis, he caught a commercial flight to Pittsburgh and had a State Police helicopter waiting for him there at midnight. "The media wondered how I got into [the prison] without them knowing about it. They forgot that my dad worked there and I knew that place pretty well. I went in through 'the old wagon gate.' I quietly made it to the warden's office and met with the inmate's committee."

Within fifty-two hours, the riot was over and the Governor walked out with the hostages one by one, avoiding further bloodshed. "The press thought I was putting on a show [by bringing the hostages out one by one], but I took them out as soon as they were given to me. The state police had ambulances waiting for them outside, because we didn't know what their condition would be. Some of the guards were crying and embracing me. One asked me, 'What the hell took you so long?' Some were offended by that comment but it didn't bother me a bit."

An inside (inmate) informant had phoned Moore from time to time, to keep him apprized of the situation at the prison, both before and after the riot. ("And you know, that informant never asked for a damned thing," Moore recalled.) He became convinced, based on these conversations and others, that there had been abuse of prisoners during the Rockefeller Administration which sparked some of the rebellion. (A 1979 breakout had resulted in the death of a prisoner and state trooper, causing "wanton physical violence [being] wreaked upon every single prisoner" by the guards, according to *The New York Times*.[1] Despite a circuit court ruling during the Rockefeller Administration, which had also required relief from overcrowding, the prison population had remained about 100 inmates over its 650 capacity. Rockefeller's administrators had tightened up dress and grooming codes and had abolished the inmate's council, which also heightened tensions.

Moore and Corrections Commissioner A. V. Doddrill promised the inmates that most of their grievances would be addressed, and that no general reprisals would occur, but that the "legal process" would be followed with regard to prosecuting those responsible for the murders.

It would take tens of thousands of dollars to replace windows and to fix other damage the prisoners had caused. It was becoming more obvious that the prison would need to be replaced.

IN HIS JANUARY 16, 1986, State of the State Address, the Governor called for the building of a new football stadium for Marshall University and assured the lawmakers that funds were available, if they chose to go forward with it. This proposal probably put Huntington Democrats like Robert "Chuck" Chambers in a quandary. They most certainly wanted the project, but the last thing they would want was for a Republican governor to get credit for something that big. (In September of 1986, Marshall went ahead and bought a $94,000 parcel of land from the Cabell County Board of Education to ready for the new structure. Governor Moore would call for sale of bonds, in his 1987 State of the State address, to finance the Marshall Stadium. In July of 1988, he would even take the unusual step of appearing before the Board of Regents to advocate for the stadium's construction. He jokingly threatened to keep the Board in Logan, where they were conducting a regional meeting, forever unless they approved his request for inclusion of the stadium in their budget.) Nevertheless, the new stadium would not be built and dedicated until after Moore's successor took office (groundbreaking ceremonies were held on July 18, 1990, and it would open for its first game on September 7, 1991).

In his speech, another of the Governor's statements would take the legislature by great surprise. "If you were made aware of the opportunity to obtain a $500 million investment in your state that would create 20,000 jobs and $150 million in new revenue, would you welcome it or wait for another time, when in fact there may not be another time?" Moore asked, rhetorically.

He had been approached by the casino gaming industry, who were trying to get legalized, casino-type gambling into the state. (Speaker Joseph Albright and House Judiciary Chairman Chambers would shoot it down, contending it would require a constitutional amendment. Yet, subsequent governors and legislatures gradually opened up the state for more and more gambling, without such an amendment.) Moore's hint that gambling could provide much-needed revenue opened the discussion, however–a door that previously had been pretty much closed to debate, until that point in the state's history.

Later that year, the Governor called a special session, asking for another thousand dollar pay raise for teachers, in addition to a six hundred dollar increase for those with twenty years of classroom experience, noting, "When the pay raise, incremental increase and retirement windfall are added together, the result is an increase of two thousand dollars for the West Virginia teacher with twenty years experience."

He appeared before the National Cancer Institute site visitation team, to lobby for a cancer research center in West Virginia (the advocacy efforts of the Governor and others would succeed; it would be located at WVU, announced in 1987).

Arch would continue to seek innovative ways to put every dime's worth of taxes to work for the State. He lease-financed new Highways equipment over a several-year period of time, just as one would do with a car or truck purchase; he could obtain additional, badly-needed equipment more quickly that way. Moore also instructed F&A to market tax-exempt "certificates of participation" to refinance old lease-purchases and to finance new equipment purchases. The legislative leadership–especially the vocal Moore critic George Farley, the House finance chairman—squawked to the news media about it, questioning its legality. Moore's Finance Commissioner, John McCuskey went full-speed ahead with the plan. The Jackson Kelly firm, along with Charleston lawyer (and Moore ally) Denny Vaughan, handled the legal end of the project, which provided $12 million (of the $40 million to be spent) in mid-1986. It was a way around an increasingly tight budget and a 1980 attorney general's opinion said spreading costs of equipment over multiple years was legal. The Democratic leadership had begun tightening Moore's finances, limiting him, however, and they did not like it one bit when he devised end-runs like the lease-purchase and refinancing plans.

A *New York Times* article of May 8, 1986, was titled, "Economy Reviving in West Virginia." For the first time since 1982, the state was not first in unemployment, it announced; Louisiana now had that "honor." The "service sector of the economy is growing significantly, creating new jobs for those who remain in the state's reduced work force," the article continued. Unemployment had dropped to 11.7 percent, compared to 7.5 percent for the national average; there were 9,500 less on the unemployment list than a year before, according to Dr. William Miernyk, the WVU economist. From Charleston there was "tentative new hope...matching the fresh, green look of spring that envelops the hills enclosing this valley capital."

The Governor was quoted as saying, "The challenge now, of course, is to shift away from the reliance on coal" as a generator of jobs, even though it would remain a major industry as far ahead as one could see. The jobs replacing coal included computer-related concerns, landscaping contractors, nursing homes, pizza parlors, social services organizations, florists, contact lens shops, and the like, the writer observed. In fact, it noted, Moore had just opened a "behavioral health center," employing 500 people in Beckley, to treat afflictions like Alzheimer's, drug abuse, alcoholism and mental retardation. The Governor told the reporter that he hoped the state's new tax incentives would lure such assets as regional corporate headquarters. He hoped the tourist industry, which had grown from $542 million in 1975 to $1.4 billion in 1984, would continue to expand. Few people thought an economic recovery would be easy, the story concluded. "Here's a state that's trying its very best to recover from a major structural shock in a national economy that is virtually not growing," said Dr. Miernyk, "and that's tough."

MOORE CONTINUED to tie up loose ends from his first two terms as governor, to complete tasks Rockefeller had neglected or failed to complete. One was the capitol dome. That Governor Rockefeller had sold the gold (that Moore had left in the vault to restore the dome) to buy a Preston County snow plow, and instead painted it, had irked Arch to no end and illustrated why he thought Jay had never fully understood West Virginia. "Governor Moore was genuinely distressed that the dome looked so pitiful; he was embarrassed," commented John McCuskey. "Arch Moore liked to do everything right, not half-assed. It was also another opportunity for him, I think, to show that Jay had done something wrong, an example of his incompetence. But he would do it right." Moore had always promised that, given the opportunity, he would re-gild the dome, just as architect Cass Gilbert had intended. To the Governor, it was just part of having pride in one's state, having self-respect, a symbol, emblematic of what he wanted those from other states or nations to think of the Mountain State. With the state no longer No. 1 in unemployment in the nation, he felt that he had a green light to go forward with the project; he decided to "go for the gold."

Gilbert had originally gilded the raised portions of the dome over the lead-copper veneer, using a design inspired by the Hotel National des Invalides in Paris, home of Napoleon's tomb. But with the techniques of the day (the capitol was built in the late 1920s and early 30s, in the depths of the Great Depression, for $10 million, then a huge sum) and the smoky, chemically-polluted Kanawha Valley air, it quickly flaked of. Senate President William Brotherton remembered, as a child, going down to the capitol and picking flakes of gold off the grounds.

So, a few months into the third term, the Governor called Commissioner McCuskey and asked him to take on the project of gilding the dome, as he had planned to do ten years before (not only was the gold available in 1976, but extensive studies had been conducted on how the dome was to be cleaned and the gold applied properly, to last a long time). "I want it done right!" he barked.

Something so extravagant during a time of tight state budgets was politically touchy, however, so a private foundation[2] was established to pay for the gilding project. Contributions came in from all over the state in $10 and $20 denominations; it was a quest many wanted to say they'd assisted. Over $140,000 was donated by Lawson Hamilton, who remained anonymous for the time. Five thousand dollars was donated by Governor and Mrs. Moore, and over $40,000 was donated for the dome restoration by taxpayers, who checked off a donation from their state income tax refund.

McCuskey took his staff with him to visit the Statue of Liberty, which was then being restored, including re-gilding the torch in her hand. He decided to hire Swanke & Hayden of New York, which was conducting that restoration, to also oversee the dome work. Their studies and testing revealed how to clean the dome before application so a patina did not form, which would cause the gold to flake off as it did in the past. Manos Tsilianios, a Greek-American from Massachusetts (who had gilded Georgia's capitol dome) won the bid to do the work, and soon his men were on ropes, down the sides of the dome in boatswain chairs, applying the cigarette-paper thin squares of gold on it, one three inch square sheet at a time. Moore chose to gild the entire dome, not just the ribs, as would be done recently; it would be similar in that respect to Atlanta's dome. It was not finished until 1991, but when completed it beautifully reflected the sun, a gleaming object of art, becoming one of the state's greatest landmarks for those passing on I-64 or up and down the Kanawha River.[3]

Moore caused other, major, changes to the capitol complex during his third term. The legislature passed a resolution authorizing the erection of a Vietnam veterans memorial on the grounds. "We had a competition to come up with an artist's design," said Alan Drescher, then deputy commissioner of F&A, who represented the Governor on the commission overseeing the project. "Veterans from other wars wanted something, too, so it became an all-veterans memorial. We had to modify the design, but the one we'd chosen easily accommodated that. It honored all West Virginia war dead from the Twentieth Century." Moore was excited about the project, Drescher recalled. "Of course, he was a veteran and that's one reason it meant a lot to him."

What would be built was a two-story, oval shape design, with statues of a World War I doughboy, a Korean War aviator, and a Vietnam War Marine on the outer walls. Private funds were raised to finance most of the project. Inside, similar to the Vietnam War Memorial in D.C., are etched names of more than 10,000 West Virginia war dead, from different wars. (Groundbreaking would not occur until June 1990 after Moore was out of office and it was not completed in its entirety until 1999, at the cost of $4 million.)

Drescher added that Governor Moore "used the memorial as a vehicle to close off the capitol campus. He combined those two things. I thought it made the capitol complex more user-friendly, nicer for the public, with more of a park-like setting." Cass Gilbert's original design had called for Washington Street to be closed off to make the capitol complex undivided by the busy street. But closing it was not without controversy; the street had been open on the east end of Charleston since the city was originally surveyed; motorist were inconvenienced and irrate until they got adjusted to going another route. "It was the only time that my life was threatened," grinned Moore. "But I turned it into a capitol complex, as had always been planned." Once they got used to it, the public preferred the closed campus, although it took away numerous parking spaces, which are always scarce there.

The State was fortunate to have on its staff at the time Beth Loflin, one of West Virginia's outstanding landscape architects. Beth, a graduate of WVU's L.A. program, designed the new campus between the main capitol building and the three towering office buildings to the rear. With its large fountain, gray squirrels and large hardwood trees, it had always been one of the nation's most attractive capitol grounds, but she made it even better and a place where large, outdoor festivities could be safely held. In a little salute to the Governor, she spelled out "AAM" with colored bricks which can still be seen from certain windows of the main capitol, a gesture that Arch got a kick out of, remembering it two decades later. Moore had been the kind of governor who literally made sure every light bulb in the capitol dome was lit, that every shrub was cut; he enjoyed the thought of leaving his initials on the capitol campus that he loved.

Arch also kept tabs on the people who worked in that capitol complex and in state government elsewhere. His knowledge of those state employees remained absolutely phenomenal. "The staff used to take the huge computer printout of the state employees roster into Governor Moore's office," recalled John Price, his former press secretary. "They would select a page at random, close their eyes and drop a finger to the page. They would read aloud to him the name on which the finger landed. The Governor would usually be able to tell, not only where the person worked, but what county they were from, and often something about their family. It was one of the most amazing things I ever saw!"

Price continued, "I remember one time when I was flying with the Governor in the King Air. He had read some papers and dozed off. He opened his eyes a little later and looked out the window. He immediately knew where in the state we were and who owned the property over which we were flying at the time." Added Price, "The man knew the state of West Virginia like the back of his hand."

DURING THE Rockefeller years, West Virginia courts had become far more activist, especially the supreme court. For example, the *Recht* decision[4] required equal funding of all state public schools, even though there was wide disparity from county-to-county in the expense of property taxes supporting them–those in counties which were expensive places to reside had to subsidize those where taxes and housing prices were low.

Another domain in which courts had been infringing on the executive and legislative branches was the prison system. Various courts began shutting down county jails because they did not find them "comfortable" enough for prisoners, forcing Moore and the legislature to provide a much more expensive Regional Jail Authority, and forcing taxpayers to spend tens of millions of dollars each year to pay for transporting prisoners to and from these modern, multi-county facilities.

These courts—including Judge Arthur Recht—were also holding that the state's prisons were antiquated and overcrowded to the point of being unconstitutionally "cruel and unusual punishment." There was insufficient funds to build all these new prisons and jails and so, in his usual fashion, Arch improvised. He set up a "reservation" system, housing convicted felons in county facilities until a space opened for them in a prison. However, the supreme court ruled in December, 1986, that his executive order was invalid. So in January, 1987, he would call it something else. He exercised his constitutional power of reprieve, which again allowed the felons to be held in county jails "until space can be found for them at an a appropriate state institution." He noted that a reprieve legally stays "the execution of a sentence for a time," and "differs from a commutation of sentence or a pardon."

Moore used a similarly crafty improvisation to protect Medicaid dollars, upon which most West Virginia physicians, dentists, hospitals and nursing homes are so dependent. There was an almost desperate need to reduce a Medicaid backlog, a shortfall. Then, as now, providing low income citizens with free health care was becoming an increasingly onerous burden for working taxpayers.

Anyone, a person or organization, could donate money to the state's Medicaid fund, the regulations provided, in which case the federal government would provide three matching dollars for every dollar donated. So Moore decided he would have medical providers and hospitals "voluntarily donate" funds to the State which were used to increase West Virginia's entitlement to federal matching funds. Essentially, these were loans to qualify the state for federal money. It was another example of Arch "thinking outside the box."

The idea actually had originated from Ed Burdette, a career Human Services employee who was then assistant to Commissioner Regina Lipscomb. Burdette convinced the Governor of the soundness of his proposal. After thinking about it, Arch decided to run with the plan. He would wring some much-needed cash from Reagan's increasingly stingy federal government, which was requiring states to provide all sorts of services but providing inadequate funding to meet those requirements.

The scheme "was legal, appropriate and smart," thought Tinder, an admirer of Burdette.[5] "We had the health care providers to make a 'voluntary contribution' to the Medicaid fund of, say $10,000. That would qualify the state for $30,000 in federal matching funds. When we received that money from the federal government, we'd then pay the provider back their $10,000."

But then other states took note of what Arch was doing and began trying it, too. "They started a run on Medicaid funds," noted Tinder. Once the federal bureaucrats began understanding what was going on, the U.S. Dept. Of Health and Human Services disallowed the scheme. So the Governor went to U.S. District Court to obtain a restraining order against them. As might have been expected, the *Gazette*, and the rest of the capitol news media which seemed to follow that paper's lead like sheep, criticized Moore's plan to no end. It will never work, they cried, it's illegal, it will cause disaster!

But in December of 1987, Moore would announce that a federal appeals board issued a decision upholding his innovative plan. The board noted that the agency had "never published any policy guidance that interprets the scope of regulation in question and gives the states guidance as to what was intended to be covered," so it was perfectly legal. The state didn't have to repay the millions of dollars to the feds as the nay-sayers had predicted.

Arch had won another one, at least for the time being, as Gino Columbo had predicted, squeezing more out of a dollar than anyone could imagine doing. He had once more out-maneuvered, outfoxed the federal government much to the advantage of West Virginians in need, and lessened the load on the state's taxpayers. "Finally, in 1988, Congress closed that loophole," Tinder noted.

ANOTHER CASE which could have–most would agree, should have caused election reform, was issued by the state supreme court in 1986. Believing it to be outrageous how Jay Rockefeller had spent tens of millions of dollars on Election Days 1972, '76, '80 and '84 , H. John Rogers had brought a mandamus action, asking for election laws to be enforced. Justice Darrell McGraw, writing for the majority, held that the secretary of state was required to promulgate rules for election expenditures, among other things, banning a candidate from spending money for election expenses unless "at a rate and for a total amount which is proper and reasonable and fairly commensurate with the services rendered."[6] In other words, the court was disallowing the purchase of elections by check, simply by pretending it was for hiring workers on election days. If they were truly election day workers, and not simply families selling their votes to the highest bidder, then they should be paid a reasonably low "wage" for such labor, Justice McGraw was requiring.

Justice William Brotherton dissented because he thought it was usurping legislative authority to allow the secretary of state to draft and enforce such regulations (which initially would limit the "wage" to $25 per worker). But Brotherton wrote, "The cost of running for public office in this state...is much too high. It is a cancer that could destroy our representative government. When the wealthy and those individuals who are able to solicit large monetary contributions are the only candidates who are capable of mounting successful campaigns, it is time to reform election laws."

(The decision and the resulting regulations would be meaningless in the next gubernatorial election, however. Moore's wealthy opponent would get around the limit by "hiring" the election day workers for three days. Secretary of State Hechler likely could have gone to court to prevent Gaston Caperton from doing that, but refused to do anything to prevent it, or to enforce the supreme court's 1986 ruling.)

DESPITE THE ADVERSE effect the flood had on the state's economy, "everything was looking pretty rosy" for the state's budget and the general business climate "two years into" Moore's third term, recalled former-Finance Commissioner John McCuskey. "The economy had been in pretty bad shape before we came in, but Governor Moore was determined, as he said many times in the 1984 campaign, to 'get the ox out of the ditch.' It had been a continuing theme of his, that Rockefeller was bad for the state, but he was good for it." In Arch's view–and a view he wanted shared by West Virginians–he would rescue and restore the state from the damage done by eight years of Jay Rockefeller.

The Democrats, obviously, did not want that to happen. They did not want to allow Moore to shine; they most certainly did not want him in office for eight years, controlling patronage, getting credit for successes, choosing the state's direction. The goal of the majority party, from Senator Byrd to the county surveyor, was to have a state run 100% by Democrats. They saw no value in a competitive, bipartisan system, especially when the opposition was led by their nemesis, Arch Moore. McCuskey thought many of them were being short-sighted, though. "They were bright men, but they weren't visionaries," he thought. "They were small-minded people who didn't understand that the game [Moore] played was a win-win situation. The [Democratic leadership] who served during his first two terms—the Boiarskys, the McManuses, the Brothertons–understood the game. Everyone believed in the [one-upmanship game Moore played] because everyone won. The state won, West Virginians won and they won re-election. It's all good, as they say. Arch's attitude was, 'I'll one-up you, but we'll both win.'

"[In the 1970s] we were no longer the butt of national jokes, the state was progressing, income was up, business was growing. Everyone loved it except the most partisan [Moore haters]." The Democratic leadership in the third term were different than those giants of the past, however. They were "willing to take 1.8 million West Virginians down the tubes just to cause Arch Moore to fail," McCuskey thought. "The Governor didn't think they could be that petty."

But they were. Or that wily and smart, if one viewed it from the opposite perspective. The Democrats finally settled on a strategy and it involved money. Cut off Moore's money supply and he could not be the hero. But how?

"The Governor would often set his revenue estimates high so he could, frankly, spend more," noted McCuskey. "It was part of his eternal optimism. It was not blind optimism, but rather calculated optimism. He would see things others did not–he could see ahead eight or ten chess moves." That Moore was always "playing" with revenue estimates did not sit well with the Democratic legislative leadership–Joe Albright, "Chuck" Chambers, George Farley, and Dan Tonkovich.

Then Moore made a flippant, disparaging remark about Farley in the press and it was a mistake. It wasn't the first time Arch had sounded off about someone in the legislature; it was a technique he had used for years. Most of the recipients had shrugged or laughed it off as partisan banter. "But for some reason, George just went ballistic," McCuskey recalled. "It was the last straw. Farley decided then and there to 'get' Arch Moore."[7]

The method the Democrats decided to use was brilliant. They would proceed to rid the state, once and for all, of the much-hated B&O tax, as had been planned for a couple of years. Because business and occupation tax unfairly taxed the gross, not net profits of all businesses, "that meant that a mom and pop business could have lost money for the year, but their gross proceeds were taxed by the state nevertheless," explained McCuskey. The tax was also unpopular with big business, including the powerful coal industry. "Speaker Albright and George Farley knew that Arch Moore couldn't oppose the abolition of the B&O tax," remembered McCuskey. It would have been quite unpopular, especially in this era of Reagan tax cuts and reforms. "They perceived, 'we have a winner here.'"

While Moore could not openly oppose it, "privately he urged those guys to think twice about [abolishing the tax]," McCuskey recalled. "He even vetoed [the abolition] once on a technicality, but they sent it back and he signed it." Coal would be subject to a severance tax, "but it is difficult to set those," the former finance commissioner noted. "And the coal industry isn't stupid. They did all they could, understandably, to keep it as low as possible. As they say, 'the devil is in the details.'"

That Moore "didn't want" the B&O completely abolished McCuskey was certain. "He knew the revenue situation would be chaotic for years, because we just didn't know, couldn't predict, what new taxes would produce." Not even Jim Boggs, the veteran Budget Director who had served numerous governors, could accurately predict the revenues based on the new tax system. "It was supposedly designed [by the Legislature] to be revenue-neutral, but it didn't turn out that way," continued McCuskey. "We lost $25 to $50 million a year from our $1.5 billion budget at the time. At the end of the day, revenue went down, even though business and the state's economy was doing pretty well. The loss of that tax caused the [political] downfall of Arch Moore. It was a calculated plan by the Democrat leaders to prevent Arch Moore from succeeding, done at the expense of all West Virginians."

But Moore's own actions may also have contributed to the cash-flow crisis. To lure new business, the Governor had urged the Legislature to adopt the investment tax credit, as other states had done. Among other things, the Japanese auto industry was placing factories in states that offered attractive tax packages. Moore felt that the Saturn plant went to Tennessee instead of West Virginia because the latter did not have an investment tax credit, to help offset the investment. Reducing taxes for an incoming business to induce them to locate in the Mountain State would more than pay for itself, by creating manufacturing jobs and all the resulting spin-off jobs, he argued.

The Legislature passed Moore's proposal and it was a tool available for his administration to bring in new industry. The problem was, as Mike Caryl had noted, the new law was not specific enough to exclude those companies already doing business in the state. It allowed all companies to ask the Tax Department for the credit, even those which simply were expanding their existing work forces, such as coal mines re-hiring miners. "We didn't know who would take advantage of it," admitted McCuskey. "As it turned out, existing businesses, including coal companies, took advantage of the credit. It ended up cutting additional revenues that would have been there otherwise. It drained the treasury of money we needed. At the end of the day, business tax revenue went down [as the result of the tax reforms during Moore's third term] even though the state's economy was doing pretty well."

The investment tax credit was something the *Gazette's* Don Marsh harped on continually, calling it a "giveaway program" for Big Business. And for once he was correct. There was no indication that it created a net increase in jobs for the state, and it caused a considerable drain on state government's revenue–again, tens of millions of dollars lost to the treasury each year.

By the end of 1986, the pain of the loss of revenue would be felt by West Virginians; it took a while for the loss to be noticed in the cash flow pipelines. For several months, there had been optimism that both tax changes could succeed, and fire up the state's economy. In December,

Auditor Glen Gainer said the treasury had only $13,000 to cover $51 million in bills, but later said it was $5 million to cover $65 million in bills. He ordered a halt to issuance of welfare checks. Moore's press secretary, John Price, said Gainer was just trying to embarrass the Governor (because Moore had threatened to remove him from office) and that the state had at least $43 million in the bank.[8] But Gainer's action was just the opening salvo of a battle that would last for nearly two years, regarding timely payment of the state's obligations. More money was obviously needed, now.

One thing that probably led to Governor Moore shying away from calling for an additional tax burden was the constant negative reaction his office received regarding the property reappraisal project. As result of the statewide reappraisal, begun under Rockefeller, real property taxes for many homeowners and business people doubled or tripled. They were furious, as could be expected. There was no indication, when the project began, that the result would be so expensive. There was also considerable question about the fairness and competency of the Ohio firm Rockefeller's administration had hired to do the job; many of their contract workers sent to do the reappraisals had little or no training or expertise; the results were somewhat arbitrary and uneven. West Virginians could always point to low taxes as a positive, when one began outlining all the negatives, but no longer; property taxes were now as high as most other states. While Moore had not started the reappraisal program, he saw the benefit that added revenue for the counties would bring, so he did not oppose it or try to reverse the results. In the minds of the uninformed, the bill came on Moore's watch, however, and so when they saw their property taxes double and triple in 1985 and 1986, it was a case of "Arch Moore raised my taxes!"

It presented a problem for him, in how to respond to angry constituents, whose letters were pouring in by the thousands. In their mind, he should do something about it. So the Governor had to be diplomatic and gentle about the controversy. His form letters to them read:

> Thank you for your letter expressing your concerns about the statewide property reappraisal. I share your concern about the accuracy of the evaluations at which the firm hired by my predecessor has arrived and can assure you that I will not allow these appraisal figures to be used until a thorough examination of their impact has been conducted and a mechanism for correcting unfair evaluation can be developed. I have

> directed the state tax department to thoroughly investigate this matter and I assure you that I will adequately protect West Virginia taxpayers from unfair or inequitable taxation. *Sincerely, Arch A. Moore, Jr., Governor.*

It wasn't a false promise. Moore's tax department did set up a system of appeals and, in some cases, property taxes were adjusted downward. In most, however, the higher tax was affirmed. The controversy showed that the public was clearly in an anti-tax hike mood. It influenced his unwillingness to call for additional state taxes to ease the coming cash flow problems.

IN MAY OF 1986, Moore again showed some prescience by proposing a state liability insurance pool for physicians. It would have also allowed other professionals, including lawyers, nurses, engineers and accountants into a $50 million fund for malpractice insurance through the state. "We're going to have to go to a state system," he said, calling for a special session to create a government-run mutual. The crisis had begun, *The New York Times* explained, when insurance companies began withdrawing their malpractice business from West Virginia because of a law which restricted their ability to cancel or refuse to renew policies. "I think they're using us as a laboratory" to see whether they can "flex their muscle" enough to bring West Virginia to its knees, Governor Moore told the paper. Consequently, he was revoking their licenses to sell other kinds of insurance in the state. "If they're not going to write malpractice insurance, they're not going to write any other insurance in West Virginia," he said. A consumer advocate thought Moore's actions would have positive "nationwide repercussions," and that the state would "set an example for the rest of the country."[9] The legislature would not grant Arch's request for a state-run malpractice insurance system, though. Had it been adopted, it may have prevented the exodus of the orthopedic surgeons, emergency room doctors and obstetricians in the late 1990s when they found they couldn't obtain malpractice insurance or that it was unaffordable. (Governor Bob Wise would get the legislature to approve such a proposal after the malpractice crisis had already done its considerable damage.)

THROUGHOUT THE 1984 campaign, Arch had witnessed the death of West Virginia's downtown business districts. Once vibrant and full of people, shopping malls, four-lane highway by-passes and job losses had turned most downtown areas into ghost towns, a bunch of dreary, empty buildings. In Fairmont, for example, almost nothing was left of the downtown. Winos and prostitutes wandered the streets. Except for local government workers, lawyers and banks, nothing much remained of what had once been a town with sidewalks full of people, and traffic-jammed streets. "Is there anything you can do about this, Arch?" was the question he frequently heard from business people and Chambers of Commerce. It was a difficult problem to solve; it required some creativity.

But Moore came up with an experiment he thought might kill two birds with one stone. He knew that the State was putting out a lot of money to rent buildings to house Human Services, DMV and other offices in those towns, money that went into landlords' pockets to the tune of millions per year. And there was nothing much to show for it. Further, every time administrations changed, a new set of landlords, who had contributed to that candidate for governor, persuaded him to relocate state offices to their empty buildings and expensive remodeling would be required; there was little permanency of location. Renting has always been expensive for government and, for the most part, impractical.

So the Governor called McCuskey into his office to discuss an innovative proposal, another big assignment. The State would seek out appropriate buildings for purchase, or lease-purchase in several suffering towns and restore and remodel them, turning them into permanent state office buildings. That would solve the rent problem and, hopefully, get some traffic moving into the downtown areas again, get some restaurants open, draw in spin-off businesses and services. The former J.C. Penney building in Parkersburg, the former Hartley's Department Store building in Fairmont, [10] an office building in Beckley, the former Sheraton Hotel in Clarksburg and the Coyles Building in Charleston (used to house the Tax Department) were among those the state bought as part of the downtown restoration project. "It was an efficient way to provide state services out of a central location and saved a lot of money which had been going to landlords," thought McCuskey about Moore's innovative experiment. "It did stem the tide of exodus from the cities; it stopped the outflow of people. And it gave the towns a centerpiece for other renovations."

IT WAS ABOUT this time that Kevin Sikora made a discovery that illustrated how Arch Moore operated, behind the scenes. "I brought a group of landlords in to see the Governor about some office space they wanted to lease to the state, to try to get his approval. They gave him their story, complaining that the leases had been held up by F&A. He picked up the phone and said, 'Audrey, get me John McCuskey.' I didn't think it was possible to talk to him because John was in Martinsburg that day and it was before cell phones. But, lo and behold, Arch's phone rang within a minute. The Governor picked it up and said, 'John, I want you to process these leases for so-and-so, right away' and hung up, assuring them it was taken care of. They got up, thanked the Governor and left the office.

"The next day, when John got back to the capitol, I asked him about the leases and he professed that he didn't know what I was talking about. I said, 'You know, the leases the Governor talked to you about yesterday.' McCuskey responded, 'I haven't talked to the Governor in almost a week!' I knew something was odd, but I couldn't figure it out."

A few weeks later, Sikora was surprised and amused to discover what had happened. He was sitting back in Governor Moore's chair one night after hours, stretching his legs out, fantasizing what it would like to be governor himself. The phone rang. He picked it up, answering, "Governor's office," but no one was on the line. "Wrong number," he mumbled to himself. When he stretched his legs out under the desk, the phone rang again with the same result. He looked under the desk well to find a foot button that, if pushed, made the phone ring.

"He'd been using that trick for years!" Sikora laughed. It was Moore's tool for getting people out his office when they'd overstayed their allotted time, or to fake a call, as he had done with McCuskey for the sake of the would-be landlords. Arch was not going to be rushed by anyone, including impatient landlords, but it was his brilliant way of handling their request politely and politically, if deceitfully. (And when they followed-up, he could say, "Didn't McCuskey handle that for you?")

But it would take more than a phone-ringer to solve another political problem he had to deal with that year.

IN THE SUMMER of 1986, Moore was involved in a nasty intra-party political battle that would cause him significant difficulties in the next election. One of his keys to success had always been the fact that he'd been able to maintain control over a relatively unified Republican party, but the results of this power struggle would leave his party split wide open, and the Governor vulnerable.

Normally, a sitting governor of either party gets to pick his or her own choice for state party chairman. It is a courtesy afforded to him almost without exception. When Republican State Chairman Kent Strange Hall announced he would not seek re-election to the post, John Raese paid a visit to Governor Moore to ask him for his support. Raese was still feeling his oats from his near victory over Rockefeller two years before, had aspirations for another run and had made a lot of friends within the GOP. But Arch smelled a skunk. Word had gotten back to him that Raese had been bad-mouthing him, particularly regarding his belief that Moore had "sold him out" in the '84 race and had soaked up available donations, depriving him of enough money to pull off what otherwise would have been a victorious quest for the Senate seat. Knowing Raese was out front, talking a lot to the press, to the party, a loose cannon, and certainly not someone he could control, Arch withheld his support. He wasn't so sure Raese wasn't after his job, when it got right down to it.

But Raese was not deterred; he campaigned vigorously for the post among state executive committee members, county chairman, promising them he would build a modern, vibrant party that could win elections. He also fanned the flames of animosity some already had toward Arch Moore. They felt he'd always appointed too many Democrats; he'd barely consulted them about appointments to vacant state jobs in the last two years. Some shared Raese's view that Moore had always run a "one-man show," and that he didn't involve others enough in decision-making. He hadn't paid enough attention to them in any of his three terms, they thought. A rebel like Raese was appealing; he was their Absalom to King David; he would listen sympathetically to their grievances against Moore. The Republicans enjoyed his vocal, slashing campaign against the hated Jay Rockefeller. Plus, as a Reaganite, Raese shared their conservative philosophy far more so than the moderate, pragmatic, less partisan Arch Moore who had always depended heavily on Democratic votes to get elected.

Not long before the Republican Executive Committee was to meet at the Charleston Marriott for the election of a state chairman, the Governor announced that his choice for the office was Edgar "Hike" Heiskell, his past workers' comp commissioner, the former secretary of state and a Morgantown lawyer. Under the direction of aide Ben Bailey, several of Moore's '84 campaign field workers, including Kevin Sikora, Nelson Robinson, Bob Duvall, Bob Chehi and Jake Reger, began working the convention for their boss. But they soon concluded that Raese had sufficient votes to win. Some of the delegates still had a sour taste in their mouths from Heiskell's resignation as secretary of state in 1975; plus, he hadn't been around for a while–many didn't know him well. On the other hand, Raese had been campaigning for their votes for some time and had proven himself as their U.S. Senate nominee. "What Arch wanted" just wasn't going to cut it.

So they went to Plan B: Moore's strategists decided that both Raese and Heiskell should withdraw and a "compromise" candidate would be chosen, also Moore's pick, state Senator Mike Shaw of Mason County. Bailey dispatched Reger to tell "Hike" the bad news. "He just said, 'Whatever the Governor wants,'" Reger recalled. "He was a team player." Robinson, no fan of Raese's, volunteered to take the message to him. "It may have been as late as one or two a.m. the night before the state meeting," Nelson recalled. "I knocked on his (Marriott) hotel door and told him Governor Moore had decided to support Mike Shaw for chairman. I could tell I had awakened him. He just looked at me angrily and said 'Thanks,' and shut the door!"

But "Kent Hall was running the thing and he was mad at Arch and wanted Raese to get it," recalled Reger. "He held a silent vote and, supposedly, Raese narrowly defeated Shaw.

"Raese was all torked up because Arch Moore tried to keep him out of it. He reminded Bob Duvall and me that he owned *The Dominion Post* and some radio stations and said, 'Tell Arch I'm going to burn him.' Bob Duvall responded, 'You'll have to tell him that yourself.'

"The vote had taken all afternoon. The Governor had planned a reception at the Mansion for the county chairmen, but few made it down, it went so long."

Raese would go on to become a vigorous, dynamic and, as expected, outspoken state Republican chairman during the next few months. And, just as Moore had feared, within less than a year Raese would be criticizing him viciously and announcing his own candidacy for the party's nomination for governor, to oppose Arch.

IT WAS difficult to believe that the third term in office was nearly half finished. The Moore Christmas card photo expanded as more and more grandchildren arrived. Daughter Shelley Moore Capito was enjoying her days playing tennis, getting involved in organizations, and being a busy stay-at-home mom as husband Charlie built more success at a Charleston brokerage. Kim was becoming a successful executive of a bank in Virginia where he and his wife had made their home. An Arch Alfred Moore IV was born in 1986 ("Alf," as he was called, would follow his father and grandfather to WVU in the fall of 2004). Lucy had married former classmate John Durbin and they were starting a paging and cell phone business in Charleston. The entire family would get together for a summer vacation in Georgia each year, at the Glen Dale home for Christmas, and elsewhere in between.

Arch and Shelley continued to enjoy playing cards, entertaining friends their age and the Governor played golf when he had time, usually at the Greenbrier. Tom Tinder, a talented tennis player, would often join the Moores for tennis often during the four years. "Arch Moore is not the best tennis player I've ever faced, but he's the most competitive," laughed Tinder. "They were both in their sixties by now, but both were still very athletic.

"And I knew it was going to be a good day when his grandchildren came to see him," Tinder continued. "They always had pictures of the grandchildren in the Mansion and at their home. Family was always very important to him. He'd always go back to the Mansion to have lunch and dinner with Mrs. Moore."

And the Governor had an undying love for WVU and the law, Tinder noted, recalling when Arch flew all the young lawyers in his administration with him up to the WVU College of Law to judge Moot Court rounds one evening. Tinder also recalled a day that they suddenly realized they needed to fulfill their continuing legal education to keep their law licenses active. "The Governor had me to see what kind of seminars were available and all I could find was the Trial Lawyers [plaintiffs' attorneys] meeting. We had to get six hours credit, so we tried to quietly sneak in the back, but the chairman, Stanley Preiser, noticed him coming in and had to announce, 'Like every other lawyer, the Governor is required to get his CLE, and is here with us today.' He asked if the Governor wanted to address the group but he declined, noting that he was there to 'get educated' like everyone else."

ON AUGUST 1, 1986, one of those young lawyers, Benjamin Bailey (who had been an assistant prosecutor for U.S. Attorney David Faber before joining Arch Moore's campaign and administration), received an interesting visit. Federal investigators, presumably with the blessing of Faber, sent individuals into the governor's office itself, to try to entrap Bailey into making a deal. The incident was the first signal that the Justice Department was continuing its efforts, initiated in the early 1970s and thwarted by his acquittal a decade earlier, to "get" Arch Moore if they could.

Mingo County Commissioners Rastie Runyon, Jr. and Ron Rumora, school board member Tom Marcum and Williamson businessman Bob Stanley had the audacity to come wearing "wires" to Bailey's office. Whether Bailey was chosen because he had been an Assistant U.S. Attorney himself before joining Arch Moore's campaign, or just because he increasingly had become the Governor's political representative, was not clear. Mingo County Prosecutor Thomas Ward would later admit the meeting had been taped as part of a federal-state investigation. Wrote the *Gazette-Mail*, "The state audit of the county reportedly was the subject of the discussion. Rumora and Runyon reportedly attempted to get the government to overlook the audit." No dummy, Bailey had read reports of investigations of Mingo County political figures and later admitted he was very cautious about what he said to these men.

"For me, the interesting notion in retrospect is the fact that there were competing investigations," remembered Bailey, nearly two decades later. "The feds had one going on, the state, in the person of Brad Russell, was running the other one. Both investigations were aligned with one of the competing factions in Mingo County[11] [They wanted] us to have the Tax Department lay off of an audit. I think they wanted to trade that for a Republican seat on the county commission, but the conversation was so general and they were all so nervous that it never quite jelled." Bailey refused their bribe and showed them the door.

Ben said he first learned that the visitors had been wired when "Russell called me about a statement made by Ron Rumora in testimony in open court, in which he claimed some sort of investigatory privilege." Bailey said he suspects he was "one of the few public employees who is actually on record telling someone 'no' when asked for a favor."

He added, "The funniest part—and the moment when I knew something was amiss during the meeting—involved our telephone system. We had installed phones with a monitor and a touch screen. Mine was behind my desk. I couldn't see it but those guys could. It had a couple of rows of dots which were speed dial buttons, and had an energy saving function which turned the screen off after thirty or forty minutes.

"I had made a couple of calls just as the meeting started, then forgot. Thirty or forty minutes later all three of those guys blanched in unison, their eyes almost popped out of their heads, and they stammered while staring over my left shoulder. I turned around and the screen had gone blank. They had seen the screen change suddenly and didn't know what was going on. I figure now they wondered if they were being bugged, since they were bugging me." Bailey said he found it "interesting where all those characters are today," noting, "Dave Faber, my boss in the U.S. Attorney's office, is a [federal district] judge; Rumora is Mingo County prosecutor and Russell moved to California and died young."

The Mingo County "swamp," as the *Gazette* called it, was getting deeper and murkier. Former sheriff and Democrat county chairman Johnie Owens had been charged with taking a $15,000 bribe to arrange a go-easy plea bargain in a murder case. In a county nine-to-one Democrat, the negative effects of the lack of a two party system were clearly evident.

The incident was an ominous warning of things to come and, in retrospect, should have alerted Moore to be extremely cautious about campaign finances in the upcoming re-election bid and especially his need to stay far away as possible from the Southern West Virginia Democratic political machines and factions. Alarm bells and flashing red lights should have gone off–these guys were trouble, they were dangerous! The feds had been investigating Mingo County politicians Gilbert Mayor Lucky Compton with receiving stolen property; seven politicos, including Johnie Owens, were charged with vote fraud, and Kermit Fire Chief Wilburn Preece and several of his relatives, with drug dealing. Runyon would eventually be indicted for not reporting $6000 he received or used in a campaign. Rumora and Commissioner Steve Adkins would later face six felony charges, including falsifying county accounts. Larry Hamrick, another party boss and former Mingo County school board president, was indicted on charges of racketeering, jury tampering, obstructing justice, intimidating witnesses, and taking money protection money from drug dealers. But getting Southern Democratic factions on his side had worked in 1972 and in other elections and it was a hard habit for Arch Moore to break; he was not confident he could win an election without his name being on at least some of those slates.

From that incident in Bailey's office forward, the *Gazette* pounded the drums incessantly, announcing every few months that "Governor Moore is being investigated." They would tell just enough to make it appear to a reader that he must be guilty of something. Observed Brenda Nichols-Harper who was in his office frequently at the time, "I don't know how he put up with that, but he continued serving as if nothing was going on. Can you imagine having to read that stuff every day? It didn't seem to bother him. I don't know how he did it. The Governor kept such a positive attitude. I never saw him not doing his job as chief executive officer of the state, even with what was going on each day."

THAT YEAR, Jake Reger left the governor's office to become director of the JTPA (Job Training Partnership Act) program, one started by Senators Dan Quayle and Ted Kennedy. It was a low-profile but important post which oversaw the Governor's Summer Youth program, which employed summer students. More importantly for the state, it provided federal funds to "retrain tens of thousands of people, including a lot of unemployed coal miners," Reger recalled.[12] "We were able to help low-income people get re-education and training for new work. Sometimes new technology would come into a plant and we could pay up to 50 percent of their salaries for on-the-job training." It was a critical program in a state where the economy was only slowly recovering from the severe recession it had suffered during Rockefeller's second term, and in which underground long-wall mining and use of larger machines on surface mines were dispensing with the need for many mine workers.

"The (JTPA) program was popular among unions," remembered Reger. "The AFL-CIO got a lot of that money for their retraining programs. When the federal funds were cut back [by the Reagan Administration], Joe Powell (state president of the union) came to my office, raising hell about it. Joe was a nice guy, but he was the old union type who would pound on your desk and try to intimidate you. I told him to go talk to the Governor about it, but he wouldn't do that. He didn't want to owe him anything."

Some of the JTPA money had gone to Mingo County's Economic Opportunity Council. Two of the operatives in that organization found a way to funnel the federal funds out to their own use; they had been forced to resign as part of the federal-state corruption investigation. Carl L. Bradford of Nitro, who had served as Moore's star director of Federal-State Relations in their first two administrations, was summoned by the Governor into service again. He would be put in charge of the program in that county. Bradford, a stout, old-school, slightly pompous man, agreed to do it, but on two conditions. He told the Governor, "I refuse to live down there [in Mingo County]. I'll commute back and forth. And I won't swim in their [expletive] pool!" (Williamson Mayor Sam Kapourales had recently caused a statewide controversy by closing a swimming pool because an HIV-positive man had been in it—at that point no one was sure how AIDS was transmitted.)

The Governor ran into Reger the next day on the capitol grounds. "Did you talk to Carl Bradford?" When Jake assured him he had, and that everything was good to go, the Governor parted with a smile, "He's not going to swim in their [expletive] pool!"

The JTPA program under Moore was scandal-free and provided millions of dollars to West Virginians who desperately needed the help. It undoubtedly prevented many families from having to leave for out-of-state jobs. It was a great success. "We were recognized for having the best job training program in the nation by the National Alliance of Businesses," recalled Reger, proudly.

AS RESULT OF THE 1973 oil crises, President Nixon had taken several measures to reduce American dependence on Middle Eastern oil. One of those had been a requirement that all states reduce their speed limits to 55 miles an hour, or lose federal highway funds. Since motorists had become used to their new Interstate highways and speeds of 70 to 90 in many cases, adapting to the lower speed felt like a slo-o-o-w crawl, a waste of time; plus, there was a question as to how much energy it really saved. It was never popular and many states reduced penalties for speeds less than 70 or police ignored violations altogether.

Ronald Reagan, who had been a two term governor of California and a strong believer in states' rights, never liked the "Drive 55" restriction. The slower speed was particularly unpopular in Western states; Montana would eventually have no speed limit on some of its long, straight, lightly traveled highways. He wrote to Moore and other governors on August 15, 1986, "For some time, I have believed that the 1973 total preemption of state control over highway speeds is no longer justified. [Nixon's speed limit] was a clear departure from the principles of federalism. Now, in view of changed conditions, I am prepared to support any reasonable relaxation of the current absolute rule, that is consistent with the need for public safety." The President continued, "I have the greatest confidence in the ability of the states to exercise this responsibility ...With Congress's cooperation, we will soon take a step toward a healthier balance between the two levels of our federal system."

Governor Moore responded to President Reagan on August 20: "I share your thoughts on this matter ... I am pleased to know of your active endorsement of this issue..."

Soon the Governor would return West Virginia's Interstate highway speed limit to 70, a move that was widely welcomed and which ceased making criminals out of tens of thousands of motorists. Interestingly, few seemed to exceed the 70 limit by much, as had been common pre-1973; new, slower driving habits had been formed. Neighboring Ohio and Pennsylvania, controlled by Democrats, balked at the change however, but eventually raised theirs to 65. (Governor Cecil Underwood would raise the speed to 70 miles per hour on portions of the West Virginia Turnpike, in the 1990s.)

DURING THE WEEK of the Charleston Sternwheel Regatta in late August, 1986, Raamie Barker, the Governor's speech writer, phoned your author, then deputy finance commissioner. "We have a member of the British House of Commons coming to visit the southern West Virginia coalfields," he said. "You want to join me in showing him around?"

"I have a full day," I replied. "It would be tough to clear everything." Barker proceeded to explain that the MP was a young, up-and-coming member of the (then minority) Labour Party and that the U.S. State Department predicted that his party was "grooming him to become the next prime minister." No one else in the Moore Administration wanted to waste a day on such a seemingly minor figure, although the Governor was going to greet him and his family for a few minutes.

"Sure, I'll do it," I relented, being a fan of British history and especially Winston Churchill. "What's his name?" Raamie looked at his letter, "Uh ... Anthony Blair."

The next morning we picked up a cheap, small, state motor pool Plymouth K-car and met him at the Charleston House Holiday Inn. "I thought that crowd of people [on Kanawha Boulevard for the Regatta, in front of his motel the night before] was here to see me," Blair joked, as we thought, "Yeah, right!" (He was completely unknown in the U.S. at the time, and a very insignificant member of the opposition party even in Britain.)

Tony, as he asked us to call him, had been over to the Charleston Department Store as soon as he got into town, to buy himself a couple pair of American Levi's. He introduced his wife, Cherie Booth (also a barrister, he explained), their nanny and infant son, who was in an expensive-looking pram. We made arrangements to get them to the West Logan Motor Lodge for their next night and headed south on Rt. 119, then not yet fully a four-lane highway.

And then Barker and I had the future prime minister and co-leader of the Free World to ourselves for the rest of the day, discussing British politics (surprising to us, he wasn't opposed to what Margaret Thatcher had done to privatize the economy), American-British relations, the power of the monarchy, and all manner of other interesting subjects, as we buzzed around in the cramped and crude state car, between his visits to UMWA leaders in Davy and other towns. Blair seemed fascinated by it all, no matter how grimy and depressed the coal town, pelting all he met with questions.

Nice fellow, we thought, very bright and engaging, but not leadership material. He had long, curly hair at the time, and seemed just too common, candid, ordinary and unpolished to reach such heights. We ended the long day with charcoaled steaks at state Sen. Earl Ray and Joanne Tomblin's secluded country home. Blair and Tomblin discovered that their districts, or "constituencies," as Tony called it, were about the same size. The future senate president kept the future prime minister in cold American beer and lively political conversation until nearly 2 a.m.

NINETEEN NINETY SIX was also a year of confrontation with the judiciary, specifically one Larry Starcher, then a feisty circuit judge in Monongalia County who had been a Legal Aid lawyer. During the Rockefeller era, the activist supreme court had required the jails to be emptied of drunks and the mental hospitals of patients who could not be proven to be dangerous. The rulings had cost taxpayers millions, as police had to transport the publicly intoxicated to mental hospitals. Many of the mentally ill now roamed the streets, carrying their meager belongings and slept under bridges, exhausting their social security disability checks early each month. Few could argue that the liberal "reforms" had been good for the victims, much less for society.

Starcher had been lowering sentences for Monongalia County convicts who were being sent to Huttonsville for violent crimes. He continued the "reforms" by ordering fifty-six Huttonsville Correctional Center inmates freed to alleviate overcrowding. Moore resisted the order, refusing to allow compliance by the Dept. of Corrections, contending that he feared for public safety if those inmates were released. He told the press, "It's a no-win position we are put into because of the judiciary's desire to invade the prerogatives of the executive branch. I don't intend to tolerate that."[13] Editorials, such as a September 24 one in the Elkins *Inter-Mountain,* denounced Starcher's actions, calling him "Let 'em Loose Larry," and an "ultra-liberal."

An inmate had complained to Starcher that he had missed a meal when he showed up late in the prison's mess hall. The judge replied, "I am not going to take this stuff. It is an insensitive son of a bitch in blue uniforms that tells them they can't eat ... And [the prison guards] ought to be fired!" Warden C. M. White responded, "With 466 people [at Huttonsville], if everyone had that attitude, we'd never get them fed."

Hyperbole abounded. William Byrne, attorney for the inmates and a Starcher favorite, told the judge, "These people have taken the constitution and thrown it in the trash!" Senate Majority Leader Si Boettner of Kanawha County screamed that Moore had a "tremendous ego problem." He complained, "It's typical of Arch Moore to turn something like this into a crisis." Del. Bill Wooten of Raleigh County contended that the state was on the verge of a constitutional crisis, which reminded him of President Andrew Jackson's defiance of the U.S. Supreme Court's order ("Now, let the court enforce it!" Old Hickory supposedly said.) Starcher threatened to find the State's sovereign in contempt of his court and eventually the order was followed. Seven of the fifty-six convicts who were released soon thereafter returned to jail, after committing more felonies.

Another unwelcome court case greeted the Moore Administration in 1986. Energy Commissioner Ken Faerber had been a lightning rod for the UMWA and environmentalists, which had contended that he had been lax in regulating the coal industry. Their accusations were not entirely unfounded; Moore's stated goal from the outset had been to make it easier and cheaper to mine coal in West Virginia, in order to restore jobs and his administration had been far more coal-friendly than Rockefeller's. Next to Moore himself, Faerber had been the *Charleston Gazette's* favorite target for constant criticism. On March 31, Kanawha County Prosecutor Charles King obtained an indictment of Faerber for donating an extra $2000 to Moore's campaign through his children, then six and eight years old. He was later acquitted, but Faerber's friend, Kevin Sikora, speculated that the stress from the ordeal was what caused his premature death from cancer.

A REVIEW OF some of the correspondence Moore received as governor[14] revealed that West Virginians wrote to him about a wide array of subjects. Typical were requests for help in getting workers' compensation benefits; welfare problems or Medicaid payments. They reported bridge and roads problems, trash along highways, damage from nearby mining operations, animal trapping, jobs. Some asked for help with visas, appointments to state and federal jobs, to academies, motor vehicles problems and social security. They reported wedding anniversaries, local political controversies, college and university matters. They sought donations for personal and public causes.

In a letter to Ted Fike of June 10, 1985, Moore had addressed an increasingly contentious subject, abortion. "As a father and a grandfather," he wrote to Fike, "I am also opposed to abortion and do not believe that state funds should be expended for abortion, except where necessary to save the mother or when pregnancy is the result of rape or incest." His sentiments closely matched the average West Virginian's at the time.

His was an efficient letter response program, undoubtedly honed during his twelve years in congress. Very few public officeholders reply to everyone who writes to him, but Arch did it, year after year. But, even in a state of only 1.8 million population, there simply were not enough hours in the day to dictate a personal response to each one; he had other duties. So a typical constituent letter was forwarded by his staff to the appropriate state employee or department where a memo to the governor was prepared for the answer or, if he trusted the employee, a response letter was prepared for his signature. And Arch did sign each and every one of them, often adding a personalized handwritten note and scratching out the salutation, to ink in a nickname. Additionally, he complied with requests for thousands of autographed photos, usually adding a personal note with gold ink. To some more honored recipients, he would offer trinkets like gubernatorial matches, coins, letter openers, cufflinks or playing cards, just as the White House does. One problem with Arch's personal touch with regard to correspondence was that, when he met a recipient out in the county of his or her residence, they expected him to remember details of its content, which was not always possible, even with his exceptional information retention ability.

THE VOTERS continued to demonstrate in November of 1986 that they were in a cranky, anti-tax mood. Although they approved a constitutional amendment repeating the federal, Second Amendment right to bear arms (by an 83.6% margin), they defeated the Better School Buildings Amendment by 52.2 to 47.8 percent, and the Highway and Bridge Improvement Amendment by 61.1 to 38.9 percent. A Warehouse Freeport Tax Exemption Amendment, which would mainly help Huntington, was passed by 57.6 percent of the voters. The defeat of the roads amendment, which would have given bond authority similar to that enjoyed by Arch Moore in his first two terms, was particularly disappointing. He and members of his administration had campaigned hard for it, calling it "one of the most important issues ever to come before the voters."

His party picked up four seats in the state senate in 1986, for a grand total of seven. The Republicans lost six seats in the House, however, down from twenty seven to twenty one delegates.

As difficult and contentious as the last two years had been, the "easy" half of Moore's third term was complete. Now the "fun" part began.

Chapter 26 Notes

1. - *The New York Times,* Jan. 4, 1986.

2. - The restoration foundation was created and overseen by your author. The project was an expensive one; West Virginia's dome is 293 feet high, five feet larger than the U.S. Capitol's dome. Another renovation project started in 2004 cost more than $5 million.

3. - The gilding failed in one spot, possibly because it had been applied during bad weather, causing an ugly, black streak. The work was guaranteed for ten years, but the streak on the backside appeared soon after the job was completed, and after Moore had been voted out of office. The

Caperton Administration did not require Tsilianios to return to repair it, for some unknown reason. "Caperton let [the gold dome] go to hell in a handbasket," Moore complained, in 2005.

4. - Richard Neely, who dissented in *Recht*, said he thought the supreme court overreached in interpreting the state constitution's "thorough and efficient education" clause to require "spending more money." Neely thought, "At the end of the day, it didn't make students any better off. The court could have just as easily used the 'thorough and efficient clause' to fire some bad teachers." The court was improperly activist, acting as a super legislature in rendering the decision, he believed.

5. - "Ed Burdette had been in the Welfare Department (later Human Services) all his career, started out in McDowell County. He was probably a Democrat. But Ed was an example of how Arch Moore operated," noted Tinder. "Ed was talented and he progressed [in state government under Moore] because of his expertise and talent. Governor Moore didn't care about political affiliation, it was a minor consideration. In the operation of government, if you had a good idea, or criticism, it wasn't filtered through who you were, who your father was, where you were from, or whether you had a "D" or an "R" after your name."

6. - *Rogers v. Hechler*, 348 S.E. 2d 299 (W.Va. 1986). Rogers had opposed Rockefeller in two Democratic primaries, as a protest to and memorial of the 1914 massacre of coal miners at a Rockefeller-owned mine in Ludlow, Colorado. He received only a small percentage of the vote ("what Richard Neely calls the 'up yours vote,'" Rogers laughed) against Jay and says he resisted the strong urge to punch Rockefeller in the face ("he'd lived a protected life and probably never tangled with anybody") as he'd done to a news reporter.

7. - Farley, a Parkersburg insurance agent, may have feared what Arch's remarks would do to him back in Republican-leaning Wood County. Such fears would not have been unfounded–Speaker Albright would be unseated by Wood County voters in November, 1986.

8. - *The New York Times* and Associated Press, Dec. 14, 1986.

9. - *The New York Times*, May 3, 1986.

10. - The Manchin family helped facilitate the Fairmont project.

11. - Wire stories would quote Russell, an assistant state attorney general, as saying a "possible aim was 'obstructing justice' and discrediting a special grand jury charged with investigating alleged election violations in Mingo County."

12. - At the time of this writing, Reger is serving as Upshur County prosecuting attorney, previously having directed the Fraud Unit of the Workers' Compensation Commission under Governor Underwood.

13. - *Gazette*, August 30, 1986

14. - Housed at the WVU Library in The Moore Collection.

Chapter Twenty Seven
"They Decided to Starve Him Out of Office"

Had the legislature cooperated, 1987 was to have been the "Year of Education." In January, Moore introduced legislation providing for sale of $75 million in school bonds, which he contended was permitted by the 1972 amendment.[1] He wanted a ten percent pay raise for public teachers to "make us competitive with our sister states." He sought approval for ten Lighthouse Schools "in which the state board of education will implement a broad range of programs exemplifying excellence in education." For teachers and staff at colleges and universities, he requested fifty percent pay raises, noting that the state was fifteenth out of fifteen in every statistic published by the Southern Regional Education Board. He asked for $45 million for physical plant improvements on those campuses. Another $1.5 million was requested for new vocational schools and the School for the Deaf and Blind.

But the Democratic leadership responded with a flat "No!" to almost all of what the Governor wanted. They contended that there simply wasn't money to do any of it and also disagreed that additional bond authority was available from the 1972 amendment. Morever, it was getting too near re-election time; the Year of Education could await a Democratic successor, in their view.

The joint venture between Moore and the Democratic legislature, such as it was, was suffering from partisan bickering; the relationship was in rapid decline. To a Bluefield State College convocation he complained, "We have worked hard, we've been innovative, and we've turned this state of ours around, and we've done it while having to move through a legislative mine-field that has, as it purpose, nothing constructive but seeks merely to inhibit our economic growth.

"This explosive field has been laid with the intention of punishing the Governor. Unfortunately, this mine field has exploded in the faces of the very people they are supposed to represent, and harmed those things which build a strong foundation for economic development–education and in this case, higher education; improvements in our roads; development of a cleaner and safer environment while not destroying industry; and peace of mind for thousands of state employees."

He also turned his anger on another favorite target, the members of an increasingly hostile press: "As a minority party governor, it is hard enough to face 72-to-22 odds in one house and 30-to-four odds in the other, but I have found there are members of the news media who feel more comfortable exercising their ability to generate heat than they are in their professional obligation to generate light."[2]

Arch showed similar frustration in a Wheeling speech in March of 1987, using his classic sarcasm and humor to make his point.

> I must admit I've taken some risk, because I've left the legislature all alone down in Charleston. Every time I do that I come back to find they've been into some new mischief. Sometimes I feel like the parent who comes home ... the cookie jar is broken...the cookies are gone ... but no one knows who did it!
>
> Are you aware there are three major parties in the West Virginia legislature? The Republican party, the Democratic party...and the cocktail party. The results of this year's session at times suggest that the third party was in control. Those guys were so removed from reality that if the Lord were governor, and a member of my party would have introduced the Ten Commandments, I am convinced our legislature, at best, would have passed only two. More likely, they'd all still be in committee.
>
> [This] administration is not going to let the legislature, or anyone else, stop us. You can steer a car if it is moving...but it is difficult to steer if it's sitting still. My administration got the car moving and we're not going to let the engine die now...our vehicle, the State of West Virginia, is going to pick up speed.

In that speech, he saluted the move of Wheeling-Pittsburgh Steel to Wheeling from Pittsburgh, bringing with it 350 jobs and a $6.5 million payroll. And he welcomed the partnership between the company and Nisshin Steel of Japan, which would create 300 jobs at a new $65 million steel coating facility in Follansbee. He also mentioned his administration's involvement in getting Eastern Associated Coal Corporation to relocate to Charleston; the AT&T regional credit management facility coming to the capital; a $5 million Variform plastics plant for Parkersburg; a $20 million modernization and expansion of the Borg-Warner Chemicals Woodmar plant; a Goodyear expansion in Point Pleasant, and Baker International's expansion in Fairmont, Bluefield and Beckley. "West Virginia is on the move! Just look at our record!" Arch shouted, with the enthusiasm of the cheerleader that he was, "At this minute, we are working with sixty companies that are seriously considering our state for job investment possibilities." One billion dollars of new economic activity had occurred in West Virginia during 1986, he claimed, more in one year than the state had enjoyed in the past six years.

At a luncheon speech in the Bellview section of Fairmont, Moore touted new C& P Telephone operating centers in Fairmont and Parkersburg that would add 150 jobs, saluted the company for relocating its directory distribution center to Martinsburg, and thanked them for their $2.1 million partnership with WVU and Siemens Switching System. He noted that an EIMCO plant in Pleasant Valley, another Marion County community, would add 194 new jobs for a total workforce of 367. Moulded Acoustical Products would soon break ground, he told the audience, with a projected workforce of 300. Marion, Harrison and Monongalia Counties would get road and bridge projects totaling $15.7 million that year.

But the problems would still outweigh the successes, however. Shorting the source of state revenues was causing serious problems.

Congressman Bob Wise told *The New York Times*, "What we've had in the last year is cat and dog government—everybody's fighting like cats and dogs instead of pushing together." House Speaker "Chuck" Chambers admitted, "We have an economy that is not that strong in the best of times, and we in state government have made it worse."[3] The article noted that, because of a $65 million revenue shortage, Moore had to slash spending, leading the Board of Regents to close state colleges for a week and cancel summer school sessions. The Governor and the legislature had "fought over a number of proposals to close the budget gap," the story said, including "raising the sales tax on food ... selling the state-owned liquor stores and wooing companies to dispose of nuclear waste and East Coast garbage." Part of the state budget crisis had been caused by a twelve dollar-per ton drop in coal prices in 1986, the paper reported, because many factories had switched back to oil. And, even though the state was mining more coal than ever, it was being done with less miners because of automation, dropping from 64,100 miners in 1976 to 34,300.

One of the worst disasters Moore inherited from the "Rockefailure Years," as a WVU political science professor called them, was the $259 million debt the state owed the federal government for unemployment benefits. The interest being charged raised the debt to $375 million. With the

West Virginia unemployment rate under Jay's second term as high as twenty percent, the state had paid out hundreds of millions more in benefits than it had collected from employers. Rockefeller had essentially ignored the crisis as it grew, leaving the crisis to his successor, whoever that would be. Under Jay's watch, West Virginia's unemployment fund had become insolvent, bankrupt. The interest alone, at a high rate set by the feds, was crushing. "The federal government came to me within days of taking office and told me, 'You're to the point where you can't issue any more unemployment checks,'" Moore said, recalling his shock that the crisis was huge and so imminent.

"I called in [union leader] Joe Powell, early in my third term," remembered Arch, "and told him, 'They left me $375 million in the hole, and I want a nickel out of [employers] and a nickel out of employees [a five percent tax] to pay it off.' He went upstairs [to the legislature] and arranged that for me. He was a first class labor leader!"

In June of 1987, Moore decided to borrow the money at lower interest (from 9.75 to 5.75 percent, an excellent rate at the time), and pay the debt off much quicker and far less expensively than had been expected. The refinancing was expected to save at least $30 million interest a year to taxpayers. In a move which he believed to be necessary but, again, won him no popularity contests, the Governor, with the Legislature's approval, levied a special tax on all wage earners beginning in 1987. The last payment on the debt to the feds was made by the end of 1991, and the state saved tens of millions of dollars through Moore's plan. Although hailed as a great financial success, and even though he had not caused the crisis, Arch took heat from taxpayers. The additional, albeit temporary, income tax added to the malaise, the general discontent of voters concerning state finances.

But he kept trying to let the public know that there was good news, that the economy truly was recovering. The Governor announced to the Weirton Rotary in July that the statewide unemployment rate had dropped to 7.7 percent, an amazing reduction from the 17.2 percent he'd inherited in January 1985 from Rockefeller. (The federal way of calculating the rate showed a drop to 9.1 percent.) Said Moore, "Many people in this country do not realize that we in West Virginia experienced a bona fide economic Depression during the early 1980s. We are still recovering from that tremendous economic shock." Arch praised the legislature for approving his Economic Development Act in 1985, which gave the state "the tools needed to compete with our sister states for jobs." By October, he was able to announce to an AFL-CIO convention that unemployment had dropped to 6.6, "the best record of improvement of all the fifty states." Over 30,000 jobs had been added since he took office, he told the union members, and there had been $1.024 billion invested in industry and development during his two years in office.

He told another group that, in 1987, the state had produced more than 135 million tons of coal, the highest production level in seventeen years. Productivity in the mines had increased 14 percent in the past two years, giving more tonnage per man working, yet fatalities in the mines were at the lowest level in state history. He attributed some of coal's comeback to the fact that he had established the Department of Energy which reduced from 210 days to 80 the average time it took to obtain a mining permit. Locks being built at Gallipolis and Winfield were providing jobs and would make river transportation of coal easier, he added.

But despite all this good news, it was generally being ignored by the public. There was general apathy, even disbelief in what Arch was telling them. Part of that was due to the public relations success of his adversaries. Having grown accustomed to running the show under Rockefeller's eight years, the Democratic legislative leadership continued their constant drum beat of opposition to Moore, on almost every topic, and the state news media jumped onto it, reporting their version instead of the Governor's. Senate President Dan Tonkovich, House Finance Chairman George Farley and others in the opposition's leadership were just beginning to crank up for the next election cycle, when they hoped to rid themselves of this pest Arch Moore.

In the 1987 session of the legislature, the leadership decided they had waited long enough for the B&O tax elimination and that it would become final on July 1, as they had agreed in their 1985 compromise with the Governor; they were eager to get it done. They didn't care that Moore was still warning them that it would cause a catastrophe, that it would compound the shortfall problems that were already appearing.

"All hell broke loose," Mike Caryl recalled, because "Governor Moore presented a budget that assumed the B&O tax would still be in place. [The tax department's] two years of data collection showed that eliminating the tax would cause the state to be about $60 to $100 million short." Moore could not conceive that the legislature would be that reckless. Surely they wouldn't do that to the state, simply for political advantage, he thought. Arch had gambled that they would be more responsible than that, but he was mistaken. Political gamesmanship won out, over the public's interest.

"The legislature did no tax modeling to determine what the elimination of the B&O tax was going to do," said Audrey Toler, who would serve in the Tax Department in subsequent administrations. "They had no clue what it was going to do to our tax base." She thought, too, that "the majority party was determined that our administration would not have the necessary resources to improve the lives of our citizens."

Larry Swann, then the House minority leader, agreed. "They [the Democratic legislative leadership] decided to starve him out of office. I asked George Farley, 'Why don't we make some minor tax increases to give the government enough money?' He told me, 'No, we're going to wait and give that to a Democratic governor.' And that's what they did. The Democrats wanted [Arch Moore] to take a hit."

When the Tax Department announced the reports, noting that eliminating the B&O would cause a budget crisis, Farley summoned Caryl and his researchers to his office and challenged the legitimacy of their studies. "He really read us the riot act. They thought we were trying to low-ball it to force the legislature to raise taxes or to spend more money on projects. But this was not some Arch Moore manipulation," insisted Caryl. The Governor was providing the Democrats with the reality of the situation, but they were unwilling to accept it. "The head of research for the tax department had very specific, objective reports showing it would cause a deficit [to replace the B&O tax with other, lesser taxes]. But they let the changes become law and we then had to scramble to find replacement revenues."[4]

The full effects of the cash flow problems brought on by the B&O tax elimination and the investment tax credits (the "Super Tax Credit")[5] began to be felt by the average West Virginian in 1987 through most of 1988. Moore imposed spending cuts by all departments (although a circuit judge ruled that education could not be reduced!) but could do little else. Even those cuts did not bring immediate relief to the cash flow problem. There were few options to keep the state budget from collapsing completely; if it had been a business it would have been near the point of filing for bankruptcy protection. "It's hard to spend what you don't have," noted McCuskey, dryly.

One desperate tactic was to delay, delay, delay as long as possible the payment of vendors doing business with the state. Large companies could tolerate it and they didn't want to abandon a customer as important and huge as the State, even if its bill-paying was delinquent. But smaller, mom-and-pop businesses (for example, family-owned pharmacies that depended heavily on Medicaid to keep them afloat) could not. Hospitals and other health care providers also were heavily dependant upon a steady flow of state payments to keep afloat themselves. "I don't know of anyone who went out of business because of it, but it was tough not getting paid on time," recalled Williamson Mayor Sam Kapourales, who owned a pharmacy there. Moore's own personal physician, Dr. William Harris, had to take out an $80,000 loan to keep his office open, because he wasn't getting his Medicaid bills paid on a timely basis, and his situation was probably common.

Calls would pour into F&A and other state agencies from irate business people, "I sent that invoice four months ago! When are we going to get paid?" Threats were made to terminate provision of goods and services to state agencies. Sour feelings were generated against the Moore Administration, from thousands who had previously supported him. If it bothered Arch, he kept his feelings well-hidden. He was doing what he had to do, given the predicament the Democratic legislature had created for him.

"That we maintained services and never laid anybody off, was amazing," noted Audrey Toler. "All of our resources had gone to flood relief; money was scarce even before the B&O tax was taken off." She added, "However, services were not curtailed. We simply did more on less." She recalled that the administration distributed "a news advisory every day on the cash balance of the state."

Sometimes, though, Moore would try to smooth feathers by promising what he could not deliver. "There was one place where he landed in a big field, surrounded by a crowd," recalled Oce Smith. "He presented a huge check for industrial development or tourism or whatever. A couple days later, when the man went to put in into their account, the check bounced all the way to Pittsburgh.

"In a helicopter appearance, the Governor off-handedly remarked that just before arrival, he had caused to be cut a nice check to pay a part of the Medicaid arrearage which the state owed a local hospital," Smith continued. "Of course, there was much cheering, clapping and jumping up and down. When someone asked him how much the check was for, he remarked, 'Substantial, substantial!' But when the check arrived it was so little it wouldn't have paid the light bill one month."

"It is quite easy to run a government, to manipulate, to trade, to offer favors and get great projects done when the money is flowing into the pump like water. However, when there is practically no money at all coming in, all the manipulating, the favors, the great projects, are dead, unless you're a helluva liar. And if you try that very often, the disobedience to the commandment will come back to haunt you very, very soon," Smith opined, presenting the Democrats' point of view to the impasse: "It was his unadulterated pride in not admitting that we were dead broke and on the brink of disaster. His pride, evidently, was too great to allow him to admit that we were in real trouble."

Surprisingly, Senator Jay Rockefeller commiserated with Governor Moore, perhaps because his last four years as governor had been so disastrous. "He's doing what has to be done," he generously stated to a Beckley paper. "I know exactly what Arch is going through."[6] So Arch's hopes, of being the "education governor" again as he had been in his first two terms, were dead on arrival. "It had education screaming," remembered McCuskey. "It gave opportunity for all the anti-Arch Moore people to say he was ruining education." Keeping enough money in pension programs or starting any new programs or building was out of the question. Moore was just trying to avoid insolvency—it was all he could do to meet payroll and keep the lights on. Anyone who had been unemployed for a period of time might sympathize with his situation.

But worst part of it, from Moore's own political, popularity standpoint, was the necessity of holding up thousands of income tax refunds. During two tax seasons refund checks were delayed, causing thousands of taxpayers to be mad as hornets. The government, which would penalize them heavily if they were late in paying taxes, was now holding up the refund of their money, without penalty, to avoid going broke. In effect, the state was giving itself an unauthorized loan. To add to the public relations disaster for Moore, it was widely publicized that Deputy Tax Commissioner John Leaberry got the Governor's tax refund expedited!

"The Governor always told me, whenever it affects someone's pocketbook, they're going to vote for a change," recalled Audrey Toler, explaining that the Moore inner circle knew that the political fallout was heavy.

"The tax department was the lightning rod for those calls," former Commissioner Caryl remembered. "Pam Steelhammer was director of Taxpayers Services and had to respond to those calls." The refund checks had been cut, but were being held up by F&A, the Auditor or the Treasurer's offices, because funds to cover their payment were not yet available, due to the budget crisis caused by the B&O tax elimination–if mail on time, the checks would have bounced. "But we took the heat for it," Caryl remembered.

Oce Smith recalled it being an unsettling time to be working in state government. "The Exxon people had picked up our credit cards. We in the legislative system were being told, when we received our [pay] checks, either to rush down to the bank to cash them immediately or wait two or three days until there was enough money in the account to cover them. It was scary." A *New York Times* story reported that the state was having difficulty meeting payroll on a timely basis for the 40,000 state employers some weeks, because "tax collections ... were $23.8 million behind estimates." The legislature refused Moore's request to allow him to borrow $100 million or even $50 million from the state investment pool, the paper noted.[7]

"There were few relief valves left," reiterated McCuskey, so even though thousands of voters were outraged by the delay, holding up the tax refunds was selected as a way to keep cash in the pipes and state employees paid. Although Arch Moore had by no means created this mess, he was getting the blame, and his political opponents smelled blood. Most harmful to his hopes of re-election or preserving his legacy, the average West Virginian did not understand the root cause of the budget crisis and really didn't care. He or she understandably just wanted his bill paid, or her tax refund in her mailbox. In his mind, that guy at the top—Governor Arch A. Moore, Jr.—was the reason for the delay, not his local senator or delegate. And the legislator quickly came to realize that, much to his glee. Herbert Hoover had noted that a chief executive gets credit for the sunshine and blame for the rain. Harry Truman had a plaque on his desk, "The buck stops here." That's the way it was for Moore in 1987 and 1988–he got the full blame for a mess he had tried to avoid and had warned would happen.

The lack of prompt tax refunds also hurt the economy, because that is generally money spent on items not normally purchased other times of the year, for appliances, furniture, even down payments on vehicles. Retailers love tax refund time. "I found out that most Southern West Virginians went to Myrtle Beach for vacations," Mike Caryl (a Martinsburg native) added. "Often they'd use their tax refunds to go down there. Someone said, 'If these tax refunds don't go out, there's going to be a depression in Myrtle Beach!'"

The Administration was sued by the school system for late payments. "That didn't help us any," noted Caryl. "It was a political disaster."

The Democratic leadership continued to snicker about Arch's dilemma. While it may or may not have been the intended result, it was an added bonus, as far as they were concerned. They had the Governor exactly where they wanted him. He was trapped in their net, struggling, squirming, unable to help free himself, and it was fun for them to watch their prey. None in the Democratic leadership lifted a finger to suggest remedying the situation by adjusting the tax system. None was responsible enough to suggest a special session (or deal with it in a regular session) to raise sufficient taxes to get the cash flow back on track. As long as the public was blaming Moore—which they were—the Democrats felt safe, even smug and gratified. "The Legislature had beaten him. There was nothing he could do about it," conceded John McCuskey. Moore finally instructed John to cease appearing for the monthly Joint Finance Committee meetings; there was nothing good for the finance commissioner to report with regard to revenues and the Democrats just used each occasion to berate McCuskey and his boss, continuing to shift the blame and the capitol reporters lapped it all up.

Said Caryl, "Farley was the [Democrats'] point man to bring down Arch Moore. It became 'us against them, circle the wagons.' They did it for purely political reasons." Echoing what Swann had been told, Caryl said, "Some of the Democrats in the legislature who were not in leadership told me privately, 'They're on a mission to bring Arch Moore down.'"

The Governor would defiantly boast, "I can run it on a dollar!" But that was whistling past the grave yard; state government desperately needed an infusion of cash. "He was a bridge player," noted McCuskey. "Arch Moore could see down the road and see what was coming, as early as 1986. You can finesse and bluff, but he took the cards dealt to him and made the best of it. He just tried to do the best he could do with what they gave him. The weed that was sown by George Farley in 1986 didn't fully blossom until near election time, which may be exactly what [the Democrat legislative leadership] planned."

Arch's successor, Gaston Caperton, within weeks of taking office in 1989, would impose the largest tax increase in state history and the state's cash flow problem quickly ended. (Caperton and his fellow Democrats in the legislature would add $900 million in extra tax burden to the second poorest state in the union, raising spending from $1.5 billion to $2.4 billion per year: "Too much of an increase, I thought," said Caryl. Caperton also got the legislature to set up a "rainy day fund," to make sure tax refunds were promptly paid under his tenure. His tax increase would be accompanied by an eventual 50-plus percent increase in workers' compensation premiums. But neither massive increase resulted in any apparent backlash from the electorate.)

So why didn't Moore do the same, when given the chance? Why did Governor Moore not bite the bullet, admit the state was in a severe budgetary crisis, quit pretending otherwise, and call the Legislature into special session for a tax bill? It was a question his supporters asked then and later.

"The Democrats were praying that would happen," was McCuskey's response to that question. "They'd stick it up his ass! He would have been done!" (Of course, he was eventually done in by failure to act, McCuskey conceded.) "Plus, it was the Reagan era of tax cuts and smaller government," so it was not a logical thing for a Republican governor to do, call for tax increases, he added.

Audrey Toler believed, in retrospect, that sufficient overtures had been made by the Moore Administration for increasing taxes to resolve the cash flow problems. "Bill Ritchie asked for a five cent tax on gasoline four years in a row," she pointed out, but the Democratic legislature "declined it, they wouldn't give it to him. Then, when Caperton came into office [in January 1989], he got it within weeks." She added, "Everything the Governor would propose for additional revenue, they would shoot down. It was the people of West Virginia who suffered, but they didn't care. We heard that what came out of the Democratic caucus was, 'We're not going to give the little gray-haired man [Moore] anything.'"[8]

House Speaker Chambers admitted to *The New York Times* that the legislature wasn't going to take the lead in resolving the cash flow crisis. The Governor was saying "it's all up to us to cut spending or raise taxes, and that's unacceptable," Chambers told the paper. "If we're going to have to eat some crow about our tax code, he's going to have to eat some about how he had run this state budget-wise."[9] The article explained that Governor Moore had warned the Democratic legislature that the $1.49 billion budget would have a $26 million deficit, because of revenue shortfalls and that the tax changes the legislature had made "taxed some businesses too much and others not enough, bringing the shortage."

Undoubtedly, Moore also remembered times in which the economy had caught up with such crises and the problems resolved themselves. Business and revenue go in cycles, sometimes with little rhyme or reason. And the state's economy was recovering, fairly quickly. Perhaps such good luck would strike once more and he would come out the hero for holding fast. Possibly he trusted the force of his own personality, his optimism, to turn it around. But Arch, in the protected bubble that even a small state's governor experiences, had become somewhat detached from the average West Virginian by now. It was difficult for him to appreciate the anger, the hostility, the disgust that existed out there, since most people were too respectful to the office to confront him directly.

But mainly it was just the result of Moore's stubbornness–some would say, arrogance. In his view, he just was not going to back down to those skunks who were willing to let the state crash just to make him fail. It had become personal, a staring contest, and he wasn't going to blink first. Unfortunately, he had run out of tricks, he could not come up with a box in which to trap the Democrats this time. "I can run it on a dollar," he kept repeating, until he began to believe it himself.[10] In Moore's view, he never raised taxes in all his years as governor. If there were to be any tax increases, they would have to be generated in the legislature, and the lawmakers weren't budging.[11]

Consequently, the administration became desperate to raise cash, to keep large amounts of dollars flowing so that bills, especially tax refunds, could be paid promptly. "We tried to aggressively settle disputed tax cases," said Caryl. "In 1986, the legislature enacted a law to govern how to settle (litigated) taxes. A lot of the cases involved disputed B&O taxes from out-of-state corporations.

"Because the Tax Department had a risk of losing those, and the delay was costing us money–Treasurer Manchin's office was supposedly getting an 18 percent return on the State's invested money–we thought it was a good economic deal to settle for eighty cents on the dollar. But the *Gazette* crucified me, said I was giving away that twenty percent![12] The *Gazette* did a Freedom of Information request to the Tax Department, demanding to know whether such a disputed tax case had been settled with CSX for $2.7 million. Because of taxpayer confidentiality laws, Caryl would not release the information to the paper, even after Kanawha County Circuit Judge Andrew McQueen ordered him to give the secret information to them. He appealed and, eventually, during the Caperton Administration, the state supreme court ruled 3-2 to reverse McQueen. It was the first FOIA case the *Gazette* had ever lost.

Another ploy the Tax Department used to raise quick cash was "Operation Thursday," in which retailers who were delinquent in paying state taxes were shut down. "The *Gazette* gave me a smiley face for that one," laughed Caryl. "I framed it and put it next to the scowling face they gave me for not releasing the information about the CSX case."

With all this negative publicity, much of which was too complicated for the average West Virginian to understand, it became impossible to present the Administration's side of the story, to show what really happened–that Arch Moore had been sabotaged by the Democratic opposition.

Moreover, Moore found his administration unable to get any good news past the "censors" in the capitol press corp. The Governor would call news conferences throughout 1987 and 1988, to announce creation of new jobs, plants that were opening due to efforts of his office, new state projects and the like, and not one word would appear in the newspapers or on the airwaves about it the next day. It would be as if no press conference, no announcement, ever took place. There almost appeared to be a conspiracy to make Arch look bad. The press corp, headed by the likes of Andy Gallagher of the Associated Press, Brian Farkas of UPI, television reporter Bob Brunner and writer George Manahan,[13] simply would not report it or, if so, barely mentioning or burying the positive news in a negative story.

If questioned about the "news blackout," the reporters and editors would often shrug it off, contending that Moore exaggerated such announcements. In some cases that was true; he did take credit for economic development prospects which were speculative at best, especially as re-election time drew nearer.[14] But the media representatives also blocked a lot of positive news for the state at a time when hope and optimism was much-needed, presumably because of their own personal feelings about Arch and desire that he not be re-elected.[15]

Whether or not these individuals were being steered and coached by Democratic leaders is unknown, but many newsmen did depend on them for news, socialized with them, and relied on them for jobs when they bailed out of the news business; there easily could have been personal incentive for doing their dirty work. Regardless of the reasons, Moore was not getting a fair shake from those who filtered his message to the people he served, and at a time he needed it most. As Ned Chilton collapsed and died at age 65 on a Washington squash court that year, the editor he had put in place at the *Gazette* continued the caustic, bombastic, sometimes vitriolic and inaccurate attacks against Arch, on an almost daily basis. The paper's gossip columnist, Fanny Seiler, did make an effort to present the truth to her readers, however, and generally gave a balanced view of the state of the state.

The Governor did not conduct any sort of organized effort to get his message out, however. Never comfortable with the media, in the third term he did little or nothing to woo them, except to grant a special interview to a favorite reporter, now and then. He continued his practice, which had begun in his first term, of releasing big news in the morning, rather than afternoon. "I did that so the *Daily Mail* and the electronic media would get the story, instead of the *Gazette*," he admitted after leaving office.

Moore's frustration with reporters was easily observed at press conferences; he would get red in the face and shout and gesture in exasperation, as if he was surrounded by fools. As did Nixon, Arch ultimately viewed them as the enemy, which was a fairly accurate assessment in his case.

Compounding the public relations difficulties was the fact that John Price, Moore's press secretary in the third term, did not have access to, or clout with the Governor as Norm Yost had in the first two terms and it showed. "Often I had to wait all day for access and might not be able to see the Governor until he left the office," recalled Price. "I would walk with him to the Mansion at the end of the day, to receive the OK to move on a [press] release or response. Meanwhile, TV, radio and newspaper deadlines passed and our version of things didn't make it into the news cycle until the following day." It was if Arch simply did not care, almost as if he thought he could do without news media coverage, or it didn't matter to the success of his programs and political future. He forgot that reporters typically just wanted a story, and if a politician makes their day, their job, easier, one is more apt to get favorable publicity. But Arch's attitude toward the news media in the 1980s almost seemed to be, "Ignore them and maybe they'll go away." Price agreed: "The Governor seemed to think of the news media as a nuisance and hindrance. His energies and priorities were focused on economic development." But instead of enlisting the press into his effort, as he might have done, he intentionally or unintentionally alienated them and contributed to their adversarial attitude.

And it wasn't as if the Governor gave Price adequate leeway and let him do some news management on his own. "Everyone who worked for him had to adjust to the fact that he was a micro manager," said Price. "This was especially true when it came to the Press Office. He gave strict orders that no statements or releases could be issued until he had personally approved them." To address the problem, Price would "tape record every public statement the Governor made. Often, when the news media sought comments, I could get something into the current news cycle by providing previous quotes from the Governor that were already in the public domain."

Moore also continued to be obsessed with preventing news leaks. "Often I was not informed of the subject matter until fifteen minutes prior to a news conference," remembered Price. "It would then be my job to prepare a new release for distribution at that news conference." Fortunately, his staff was so strong, he was always able to pull something together, but it was far from being an ideal public relations situation.

A GROUNDBREAKING ceremony of which Governor Moore was proud was for the Mary Babbs Randolph Cancer Center at WVU. The federal government was searching for a site and Moore committed $10 million of state funds as seed money. Arch was pleased that it was named in memory of the late wife of his one-time opponent and former Senator Jennings Randolph, with whom he had a lot in common and remained friendly. Randolph had also been instrumental in funneling money to the project.

Arch also had the privilege, on September 2, 1987, of cutting the ribbon on the West Virginia Turnpike. Begun in 1954 as an expensive, winding two lane, sometimes three lane highway, it had been the site of many terrible crashes and fatalities. After a fourteen year upgrade (which Moore had begun in 1973) to all four- and six-lane, and bypassing the defunct Memorial Tunnel, the 88-mile stretch of road would be much safer, although not trouble-free. The many trucks which traversed the road, now part of I-77, would often take the sharp curves too fast, and overturn. The following year, Moore would designate another road in Southeastern West Virginia, U.S. Route 60, as a Scenic Highway.

IN ONE of the most insightful articles it ever wrote about him, the *Sunday Gazette-Mail* did a third-section cover story on Arch Moore in which its sub-headline called him a left-winger and populist. For that paper, those normally were complimentary terms, but not when it came to their constant target. Their reporter wrote, "Most people have traditionally seen Moore as a pro-business Republican. He's proud that he used tax breaks to help lure corporate giants like AT&T, CSX and Eastern Associated Coal...Environmentalists and coal miners complain that his Department of Energy favors unsafe coal operators and polluting strip miners."

But they quoted former WVU economist William Miernyk as characterizing what Moore had been doing in his third term as "state socialism," and the reporter called it "ideological schizophrenia...a despot, a shrewd politician, a governor carrying a big stick and a man trying somehow to confront economic disaster." (Reluctantly, the writer conceded that unemployment had been cut in half during his three years in office.)

They cited several examples of "this left-wing Moore...a new creature that was not sighted during Moore's previous administration." Exhibit One was how he treated the half-billion dollar Newell Company, which was closing the Anchor Hocking plant, causing 940 Harrison County jobs to be lost. They noted how Arch initially had offered to return $2.5 million in checks from Newell, but when that didn't stop them from closing the factory, then sued them for $614 million because they'd received a low-interest loan from the State, which Moore suggested obligated them to stay in West Virginia for twenty years.

Another "left wing project," continued the November 8, 1987, article, was Moore's plan to offer physicians state-sponsored medical malpractice insurance when out-of-state insurance companies threatened to leave the state (interestingly, the paper was not in opposition to such a program when Governor Bob Wise and the Democratic legislature put it into action fifteen years later). Another "radical move" was Moore's proposal for State-owned electric power plants–to build and operate four coal-fired generating units—which the writer admitted was reminiscent of Franklin Roosevelt's Tennessee Valley Authority project. He also acknowledged that Moore got approval for the Public Energy Authority and that "Appalachian Power Co., which initially fought the proposal, [had] dropped its opposition."

Most offensive to the business community, writer Bob Geiger opined, was an incident in 1985, in which Governor Moore replaced two of the three Employment Security Board of Review members, reversed their denial of benefits to striking Wheeling-Pittsburgh Steel employees, and personally handed unemployment checks to the workers, who claimed they had been locked out. They quoted a Wheeling-Pitt lawyer who said Moore's move "violated every known concept of due process."

H. John Rogers, on the left end of the spectrum himself, would refer to the Governor as "The Great Helmsman" and "Chairman Mao," independent of the *Gazette-Mail* story. "Who is he?" he asked of Moore's ideology. "According to the ADA, he's a conservative. But for West Virginia, he was very much a populist. He was our Huey Long, without the hard, kick-ass side to him." Richard Neely thought Moore could best be described as a pragmatist, neither a conservative nor a liberal. "But he would not feel at home with today's [more conservative] Republican Party," he added.

The point the article made was correct, but it failed to realize this behavior was nothing new; it had always been Arch's style. He was a pragmatist. He constantly pushed the envelope. Courts or the legislature could stop him if they didn't approve. Moore was never one to box himself into being a pro-business conservative; privately, he even denounced Reaganomics; he always saw himself as a man of the people, looking out for the interests of the "little guy."

But, of course, the paper portrayed it all very negatively, with terms like "bizarre" and "Moore's many faces," and "confusing" in the sub-titles. Geiger correctly wrote, "When Moore has confronted business it is often because business has angered him. The carrot has failed and it's time to turn to the stick." He was accurate in that regard; that was Arch's modus operandi. He added, "Moore knows his behavior is raising eyebrows. He recently told a crowd of industry and environmental regulatory officials, 'Somebody's going to look at me and say, Arch, where is your political philosophy? Well, you know, my political philosophy occasionally might very well run counter to what you would consider a certain definition of a political philosophy.'"

As to be expected, the opinion piece led with harsh criticisms of Moore by the Newell CEO. And the WVEA's Perry Bryant said he thought many of Moore's proposals, like the power plants, were "pie in the sky" because they would cost billions and state government was "running deficits." But it quoted his admission that Arch was thinking and acting outside the box for "West Virginia's economy, which is going to need very active intervention." WVU's Fred Zeller was quoted as noting that Moore was governor "of a state that is troubled. From time to time, his assessment of those troubles may be such that they break through the ideological armor that some of us have." About the Anchor Hocking situation, John Hurd of the state's Chamber of Commerce conceded that he could understand Moore's "anxiety and trying to combat the situation the best way he could." No one could be sympathetic to corporations which gladly took state subsidies, but then were quick to leave employees out of jobs when their market dipped or they could make their products cheaper in China. In suing the company, Arch was championing what others would like to have done to them.

Another WVU professor mentioned the obvious political factors: "Employers don't elect Arch Moore. Workers elect Arch Moore. He is showing he is for the worker...I think he's an astute politician." Others noted that he had to attract Democratic voters unlikely to be offended by his populist positions.

The article, which displayed a caricature of Arch with a menacing scowl, changing from white to black gloves, explained the Governor's third term posture—the character of his entire career, actually— better than almost anything that had been written during that period. It also prophetically explained why Arch would experience very serious problems and desertions within his own party in the coming months, due to his failure to follow traditional conservative dictates.

AFTER A good start early on, in the middle of Arch's third term there was almost no net job growth. Without the efforts of Moore's people in bringing in some new plants, and particularly the growth in the eastern counties, there would have been a net loss. Heavy industry and manufacturing continued to decline, as it would under every governor who succeeded Moore. The Governor often was left to struggle with seeking concessions from companies set to close their doors, as Rockefeller and Byrd had done time and again during the late 1970s. For example, he obtained a parting bonus, a few hundred dollars each, for laid-off Anchor Hocking employees, about the best he could wring out of Newell. He went to Clarksburg to personally hand out those checks to each worker. The Governor was greeted politely, but without enthusiasm, by glass workers who had hoped his administration could have done more to save their jobs. They had higher expectations of Arch than they seemed to have when it came to, say Byrd, Rockefeller, or others who were equally unable to wave a magic wand and create or preserve employment.

"We worked real hard," observed Lysander Dudley about the Moore Administration's efforts to get jobs into the state in the 1980s. "But things are constantly changing." The nation was witnessing a continuation of outsourcing of its skilled, blue collar jobs to third world countries with near-slave wages, although Ohio and the Carolinas would not suffer as West Virginia did until a decade or so later. "In the 1970s [the Moore Administration] was able to bring in Kinney Shoes plants in Glenville, Romney and Kingwood. But those are all closed now; those shoes are made in China." But there were other reasons why West Virginia was having a tougher challenge than most states in attracting new employers, Moore's industrial recruitment guru noted.

"We always had working against us the [bad] labor [relations] image, the workers' comp thing [higher rates and more generous benefits than other states]–those really hurt us," continued Dudley. "We had to just fight, fight, fight!" As often was the case, the workforce of these West Virginia plants were often middle aged, limited in skills and education, with no other immediate employment prospects. It was not a pleasant task to watch the results of such job losses, nor one which won Governor Moore any much-needed popularity.

In ancient times, men would have concluded that the gods were now frowning upon Arch Moore, having smiled brightly upon him during the first two terms. Even the weather did not cooperate. While there were no more catastrophic floods as had greeted him in 1985, multiple forest fires plagued the southern half of the state in the unusually dry, rain-free autumn of 1987, covering the region with a heavy, smelly, literally choking smog that would not abate until the first winter frosts arrived. The inescapable smoke from the leaves and trees permeated one's sinuses, clothing, even cars and homes. It seemed to symbolize the state's mood, certainly those who worked in Moore's administration, who began to see the handwriting on the wall–that their time in office was limited.

Only a miracle was going to turn it around, and give the Governor a fourth term. But no miracle was anywhere in sight.

What was in sight was John Raese. The young Morgantown millionaire, who had nearly defeated Rockefeller for U.S. Senate in 1984, whom Moore had tried to block from becoming Republican state chairman, was making the rounds again. He was speaking at nearly every service club luncheon or GOP function to which he was invited. Despite the fact that Arch was the state's chief Republican, normally one strongly defended by a party chairman, there was no forgiving or forgetting. Raese was in a full rebellion mode and he had Moore in his sights, ready to pull the trigger. His message was simple and consistent: the state was in a big mess and it was all Rockefeller's and Moore's fault, mainly the latter. And his audiences were attentive and receptive to the message. The fact that he'd nearly defeated Jay in 1984 gave him credibility he otherwise would not have enjoyed.

State Republican leaders were still angry at Arch because Democrats still held most state jobs. "I didn't have buckets of jobs to hand out like I did in 1969," admitted Arch. Some GOP leaders were desirous of an alternative gubernatorial candidate who would listen to their demands.

With an ego that rivaled Moore's, and with no other contender stepping up as a challenger, Raese anointed himself as that other candidate. And he was finding that there were plenty of Republicans in the state—who were philosophically to the right of the populist Moore and who resented his longtime alliances with Democrats—eager to have an alternative.

The year 1987 also brought onto the stage another player who eventually would cause Arch Moore considerably more grief than even Raese would generate. In April, Michael Carey, an Assistant U.S. Attorney for the Southern District of West Virginia, finished a 120-day interim term as head of that office. The U.S. Attorney's office had subpoenaed Moore's 1984 campaign reports from Secretary of State Hechler. Carey reportedly was overseeing an investigation and potential prosecution of the Governor and other public figures.

Suspiciously, given the circumstances, Chief U.S. District Judge Charles Haden, along with the agreement of the four other federal judges in the district, replaced Carey with Charlotte Lane. It was immediately questioned, because Lane was formerly a Republican delegate who had been appointed to the Public Service Commission by Moore. The May 28 edition of *The Washington Post* reported that the career bureaucrats in the Justice Department strongly opposed the judges' decision to appoint Lane. "Carey's brief term expired before the [Reagan] administration got around to nominating him for the permanent post," the paper wrote, explaining why Haden got involved.

The Justice Department made sure Lane was locked out of any investigation information concerning Moore or Charleston Mayor Mike Roark (also a Republican, being investigated for cocaine use). Senate Majority Leader Robert Byrd rushed in to make sure Carey was quickly nominated and confirmed by the Democratic U.S. Senate, in order to block Lane completely.[16]

Carey and Raese would play prominently in the next three years of Arch Moore's life.

Chapter 27 Notes

1. - Because a considerable portion of those bonds had been paid off, he viewed it as a line of credit, to be drawn on again, an innovative concept, to say the least. The legislative leaders weren't buying Moore's inventive notion and it is doubtful it would have held up in court at the time, if challenged. It wasn't a revolving fund, they contended.

2. - *Third Term,* Ibid.

3. - *New York Times,* May 19, 1987.

4. - Reagan had just cut federal income tax and one option for the state was to "take advantage of that windfall with a state personal income tax increase," Caryl said, but "no one, including Arch Moore wanted to stand up and say that windfall should be used to balance our budget." The legislature did eliminate and narrow several sales tax exemptions in 1987. For example, contractors had to begin paying tax on materials they purchased. Moreover, the B&O tax was not eliminated on power plants. "But it didn't help, obviously," Caryl said.

5. - Caryl did not think the investment tax credit was all that responsible for the cash crunch, but others disagreed.

6. - *Beckley Register-Herald,* Aug. 27, 1987. Several months after moving to Washington, the Rockefellers bought a house there costing $6.6 million and spent nearly as much renovating it. It had 21,300 square feet of living space and a 2000 square feet garage into which a typical West Virginia home could have fit. The Detroit Free Press was noting the irony that a state, in which the per capita income was $10,000, the second poorest in the nation, had sent such a wealthy man to represent it. Jay and his cousins were worth $3.5 billion, according to a Fortune magazine article in 1986, or an average worth of $40 million per cousin.

7. - *The New York Times,* Dec. 16 and 17, 1987.

8. - Toler, Aug. 21, 2005.

9. - *The New York Times,* Dec. 3, 1987.

10. - When asked by your author, on August 19, 2005, whether he would have done it differently in retrospect, Moore answered in the negative. "There was no other way to do it!" he shouted. It was a misconception, a myth, he thought, that Caperton later solved the cash flow problem with the mammoth tax increases of 1989. Because of the tax increases the year after Moore was gone, his Democratic successor would have at his disposal, during his eight years, $5.5 billion more to spend, he noted. "When Caperton came in, he didn't have money to play with. He had to create a fiction. He had to pay back labor, who had got him elected." Moore continued, "That's what happened to Workers' Comp, too— Caperton greatly increased benefits to claimants and broke the bank." He added, "I left Rockefeller $720 million in the bank [in 1977] and he took the tax off food. Caperton put it back on,

apparently acknowledging that Rockefeller had made a mistake."

11. - If there was justification for the Democrats' failure to propose tax increases to avert the cash flow crisis, it might have had its roots in the hard feelings caused by Moore's "on again, off again" support of the property tax reappraisal. They may have feared that, if they had proposed a tax increase, the Governor would have come out against it to score points with voters. They may have not trusted him to "play fair."

12. - As it would be discovered in 1990, Treasurer Manchin's office was not earning such a good return on the state's invested money. It was an illusion.

13. - Interestingly, most of these news men who had been so critical of Republican Moore would be rewarded with high-paying state jobs in the Democratic Caperton Administration, soon after he replaced Arch.

14. - Once, when confronted by an obviously exaggerated figure on some job development statistic by Moore, Lysander Dudley smiled to a reporter, "Well, he needs to go back and sharpen his pencil on that one."

15. - Gallagher's allegiance would become more obvious in years to come. For example, he worked as PR man for the Warren McGraw re-election campaign in 2004 (McGraw was the "local leftist icon," according to *Graffiti* magazine). *Gazette* Editor Don Marsh, nee Donald Segal, a Logan County coal camp native, confessed to this author in 1988 that he was printing untruths and distortions about Moore but with a devilish laugh added, "If you quote me, I'll call you a liar." So much for an independent, objective press. Virtually all writers, broadcasters and publishers have an agenda, and anyone who thinks otherwise is naive or in denial. That year, most of them were obviously ganging up on Arch Moore.

16. - Although then blocked from being the U.S. Attorney, upon the recommendation of Congresswoman Shelley Moore Capito, Lane would later be appointed by President George W. Bush to the U.S. Securities and Exchange Commission for a twelve-year term.

Chapter Twenty Eight
Up Against Millions, Again

So Moore entered the next election cycle with the paradox of having a much improved private sector economy, but with a continuing governmental financial crisis. On January 20, 1988, Tax Commissioner Caryl confirmed that he would not yet certify the real property tax reappraisal that had started in 1983, as result of the 1982 amendment. "That is my opinion, and that's the way it will be unless the legislature changes the law," he told reporters. County commissioners were to begin hearing appeals from taxpayers for the 87-88 tax assessments in February. Certification would have to wait until after the next election.

Clyde See's hometown paper, was outraged. "The governor is still playing games...According to several news accounts, the tax commissioner has no plans to certify that reappraisal. He suggested that the legislature do the job. Talk about passing the buck!"[1]

Early that year, Governor Moore made a trip to Asia with particular focus on Japan, trying to persuade them to invest in West Virginia. The Japanese had local auto and other manufacturing plants in nearby Kentucky and Tennessee, as well as throughout the Midwest, so he saw no reason for West Virginia to be ignored. No firm commitment was made but, upon return, Lysander Dudley announced that Moore's confidential records would be furnished to Senator Rockefeller for follow-up. Dudley said he knew nothing of an alleged feud between Moore and Rockefeller and believed it was in the state's best interest for their offices to cooperate.[2]

Highways Commissioner Bill Ritchie reported that road building and repair was proceeding, thanks to the $54 million per year provided by a five cent tax on gas which had been passed by the legislature in 1983. He had cut overall highway spending though, and the amount of Highways employees had dropped from 7,750 in 1980 to 5,531 in 1988.[3] He continued to seek another nickel-per-gallon tax which would not be given him; the legislature would wait until a new governor took office.

But, on February 24, the battle between the three branches of state government entered a new phase, as the state supreme court declared the $1.49 billion budget unconstitutional because it contained a deficit. State Auditor Glen Gainer, who had been an increasingly caustic Moore critic, said he would stop all state spending. A spokesman for Governor Moore agreed with the court: "The Governor has been saying it's unconstitutional since June [of 1987]." The court's ruling came as result of a lawsuit filed in 1987 by the West Virginia Education Association,[4] which had challenged $13.5 million in cuts in education spending and demanded that the court order Moore to call a special session. The decision, written by Justice Darrell McGraw, said the court could not tell the other branches how to deal with the question of spending or the deficit. Moore and legislative leaders worked out a compromise in response to the order, and Gainer resumed release of checks.

AS EXPECTED, on January 24, 1988, the 38-year-old John Raese announced his candidacy for governor, from the 600-acre Greer Mansion estate he'd inherited from his grandmother, high up on a hill overlooking Cheat Lake. He appeared in jeans, cowboy boots and a casual, short sleeved, open neck shirt, apparently to give it a Reagan-at-the-ranch touch. Referring to the Governor, he charged that West Virginia Republicans "don't have much of a party. We have a one-man party." In the announcement (that was well publicized by Morgantown's *Dominion Post,* owned by John and brothers David and Richard Raese) he vowed to take only one dollar a year for salary as governor, donating the rest to promote the state. "I'd love to go on Monday Night Football and tell everyone about West Virginia." He renewed his call for right-to-work laws and the construction of a coal slurry pipeline through Maryland and Virginia, to transport West Virginia coal to eastern seaports. Raese didn't explain where the billions needed for such a project would be raised. He called for a lowering of the sales tax and wanted downsizing of state government and privatization of government functions. *The West Virginia Blue Book* was "twice as thick as it used to be," he charged, "because of runaway government."[5] He said West Virginia had too long been known as "the welfare state," which he intended to remedy. To the disbelief of those who knew him, Raese pledged that he would not be critical of Governor Moore or Senator Rockefeller, but would be "critical of the last twenty years in West Virginia."

Unlike Underwood and Moore, Raese was not a liberal or moderate Republican—he was strongly and proudly conservative, and unabashedly pro-Big Business of which he was a part. He drew national speakers to help him at fund raisers. For example, the Vice President's son, George W. Bush, came to speak for Raese at a Beckley fund raiser. He also attracted conservatives in his party who agreed with many of his views.[6]

Raese, whether by design or not, was colorful and quotable. He made good copy, as they would say in the newspaper business. For example, he told the *Gazette's* Don Marsh that he slept with .44 magnums "right beside my bed on each side, both Smith & Wessons. I don't have bodyguards like a lot of wealthy politicians ... but I believe in defending myself." One of the handguns belonged to wife Liz, he added, and "she's a great shot."

Although not in the same league as Rockefeller, Raese had been born to great wealth. His maternal grandparents, the Greers, owned Greer Steel, Greer Limestone, Preston County Coal & Coke, West Virginia Newspaper Publishing *(The Dominion Post)*, West Virginia Radio Corporation (which included a 50,000 watt Morgantown station, and stations in Charleston and elsewhere), the MetroNews Radio Network, Buckeye Construction, and Seneca Caverns Co. Because his parents divorced when he was six, John and his two brothers were raised by his father, Richard "Dyke" Raese, a friendly, popular Morgantown coach and friend of Arch Moore's. John played basketball and baseball at Morgantown High and got a degree in education at WVU in 1973, where he was often seen tooling around in his Corvette. John and his brothers had inherited the Greer empire when grandmother Agnes Greer died at 92. Morgantown politicians feared him because of his media outlets and great wealth.[7] Raese released his tax returns in January, which revealed he'd made more than $3.2 million in the past decade. Some thought that figure sounded low.

The Morgantown millionaire would quickly prove to be a real threat to Moore. At age 34 and with a fairly weak and disorganized campaign, Raese had come within 29,000 votes of defeating Jay Rockefeller for U.S. Senate in 1984, despite the fact that Jay had spent $13 million to his one million. The Democrats couldn't contain their glee at seeing a Republican intra-party fight. Clyde See said he "was snickering a little bit" by the news that Moore would have a primary opponent. "I wouldn't be candid if I didn't say it kind of tickles me in some respects. [The Republicans might be] having their own little blood bath." Raese's candidacy would be "the best thing that could happen to the Democratic Party in this state," See accurately predicted.

Raese's *Dominion Post* would step up its editorial pounding of Arch Moore, which had started in 1986 and would continue for the next two decades.[8] As had begun in 1987, John Raese appeared at every civic or political function to which he'd been invited, big or small. He dressed in expensive Italian, double-breasted suits with bright ties, and with his slicked-back thinning hair and Caribbean suntan, looked like a GQ model or a French politician. He spoke in smooth, comforting, conversational tones that Mrs. Moore, for one, thought made him appeal to Republican voters. A March poll published in the *Gazette* showed Raese at 49 percent to Moore's 36 percent, similar to Raese's internal polls. Sixty eight percent said Moore did not deserve to be re-elected. (Clyde See, the presumed Democratic nominee again, was leading Gaston Caperton, 28 to 17 percent at the time.) Raese ran half-page ads in state newspapers, in which he was depicted wearing a suit and tie, but holding a musket, with the caption, "Help me hit the bull's eye."

When asked in Parkersburg if he'd debate Raese, Moore replied, "What for? This individual has never voted on a bill and doesn't have a record." They did end up sharing the podium at Lincoln Day dinners in Fairmont and elsewhere, however. The one in that town got so heated that the master of ceremonies called a recess after Raese unleashed his caustic attacks, to afford Moore and his supporters several minutes to cool off before the Governor responded.

Moore's people knew he was in trouble. Some thought he might spare himself the grief by retiring and not having to go before the electorate that year. Part of the problem, supporters such as Dick Barber warned them, was the perception that the Governor had lost touch and wasn't solving constituent problems as well as he had done in the past. The "Arch the Problem Solver" image was tarnished during the past three years; people "out in the counties" were feeling ignored. Moore was listening to people as he always had done but, even with his computer-like memory, he was unable to recall everything they were asking him to do and had insufficient time to follow-up on it. So they decided to pull Kevin Sikora from F&A and have him accompany Moore everywhere he visited, recording in his "black book" all complaints and problems anyone voiced to the Governor along the way–perhaps a road with pot holes needing patched, a workers' compensation matter that wasn't being quickly resolved, a bill the State hadn't paid, or a myriad of small matters that meant much to the respective requesters. Each evening, Sikora would summarize the requests, usually at least twenty per day, to Candy Price of the Governor's Office and she would then contact the various department heads to try to get a prompt answer. This put Moore back on track with voters, Sikora said, and did a lot to regenerate much of the good will he had lost.

The Robert Goodman Agency once again prepared TV spots, touting Moore's tax cuts, finishing the Interstate highway system, rebuilding after the '85 flood, getting the prison hostages out alive, bringing thousands of jobs to Elkins, Charleston and elsewhere. Arch was the "best friend we've ever had and we're going to keep him," the ads proclaimed.

A Bell Atlantic business research report released in May provided a very bright forecast for continued improvement of the state's economy. *The West Virginia Economic Outlook* announced that West Virginia's new business, job expansion and reduction in business failures (down 60 percent since 1985) was encouraging. It projected continued economic growth of at least two percent or better each year for the next five years, estimating that employment would increase from 652,000 to 733,000 by 1993. The exodus of workers to other states to seek jobs was over, it opined, adding, "The possibility of West Virginia retaining its younger adults looks better than it has at any time in the recent past." It projected a 13.5 percent increase in personal income in the state during the following five years. About the glowing report, Governor Moore said that it confirmed "what I have been telling West Virginians for months. Our economy is getting stronger. You can see it; you can feel it; and now the statistics confirm it."

To an AFL-CIO convention, Moore announced that I-64 would be completed in July. He noted that $70 million was being let in contracts to finish a Boone County stretch of Corridor G (U.S. 119) and that the Alum Creek-Charleston stretch had already been opened. Five million dollars had been approved to begin a Logan County phase of the four lane. Nineteen million had been spent recently to build a new mental hospital near Weston, he mentioned. He had lots of good news to offer when he went on the road in the weeks before the primary, to tout the successes of his third term.

IN MAY OF 1988, the Governor had another type of publicity, however, that wasn't a bit welcome. In fact, it was the beginning of a disastrous two years for him. Chief U.S. District Judge Charles Haden had sentenced long-time Mingo County Democrat boss Johnie Owens to fourteen years in federal prison for extortion, vote-buying and tax evasion. "He sent me straight to jail; I didn't even get to go home until time to report. And I'd plea-bargained for eighteen months," remembered a still-embittered Owens, years later. Owens viewed Judge Haden and Arch Moore as one and the same ("they were bedfellows"), even assuming that Haden was taking orders from Moore, because the judge had worked in Moore's first administration and Moore asked President Ford to appoint him to the federal bench. Plus, according to Johnie's version, Haden had been involved in the vote-buying process himself in the 1972 race.[9] The former Mingo County sheriff felt that other local politicos were going free while he was getting an excessive sentence. ("I thought I'd probably die in prison.")

So, after going to the federal penitentiary, Johnie summoned a lady friend who worked for an NBC affiliate and told her Moore had attempted to give him $12,000 to buy onto his slate. The interview was carried nationally, even though the inflammatory allegation apparently was not corroborated by an independent source. What made the tale sound particularly sordid was his allegation that Arch made the offer in the back of a car and that, when passing headlights had shown on them, Moore would slump down to avoid being recognized. The news media made the meeting, which allegedly occurred near an armory in Boone County, sound like it occurred in 1972; some viewers probably even thought it was recent. Col. Donohoe said it was an impossible scenario, though, because the Governor always had state police drivers anywhere he went.

(In an interview for this book, Owens got around the State Police superintendent's rebuttal by claiming the press had the date wrong. He now claimed the covert meeting actually occurred during Moore's 1978 campaign against Randolph when Arch was a private citizen, unescorted by state troopers.) [10]

Moore's spokesman called the charge "a piece of garbage," but Owens challenged Arch to take a lie-detector test. The Governor personally responded: "Johnie Owens is a convicted felon and an experienced liar. There is not one ounce of truth in anything he says. He and his fellow criminals in Mingo County have, for their own desperate reasons, hurled ridiculous accusations [at me]. My family and I should not be forced to respond to such outrageous, premeditated assaults on my integrity. The fact is that the conviction of Johnie Owens was one of the best things to happen in West Virginia this year."[11] This statement by Arch, Owens said many times thereafter, just made him hate Moore all the more, and caused him to seek revenge.

With regard to Judge Haden, columnist Adam Kelly wrote at the time, "West Virginians who know Chuck Haden regard him as the absolute epitome of fairness and integrity on the bench." He noted that the judge had called Owens "one of the most immoral men he had ever met." Kelly thought Owen's "veracity on this, as well as most any other matter, is subject to a good bit of question." He ended his column, "I don't know what, if anything, Johnie will try as an encore for the November election, but it is devoutly hoped that news organizations use better judgment than NBC in airing such worthless trash."[12] But the Owens story got major play in the *Gazette* and other news outlets. Editor Wally Warden of the *Williamson Daily News* began a crusade of numerous front-page, anti-Arch Moore stories.

Worse (for Arch) than his going to the news media to vent, Owens also volunteered to testify against him before a federal grand jury in Charleston. He clearly enjoyed his sudden celebrity status and the fact he was getting revenge. "If they'd left me alone, I wouldn't have bothered them," he said years later. "Arch could have picked up the phone anytime and got Haden to allow me parole," he complained, adding that Williamson's leading citizens asked that he be released early, but Haden's sentence wouldn't permit it.[13]

ANOTHER NEWCOMER to gubernatorial politics was a Charleston millionaire who ran as a Democrat. Gaston Caperton had grown up on the east and west sides of downtown Charleston, grandson of the owner of a coalmine in Slab Fork and son of a successful insurance man. Graduating from Lincoln Junior High School on Charleston's west side, he had been sent off to a private Episcopal school out-of-state, where the six foot, three inch tall student played basketball and football. He later graduated with a business degree from the University of North Carolina, overcoming dyslexia. He'd registered as a Republican when he turned 21, but switched parties after college, explaining, "I just liked the Democrats I knew in Charleston, like Bill Brotherton and Ivor Boiarsky." As a college student in 1964, Gaston had worked for Hulett Smith's campaign for governor. (Caperton's father was a friend of Smith's, both insurance men who had grown up in Beckley.)

After working for the company about a decade, Gaston bought out his father's McDonough-Caperton-Shepherd insurance group in 1976, and then "went at it like gang busters," according to Charleston lawyer Robert Elkins. "Before you knew it, he was buying up other fairly large insurance agencies throughout West Virginia, including the Paull firm in Wheeling, and in other states, too." His connections with Governor Rockefeller had helped his firm secure the lucrative state employees' health insurance contract. Soon his company had 550 employees in several states and a gleaming 26,000 square foot building on the hill above the state capitol complex. His success could be traced to "surrounding himself with good people, like Marty Becker," thought Elkins. "I initially wondered if [McDonough Caperton] was a house of cards because we'd had many companies like that go under. But I was absolutely wrong. He had success like I didn't dream you could have in the insurance business. He had an excellent reputation for being honest, upright, hard-driving, and was well-liked."[14] Caperton had married the former Dee Kessell, a runner-up to Miss America, active in Democratic politics and daughter (ironically) of conservative Republican Circuit Judge Oliver Kessell of Jackson County.[15]

"They bought a farm in Jackson County and Dee introduced him to influential Democrats there, like the Goodwins, Russ Isaacs and the Hardestys," said Elkins. Soon, in addition to heading up all sorts of Charleston civic organizations, Caperton was getting more involved in Democratic politics and was even treasurer for the campaigns of Governor Rockefeller and Senator Byrd.

"Gaston used to come into the Marvin Midtown [Motel] for breakfast each morning, often alone," remembered Elkins. "But [in 1987] I noticed he was having breakfast with political people, like Harley Mooney, Charlie Jones and Kemp McLaughlin. Before I knew it, he was announcing that he was running for governor." Dee Caperton had won a seat in the House of Delegates in 1986, and with her good looks, charm and wealth, drew a lot of media attention.[16]

"I started in August of 1987, and for a year and a half ran hard for governor, twenty-four hours a day, seven days a week," recalled Caperton. "I was new at campaigning. People didn't know me. I had to go into neighborhoods, spend a lot of time one-on-one. It was very hard work." Why did one who had made a fortune, had such success in the private sector, want to get into politics? "I loved being in business. It was a wonderful time of my life. But I thought my life could be more purposeful [if I served as governor]. West Virginia was in bad shape–I thought it needed new leadership."

The 48-year-old, who had never held any public office, would recruit Lloyd Jackson, a state senator from Lincoln County (from a political family—his father had been senate president and had great oil and gas wealth) to chair his campaign, to get him through a primary in which southern counties would be key. "Lloyd also worked hard, 24 hours a day, seven days a week," said Caperton. "I was very lucky to have Lloyd–he was brilliant." The effort would be managed by long-time West Virginia Education Association lobbyist Steve Haid. They were able to get him the UMWA endorsement, despite his family history of owning Slab Fork Coal Co. Naturally, Haid got the WVEA endorsement for his candidate. The organization said they abandoned Moore because he hadn't been able to produce as many teacher pay raises as they expected and because the Teachers' Retirement system was "all screwed up."

Caperton retained Frank Greer's public relations firm to do his media. "They had been recommended to me by my friend Brer Jones, the lieutenant governor of Kentucky."[17] The agency would intrude more and more into the day-to-day operations, managing every statement, just as David Garth had done for Jay in 1980. His campaign leadership was rounded out by Bill Clinton look-alike, Chuck Smith. "I had a great team helping me," said Caperton.

Huntington Mayor Robert Nelson, who had earlier thought of throwing his hat into the race, accused Caperton of "using Rockefeller tactics" in getting early support. "It is clear to everyone where Mr. Caperton is coming from in that he has been anointed by Rockefeller to be the Democratic nominee for governor and to hell with the people of this state. This is terrible because it pretty much means business as usual."[18]

Nelson's perception was incorrect, said Caperton in an interview for this book. "I didn't even talk to Governor Rockefeller, nor Senator Byrd, about [running for governor] until I'd already announced. They did not get involved [in primary battles] and I respected that." There was no "Rockefeller organization" per se, said Caperton. "I couldn't go to some boss and say, support me because of Rockefeller." He had met a lot of the same people key to Jay's victories in the past, as Rockefeller's and Byrd's treasurer, "but it's different when you are the candidate," he pointed out. He did use Jay's pollster, Peter Hart & Associates, but "I was very independent [of Rockefeller]," Gaston insisted. Was he a Rockefeller protege or clone, as Nelson and others believed? "Not at all."[19]

At first Caperton remained unknown, trailing Clyde See, state Senators Mario Palumbo and Dan Tonkovich, and Agriculture Commissioner Gus Douglass in the polls. But he began to catch up quickly, with the help of saturating the airwaves with ads, *a la* Jay Rockefeller. As late as the end of April, a New York polling firm showed See leading Caperton by 35 to 29 percent. But as Caperton pumped his seemingly inexhaustible personal funds into the primary race that situation changed, especially when the effects of what he'd budgeted for election day became evident. Caperton had taken a lesson from Jay Rockefeller on how a wealthy candidate could win a statewide election. His paid voters and, hopefully their families, would make the difference; it was all about turnout.

State Republican Chairman Edgar "Hike" Heiskell of Morgantown accurately predicted, "I think you're going to see cascades of money being spent by Gaston Caperton ... the same as Jay Rockefeller did to influence voters in 1980 and 1984. Caperton is using the same Rockefeller organization."

With a badly wounded Republican incumbent, the primary battle for the Democrat nomination for governor meant that the candidates were seeking a valuable prize. Accordingly, the fighting got down and dirty. Snarled Clyde See about Caperton's much-touted success as an insurance executive, "If I got a sweetheart contract for $2.8 million with the State of

West Virginia, hell, I might be a roaring success." See tried to make McDonough Caperton an issue. "When the PEIB audit came out the other day and disclosed that $100,000 had been paid to people who weren't even members of the system, when 25,000 people had possibly been paid twice and one out of every four claims that were processed was in error, I mean, if that's Caperton's business success story, think what he will do to West Virginia!"[20] At a Star City rally, See also criticized Governor Moore for going to Japan to "look for exotic industry." The *Sunday Gazette-Mail* reported that See, whom they characterized as a conservative who'd served as a lawyer for Pittston Coal Co., was "a bitter UMW foe [and] has all but written off labor and union support."

Clyde See told the *Guyandotte Voice*, "I think I'm the only Democrat who has the ability, knowledge and the guts to take that guy [Arch Moore] on. He's a tenacious son of a gun and he's going to continue to be. Those who think he's going to be duck soup in November had better understand that he has never been and never will be an easy opponent." To Marshall University's paper, See said, "In 1984, I had a personal statement.. . 'Where's the cash, Arch?' [This year], I want to change it a bit: 'Where's the truth, Arch?'" The reference was to Moore calling for a ten percent pay raise for teachers, but not including enough money for it in the budget.

See had a bit of scandal in his own camp. Former Keystone Mayor Robert Boggs, on trial for mail fraud, was implicated for funneling flood relief money into See's campaign coffers.[21] However, U.S. Attorney David Faber would report that there was "not one shred of evidence" linking See or his campaign manager to the scheme.

On April 23, the *Beckley Register-Herald* reported that a coal operator who had been indicted for murder, H. Paul Kizer, was spreading his wealth around, apparently hedging his bets, like many big money donors do. Kizer donated to the election efforts of Clyde See, Gaston Caperton, Arch Moore and Supreme Court candidates Margaret Workman, Fred Fox and John Hey. Kizer's name would be in the news again soon.

See and Caperton, the emerging front runners, called press conferences to question each other's honesty. Taking offense at Caperton's TV ads which had portrayed See as a Pinocchio with a growing nose, the former House speaker said it was Caperton who was a liar. He said Gaston was trying to buy the election. The ad had countered See's charges that Caperton was barred from coal mining in West Virginia.[22] See also charged that Caperton was bypassing the $35-a-day limit on campaign workers by hiring them to work three days. Noting that Gaston had already spent $1.8 million of his own money by April, See thought, "People are disgusted with the amount of money being thrown around" but apparently not enough of them were disgusted.

Novice Caperton was the big Democratic winner with 132,435 votes to veteran See's 94,364.[23] The former Speaker, realizing it was the end of his political career, was openly bitter. See's campaign manager, Dave Callaghan, told the *Gazette*, "There's only one factor that affected the outcome of this race and that's money, two and one half million bucks [what Caperton spent to win the primary]. On a level playing field, it would have been a different outcome." See told the *Daily Mail*, "Gaston Caperton refused to sign the campaign code of ethics and thumbed his nose at the state election commissioner. He said, I'll spend whatever amount I want, then went on to spend millions of dollars to buy the election, saying he was a successful businessman. As far as I'm concerned, he's running a fluff campaign while a group of people sing about his program on TV. Come on now, that isn't what this state needs in a time of crisis." See said of Caperton's victory, "I'll say one thing, he bought the election fair and square."

RAESE HAD held his lead over Moore in the polls from late 1987 through the end of April of 1988. It appeared to all that Moore would become a lame duck seven months before his term ended. Many of the second tier level members of his administration took vacations to go back out into the field, to work the campaign. What they were hearing was frightening. The state's cash flow problems, the unfavorable wire stories and Raese's constant attacks had taken a tremendous toll. The mood outside Charleston was bleak; people felt Arch hadn't performed the economic miracle they'd expected in the past three years and that he was even out of touch. Phone bank callers were getting irate, negative responses from Republicans when they were asked if they would support Moore. Nevertheless, the Governor kept his chin up, running an intensive campaign schedule, as if he still had a chance. At 65, it wasn't as easy or as much fun as it once had been—it became a chore for Arch, another tiring, uphill battle to be fought against what he considered an inferior, untried opponent.

Then something happened in those final weeks of the primary campaign, a shift in sentiment, the cause of which was never completely clear. Perhaps it was the fact that Governor Moore and his organization were "out in the counties" renewing friendships, asking for help, reminding voters that he had been a good governor despite tough times and had almost always delivered for the GOP. But some thought it was John

Raese's image and temperament that turned the tide toward Moore in the end and that interest in the challenger was quickly wearing thin. Others thought it was John's wife Liz, from the wealthy Solomon family of Morgantown, who killed his chances of being governor, with an interview she gave the *Gazette*. In a May 4 article, Liz Raese said she was frustrated that her husband had been tagged with the reputation of being a spoiled kid, a hot tempered "party animal." She insisted that John did not spend all his time racing fast cars and boats. "The press makes an issue about his cigarette boat [which Raese liked to race in Florida waters] ... the boat is used as much for fishing as racing. Sure, John loves fast cars and fast boats. When he gets stressed out, that's his release."

Then Liz added something that made John's conservative supporters squirm. "In fact, we have our best love affairs in the middle of the ocean. There is a solitude out there. We're alone. The ocean is special to us. Why make such a big deal out of it?" She said when she found out how much money her husband made (he'd released his income tax returns, challenging Moore to do the same), she was angry and embarrassed. Because of it, she asked John, "Why do you want this job? Our life before was so easy." He responded, she relayed, "Liz, how many suits can we buy? How many planes can we fly? How many parties can we attend? There must be more to life than this."

The *Gazette's* Fanny Seiler rather liked Arch Moore and even clashed with publishers and editors at her paper over her continued respect and affection for him. A native of Preston County, near the Greer Empire, she clearly did not like the Raeses. In a November, 1987 column, Fanny had noted, "The average West Virginian can't jet to Florida and back every week or two and maintain one or two condominiums on the ocean front where he has an expensive cigarette ocean racer docked. But that's the lifestyle of Republican gubernatorial hopeful John Raese and his wife, Liz, who probably spends as much time in Florida as she does in West Virginia." Seiler proceeded to tell a story of Raese's hundred-mile-an-hour boat, with its "three decks" and three engines, with a "price tag in the six figures," and how John struck another's boat and paid him in cash on the spot for the damage after the two "exchanged insults." Fanny concluded, "One wonders if Raese would spend as much time in Florida if he were governor," plainly suggesting he would.

Word also began getting out that Raese had a very short fuse and often fired employees. One of them, a disgruntled former chief of staff (who'd been fired for calling Liz Raese a liar), defected to Moore's side and became vocal about it.[24] Steven Canterbury asked the *Gazette-Mail,* "Who would be listening to Raese if he didn't have a million dollars? John is packaged well. He can make the most empty statements sound good. But he never wanted to do his homework. He'd rather talk about sports or watch a movie." Canterbury continued, "Some of his statements were irrational. He can be a charming man, but he can be brutal. He got very angry after I mentioned he had missed some campaign appointments. He's not used to following a schedule."

In the same article Raese's high school friend, Jim Manilla, was quoted as saying John would get very upset if he didn't win a basketball game. "John was a nice guy, but you didn't want to mess with him. He was big and he has a temper." In the interview, Raese seemed to blame his shortcomings on the fact that his parents divorced when he was six. "Obviously, I've had family problems. But we had a lot of governesses to take care of us and my grandmother helped out a lot."[25]

And word started getting out that Raese's proposals were unrealistic. Tax Commissioner Mike Caryl and House Finance Chairman George Farley pointed out that Raese's proposal to cut sales tax would deprive the state of $70 million in much-needed revenue.

Lastly, Republican voters began getting reminders that Moore had performed better than for which he was credited. In a May 3 editorial, the *Daily Mail* endorsed Arch Moore with praise:

> When Arch Moore returned to the governor's mansion after an absence of eight years, the judiciary had been allowed to take control of education, prisons and mental hospitals. The state had lost revenue from the sales tax on food, had been saddled with $300 million dept from unemployment compensation, and was hemorrhaging from an out-of-control program for public employees' health benefits. Tens of thousands of mining and manufacturing jobs had been lost and the state's programs did not encourage the creation of new ones. Moore correctly made jobs his highest priority. The legislature passed his programs for attracting new industry. The unemployment debt, a disincentive to employers, was refinanced. Those programs are clearly working; the Volkswagen Stamping Plant in South Charleston, the AT&T office in downtown Charleston, the CSX consolidation in Huntington, the Bruce Hardwood flooring plant in Elkins, the

> Wheeling-Pitt move to Wheeling ... Moore has made a good many things happen.

Arch would snatch victory from the jaws of defeat one final time in his political career in May. Republicans would rally around their embattled Governor by a narrow margin.

One would have thought that the Moore forces would have rejoiced at the bitterly divided Democratic party, that it would give them hope. But the Governor had problems in his own party, as his primary election result demonstrated, with deep wounds that would never be healed. He won by about 53 to 47 percent over Raese,[26] but that was not a promising sign for Moore, who'd always counted on 90 percent of the GOP sticking with him in the general election.[27]

One could almost see the disappointment in Moore on primary election night (he'd flown down from Glen Dale to speak to supporters at the Charleston Marriott at 12:40 a.m.). The 65-year-old Governor's shoulders sagged, he looked tired—he had the look of one who barely escaped a close call, which he had. "We look forward to the opportunity to carry our party's banner in November. That's what it's all about." He tried his best to be enthused and optimistic in his acceptance speech that night, but it was apparent to those who knew him that he was disgusted to have been forced to battle for his own party's nomination, disappointed that it wasn't a stronger margin of victory and worried about the next one. Clyde See he knew—he had an extensive file and speaking points on his '84 opponent. See's funds were limited; he had defeated him once and knew how to do it again. But instead he now had to oppose another tall, wealthy newcomer, Caperton, who like John Raese had never served in office and thus had no public record, no controversial votes or actions to defend, and few enemies except for See. It was going to be tough. Asked to comment on the pending race, Arch paused and then said, "I'm going to bed."

When the reality of another defeat sunk in, a shocked and angry John Raese sulked off from the main area of his campaign headquarters, ceased giving interviews and cancelled a Wednesday morning press conference. His press assistant said he and Liz were going to a White House dinner with Reagan. He released only a written statement, saying he would "go back into business and make little rocks out of big rocks," referring to the quarry at Greer Limestone.[28] Despite his youth, other attractive opportunities, and a relatively large and loyal following, Raese did not reenter politics until 2006, when he ran again for the U.S. Senate.

But Raese's challenge had forced Moore to spend $796,600 to win his party's nomination, money he desperately needed to ward off the next threat. By the same token, it brought the Governor out onto the campaign trail earlier than he otherwise would have arrived and he needed to do that.

It was difficult for Moore to get pumped up for what lay ahead, however. He had been through the meat grinder, not only in the primary race, but also during the past three years in office. He was having increasing difficulty coming up with any new solutions, either for the campaign or running a difficult ship of state. Some likened it to the scene when the curtain was pulled back and the Wizard of Oz was revealed to be a mere mortal. The Arch Moore magic was no longer working. His bag of magic tricks was depleted.

"A lot of energy went out of Arch Moore in that third term," conceded Arch's friend, Charles Ryan. "I think he always regretted not running for the Senate [in 1984, the year Rockefeller won the seat]; he really wanted to be in the Senate, not governor again. I always felt that his heart was not fully into it during that third term." (But Moore chose to run for governor "because the money scared him off," thought Ryan—the millions of dollars Jay and Raese would have spent to deny him that Senate seat in '84.)[29] His campaign manager, former deputy tax commissioner and Workers' Compensation Commissioner John Leaberry, could not seem to get out of first gear. Little was happening in the counties, with regard to organizing the re-election bid. Money was not coming in as it should, especially for a sitting governor. It was tough to know whether the problems were Leaberry's fault or just the result of growing disenchantment with his boss. First Daughter Shelley Moore Capito began showing up at headquarters, trying to organize and help out with her father's efforts.

More than the usual amount of attention was paid to the size of state government's payroll, especially since Raese had made smaller government a pledge. In mid-year it was revealed by the state auditor that there were 46,350 people working for the State, versus 40,450 a year before. Moore's spokesman, John Price, contended that Employment Security records showed that the amount of people on the state payroll had dropped from an average of 44,900 to about 39,000 under Moore's third term, however. Like the Democrats before and after him, Moore's administration had made use of six month "exempt" employees (any employment longer than that required civil service) to satisfy political demands. The payroll would continue to grow under subsequent governors.

CAPERTON'S CAMPAIGN centerpiece was a plan he called "The

West Virginia Partnership for Progress." The proposal again seemed to take a chapter from successful Rockefeller campaigns: platitudes repeated over and over that sounded good to unsophisticated voters. The plan seemed to be from the KISS Method ("Keep it Simple, Stupid"). It contained seven goals: "Support industrial modernization, encourage small business development, improve our industrial recruitment strategy, renew our physical infrastructure, encourage greater cooperation between management and labor, invest in education and training, and improve our quality of life."[30] Those were things his administration was already doing, a scoffing Moore countered. "Frank Greer, Lloyd Jackson and Chuck Smith came up with it," said Caperton, who remained proud of the proposal years later. "They felt you had to have a plan. We [later] followed it and it was effective."

William Miernyk had served as a distinguished economics professor at WVU until 1983. He spoke out against Caperton's "Partnership for Progress," saying there was nothing new about it, that it was not "a strategy for economic development," but "simply a wish list." Everyone agreed that better education and new industrial jobs were needed, Professor Miernyk said. Caperton wasn't "offering any alternatives in the event that some of these goals can't be achieved," he complained. The Benedum professor said the Caperton plan resembled cotton candy. "I can remember the first one of those I ever tasted. What anticipation for the first bite into what appeared to be a lovely and substantial confection; what bitter disappointment to discover that it was simply a bite into nothingness." The "Partnership for Progress" proposal "is packaged beautifully by the best public relations and media consultants a lot of money can buy. But inside is nothingness." The economist said he found no fault with Moore's record, considering the external conditions and that the state had not yet fully recovered from the deep recession which began under Rockefeller. "I would say [Arch Moore has] done as good a job as any reasonable person could expect. I'm constantly surprised at his knowledge of some of the fine details about the state economy, which one wouldn't expect a political leader to know. He probably knows as much about the economy as most of us who devote a good part of our working day to pouring over figures and other information about the state."[31]

Editor Adam Kelly was another critic. The Country Editor wrote that Caperton's "Partnership for Progress" parroting reminded him of Rockefeller's earlier campaign in which "he declared in as firm a voice as possible, 'Coal.' Rockefeller's profound pronouncements coincided precisely with the virtual demise of mining in West Virginia ... Caperton's

'Partnership for Progress' came right out of the same mold. [It] really doesn't mean a damn thing. It's only a political ploy to elect a man of wealth with no credentials as governor of West Virginia. Of course, it might work [to win an election]. It has before."

About his opponent's plan, Arch Moore told a union audience, "Now comes an upstart, who has mirrored and championed that goal which I set for West Virginia in 1984 and 1985. I don't know whether to sue him for plagiarism or congratulate him for endorsing the plan I already have in motion." He continued, "I can only say to him and to the people of West Virginia that we have done the work others are only beginning to talk about. We've laid the foundation for the future and we are ready to move forward the next four years building on the good work that has already been done, preparing West Virginia for entry into the next millennium."

Even Associated Press columnist and Arch Moore critic Andy Gallagher questioned Caperton's sincerity in reforming state government. He noted that the Democrat had criticized Moore for failing to implement $384 million in cost-cutting measures Arch's task force had recommended in 1986. But even Caperton would not publicly support $240.3 million of those cuts which would have been achieved by cutting back the amount of workers on state payrolls by twenty percent, a proposal highly unpopular with unions. AFL-CIO President Joe Powell had called the task force report a "sham" put together by "corporate vultures." F&A Deputy Commissioner David Stamm had noted that about half of what Moore's task force had recommended required legislative action (that would never happen because of political risk).

Nevertheless, Caperton was increasingly viewed as the reform candidate, the clean outsider who would set things right for the state. That was supreme irony, because Arch Moore had been perceived the same way when he first ran for governor, exactly twenty years earlier.

As part of the National Governors' Association, of which he'd once been chairman, Governor Moore (with the help of aide Ben Bailey) prepared a Comprehensive Energy and Natural Resources Policy Statement in 1988, a blueprint that if followed "would have saved us a lot of trouble today," Bailey observed. As expected, the Governor placed heavy emphasis on better, and increased use of, American coal to combat oil shortages and ever-increasing oil prices. He wanted the federal government to mandate reconversion to coal-capable boilers in electric power plants and for other industrial energy users; streamline federal rules for coal production; accelerate development of synthetic fuels (again, using coal); improve roads, rails and waterways for transportation of coal; and provide emergency assistance to "boom and bust" energy-dependent towns. Increases in the strategic petroleum reserves to four months' worth of oil was proposed. "The plugging of currently producing" oil wells because of the Windfall Profits Tax should be stopped, it said. Federal assistance for utilities and others to build pollution controls was suggested, as well as federal power projects (both, so more coal, and less foreign oil could be used). It also talked about nuclear power, solar, wind, hydroelectric and other clean power sources. Conservation and environmental standards were discussed. Use of alcohol fuels for vehicles, made from American corn, was pushed.[32] Moore's recommendations were sound, not far-fetched, but Washington was not listening. Jimmy Carter had favored much of what was in the proposal, but Republicans Reagan and Bush generally had a hands-off attitude toward national energy, preferring to allow the free market to take its natural course.

To Moore, the future for coal and the West Virginia economy could and should be a bright one; he was optimistic. But short term, things were not going well for his government. More bad financial news was generated by the end of the fiscal year in 1988. Moore had contended that the year ended with a balance of $34.7 million in the bank, but the state auditor's office had an actual shortage of $170 million. It depended on whose math one believed.

During the campaign, Arch had claimed that there had been $5.1 billion in economic development during the past three and a half years. When challenged by reporters to back up the boast with detail, his campaign staff pointed to five power plants which supplied Virginia Power, an investment of $825 million; a planned American Electric Power plant near New Haven; a $150 million plant in Morgantown; plus facilities in Grant Town, Marion County (a project in which coal was extracted from a slag pile) and in Grant County. "We used state bonds to cut the interest rates for private investors to make those projects possible," Moore explained, years later.

One of the jewels in his economic crown for the third term was the Bruce Hardwood Plant, near Beverly, Randolph County. He broke ground on July 16, 1988, noting that $40 million had been invested, that it provided 700 jobs and "possibly thrice as many more jobs in related support industries." Noting that he had competed with eight other states for the facility, Moore told the group, "Our economic development program is paying off. West Virginia has the good fortune to witness the beginning of another success story." The heavily Democratic Randolph County would be one of the few to remember him with gratitude on Election Day 1988, giving him a majority of its votes.

Arch would get so frustrated by the nay-sayers in the news media and elsewhere, however. "One can only wonder what accountability it will take to get some to see the light," he told a Labor-Management Council in Charleston. "The light of 30,000 new jobs, $3 billion in new business development, and reduction of unemployment by over fifty percent to 6.3 percent." Moore was correct–very little of the good news was being filtered out to readers or viewers of news in 1988; it was all doom and gloom that had little basis in reality. It was clear to anyone who knew the facts and observed the way the news media was reporting them that the story was being told in such a fashion as to hurt Moore and help his opponent. The public was not getting the truth, but there was virtually nothing the Governor could do about it; his credibility, because of the cash flow problem, was at an all-time low.

Perhaps more central to Caperton's strategy of winning the election, however, was the math. There were more than twice as many registered Democrats in the state as Republicans (632,087 to 293,659).[33] If a candidate can get most of the majority party's votes, he has won, pure and simple. So Gaston and his party's leadership began spreading the word to Democrats: Vote a straight ticket! "Sure—where it was effective [to push straight ticket voting] you always do that," Caperton admitted. "You try to get every Democrat vote you can—Republican, too, for that matter." And that was where Caperton's vast money advantage was going to help him defeat the incumbent. Using the Rockefeller method, he would simply "hire" enough Election Day workers to get the maximum amount of Democrats out to vote for him. It would be legal, it would be done by checks, it would be reported, but many agreed with Clyde See that it was nothing less than buying an election.

Mavericks were threatened, too. Democratic party leaders and business people were warned: there would be hell to pay if they discovered that any of them supported Moore's re-election. Defectors would not be forgiven this time; favors and patronage decisions would be denied them; they would be ostracized if they stuck with Governor Moore. The Manchin family in Marion County was one of the few to bravely ignore those warnings; they loyally maintained allegiance to their long-time friend. They did not turn their backs on Arch Moore.

NOTHING COULD be said about the record of Moore's opponent, because he had none. There were no policy decisions, speeches, votes, gaffes or political deals to criticize because he had never held any public office. But a few were talking about the candidate himself, his southern twang and sometimes prissy manner of speaking, which contrasted with the Governor's personal style considerably. Charleston pundit, lawyer and sometimes-candidate for governor Jim Lees discussed Caperton's image in an article he wrote at the time. "The truth was, the West Virginia electorate thought Gaston Caperton was—a wimp! This impression was apparently the result of people throughout West Virginia actually hearing Caperton speak, particularly in an introductory television commercial. [An] unnamed consultant racked his brain attempting to deal with the 'wimp factor.'"

Lees wrote that Caperton's consultant decided to the way to overcome the "wimp factor" was to mimic the Spartans who guarded the gates, and Greece itself, against the Persians: Gaston would have to be portrayed as defending West Virginia against some type of "foreign invader." He found such an issue in the Eastern Panhandle where a local issue involved whether to allow out-of-state garbage to be dumped in local landfills. "So a commercial was made with Caperton at the gates of a landfill, while the announcer intoned dire warnings of the soon-to-be tidal wave of out-of-state garbage that most assuredly would descend upon us. And who was the man to stand firm against the invasion? Gaston Caperton, of course. The commercial ended with a manly Gaston literally slamming the gates on out-of-state garbage. Caperton quickly rose twelve points in the polls..."[34]

The perception of the Democratic nominee was enhanced in his lone debate with Moore when Caperton scolded Moore for "pooh-poohing my Partnership for Progress" plan, erupting guffaws and snickers from Arch supporters.

Governor Moore couldn't resist having a little fun with his opponent's image at a stop in Pineville. Moore was presenting a grant at the Wyoming County courthouse there, after which he invited questions from the crowd. A good ole boy in a hunting cap raised his hand and broached the subject about which many had been whispering but none spoke too loudly. "Uh, Governor, 'bout this guy who's runnin' against you," he asked Moore, "Is it true he's a little...?" As he asked the question, he did a limp-wrist gesture.[35]

Standing in the middle of the crowd, Moore's assistant Kevin Sikora cringed, wondering how his boss would handle the question.

The Governor, with a serious expression, paused for effect and then responded, "Let me just tell you this: He's a neophyte."

The crowd burst into laughter and the inquirer chortled, "Yup! Yup! I knew it! I knew he was one!" obviously ignorant of what the word meant.

Campaign manager John Leaberry got a good laugh when Sikora relayed the story. He passed it onto wealthy Democratic businessman Bernard Folio in Clarksburg, a long-time Moore supporter. Folio liked it so well that he bought several billboards with a slogan, "Don't Elect a Neophyte!"[36] (Reportedly, Caperton never forgave Folio for doing that, shutting him out of state government favors for eight years and wouldn't speak to him, even though the personal jabs ultimately never seemed to gain traction or harm him in any significant way with the electorate.)

Moore couldn't resist another little poke at Caperton again in October 1988 in a speech in Fayetteville, at which the news media was absent and by which time his poll numbers were so bad that he had nothing to lose and could say what he pleased. "My opponent says I've attacked his wife and next I'll attack his dog," Arch told his audience, in a grave tone. "But ladies and gentlemen, I solemnly assure you: I will never attack a poodle!" The crowd erupted in laughter and hooting. On one occasion, Arch accused Caperton of "tip-toeing through the tulips" with regard to an issue (invoking memories of Tiny Tim). Another time, Moore caught some flack from the news media when he said Caperton was "coming out of the closet on the issues." But, despite these few fun-poking comments, Moore usually kept the debate on a higher level. There was no love lost between the two opponents, however.

The public seemed to more concerned that electing Caperton would be inviting another "Rockefailure" era. A letter writer to the Huntington *Herald Dispatch* criticized Rockefeller's support of "his protege Gaston Caperton" saying people had short memories. Noting that Jay had promised 50,000 additional jobs but lost 34,000 manufacturing ones, the writer noted that employment under Moore's third term had actually increased, from 633,100 to 662,200 in 1988. "That's a darn good record" for a "one man show" or a "lone ranger," as the Dems had been calling Moore, thought the writer. Arch had to be a loner because none of the Democrats would help him, he suggested.[37]

In Beckley, the Governor gave a rare but heart-felt public commendation to his wife. Pointing to the First Lady, he said, "I've got a whale of a girl there. Who else would have put up with a fellow running 28 times?"

He admitted he was running scared, not only because of the Democrats' vastly superior numbers but also because of the overwhelming money difference. Reminding the audience that Jay had outspent him by $12 million to $1 million in 1980, he noted that his "newest long-legged millionaire" opponent, Caperton, had already spent more than $2 million on the primary.

In an obvious attempt to embarrass the Administration, claimants' lawyers organized pickets in front of the Workers' Compensation Fund offices (then located in a former chicken warehouse on Morris Street in Charleston). The marchers, off work and on compensation checks, carried signs for the news media's benefit and chanted that their claims were not being addressed promptly enough to suit them. Commissioner Nelson Robinson, the GOP nominee for state auditor and a fierce defender of Governor Moore, charged that theirs were politically motivated attacks. When Moore took office it was taking twenty months to get a claim to the Occupational Pneumoconiosis Board, he noted. That had dropped to seven months. Dependent's benefits were being processed within 90 days, as opposed to two years under Rockefeller. Payment of medical bills had dropped from 60 days to one week, he contended. Hearing loss claims were being processed in six weeks, as opposed to two years under Jay's administration. The black lung fund had $333.2 million and a surplus of $230 million, Robinson alleged.[38] But because the Fund was taking in $38 million per year less than it paid out, something (a premium increase) would have to be done in 1989, he conceded.[39]

The tax refund fiasco continued, despite the best efforts to get them paid in a timely manner. The cash flow crisis simply didn't allow it. Governor Moore had promised in a June press conference that all state tax refunds would be paid by July 1. By July 6, there were 30,000 taxpayers awaiting checks, however. The situation was looking somewhat promising, though: tax collections for July were $2.5 million ahead of projections and Moore thought August's goals would be met. He believed that money for the Marshall stadium could be found, despite the shortfalls. But the Teacher's Retirement Fund and other large accounts were being neglected by the shortfalls; there truly was no extra money for anything, only a deficit, a point Caperton and the Democrats stressed at every opportunity.

Additionally, the property tax reappraisal controversy was still fresh in voters' minds in 1988, and many were still not sure Arch Moore wasn't the instigator, since they received their first whopping bill after he took office. Many forgot that it had been approved in 1982, long before Arch's third term began. Moore's TV commercials tried to deflect criticism that was being heaped upon him from this Rockefeller tax hike—they accused Caperton of supporting the reappraisal, which had been required by a 1982 constitutional amendment, saying it would cost taxpayers $300 million. Caperton didn't respond directly—he and Moore both knew the unpopular, higher taxes would be helpful to state and local governments, but couldn't concede that publicly. The Democratic nominee deftly turned the focus of that red hot issue back onto the Governor in October by accusing his brother, Harry Moore, of being a paid lobbyist for the Ohio-based firm that performed the study (which had begun and was completed under Rockefeller). There would have been nothing improper if he had, but Harry Moore denied ever working for Cole, Layer, Trumble Co. (and it was unclear as to how Arch's brother could have helped get the company a contract with the Rockefeller Administration, which chose the controversial company). Caperton had refused to be drawn into the legislative debate on the issue earlier in the year, telling Beckley reporters, "If things don't get passed, people will blame me. If it does get passed, they will blame it on me. I refuse to get involved." He later did affirm his support of the program, which he termed "not perfect, but fair."[40] In the meantime, the Democratic nominee went about calling for a $100 million cut in the cost of state government but was extremely vague about programs he would pare, other than to say he'd make state government more efficient. (Government actually would continue to grow in personnel during his eight years and administrators' salaries would greatly increase.) At the same time, Caperton promised an across-the-board pay raise for all state employees. He said he would not consider a plan, which was in vogue at the time, to merge all institutions of higher learning into three state universities, to save money and make them better. He kept pounding his theme to every crowd that the state was "a basket case," and contended (contrary to statistics) that Moore had lost 40,000 West Virginia jobs since 1985.

In August, Lloyd Jackson departed Gaston's campaign to become Democratic State chairman. Rudy DiTrapano assumed chairmanship of Caperton's campaign. That month they brought a little-known Arkansas governor in to campaign for Caperton, at the Charleston Civic Center. Bill Clinton told the crowd that "perhaps no two states in the nation have problems as similar as Arkansas and West Virginia." Jay Rockefeller also told the 1700 Democrats at that Jefferson-Jackson Day dinner, "We are tired of Arch Moore's lies! Aren't you tired of Arch Moore taking credit for things he didn't do? It's time to say goodbye to Archie Moore and Ronnie Reagan!" When it came his turn, Caperton said Moore "has taken the state into bankruptcy, he offers us bankrupt leadership and no vision for the future, no plans."

At the Republican convention, the Governor had some fun with his opponent's name. "It will be new signs, new slogans, but the same old Gas. We're going to have a lot of Gas between now and November." He also tried to coin a new nickname for Caperton, "Cash-Dash and Spend-a-ton." He reminded the delegates of the great mess he'd inherited from Rockefeller and noted his own accomplishments since 1985: cutting taxes, fixing three thousand miles of highway, completing I-64, repairing a thousand bridges, restoring lost business and bringing in more than $3 billion in economic development. What was offered in November was the "tried and true" vs. money and inexperience, he said. Moore noted that Caperton had spent an unprecedented $2.15 million to win the primary and predicted he'd spend another ten million to win the general. He offered an olive branch to Raese, contending that the bitter primary battle had tested the mettle of the GOP and that it had come out stronger.[41]

As it would turn out, the ribbon-cutting ceremony for the completion of I-64 on July 15, 1988, was the last major event over which Moore would preside as governor of West Virginia. It was fitting, because–while other governors, senators, congressmen, presidents and federal and state administrators had been involved in the funding and planning–Arch Moore had done more than any single individual in bringing the modern Interstate highway system to fruition in the Mountain State. He had ridden herd on the project, cracking the whip, from those early days in 1969, to get it funded and completed quickly but at the highest standards. Without his persistent, occasionally frantic effort, it may have not been completed for decades, or ever.

So, as the last 36-mile link was to be opened, providing motorists 1,125 miles of four-lane from St. Louis, Missouri to Norfolk, Virginia, it was a day of pride for Moore, Ritchie and the remainder of their team. Arch invited former Governors Hulett Smith and Okey Patteson, and the congressional delegation, including Byrd and Rockefeller. It was a hot, summer day, and Arch knew the crowd would not appreciate endless, lengthy speeches by political windbags, all of whom wanted to take credit for the accomplishment. But that didn't stop some from trying and some childish pouting when it became clear that he wouldn't allow it.

Robert C. Byrd's egomania had not yet become as chronic and full-blown as it soon would, but his autobiography made it clear that the senior senator thought he should have presided over the ceremony, that it should have been his big day, not the Governor's. He wrote:

> *As a crowd of about ten thousand watched, the governor cut the ribbon to open Interstate 64. He declared: "It is indeed a personal achievement. It is a monument to progress. It is a highway for tomorrow. With determination and imagination, this is a reality. Congratulations, West*

Virginians. This your highway."

Moore, a phenomenal politician who always received many Democratic votes, was an individual who operated as a one-man show. Hence, as far as participating in the speaking portion of the program marking the completion of I-64 was concerned, Democrats were virtually shut out by Moore. A day or so prior to the ribbon-cutting ceremony, I had called the governor from Washington to request that Senator Rockefeller and I be included in the program, if only for a brief few minutes.

Moore's response was that he wanted to keep the program short. I reminded the Governor that I-64 was a federal-state undertaking, with the federal government having picked up 90 percent of the overall cost, and I pointed out that I had supported the interstate program through the years from its inception, going back to my service in the House of Representatives during the Eisenhower administration. I also emphasized that, as a member of the Senate Appropriations Committee, I had supported the funding for I-64 and other interstate routes, to all of which Governor Moore turned a deaf ear. He simply repeated what he had already said, namely, that there would be a short program, some music, a brief speech by himself, and that would be it. Period.

Moore was rather curt, and so was I. My closing words: "Okay, Arch. I get the message. Goodbye!" Although Rockefeller and I were unable to participate in the program, we both joined, along with Moore and others, in the cutting of the ribbon.[42]

What Byrd failed to realize—or more likely he did realize and didn't care–was that Moore was in a fight for his political life and was trying to remind voters of everything he had done for them during his three terms, including highway completion.

Bringing teachers' salaries up to national standards was another accomplishment of Moore's and he wanted them to know that it wasn't for trying that they had not received one in 1986 and 1987. At a Teachers' Forum in Charleston, the Governor reminded them that there had been few of the "Arch Moore years ... that teachers did not receive salary increases ... That is, until the legislature the past two year rejected my proposals."

Referring to Caperton and his party, Moore said he found "it quite ironic that the party that touts the support of the WVEA is the party that killed those raises...and I believe set education back another decade. I also find it quite ironic that my opponent's wife [Del. Dee Caperton, D-Kanawha] and one of his closest aides [Sen. Lloyd Jackson] cast the deciding votes against those raises. When they tell you the money was not there for it, I can only say that I pointed the way, but they chose another. They call it confrontational politics. I call it cowardice." Parents and students know what they want and teachers know what they need, he said, but the legislature stood in the way of progress. He added, "As a columnist said this week, 'I guess they just didn't want Arch to look too good.' Well, I'm not interested in how I look as I am in how those test scores will look in the years to come ... My greatest nightmare as governor is not a natural disaster, although they are bad. It is not a fiscal crisis or even losing an election, though that would be bad. But it would be to get a failing grade from that next generation because we let them down by not providing the best education and opportunities possible. That would be a curse upon us all, an indelible stigma which we would be unable to erase for as long as time stands."[43]

The Wall Street Journal, normally a bastion of Republicanism, surprisingly weighed in against Moore in a late September, 1988 issue, in an article headlined, "State of Despair." Playing to the East Coast's stereotypes, the paper alleged that West Virginia was a state full of shacks, chronic unemployment, political corruption, teachers fleeing the state in droves and the worst population exodus in the nation. Moore, always a defender of the state's image and especially now, was livid. He called the article an outrage and said it represented the past. He noted that there were people in New Jersey living in a dog house and there were "people living in cardboard boxes on the streets of New York" that the *Journal* ignored, in order to pick on the Mountain State. The newspaper was not widely read among West Virginia voters, but the article was an unfair, low blow.

The Governor smelled a skunk. He blamed the article on Caperton, whom he suspected of planting it. "I run against the doom and gloom candidate of the century," the Governor told a Bluefield crowd, referring to his Democrat opponent. "That article yesterday adds material to his very heavy portfolio." To the Conference on Small Business, Moore labeled the *Journal* as the "Northern Sick Call" (as opposed to the *Gazette,* which he called simply the Sick Call). With a burst of populist rhetoric, he complained that it was a newspaper "which feeds unmercilessly off the profits of hard working small businessmen so others can get rich doing nothing from the toil of those who do."

Not all the press was negative, however. A September editorial in the Elkins *Inter-Mountain* noted that "so far in every month this year have been more West Virginians employed than during the same month a year ago. That, together with a state reduction in unemployment, tells us that the economy of our state is growing." The paper noted that manufacturing, construction and trade had grown by 1400 jobs and that there were 8,600 more people employed in July 1988 than a year before. Unemployment was remaining at 6.7 percent in July (a vast improvement over its peak 20 percent rate under Rockefeller) and employment had expanded by 2,700 jobs that month.

Moore told a business convention in Charleston that he was reminded "of the time when I was a boy and an evangelist came to our town to hold a series of revival meetings."

> *After the revival was over we all assembled at the river to watch the baptismal service. We were especially interested because the town reprobate, a man named Abner, was going to be baptized. Abner waded out into the water in his very best blue serge suit. When he got in as deep as his trouser pockets, the jack and ten of spades came floating out on the water. That caused some snickering along the river bank. And it really embarrassed Ab's wife Vern. When the water got to Ab's vest pockets the king and queen of spades floated out on the water. This brought a little stronger reaction from the riverbank crowd. Just as Ab reached the preacher the ace of spades floated out from his inside coat pocket. There was a great roar of laughter from the riverbank and poor Vern couldn't stand it any longer. She shouted out to the preacher, "Parson, there's no use foolin' with Ab. He's lost!...lost!...I tell, you lost!" The evangelist turned, looked straight at Vern and said sternly, "I'm ashamed of you, Sister Vern. How in the hell could he be lost with a hand like that?"*

Arch made a point from his parable: "The excellent working relationship we have forged between government, business and education has given the state of West Virginia cards in every pocket! And we just can't lose with a hand like that!"

In that speech, he recounted the increase in jobs, new businesses and factories his administration had helped create in three years, adding that he and Governor John Sununu of New Hampshire were working on a cooperative in which coal-fired power plants in West Virginia would provide electricity to that northern state (with complaints coming from Canada about air pollution that was drifting across the border).

Arch added, "Some people look at this Governor and say, 'He's an optimist.' Unfortunately, they don't mean it as a compliment! But I am an optimist and I think our progress the past four years gives me ample reason for optimism. And those who are objective in their view of the State of West Virginia will agree with me."[44]

Despite the fact that the economy was rebounding, and a lot of that was because of Moore's efforts, he found long-time supporters abandoning him like never before. The "South of Route 60" crowd, the Democrats who could be bought, were running away from him, like rats fleeing the sinking ship. Arch was far from a good bet in '88 and they weren't about to risk problems with state party bosses and jeopardize their power and control over patronage by supporting this Republican again. But even Dick Barber walked this time. He'd been with him in '84, making deals with Southern Democrats, but late in '88 he went to California, claiming he had to be away for his beer distributor business. Before he left, he was heard lamenting the fact that Moore was even seeking a fourth term. "He's like an old prize fighter, going into the ring one too many times!" he told political friends.

Nominee Caperton was joined for a three-city tour by New Jersey Senator Bill Bradley. He complained that every time he would "go to a community, [Governor Moore] follows right behind me and offers them a $5000 or a $100,000 grant. I think people are tired of that!" He said that "we have no participation in government, we've got a king." Moore retorted, "That's not true. I am a leader. I am an impatient person for the future of this state and I don't have to learn. We built a base. We're ready to go." The Governor reiterated that, if one looked at Caperton's "Partnership for Progress," he would see that "every one of those single points have been in operation in West Virginia for years."

Moore did his best to engender optimism wherever he campaigned. In Clarksburg and Martinsburg, he announced 185 new jobs and in Huntington told his audience that the "nay-sayers won't be able to stop" the building of a new, 30,000-seat football stadium for Marshall University. In October, the new state office complex in Fairmont was dedicated, named the Arch A. Moore, Jr. Office Complex. "I tried every way in the world to keep them from naming this building after me," the Governor insisted to the audience. (Naming it for Arch was the idea of the Manchin family, who controlled Marion County politics. The Governor had allowed state Senator Joe Manchin to share credit for the building.)

As in 1980, there simply was no way for Moore to match the personal funds of a multi-millionaire willing to spend his fortune on a victory. As he did in the primary against See, Caperton flooded the airwaves with advertising and the election workers network with tons of money. Officially, he spent almost $4.6 million to Moore's nearly $2.5 million in the general election.[45] But Arch's Democratic friends came to him with news far more disturbing: Caperton was planning to dump tons of money in the last days, out into the counties, to the hills and hollows, to buy a huge, friendly voter turnout. From the Republicans' point of view, what Caperton planned to do was illegal.

Moore called upon Secretary of State Ken Hechler and the State Elections Commission to enforce the $35 limit on buying election workers, saying it was needed to "stop the millionaires from buying" the elections. Caperton had circumvented the rule in the primary, paying far more than that, by paying for three days' "work" from each recipient, not just for services rendered on one election day. He planned to use the same tactic against Moore in November. If there was a cause in which Hechler was interested, he didn't hesitate to act boldly. But now he weakly questioned whether he had authority to do anything about it (even though the state supreme court had ruled, in *Rogers v. Hechler,* that he had a mandatory duty to put the election reforms into effect). Perhaps his party's leadership was pressuring Hechler to turn a blind eye. He had always been a maverick, frequently had shown courage, but this time he yielded. The Secretary of State sat on his hands and did nothing. Hechler had been running on the issue of clean elections for 45 years, Moore bitterly observed, but ducked the chance to do something about it when he had the chance. "I think Hechler proved he was a fraud,"Arch told the *Daily Mail* on October 13. The Governor filed suit in the supreme court to force Hechler to do his duty, but it was too little, too late. The Democratic Machine most certainly was not going to police itself, not in 1988, at least. Their idea of reform was to get rid of the Republican governor.

Arch the Candidate tried to link Caperton to the national Democrats and to tie him especially to gun control, a crucial issue in a state full of hunters and rural homes where police protection was almost non-existent. But Gaston pretty much ignored Moore's efforts to draw him into battle.

Apparently upon recommendation of his handlers, Caperton was so comfortable with his lead in the polls that he withdrew from reporters and rarely made a public, unrehearsed statement. He became almost completely inaccessible, lest he say something stupid and blow the election. Reporters complained, but they did not turn on the Democrat. Moore's gun control TV and radio spots were running up Caperton's negatives a bit, however, so he sent letters to voters in the waning weeks of the campaign, assuring them he would not try to take their guns away.

In the sole debate between the men, broadcast live on October 10, 1988, from a theater at West Virginia State College in Institute, each with his partisans cheering him on, Arch tried to score some points. The Governor charged that Caperton's plan was "nothing but paper, empty words." He repeatedly tried to illustrate that his opponent was inexperienced, untried, unpredictable, with no record. Caperton, in turn, retorted, "The Governor always wants to blame somebody else for the problems–the legislature, the media [and] lately he has even blamed my wife and campaign manager."

Arch stuck to his theme, that the overall situation was much, much better than the media or the Democrats would acknowledge. They wanted to return to "politics of the past," he charged. "The opposition is suffocating good news. The opposition absolutely fails to recognize that there is tremendous regeneration in the mineral and energy fields and...manufacturing." But Caperton continued to repeat an inaccurate and unsubstantiated claim that "the reason unemployment is going down is that the state has lost thousands of workers to other states" which rang true to disillusioned voters.

The two were given a chance to ask each other a question. Caperton asked Moore why his administration had "forgiven millions of dollars" in unpaid workers' compensation premiums. The Governor, visibly peeved, insisted all the settlements were legal and used the opportunity to remind viewers that Caperton's insurance firm had collected $3 million a year from state government. "You've lived off the government all your life," he snapped. Caperton's retort was that his insurance company just processed claims and that the insurance program was in trouble because it was underfunded by $50 million. He noted that he'd been in the private sector all his career while Moore "has been living off the government all his life."

Arch asked Caperton why he supported Democrat Senator Lloyd Benson for vice president. Gaston fell into the trap, contending that the nation needed someone old enough, experienced enough, to lead the nation if necessary. Moore grinned and said, "I think he answered my question. He is going to competence and experience and that's what I'm all about." When Caperton said he'd cut costs by curbing executive helicopter rides and streamlining the Lottery Commission, Arch said, "Mr. Caperton does not understand state government."

Toward the end of the debate Caperton expressed certainty that he would win the election to which Moore said, "I would suggest that you don't bet too much of your money on that one." In a response that would be more fully appreciated in November, Caperton responded, "I already have."

But Moore's methods in the exchange–such as calling Caperton "young man"—did not go over well; they made the Governor look old, cranky, even desperate. "Governor Moore changed his debating style and approaches about three times in that debate, like a boxer, trying to see what would work," thought Caperton. "Because he was such a good debater and always in command of the facts, I think he underestimated me, he didn't take me seriously. But once he got into it, he realized I was better than he expected."

Apparently remembering how Nixon's appearance caused him to lose the first 1960 debate to Kennedy, the producers of the Moore-Caperton debate pulled out the stops to cause Arch Moore to look bad. They put a camera on the Governor that made him look bleached-out, and which created a fuzzy picture. They superimposed a caption on the screen, "The problem is not with your set." It clearly was done on purpose, because it would have been very easy to substitute another camera had it simply been a "technical difficulty." Noted veteran newsman Raamie Barker, "Their caption implied, 'The problem is with the *Governor.*'" It may have been the dirtiest trick of the campaign, and it was effective.

Caperton had conducted an intense mock debate beforehand, with Joe Bob Goodwin acting as Moore. "There's a certain amount of facts and figures you want to have in your head. And you want what you say in the debate to be consistent with what you've said in the campaign," Caperton pointed out. But the entire day of the debate, Caperton went into seclusion and just silently contemplated what he wanted to say. "I sat quietly by myself and thought about why I wanted to be elected, what I believed in. People watch enough television—they know if you're being sincere. And I think I came off as sincere."

Caperton did well in the debate, at the very least holding his own against the incumbent governor, which is all he had to do with such a huge lead in the polls.

Moore challenged Caperton to another debate on October 30, but the

Democratic nominee refused. His spokesman, Steve Cohen, said, "Now that [Moore] badly trails in the polls he may be getting nervous. In a panic he suddenly wants a last-minute debate." Moore's Ed Esposito countered, "Why is [Caperton] afraid to face Arch Moore?" But there would be no risk taken by another debate; he continued to ignore the request.

The economy continued to be subject of an ongoing public exchange between the two. The Governor took credit for taking the unemployment rate from the nearly 18 percent he had inherited from Rockefeller to 5.9 percent in 1988. Official records bore witness to the truth of his boast. But Caperton convinced listeners that it wasn't correct. "Moore has created a lot of jobs for West Virginians–in North Carolina and Virginia," he would continue to allege.[46]

The Charles Ryan-Samples Research poll showed that Caperton's Labor Day lead over Moore, of 60 to 31 percent , had tightened to 52 to 36-percent in mid-October. Arch's job approval had risen from 19 percent in April to 31 percent, still quite dismal for the incumbent. Interestingly, 31 percent thought Moore had won the debate, 14 percent thought Caperton and 41 percent said there was no clear-cut winner.

Both campaigns focused their efforts, energy and funds on ten counties—Kanawha, Cabell, Fayette, Harrison, Marion, Mercer, Monongalia, Ohio, Raleigh and Wood—which contained half of the state's population and were 68 percent Democrat. Historically, the candidate who won a majority in those won the statewide election.

A well-publicized and attended "Salute to Arch Moore Day" was held in Marion County, arranged in part by John and Joe Manchin, but such events were rare. (Moore would not carry that county in November, despite economic revitalization efforts there which he had engineered during his term–Marion Countians had quickly forgotten what an economic Depression they had suffered under Moore's predecessor, whom they had thrice supported for governor.) After the success of that day, one of Moore's friends told him sarcastically, "Now you just need fifty-four more of these!"

Editorial support of newspapers meant far less than it did in elections past. People had pretty much decided early on how they were going to vote; what a writer opined mattered little. The Governor received the endorsement of nine of the twenty-one state dailies, including the *Register-Herald* of Beckley, Elkins' *InterMountain*, Huntington's *Herald-Dispatch*, Martinsburg's *Evening Journal*, *The Parkersburg News*, *The Welch Daily News*, Wheeling's *Intelligencer* and Clarksburg's *Telegram*. *The Charleston Daily Mail* gave him a lukewarm, short endorsement, and waited until just a day or two before the election. A few, such as the *Montgomery Herald*, did begin questioning the vague and ambitious promises of Caperton to balance the budget (with no specifics on how much, if any new taxes) and cutting government spending and creating jobs (again, with no specifics offered). The Democrat talked in "generalities, [but was] weak on specifics," the paper wrote.

No one who observed his frantic 1988 campaign schedule could say that Arch didn't want a fourth term. The blades of the state helicopter rarely ceased their rotation. He campaigned long, hard days, especially in those last six weeks. He took off a day only to go see his Redskins.

Kevin Sikora was with the 65-year-old warrior continually in those final days. "He would just be exhausted, sleeping between campaign stops. I would have my doubts whether he could keep up the pace." But after a power nap, Sikora remembered, "He would spring from the helicopter, his usual self, with, 'Arch Moore's the name!' shaking hands and campaigning enthusiastically." Sikora, athletic and forty years younger, could not keep up with him. "I'd be exhausted at the end of the day. The Governor had boundless energy."[47]

In the closing weeks of the campaign, Governor Moore told anyone who would listen that, contrary to what the news media was portraying, the state was actually "on fire economically." He claimed a figure of $5.1 billion in economic development during his three-plus years in office. He pointed out that his administration had greatly reduced the unemployment rate.

But Caperton attacked his credibility, repeating his contention that the rate had dropped because people were leaving the state for jobs. He charged that tax refunds had been held up to balance the budget. And Caperton's message stuck. He convinced them it was time for a change. Even though much of what he said about the improving economy was true, unexaggerated, few believed Arch anymore. Polls showed voters did not blame the Democratic legislature for the cash flow problems; they blamed the Governor for the impasse and the problems it generated. Another cause of the PR failures was that Arch exaggerated his successes, to the point in which many refused to believe any of it. "He took credit for a gallon when only a pint would do," wrote columnist Tom Miller. "Voters elected him four years ago because they wanted to return to those 'wonderful days of yesteryear,' but Moore wasn't able to deliver. The heralded move of hundreds of CSX Transportation, Inc. workers to Huntington was a prime example that was more smoke than fire."[48]

Moore repeated his charge to a Wheeling Rotary club, that Caperton was a "neophyte" and a clone of Jay Rockefeller, predicting that the state would be "dead in the water" if they elected him. The Democratic nominee had become rich from state insurance contracts Rockefeller had arranged for Caperton, he charged. He told them Caperton's company had received those lucrative contracts as result of the "buddy-buddy system" obtained "in a political climate, for political reasons, for political favors, because of his political connections." He said Caperton's firm had been fired (by Moore) from handling the PEIB contract because of a twenty five percent error rate in handling health insurance claims. (Lloyd Jackson said that Caperton had simply chosen not to bid on the contract again, however.)

The *Gazette* moved in for the kill, unleashing its fury upon Moore as it hadn't done since 1972. They quoted on their front page Caperton's allegation that the Governor used the state helicopter to fly from the Mansion the short distance to Yeager Airport. "I don't know where they got that; that's not a correct statement at all. We never have," insisted Wayne Childress, the state trooper in charge of aviation. But the damage was done; the wild story became accepted by many as fact.

The Governor's hometown paper asked him to make a prediction on the election's outcome. In a rare example of candor about the subject, he told the reporter, "Honesty compels me to say I'm scared to death." He noted that his opponent was from Kanawha County and "that in and of itself poses a problem. There's always the tendency for the county to support the person of that county."[49] Although the official line from campaign chairman John Leaberry and others was that her dad was slightly ahead of Caperton, Shelley Moore Capito was straightforward. "It doesn't look good," she would admit to friends, when asked directly.

As was their custom, the Moore clan listened to the returns from his Moundsville office. It was bleak; there was no good news. He "got his clock cleaned," as Nelson Robinson would put it the next day. It was tough, very tough–this was Arch's first defeat as an incumbent, and the worst loss he had ever suffered in terms of numbers, 382,421 to 267,172, or about 59 percent to 41 percent. The Governor won a mere ten counties only two of which, Randolph and Fayette, were heavily Democrat. Even many traditionally Republican counties went for Caperton. The rejection by the majority of voters of Moore's third term (and their desire for no fourth term) was clear; it was not simply that his Democratic opponent had bought the election or that the Democrat machine had succeeded in getting tens of thousands of straight ticket votes cast.

"We've finally driven a stake into that bastard's heart!" Rudy

DiTrapano was heard to exclaim.[50]

Even though it was not unexpected–the polls had been horrible for Arch throughout the year–there were tears nonetheless. The Governor released a statement, "The people of West Virginia have been very kind to the Moore family and their public service. We believe, as a family, we gave them our heart and soul all the years of our services. For West Virginia today is decidedly better than a few brief years ago. This progress must be continued. We wish our successor well in that effort."

The continued disunity of his own party was a contributing factor to the huge margin by which Arch Moore was defeated, his campaign spokesman believed. "We got some Clyde (See) votes but not enough," Ed Esposito told the Associated Press. "My gut reaction is that we were not the beneficiaries of a united Republican Party." The damage caused by the Raese challenge destroyed Arch's chances of keeping his coalition together.

State GOP Chairman "Hike" Heiskell thought that straight Democratic ticket voting killed Moore's chances, which of course had been Caperton's strategy. "When the Democrats are running out 70 percent of the Democrats voting for Democrats, the Republicans are going to take a whipping because of the two-to-one registration the Democrats have."[51] Hike noted that there had been 12,000 straight Democrat tickets voted in Kanawha County alone. The straight ticket voters allowed Massachusetts Governor Michael Dukakis, one of the least illustrious candidates the Democrats ever nominated, to win West Virginia by 31,000 votes, even though he was pro-abortion, anti-prayer in schools, pro-gun control—positions contrary to those of most voters in the Mountain State. Clearly, many voted their party, not their convictions.

Dave Peyton, another columnist hostile to Moore, blamed the defeat on the Governor's style. He had an autocratic, imperialistic haughtiness, Peyton charged, a Nixonian "them against us" bunker mentality. Moore thrived at shaking his finger at members of the press and the legislature, wrote Peyton, and "a substantial number of people got tired of that." The Governor "tried to convince dejected and beaten people that things were improving and subtly suggested that if they didn't believe him they were part of the problem. Moore was not to blame for our economic collapse," he ended. "But he is guilty of not responding to the victims in a kind and gentle way."[52]

Governor Moore made emotional, comforting remarks to his staff and administration at a Christmas reception in his office. All were dignified good-byes, but had a definite air of finality about them. Few felt that he would ever return to public office; this was the end. He told the group assembled that several of them were worthy and capable of following him as governor (none has) and that he hoped he would see that come to pass.

On January 11, 1989, he followed tradition in making a farewell address to the legislature, which was respectfully, even enthusiastically, received. It was one of his most heart-felt speeches and one in which he was entirely candid and blunt about the state's future. More than a few in the audience were wiping their eyes. "This may have been his finest speech ever," thought Tom Tinder. "He was very prophetic, telling the legislators that rising health insurance costs would become the biggest problem they would deal with in coming years. He also mentioned that land fills, disposing of garbage, would become an increasing challenge."

Undoubtedly realizing that it would be his final speech as a public person, Moore allowed some sentimentality and personal feelings to show. "There is a line from one of the great Broadway plays...in which an expression is made by Rex Harrison to Eliza Doolittle ... [He] uses the term, "I've grown accustomed to your face." And I think that lyric goes on to say, "It's like breathing out and breathing in." Mr. Speaker, Mr. President, I've grown accustomed to this place. It's been my life, and truly, it's like breathing out and breathing in."

The Governor admitted that he often had called for programs and improvements, not always knowing from where the funds would come to pay for them. "It takes no special talent in politics to say 'no' because then you don't have to perform," he told the solons. " The great talent in politics is to say 'yes,' and try to figure out how you can perform, because you place this special burden upon yourself."[53]

With no inkling that his successor would request, and they would grant, the largest tax increase in the state's history within a matter of weeks, Moore warned the lawmakers that "you are in a hopeless circumstance as it relates to remaining current." Medicaid alone was going to add $40 million a year, he noted. "In 1988, we spent $269 million in Medicaid claims. We estimate that those claims are going to be over $650 million in the next four years." Other federal programs were making more and more demands on the states, he said, adding that they impose sanctions if a state does not follow their demands, such as withholding highway funds, "giving us much more federal benevolence than we can afford," he suggested.

Noting that coal employment in the state had risen to 34,000 and would have difficulty staying at that level, he advised against tinkering with the Department of Energy, as the liberals were proposing. They would be "rolling the dice" to do so, he cautioned, "and the regeneration of this industry will be severely jeopardized."

He told the legislators that he was leaving them with money in the bank. An audit had revealed the treasury was $25 million richer than had been thought. Bond indebtedness had been reduced by $110 million during his term, he claimed. Department of Highways reserves had been $45 million when he took office; he was leaving them with $165.5 million in reserves in that fund. Employment Security had owed the federal government $375 million when he took office; now that debt "has been paid off," and a reserve of $129 million was available, "as solvent as that fund has been in modern history."

Altogether, he estimated that $7 billion in new economic investment by the private sector had occurred during his third term. "I believe that the full benefits of those results are going to come further down the line, because of the necessity to create, to build, to bring the jobs on stream." (And he was correct about that.) "I believe we have done a respectable job–not to the satisfaction, perhaps, of a lot of people...[but] you have nothing to be ashamed of..." He ended his speech with the finality and poignancy it deserved from someone who had been a public *servant* for most of his career.

> *[There] are some who suggest that Arch Moore can play a crowd like a banjo. I don't mean to take you down that path at all. But literally thousands of letters have been received by the Moore family following November 8, 1988. And we have responded to those letters very simply as I respond to you today and I respond to my fellow West Virginians: For thirty five years the people of the State of West Virginia have been very good to the Moore family. We have given you our heart and soul. We have never regretted one day in our public service to the people of our state. Should we as a young couple, as we did, make a decision that public service was really our way of life–if that decision were to be given to us again today, knowing all the things we know—we would still choose to try to serve the people of this state. My children have grown up in the hot climate of political debate. Mrs. Moore and I are tremendously rewarded by their character, their stature and their commitment as our children to the state of West Virginia.*
>
> *We will be around, Mr. Speaker and Mr. President, in any way that we possibly can, to add, to help, to ease and to*

suggest, only perhaps more quietly than in the past, the direction we should go. For you see, Mr. Speaker and Mr. President, we're West Virginians. And we always will be. Thank you, and goodbye.[54]

He and Mrs. Moore attended the inauguration, but (as they had done in 1977, when Rockefeller became governor) departed before Caperton's speech began. It was more than he could do to sit and listen to more negative, somewhat inaccurate rhetoric from his successor: "[There] are many people suffering as did those in the Depression...Our education system has not kept pace, our economy has not created the needed jobs, our environment has not been protected, and our government has not functioned responsibly."

Moore and Ken Faerber would establish an office on Kanawha Boulevard in Charleston, with Audrey Toler, his loyal secretary, sticking with him. Arch hoped to use his contacts to re-establish a law practice.

An Arch Moore government-in-exile was not to be. Things would go from bad to worse for our subject—much, much worse, now that he was out of office. The underlying storm that had been brewing for two years–perhaps since the 1968 campaign–would soon be bursting out in full force and fury.

Chapter 28 Notes

1. - *The Moorefield Examiner,* January 27, 1988.

2. - *Register-Herald* Jan. 8, 1988. Rockefeller would later succeed in getting Toyota to build a large plant in Putnam County, which spun off additional manufacturing and service jobs and continued to expand, likely his greatest (some would say only) achievement during his years as governor and senator.

3. - *Montgomery Herald,* Feb. 3, 1988.

4. - The WVEA had become more radically partisan in recent years, fighting Moore at every opportunity, even though he had given teachers more pay raises than any other governor in history. Instead of helping him accomplish more for education in the legislature, it seemed to be their clear goal to drive him from office. One of the organization's leaders showed his true colors when he joined the Caperton campaign and, later, became a cabinet member in his administration.

5. - *Sunday Gazette-Mail,* Nov. 15, 1987.

6. - When Vice President George H. W. Bush, the presumed GOP presidential nominee, appeared in Morgantown in his drab gray suit that Spring, he suspiciously refused to be seen with Governor Moore. Some thought it was in order not to take sides in the divisive primary race. Others saw something more ominous in the snub, thinking it signaled what they suspected: that the Justice Department was targeting Moore and that the Vice President had been warned to stay away from him, not to be photographed with him, because the Governor was contaminated.

7. - *The Dominion News* once went after former Monongalia County Prosecutor Joe Laurita, a Republican whose Jaguar was bombed by criminals, with a series of articles harshly derogatory to him. He was nearly the only one to fight back. Laurita's family had enough coal money to mount a counteroffensive so he started a full-circulation tabloid, *The Better Times Weekly,* which went to 57,000

households and, for several years, competed with Raese's daily for advertising dollars before a peace treaty between Laurita and Raese was consummated.

8. - On Primary Election day, a disc jockey on Raese's WVAQ would urge listeners to go out and vote for a "new governor." Interestingly, Caperton and Raese met each other, for the first and last time, on Primary Election day, at an airport. They wished each other luck, according to Caperton, but didn't discuss Moore.

9. - The reader should note that ex-convict Owens' hatred for Haden remains bitterly intense and the Judge is no longer around to defend himself; you can believe his allegation or not.

10. - Owens claims that, for the past two decade, even while in prison, he has always received a Christmas card from Senator Rockefeller and that, at a Mingo County Democratic function, Jay came out of his way, into the crowd to specifically shake Owens' hand and give him a hug. He showed the author several photos of himself with Rockefeller, which were inscribed with affectionate comments to him by Jay, in Rockefeller's handwriting and signed by the Senator.

11. - Associated Press story, May 16, 1988.

12. - *The Inter-Mountain*, May 14, 1988.

13. - Owens, July 18, 2005.

14. - Elkins, March 4, 2005.

15. - Governor Moore appointed Judge Kessell to the state supreme court to fill a vacancy.

16. - Dee and Gaston would divorce, the first time that had happened to a West Virginia governor. Her run for secretary of state was unsuccessful. Caperton's colorful and sometimes controversial courtship and second marriage to Rachael Worby would serve as fodder for national news stories.

17. - Jones also was from a West Virginia Republican family.

18. - UPI, Sept. 20, 1987.

19. - Caperton, March 9, 2005.

20. - *The Herald Dispatch,* April 20, 1988.

21. - *Daily Mail*, Feb. 19, 1987.

22. - Energy Commissioner Ken Faerber confirmed that Caperton was ineligible for a mining permit because the state had to spend more than $360,000 to clean up the Slab Fork closed mine, because it owed the Dept. of Energy $118,000 in fines, had forfeited bonds totaling $74,195 and owed the UMWA's health and retirement fund $3.5 million. *Charleston Daily Mail,* May 9, 1988.

23. - Mario Palumbo won 51,722, Gus Douglass 48,748, and Dan Tonkovich 14,916, with two minor candidates getting the remainder.

24. - Raese, Steve Canterbury contended, exploded, telling him that if he wasn't out of the Greer Mansion in five days, "he would throw my ass out the window and would throw my [expletive] bird against the wall. I have a pet parrot." He added, referring to an incident at the 1984 Republican Convention when Raese hit a Charleston reporter, "I think he might have knocked me around, too." *Herald-Dispatch,* April 29, 1988.

25. - *Gazette-Mail,* April 17, 1988.

26. - 78,495 for Moore, 68,973 for Raese.

27. - Sixteen delegates were selected for the Republican National Convention, statewide. Normally the top vote-getting in any such contest, Moore came in a dismal 15th place while Underwood finished 16th.

28. - *Gazette,* May 12, 1988.

29. - The Governor rarely would consider adventurous or politically risky ideas. For example, some suggested that, with the creation of the Regional Jail Authority and building of new prisons and jails around the state, it would be a perfect time to consider privatizing some of the prison work, contracting it out to professional, non-state employees as other states had done, saving money and obtaining a better system. Moore would not give the suggestion a glance.

30. - *The Caperton Years,* 1989-1993.

31. - *Martinsburg Journal,* Oct. 1, 1988.

32. - *National Governors' Association Policy Positions 1988-89,* pp. 101-103.

33. - *W. Va. Blue Book,* 1987, p. 686.

34. - Jim Lees, *Graffiti Online,* undated.

35. - Gaston Caperton was a confirmed heterosexual, one of his state police bodyguards insisted.

36. - Kevin Sikora, November 2, 2003.
37. - *Herald-Dispatch,* Sept. 27, 1988.
38. - *Daily Mail,* Oct. 18, 1988
39. - *The Herald Dispatch,* Oct. 8, 1988.
40. - *The Register-Herald,* June 28, 1988.
41. - *The Dominion Post,* July 24, 1988.
42. - Byrd, Ibid.
43. - *Third Term,* Ibid.
44. - *Third Term,* Ibid.
45. - Secretary of State's Office.
46. - *The Daily Athenaeum,* Oct. 24, 1988.
47. - Sikora, April 9, 2005.
48. - *Huntington Dispatch,* Nov. 13, 1988.
49. - *Moundsville Echo,* Nov. 8, 1988.
50. - H. John Rogers, July 27, 2005.
51. - According to the 1989 *West Virginia Blue Book,* the Democrats had 640,255 on their roles in the 1988 election, the Republicans had only 303,061 and 25,303 were registered as independents or "others." That was 56,000 less Republicans than the state had in 1972 when Arch beat Jay. Thirteen thousand less Republicans were on the books since the 1984 election, but the Dems had lost 44,000 of theirs in that same four year period. Part of that loss for both parties, undoubtedly, was due to a clean-up of the county clerks' records, expunging dead voters or those who had moved away.
52. - *Huntington Herald Dispatch,* Nov. 11, 1988.
53. - *Third Term,* Ibid.
54. - *Third Term,* Ibid.

Chapter Twenty Nine
The Feds vs. Arch Moore

Driving southbound on I-79 in late 1989, Charleston businessman Bill Ellis noticed the blue lights of a State Police cruiser flashing in the rearview mirror of his Cadillac. He thought that maybe he'd been speeding. He was shocked when the trooper asked to see his driver's license and then informed him he was under arrest.

Ellis had been managing a Cross Lanes dog racing track of which he was part-owner. It was trying to evolve into a casino and needed legislation to make that happen. At the time of his arrest, he was returning from a visit to Sam D'Annunzio, a Clarksburg beer distributor. Closely connected with Democratic politics, D'Annunzio was the go-to guy when one wanted a bill passed in the legislature. He demanded cash for his assistance, lots of it, and didn't explain what it was to be used for. It was just known, "Sammy D" will get it done; one didn't ask too many questions.

As with others who would be caught in his web, Ellis was unaware that Sammy had been under investigation by the FBI for several months. In exchange for immunity from prosecution for his role as the legislative leadership's bagman, Sammy had agreed to wear a wire and the feds were recording his telephone and in-person conversations.[1] Accused of being in on Sammy D's cash-for-influence scheme, Bill Ellis was indicted by federal prosecutors in December 1989 and tried in February 1990. It was alleged that he, too, was delivering payments from the racetrack to powerful senators for passage of favorable legislation.

It was a strange and traumatic time for the state, difficult for many to grasp, to understand, to sort out. From the mid-1980s through 1991, the web of political intrigue and corruption just seem to widen, ensnaring more and more West Virginia politicians and businessmen. The tangled web would eventually eclipse the investigation and punishment of the Barron Gang in the 1960s.

Coincidentally, the headlines were also filled with news of another scandal of a more costly nature, but unrelated to the criminal investigations. A. James Manchin had illustrated the Peter Principle when he assumed the office of state treasurer (or, "Treasurer of State," as he preferred to call himself). Manchin freely admitted he knew nothing about finances, the most important function of the office he'd just won. He hired Rockefeller's F&A commissioner, reputed whiz kid Arnold Margolin, as assistant treasurer to manage that end of the office. For the first couple years, Arnie Margolin was drawing complimentary headlines for the huge returns he supposedly was earning the State. But then his house of cards collapsed and taxpayers discovered he had been engaging in a highly risky, and ultimately disastrous, handling of their funds.

Chronicled Professor Rice, "[When] the public learned of the enormous losses to the state through reckless investment of moneys in the Consolidated Investment Fund...[blame] fell heavily upon Manchin, who was lacking in knowledge of such financial matters, but who had entrusted the investments to Arnold Margolin...Margolin was regarded as a financial genius, but in 1987-1988 his advice resulted in the loss of $279 million to West Virginia and placed the shaky finances of the state in an even more precarious condition. Ultimately, Margolin was sentenced in federal court to one year in prison [and received a $10,000 fine] for hiding these enormous losses."[2] The mismanagement of the State's money also spelled trouble for one of West Virginia's most enduring politicians. The House of Delegates impeached Manchin on March 23, 1989.

At first, Manchin seemed prepared to demand a trial in the Senate and fight conviction and removal from office, but then called a press conference to announce he would retire on July 9, 1989. (The arrangement was allowed by Democratic legislators so A. James could keep his $2000-a-month state pension.)[3]

The financial scandal fed the overall malaise and outrage felt by West Virginians about their state's government, coming so close on the heels of the cash flow problems that had slowed tax refund checks for two years. (Perhaps because of Manchin's connection in his days as REAP director in the 1970s, some of the ill feelings rubbed off on former Governor Arch Moore, even though the latter had nothing to do with the investment mess. To the contrary, Moore's finance commissioner, John McCuskey, had offered numerous warnings, loudly and clearly, that Margolin's investment practices would prove disastrous. But those went unheeded by the news media at the time—Arnie, a likable individual, a marathon runner, was a Democratic media hero, as he had been during his service as Rockefeller's finance commissioner.)

Even the new governor, Gaston Caperton, was not held in high regard at this point. A front-page story in *The Charleston Daily Mail* on March 21, 1989, featured a Ryan/Samples Research poll which indicated that, if the election had been held again, Arch Moore would defeat him 43 percent to 36 percent, with a fifth of those interviewed undecided. One in three of those polled then called Caperton's performance only fair, while 30 percent thought he was doing a poor job. The poll revealed that a whopping 73 percent of those surveyed said Caperton broke a campaign promise by asking the Legislature for record tax increases.

It was neither a good time to hold statewide public office in West Virginia, nor to face an investigation or prosecution. Reagan's Justice Department brought in "law and order" types who were tired of the excesses of the past two decades of "anything goes." They gave the green light to federal agents to crack down on public corruption and especially drugs. Since the mid-1980s, federal investigators, mainly FBI, DEA and IRS agents, had been busy in West Virginia pursuing public officials. Although much of their activity was in corrupt southern counties, northern ones were not spared. In longtime Democrat Machine-run Marion County, for example, the prosecuting attorney, a magistrate and the sheriff were busted for taking bribes from gamblers and drug dealers. Cocaine, easily obtainable in West Virginia cities in the late 1970s and 80s, brought down Republican Mike Roark, a popular former Charleston mayor and prosecutor. In the U.S. Southern District alone, a three-year investigation yielded seventy-eight convictions. They had not yet been able to bring down a "trophy" defendant, however, a conviction of the magnitude that would gain them big headlines.

Nothing excites prosecutors more than sending celebrities to jail, whether it be Leona Helmsley, Michael Milliken, Jim Bakker, Martha Stewart or, in West Virginia, someone like a former governor. A lesser-known citizen might get a fine, probation or be required to perform restitution and public service, while a prominent person charged with an equal offense goes to prison. Woe unto you, as Tom Wolfe illustrated in *Bonfire of the Vanities,* if your name is well known and you're accused of a crime. In part, they do it to send a well-publicized message to other would-be offenders. But part of it, no doubt, is to humiliate, embarrass and show them "you're no better than the rest of us," and because they tire of seeing few except drug and gun offenders in their courts.

JOE SAVAGE WAS your stereotypical brusque, bulldog Boston lawyer, a Harvard and University of Virginia graduate. Formerly an assistant to U.S. Attorneys Bill Weld and Rudy Guilliani, Savage had been a campaign worker in Democrat Michael Dukakis's second bid for governor of Massachusetts in 1982. He came to Charleston in July of 1985 to work on a team that had several criminal investigations heating up. Word on the street was that he was brought down to West Virginia to build a case against Governor Arch Moore, to send him to jail. (Savage subsequently denied that the Justice Department assigned him to West Virginia to "get"

Moore, contending, "When I came to West Virginia, I didn't know Arch Moore from a stump.")

Among other things, the U.S. Attorney's office was investigating vote buying in Mingo County. They eventually prosecuted numerous public officials there, including the mayor of Kermit. The former sheriff and Democrat chairman, Johnie Owens, would get fourteen years in prison for tax evasion and bribery (he had also been sentenced for selling his sheriff's office, a moneymaking enterprise, to another man for $100,000). Two former Logan County sheriffs, Oval Adams and Earl Tomblin, would get prison terms, as would former McDowell County Sheriff Clark Belcher.

Initially, the investigation/prosecution team included Assistant U.S. Attorneys Michael Carey, Larry Ellis and Nancy Hill; Tom Kuhn and Chuck Little of the IRS; plus a few FBI agents. John Campbell, of the Public Integrity section of the Justice Department, was calling the shots from Washington. After he became governor, Caperton would add the state police to the team.

John Weaver, a pleasant, quiet man, was another veteran IRS investigator in the middle of the complex investigation. "It originally started in 1986 when Joe Savage sent us [to Mingo County] on a drug case," he explained. "We had no idea it would result the way it did. But we started hearing stories from all of those guys about money given by coal companies to local officials and we started looking into that. When we followed the money trail, it came back to [Charleston]." The local politicians were telling the federal investigators that they were not alone, that cash was going into Arch Moore's campaigns, among others. This development made the federal investigators salivate. "Could we actually bring down a governor?"

When the Justice Department had prosecuted officers of Marrowbone Coal Company in 1987 in an unrelated matter, they testified that they had donated $100,000 in cash to multiple political campaigns, which had included Moore's. State law prohibited corporations from giving campaign donations and individuals were limited to no more than fifty-dollar cash donations. So this testimony, too, got the feds very interested.[4] So interested, in fact, that they soon thereafter seized all of the 1984 Arch Moore campaign expenditure records from Secretary of State Hechler's office, began digging through them to see what they could find, and never returned them. They also began subpoenaing before a grand jury people who claimed they'd given cash to Moore's campaign. (For some unexplained reason, Moore's seemed to be the only campaign they pursued regarding the cash raising issue, however. Although many donors were known to split their money on both sides to hedge their bets, it never appears that the feds investigated Clyde See.)

There was no indication that the donations made to any of these office holders were extortion in the strictest sense—they weren't necessarily forcing or leaning on these coal operators to contribute. It was just a long-established, normal course of business in Southern West Virginia to give payments (usually, cash) directly to those whose help, cooperation and/or good will they sought.

It extended to every level of society. The coal companies had lots of money and their owners knew they were expected to share it. Union railroad workers would not move a trainload of coal, Weaver discovered, unless they were provided a bottle of Maker's Mark and some KFC by the coal company. The companies, some non-union, were seeking law enforcement protection when they needed it, leniency from mine inspectors and similar favors, he speculated. ("That place was a cesspool," Arch would later observe, regarding the southern coalfields.) The IRS was very close to being able to arrest one or two of the very prominent, high profile coal operators when the Justice Department pulled the plug on their investigation, Weaver added ruefully, noting that tax violation investigations often take longer than prosecutors are willing to wait. "They like to wrap up their cases quickly, get the headlines and move on to something else."[5]

State Senator Larry Tucker, a nineteen-year veteran legislator from Summersville and Senate President Dan Tonkovich of Marshall County, would eventually be charged with extortion, unrelated to the Southern West Virginia investigations. (Tonkovich's own secretary turned him in!) Tucker pled guilty in 1989 and was sentenced to six months incarceration for accepting a bribe from racetrack officials in return for favorable senate votes (relating to the money allegedly supplied through Ellis and D'Annunzio). Later, Tucker admitted he had been untruthful to a federal grand jury and obstructed justice during that first trial and received an additional thirty-seven months in prison. Tonkovich, who had been so destructive of Governor Moore's programs in his third term, pleaded guilty in 1989 to extorting money from gambling interests. Prosecutor Carey charged that Tonkovich had "used his office as a racketeering enterprise, doling out favors in return for money." He was sentenced to prison in December 1989.[6] Sen. John "Si" Boettner, a former majority leader, and a long-time Moore antagonist, would get probation for tax evasion. The three Democrats would lose their offices and Tucker and Tonkovich would be led off in chains to federal prisons.

The plot thickened when disgruntled employees of the Workers'

Compensation Fund began alleging that there was something fishy going on there. At least one of those employees (who, interestingly, later would be given a high-paying federal job) urged federal investigators to look into the situation. John Leaberry, a lawyer (and Moore's second of three workers' comp commissioners in the third term), had left the Moore Administration in 1987. He began representing coal companies and other employers, seeking refunds and penalty waivers for them from the two departments he'd recently left (producing a few six-figure fees for himself). Many career Fund employees were suspicious of what Leaberry was doing and likely resented the easy money he was making. It interested the feds, who subpoenaed boxes full of workers' comp financial records.

As an inducement to keep West Virginians employed and businesses up and running in a tough economy, administrations including Moore's often had waived penalties for past-due workers' compensation premiums. The Rockefeller Administration and others had done the same. But Nelson Robinson (Moore's third and last comp commissioner in his third term) noted that the federal investigators "looked at every forgiven penalty" during Moore's third term, trying to link financial breaks afforded to companies that had contributed to Moore's campaigns. Among those they reviewed were the LeRose family, active in Republican politics for years, who owned a Summersville car dealership they had taken out of bankruptcy (that had unpaid comp premiums and penalties) and an Eastern Panhandle stone quarry client of Hoy Shingleton's.

Another item that interested the feds was the refund of premiums paid to the Coal Workers Pneumoconiosis (CWP) Fund. One of Rockefeller's early comp commissioners, knowing that the CWP Fund was overfunded by about $200 million, allowed coal companies that chose to become self-insured to obtain refunds of all the premiums they had previously paid into that fund (for federal black lung claims) upon confirming they were financially sound. They were allowed to "retroactively insure" their companies. It was a shockingly generous policy that was understandably popular among coal operators.[7]

The West Virginia Workers' Compensation Fund was merely an overseer or local manager of the CWP fund for the federal government, however. It was actually an insurance system controlled and regulated by the U.S. Department of Labor (DOL). It was a federal program. The refunds were given routinely; if a company was deemed by the DOL to have sufficient assets to become self-insured for federal black lung awards, the federal agency approved their applications for change of status. Noted one of Rockefeller's comp commissioners, "Truth of the matter was, there was nothing that Arch Moore or any governor, for that matter, could have done to influence a [CWP] refund." Not even a governor's appointed Workers' Compensation Fund commissioner could grant or deny the application; he or she simply honored the DOL order and paid the particular coal company the refund to which it was entitled.

H. Paul Kizer, a Beckley coal operator who was under indictment in a murder case,[8] was one of those who received such a refund in 1985, for his company, Maben Energy.

As part of the overall investigation, federal agents asked Arch about a large item of income, $523,721, after he produced financial documents they'd demanded to see. He told them it was for work he had done in his private practice of law for Kizer, prior to becoming governor in 1985. It primarily related to processing the application for Maben and other Kizer companies to obtain self-insured status and CWP Fund refunds (about $2 million). "I'd been his attorney beginning in 1983," Moore told the auditors, producing documents to prove it. Later Arch would say of himself, "If [the $523,721 had been a bribe], you're looking at the world's biggest dumb-ass, because I freely reported it as income on my personal tax return."

When the feds pressed him for proof of his explanation, Moore produced two more documents. An authentic-looking letter of December 28, 1984, signed by Attorney Bill Loy, to Samuel Davis, director of the CWP, was stamped in as received by the CWP Fund on the same date. In it, Loy represents himself to be the attorney seeking the refunds for Kizer's companies, including Maben Energy, Jet, Half-Way, Inc., Barrett Fuel and Turkey Branch. In the letter (which contains odd typographical errors), Loy asks that Kizer's CWP refund be processed before January 1, 1985.

"As a sole practitioner, I didn't have the luxury, after being elected governor, of referring my work to a partner of my firm and letting that firm give me my share of the income it produced, as others have done when they went into government," explained Moore. The 1989 Ethics Act, for the first time, would require governors and others to put such income-generating matters, which had a potential for conflict of interest or appearance of impropriety, into blind trusts (and all since Caperton have done that). But for Moore in December 1984 (before he took office in 1985), there was no state ethics law to require a formal arrangement so, in his mind, Bill Loy became his "blind trust." Loy would continue to handle a couple dozen case files for him with the understanding that Moore would receive portions of fees for legal work he had started. The plan was that he would then take the clients back when he returned to private life.

Arch also provided the federal investigators with an affidavit signed by his Moundsville office secretary, Mary Louise Lipsky, dated December 1, 1989. Mrs. Lipsky confirmed that numerous of Moore's files (which she detailed) had been transferred for handling by the Loy, Shingleton & Caryl firm of Martinsburg, before Moore took office in January of 1985 or soon thereafter. She had personally delivered many of the files to Loy, she swore, in order "for Mr. Loy to make final disposition of the pending legal matters."

When the feds approached Kizer, he told them essentially the same story. He confirmed to them that Arch had been his lawyer prior to becoming governor in 1985, and that the half million dollars-plus that he'd conveyed to Moore represented a lawyer fee. He assured them that it was not a bribe and that no one had been involved in any extortion scheme. All the refunds and tax credits his coal companies had received were proper and legal, Kizer assured his interrogators. Kizer gave the same testimony to the grand jury on two occasions.

But they didn't want to believe that. They were getting exasperated. It was the government's theory that Moore and Kizer had concocted the story after the fact, that the money was payment for services Moore had rendered as governor (because Kizer didn't receive his refunds until after Arch took office). In drawing such a conclusion, they essentially ignored the fact that a governor had no control, no personal jurisdiction over who did and did not receive CWP Fund premium refunds. They ignored the fact that the decision to allow self-insurance/refund was made by their own federal government, not the governor nor anyone under his command. [9]

Without Kizer making an admission of guilt, and with him corroborating Moore's position, the feds knew their case against the former governor would be very weak. So, in early 1990, they sent two FBI agents to Kizer's personal gym at his coal company office to make him an offer he couldn't refuse. "Either admit to us that it was a bribe, or we're going to charge both you and Moore with extortion," they threatened him. "You'll be looking at ten years in prison," they warned the 48-year-old coal operator. "But you'll get off with no jail time or even a fine if you cooperate with us," they promised him.

Kizer (whose companies would later go bankrupt) then lived in a manner of the rich and famous. He flew around the state in a fast, sleek, black helicopter. One of the nation's top twenty coal producers, he had more than a thousand employees on his payroll, which paid $1.8 million every two weeks. Kizer was one of those who had no particular loyalty to a party or individual; it was all business to him. He'd contributed to Clyde See, Dan Tonkovich, Gaston Caperton and other Democrats, in the fashion of those in "the permanent government" who want doors open to them wherever they may need favors. He claimed that even Jerry Bradberry, enforcement officer for the Tax Department, had solicited funds from him. He'd also paid John Leaberry, as a private attorney, what he called a "consulting fee" of $211,542. After Moore left office in 1989, Kizer was paying Caperton allies huge fees to secure $60 million in Super Tax Credits for his companies. "You can't do nothin' in West Virginia without someone putting their hand in your pocket," Kizer grumbled to his buddy at the *Gazette*, Paul Nyden.

Kizer anguished about the noose the feds were tightening around his neck, but he realized what he had to do. He reportedly told confidants, "I hate to do this to Arch, but if I go to prison, I'll lose everything I got and my employees will be out of work."

He accepted the feds' offer of immunity and told the grand jury that he'd paid Governor Moore a bribe to secure his CWP refund. Moore had demanded the "fee" in October of 1985, after he was in office for eight months, to get Kizer his refund, the coal operator told the grand jury and Nyden, thereafter. (Kizer would recant in 2002, saying it had all been untrue, returning to his original position that Arch Moore had never extorted him.)[10]

Audrey Toler, Moore's assistant, was frantically trying to get many of his former donors to provide affidavits, explaining their contributions, to protect her boss. "Some of [Moore's] supporters signed affidavits saying they had given him money gifts. They were harassed. They had to get their own attorneys because several were called before the grand jury."

Toler noted that Arch was trying to shield his family, telling them as little as possible at this point. He had been so successful that his son Kim first learned of his father's legal problems when a business associate in Virginia told him about it. ("I hope everything works out for your dad," he remembered him saying. When Kim asked him what he was talking about, the man said, "Oh, he's got some issues with Maben and Paul Kizer." Kim said, "I had to hear about it 200 miles away. I called [my father] and he confirmed that he was a target.") Arch used Toler as his primary sounding board. "These were very, very tough times," she recalled, with softness and sadness in her voice.

Of course, Moore retained legal counsel. Noted Kim, "I tried to get him to hire Alan Dershowitz, who'd helped defendants with similar situations." But Arch returned to the lawyer whose services had been so beneficial in his previous tax situation, William G. Hundley. Bill Hundley had represented Attorney General John Mitchell, had headed the Organized Crime and Racketeering Section of the Justice Department under Eisenhower, had worked in JFK's 1960 campaign, and was Attorney General Robert Kennedy's special assistant. Hundley reportedly still had good connections inside the Justice Department, at the levels where big decisions were made, the kind of "access" for which clients pay big fees.[11] The feds were bringing in for questioning, not only his political allies and contributors, but also close personal friends of Moore's, a few who had worked in his administration, and even family members. Reportedly, they harassed them more harshly than Jack Field had done in 1976.

Arch's buddy, Dr. Tom McCoy, was among those they harassed. They audited his urological practice. "They were trying to find out whether my corporation had ever given [Moore] a donation. But they found nothing, of course." Nevertheless, they summoned McCoy three times. "I'd go in there in my gardening clothes, looking like a tramp" just to show his disdain for them, he laughed. "They were just pick, pick, picking. At one time, Larry Ellis (one of the prosecutors) asked me about our golf games. "Did you [and Moore] ever play for money?" Ellis demanded. "Oh, yeah, one time we played for two dollars," the physician told him, sarcastically. "I finally brought Tom Ciccarello (a respected Charleston criminal lawyer) with me the third time and he put a stop to it. Ellis left the room, I guess trying to catch us on tape saying something [incriminating] but we talked about the WVU-Pitt game. He left me alone after that meeting."

Kevin Sikora also had some fun with the U.S. Attorney's inquisition. "They called me into their office twice for interviews. I took a lawyer with me the second time and he objected to the line of questioning, agreeing with me that they were trying to put words in my mouth." Sikora, who'd been a Moore aide, continued, "They were trying to get me to incriminate Dickie Barber and I kept insisting that my dealings with him had all been honorable. Nancy Hill would scream at me, 'But he's a convicted felon!' I'd reply, 'That may be so, but I've never known him to do anything illegal.' She said, 'Fine, we'll just subpoena you before the grand jury,' and they did. In there, when I pointed out that two of the grand jurors were sleeping instead of listening to my testimony, [Hill] got red in the face, all flustered. My lawyer told me later, 'They will put you on a train to Canada! They won't want you testifying at the trial!'"[12]

Audrey Toler, who was called before the grand jury six times, thought "Nancy Hill wasn't nice, but I realize she was doing a job. Larry Ellis was very kind. Most of [the federal attorneys] were very respectful, but Joe

Savage was a monster. He and Hill tried all the time to make you feel like you were a criminal." Toler said Moore's Moundsville law office secretary of many decades, the very gentle lady Mary Louise Lipsky, was also called to the grand jury several times, bringing with her Arch's financial documents from that office. "They were always trying to prove he didn't properly file his income tax returns," Toler explained. Arch admitted that many of his client relationships were based on a handshake, with little documentation, sometimes no paper trail, so Mrs. Lipsky's task must have been very difficult at times.

Some viewed it as a witch-hunt. Others identified it as a fishing expedition, that the U.S. Attorney's office assumed that they would eventually catch something if they brought enough people in and worked them over hard enough. Savage denied that had happened. "The drill is, you get one piece of evidence and then it leads to other questions. You don't know till you ask them."

Nevertheless, the FBI and IRS agents were on the streets everywhere, working hundreds of hours, trying to find some dirt on the Governor. "I was shocked when two agents flashed their badges at me and demanded to know if Arch Moore had ever paid cash for suits," recalled Tony Paranzino, owner of a Charleston men's clothing store. "I was shaken up by it." He told them Moore had never even been in his store. (When IRS investigators suspect that income is not being reported on one's tax returns, they often search for cash expenditures, such as expensive clothing or oriental rugs purchases, for example—something that doesn't show up in a bank or credit card transaction. Although they struck out with Paranzino's, they did discover that Moore had spent $13,000 in cash for Oxxford suits from Schwabe-May, an exclusive Charleston men's clothing store, in 1984 and another $21,000 there in 1985.) There may never have been any investigation so extensive, intense and widespread in West Virginia history. It was as if they were trying to find a terrorist with a nuclear bomb. The feds wanted Arch badly and were going to make sure they nailed him this time.

The honest, respectable Mary Ann Winter, who had done such an outstanding job restoring the Governor's Mansion, also was called in several times and the feds seized all the Mansion Foundation's receipts and never returned them. "They didn't find anything because there was nothing there," she noted. Among those summoned were even a few Rockefeller holdovers, who were shocked to have U.S. Marshals come to their offices, flash badges and hand them subpoenas.

"They tried to intimidate people," Audrey Toler thought, adding that she believed the stress federal prosecutors put on former Boone County Sheriff and GOP Chairman Vernon Harless actually killed him.[13] "They threatened him about the [campaign] cash all the time, but he couldn't tell them anything. I think they did that to a lot of people. They talked to a number of [Republican] county chairmen."

The feds then focused their attention on Moore's family. They questioned Mrs. Moore multiple times. They interrogated his youngest daughter, Lucy Moore Durbin, asking her about a carpet that had been in the Mansion (that belonged to her parents), for example, and the circumstances of the purchase of their house (Bill Ellis's wife was the realtor who sold it to the Durbins). All of that came to naught; they had no proof that Lucy had done anything wrong. It greatly distressed Arch Moore to hear daily what the feds were doing to his friends, family, supporters, and former employees and perhaps that was what the feds intended.

When they brought Huntington lawyer Tom Craig, who'd been Moore's 1984 campaign manager, before the grand jury to testify he assured them there had been no cash raised or spent in that campaign. When he heard how Craig had testified, an alarmed Moore let him know that he already had told the feds that the campaign had spent cash. (Moore may have thought the statute of limitations had run on that campaign.) Arch urged Craig to go back in to the grand jury to correct his testimony for his own safety, which he did.

But now the feds had a perjury charge they could use as leverage on Craig to get him to cooperate. Moreover, his name was signed to all the 1984 Moore campaign expenditure reports that had been mailed to the secretary of state's office and those had made no mention of the cash receipts or disbursals. So they also could use the old, trusty federal "mail fraud" charge against Tom, if need be.

Kizer's statements regarding his dealings with John Leaberry had brought the latter into the case. The IRS had enough to bring criminal charges against Leaberry for failure to report income from Kizer.[14]

With their leverage on Leaberry, the feds demanded that he and Craig cooperate with them, if they wanted leniency. Two dominos had fallen; they wanted the third, Big Domino.

The feds even believed that they already had enough to use on Arch to get an indictment from the grand jury, but they remembered how he had beat them at trial in 1976 and it made them nervous. They knew that, if they didn't trap him in very, very tightly, he would wiggle free once again and make monkeys of them like he'd done to Jack Field. They needed a Judas, someone who had Moore's confidence, who could get close to the former governor, to help them nail him down.

Earlier, the feds had sent Bill Ellis to Moore's office to try to trap him into saying something incriminating, or which they could claim to be obstruction of justice. But Arch said no such thing, Ellis said. He left Moore's office empty-handed and the feds were furious. They would show Bill no mercy after that failure.

Ellis having failed, John Leaberry was the one they chose to get close and bring in their prey.

After Arch had left office, Leaberry had agreed to share Kanawha Boulevard office space with Moore and Ken Faerber, by then a Charleston developer. Leaberry was loosely what one would call Moore's law associate. But John hadn't come around that office very much recently. Reportedly, Leaberry had become somewhat bitter toward Arch because he believed Moore should have shared the growing wealth of the law practice with him but had not done so. For example, Arch had earned a million-dollar fee for handling the sale of Lawson Hamilton's coal holdings, but shared none of it with anyone. The feds may have approached John at a vulnerable time when turning on his former boss wouldn't cause him to lose any sleep.

Leaberry had "always been more interested in making money than serving in government," his former friend and roommate Nelson Robinson noted. In the past four years, Leaberry had worked as deputy tax commissioner, workers' compensation commissioner, Moore's campaign manager and private attorney. The darkly handsome bachelor had remained somewhat aloof from most of the other young people who worked for Moore. Generally, Moore's employees had been living modestly, from paycheck to paycheck, driving older cars, often with young families and living in modest dwellings. But John, on the other hand, had expensive tastes in clothing, drove a new, red Saab convertible, played a lot of squash, often dined with "players" around the state, and sometimes spoke in tones as if he'd come from old money or an elite college.

A few Moore loyalists, including Robinson and Sikora, had warned Arch that he could not fully trust Leaberry, but he ignored them, to his detriment. "I trusted him implicitly," Moore later confessed, sorrowfully. "He had been in my administration."

Some would later wonder why the U.S. Attorney and the federal investigators were so frantic, so intense, about going after Moore's head, especially since he was now out of office in 1989 and was unlikely to ever return to public life. Why did they want him so badly? Larry Tucker thought he, Tonkovich and Boettner had been caught in a net designed to get Moore. He believed the federal prosecutors' hatred was intensified against Arch in 1987, when U.S. District Judge Charles Haden had appointed Charlotte Lane, Moore's former Public Service Commissioner and a former Republican delegate, in as interim U.S. Attorney after David Faber was elevated to federal judge. Although the chief judge can do that when there is a vacancy, Haden was (rightly or wrongly) viewed as doing Moore's bidding in appointing Lane. The Justice Department had literally banned Lane (who would later be appointed by President George W. Bush to the U.S. Securities and Exchange Commission) from touching the Moore investigation. Alarmed that Lane might actually block the efforts to put his old rival Arch Moore in jail, Senator Byrd intervened and got President Reagan to name Mike Carey as the U.S. Attorney. Once Carey was sworn in as the U.S. Attorney, "that's when they really came after Arch," thought Tucker, an astute politician in his day. "They perceived that Moore had intervened in their internal affairs" and were more determined than ever to get him.

Arch Moore, on the other hand, always felt that the crusade by the feds to get him "came from the *Gazette*" and no other factor, a notion that the late Ned Chilton undoubtedly would have relished.

Tucker simply blamed the pursuit of Arch Moore on the ambition of the pursuers, contending that they wanted a trophy to boost their respective personal career prospects. "Mike Carey wanted to be a federal judge or governor," he believed. "Nancy Hill wanted to be the U.S. Attorney. Joe Savage had national Democratic ambitions. Chuck Little wanted to be the U.S. Marshal."

Former Chief Justice Richard Neely, a Democrat who had often been antagonistic to Moore, agreed with Tucker. "Was the prosecution of Arch Moore political? Absolutely!" He explained his view: "Very little meaningful law enforcement is done by the U.S. Attorney's office. Over the past twenty-five years, they have spent an enormous amount of money on drug enforcement with little success. They are always looking for a high-profile case." Neely continued, "Arch Moore did certain things as a lawyer and, then when he was elected governor, he followed through with them without paying attention to the niceties, without disqualifying himself or dealing with the conflicts of interest." Neely viewed Mike Carey, who had been interim U.S. Attorney, as "a person who wanted to stay on as U.S. Attorney and thought if he prosecuted Arch Moore, there was some likelihood he'd be asked to stay."

Believing it "was an exercise of little people trying to bring down a great person," Neely said he was reminded of what the Duke of

Wellington's mistress told him: "You will be remembered as the one who brought down Napoleon. Napoleon will be remembered for himself."

Joe Savage denied that the Justice Department had any personal agendas or received any political pressure to take out Arch Moore, although he admitted there were powerful forces who wanted him gone from the political arena. "There was zero pressure. Did people have strong feelings both ways? Absolutely. But it would have been a risk for someone like [Byrd or Rockefeller] to push for it." He also denied that the *Gazette* fueled the U.S. Attorney's crusade to convict Moore. "For every *Gazette* thing, there was the *Daily Mail* writing that Moore was the best thing since sliced bread." John Weaver also denied that the investigation was designed to target Moore. He insisted that the feds quit watching the Governor after he was acquitted in 1976 and had left him alone until new allegations were raised in the late 1980s.

But Moore's "greatest sin was to beat the rap in the 1976 trial," thought former State Police Superintendent Fred Donohoe. Donohoe was one who believed Arch Moore did wrong, "But worse than other [state politicians]? I don't know." Donohoe insisted that all of the governors under whom he had served probably violated election laws in different, or even similar ways. "I was a career law enforcement officer. Nobody lied about [Arch Moore during the investigation] but rules were changed about how strictly to enforce federal law [in order to prosecute Moore]."[15]

And did the feds spend millions to "get" Arch Moore, as was widely rumored when it was over? "I think it's a conservative estimate to say [the IRS and Justice Department] spent $5 to $10 million," thought Col. Donohoe. "And they did a fine job in accomplishing what they set out to do: put Arch Moore's ass in jail. But they could put anybody in the federal pen, for the amount of money they spent to get Governor Moore." Savage refused to confirm or deny the figure, asking rhetorically, "How can you put a price tag on an investigation like that? How do you segregate out what was spent, how many hours, between Arch Moore and the others they were investigating?"

But Moore had not learned caution even as he was hearing bits and pieces of the extensive investigation. He surely had to have considered that the feds were watching him like hawks. But when one campaign worker expressed concern about federal investigators, Arch Moore reportedly responded to him, "We are smarter than they are." He apparently believed that, when it came right down to it, he could beat any charge they might bring against him.

But then again, Arch hadn't counted on them using someone he trusted against him. H. John Rogers thought, "Arch trusted people too much." He noted that Moore had a naive, almost gullible belief that everyone was good and could be trusted, even hostile judges and lawyers. "It belies the notion that Arch was a con-man, because con-men are the most suspicious people you know; they're on their guard all the time." Rogers continued, "Arch thinks positively, like a businessman. He's looking at 'what dogs will hunt, what ducks will fly.' Lawyers, on the other hand, think about what can go wrong. Moore thought more like the businessman than the lawyer, sometimes to his disadvantage."

SO, IN EXCHANGE for a promise of extreme leniency, John Leaberry agreed with the feds to wear a wire and try to trap Arch Moore into saying something incriminating on tape. On a snowy January 8, 1990, afternoon they met in a parking lot near Mackey's Exxon in

Parkersburg, chosen because it was about halfway between Moore's Moundsville office and Leaberry's Charleston base. Leaberry, who recently had undergone gall bladder surgery, called the former governor and pretended that he needed to talk to him before appearing before the grand jury. Upon instructions of his federal handlers, John had allowed Moore to choose the rendezvous site, so as not to raise suspicion. They didn't want him to fail, as Ellis had done.[16]

"We went to Leaberry's attorney and asked if he'd be interested in cooperating," contended an Assistant U.S. Attorney, who saw nothing dishonest about the government's deception, the luring of Moore into their lair. "It was [Leaberry's] opportunity to prove he was acting in good faith."

The tape of that January 1990 conversation between John Leaberry and his former boss would be the centerpiece of the government's prosecution of the former governor. "I have to think [Arch's] attorney was telling him not to talk to anyone, that if you need to talk about the investigation, call your lawyer," said a prosecutor, remembering that they were utterly astounded that Moore would discuss matters with, not only Leaberry, but also Paul Kizer. The transcript of the tape the federal investigators made is 63 pages long, and makes for fascinating reading, exposing Moore's thought processes at the time.

Interestingly, contrary to their later charge that he was "obstructing justice," the transcript reveals that Moore emphatically urged Leaberry throughout the conversation, "You tell them the truth, period," and, "John, it's not a question of what I want you to do," and "You got to tell them the truth," and "[You] only tell it like it is," and even urged him, "Stay away from Kizer." At no point in that conversation does Arch specifically urge

Leaberry to lie or cover-up anything.

However, there was considerable discussion between the two men about what "the truth" was, and clearly an effort by Moore to "get their stories straight" to avoid either of them getting charged with felonies. But there was no indication of panic, only Moore's controlled emotions, his analytical mind working, planning, and trying to think through how they would respond to issues. When Leaberry warned him he couldn't "take a felony," Moore agreed, and indicated he expected only a state charge, perhaps just a misdemeanor, would result. But it was obvious that he was in some anguish about the possibilities that it could be much worse. He mentions to John that the feds "have gone through me with a fine toothed comb."

Deeper into the conversation, Arch discusses that $100,000[17] in cash had been spent in the 1984 gubernatorial campaign. "They've got people that have indicated they gave me cash," he warns Leaberry. He wanted to disclose that figure to the government, to demonstrate that he was acting in good faith (and he probably incorrectly thought it was outside the statute of limitations for prosecution, a prosecutor speculated). He and Leaberry questioned their memories as to whether there had been any campaign cash spent in the 1988 campaign and went back and forth on the issue, finally deciding that only about $7000 to $20,000 had been used. Moore mentioned that cash donations had been funneled through a Republican national organization for gubernatorial candidates (much like the method that would get House Majority Leader Tom Delay in criminal trouble in 2005-06) for use in his 1988 campaign and suggested the federal prosecutors be told that, as well.

Leaberry played dumb, acting as if he was afraid to disclose certain things to the feds (all the time, knowing they were listening to that very conversation). His acting skills were so good that Moore apparently didn't suspect a thing, not even when John got twisted up on when his grand jury appearance was scheduled.

They discussed that they both had represented Paul Kizer and had accepted fees. They fretted over whether the $2 million CWP Fund refund Kizer received as result of their actions as was disbursed within the legal time frame permitted by the workers' compensation legislative regulations and decided they would research that issue. (They determine later that the refunds had been permissible until the rules changed in mid-1986.)

On several occasions in the Leaberry conversation, Arch repeats his concern that he will be falsely accused of personally keeping cash which had been accepted by his committee and used in the "underground" or "sub rosa" campaign, as he calls it, and risk IRS prosecution for not reporting it as personal income. The two men agree that the cash was never used to buy votes, but rather to pay poll workers and drivers in Harrison County and elsewhere. Because it was such a common practice among candidates, they do not even talk about why cash was necessary for that purpose.

Col. Donohoe, among others, saw little in the "Leaberry transcript" that was particularly incriminating. "The prosecutors took that to mean Governor Moore was threatening a grand jury witness [Leaberry], but I didn't see it that way. Did he violate the law?" the former State Police commander asked, rhetorically. "Maybe. It was an accepted practice to accept campaign contributions outside legal parameters. I have no doubt it went on before. Did he do wrong? I don't mind saying, yes. Worse than others? I doubt it. He may have known that his campaign manager was keeping a separate set of books [to raise and spend cash on Election Day]. The federal prosecutors got Leaberry over a barrel with something they had on him. It was quid pro quo: 'get Arch Moore for us and you go free.'"

But the surveillance product was important to the feds in several ways. Among other things, although he had admitted cash expenditures in the 1984 campaign in sworn interviews, now they had Moore's voice on tape admitting that at least some cash was spent in 1988, as well. And of course the campaign spending reports, which had been mailed to the secretary of state, made no mention of cash being raised or spent, because such fundraising and expenditures were illegal. Now they needed only to play the tape to a jury if he tried to explain it away. Moreover, they had him talking to a grand jury witness about prospective testimony, which they could label as obstruction of justice. He'd handed them a very, very valuable tool with his lack of discretion.

Leaberry may also have tried to get at least one of Moore's former assistants on tape. Out of the blue, Kevin Sikora got a phone call from Leaberry, wanting to meet with him. "We sat in his car on a warm day with the windows up and the engine off. He started asking me odd, off-the-wall questions about cash used in the '84 campaign," remembered Sikora. "He was acting very nervous, perspiring heavily. I laughed at him and asked, 'What's wrong with you, John? What are you talking about?' and he'd say, 'You know, the cash we used to get onto Democrat slates.' I was certain he was wearing a wire at the time." Sikora was more cautious, skeptical and sensitive to the "strange vibes" from Leaberry than Moore had been; he feared John was trying to set him up, or at least corroborate what Leaberry had told the feds. Sikora replied, "I don't know what you're talking about, John," and the mysterious conversation ended abruptly.

Two days after the meeting at the Parkersburg Exxon, Arch was questioned under oath at the federal building. (Again, why Moore continued to allow them to interrogate him, and not exert his Fifth Amendment rights, is another baffling mystery. One must assume it was the "we're smarter than they are" mentality.) When asked specifically by the federal prosecutor whether he'd ever had a discussion with Leaberry about cash in the campaign, he denied it. He also stated, "I know of no one who was involved in cash in the '88 campaign." Moore also denied any conversations with Paul Kizer about the investigation although he admitted that he communicated with him about continuing legal work he was performing for him.

With that, the feds had him! They at least had him on perjury, the same charge that would later get Bill Clinton impeached. Leaberry had "done good."

But just to make absolutely sure, they had Leaberry phone Arch the day after the deposition, again with tape recorder running. Leaberry skillfully play-acted a second time, telling Moore he was going before the grand jury and, "Uh, is there anything I need to know before I go in there?" Moore warned him that he had denied any cash expenditure in the '88 campaign, adding, "And that is a fact, right?" to which Leaberry responded, "Right." He reminded John of his position that '88 cash had been run through "the mechanism of the Republican Governor's Association." When Leaberry asked, "Do I still maintain the same position?" Moore answered, "Well, yeah, you do because that's in fact what would have occurred. It went indirectly probably through the course up to the, you know, the Republican Governors [Association] and back." Moore also warned him that he'd told the feds that they had not talked to each other, clearly signaling that should be Leaberry's position also.

Regarding the Kizer CWP Fund refund, Moore indicated in the phone conversation that he had learned "there is some inconsistency in the regs on the question of withdrawal." He also called Kizer "Mr. Loy's client," reiterating his position that he had handed Kizer's case file over to Loy before Moore became governor. Arch repeated to Leaberry what he'd said to others—he noted that, while those in big law firms could simply hand over a client or account to a partner and not lose the fee when there was a potential conflict of interest upon taking public office, he had been unable to do so as a sole practitioner. In this conversation, Arch again gave no clue that he suspected or mistrusted Leaberry; he was speaking freely to him as a trusted confidant.

The feds took Moore's testimony again on April 9, 1990, nailed him down some more and a few days thereafter disclosed to Hundley that they possessed the Leaberry/Moore tapes. Interestingly, the U.S. Attorney's office was not confident enough to allow Arch Moore to listen to his own tapes, to see if he agreed there was "obstruction of justice," as they now were contending. They weren't going to show him the cards they were holding and, unlike in civil litigation, no judge would force them to do so. It was time to put the squeeze on.

The feds gave Hundley an ultimatum. They told him if Arch didn't concede and sign a plea bargain within twelve hours, which included that night, the grand jury would indict him the next morning on twenty-eight felony counts. ("They had an [indictment] document about a foot or two in thickness," remembered Moore's secretary, Audrey Toler.) But if Arch wouldn't force them into a risky and time-consuming trial, they would go with less. His client would probably only get a maximum of six months in jail, they assured Hundley, in an effort to persuade him to accept the deal. Hundley was overwhelmed by what they presented.

So the veteran lawyer came to Moore explaining, "They have five points." After reviewing the five charges the feds intended to bring against him, Arch replied to his lawyer, "Bill, none of these are (sic) adverse to me." He told Hundley, as he would thereafter repeat time and again, "I haven't done anything wrong." He considered Kizer's payment a legitimate legal fee and, because he had no direct control as governor over the CWP Fund, how could it possibly be extortion?[18]

"Well, because you were the sitting governor when Kizer got the money," Hundley told him. And with regard to accepting and distributing cash in campaigns, Moore told his lawyer that, "at most I was a conduit; I never knowingly, at least, took cash from anyone." (Arch told him that, when people would come up to him with envelopes when he was governor, he would ask them to give it to the trooper. If it happened to be cash or a check, he would pass it along to Tom Craig or a member of his campaign finance committee.) Hundley acknowledged then and publicly that Moore was simply playing the Democrats' cash game, which was as old as anyone could remember. But he was concerned, as a defense attorney, about the tapes and the extensive, adverse testimony given by many witnesses to the grand jury. Those, coupled with Arch's later sworn statements, at the very least would put doubt in jurors' minds about Moore's veracity and trustworthiness, he knew. Some of it would be bound to stick if they went to trial, he thought. It would be difficult to get an acquittal with those tapes in the government's possession, Hundley was certain. But he had an extremely reluctant client who didn't want to plead guilty. "I haven't done anything wrong," Arch kept insisting.

To coax Moore into accepting the government's offer, Hundley assured Arch that four of the five were "throw-away counts." Only the obstruction of justice count carried any mandatory jail time, Hundley explained to him, and that could be as little as six months. Maybe he'd even get off with just a fine or probation, given his history of public service and war record.

Hundley also used another technique on that high-pressured afternoon to persuade his reluctant client to accept the government's offer. According to Moore, he suggested that he sign the agreement and "then we'll get their case, find out what they have, and then we'll withdraw the plea and go to trial." In other words, Moore claimed Hundley proposed using a guilty plea as a discovery measure, which Arch believed was a strategy "not unusual for old-time lawyers."

Moore was intrigued. If nothing else, it gave him some hope that the predicament wasn't as dire as it seemed. "Can we do that?" he asked. Hundley assured him that it would be "as easy as falling off a log," Arch recalled.

A federal prosecutor admitted that the government's case was not fully disclosed to Arch, that Moore never got to hear the tapes, but she insisted that Hundley heard them and summarized them for his client. "He spent all the time he wanted. He told Arch Moore everything he needed to know to make a decision." (But the question remains, why didn't they let Arch hear the tapes for himself? Why did the feds not disclose details of the multiple counts they planned to drop on him if he didn't enter a guilty plea? Why didn't they give him more than twelve short hours to make this huge decision? Did they think that, if they played fair, he would not enter into a plea agreement? If they had such an airtight case against Moore, what was it they were they afraid of?)

"You have no choice" but to plead guilty, Toler remembered Hundley telling Moore, very simply. Arch would later testify that Hundley told him, "I think you *are* guilty of obstruction of justice." (It was the same offense that had sent most of the Watergate figures to jail: an attempt to cover-up prior illegalities.) After an agonizing afternoon and early evening, Arch finally decided he would comply with his lawyer's advice. Against his better judgment, he would sign a plea agreement but then they would move to withdraw the plea before sentencing and go to trial. At least that gave him some hope. But it was going to be very ugly, very unpleasant, nevertheless.

Toler, who admitted that Arch "had been like a father to me," said it was the "worst day of [her] life." She added, "I tried to be strong for him. I don't remember crying in front of him but I did after I left his office."

Arch then broke the somber news of his plans to his spouse. Mrs. Moore could remember him saying simply, "This thing is not going to get any better." She had heard and read about what was being speculated, and had undergone questioning herself, but this was the first she heard the ultimate bad new from her husband's lips.

Mrs. Moore later admitted that she went into a state of shock ("I just numbed it out") because of what was happening to their world. Her mind and emotions were shutting it all out, so unbearable it was to accept. Her earlier fears—of what would happen if they remained in the political arena past 1976—were becoming reality. Their political and personal life as they had known it since 1956 was under siege. It was a worst case scenario, unfolding before their eyes. She was crushed. "Mother was just like a clam shell closing, she just clammed up," recalled daughter Shelley Moore Capito. "She was very emotional. But I never saw her turn on him or turn away from him for any reason. We didn't either." Like the Kennedy Clan, the Moore family had always been extremely loyal to each other, through thick and thin, victories and defeats. It would not change.

Mrs. Moore had son Kim accompany her on a flight to their Florida condo, to get away from all that would be coming down that week. She didn't want the phone calls, to see the headlines or the TV coverage regarding what would be blockbuster news. Perhaps she was even in denial, as they say. The flight from Pittsburgh to Florida was silent, Kim recalled.

Arch had spent time with his two daughters and their husbands at their respective Charleston homes that evening, informing them in great detail of all he knew and what he was going to do the next morning. He "came to each of us privately," Capito remembered. "He was extremely apologetic to the family. He was shaking his head a lot. He kept saying, 'I'm sorry...I'm sorry'— not so much about the details, but just that this was happening. He pretty much just laid it all out." He answered all their questions.

"He was pretty rattled," agreed daughter Lucy Durbin.[19]

"He said, 'I'm in a whipsaw.' He only had a few hours, most of them sleeping hours, to make the biggest decision of his life. They had him in a box. If he didn't plead guilty, they told him, he would go to prison for the rest of his life, that they would bring numerous charges against him. He looked white as a ghost, all the blood was drained from his face. He'd had no idea that he'd been wiretapped; they'd just disclosed that to him." Durbin noted that it is a very unsettling thing to discover, as she did later on, that you've been under surveillance.

"You could see it coming, by what we'd all been reading in the papers, but it was such a dark day" when he told the family he was pleading guilty to the charges, recalled Shelley Moore Capito. "Our kids were old enough to know what was going on, and we had to tell them, which was rough, too. That part was tough for him. He had been an idol in everyone's eyes." Siblings Lucy and Kim echoed that: "Shelley's kids had a very difficult time of it." Capito had to shut it all out for a while for herself, as well. She cancelled the newspaper. The headlines were just too much for her to bear. She loved and respected her dad and it hurt deeply.

But after his decision was made, "we zipped up our rubber suits and put a smile on our face; that's what we all did," remembered Lucy. Dad and Mom had taught them to be stoic.

Arch also had dined the night before he signed the plea at Steak & Ale in Charleston with close friends Lysander Dudley and Dr. Tom McCoy. "Arch plays everything pretty close to his vest and [at dinner] you wouldn't have known that anything was wrong. Nothing came out," remembered McCoy. But when, as he often did, Arch retired to the McCoys' Fort Hill residence to spend the night ("He had the upstairs to himself and I had the downstairs to myself," with both wives in Florida), Moore broached the subject. "Tom, there's something I want to tell you. Tomorrow I'm going to plead guilty to those charges."

Even though he had known it was closing in for his friend, McCoy exclaimed, "Gosh, almighty!" After it sunk in, Tom told him he was disappointed for him, but reassured him that he was his friend and he always would be. "I was probably more shook up about it than Arch was. He was very calm." Before turning in for the night, the two spent the evening reminiscing, making small talk, and avoiding the Big Subject. "I didn't give advice."

KNOWING WHAT a fighter he'd always been, some wondered with what the feds threatened Arch Moore to get him to plead guilty so quickly. Savage flatly denied that a threat against family members was made and Mrs. Moore verified that she was never actually targeted. "We put a lot of pressure on him to plead guilty by simply showing him what his penalty would be if he was found guilty at trial," Savage insisted. About Mrs. Moore, "She would have needed knowledge that the tax returns were inaccurate" for there to be criminal intent, he noted, and there was no such indication of her foreknowledge.

The feds' investigation of daughter Lucy Moore Durbin undoubtedly sent a signal to Arch that they might go after other family members, however, if he did not roll over. Toler had signed documents as campaign treasurer; perhaps Arch feared for her, as well, and she was like family to him. He couldn't drag these loved ones into it. "I always felt he [pleaded guilty] because of his family," said Toler. Tom Tinder was certain that the "family factor" played a role in Moore's guilty plea. "I think they were threatening to go after his daughter [Lucy]. He was going to take the fall. If federal prosecutors want you, they'll get you. And nothing is more precious to Arch Moore than his family." Agreed Lucy, "Pressuring the family was a huge reason he pleaded guilty. Mother was in there a lot [being required to undergo questioning by the government]; it was a pressure point."

Dr. McCoy said that Arch actually admitted "his guilty plea was an attempt to get the government off the backs of his family and friends. They were pestering Lucy and [Mrs. Moore]. He felt he would take the shot and get everyone out from under the heel of the government. He's nobody's coward. He'd beat 'em before and he could beat 'em again. And I think he'd been led by Hundley to believe it was [good strategy to enter a plea]."[20]

Shelley Moore Capito was another who agreed that it was a factor, noting that within two weeks of her mother and sister being called in by the feds for questioning, her father decided to enter the guilty plea. She believed that the U.S. Attorney was bringing in family members to pressure him to cave in. "The prosecutors had beaten him down through different methods," thought his daughter.

THE FIRST felony charge, or count, to which Moore pled guilty was mail fraud. In it the Justice Department alleged that Moore's campaign manager, Tom Craig, had received and spent $100,000 during the 1984 election without reporting it, and that he and Moore had signed three inaccurate campaign expenditure reports. They had mailed them to the secretary of state, thereby giving the Justice Department jurisdiction over what could be a state charge only, had someone hand-delivered the documents. State law allowed an individual to contribute no more than $1000 per candidate and it was illegal for corporations to contribute, the "count" noted. Only $50 in cash could be donated by anyone.

Count Two alleged that Moore had extorted H. Paul Kizer and his coal company, Maben Energy, in return for Moore's assistance in obtaining the two million dollar refund from the West Virginia Coal Workers'

Pneumoconiosis Fund and backdated his contingent fee document "to cover up this extortion." The feds alleged that it was in the weeks following his 1984 election that Arch had entered into a twenty-five percent fee arrangement with Kizer to obtain his refund. Moore also had kept the DNR from enforcing environmental regulations against Kizer's company, they claimed. He had given $50,000 to another lawyer to transact the fee in 1985, the count stated.

Count Three alleged that Moore failed to report on his 1984 income tax return $10,000 accepted from Sammy D'Annunzio and $10,000 from "individuals associated with Island Creek Coal Company."

Count Four claimed he failed to report on his tax return $52,000 received in 1985 from an agent of Marrowbone Development Company and $2500 from Robert Gillian of Logan. Apparently, because no one had proven that those cash donations went into the campaigns, Arch was "stuck" with them for tax purposes, as if they had been converted to personal use.[21]

Count Five was for obstruction of justice, the only one that carried mandatory jail time. They claimed that Moore planned a cover story with Kizer, had created and backdated letters to support their story, had given false testimony, had lied to investigators, and had attempted to persuade other witnesses to lie to the grand jury.

So it was, on April 12, 1990, that Arch Alfred Moore, Jr. formally signed an agreement pleading guilty to all five counts. Nancy Hill, Larry Ellis and Joe Savage, Assistant U.S. Attorneys, and John Campbell, of the Public Integrity Section of the Justice Department, signed on behalf of U.S. Attorney Michael Carey.

The agreement boilerplate stated, "There have been no promises or representations whatsoever made to Mr. Moore by the United States or any of its agents as to what the final disposition in this matter will be." He was required by the agreement to cooperate with the ongoing investigation. (He and Senator Tucker would testify in Bill Ellis' trial; the unfortunate Ellis would end up getting more prison time than any of them.)

After he signed the document, Arch phoned his wife in Florida to tell her "it is done." Kim comforted his mother for four days, getting her through the worst of it, before flying back to his own family and job in Virginia. "He was between a rock and a hard place," Kim said of his father's legal position. "He thought it was the best thing to do for himself and his family. 'That's the way it's going to be and we're just going to have to handle it,'" is how Kim remembered his father presenting it to the family. Mrs. Moore was as grieved as if her husband had died, maybe more so.

Her weeping was so loud it could be heard in the Yoho's nearby condo.

Moore would verbally repeat his intent to enter guilty pleas on all counts at a Charleston hearing before U.S. District Judge Walter E. Hoffman[22] on May 8, 1990, going through each one, answering, "I understand, your honor," and "Yes, your honor," to the litany of mandatory questions. "It was hell to see him standing in front of the judge," remembered Kim Moore. "He was so ashamed, so devastated, because of what it meant to all of us, especially to Mom."

Arch Moore recalled: "I could not bring myself to say 'Guilty.'" Indeed, there was long, long pause between the judge's question and Arch's response and the packed courtroom was dead silent, awaiting his answer. "I just stood there. I was halfway in tears. Hundley then pulled on my coattail."

The public, although shocked by the sensational outcome of the investigation, seemed largely supportive of, if saddened and disgusted by, the conviction of their former three-time governor. Julia Clements, who at that time worked as a legislative staff member, probably spoke for many with her observations: "I was pleased that Mike Carey, a Republican, did not hesitate to prosecute Moore." But, also likely typical of public sentiment, she added: "Moore was one of the best governors we ever had and probably could be re-elected."

Moore's adversary, the *Charleston Gazette*, wasn't talking about re-election. For them, it was Christmas, New Years, the Fourth of July, and everybody's birthday all combined! The paper had won the big battle! In their view, Ned Chilton's crusade, begun more than two decades earlier, had succeeded beyond their wildest dreams. They could not contain their delight; they splashed the story over several pages, for days, in a "Ding dong, the wicked witch is dead" style of journalism. It was a time of great rejoicing for the capitol press, which had become so hostile toward the feisty governor who had never bowed to them. It mattered not that very prominent Democrats, who remained in high federal and state office, also had operated cash campaigns and got away with it. They saw no injustice or inequity to that. It was a day to celebrate!

Likewise, Moore's enemies, previously quiet for fear he might return to power some day—poured out of the woodwork to say nasty things about him. Even some old "friends," even some co-conspirators in the cash politics game, suddenly realizing he was a liability instead of an asset, joined in the chorus of bad-mouthing Arch, hypocritically professing that the "underground cash campaign" was quite a surprise to them. Some, who had prospered or received honors as result of their relationship with him over the years, would literally turn their backs on him, snubbing him when they saw him in public. (Many others would not, however. "He's always been my best friend," said Dr. Yoho. "I couldn't help but stay with him.")[23]

On the front pages of the Charleston papers, Jim Love, president of C&O Motors, suddenly began demanding return of a 1984 Oldsmobile 98 Regency that Arch Moore had been given to test drive before the election that year, and which he not yet returned.[24] Even previously-friendly Richard Grimes sat with other reporters, including Tom Miller, on their weekly TV talk show, snickering at how dumb West Virginians could have been to have elected Moore a third time, suggesting his victory in 1984 had simply been due to nostalgic feelings about the 1970s.

But the comments were not uniformly negative. Dr. Jim Whisker, then a WVU political science professor and a Pennsylvanian who came to admire Moore's work as governor after bringing scores of students to the capitol to serve as government interns, assured *USA TODAY*, "There was a greatness about the man."

There were the inevitable comparisons to Governor Barron, but H. John Rogers (who admitted to voting for Moore only once) was one who thought those were unfair and inaccurate. "Wally Barron was in it for himself," Rogers thought, but "Arch actually cared about people; he would worry over their problems, ponder them. He'd call people to see how he could help. Arch's 'corruption' [raising and using cash in campaigns] was a means to an end. He was playing the game by the local rules. You have to raise at least a million dollars to be in the game and you don't get that from twenty five dollar contributions; you get it from the Kizers of the world."

Rogers added that, although many people thought Moore was "really slick," he could actually be a very forgiving and generous individual toward his most vicious enemies. "There's something almost Biblical about that attitude. Wally Barron, Bobby Kennedy or George W. Bush wouldn't have done that!" (Indeed, many believed that Moore had treated his enemies better than he had his friends, in many cases over the years; the latter he often took for granted.)

In addition to the emotional trauma suffered by his biological family, Moore's "extended family," those hundreds of men and women who had served in his three administrations, were also hurt, embarrassed and grieved by the situation. In almost every instance, they had chosen to work for him simply because they wanted to build a better state, not for personal gain. In fact, many had sacrificed part of their own careers to work long, tiring hours for Arch Moore's government. Moreover, almost all had been honest beyond reproach, not even accepting a free cup of coffee from a favor-seeker.

"When I went to work for Governor Moore in September of 1985, as the deputy labor commissioner, I advised him that I would never do anything dishonest," Raamie Barker remembered. "He looked me in the eye and said, 'Don't you ever do anything that will get you in trouble. If you do, you're on your own!' And he never asked me to do anything dishonest." Barker's recollection was typical of those who worked for Moore. When a state vendor innocently and thoughtfully presented Moore's F&A commissioner, John McCuskey, with a gift photo of his hero Abraham Lincoln, he refused to accept it—years before a state ethics law existed. And there were hundreds of other examples. Yet even Barker would muse when all the dirty laundry was aired in 1990, "I wonder if we [honest appointees] were just window dressing?"

Now they now found themselves suspect, tarred by the same brush as their former boss. Ironically, the three Moore Administrations as a whole had been extremely clean ones, populated by some of the most honest, dedicated people who ever served West Virginia. Now there was a stigma to having worked for Arch Moore. Fortunately for them, almost all of his former associates had moved into other good careers and professions by mid-1990, or they might have had difficulty finding employment. They also grieved for the Moores. More than others, these former employees had witnessed up close the daily lives of Arch and Shelley during those twelve years of service; it hurt them to witness the family's disgrace. Despite Arch's ethical failures, they knew that the Moores had been tirelessly dedicated to the betterment of the state.

Arch would raise the question, for years thereafter, as to whether he received good legal advice when he agreed to the plea bargain. Some thought he did not. "When Hundley reviewed the evidence I think he may have failed to see avenues of escape and very well may have convinced Governor Moore to make a plea he was later sorry he made," thought Col. Donohoe.[25]

It would get worse. Hundley filed the motion to withdraw the guilty plea, as Moore had insisted, but did not so until several weeks after the plea agreement had been signed. The federal judge did not respond and Arch was getting antsy. Then, "two days before the sentencing hearing, Hundley called me and said there's been a change in the law, but not to worry about it. He'd submitted an affidavit and remained confident that I'd be able to withdraw my plea." The feds' view was that Moore was reneging.

The judge was a tough old bird. Hoffman, a Virginia Republican, had sentenced Charleston Mayor Mike Roark to prison for cocaine possession. He'd given U.S. District Judge Clairborne of Las Vegas two years in prison on corruption charges and he'd presided over Vice President Agnew's guilty plea and sentence. He was not a hanging judge like John Sirica had been with the Watergate defendants, but he wasn't known to be lenient, either. "I was afraid Arch would get so much time, he'd die in prison," admitted H. John Rogers. Moore was facing the maximum sentence of thirty-six years in prison and $1.2 million in fines, although no one really expected that.

Hundreds of people had written to Hoffman, requesting leniency due to Arch's record as governor, because of his age, his combat service and record of service to his community. The letter writers who asked for mercy included some of the most prominent lawyers, law professors, judges and business people in the state. Some asked that he be allowed to perform community service, perhaps free legal work for the poor, rather than go to prison. Rogers was one who wrote to the judge, asking for leniency. "I knew Hoffman from the days when I'd clerked for Judge Maxwell. In effect, I explained to him that Arch 'was playing by the rules in West Virginia.'"

But others had detested Moore before the plea and their hatred was now intensified; indeed, it would never be satiated. They wanted Hoffman to lock him up and throw away the key.

Dressed in a blue suit, white shirt and red tie, Arch appeared with his wife and Hundley at the federal courthouse on July 19, 1990, for the sentencing hearing.

Hundley brought an associate along to cross-examine himself, anticipating that he would be given a chance to testify regarding his motion to withdraw his client's guilty plea, an affidavit he'd submitted, and regarding Moore's reliance on his advice that he could withdraw the plea up until sentencing.

Before allowing his argument on the motion, Hoffman gave Arch "an opportunity to fire Hundley." Arch noted, "A lawyer in the courtroom later told me I lost [my chances] then and there, when I assured the judge I wanted to keep Hundley."

Judge Hoffman peevishly asked Hundley, "Why would you wait until the day of sentencing to file a motion to withdraw the plea?" Hundley reminded him that the written motion had been filed a week before. "You had two months to file that and gave no indication you were going to do this," insisted the judge. (In his affidavit, Hundley admitted that Moore had instructed him in June to go ahead and withdraw the plea.)

To Moore's shock and disappointment, Hoffman denied the motion. There would be no testimony regarding the motion; it was dead. The Judge would not allow a withdrawal of the plea; he would go forward with the sentencing. Unbeknownst to Hundley, judges no longer automatically allowed withdrawal of guilty pleas. "Hundley didn't even know what the sentencing guidelines were," H. John Rogers added. Many West Virginia lawyers scratched their heads in wonder, as to why Arch had paid big bucks to a Washington inside-the-beltway attorney who seemingly didn't do him much good.

It then fully sunk into Arch Moore for the first time that he was heading for prison. It was a kick in the gut. Until then, he held out hope that he could go to trial, or perhaps negotiate further. "I absolutely froze," Moore recalled about that moment, sitting in the courtroom. "I was not prepared for it, my family was not prepared for it." He insisted, "I cared nothing for myself...My family and the people who'd placed their confidence in me were all that were on my mind."

So it was on to the sentencing phase, ready or not.

Not satisfied that they'd won a big victory with the judge's ruling, the feds continued to try to hammer him, nonetheless. Throughout the lengthy hearing, Hoffman had to swat down Joe Savage repeatedly as he tried to inject items deemed irrelevant to the sentencing, such as the Moores' six-year test drive of the Oldsmobile. Moore did not speak throughout the hearing but frequently grimaced, shook his head and nudged Hundley to object, as Savage continued to make these statements to the judge that were outside the plea agreement, even outside the official record. Noted a prominent newspaper editor, "There's no question the government played dirty."[26]

Hundley told the judge that virtually the entire case against his client—the alleged tax evasion, the obstruction charge, the so-called extortion— revolved solely around the underground campaign, the raising and spending of cash on election day. Hundley, the old Kennedy supporter, advocated to the judge, "I'm not saying it was right ... but underground campaigns in West Virginia were going on back when Jack Kennedy ran in the primary and I was working for him down here. Both parties have used [cash in campaigns] ... They counter balance." He said the $50 cash donation limit had "been honored in the breach."

Judge Hoffman agreed totally, complaining that West Virginia didn't enforce its election laws and "then they dump everything on the federal government and they become the most unpopular people in the world." When Savage begged for a long prison term (thereby violating the government's agreement not to argue for any particular sentence, specifically not a severe one), Hoffman asked him if Moore had been cooperative and truthful. Savage conceded, "I believe his testimony was truthful." Arch had done everything the feds had demanded except apologize profusely, Savage admitted. So Hoffman refused to use the higher sentencing guidelines reserved for non-cooperative defendants.

Savage shouted, "Let there be no mistake, Arch Moore is a criminal! This court's sentence needs to reflect that central fact!" Judge Hoffman seemed sympathetic throughout that Moore's organization was simply playing a cash political game that others had done for decades. He asked Savage, "You think I should penalize Mr. Moore for the acts of others that have [done in the past]?" Savage responded that Arch should get a stiff sentence because he was "a leader of the pack." He wanted Hoffman to make it clear that "cash and carry politics is now relegated to a bygone era." Others would say the "governor did the same thing and got away with it," he contended, if Hoffman let him off lightly. As compassionate as Hoffman seemed to be with Arch's plight, and as irritated as he seemed with the prosecution's overzealous advocacy, their over-reaching, he nevertheless seemed to agree with Savage that a sentence of a mere few months, or just a fine, was insufficient.

So Hoffman handed down a sentence somewhere between what Moore's friends and enemies were advocating: five years and ten months confinement in a federal facility (which would turn out to be thirty-three months with good behavior) plus a total fine of $170,000.

"It's an unfortunate situation for you to face the inevitable," Hoffman told Moore, in a kindly fashion. The former governor, whose family sat behind him, was composed and exhibited no emotion when the sentence was pronounced. He left the federal building with Mrs. Moore and refused to comment as he brushed past the throng of reporters and photographers and got into their car.

The New York Times wrote, "In West Virginia politics, they do take prisoners ... Governor Arch A. Moore, Jr. was sentenced to become one ..."[27]

While it could have been worse, it was a harsher sentence than the prosecutors had lead Hundley to believe would be given. There certainly were no "throwaway" counts, as his lawyer had promised Arch. (Moore would later testify that the feds had promised to seek no more than six months "away from [my] family and Mrs. Moore" for the entire sentence, on all five counts. However, Hundley had warned him that the obstruction charge, alone, could carry up to five years. "Don't worry about the other four counts," he quoted him saying.)

Hoffman announced that he would recommend that Arch be allowed to serve his time at a very minimal security prison camp in Virginia, not too far from home (Moore would chose to go to Maxwell Air Force Base in Alabama, instead). He also assured Moore that he would be immediately eligible for parole on each of the five convictions, but warned him that a parole board likely wouldn't see it that way, because they apply the "guidelines very ritualistically."

In Moore's favor, Hoffman turned down a request by an assistant to state Attorney General Roger Tompkins that Moore be required to set up a trust fund and pay the State four million dollars. Since there was no proof of anything Arch needed to repay (no one ever alleged that he'd taken a penny from the State; the cash had all been from private donors), Hoffman told her she could file a lawsuit if she disagreed. (They did and basically failed.)

Arch was afforded a few weeks to report to prison, to get his affairs in order. "During the weeks before I went to Alabama the U.S. Marshals were very kind to me," he recalled.

But Moore was bitter about what had happened, and psychologically traumatized. He would never quite be the same. "For the next three years, I lived in a vacuum. I just didn't accept what had happened to me, because I knew my country would never, ever do anything like this to one of its citizens."

The reaction by prominent West Virginians to the sentence was mixed, but most seemed to think it was fair. John Raese, still stinging from his 0-2 record at the polls, crowed that it marked the end of the Arch Moore era. GOP Chairman "Hike" Heiskell said he hoped it would be a lesson to others involved in corrupt activity. Governor Caperton graciously commented, "This is a difficult time for West Virginia, but a particularly painful time for former Governor Moore's family. My sympathy is with them."[28] Even George Farley, who had blocked so many of Moore's reforms in the third term and had orchestrated the effort to "starve him out of office," conceded, "It's really a sad ending to a man who had tremendous talent."

BUT AFTER the initial shock of the sentence subsided, "it then became a fight," as daughter Shelley Moore Capito put it. Her father told the family, "We'll fight it!" And so he did, by filing motions and appeals.

Hundley argued that the sentence should be overturned because the feds had advocated twenty years in prison, in violation of their promise that they would ask for no specific sentence. He also based the appeal on the fact that Arch had not been allowed to withdraw his plea and go to trial, and for other technical reasons.

As to be expected, the U.S. Attorney's office opposed his request for a trial. "Moore claimed [in his appellate briefs] that there would be no prejudice to the government if he was allowed to withdraw his guilty plea and go to trial," said a former assistant prosecutor who worked on the case. "But that train had left the station. We had the files stored in cabinets in different locations and had broken up the [investigation and prosecution] team, sending them all over the country. It would have been difficult to reassemble all that for a trial."[29]

The Fourth Circuit denied the appeal, writing, "There is no substance to Moore's claims. It would be pointless, perhaps even unjust, to allow him to relitigate."[30]

Demonstrating that it was still very "personal," Savage even tried to prevent the former governor from being eligible for parole during his five-plus years, but Hundley went to bat and got Hoffman to block that end-run manuever. "That's one thing he did do for me," admitted Arch.

Having lost his general appeal, on August 1, 1991, Moore again would move for withdrawal of his plea and an opportunity to go to trial, this time on the basis that he'd received ineffective assistance of counsel. He argued that Hundley had given him bad advice by telling him he could withdraw the plea any time up until sentencing. He also filed as exhibits the June 27 and July 9, 1990, affidavits by Hundley. In those sworn affidavits, the Washington lawyer admitted that he based his recommendation that Moore plead guilty even though his client was not given a chance to hear the tapes of his conversations with Leaberry and without giving the two more than a few hours to review the government's evidence. Hundley had also stated that Moore had never, ever received the $50,000 alleged to have been accepted from Marrowbone Coal Company. No such money had been conveyed to Moore or his campaign, Hundley swore. His lawyer stated that he had asked the prosecutors for a day or two "to discuss this important decision in detail and without due pressure," but they refused.

Further, Hundley wrote, the feds had promised to "structure the indictment so that the obstruction of justice count was the only count within the sentencing guidelines [and the only one for which Moore would face jail time]," but they reneged once Arch had signed the agreement. His client had been put under "anxiety and pressure" and "really did not have an opportunity to absorb the contents of the statement before, on my advice, he entered the plea the following day," his lawyer wrote. "If he had, in my opinion, he would not have pleaded guilty."

Hundley added that Moore "vehemently" denied the version of the "extortion" given by Paul Kizer, whom he reminded the court was "an immunized government witness." Essentially, Hundley accused the federal prosecutors of playing dirty, unfairly—unduly pressuring Moore to quickly entering a plea without having time or opportunity to determine what accusations they prepared to use against him. That was why, Hundley continued, that there was "a long pause by Mr. Moore before he answered the judge's question as to whether his plea had been the result of duress or coercion."

But, on February 24, 1992, U.S. District Judge Richard Williams denied Moore's motion. Arch would try one more time to withdraw the plea, this time representing himself before the court in April of 1994, but it had the same result.

Even after striking out again and again, Moore continued for years to research the law, excited when he'd find U.S. Supreme Court case law that seemed to support his position. One case in particular held that a public official could not extort a favor-seeker for something he had no control over, which fit to a tee the Kizer refund situation. He had also found case law that held, if there was a plea agreement and the judge does not abide by that agreement, then he cannot deny a defendant the right to withdraw his plea—another decision that applied to his circumstances. Arch had explanations for all the accusations that he believed were plausible. That his motions were denied ate at him continually, almost as much as the disgrace of the penalty; he believed he had not received justice. Whether anyone else agreed or understood his position did not matter; he'd convinced himself that he had been railroaded. "I may take a third stab at [at getting the verdict set aside and a trial on the merits]," he was saying in late 2005. He even held a secret affidavit (concerning the Kizer episode) that he apparently planned to use as a trump card, if he ever filed that new motion.

Most who read or heard about Moore's continuing quest to withdraw his plea scoffed at it. They did not understand where he was coming from and assumed he was simply reneging. "How could a lawyer as smart as Arch Moore be convinced to plead guilty if he didn't really want to do so, if he wasn't convinced it was the best deal he could possibly get?" was the question normally heard. They simply couldn't believe that his appeals were offered in good faith; they weren't buying his assertion that the guilty plea had been entered solely as a "discovery measure." But "he was deadly serious about withdrawing his plea," insisted son Kim Moore. "He's worked harder against that than anything else he's done in recent years." It absolutely has not been a public relations effort, an attempt to plant doubt in the public's mind about his guilt, Kim insisted. But he admitted that his father's appeals had "also been a disaster and a waste of money."

A common-sense question loomed over and above the guilty plea issue, nonetheless: Why in the world did Moore allow cash to be solicited and spent in the 1984 and 1988 campaigns, especially when common sense told him the feds were watching, just waiting for an opportunity to pounce?

"I think when Bill Loy was gone, Dad lost his anchor," speculated Shelley Moore Capito. After a thoughtful pause she added, "It's sort of inexplicable." In fact, she said she had warned him against allowing cash transactions, reminding her father, "It's illegal!" She noted that, later on, when the Capito children got older, they demanded details about what happened. "I told them, 'Well, he kinda screwed up, but not as bad as they said.'"

As part of the guilty plea, the former governor agreed to cooperate with the on-going investigation. Savage and the other prosecutors met with him in his Charleston law office for interviews. On the way out of his office, the government lawyers admired all the certificates, commendations, awards, and photos of Moore with presidents, various celebrities and sports figures, which he had displayed on his walls.

"Some day I'm going to write a book," Moore told them, referring to his illustrious career. "But none of you are going to be in it!" Even they had to laugh at that one.

Chapter 29 Notes

1. - The guilt of implicating his friends and associates may have been too much for him to bear. D'Annunzio would commit suicide when the results of the investigation began producing arrests. His comments to investigators, however, would be allowed into evidence by the judge in the trial that eventually sent Ellis to jail.

2. - Rice, Ibid.

3. - In 1998, A. James Manchin would return to the capitol where he had begun his career, as a delegate from Marion County, and would remain in the House until his death in 2002.

4. - Moore later said he thought Marrowbone officials made the contribution to his campaign in appreciation for a coal strike he'd helped settle.

5. - John Weaver, May 5, 2005.

6. - *Daily Mail,* April 13, 1990.

7. - "I think John McClaugherty [a Charleston lawyer] talked him into doing that," speculated one of Jay's later comp commissioners. For the coal companies, "it would be like going to State Farm and saying, 'I haven't had any car accidents in the past ten years, so I'd like a refund of all the premi-

ums I paid during that time. I want to be self-insured.'" But as long as the CWP Fund was solvent, the Department of Labor didn't care about the generous refunds, which were given to scores of coal companies during the Rockefeller and Moore Administrations. And, after all, it was money that the coal companies had been forced to pay in premiums to begin with. The system was overfunded because there hadn't been as many federal black lung claims as they'd projected. It was the coal companies' money, a mutual fund, despite what the news media would later try to portray to the contrary.

8. - Kizer and his bodyguard, James Bonham, were charged with murder for the March 16, 1986 shooting death of a 31-year-old Boone County man, Jimmy Vickers. Kizer had been accused of paying a thousand dollars to two men to "whip" Jimmy, after Vickers had struck him (Vickers had found Kizer with Vickers' girlfriend). But the hired thugs had gone overboard, shot into his mobile home and killed Vickers. Bonham was convicted in November 1989 and was sentenced to two years in prison for voluntary manslaughter and conspiracy to commit malicious wounding. But Kizer, who'd hired high-powered Morgantown lawyer Clark Frame, was acquitted by the Cabell County jury. Kizer would later claim that he made a contribution to a Republican national governors' campaign committee in order to win favor, insurance in case he was convicted of murder and had to ask Governor Moore for a pardon.

9. - "Whether a half million dollars was an excessive fee for Moore to have charged Kizer for processing the application is another issue," noted one of Rockefeller's workers' compensation commissioners, "but it would be a matter between the lawyer and his client, not a criminal matter." He noted that most firms would have charged a client only a few hundred dollars to file the self-insurance application and see it through.

10. - In a December 10, 2002 *Gazette* article, Kizer told Paul Nyden that he "needed to set the record straight" about the "$573,000 so-called kickback" to Moore. He then admitted to Nyden, "I deserved every credit I got." Kizer, then running an unsuccessful campaign to become the Republican nominee for governor himself, said he wanted Arch to get his law license returned, noting that Moore "was an excellent governor and has my support in his future endeavors." Back in 1990, Kizer "repeatedly told reporters he was a victim of various Moore administration extortion schemes," Nyden wrote in 2002, but now Kizer confessed that the allegations were "untrue." He admitted that he actually had been "legally entitled" to every credit and refund he'd received during the Moore and Caperton administrations. He specifically told Nyden that he did not bribe Arch Moore. Kizer admitted that accusations his lawyer, Fred Fahrenz, had made against Arch (that he'd demanded payments even after he went to prison), were also totally untrue. The article noted that Kizer's twenty-some companies went bankrupt during the Caperton Administration in 1992, leaving a $44.6 million debt to the Workers' Compensation Fund. He had sold a billion dollars' worth of coal between 1983 and 1993, and he still owned 100 million tons of high-quality coal. Moore's Super Tax Credit program was "the single most important factor" to allow him to expand his mines and keep 1022 employees working for a decade, he told the *Gazette*. But the damage had been done to Arch Moore twelve years earlier. The egg had been broken and couldn't be put back together again.

11. - Hundley also would represent Clinton buddy Vernon Jordan during that President's scandals. He had started his career prosecuting Communists as part of the Justice Department's Internal Security Division during the McCarthy Era but as a liberal Democrat didn't like doing that. He'd been a special assistant to NFL Commissioner Pete Rozell. Hundley joined Washington "fixer" and former Democratic Chairman Robert Strauss' law firm and was there when Arch retained him. He'd successfully represented Maryland State Senator Dale Hess in Governor Marvin Mandel's scandal. He got Tongsun Park, a South Korean operative who bribed U.S. Senators and Congressmen, off the hook. He also got Warren Trepp, Michael Milken's bond trader, acquitted. But he admitted to *The Washington Lawyer*, "I've had a lot of losses, too. At one time they used to refer to a 'Hundley Wing' at Allenwood [Prison]." Hundley said he'd learned not to get personal feelings involved in criminal defense, not to get worried as long as his name wasn't in the style of the case, as the defendant.

12. - Sikora, March 25, 2005.

13. - Harless died on December 21, 1990. He was in his sixties.

14. - Leaberry, 38, would be charged by the U.S. Attorney with failure to disclose all sources of his income to the IRS in 1988, including $5000 income from Kizer. They also said he claimed a deduction of $12,029 for non-existing accounting and engineering expenses of Left Coast Inc., which he'd set up. He pleaded guilty on September 11, 1990 before Judge John Copenhaver, paid a fine and was given

probation. He did not serve any prison time. In December 1990 the state Supreme Court allowed him to keep his West Virginia law license. Only Justice William Brotherton voted to suspend Leaberry's license. Leaberry moved to Clearwater, Florida, married and began his own law practice there.

15. - Donohoe, April 14, 2005.

16. - An aggravation to Moore when the story was told by the news media was the allegation that he had "slumped down" in his seat of his car during the conversation with John Leaberry. "I'm not a tall man," he said. "My head was blocked by the headrest. I wasn't slouching down!" His son, Kim Moore, laughs that his dad always claimed to be five feet nine and three quarters, but "he's my height, and that's five feet seven. His suits fit me like a glove."

17. - Which Moore contends had been left over from an earlier campaign.

18. - The definition of "extortion" was not merely an esoteric debate in Moore's case. While *Black's Law Dictionary*, the lawyer's "bible," defines extortion as "unlawful obtaining money from another," courts have defined it differently over the years, in different jurisdictions. Recent court decisions, however, held that extortion by a public official could occur only if he or she had control over the "favor" that was being given to the one offering the bribe.

19. - Mrs. Durbin said that her father's guilty plea did not come as a complete shock to her. "I knew something was going on. That previous December, I'd been served with a subpoena," recalled Lucy. "I went to Dad and he told me, 'Go in there [to the grand jury or federal interrogation] and be honest, but don't tell your mother about it.' He was trying to protect Mom from all of that. Joe Savage was a good interrogator but he has no heart. He wanted to know about gifts we took, trips we took, carpet in my basement—which had come from the Mansion, but belonged to my parents. So I knew something was up. Dad had been to the federal building." Further, the feds had interrogated Lucy regarding the house bought through Wilma Ellis (Bill's wife), although nothing improper could ever be established.

20. - McCoy, July 26, 2005. Dr. McCoy had a difficult time speaking of this portion of his friend's life, often choking up and having to stop. "I love that man," he said, several times.

21. - Moore had reported personal income of $949,453 in 1985, the indictment said. He reported $189,101 in 1984. In reviewing this report for accuracy, Arch wrote, "This is not so," but, again, provided no contrary figures.

22. - Hoffman, was U.S. District Court for the Eastern District of Virginia (Norfolk), an unsuccessful Republican candidate for Virginia attorney general in 1948. Eisenhower appointed him to the federal bench in 1954 and he served until his death in 1996.

23. - Others were persecuted for their loyalty to Moore. Arch's family physician, Dr. William Harris, had performed a lot of free medical care for state employees and other pro bono projects, for which the Governor had presented to him a Distinguished West Virginian certificate. He prized the document and had it framed, along with a photo of himself with Moore and hung it proudly in the reception room of his Kanawha City office. He came out one day to discover that someone had drawn prison bars with a Magic Marker on the display. "It was ruined," Dr. Harris said, with sadness. "I had to dispose of it." Some people even suffered loss of business and income because they would not turn their backs on Arch, because they refused to remove his photo from their office walls.

24. - An IRS agent would testify on July 10, 1990 that Love had loaned the car to Moore prior to his election as governor, and that there had been on-going negotiations about a lease or purchase price, but Moore had never returned the car used by Mrs. Moore, and never paid for it until April of 1990. However, the IRS agent would testify that Moore had on several times told Love, "Let me know how much you want me to pay and I'll pay for it." Judge Hoffman would say, "[It is] then the over-exuberance of the Internal Revenue Service to say 'it is not paid,'" and dismissed it as nothing.

25. - Arch said he paid Hundley over $40,000 for his work in the case. Had Moore thought of bringing a malpractice action against Hundley? Moore said he did, "but Hundley's firm began papering their files to defend against that," and he decided not to pursue such an action. Besides, that would not have gained him his freedom even if he prevailed. In his darkest moments, Arch suspected that perhaps Hundley may have even "traded him" to the Justice Department for the freedom of a Wall Street client in an SEC case because "he had a friend in the Public Integrity Section" but, again, he never made any formal allegations regarding that belief, lacking solid proof.

26. - Bob Kelly, November 28, 2005.

27. - *The New York Times*, July 15, 1990.

28. - *Gazette*, July 20, 1990.
29. - Nancy Hill.
30. - *U.S. vs. Moore*, 931 F. 2d 245 (4th Cir.)

Chapter Thirty
"My Sabbatical"

Arch was permitted to remain free for a few weeks until time to begin his sentence at Maxwell Air Force Base, near Montgomery, Alabama, where by choice he was assigned.[1] The Governor's brother and sister-in-law drove the Moores to Alabama,[2] to report to prison. "That was the worst day of my life," said Harry Moore. ("Dad and his brother are so close, when one hurts the other hurts," noted Kim Moore.)

Despite the reason for the journey, both Arch and Shelley remained characteristically upbeat, however. "They didn't reveal their inside feelings," remembered Harry. A casual observer might have thought they were on a family vacation, as they pleasantly chatted away about light subjects, all the way to Montgomery.

The scene changed a bit when, at the appointed time, Harry delivered his brother to Maxwell on August 7, 1990. Mrs. Moore remained behind, "I just fogged the entire thing out," she would later say, "just blocked it out of my mind, until I can't even remember it." His brother took him to the gate, and shook his hand before he walked into the facility alone. Despite promises to the contrary, prison officials allowed news media reps in for Moore's entrance. Warmed by the Alabama sun, Arch carried his suit jacket in one hand, a suitcase in the other. He had to endure another round of photos and questions shouted to him, which he silently ignored. A few inmates taunted him. "It was a disgrace," thought Harry. "I complained to a guard. It was especially upsetting that they allowed the press in."

Then West Virginia's only three term governor, once considered presidential material, officially became Prisoner No. 02928-088, which had been the number assigned to his federal criminal case.[3] And No. 02928-088 would be locked up for five-plus years unless paroled early or eligible for "good time" which cut weeks off the sentence automatically.

He gave up his street clothing (although allowed to wear those for family visits), and got into the boots and the Kelly green, government-issue uniforms the inmates were assigned (they wore tennis, street, or work shoes, whatever they preferred). He was searched, taken for extensive paperwork and processed. He was treated like any other inmate at the facility, eighty-five percent of whom were drug offenders, the remaining fifteen percent white collar criminals and "property offenders," all non-violent criminals.

After a final, emotional goodbye, Harry then drove the former First

Lady to her brother's home in Georgia. At that point, Mrs. Moore dropped the brave face she'd maintained for her husband's sake. "She cried almost all the way over there," recalled Harry Moore. "It was very, very sad." It was not just the disgrace, the end of dreams, but also the first time since they were married that they would be separated for so long. Arch had even come home for lunch when he was governor.

While there were no fences or walls, Arch's new place of residence was not the country club that some supposed. The new prisoner was assigned to a barracks-style room in a cinder block structure that was, mercifully, air conditioned. The one large room, with walled (but not barred) block partitions, housed about forty men, each of whom had a bunk bed and personal locker.

Once the processing is completed, and you settle in, it hits you: I'm in prison! It certainly wasn't the "fourth term" he'd sought.

Kim Moore said the family phoned his father several times "to see if he was OK," but in those first 48 hours it was almost impossible. "He was emotional, crying ... it really wrung him out. You couldn't carry on a conversation with him. It hit him so hard. I guess that's part of the punishment."

Bill Ellis recalled his thoughts in his first day of six years of incarceration. "The fear of the unknown is a whole lot worse than what it turned out to be. Actually it was a camp-like environment. There were no guns, handcuffs, gates or fences. The food was institutional. You got used to the routine." After the trauma of the situation subsided, Ellis realized it could be a whole lot worse. "I felt safer in prison than I do on the streets [of Charleston]. Not once was I threatened by any staff or inmates."

The routine was the same each day: up at five a.m., breakfast at the cafeteria (the prisoners ate in shifts), after which it was work time for the remainder of the morning; they were kept very busy. Many of the prisoners did grounds-keeping and maintenance, which meant they mowed, trimmed and cleaned up the golf course and other areas of the base. "I flew in and out of there many times during that period," remembered Randy Dell, who served with the U.S. Marshal Service and the Joint Chiefs of Staff. "Being from West Virginia myself, I always tried to spot Governor Moore, but I could never pick him out." Prisoner Moore was initially assigned to the task of picking up litter and such but, in deference to his former position and age, was soon transferred to conduct his work assignments in the kitchen and prison library.

For their hard work, the inmates received eleven cents an hour. The pay could rise as high as forty cents if the work one performed was skilled, such as meat cutting. In addition to grounds-keeping, the convicts kept busy in the food service areas, cleaning, mopping, peeling potatoes, cooking, preparing the salad bar. By all reports, Prisoner Moore took to his assigned tasks with enthusiasm and vigor, just as he'd handled every phase of his career since he began carrying newspapers as a boy. "I'm here, so I might as well make the best of it," seemed to be his unspoken motto. And another: "Never let them see you sweat."

His son reported that Arch baked a lot during his kitchen work at the prison. "When Mom and I would visit, he'd bring out some warm cinnamon rolls he'd just baked. Sometimes he'd work as a bus boy." Jerry Scott, food service foreman there, would later report, on March 29, 1992, that Prisoner Moore had "excellent performance" for the seventeen months he'd been on kitchen detail. "He takes pride in his work," and "tries to make a difference." He was "very well-liked by both the staff and inmates."

"There's never an hour of the day that you're not aware of where you are and how you got there," recalled Arch. "But I stayed busy and tried to keep my mind off of it. I dealt with it by dedicating myself to others. That's the way you work through it. But you can't completely get your mind off yourself and your circumstances." He added, quietly, "And there's never been a day [since he left prison] that I haven't thought about it—often many times a day. That's not something you turn off and on."[4]

He added, "I knew that, if fairness had prevailed, I would not be there. But I knew my Lord was going to see me through this and I was going to continue to be everything I represented myself to be." Observed his son-in-law, "They tried to break his spirit in there, but he had the mental determination, the strength to push through it. He just plowed through it."[5] According to all witnesses, he remained the "same Arch Moore" he had always been; he succeeded in maintaining his mood, his dignity, his self-confidence and, most of all, his commitment to being useful.

Between ten and eleven, the prisoners ate lunch and then it was back to work, for at least seven hours per day. At four p.m., they had to stand by their bed for the daily "count." There was school in the evening for those who needed it, and recreation—basketball, softball, other games—for those who didn't. There was no mandatory bedtime, "as long as they were quiet," said Shelan Moore (no relation to Arch), of the prison's staff. "Arch spent a lot of his free time there playing cards," said Ellis, who remained friendly with, and defensive of, the former governor, even though Arch had testified in Ellis's trial. Local pastors provided chapel on Sundays and sometimes during the week. "I played shortstop on the baseball team," Arch recalled. "I played tennis all the time. We'd get a crowd around [watching them play]." He was able to "use the phone anytime I wanted to. I called my wife every night, and my children every Sunday night, as I always have done."

The building in which Arch and his fellow inmates were housed "was a three story building; it looked like a high school," recalled daughter Lucy Durbin. "They make it sound like a country club, but it was not." She noted that the base housed about 800 to 900 inmates at the time, eighty percent of whom were African-American. (Many of the Alabama prison's administrators also were African-American. Few probably realized they were guarding a man who had helped author and pass several Civil Rights bills.) The black inmates "loved him," said Lucy. "My parents taught me we're all the same." Her father was not a racist, nor did he look down upon lower income people. "If you don't have two nickels to rub together, he'll still talk to you. He'll be your friend," she noted, with an appreciative grin.

"They had vending machines in the visitors area. It was so hot down there, we usually visited outside. They had a patio area, with [outdoor] patio furniture. That's where we usually met him. He'd bring us a candy bar, pull it out of his pocket." Lucy wept as she added, "The [visitor's area] was always packed, just crowded with people, but he made us feel like we were all alone."[6]

The prisoners also had access to the law library, where the former governor spent much of his time. "Inmates were always asking him legal questions, with which he would try to help them," said brother Harry. Not only did he give advice to convicts, but the prison staff, even administrators, would quietly come to Moore for advice on their own careers, or how to handle a particular problem. He became known as a sage who was easy to talk to, who would listen with sympathy, who always seemed to have sound advice for anyone. "I could have been elected mayor [of the prison] by the time I left there," joked Moore.

One of his bunk mates was a large black man named Luther. Luther came to him one day and said, "Governor, I write songs. Could I sing one for you?" When Arch eagerly agreed to listen, Luther sat down in front of Moore's bunk and sang him a love song. Kim Moore got a kick out of that story, visualizing the scene, which he thought was a comical one.

Arch "volunteered hundreds of hours to the library and its staff," wrote Angela Crosby, college coordinator at the facility, on March 30, 1992. He went "beyond his regular work assignment, had provided tutoring to inmates in the area of their educational requirements," and "taught the library stewards, who in turn are helpful to the population in general at Maxwell." She added that Prisoner Moore "volunteered his special efforts in reorganizing the law library which is now more easily used." She noted that Arch had helped inmates get their GEDs and others to complete their college courses at Troy State University. She concluded that the former governor "demonstrated his caring and concerned attitude in any request made of him."

But in much of his spare time in the library, Arch also continued to research court case law for himself, trying to find a way out of his nightmare. For more than a decade after his incarceration, Moore almost obsessively continued to research the law to find a basis for overturning his conviction and restoring his honor. (That he might actually be successful on appeal but be tried, convicted and receive a greater sentence, never seemed to concern him.) Although he accepted his punishment–he didn't have a choice–he never accepted that he was pronounced guilty of felonies, by his own plea agreement.

THEY SAY that the family serves the sentence along with their loved one, which certainly was true of the tight-knit Moore family. It's not uncommon for some to turn their back on a spouse at a time like this, in shame, disgust or weariness. When some men go off to prison their wives even divorce them. But Shelley Moore was the most faithful, loyal partner one could ever hope for. As her daughter would say, she "never turned away from him." To the contrary—the couple had always been a team, through thick and thin, and that was not going to change now when Arch needed her the most. "She flew down to Alabama every week to visit Arch," confirmed Harry Moore, who often drove Mrs. Moore to the airport. "That was the best thing that ever happened to Arch—the day he met her." The former governor confirmed her loyalty, her visitation pattern, choking up, "She was with me every weekend." Both would forever take the disgrace very, very seriously. But with characteristic humor, Shelley and Arch would euphemistically refer to the 33 months he was incarcerated as his "sabbatical" and the whole affair as "my problem." It could accurately be said that, even though Mrs. Moore was never charged with anything, the prison sentence was served by both of them. Her "other half" was in jail and she missed him terribly, cared about him intensely, and he for her. But were both of hardy stock and, if anything, the terrible ordeal seemed to strengthen their marriage, their bond.

During weekdays, the former first lady stayed busy in Glen Dale and Moundsville, with her usual social and church activities. "She spent a lot of time with us and my sister," recalled Harry. "She stayed occupied, kept her mind off what had happened." Moundsville neighbors and friends would see her from time to time, at a gas station or shopping, and offer their condolences, their support to a lady they still loved dearly. "I was treated very well," she confirmed. Shelley could not help but be tearful with many, unable to even talk. In many ways, the experience was much tougher for her to handle than it was for her husband.

"I talked to my mother by phone more than I ever had before," her son recalled. "Dad was always the leader of the band, but she was the leader of the band those three years." Said Dr. McCoy, "It was important to let Arch know his friends were still his friends. If you're my friend, that's it." They and other family friends kept in touch with Arch, through Mrs. Moore.

It was terribly difficult to accept that their father was in prison, daughter Shelley Moore Capito remembered. "The first time I visited him down there, it was really, really hard." But Capito began to see that something positive could be derived even from this traumatic episode. "For the first time in my life, I had my dad's undivided attention for five hours. So there is always something good." Kim Moore, who visited him four times a year, agreed. "It was sad. But we played Hearts and joked around. It wasn't like, 'Woe is me, it's the end of the world.' He was always looking at the next step. And Mom was a real strength for him."

Some of those who had benefitted greatly from Arch Moore administrations would never again speak anything but ill of him and shunned him if he was in a public place. But that was far from the norm. Although greatly disappointed by the turn of events, the disgrace Moore's guilty plea and sentence had brought to them and their state, many of his former supporters and friends remained true to him, showering him with small gifts, notes and cards. They wanted him to know that not everyone had abandoned him, that they still remembered the positive impact he'd made on the lives of West Virginians in years past. They phoned often to check on Mrs. Moore.

For his part, Arch never corresponded with anyone while in the prison; he communicated with the "outside" through his wife, as needed. Nelson Robinson, by now a successful lobbyist, was one of the faithful who wrote to his former boss while he was in prison, keeping him up-to-date on politics of the state. "Mrs. Moore told me not to expect to hear back from him. I don't think he ever wanted to factually admit where he was. I don't think he wanted to correspond with anyone with a postmark from a federal institution." He didn't want to give someone a souvenir, in other words. It was part of Moore's denial, perhaps, pretending in his own way that this terrible situation didn't really exist. Possibly it was his ongoing compartmentalization of his life that had been so successful in the past.

None but family was allowed to visit Arch while he was incarcerated. An exception was not even made for close friend Dave Yoho or "family member" Audrey Toler. "He didn't want me to see him like that," said Toler, softly. She would send the former governor newspaper clippings throughout his months of confinement, to keep him up-to-date on state affairs and politics. (He particularly enjoyed those when they showed his successor having difficulties.) She occasionally talked to him by phone, such as during the time she was closing his Charleston law office ("That was the second hardest day of my life") forever.

"He did phone me a couple times when he was there," chuckled Dr. Yoho, about one of the calls. "He was talking in code one time, asking me to play some specific numbers for him on the Florida lottery." (Yoho figured out what he was talking about. Moore did not hit the lottery, however.)

In all, Moore received more than eight thousand cards and letters from well-wishers and sympathizers, while in federal custody. He kept every one of them. He was even "called in" to the warden's office where he was instructed to have his correspondents to cease referring to him as "Governor" on the envelopes. "How do I know who's going to write to me?" countered Prisoner Moore. "You've got a point," the administrator admitted, and overruled the complaining mail clerk. "From then on the guy who would hand out the mail would emphasize '*Governor* Arch Moore!'"

Harry visited his brother three times while he was in the Alabama prison and twice after he was transferred to a less secure facility. "Arch was usually dressed in a sweater and casual slacks," he recalled of those visits. "We just caught up on things. He was always upbeat."

Shelley Moore Capito recalled that her sons, still small, had not seen their grandfather for more than a year when she took them with her to pick him up at Yeager, when he was on furlough to testify in court. They missed him terribly. She had not told them where they were going, keeping it a surprise. Her voice halting with emotion, Capito recalled that, upon sight of his grandfather, her eldest son, Charles, ran and clung to him "for what seemed like an hour. It was a very touching moment."

For her weekly visits, the former First Lady would drive to Pittsburgh, fly to Columbus, Georgia to lodge with family (her brother was a retired Army colonel who had been stationed at nearby Fort Benning), and take a car, which they had left there, on to Montgomery to visit her husband. "We just had light conversation," Mrs. Moore recalled, of the weekly visits. "It was always so wonderful to see him. He did very well, health-wise, while in there–they kept him doing therapeutic things.

"He'd have things he would need me to tend to, to check on. He'd always come out [for the prison visits] with a smile. He would never burden us in any melancholy way." Her brother and sister and their families were "very close" and supportive of her during these traumatic times, Shelley recalled, adding, "I was just thankful that our parents were gone and didn't have to go through that." Her children "continued to be a part of my life and were very sweet." She would spend a lot of time at her son's home in Virginia or in Charleston at her daughter's (Shelley Moore Capito's) home.

"My mother had a saying, 'Nothing is so bad that it couldn't be worse.' I've always lived by that," said Mrs. Moore. She found that axiom to be true once again on August 31, 1992, while Arch was still in confinement. The family was disgraced and embarrassed once again when son-in-law John Richard Durbin and daughter Lucy, by then 36, were arrested for selling a fourth of an ounce of cocaine for five hundred dollars. U.S. Attorney Mike Carey announced that their arrest, along with two others, was part of a six month "sting" operation.

The Durbins' lawyer was critical of the way it was handled. Although the Durbins were well-known Charlestonians, and undoubtedly would have responded to a summons (the magistrate released them on a recognizance bond) two huge policemen went to Lucy's office at C&P Telephone, where she had worked for thirteen years.[7] They handcuffed the tiny, petite young woman and took her to the courthouse as if she was a dangerous criminal.

"Her sister would confront Lucy [about the rumors of drug use]," recalled Audrey Toler, "but she'd always deny it." The arrest "took a toll on" Mrs. Moore, in particular, Toler added. Mrs. Moore "is the one who's been affected the most by all of this."

Carey refused to reduce Lucy's charge to a misdemeanor, after she insisted to Joe Savage that she could not identify other cocaine users in Charleston. ("He thought we'd implicate doctors, lawyers and businessmen but there was nothing there. We were just partying.") In Huntington on March 12, 1993, U.S. District Judge Robert Staker would place Lucy on three years probation for "aiding her husband" in the illegal drug sale. Their car was seized by the government. "They just destroyed my home," Lucy added, noting the agents "tore things up so badly that it looked like a hurricane had struck–and they found nothing." After apologizing to the Moore family and his own family, Lucy's husband was sentenced to a year and a day (in excess of a year, so he would not have to be housed in a county jail).[8]

It was Lucy's niece's first day of school when the news of her arrest had come out. Shelley Moore Capito was "so pissed off at me," Lucy recalled. "She asked, 'How could you do that?' She had to drive up to Pittsburgh to meet Mom at the airport [who was returning from a visit to Arch in Alabama] to tell her before she heard it or saw it on the news." Lucy's father, too, was very angry. He blamed it all on son-in-law John Durbin and refused to speak to him for some time. Arch then cooled off and his relationship with John was restored. ("He finally forgave him.") Lucy remained certain that she was targeted because of her father's situation. ("There's no doubt in my mind.") Perhaps the prosecutors were using this as a tool to fight back, because Arch continued his appeals and requests for a trial; unable to punish him more, they lashed out against a family member. Or perhaps it was all just a coincidence. Whether or not, the Moore clan severed all relations with Carey, who had been in the Capitos' wedding party and had been a long-time friend of Charlie Capito.

FOR THE LAST few months of his sentence, Arch was allowed to serve his remaining time a little closer to home, in another minimum security federal prison camp in Ashland, Kentucky beginning on April 8, 1993. He was provided a Greyhound bus ticket and allowed to transfer from Alabama on his own without supervision, but basically with nothing but the clothes on his back, with no money, food, or personal items. (Arch's old adversary, Johnie Owens, already there, was called in by the administrators to see if he'd object to Moore being in the same facility with him. "I said no, this place is big enough for the both of us. I'd have been shipped off to Timbuktu if I'd said no, and I liked being in Ashland; it was close to home.")[9]

There the men were assigned to barracks, Appalachian 1 or 2, or Bluegrass 1 or 2. Generally two prisoners were assigned to each cinder block cell, but Arch had one to himself. "Deference was given to their age, former position and nature of their offense," explained Ellis, who served there with him.

Moore found other West Virginia politicos among his ranks. Former state Sen. Larry Tucker was an inmate in the Ashland facility,[10] as was former Logan County Sheriff Earl Tomblin and Owens (who would serve 98 months). "Tomblin and Moore, being former administrators, would sit and discuss ways the prison system could be run more effectively," laughed a Logan Countian who knew the former sheriff. It was a West Virginia reunion.

Owens described the prison camp at Ashland as "like a town, with a commissary, post office, a doctor's office, visiting rooms," and even a motel across the street where some of the inmates would sneak off to spend time with girlfriends or wives. "It wasn't that bad," Owen insisted. "It's just what you make of it. Your family suffered more than you did. You'd get up at six a.m., have bed check at 10:30 p.m. Warden Dove would walk through to inspect twice a week. The food wasn't bad except they burned me out on rice–they'd fix it a different way, seven days a week."

By now, Bill Ellis was a camp clerk, given a typewriter, "lots of privileges," and was allowed to drive a van around town. He was even given bookkeeping and management duties of the prison industries, which fit his business background. "For a prison, I couldn't have asked for a better situation," he would later smile. Tucker agreed. "If you'd been in the military like Arch and I had, it wasn't all that different. You can be an a–hole, or you can chose to get along, and Arch and I did."

The inmates at Ashland wore surplus military fatigues, either olive or khaki and Arch wore tennis shoes "for comfort." The inmates always know what's going on in the prison system even before the administrators do, noted Tucker, and "there was a long, long line of men waiting to greet Arch when he arrived at Ashland. I was going to greet him myself, but the line was too long." Tucker said when he saw Arch the next day, he asked, "How'd your fund-raiser go last night?" to which he laughed.

Again, every inmate had assigned tasks, chores. The former governor was given light duty work at the Ashland prison camp. He basically worked as a bus boy, keeping salt, pepper and napkins on the tables of the dining hall, and cleaning them after meals. For this menial task, Arch earned between ten and fifteen cents per hour, never more than eight to ten dollars per month. Still steaming because he believed that Moore could have (via Judge Haden) got him out of prison or kept him from going there in the first place, Owens relished the sight of the former governor being in prison with him. "I always had an extra cup of coffee so I could watch him burn, as he walked around in his apron, clearing tables."

Owens reportedly was the exception. There was a special respect among the inmates for Moore, thought Tucker, because he had served with distinction in the Congress and as governor, had become a senior citizen, and because he had been kind and accessible to other prisoners.

But there was another reason, too. When the feds went after him,

Arch had practiced what the Mafia calls omerta, the code of silence. It wasn't in his personal code of conduct to squeal on other major state politicians just to save his own skin.[11] "Arch knew a lot, but didn't tell," noted Tucker, to whom such a trait was a mark of honor. "He handled it like a man. Others would have run to the courthouse to tell on everyone they knew [to obtain a lighter sentence].

"Arch knew enough to send almost every politician in the state to jail, and could have got a bunch of big contributors in trouble, but he kept silent. He was far from being the only one who had used cash [to buy onto Democrat slates to get elected]. Everyone was doing it. But he didn't hurt anybody. He chose to take his licks. Whatever Arch knows [about the others] he'll take to his grave with him."[12]

"He always was 'The Governor,'" in his look and demeanor, remembered Tucker who was Moore's best friend while they were both confined. "Arch was always neat, clean-shaven, upbeat, friendly to everyone, staff or fellow inmates." Arch's mood continued to be uplifted by the frequent visits from Mrs. Moore, his children and grand-children, Tucker remembered.

As in Alabama, the former governor spent most of his free time in the prison library, working on his own appeal. And he and Tucker help other convicts with their appeals. Scores of inmates, mainly young black drug offenders, would ask Arch for legal assistance and he turned none away. "He would prepare their briefs and I was good at typing, so I'd type them up," laughed Tucker. "At one point, Arch worked for me, because I did clerical work and he was a kitchen helper," he added.

Tucker said Moore never talked to him directly about his motives for his legal research, his constant pursuit of a reversal of the sentence, but he believed it was because Arch thought he had received an unjustly harsh sentence from the federal court. "We looked at that New Jersey senator who got in trouble," noted Tucker, "and he was simply allowed to resign. No indictment, no conviction, no jail time. He 'walked.' [The New Jersey senator] even got to keep his pension. So we felt there was a double standard."

One observer had another theory: "It gave Arch some hope for possible restoration of his honor, to think he might [get his sentence reversed]. The pursuit of appeals gave him something with which to occupy and divert his mind, something to cling to. It wasn't about getting out of prison early, it was about restoring his respect among the people of West Virginia, to somehow end his disgrace."

His appeals and arguments would continue, even after he would be released.

One of Arch's greatest fears about the prison sentence was that his many fans, friends and supporters would all turn their backs on him, hate him, never forgive him, shun him. And Moore desperately "liked to be liked," as Linda McCartney once said about husband Paul. Arch couldn't bear the thoughts that he would lose all those relationships, friendships he'd acquired over sixty-some years. He didn't know what to expect. But while the experience weeded out those who'd just been using him and left the true friends, Moore was pleasantly surprised to learn that thousands did not abandon him; some forgave him; some didn't but still loved him for what he'd done as governor. More than a few even believed that he'd got a raw deal, that he had been punished for something others had done but still remained in office. The initial rage at him calmed down, as time healed the anger and it was all put into perspective. The realization that he still had many friends became clear as the mail continued to reach him, in such volumes that prison authorities would get irritated by it. And it was not easy for one to send him correspondence–it took an effort to even discover his address.

Governor Moore would often receive letters of consolation and gratitude from some of the thousands of West Virginians he had helped while serving as governor. It seemed that they wanted to lessen his misery by reminding him of how he had lessened theirs at one time or another. Many stories he had never heard before; they were the "... and this is what happened afterward" type of revelations that few had ever followed up on before now. They brightened his day immensely; he would beam as he told a guest about the latest one. "They often came after [the *Gazette*] had blasted me about something else," he chuckled. "People wanted me to know they still cared about me, and appreciated what had been done for them." Some of the letters and cards would bring tears to the man's eyes, softening his heart.

A typical hand-written letter came from a woman who reminded Arch that, when she was sixteen years old and he was governor, she had a rare, life-threatening medical condition for which she could be treated in a Cincinnati hospital. Her mother frantically phoned Governor Moore at the Mansion the evening before she was to go there. He took the call and asked how he could help her. She was a single mother, she explained, she didn't know how to get around in that big Ohio city, and she had no transportation. But she desperately wanted to help her daughter. Could he please suggest something, could he help them?

"You asked my mom if she could get to the Charleston airport and she said she could," the letter writer explained. "You had your state plane waiting to take us, and also had a state trooper go along with us, to make sure we got to the hospital. What you did saved my life, Mr. Moore, and we will never forget it." There would be numerous such affectionate letters, "We haven't forgotten you." He kept them all, storing them in boxes in the dusty, third floor warehouse of his office building in Moundsville. Those cards and letters had kept him going, reminding him of who he was in the past, giving him hope for the future.

Others remembered him to the Almighty. "His church in Moundsville prayed regularly for him and Mrs. Moore while he was in there," noted H. John Rogers, who was touched by that gesture.

Several months were cut from Arch's prison term for good behavior and soon his thirty-three months of confinement were over. He had paid his debt that the federal court had demanded. Whether or not the sentence was fair, he had fulfilled it.

In late July, the warden at Ashland advised Prisoner Moore that he'd learned he would receive an early release very soon, any day now. He warned him to tell no one, though, for fear that the U.S. Attorney's office would get wind of it and try to block the release somehow. So Arch disclosed it to no one in the facility, giving a "heads-up" only to his wife and daughter. He got packed up and ready, so he could depart quickly when allowed to do so.

A steamy August 4, 1993, was the final day of Moore's confinement. Earlier that week, "he'd asked me to be on stand-by, because he might be released any time," recalled daughter Shelley Moore Capito. "All of a sudden, that day, I got a call from him, 'Come get me!' He wanted to get out of there before reporters heard about it and showed up [with cameras and microphones]."

When she pulled up in front of the Ashland facility in her large family station wagon, "he came flying out of there with his knapsack, jumped into my car and said, 'Let's get the hell outta here!'"

Eastbound on I-64, Capito kept apologizing to her father because the air conditioner on her car wasn't working and it was a sizzling, muggy Kanawha Valley day. "He said, 'I don't care! I'm *out!*'"

Arch quietly slipped into his grandsons' bedroom and sat on the floor. Soon, Charles Capito awoke and shouted, "Pap-paw!" Mrs. Moore would meet them in Charleston and the reunited couple would return to their Glen Dale home, quietly holing up there for a while, regaining their bearings. Without stopping to talk, the Moores drove past a throng of TV news reporters to get into their garage and quickly closed the door, but they couldn't help but notice that their lawn was covered with flowers from dozens of well-wishers.

"And then they had a slow assimilation back into life," said Capito. "That was hard. They went to a WVU football game that fall. That's their love." They feared how he would be treated, "but people were happy to see him," she noted.

Did Arch and Shelley ever consider doing what others, including the Barrons, had done—move to Florida, get forever out of the limelight, avoiding the bad feelings many had toward the former Governor? "Heavens, no!" exclaimed Harry Moore. "They never had any intent of leaving West Virginia. That's where their family, friends and memories are." (Arch and Shelley own a small condo at Riviera Beach, Singer Island, Palm Beach County, Florida, which they use about four times a year.)

The Moores were true West Virginians and they would live and die in their beloved Mountain State, no matter what.

Her father's release was a bittersweet time for Lucy. Her husband, John Durbin, was sent to the same Ashland facility to serve eight months for the cocaine charge, almost immediately upon Arch's release. "They were joking about that on the radio," she laughed, "that Dad and John passed each other on I-64—one headed westbound, the other eastbound." (The months there were therapeutic for her husband, she said. "He was in the best physical shape he's ever been in," she noted, despite the fact that Durbin and fellow inmates would occasionally sneak across the street for a Big Mac. Said family friend Mary Ann Winter, "The Moores thought the arrest was a blessing in disguise. It caused a change in lifestyle for the couple." Lucy admitted, "I emerged from all that a stronger person.")

New Martinsville lawyer H. John Rogers paid Arch a courtesy visit at his Moundsville office "a month or two after his release." He was pleasantly surprised at what he observed. Moore was not hardened or bitter; there was no hostility toward anyone. "I never knew anybody who came [out of prison] better than when they went in. But Arch was grateful for his wife's many trips to visit him. He was sad to have left Larry Tucker in there—said he was one of Larry's few friends there. He had an overwhelming gratitude to be out. He even took no pleasure that John Field [his prosecutor in 1976] had been imprisoned. I was just amazed at his whole attitude."

As a footnote to this story, it should be noted that, if the feds thought sending Governor Moore to prison would stop vote-buying in West Virginia, they were sadly and naively mistaken. Even as this book was being written, dozens of Democratic politicos and lawyers—some quite wealthy and prominent—in Logan, Lincoln Counties and elsewhere, were being indicted and sent to prison for vote-buying. It was like weeds—pull a few and others pop up in their place. Or like a moth, who could not resist getting too close the flame. There was too much money and power involved not to attract replacements—possibly compared to a lucrative crack cocaine concession in the inner cities. "It's a way of life," agrees Johnie Owens. "After they ousted me, they talked about how clean [Mingo] County was. But most of them who replaced me were indicted and put in prison, too." Using cash and buying elections? "It's always been that way. And it probably will be for a long time."

Chapter 30 Notes

1. - "At least, they never put Arch in chains to transport him. They like to embarrass [white collar, non-violent criminals] that way, even though there's no need to do that. But, thankfully, they spared him the humiliation of that," noted former state Senator Larry Tucker, who was serving his sentence at the same time (and who was not spared that shame).

2. - Moore wanted Maxwell because that was where former Attorney General John Mitchell had served his sentence, in teh Watergate cover-up. He'd heard it was one of the better federal facilities.

3. - Source: U.S. Bureau of Prisons. Prisoners generally were not called by their numbers in these non-violent offense prisons, however, but were treated respectfully and addressed as "Mr. Smith," or "Mr. Moore."

4. - He continued, forever, to blame his plight on the *Charleston Gazette's* crusade against him. "I never had a newspaper threaten me like that in my life. I was one who was not frightened of them and that irritated them all the more. I kept thinking that all of West Virginia was in the same canoe, but that newspaper was far beyond that." Moore, April 22, 2005.

5. - Charles Capito, Aug. 24, 2005.

6. - Durbin, Aug. 2, 2005.

7. - Lucy would lose her job as result of the arrest, but was able to take advantage of an early retirement provision.

8. - *Gazette*, Sept. 1, 1992 and March 13, 1993.

9. - During his long prison term, Owens said he did time in multiple federal prisons and had among his fellow inmates Televangelist Jim Bakker and baseball's Pete Rose. Owens said Rose received no special treatment, but was a "snob."

10. - "Larry claimed he couldn't have made it through that ordeal without Arch Moore," recalled Audrey Toler.

11. - Mentioning omerta to a jury was apparently so unpopular that it landed Ed Rebrook, a Caperton Era politico, in jail for insider trading.

12. - Dec. 10, 2004 interview of Larry Tucker.

Chapter Thirty One
"He Has Been A Great Father"

Among the several humiliations and penalties the former governor would receive for his guilty plea was loss of his state pension, which he had earned as part of his compensation package for twelve years of service as governor. It mattered not that most of those years represented at least six tiring, fourteen-hour days per week.[1]

As another part of his overall punishment package, Arch Moore had been disbarred on October 31, 1991. He would never again be allowed to practice law, the profession for which he was schooled for several years, following his military service.

In the late 1990s, Moore began an intense, but ultimately futile, quest to regain his law license. He would explain to friends, "I began my career as a lawyer, and I'd like to end it as a lawyer." Since his freedom was restored, he had been doing consulting work, and working for other attorneys as a paralegal, but he wanted to represent clients on his own.

Some West Virginians supported it, noting that he had served his sentence. On September 18, 1998, his own Marshall County Bar Association passed a resolution in support of reinstatement. Dozens of prominent lawyers, including a few law professors, even a Democrat later elected to the supreme court, supplied letters recommending that he be allowed to resume his practice of law. But there were others who thought his crime and disgrace to himself and the state had been too great for restoration.

Yet others were supportive, but could not understand why he would subject himself to more years of public scrutiny, humiliation, personal attacks, a re-airing of the dirty laundry, by filing such a petition. He retained his long-time adversary, Rudy DiTrapano, to handle the petition (although Sean McGinley of his office appeared to do most of the work in the case), apparently believing that the Charleston lawyer could persuade the supreme court, all but one of whom were Democrats (by now, Moore's former F&A chief, John McCuskey, had been appointed by Governor Underwood to fill an unexpired term).

Moore made several arguments in support of that petition. One argument was that the federal court, in the State's civil action against him for monetary damages, had largely cleared him of wrongdoing.[2] Second, his position was that, even if he had committed crimes, they had not arisen in his capacity as a lawyer, but rather as a public officeholder. The process dragged on for years, with long periods of inaction, far longer than most such petitions seem to require. Most observers thought he was wasting his time, given who would be making the decisions. However, Arch had an almost naive faith in the system; he remained confident that he could regain his license and, with it, restore another portion of his dignity and respect.

The panel which eventually heard the matter was chaired by ACLU and plaintiffs' lawyer Al Karlin of Morgantown, one not known to be a friend of Moore's, to put it very mildly. Even before Nancy Hill, now a private citizen, presented arguments against restoration (and asked to release the Justice Department's entire, sealed case against the former governor, armed with an order from U.S. District Judge Robert "Chuck" Chambers allowing it), the deck was heavily stacked against Arch and the outcome was a foregone conclusion. The hearing panel recommended to the West Virginia Supreme Court that the petition be denied. "I think he believed that he was going to get his license back but there was never a chance," said Tom Tinder.

Justices Joseph Albright (who had publicly supported reinstatement) and Warren McGraw (a long time, rough-and-tumble opponent of Moore's from the left) recused themselves from hearing the matter, assigning two circuit judges, Andrew Frye and David Pancake, to hear the petition along with the three remaining justices.

Governor and Mrs. Moore quietly sat in the Cass Gilbert-designed courtroom for the final hearing. The questions and comments they heard from the bench were not in the least encouraging. They all pointed in one direction and it wasn't up. In an order of November 18, 2003, the court unanimously rejected his petition. Quoting a previous case, regarding the loss of license by former Charleston mayor and Kanawha County prosecutor Mike Roark, they reiterated their position that "misconduct by lawyers who are public officials is more egregious than that of other lawyers because of the betrayal of the public trust." The court added that "the nature and severity of the original offenses, standing alone, is sufficient to deny reinstatement. Moreover, the fact that Moore continues to speak less than truthfully about the events that led to his disbarment, along with his continued failure to acknowledge and accept responsibility for what he has done, further supports the Panel's conclusion."[3]

If a poll had been taken, it likely would have shown that a majority of the public, even of other state lawyers, supported the court's decision. But some thought Arch Moore had been dealt harshly by the process. After all, the court had restored the law licenses of Democratic politicos after they served time for felonies, including state Senator W. Bernard Smith of

Logan County and, more recently, Caperton appointee Ed Rebrook.[4]

At least a few people believed there was a double standard, based on political affiliation. A humor columnist, who was giving away imaginary gifts to the newsworthy, had one for former Governor Moore for Christmas 2003: "A copy of John Hey's book, entitled, "How to Get Your Law License Back." Hey's book, joked the columnist, was "291 pages long but has only four words: "Register as a Democrat."[5]

"Two or three supreme court justices told me that, if Arch had just been a little bit contrite, admitted he'd done wrong, they would have restored his license," said Ken Hechler, who had been among those who signed the petition in support of Moore's reinstatement. "The fact that he'd continued to insist that he was innocent and that he'd been mislead by his lawyer just didn't sit well with them." A prominent lawyer who knew the inner workings, the thoughts of the court, agreed. "They wanted him to apologize some more, admit he was wrong, and he just wasn't going to do that."

Hechler noted that Arch Moore knew how to act humble when he wanted to do so; he had observed that acting ability on several occasions while Moore was a congressman and governor. "He just seemed to lose his direction [since leaving prison]. You can fake [humility] if you need to, but Arch wouldn't do it."[6]

No doubt, Arch wasn't going to grovel for one big reason: he had done something thousands of other successful officeholders had also done in West Virginia—raised and spent cash to get onto Democratic slates. Many were still in office who had done so, enjoying their prominence and power and keeping their law licenses. Even some supreme court justices had got there by that mode, over the decades. It was a practice more common than not, particularly for statewide candidates.

A concurring opinion in the high court's order, by Justice Elliott "Spike" Maynard, seemed to corroborate what Hechler had heard from the justices. In what read like a dissent, Justice Maynard wrote that he "reluctantly [concurred] with the majority to deny the reinstatement of Governor Moore's license to practice law," but he admitted the case required comparison to the reinstatement of W. Bernard Smith to the Bar. He reminded the court that Smith was a former state senator, Governor Barron's welfare commissioner, part of the "Logan County Five," indicted for bribery and "witnesses told of delivering bags of cash to Smith and others at the capitol." Smith had been charged with stuffing the ballot box, Maynard added. A fair observer would find no difference in Smith's case compared to Moore's, he offered, adding, "Both continued to assert post-conviction that they were innocent or had been the victim of some miscarriage of justice." Justice Maynard, a politically savvy Democrat from Mingo County, summed up what his Court was doing: "Frankly, a fair-minded person may conclude that the only real difference in the Bernard Smith case and the Arch Moore case is that Arch Moore is a Republican and Bernard Smith was a Democrat who could deliver thousands of Democratic votes on election day. And, oh yes, Smith got his law license back and Arch Moore did not."

Justice Maynard concluded his opinion by saying some complimentary things about Moore.

> *Certainly enough has been said at this point, but I cannot lay this pen aside with expressing the sadness and regret many West Virginians feel about this tragedy. And it is a tragedy. Governor Moore is a war hero who was horribly wounded in combat fighting for this country in World War II. If you erase, just for a minute, his now very public failings, and look at his tremendous accomplishments as a congressman and governor, they are truly remarkable.*

Tom Tinder, who has served as the popular executive director of the State Bar since leaving Moore's service, said he "really wished he would have been successful [in getting his license restored]. I know that meant a lot to him." Tinder, a gracious and gentle man, had speculated that perhaps a compromise could have allowed Arch to get his license back but go into inactive status, moreorless as a restoration of his dignity, if they didn't think it advisable to allow him to practice law. But it was not to be.

Oce Smith probably spoke for many of his fellow Democrats who knew Arch Moore. "Really, a man with Arch's financial resources and being past eighty years old, isn't going to do much damage in the courts of law from here on out. He just wanted his license to hang on the office wall again." Smith said he wanted the Bar "so very, very much to give him back his law license." He added, "The state and federal authorities could well have nailed Arch on countless of whatever nefarious deeds which they didn't bother to bring and I for one am glad they didn't. Because, once a man's career, his legacy and his reputation has been ruined, there is no reason to rub his nose into the sand any longer. Even as popular as he still is, his future as a public official is emasculated and all he can do is get on with his life from this point."

The failure to regain his status as a member of the Bar was personally painful to the former governor but he noted that, after every setback or every adverse headline, he would receive yet another flurry of letters and phone calls from well-wishers, who would thank him for past assistance and commend him for his kindness and help to them in the past. That seemed to keep his spirits from sagging, to know that there was a large portion of the population which still remembered him with fondness and gratitude.

Arch was sentimental about one of those letters; he would choke up with emotion when reading portions of it. In his final months before cancer took his life, Chief U.S. District Judge Charles Haden had written to his mentor, expressing appreciation for the opportunities for public service Moore had given him: "[Thank] you, thank you, thank you for the wonderful experience." He reminded the former governor, "You were the one who appointed me to ... the State Supreme Court ... and you were the one who gave me the opportunity in 1975 to become a federal judge, a position which has come to fit me like an old shoe...As Jay Rockefeller once said about me in describing our relationship, 'I owe my good fortune to you.' Clearly that remains true."[7]

As he became an octogenarian, Arch found that he was surviving many of his contemporaries and even those such as Loy, Hallanan and Haden, who had served in his administrations. When another, A. James Manchin, died his nephew Joe asked the former governor to give the eulogy. This one he could not do; it was emotionally just too difficult for him, at this point. "I can no longer handle funerals of friends," Arch explained, looking at the photo of A. James he keeps on his credenza. "And [A. James] was my friend since the day he ran for class president at West Virginia University. His family were devoted Democrats and his brother [John] effectively headed Democrats for Moore. There is a side to me," continued Arch, "that is really attributable to how my mother and father raised me. I have a deep, deep commitment to people. It is hard for me to take the loss of a friend, a family member or a son killed in war. My personal emotions take over. I don't apologize for that. People think I'm hard as a rock. I told Ivor Boiarsky that, once you get to know me, I'm as soft as a ball of putty. He responded that, 'Yes, but if you drop that putty into a bucket of water, it becomes hard as cement.'" Moore laughed, acknowledging that it, too, may be true.

THERE WAS one rare bit of good news, among the fallout from his guilty plea. On top of everything else, the state attorney general had sued Moore, claiming he illegally used his office as governor to enrich himself.

They wanted the court to force Arch to pay back the salary he'd received as governor, among other penalties. A July 28, 1995, front page headline in the *Charleston Daily Mail* read: "Judge drops some charges against Moore." The story explained that U. S. District Judge Richard Williams "threw out several major allegations by the State lawyers against Moore" in the state's lawsuit against him and Paul Kizer, seeking $2.2 million in damages from the refund Kizer had received. The judge dismissed with prejudice (preventing the State from ever filing them again) seven allegations against Moore, including civil racketeering and fraud. He ruled that the State had "not established that it was in fact damaged by the Kizer refund or that it paid this refund on reliance" of Moore's activities. He would not grant Arch's motion to have the entire suit dismissed, however. Among other things, a court was finally acknowledging something neither the press nor very many members of the public seemed willing to recognize: that Kizer's refund was legitimate; it was his company's money. In Moore's view, it also enforced his position that he hadn't extorted anyone. "Judge Williams dismissed twelve out of the thirteen counts against me," was how Arch remembered the case.[8]

Moore remained active in political affairs after his release, remaining connected to what was going on around the state as well or better than anyone. He couldn't resist some behind-the-scenes assistance to Democratic gubernatorial nominee Charlotte Pritt in her unsuccessful 1996 campaign against his old rival, Cecil Underwood, but was not displeased when the former governor prevailed, especially after Underwood graciously showed kindness to Moore's daughter and former appointees.

That Arch stayed plugged into the political network served the family well, as daughter Shelley Moore Capito served two terms in the House of Delegates from Kanawha County and then, in 2000, sought the 2nd District congressional seat vacated by Bob Wise, who narrowly defeated Governor Underwood that year. Shelley was up against a former Kanawha County state senator, Jim Humphreys, who had made a huge fortune from getting clients awards from the manufacturers of asbestos, one whose ads were on TV all the time. Despite being outspent about ten-to-one, and receiving some of the nastiest negative attacks a candidate could endure, Shelley twice defeated the Charleston Democrat. She developed a friendship with President George W. Bush, whom she brought to the state on numerous occasions. Their alliance helped Bush win the heavily Democratic state in two very close elections in which its five electoral votes were critical.

Although Arch was prohibited from holding office again himself, and prevented from practicing law, the success of his daughter, the affection that was poured upon her by thousands of people, was very gratifying to him. "It let me hold my head high once again," he said. His office remains full of photos of his daughter, including one of Shelley exiting Air Force One with the President. That she was loved and accepted helped him feel vindicated, to some degree. And certainly he was with her every step of the way, giving advice, making phone calls, analyzing problems and poll numbers, and planning, when asked to do so. And fifty years of observing how her dad did it probably helped the Congresswoman more than even she realized. No doubt she learned from his mistakes. Shelley Moore Capito is softer, quieter, perhaps a better listener, more candid, with less rhetoric and ego than the politicians of the past, more in tune with the conversational, personal style of politics today, practiced by Bill Clinton and George W. Bush.[9] To some degree, her parents were able to live vicariously in their retirement years through Capito's experiences and accomplishments.

However, her parents' response to her political career differed, noted Capito. "My mother is a very kind, considerate person. She is the epitome of unconditional love. If I give a speech, my dad will say, 'That was good, but...' Mom, on the other hand, will always say, 'That was the best speech I've ever heard!'" (Mrs. Moore is also a very emotional person, her daughter noted, "like her father, who cried all the time. She's close to the surface. But she's also a very competitive person. Most people don't know that.")

Most people incorrectly assumed that Arch Moore was calling the shots of her political career, Congresswoman Capito mentioned. "People think he tells me what to do." But her father "has never once given me advice unless I've asked him for it," she insisted. "He is always very respectful of my decisions, what I'm doing." About his mental skills, "He knows the answer before you even ask the question."

Those who know her well realize Shelley Moore Capito is an "unpolitician." You get the feeling that she enjoys her work in Washington, takes it very seriously, but she doesn't have to be in politics—she could walk away or lose an election and happily return to her former, private life. She's very comfortable in her skin, as they say, and she is genuine.

But to her father she has occasionally expressed doubt about her abilities, especially in serving as her party's leader in West Virginia. "I've told him, 'The party wants me to do this, or that. I don't have the strength to lead like you did. I'm not the leader you were.'

Arch replied to his daughter, "First, you have to remember that I'd been at it for twenty years [when he became the state party's leader]. And you know what? Sometimes I *faked* it!'"

Moore made it clear that he wanted his daughter to challenge his long-time adversary and rival for attention, Senator Byrd, in 2006, but it was not to be. He lit up when reporters suggested she might eventually become the state's first female governor, if not U.S. senator.

His role as "Shelley's dad," plus his own exceptional personal record of service, made it easier to reintegrate the former governor into political and public life than would have been possible under different circumstances. Not only did Arch often substitute for his daughter at political dinners as she'd once done for him, but he was almost always there for events such as the President's visit to Woodburn Circle, WVU, on July 4, 2005—on stage, front and center (in his Marshall University green sport jacket, just to be ornery), just like old times. Mentioned Audrey Toler, "When he does Lincoln Day dinners, they are always sold out immediately. He's still such a force! People ask me about [Governor and Mrs. Moore] all the time; I often hear, 'If he was on the ballot today, I'd vote for him!'"[10] Charles Capito noted that his children, like those of their generation, "have never known anything but the negative stuff," about their grandfather, and "so they are amazed when they see crowds enthusiastically drawn to [Arch Moore] when he attends public events."[11]

After his "sabbatical," the Moores spent more time, especially in winter months, enjoying their condo at Singer Island, Florida. "It's on the ground floor of Sugar Sands across the street from the ocean," said Lysander Dudley. "He invited us to relocate there, too, so we bought a place there in '83. Dr. David and Betty Jane Yoho also live nearby. Most of their friends in Florida are old friends from WVU or fellow congressmen." The Dudleys and Moores continue to socialize in Florida, as they'd done since 1969. "We play a lot of bridge, we like to go out to eat, we used to sit on the beach. Arch is a big tennis player and plays with Dr. Yoho and, until recently he and Shelley played with other couples. It's fun to be with him. Occasionally, someone from West Virginia will spot him and yell, 'Hey, there's Governor Moore!'"

Son Kim says that Arch loves the beach, just sitting under an umbrella, watching the waves come in. "He'll usually have a crossword puzzle. His dad [Arch, Sr.] also did crossword puzzles all the time, but he'd get to the end and just put any letter in. Dad finishes his. If there was such a thing as a crossword tournament, he'd be the world champion!" And while his dad is a "great tennis player," he "can't swim at all," Kim disclosed. "He sinks like a rock." Although Moore has played a lot of golf in recent decades, his son says he's not that accomplished at it. "I've asked my son,

Alfie, 'Do you notice that your grandfather always wins by at least one point?' He came back after one game with him and said, 'Hey, you're right. If I shot a six on that hole, he would have a five.'" Arch always kept the scorecard.

When the Moores visit their Florida condo, it is for a week to ten days, during the winter months, said Mrs. Moore. "We sleep in late, sit by the pool, go shopping or play bridge. We visit the Yohos a lot." The extended Moore family gets together for a summer vacation at Sea Island, Georgia each year, she noted. "We just hang out on the beach, play some golf, go out to dinner. Each family takes turn fixing dinner one night," said daughter Lucy. Mrs. Moore's family, the Rileys, live in the South, so they sometimes have reunions at Pipestem State Park.

When in their Glen Dale home, the couple enjoys watching Steelers football and Pirate baseball, "all kinds of sporting events—football, basketball, tennis, golf," the Fox News channel and "we never miss a Seinfeld rerun." In the summer months, Arch enjoys working in his Glen Dale flower garden ("I'll bet a lot of people would be surprised to know that about me"). According to Lucy, her father usually has a TV going, but is doing something else at the same time. "He reads *The Wall Street Journal*, the Moundsville and Wheeling papers, no Charleston papers, *USA TODAY, Time* and *Newsweek*. My mom reads books all the time; he does not."

Lucy repeated what others say—that Arch and Shelley are intensely competitive. "Even when the family plays backgammon, Hearts or tennis, they want to win, especially Mom. She does not like to lose, especially to Dad."

Although wealthy by any standard (he is a major stockholder of BB&T), Arch is very frugal, admits daughter Lucy Durbin. "Even their condo in Florida is very small and they've had it for years. He brags about spending less than ten dollars on his monthly haircut. His only other expense is gas he puts in his Chevy." (Moore drives an unassuming, two-door, gray Monte Carlo, with a "Shelley Moore Capito" sticker on the dash, and a current State Troopers Association sticker on the back window.) Dr. Yoho agreed that Arch is not one to spend excessively: "He does spend a lot on his family. I remember, for example, when we were on vacation with them one time, he took everybody—and it was a lot of people—to the Cloisters [an expensive restaurant] and picked up the tab." One of the few luxuries the couple allows themselves is travel. "I went with Arch to the Soviet Union several time," Mrs. Moore remembered. "We've been to England, Scotland, Ireland, Germany, just about covered it all." She added that, "any time I could go I went" when he was making overseas trips as a congressman or governor.

But clearly their favorite activity is their children and grandchildren. If someone visits Shelley Moore, she shows photos—their home is full of them–of each grandchild and updates them on their latest status.[12] "When Arch had his first grandson, Riley Moore, he was down on the floor making baby noises," said Dr. McCoy, remembering when he visited the Moores at a cottage at the Greenbrier. "Moore Capito has a lot of his grandfather in him," said McCoy, noting what others observed. "He's looked and acted like him since he was a little guy."[13]

"Christmas is big in the family," noted Lucy. "Dad is Mr. Christmas." After gift exchange and dinner, Arch gives what grandson Moore Capito calls "The State of the Family Address." The former governor "gives a spiel on how things are going, what's going on in the family financially, then the family vacation plans for the summer. Then Mom says a few words."

They are proud of the success of their children and grandchildren. As this book went to press, Lucy was busy with her daughter and her husband's business ventures—cell phones and paging systems, plus a sports bar in the Kanawha County area. Arch continued to phone all three of his children every Sunday evening, no matter where they are at the time. It is his ritual of a weekly family reunion, a way for all of them to stay connected. (It seems to be a call to which they look forward; both Kim and Shelley mentioned it several times.)

And the couple remained loyal and very close to each other. In 1999, Arch and Shelley celebrated their fiftieth wedding anniversary. "I define love as what's left over after fifty years of marriage," said H. John Rogers. "And it was true about the Moores; they're really devoted to each other." Observed Dr. Yoho, their best friend of many decades: "I have never heard Arch or Shelley say one bad word about each other. They have a very good marriage."[14]

Their public appearances were rare after the prison term. They were at the capitol in January 1997 to celebrate when Shelley Moore Capito was sworn in to her first term in the House of Delegates. "My generation [of mothers] stayed home," noted Mrs. Moore, who was not certain whether serving in public office would be conducive to good family life for her daughter. "I didn't have any idea that Shelley was even interested in politics [before she ran for House of Delegates]. I questioned her, 'How does Charlie feel about this?' I asked Moore [Capito, her grandson] what he thought of his mother getting into politics and he said, 'Oh, that's ok.' I asked, 'Well, what if she later goes to Washington?' and he said, 'We'd move over there.' When I asked what his father [Charlie Capito is a successful stock broker in Charleston] would do, Moore answered, 'Oh, he could find something to do over there [in Washington].'"

In Capito's 2000 and 2002 campaigns for Congress, her father guided her through the channels of getting connected to big names in Washington GOP circles and to the donors it required to twice defeat her very wealthy, plaintiff lawyer Democratic opponent. Her father's legal problems caused a few of her own party to abandon her. But, overall, the name (she's always gone by Shelley Moore Capito) was still magic, a trusted product brand, gave her instant credibility, and helped her get elected and re-elected several times.

"Arch is very energized by [his involvement with his daughter's public service]," thinks "Hike" Heiskell. "It keeps him reading the national press, staying up on things."

When Democratic legislators re-districted the state in 2001, it was assumed they would reconfigure the district to make it more difficult for the state's lone Republican member of Congress to win re-election. But they did just the opposite–they removed two heavily Democratic counties from Capito's district. "Tell Arch we took care of him," said a Democratic senator to one of his friends.[15] They viewed helping Shelley as a little salute to Dad.

Capito's success reflected well on her parents, on the way they had brought her up, and also on the dedication her parents had given to the generation before. When Larry King asked Barbara Bush on his TV talk show in 2003 whether there was a "Bush Dynasty" (given that her father-in-law, husband, two sons and a grandson were in the national political spotlight), Mrs. Bush laughed it off, deflecting the question by suggesting instead that there was a "Moore dynasty in West Virginia." But neither Arch nor his daughter saw it that way; Shelley Capito was simply carrying on the same good government her father always strived for.

Mrs. Moore thought her daughter learned a lot from the way Arch conducted himself as a congressman. As her father had done in 1957, Capito would bring in a hard-working, knowledgeable staff, which included long-time political pro Anne McCuskey (wife of former Justice John McCuskey). In her dad's style, a lot of personal attention would be given to the old-fashioned concept of taking care of constituent needs. She busied herself getting federal dollars into the district, especially ones for highways and job development. Shelley spent a lot of time in public meetings, listening to views about such controversial subjects as social security reform. Even those who opposed her on a political or ideological basis had to admit that Shelley was very likeable, very open to them, a good listener. And she was down to earth—they may bump into her at the local high school or Kroger or Foodland store.

"Shelley will phone me to let me know she's going to be chairing a committee meeting and is going to be on C-Span," chuckles Mrs. Moore. "She'll ask later, 'Did I look all right, Mom?'" The former First Lady thinks her eldest daughter "has a lot of personality traits" like her mother. "We both stand up for our beliefs. She's a very truthful person. I tell people, 'If she doesn't treat you right, talk to me,'" Mrs. Moore laughs.

But the Moores were equally devoted to their other children and grandchildren. Said daughter Lucy, "When we'd go on the annual family vacation [which Arch and Shelley would sponsor], Dad makes sure he spent some time with every member of the family, individually, to find out what is going on in their lives." She continued, "He is such a good father. He's pulled me out of so many fires, you wouldn't believe. He loves to solve problems for people. I'll call him with problems, feeling down, and he'll quickly turn it around. He's very positive, a motivator. Even when he was incarcerated he was making the best of a bad situation, keeping his sense of humor."

When Arch turned 82 in 2005, his wife asked him when he thought he might retire.[16] "He looked at me like I was crazy," she laughed. It is not so much that Arch is a workaholic, but rather that he wants to remain useful to others, to stay engaged and plugged into the state's political scene and keep his mind and body active as he finishes "the fourth quarter" of his life, as he put it. She admitted that he stays very busy. "He was brought up to believe that you use the most of what you were God-given. People come to him for advice because he's a wealth of knowledge in so many areas. He's especially glad to help young people." In recent years, Mrs. Moore guessed that he has made public speeches about a dozen times per year.

Arch remained almost obsessed about one issue, however. He could never get out of his mind the possibility of some day, some way, clearing his name and restoring his honor. "I may take yet another crack at [getting a judge to set aside his guilty plea]," said the former governor in 2005, noting that he continued to find favorable case law supporting his position. He insisted that, if he could just get a trial, he would be acquitted for the charges that sent him to prison for 33 months. It hurt him deeply that, despite his phenomenal accomplishments and good he had done for his fellow West Virginians, his obituary would nevertheless some day repeat that hated, shameful description, convicted felon. "But my wife and all my kids tell me, 'Dad, West Virginians love you, no matter what. Let it go."

He knew it was true, but difficult to accept that advice when you've always been a fighter.

And love him they do, at least many of them. Said H. John Rogers, "I once wrote a column contending that Marland was the No. 1 governor—for what he'd set out to accomplish, not what he'd accomplished—and that Arch Moore, whom I called The Great Helmsman, was No. 2. Arch was not just an empty suit. Many die-hard Democrats said they agreed with me, but thought Arch is first, that he's the best governor we ever had." Rogers said he worked with Moore on a lawsuit involving Wal-Mart in recent years and that his wife had attended church with the former governor. "I'd trust Governor Moore with my life, but not my wallet,"[17] he grinned.

This should not be taken to mean that Moore has lived in the past since leaving office, however. Many people in their eighties may be sitting in the rocking chair, enjoy reminiscing, comparing how much better it was in their day as compared to now, resting on their laurels. One does not have to be around Arch more than a few minutes to know just the opposite was the case with him. He keeps the pace of a man decades younger and was constantly looking to the future. And despite how things ended for his own career, the sadness he always carries about his period of personal embarrassment, he never seems to lose his affection for West Virginia and its people. He is thinking constantly about how the future could be brighter. He stays young in mind and body by thinking incessantly of "the next big thing," another opportunity or newest challenge—reading, reading, listening, listening, studying, researching, reviewing—keeping current on as much information as possible. His passion and enthusiasm for life, for politics, seemingly has diminished little with years; he remains excited, involved, interested, curious, thinking about solutions. He quietly advises a few subsequent governors, gubernatorial candidates, even a couple dozen leaders across the nation.

His physical health appears to have suffered very little with age; if he is becoming old and decrepit, he keeps it well-hidden. Moore is still bouncing around like a forty-year-old, running up and down stairways, traveling, looking as fit and lean as he'd been for decades, still not even needing reading eyeglasses, with no hearing problems or other limitations. "He does exercises in bed every morning," said daughter Lucy. "He runs up those steps in his office every morning, and occasionally he and Mom go on walks." His long-time family physician, Dr. William Harris, of Charleston, agreed that Moore has always been blessed with good health. "He has always been very disciplined about exercise and keeping his weight down. The man is in tremendously good physical shape. He's a joy to take care of."[18]

Yes, his great intellect may have landed him in trouble a few times and sometimes his actions demonstrated that he had not exercised wisdom or even the ethics his parents had instilled in him. But, as he said about the uncle who mentored him, many could also say about Arch Moore, "*He was the smartest man I ever knew*." They might even have added, "He was the most *caring* individual I ever knew."

Said "Hike" Heiskell, now practicing law in Virginia, "I don't think that Rockefeller, Byrd and Caperton, combined, did as much for West Virginia as Arch Moore did in that first term." Moore fell because of the "arrogance of power," Heiskell believed. His gradual loss of humility got him into trouble, he thought—he was a victim of his own success. Nevertheless, "No one had a more profound influence on the people of West Virginia in the Twentieth Century than Governor Moore," he continued. "The term 'leadership' became synonymous with his name. The dynamics of his governance provided lessons for every serious student of political science."

Said Richard Neely: "Arch Moore did more for West Virginia when he wasn't paying attention than all the people who brought him down, put together—starting with the self-promoters at the U.S. Attorney's office and ending with the lickspittles at the *Charleston Gazette*, who continue to hound him to his grave."

Arch's son, Kim Moore, summed it up well: "He's hit a few bumps in the road, the last one the worst. He may have squandered some opportunities. If you take those out of the equation, he had the talent to be president. It was always the politician versus the statesman and sometimes the politician won out. That's what tripped him up. But he has been a great father."

"There will never be another Arch Moore," observed Parkersburg editor Jesse Mancini, echoing what thousands of others had said.

In the words of Hamlet: *"We shall not look upon his like again."*

Chapter 31 Notes

1. - Moore's pension was stripped from him and not another penny paid, despite the fact that Democratic officeholders who had been convicted of crimes kept their government pensions. Again, a double standard seemed to be applied. Marion County Sheriff Charles Dodd, boss of the old J. Harper Meredith Democratic Party machine, was an example of an officeholder of that same era whose pension was not taken from him. Another example was former Kanawha County Circuit Judge John Hey, also a Democrat, who pleaded guilty to two counts of battery and stepped down under pressure to resign in 1994. His law license were restored by the Supreme Court and ended up getting more retirement pay—$87,000 per year—than he'd earned as a judge. *Daily Mail*, May 16, 2005.

2. - *West Virginia v. Moore,* 895 F. Supp. 864 (S.D. W.Va. 1995). The West Virginia Supreme Court would find, however, that the federal judge did not conclude "that Moore was an innocent man. Rather, [Judge Williams] concluded that the State failed to demonstrate that it had actually suffered a financial loss as a result of Moore's criminal conduct." *Lawyer Disciplinary Board v. Moore,* (No. 25794, Sept. 2003)

3. - *Lawyer Disciplinary Board v. Moore,* Nov. 18, 2003.

4. - Rebrook was alleged to have violated insider trading laws by disclosing to Sammy D'Annunzio that the state was going to be in the market for slot machines.

5. - *Daily Mail,* December 19, 2003. But it wasn't purely partisan–Republican former mayor and prosecutor James E. Roark's law license was restored by the supreme court in 1997, after he had lost it due to pleading guilty to six counts of federal misdemeanor charges of possession of cocaine. Roark had even been arrested twice in North Carolina on misdemeanor charges, subsequent to his loss of licence.

6. - Hechler, Jan. 29, 2005

7. - Charles Haden letter to Arch Moore, June 23, 2003.

8. - Moore, August 22, 2005.

9. - When asked why he never had any interest in following his father in politics, the quieter Arch "Kim" Moore III said about himself that he always "had an independent streak and felt that making my own way was the way I wanted to go. I loved a lot of it— it was heady stuff, even for a youngster." He saw what a successful political life required and didn't want it for himself or his own family. "As my sister has discovered, it's so time-consuming; you're always on someone else's schedule. There is no down time, you're always 'on,' immersed into it seven days a week."

10. - Your author observed this phenomenon on August 20, 2005, at a Cultural Center retirement party for JoAnn Humphreys Calhoun, who served four governors in the press office. Governor Underwood and other dignitaries present were treated respectfully, but it was Arch and Shelley Moore that the crowds circled around, with scores wanting to greet them. The charisma and magnetism of former Governor Moore was quite evident. After a brief, but dynamic, energized speech there, several were heard to exclaim, "He's still got it!"

11. - Charles Capito, Aug. 24, 2005.

12. - The Moores have seven grandchildren. Kim's are Riley, Gena (named for Genevieve, his grandmother), and Arch Alfred Moore IV ("Alfie," a tall, thin, handsome lad who looks like his mother). Congresswoman Shelley Capito's children are Charles Lewis, Arch Alfred Moore Capito (known as "Moore," who looks and acts most like the former governor) and Shelley Eskew Capito. Lucy's daughter, Sydney, was born in 1995.

13. - Raamie Barker, who works each year as a counselor at Boys State at Jackson Mills, took note of Moore Capito the year he attended and was elected senate president. "He has a lot of charisma and political ability. He is athletic and he's smart. He would make an attractive candidate some day." Arch predicted that either Arch IV or Moore Capito will follow him in politics.

14. - Yoho remembered that Arch Moore was always protective, polite to women, especially his spouse. Although not a prude, that "protection" included subjects of conversation. "When he was in Congress, he took our entire bridge group with them to the Congressional Country Club for dinner. One of the physicians was telling dirty stories to the women. Arch didn't care for that–he put a stop to it!"

15. - Barker, 2001.

16. - At the time of this writing, he continues to dress like he's running the state, driving to his Moundsville office for full days of phone calls, visitors, media interviews, financial management and correspondence. About the seemingly endless calls, the requests for help on this or that problem, Arch pretends to grumble, "You'd think I was still running the show!" But one doesn't get the sense that it's an annoyance, that instead he's pleased to be asked.

17. - Rogers, June 29, 2005.

18. - Dr. Harris, August 2, 2005. For years, Harris would get phone calls from obnoxious reporters about Moore's health which, of course, he would not answer due to privacy constraints. "When he came back from China, they wanted to know if he had encephalitis! They were always asking if he had some kind of mental illness."

Afterword

Few people are ambivalent toward former Governor Arch A. Moore, Jr. Some speak of him in the awed tones usually reserved for heroes of epic poems; others dislike him with equal passion.

Arch Moore was a masterful politician and such men inspire strong judgments. He understood how to use power when he had it, and how to bluff when he didn't. He recognized the inherent tendency toward inertia–toward doing the "safe" thing–that characterizes bureaucracy, and he found ways around it. He frustrated his enemies and delighted his friends, or he frustrated his friends and delighted his enemies, sometimes simultaneously, always in the service of his agenda for West Virginia.

The Modern Budget Amendment, an important new law, gave the Governor line-item veto authority over appropriations and made him chief planning officer of the State for the first time. The strengthened executive branch was a perfect match for the leadership and political skills brought to the office by Governor Moore. He freely wielded his veto power to hold state agencies in line with the executive budget, while using his knowledge of federal programs acquired during his years in Congress, to maximize the use of federal dollars for the state. To raise the state funds necessary for the Governor's work plan, severance taxes and property taxes were raised on extractive industries, and bonds were issued with voter approval, to secure low-cost, long-term financing.

The results are indisputable: 225 miles of Interstate highways opened with many more under construction by the end of his second term; construction of the New River Gorge Bridge, the second longest steel arch span in the world; funding of more than thirty rural primary health care centers; increases in teachers' salaries; the beginning of two additional medical schools to provide physicians for rural areas; construction of a Science and Cultural Center, which focused efforts to preserve and treasure West Virginia's cultural heritage; a coordinated statewide public library system; and new infrastructure, seemingly around every bend in our winding roads, from vocational-technical education centers to water and sewer systems.

The Moore years comprise a "perfect storm" of governance—a state hungry for progress, institutions desperate for leadership and a Chief Executive who approached problems with creativity, resolve, resilience and humor. A man who used to rub his hands together and say, with a gleam in his eye, "Ahhh, controversy—it's the reason I get up in the morning."

Whether ally or adversary, few will dispute that Arch Moore was a persuasive, energetic and optimistic leader. His impact will be felt for decades to come.

Hon. Judge Ronald G. Pearson
Charleston

Author's Note

Sitting in an evening political science class in WVU's Woodburn Hall in the early 1970s, my classmates and I were jolted awake by something the instructor said. Bill Ross expressed his opinion that the disgraced W.W. "Wally" Barron had been West Virginia's greatest governor.

Whether or not we agreed with his assessment (I, for one, did not), it was the first time we had ever considered that an individual could be a law-breaker but also retain greatness and worth; the two seemed paradoxical and incompatible. It was a new concept to me but one I more fully comprehended and accepted when Governor Moore pleaded guilty to five felonies and went off to prison.

For, despite his crimes and ethical lapses, which may well have been extensive and certainly disappointing, arguably no other person did more to improve the quality of life for West Virginians than Arch Alfred Moore, Jr. When one considers the vast improvements he made to transportation, education, health, welfare, medical education, insurance, libraries, teachers' and state employees' pay, and in so many other fields, the numerous jobs he created and retained for the state, he must consider that Rogers might just possibly be correct: Moore is the "GLWV," The Greatest Living West Virginian. Why, just getting rid of the "flower funds," that had existed for decades, alone should earn him some accolades. His tenure certainly was not without mistakes, but, essentially, Moore ushered his state into the modern age.

Because of his guilty plea, however, his unmatched record of accomplishment was almost forgotten. Books and Internet articles had reduced Moore to a sentence: "The governor who went to prison." His adversaries removed his name from every possible location, much like Stalin would do to his rivals he had shot; Arch was being erased from history. His contemporaries understood that was not the sum of the man, that there was far more. But there was a danger that younger people, who never witnessed the "before and after," would never understand and appreciate his significance.

Quite frankly, I waited for years, thinking that surely someone more qualified and skilled than myself, someone closer to Moore, who knew more about him and his circumstances, would write his biography. Those of us who worked for him at various times in his career would repeat some of the stories, laugh, and end the conversation with, "Someone ought to write a book!" But when that appeared increasingly unlikely, I phoned him in late 2003, to ask if he would be willing to help me tell his story. Only he could provide a few of them, such as his war story, in any detail.

He was quite reluctant at first; he had to be convinced. So much ugly stuff, some untrue, had been written about him that he saw nothing but risk. Mrs. Moore, hurt more than any of the clan, was particularly hesitant about rehashing all that. But I'd known the Governor since I was fourteen (in his 1968 campaign), had supported him as a Young Republican and had served in state government as a second-tier administrator during his third term. I had witnessed first hand much of his post-1968 story. After his legal troubles, I let him know that my wife and I were among the thousands who continued to care about him and Mrs. Moore on a personal basis.

As he began relaying the stories, of past campaigns, of his ancestors, his adventures, I think he realized that it was a story well worth preserving, despite the fashion in which his career ended. Arch Moore remains a polarizing figure, just as Nixon, Bush or Clinton were. Some love him. Others despise him and always will. One could not write negatively enough about Moore to ever please them. They will never, ever forgive him.

While certainly not defending Governor Moore's ethical lapses, I think this book explains why most of them arose. He did not invent the game that caused his political demise; it was one devised by the opposition party and in which presidents, senators, congressmen, other governors and local and state officeholders willingly participated and succeeded. Hopefully, today's politicians have learned from the consequences Arch Moore and others suffered, making similar misdeeds less likely in the future—*but don't hold your breath*. One suspects that there will always be ethical problems and crimes as long as money is involved in political campaigns. Indeed, if all who committed the crimes of which Moore was accused were penalized in the same fashion, the prisons could not have held them all and several top public offices in West Virginia would have been vacant.

I will add, as an aside, of all the scores of people I have known who either worked or dealt with Arch Moore, none has indicated that he ever asked them to do anything illegal or unethical; to the contrary, he would urge them to comply with the law, to tell the truth. If his appointees got into trouble, it was by their own choosing. With a couple of exceptions, those I've known who served in his administrations were highly ethical, honest men and women who cared deeply about the people of their state. I was very proud to have spent four years with them.

It would be a wonderful development if we could somehow, fairly limit campaign fund-raising and spending. (Arch likely would agree; he probably would have won all his elections, if he'd had a level playing field with regard to money. He proposed more campaign reform bills than any other governor.) As long as we have the First Amendment, true election reform will be an ideal that is virtually impossible to achieve. It would be ideal, too, if we could somehow guarantee that favor-seekers never again buy government contracts, services and favorable legislation, through legal or illegal means. Is anyone really confident that we can do that? Offenders always seem to find loopholes. And prosecutors continually harvest a new crop of corrupt politicians but, like weeds, others just pop up in their place, with the next rain.

Governor Moore clearly accepted money he should have declined, both from a legal, ethical and moral standpoint, probably on more than one occasion, and there's no defending or excusing that. But with regard to vote-buying, is there any moral, ethical, difference between paying cash to political leaders to accomplish that vs. buying votes with checks, under the pretense of paying for election day work? Both methods are clearly wrong and should not be tolerated, yet the practitioners of the first method go to prison but those in the second category are honored.

Whether you're a Moore-hater, a fan or somewhere in between, you have to admit: his is a fascinating, gripping story. It spans nine exciting decades and he was at the center of many of the events that made national headlines. This book could have been two or three times in length and still not have contained all the interesting stories and accomplishments. For those who want more information about him, I direct you to his official papers, which are contained in several volumes and available in many libraries.

MANY THANKS go to Julie Bupp, Raamie Barker and Sally Crouser for several hours of editing and suggestions; to my secretary, Sherry Belcher, for help with the photos; the George brothers for hospitality during my Morgantown research; to Barker, Allen Prunty, Kevin Sikora, Tom Sweeney, Herb Rogers, Wesley Crouser, Ann Rembrandt, Mrs. Bupp, Secretary Ken Hechler and Dr. Jim Whisker, for being sounding boards; to Sam Kapourales, Mary Louise Lipsky, Keith Davis, Dave Barnes and Sikora for assistance in arranging interviews; to Elizabeth Chilton, Earl Benton, Audrey Toler Pennington, the Dwight D. Eisenhower, John F. Kennedy, Lyndon Johnson, Gerald Ford, Ronald Reagan and George Bush Presidential libraries, and Governor and Mrs. Moore for permission to use photos; to West Virginia University Library for making the Moore Collection available, to the Kanawha County Library and the West Virginia Archives and History for use of microfilm, and to the scores of interesting and brave people who gave their time for interviews, especially Governors Underwood, Caperton, Manchin, Congresswoman Capito, Coach Bobby Bowden, former Justice Richard Neely and, most of all, Governor Arch and Shelley Moore. I also must thank my fellow members of Jackson Kelly PLLC for allowing me time in which to research and write this book, while still conducting my practice of law in 2003 through 2005.

Obviously, this book would have been better had I been able to interview individuals such as the late Bill Loy, Jim Sprouse, Charles Haden and A. James Manchin. The latter two had agreed to interviews but passed just weeks before that could be accomplished. I never had the privilege of meeting Loy. For others, such as Bob Mellace (who died in September, 2005), age sadly had robbed them of their memories. There's no doubt they could have added some very interesting stories and insights. Before the reader becomes too critical of how certain stories were related, he should know that many other prominent figures discussed on these pages declined requests to be interviewed, despite persistent efforts by your author. Those included Senators Byrd and Rockefeller, Michael Carey, John Raese, Tom Craig and John Leaberry.

I simply followed along with my legal pad and pen and allowed this story to tell itself; I was never sure what direction it would take—that was part of the fun of researching it. Some of the stories I had never heard before and they surprised and fascinated me. Despite how an author may try to disguise that fact, a biography is heavily dependent upon who will and will not provide their stories. For the most part, however, people were eager to talk about Moore and their part in his story, so many in fact that there was insufficient time to interview everyone. As Mrs. Lipsky (in her sixth decade as Moore's secretary in his Moundsville office) and I discussed, one could spend a lifetime researching and writing this story, but there comes a point at which you must send it to the publisher. I hope you have enjoyed reading about Arch Moore as much as I did in researching and writing it.

Brad Crouser, January, 2006

Bibliography

Alexander, Bevin, How Hitler Could Have Won World War II, NY: Crown, 2000.

Ambler, Charles H. and Summers, Festus P., West Virginia the mountain state, NJ: Prentice-Hall, 1958.

Ambrose, Stephen, Citizen Soldier, NY: Simon & Schuster, 1997.

Byrd, Robert C., Robert C. Byrd Child of the Appalachian Coal Fields, WV: West Virginia University Press, 2005.

Caro, Robert A., The Years of Lyndon Johnson: Master of the Senate, NY: Random House, Inc., 2002

Dallek, Robert, An Unfinished Life: John F. Kennedy, NY: Little, Brown & Co., 2003.

Davis, F. Keith, West Virginia Tough Boys, WV: Woodland Press, 2003.

Erickson, Kai T., Everything in its Path, NY: Simon & Schuster, 1976.

Ford, Gerald R., A Time to Heal, NY: Harper & Row, 1979.

Frasure, Carl and Leonard Davis, Ed., Eight Years: Official Statements and Papers of the Honorable Arch A. Moore, Jr., Governor of West Virginia 1969-1977, WV: State of West Virginia, 1978.

Grimes, Richard, Jay Rockefeller Old Money New Politics, WV: Jalamap Publications, 1984.

Keefer, Louis, Scholars in Foxholes, VA: Cotu Publishing, 1999.

Kelly, Richard A., Outstanding West Virginians of 1969-1970, WV: Bold Enterprises, 1969.

Morgan, John G., West Virginia Governors, WV: Charleston Newspapers, 1980.

Nixon, Richard M., Six Crises, NY: Doubleday, 1962.

Nugent, Tom, Death at Buffalo Creek, NY: W.W. Norton, 1973.

O'Neill, Thomas P., Jr., Man of the House, NY: Random House, 1987.

Ralph, James R., Jr., Northern Protest: Martin Luther King, Jr., Chicago and the Civil Rights Movement, MA: Harvard University Press, 1993.

Rice, Otis K. and Stephen W. Brown, West Virginia, A History, KY: University of Kentucky Press, 1995.

Schlesinger, Arthur M., A Thousand Days, NY: Houghton Mifflin, 1965.

Sidey, Hugh, John F. Kennedy, President, Schribner, NY: 1963-06.

Stern, Gerald M., The Buffalo Creek Disaster, NY: Random House, 1976.

Theroux, Gary, The top ten, NY: Fireside, 1962.

Tinder, Thomas, Ed., Third Term: The Official Papers of the Honorable Arch A. Moore, Jr., 30th Governor of the State of West Virginia, WV: State of West Virginia, 2002.

Williams, John Alexander, West Virginia A History, WV: West Virginia University Press, 2001.

Willis, Todd C., Ed., et al, West Virginia Blue Book, WV: West Virginia State Senate, 1939-2002.

White, Theodore, The Making of the President, 1960, NY: Atheneum, 1961.

PERIODICALS and NEWSPAPERS

The Atlantic Monthly, Associated Press, Beckley Register-Herald, Bluefield Daily Telegram, Charleston Daily Mail, Charleston Gazette, Charlotte Observer, Congressional Quarterly, Daily Athenaeum, Detroit Free Press, Dominion News, Dominion Post, Elkins Inter-Mountain, Fairmont Times, Fortune Magazine, Graffiti, Grafton Sentinel, Huntington Herald-Dispatch, Intelligencer, Kanawha Valley Leader, Library of Congress, The Logan Banner, Maroon and White, Martinsburg Journal, Montgomery Herald, The Moore Collection, West Virginia University Library, Moorefield Examiner, Morgantown Post, Moundsville Echo, Mountaineer Spirit, New York Times, Richard M. Nixon Presidential Library, Parkersburg Sentinel, Point Pleasant Register, Republican Delta, Saturday Evening Post, Sunday Gazette-Mail, United Press International, USA TODAY, U.S. News & World Report, Wall Street Journal, Washington Post, Washington Star, West Virginia State Bar, Office of Disciplinary Counsel, Wheeling New-Register, West Virginian, and The Williamson Daily News.

AUTHOR'S INTERVIEWS

Vivian Ashcraft, Dave Arnold, Benjamin Bailey, F. Raamie Barker, David Bartlett, Bobby Bowden, Sue Browning, Will Brotherton, Governor Gaston Caperton, Charles Capito, Hon. Shelley Moore Capito, Michael Caryl, Raymond Chafin, John Charnock, Jim Cochran, Harry Cronin, Elaine Davidson, John Davidson, Randy Dell, Fred Donohoe, Alan Drescher, Lysander Dudley, Lucy Moore Durbin, Robert Elkins, William Ellis, Edwin Flowers, Steve Goode, Brenda Nichols-Harper, Ken Hechler, Edgar F. "Hike" Heiskell, Nancy Hill, Beth High, John Hoblitzell, Sam Kapourales, Bob Kelly, Sam Kusic, Ira "Sandy" Latimer, Jr., Governor Joe Manchin, John Manchin, James McCartney, Maggie McCoy, Thomas McCoy, John McCuskey, Sean McGinley, Hon. M. Blane Michael, Governor Arch A. Moore, Jr., Arch A. "Kim" Moore III, Harry "Moo" Moore, Shelan Moore, Shelley Riley Moore, James "Tiger" Morton, Richard Neely, Larry Nelson, Johnie Owens, Tony Paranzino, Henry Payne, Hon. Ronald G. Pearson, Audrey Pennington, Thomas Potter, John Price, Paul Prunty, Hon. Jacob Reger, Lester S. Regillo, John Roberts, H. John Rogers, Carl Roncaglione, Nelson Robinson, Richard G. Rundle, Charles Ryan, Joseph Savage, Fanny Seiler, Hoy Shingleton, Jr., Joy Moore Sievertson, Kevin Sikora, Bill Smith, Oce Smith, James Snoderly, Larry Swann, Thomas

Sweeney, William "Pete" Thaw, Tom Tinder, Gary Joseph Triplett, Larry Tucker, Dave Tyson, Dick Tyson, Governor Cecil Underwood, Warren Upton, H. Gerald Warren, John Weaver, James B. Whisker, Frances Whiting, Mary Ann Winter, Dolly Withrow, David Yoho, and Norman Yost.

About the Author

Brad Crouser grew up in rural Marion County, West Virginia, working as many as three jobs at a time to put himself through the West Virginia University School of Journalism and College of Law. During his undergrad years, he observed the Moore Administration for a few weeks while serving as an intern to House Minority Leader George "Bud" Seibert and later to Secretary of State James McCartney. From age sixteen, Brad was creating weekly political cartoons and, later, political columns for seven daily and weekly newspapers around the Mountain State, which he continued into law school days. While in law school, he managed and edited *The Better Times Weekly*, a four-county tabloid that went to 57,000 households. In recent years, he's written an occasional column for *The Charleston Daily Mail*. He was elected in 1980 to a term as magistrate of Marion County, at that time only the second Republican to hold a full time office there since the 1920s. It was in those early political years that he came to know and respect the work of Congressman and Governor Moore. In 1985, Crouser had been accepted to become an FBI special agent but, instead of reporting to Quantico for training in February of 1985, he declined the appointment to work in the Moore Administration. He served as deputy finance commissioner, executive secretary of Workers' Compensation and, briefly, as the State Tax Commissioner. He was elected as a delegate for President George H. W. Bush to the Republican National Convention in 1988.

Since then, Crouser has practiced law as a member of *Jackson Kelly PLLC*, a national firm based in Charleston. He was appointed in 1997 by Governor Cecil Underwood to the West Virginia Ethics Commission, of which he was vice chairman until 2005. He also chaired the Committee on Open Governmental Meetings for several years. In 2005, he was appointed by Governor Joe Manchin to the Probable Cause Board, of which he is chairman.

He and wife Sally live in Charleston and have two children of whom they are very proud, Wesley and Julie. Brad has also authored *What's My Excuse For Not Being a Christian?*, a Christian apologetics book, published by *Woodland Gospel Press*, a division of *Woodland Press*.

Arch Moore, August 2005, with the author. —Photo by Mrs. Harry (Alice) Moore

—*Photo by the late Leo Gardner, March 1985, courtesy Audrey Toler Pennington.*

PUBLISHED BY

Woodland Press, LLC

In Conjunction With Logan Novelties and Books, LLC

Other Award Winning Titles by Woodland Press:

The Tale of the Devil:
The Biography of Devil Anse Hatfield
Dr. Coleman C. Hatfield and Robert Y. Spence
(Dr. Hatfield was named Tamarack Author of the Year 2004)
ISBN 0-9724867-1-2

West Virginia Tough Boys
Vote Buying, Fist Fighting And A President Named JFK
F. Keith Davis
ISBN 0-9724867-2-0

Mountain Boy
The Adventures of Orion Saddler
Norman Mullins
ISBN 0-9724867-4-7

What's My Excuse For Not Being A Christian?
Brad Crouser
ISBN 0-9724867-5-5

Prickett's Fort
Bill Hawkins
ISBN 0-97248-677-1

www.woodlandpress.com
www.woodlandgospel.com